Praise for Peter Frankopan's

The Silk Roads

"This provocative history challenges the view of the West as heir to a pure Greco-Roman culture. . . . Frankopan marshals diverse examples to demonstrate the interconnectedness of cultures, showing in vivid detail the economic and social impact of the silk and the slave trades, the Black Death, and the Buddhist influence on Christianity." —*The New Yorker*

"Frankopan has created something that forces us to sit up and reconsider the world and the way we've always thought about it. . . . The book takes us by surprise right from the start." —NPR

"This is deeply researched popular history at its most invigorating, primed to dislodge routine preconceptions and to pour in other light. The freshness of . . . Frankopan's sources is stimulating, and their sheer range can provoke surprising connections. He likes to administer passing electric shocks." —Colin Thubron, *New York Review of Books*

"An ambitious book. . . . By spinning all these stories into a single thread, Peter Frankopan attempts something bold: a history of the world that shunts the centre of gravity eastward. . . . Mr. Frankopan writes with clarity and memorable detail." —*The Economist*

"Dazzlingly rich and accessible. . . . By reorienting the history of the last few millennia to the east, and by resolutely keeping the camera rolling there, Frankopan unhooks us from the usual story of 'Western Civ' and gives us a startling and brilliant perspective on events that may once have been familiar—and plenty that aren't." —*The Philadelphia Inquirer*

"This is history on a grand scale, with a sweep and ambition that is rare. . . . A remarkable book on many levels, a proper historical epic of dazzling range and achievement." —*The Guardian*

"Superb. . . . Peter Frankopan is an exceptional storyteller. . . . The lands of the Silk Roads are of renewed importance, and Frankopan's book will be indispensable to anyone who wants to make sense of this union of past and present."
—*The Dallas Morning News*

"A very well-written and wide-ranging study, founded on reading of staggering breadth and depth. . . . Strikingly up to date. . . . No one could read it without learning a great deal, or without having their conception of the course of history radically challenged."
—*The Times Literary Supplement* (London)

"Underlying the tightly researched history is a grander human truth. As a species, we are motivated by stories. . . . This invigorating and profound book has enough storytelling to excite the reader and enough fresh scholarship to satisfy the intellect. . . . Charismatic and essential."
—*The Daily Telegraph* (London)

"Not only the most important history book written in years, but the most important written in decades."
—*Berliner Zeitung*

"Many books have been written which claim to be 'A New History of the World.' This one fully deserves the title. . . . So ambitious, so detailed and so fascinating. . . . *The Silk Roads* demonstrates why studying history is so important."
—*The Times* (London)

"Essential in shifting Eurocentric views—and is also a thumping good read."
—*Sunday Times* (Johannesburg)

"A dazzling piece of historical writing."
—*South China Morning Post*

Peter Frankopan

The Silk Roads

Peter Frankopan is a historian based at Oxford University. He is the author of *The First Crusade: The Call from the East*, a major monograph about Byzantium, Islam and the West in the eleventh and twelfth centuries. He is a senior research fellow at Worcester College, Oxford, and the director of the Oxford Centre for Byzantine Research at Oxford University. His revised translation of *The Alexiad* was published in the United States in 2009.

www.peterfrankopan.com

ALSO BY PETER FRANKOPAN

The First Crusade: The Call from the East

The Silk Roads

A New History of the World

PETER FRANKOPAN

VINTAGE BOOKS
A Division of Penguin Random House LLC
New York

FIRST VINTAGE BOOKS EDITION, MARCH 2017

The Library of Congress has cataloged the Knopf edition as follows:
Frankopan, Peter.
The Silk Roads : a new history of the world / Peter Frankopan.—First US edition.
pages cm
1. World history. 2. Silk Road—History. 3. Trade routes—History.
4. East and West—History. 5. Imperialism—History. 6. Culture conflict—History.
7. Acculturation—History. I. Title.
D21.3.F73 2016 909—dc23 2015013264

Vintage Books Trade Paperback ISBN: 978-1-101-91237-9
eBook ISBN: 978-1-101-94633-6

Author photograph © Michael Lionstar
Maps by ML Design
Book design by Soonyoung Kwon

www.vintagebooks.com

Printed in the United States of America
12 14 16 18 20 19 17 15 13

To Katarina, Flora, Francis and Luke

We halted in the country of a tribe of Türks . . . we saw a group who worship snakes, a group who worship fish, and a group who worship cranes.

—Ibn Faḍlān's *Voyage to the Volga Bulghars*

I, Prester John, am the lord of lords, and I surpass all the kings of the entire world in wealth, virtue and power . . . Milk and honey flow freely in our lands; poison can do no harm, nor do any noisy frogs croak. There are no scorpions, no serpents creeping in the grass.

—Purported letter of Prester John to Rome and Constantinople, twelfth century

He has a very large palace, entirely roofed with fine gold.

—Christopher Columbus' research notes on the Great Khan of the East, late fifteenth century

If we do not make relatively small sacrifices, and alter our policy, in Persia now, we shall both endanger our friendship with Russia and find in a comparatively near future . . . a situation where our very existence as an Empire will be at stake.

—Sir George Clerk to Sir Edward Grey, British Foreign Secretary, 21 July 1914

The president would win even if we sat around doing nothing.

—Chief of Staff to Nursultan Nazarbayev, President of Kazakhstan, shortly before 2005 elections

Contents

Note on Transliteration

Historians tend to become anxious over the issue of transliteration. In a book such as this one that draws on primary sources written in different languages, it is not possible to have a consistent rule on proper names. Names like João and Ivan are left in their original forms, while Fernando and Nikolai are not and become Ferdinand and Nicholas. As a matter of personal preference, I use Genghis Khan, Trotsky, Gaddafi and Teheran even though other renditions might be more accurate; on the other hand, I avoid western alternatives for Beijing and Guangzhou. Places whose names change are particularly difficult. I refer to the great city on the Bosporus as Constantinople up to the end of the First World War, at which point I switch to Istanbul; I refer to Persia until the country's formal change of name to Iran in 1935. I ask for forbearance from the reader who demands consistency.

Preface

As a child, one of my most prized possessions was a large map of the world. It was pinned on the wall by my bed, and I would stare at it every night before I went to sleep. Before long, I had memorised the names and locations of all the countries, noting their capital cities, as well as the oceans and seas, and the rivers that flowed in to them; the names of major mountain ranges and deserts, written in urgent italics, thrilled with adventure and danger.

By the time I was a teenager, I had become uneasy about the relentlessly narrow geographic focus of my classes at school, which concentrated solely on western Europe and the United States and left most of the rest of the world untouched. We had been taught about the Romans in Britain; the Norman conquest of 1066; Henry VIII and the Tudors; the American War of Independence; Victorian industrialisation; the battle of the Somme; and the rise and fall of Nazi Germany. I would look up at my map and see huge regions of the world that had been passed over in silence.

For my fourteenth birthday my parents gave me a book by the anthropologist Eric Wolf, which really lit the tinder. The accepted and lazy history of civilisation, wrote Wolf, is one where "Ancient Greece begat Rome, Rome begat Christian Europe, Christian Europe begat the Renaissance, the Renaissance the Enlightenment, the Enlightenment political democracy and the industrial revolution. Industry crossed with democracy in turn yielded the United States, embodying the rights to life, liberty and the pursuit of happiness."[1] I immediately recognised that this was exactly the story that I had been told: the mantra of the political, cultural and moral triumph of the west. But this account was flawed; there were alternative ways of looking at history—ones that did not involve looking at the past from the perspective of the winners of recent history.

I was hooked. It was suddenly obvious that the regions we were not being taught about had become lost, suffocated by the insistent story of the rise of Europe. I begged my father to take me to see the Hereford Mappa

Mundi, which located Jerusalem as its focus and mid-point, with England and other western countries placed off to one side, all but irrelevancies. When I read about Arab geographers whose works were accompanied by charts that seemed upside down and put the Caspian Sea at its centre, I was transfixed—as I was when I found out about an important medieval Turkish map in Istanbul that had at its heart a city called Balāsāghūn, which I had never even heard of, which did not appear on any maps, and whose very location was uncertain until recently, and yet was once considered the centre of the world.[2]

I wanted to know more about Russia and Central Asia, about Persia and Mesopotamia. I wanted to understand the origins of Christianity when viewed from Asia; and how the Crusades looked to those living in the great cities of the Middle Ages—Constantinople, Jerusalem, Baghdad and Cairo, for example; I wanted to learn about the great empires of the east, about the Mongols and their conquests; and to understand how two world wars looked when viewed not from Flanders or the eastern front, but from Afghanistan and India.

It was extraordinarily fortunate therefore that I was able to learn Russian at school, where I was taught by Dick Haddon, a brilliant man who had served in Naval Intelligence and believed that the way to understand the Russian language and *dusha*, or soul, was through its sparkling literature and its peasant music. I was even more fortunate when he offered to give Arabic lessons to those who were interested, introducing half a dozen of us to Islamic culture and history, and immersing us in the beauty of classical Arabic. These languages helped unlock a world waiting to be discovered, or, as I soon realised, to be rediscovered by those of us in the west.

Today, much attention is devoted to assessing the likely impact of rapid economic growth in China, where demand for luxury goods is forecast to quadruple in the next decade, or to considering social change in India, where more people have access to a mobile phone than to a flushing toilet.[3] But neither offers the best vantage point to view the world's past and its present. In fact, for millennia, it was the region lying between east and west, linking Europe with the Pacific Ocean, that was the axis on which the globe spun.

The halfway point between east and west, running broadly from the eastern shores of the Mediterranean and the Black Sea to the Himalayas, might seem an unpromising position from which to assess the world. This is a region that is now home to states that evoke the exotic and the peripheral, like Kazakhstan and Uzbekistan, Kyrgyzstan and Turkmenistan, Tajikistan and the countries of the Caucasus; it is a region associated with regimes that are unstable, violent and a threat to international security, like Afghanistan, Iran, Iraq and Syria, or ill versed in the best practices of democracy, like Russia and Azerbaijan. Overall, it appears to be a region that is home to a series of failed or failing states, led by dictators who win impossibly large majorities in national elections and whose families and friends control sprawling business interests, own vast assets and wield political power. They are places with poor records on human rights, where freedom of expression in matters of faith, conscience and sexuality is limited, and where control of the media dictates what does and what does not appear in the press.[4]

While such countries may seem wild to us, these are no backwaters, no obscure wastelands. In fact the bridge between east and west is the very crossroads of civilisation. Far from being on the fringe of global affairs, these countries lie at its very centre—as they have done since the beginning of history. It was here that Civilisation was born, and where many believed Mankind had been created—in the Garden of Eden, "planted by the Lord God" with "every tree that is pleasant to the sight and good for food," which was widely thought to be located in the rich fields between the Tigris and Euphrates.[5]

It was in this bridge between east and west that great metropolises were established nearly 5,000 years ago, where the cities of Harappa and Mohenjo-daro in the Indus valley were wonders of the ancient world, with populations numbering in the tens of thousands and streets connecting into a sophisticated sewage system that would not be rivalled in Europe for thousands of years.[6] Other great centres of civilisation such as Babylon, Nineveh, Uruk and Akkad in Mesopotamia were famed for their grandeur and architectural innovation. One Chinese geographer, meanwhile, writing more than two millennia ago, noted that the inhabitants of Bactria, centred on the Oxus river and now located in northern Afghanistan, were legendary negotiators and traders; its capital city was home to a market where a huge range of products were bought and sold, carried from far and wide.[7]

This region is where the world's great religions burst into life, where Judaism, Christianity, Islam, Buddhism and Hinduism jostled with each other. It is the cauldron where language groups competed, where Indo-European, Semitic and Sino-Tibetan tongues wagged alongside those speaking Altaic, Turkic and Caucasian. This is where great empires rose and fell, where the after-effects of clashes between cultures and rivals were felt thousands of miles away. Standing here opened up new ways to view the past and showed a world that was profoundly interconnected, where what happened on one continent had an impact on another, where the after-shocks of what happened on the steppes of Central Asia could be felt in North Africa, where events in Baghdad resonated in Scandinavia, where discoveries in the Americas altered the prices of goods in China and led to a surge in demand in the horse markets of northern India.

These tremors were carried along a network that fans out in every direction, routes along which pilgrims and warriors, nomads and merchants have travelled, goods and produce have been bought and sold, and ideas exchanged, adapted and refined. They have carried not only prosperity, but also death and violence, disease and disaster. In the late nineteenth century, this sprawling web of connections was given a name by an eminent German geologist, Ferdinand von Richthofen (uncle of the First World War flying ace the "Red Baron") that has stuck ever since: "Seidenstraßen"—the Silk Roads.[8]

These pathways serve as the world's central nervous system, connecting peoples and places together, but lying beneath the skin, invisible to the naked eye. Just as anatomy explains how the body functions, understanding these connections allows us to understand how the world works. And yet, despite the importance of this part of the world, it has been forgotten by mainstream history. In part, this is because of what has been called "orientalism"—the strident and overwhelmingly negative view of the east as undeveloped and inferior to the west, and therefore unworthy of serious study.[9] But it also stems from the fact that the narrative of the past has become so dominant and well established that there is no place for a region that has long been seen as peripheral to the story of the rise of Europe and of western society.

Today, Jalalabad and Herat in Afghanistan, Fallujah and Mosul in Iraq or Homs and Aleppo in Syria seem synonymous with religious fundamentalism and sectarian violence. The present has washed away the past: gone are the days when the name of Kabul conjured up images of the gardens planted and tended by the great Bābur, founder of the Mughal Empire in India. The Bagh-i-Wafa ("Garden of Fidelity") included a pool surrounded by orange and pomegranate trees and a clover meadow—of which Bābur was extremely proud: "This is the best part of the garden, a most beautiful sight when the oranges take colour. Truly that garden is admirably situated!"[10]

In the same way, modern impressions about Iran have obscured the glories of its more distant history when its Persian predecessor was a byword for good taste in everything, from the fruit served at dinner, to the stunning miniature portraits produced by its legendary artists, to the paper that scholars wrote on. A beautifully considered work written by Simi Nīshāpūrī, a librarian from Mashad in eastern Iran around 1400, records in careful detail the advice of a book lover who shared his passion. Anyone thinking of writing, he counsels solemnly, should be advised that the best paper for calligraphy is produced in Damascus, Baghdad or Samarkand. Paper from elsewhere "is generally rough, blotches and is impermanent." Bear in mind, he cautions, that it is worth giving paper a slight tint before committing ink to it, "because white is hard on the eyes and the master calligraphic specimens that have been observed have all been on tinted paper."[11]

Places whose names are all but forgotten once dominated, such as Merv, described by one tenth-century geographer as a "delightful, fine, elegant, brilliant, extensive and pleasant city," and "the mother of the world"; or Rayy, not far from modern Teheran, which to another writer around the same time was so glorious as to be considered "the bridegroom of the earth" and the world's "most beautiful creation."[12] Dotted across the spine of Asia, these cities were strung like pearls, linking the Pacific to the Mediterranean.

Urban centres spurred each other on, with rivalry between rulers and elites prompting ever more ambitious architecture and spectacular monuments. Libraries, places of worship, churches and observatories of immense scale and cultural influence dotted the region, connecting Constantinople to Damascus, Isfahan, Samarkand, Kabul and Kashgar. Cities such as these became home to brilliant scholars who advanced the frontiers of their subjects. The names of only a small handful are familiar today—men like Ibn Sīnā, better known as Avicenna, al-Bīrūnī and al-Khwārizmi—giants in the fields of astronomy and medicine; but there were many more besides. For centuries before the early modern era, the intellectual centres of excellence of the world, the Oxfords and Cambridges, the Harvards and Yales, were not located in Europe or the west, but in Baghdad and Balkh, Bukhara and Samarkand.

There was good reason why the cultures, cities and peoples who lived along the Silk Roads developed and advanced: as they traded and exchanged ideas, they learnt and borrowed from each other, stimulating further advances in philosophy, the sciences, language and religion. Progress was essential, as one of the rulers of the kingdom of Zhao in north-eastern China at one extremity of Asia more than 2,000 years ago knew all too well. "A talent for following the ways of yesterday," declared King Wuling in 307 BC, "is not sufficient to improve the world of today."[13] Leaders in the past understood how important it was to keep up with the times.

The mantle of progress shifted, however, in the early modern period as a result of two great maritime expeditions that took place at the end of the fifteenth century. In the course of six years in the 1490s, the foundations were laid for a major disruption to the rhythm of long-established systems of exchange. First Christopher Columbus crossed the Atlantic, paving the way for two great land masses that were hitherto untouched to connect to Europe and beyond; then, just a few years later, Vasco da Gama successfully navigated the southern tip of Africa, sailing on to India, opening new sea routes in the process. The discoveries changed patterns of interaction and trade, and effected a remarkable change in the world's political and economic centre of gravity. Suddenly, western Europe was transformed from its position as a regional backwater into the fulcrum of a sprawling communication, transportation and trading system: at a stroke, it became the new mid-point between east and west.

The rise of Europe sparked a fierce battle for power—and for control of the past. As rivals squared up to each other, history was reshaped to emphasise the events, themes and ideas that could be used in the ideological clashes that raged alongside the struggle for resources and for command of the sea lanes. Busts were made of leading politicians and generals wearing togas to make them look like Roman heroes of the past; magnificent new buildings were constructed in grand classical style that appropriated the glories of the ancient world as their own direct antecedents. History was twisted and manipulated to create an insistent narrative where the rise of the west was not only natural and inevitable, but a continuation of what had gone before.

Many stories set me on the path to looking at the world's past in a different way. But one stood out in particular. Greek mythology had it that Zeus, father of the gods, released two eagles, one at each end of the earth, and commanded them to fly towards each other. A sacred stone, the *omphalos*—the navel of the world—was placed where they met, to enable communication with the divine. I learnt later that the concept of this stone has long been a source of fascination for philosophers and psychoanalysts.[14]

I remember gazing at my map when I first heard this tale, wondering where the eagles would have met. I imagined them taking off from the shores of the western Atlantic and the Pacific coast of China and heading inland. The precise position changed, depending where I placed my fingers to start measuring equal distances from east and west. But I always ended up somewhere between the Black Sea and the Himalayas. I would lie awake at night, pondering the map on my bedroom wall, Zeus' eagles and the history of a region that was never mentioned in the books that I read—and did not have a name.

Not so long ago, Europeans divided Asia into three broad zones—the Near, Middle and Far East. Yet whenever I heard or read about present-day problems as I was growing up, it seemed that the second of these, the Middle East, had shifted in meaning and even location, being used to refer to Israel, Palestine and the surrounding area, and occasionally to the Persian Gulf. And I could not understand why I kept being told of the importance of the Mediterranean as a cradle of civilisation, when it seemed so obvious that this was not where civilisation had really been forged. The real crucible, the "Mediterranean" in its literal meaning—the centre of the world—was not a sea separating Europe and North Africa, but right in the heart of Asia.

My hope is that I can embolden others to study peoples and places that have been ignored by scholars for generations by opening up new questions and new areas of research. I hope to prompt new questions to be asked about the past, and for truisms to be challenged and scrutinised. Above all, I hope to inspire those who read this book to look at history in a different way.

Worcester College, Oxford
April 2015

The Silk Roads

1

The Creation of the Silk Road

From the beginning of time, the centre of Asia was where empires were made. The alluvial lowlands of Mesopotamia, fed by the Tigris and Euphrates, provided the basis for civilisation itself—for it was in this region that the first towns and cities took shape. Systematised agriculture developed in Mesopotamia and across the whole of the "Fertile Crescent," a band of highly productive land with access to plentiful water, stretching from the Persian Gulf to the Mediterranean coast. It was here that some of the first recorded laws were disseminated nearly 4,000 years ago by Hammurabi, King of Babylon, who detailed his subjects' obligations and set out fierce punishments for their transgressions.[1]

Although many kingdoms and empires sprang up from this crucible, the greatest of all was that of the Persians. Expanding quickly in the sixth century BC from a homeland in what is now southern Iran, the Persians came to dominate their neighbours, reaching the shores of the Aegean, conquering Egypt and expanding eastwards as far as the Himalayas. Their success owed much to their openness, to judge from the Greek historian Herodotus. "The Persians are greatly inclined to adopt foreign customs," he wrote: the Persians were prepared to abandon their own style of dress when they concluded that the fashions of a defeated foe were superior, leading them to borrow styles from the Medes as well as from the Egyptians.[2]

The willingness to adopt new ideas and practices was an important factor in enabling the Persians to build an administrative system that allowed the smooth running of an empire which incorporated many different peoples. A highly educated bureaucracy oversaw the efficient administration of the day-to-day life of the empire, recording everything from payments made to workers serving the royal household, to validating the quality and quantity of goods bought and sold in market places; they also took charge of the maintenance and repair of a road system criss-crossing the empire that was the envy of the ancient world.[3]

A road network that linked the coast of Asia Minor with Babylon, Susa and Persepolis enabled a distance of more than 1,600 miles to be covered in the course of a week, an achievement viewed with wonder by Herodotus, who noted that neither snow, rain, heat nor darkness could slow the speedy transmission of messages.[4] Investment in agriculture and the development of pioneering irrigation techniques to improve crop yields helped nurture the growth of cities by enabling increasingly large populations to be supported from surrounding fields—not only in the rich agricultural lands to either side of the Tigris and Euphrates, but also in valleys served by the mighty Oxus and Iaxartes rivers (now known as the Amy Darya and Syr Darya), as well as in the Nile delta after its capture by Persian armies in 525 BC. The Persian Empire was a land of plenty that connected the Mediterranean with the heart of Asia.

Persia presented itself as a beacon of stability and fairness, as a trilingual inscription hewn into a cliff face at Behistun demonstrates. Written in Persian, Elamite and Akkadian, it records how Darius the Great, one of Persia's most famous rulers, put down revolts and uprisings, drove back invasions from abroad and wronged neither the poor nor the powerful. Keep the country secure, the inscription commands, and look after the people righteously, for justice is the bedrock of the kingdom.[5] Tolerance of minorities was legendary, with one Persian ruler referred to as the "Messiah," and the one whom the "Lord, the God of Heaven" had blessed, as the result of his policies that included the release of the Jews from their Babylonian exile.[6]

Trade flourished in ancient Persia, providing revenues that allowed rulers to fund military expeditions targeting locations that brought yet more resources into the empire. It also enabled them to indulge notoriously extravagant tastes. Spectacular buildings were erected in the huge cities of Babylon, Persepolis, Pasargadae and Susa, where King Darius built a magnificent palace using the highest-quality ebony and silver from Egypt and cedar from Lebanon, fine gold from Bactria, lapis and cinnabar from Sogdiana, turquoise from Khwarezm and ivory from India.[7] The Persians were famous for their love of pleasure and, according to Herodotus, only had to hear of a new luxury to yearn to indulge it.[8]

Underpinning the commercial commonwealth was an aggressive military that helped extend the frontiers, but was also needed to defend them. Persia faced persistent problems from the north, a world dominated by nomads who lived with their livestock on semi-arid grassland belts, known as steppes, stretching from the Black Sea across Central Asia as far as Mongolia. These nomads were famed for their ferocity—they were said to drink the blood of their enemies and make clothes of their scalps, and in some cases to eat the flesh of their own fathers. Interaction with the nomads was complex though, for despite stock descriptions of them as chaotic and unpredictable, they were important partners in the supply of animals, and especially fine horses. But the nomads could be the cause of disaster, such as when Cyrus the Great, the architect of the Persian Empire in the 6th century BC, was killed trying to subjugate the Scythians; his head was then carried around in a skin filled with blood, said one writer, so that the thirst for power that had inspired him could now be quenched.[9]

Nevertheless, this was a rare setback that did not stall Persia's expansion. Greek commanders looked east with a combination of fear and respect, seeking to learn from the Persians' tactics on the battlefield and to adopt their technology. Authors like Aeschylus used successes against the Persians as a way of celebrating military prowess and of demonstrating the favour of the gods, commemorating heroic resistance to the attempted invasions of Greece in epic plays and literature.[10]

"I have come to Greece," says Dionysus in the opening lines of the *Bacchae*, from the "fabulously wealthy East," a place where Persia's plains are bathed in sunshine, where Bactria's towns are protected by walls, and where beautifully constructed towers look out over coastal regions. Asia and the East were the lands that Dionysus "set dancing" with the divine mysteries long before those of the Greeks.[11]

None was a keener student of such works than Alexander of Macedon. When he took the throne in 336 BC following the assassination of his father, the brilliant King Philip, there was no question about which direction the young general would head in his search for glory. Not for a moment did he look to Europe, which offered nothing at all: no cities, no culture, no prestige, no reward. For Alexander, as for all ancient Greeks, culture, ideas and opportunities—as well as threats—came from the east. It was no surprise that his gaze fell on the greatest power of antiquity: Persia.

After dislodging the Persian governors of Egypt in a lightning strike in 331 BC, Alexander set off for an all-out assault on the empire's heartlands. The decisive confrontation took place later in 331 on the dusty plains of Gaugamela, near the modern town of Erbil in Iraqi Kurdistan, where he inflicted a spectacular defeat on the vastly superior Persian army under the command of Darius III—perhaps because he was fully refreshed after a good night's sleep: according to Plutarch, Alexander insisted on resting before engaging the enemy, sleeping so deeply that his concerned commanders had to shake him awake. Dressing in his favoured outfit, he put on a fine helmet, so polished that "it was as bright as the most refined silver," grasped a trusted sword in his right hand and led his troops to a crushing victory that opened the gates of an empire.[12]

Tutored by Aristotle, Alexander had been brought up with high hopes resting on his shoulders. He did not disappoint. After the Persian armies had been shattered at Gaugamela, Alexander advanced east. One city after another surrendered to him as he took over the territories controlled by his defeated rivals. Places of legendary size, wealth and beauty fell before the young hero. Babylon surrendered, its inhabitants covering the road leading to the great city with flowers and garlands, while silver altars heaped with frankincense and perfumes were placed on either side. Cages with lions and leopards were brought to be presented as gifts.[13] Before long, all the points along the Royal Road that linked the major cities of Persia and the communication network that connected the coast of Asia Minor with Central Asia had been taken by Alexander and his men.

Although some modern scholars have dismissed him as a "drunken juvenile thug," Alexander appears to have had a surprisingly delicate touch when it came to dealing with newly conquered territories and peoples.[14] He was often emollient when it came to local religious beliefs and practices, showing tolerance and also respect: for example, he was reportedly upset by the way the tomb of Cyrus the Great had been desecrated, and not only restored it but punished those who had defiled the shrine.[15] Alexander ensured that Darius III was given a funeral befitting his rank and buried alongside other Persian rulers after his body had been found dumped in a wagon following his murder by one of his own lieutenants.[16]

Alexander was also able to draw more and more territory under his sway because he was willing to rely on local elites. "If we wish not just to pass through Asia but to hold it," he is purported to have said, "we must show clemency to these people; it is their loyalty which will make our empire stable and permanent."[17] Local officials and old elites were left in place to administer towns and territories that were conquered. Alexander himself took to adopting traditional titles and wearing Persian clothing to underline his acceptance of local customs. He was keen to portray himself not so much as an invading conqueror, but as the latest heir of an ancient realm—despite howls of derision from those who told all who would listen that he had brought misery and soaked the land with blood.[18]

It is important to remember that much of our information about Alexander's campaigns, successes and policies derives from later historians, whose accounts are often highly idealised and breathless with enthusiasm in the coverage of the young general's exploits.[19] Nevertheless, even if we need to be cautious about the way the collapse of Persia is covered in the sources, the speed with which Alexander kept extending the frontiers further east tells its own story. He was an energetic founder of new cities, usually named after himself, that are now more often known by other names, such as Herat (Alexandria in Aria), Kandahar (Alexandria in Arachosia) and Bagram (Alexandria ad Caucasum). The construction of these staging posts—and the reinforcement of others further north, stretching to the Fergana valley—were new points running along the spine of Asia.

New cities with powerful defences, as well as standalone strongholds and forts, were primarily built to defend against the threat posed by tribes of the steppes who were adept at launching devastating attacks on rural communities. Alexander's programme of fortification was designed to protect new areas that had only recently been conquered. Similar concerns met with similar responses further east at precisely this time. The Chinese had already developed a concept of *huaxia*, representing the civilised world, set against the challenges of the peoples from the steppes. An intensive building programme expanded a network of fortifications into what became known as the Great Wall of China, and were driven by the same principle as that adopted by Alexander: expansion without defence was useless.[20]

Back in the fourth century BC, Alexander himself continued to campaign relentlessly, circling back through the Hindu Kush and marching down the Indus valley, again founding new strongholds with garrisons—although by now meeting with regular cries of protest from his weary and homesick men. From a military perspective, his achievements by the time he died at the age of thirty-two in Babylon in 323 BC, in circumstances that remain shrouded in mystery, were nothing short of sensational.[21] The speed and extent of his conquests were staggering. What was no less impressive—though much more often ignored—is the scale of the legacy he left behind, and how the influences of ancient Greece blended with those of Persia, India, Central Asia and eventually China too.

Although Alexander's sudden death was followed by a period of turbulence and infighting between his senior commanders, a leader soon emerged for the eastern half of the new territories: an officer born in northern Macedonia named Seleucus who had taken part in all the king's major expeditions. Within a few years of his patron's death, he found himself governor of lands that stretched from the Tigris to the Indus river; the territories were so large that they resembled not a kingdom but an empire in its own right. He founded a dynasty, known as the Seleucids, that was to rule for nearly three centuries.[22] Alexander's victories are often and easily dismissed as a brilliant series of short-term gains, his legacy widely thought of as ephemeral and temporary. But these were no transitory achievements; they were the start of a new chapter for the region lying between the Mediterranean and the Himalayas.

The decades that followed Alexander's death saw a gradual and unmistakable programme of Hellenisation, as ideas, themes and symbols from ancient Greece were introduced to the east. The descendants of his generals remembered their Greek roots and actively emphasised them, for example on the coinage struck in the mints of the major towns that were located in strategically important points along the trade routes or in agriculturally vibrant centres. The form of these coins became standardised: an image of the current ruler on the obverse with ringlets held by a diadem, and invariably looking to the right as Alexander had done, with an image of Apollo on the reverse, identified by Greek letters.[23]

The Greek language could be heard—and seen—all over Central Asia and the Indus valley. At Ai Khanoum in northern Afghanistan—a new city founded by Seleucus—maxims from Delphi were carved on to a monument, including:

> As a child, be well-behaved.
> As a youth, be self-controlled.
> As an adult, be just.

As an elder, be wise.
As one dying, be without pain.[24]

Greek was in daily use by officials more than a century after Alexander's death, as tax receipts and documents relating to soldiers' pay from Bactria from around 200 BC show.[25] Indeed, the language penetrated deep into the Indian subcontinent. Some of the edicts issued by Maurayan ruler Ashoka, the greatest of the early Indian rulers, were made with parallel Greek translations, evidently for the benefit of the local population.[26]

The vibrancy of the cultural exchange as Europe and Asia collided was astonishing. Statues of the Buddha started to appear only after the cult of Apollo became established in the Gundhara valley and western India. Buddhists felt threatened by the success of new religious practices and began to create their own visual images. Indeed, there is a correlation not only in the date of the earliest statues of the Buddha, but also in their appearance and design: it seems that it was Apollo that provided the template, such was the impact of Greek influences. Hitherto, Buddhists had actively refrained from visual representations; competition now forced them to react, to borrow and to innovate.[27]

Stone altars adorned with Greek inscriptions, the images of Apollo and exquisite miniature ivories depicting Alexander from what is now southern Tajikistan reveal just how far influences from the west penetrated.[28] So too did the impressions of the cultural superiority brought from the Mediterranean. The Greeks in Asia were widely credited in India, for example, for their skill in the sciences: "they are barbarians," says the text known as the *Gārgī Samhitā*, "yet the science of astronomy originated with them and for this they must be reverenced like gods."[29]

According to Plutarch, Alexander made sure that Greek theology was taught as far away as India, with the result that the gods of Olympus were revered across Asia. Young men in Persia and beyond were brought up reading Homer and "chanting the tragedies of Sophocles and Euripides," while the Greek language was studied in the Indus valley.[30] This may be why it is possible that borrowings can be detected across great works of literature. It has been suggested, for instance, that the *Rāmāyaṇa*, the great early Sanskrit epic, owes a debt to the *Iliad* and to the *Odyssey*, with the theme of the abduction of Lady Sita by Rāvaṇa a direct echo of the elopement of Helen with Paris of Troy. Influences and inspiration flowed in the other direction too, with some scholars arguing that the *Aeneid* was in turn influenced by Indian texts such as the *Mahābhārata*.[31] Ideas, themes and stories coursed through the highways, spread by travellers, merchants and pilgrims: Alexander's conquests paved the way for the broadening of the minds of the populations of the lands he captured, as well as those on the periphery and beyond who came into contact with new ideas, new images and new concepts.

Even cultures on the wild steppes were influenced, as is clear from the exquisite funerary objects buried alongside high-ranking figures found in the Tilya Tepe graves in northern Afghanistan which show artistic influences being drawn from Greece—as well as from Siberia, India and beyond. Luxury objects were traded into the nomad world, in return for livestock and horses, and on occasion as tribute paid in return for peace.[32]

The linking up of the steppes into an interlocking and interconnecting world was accelerated by the growing ambitions of China. Under the Han dynasty (206 BC–AD 220), waves of expansion had pushed frontiers ever further, eventually reaching a province then called Xiyu (or "western regions"), but today known as Xinjiang ("new frontierland"). This lay beyond the Gansu corridor, a route 600 miles long linking the Chinese interior with the oasis city of Dunhuang, a crossroads on the edge of the Taklamakan desert. At this point, there was a choice of a northern or a southern route, both of which could be treacherous, which converged at Kashgar, itself set at the junction point of the Himalayas, the Pamir mountains, the Tien Shan range and the Hindu Kush.[33]

This expansion of China's horizons linked Asia together. These networks had hitherto been blocked by the Yuezhi and above all the Xiongnu, nomadic tribes who like the Scythians in Central Asia were a source of constant concern but were also important trading partners for livestock: Han authors wrote in the second century BC of tens of thousands of head of cattle being bought from the peoples of the steppes.[34] But it was Chinese demand for horses that was all but insatiable, fuelled by the need to keep an effective military force on standby to maintain internal order within China, and to be able to respond to attacks and raids by the Xiongnu or other tribes. Horses from the western region of Xinjiang were highly prized, and could make fortunes for tribal chieftains. On one occasion, a Yuezhi leader traded horses for a large consignment of goods that he then sold on to others, making ten times his investment.[35]

The most famous and valuable mounts were bred in the Fergana valley to the far side of the spectacular Pamir mountain range that straddles what is now eastern Tajikistan and north-eastern Afghanistan. Much admired for their strength, they are described by Chinese writers as being sired by dragons and are referred to as *hanxue ma* or "sweating blood"—the result of their distinctive red perspiration that was caused either by a local parasite or by the horses' having unusually thin skin and therefore being prone to blood vessels bursting during exertion. Some particularly fine specimens became celebrities in their own right, the subject of poems, sculpture and pictures, frequently referred to as *tianma*—heavenly or celestial horses.[36] Some were even taken with their owner to the next life: one emperor was buried alongside eighty of his favoured steeds—their burial place guarded by statues of two stallions and a terracotta warrior.[37]

Relations with the Xiongnu, who held sway across the steppes of Mongolia and across the grasslands to China's north, were not always easy. Contemporary historians wrote of the tribe as barbaric, willing to eat raw meat and drink blood; truly, said one writer, they are a people who "have been abandoned by heaven."[38] The Chinese proved willing to pay tribute rather than risk attacks on their cities. Envoys were regularly dispatched to visit the nomads (who were trained from infancy to hunt rats and birds and then foxes and hares), where the Emperor would politely ask after the health of the supreme leader.[39] A formal system of tribute developed whereby the nomads were given luxury gifts including rice, wine and textiles in return for peace. The most important item that was given was silk, a fabric that was treasured by the nomads for its texture and its lightness as a lining for bedding and clothing. It was also a symbol of political and social power: being swathed in voluminous quantities of precious silk was an important way that the *chanyu* (the tribes' supreme leader) emphasised his own status and rewarded those around him.[40]

The sums paid in return for peace were substantial. In 1 BC, for example, the Xiongnu were given 30,000 rolls of silk and a similar amount of raw material, as well as 370 items of clothing.[41] Some officials liked to believe that the tribe's love of luxury would prove its undoing. "Now [you have] this fondness for Chinese things," one envoy brashly told a tribal leader. Xiongnu customs were changing, he said. China, he predicted confidently, "will in the end succeed in winning over the whole Xiongnu nation."[42]

This was wishful thinking. In fact, the diplomacy that maintained peace and good relations took a toll both financially and politically: paying tribute was expensive and a sign of political weakness. So in due course the Han rulers of China resolved to deal with the Xiongnu once and for all. First, a concerted effort was made to take control of the agriculturally rich western regions of Xiyu; the nomads were driven back as the Chinese took control of the Gansu corridor in a decade-long series of campaigns that ended in 119 BC. To the west lay the Pamir mountains and, beyond them, a new world. China had opened a door leading on to a trans-continental network; it was the moment of the birth of the Silk Roads.

The expansion of China saw a surge of interest in what lay beyond. Officials were commissioned to investigate and write reports about the regions beyond the mountains. One such account survives as the *Shi Ji* (Historical Records), written by Sima Qian, son of the imperial court's Grand Historian (*Taishi*), who continued to work on this account even after he had been disgraced and castrated for daring to defend an impetuous young general who had led troops to defeat.[43] He carefully set out what he had been able to discover about the histories, economies and armies of the peoples in the Indus valley, Persia and Central Asia. The kingdoms of Central Asia were weak, he noted, because of pressure from nomads displaced by Chinese forces who had turned their attention elsewhere. The inhabitants of these kingdoms were "poor in the use of arms," he wrote, "but clever at commerce," with flourishing markets in the capital Bactra, "where all sorts of goods are bought and sold."[44]

Trade between China and the world beyond developed slowly. Negotiating the routes along the edge of the Gobi desert was not easy, especially beyond the Jade Gate, the frontier post past which caravans of traders travelled on their way west. Passing from one oasis to another across treacherous terrain was difficult whether their route took them through the Taklamakan desert or through the passes of the Tian Shan mountains or through the Pamirs. Extremes of temperature had to be negotiated—one reason why the Bactrian camel was so valued. Hardy enough to brave the harsh conditions of the desert, these animals have advance knowledge of deadly sandstorms, one writer observed, and "immediately stand snarling together"—a sign for the traders and caravan leaders to "cover their noses and mouths by wrapping them in felt." The camel was clearly a fallible weathervane, however; sources talk of passing large numbers of dead animals and skeletons along the routes.[45] In such tough circumstances, rewards had to be high for the risks to be worth taking. Although bamboo and cloth made in Sichuan could be found for sale thousands of miles away in the markets of Bactria, it was primarily rare and high-value goods that were transported over long distances.[46]

Chief among these was the trade in silk. Silk performed a number of important roles in the ancient world apart from its value to nomadic tribes. Under the Han dynasty, silk was used alongside coins and grain to pay troops. It was in some ways the most reliable currency: producing money in sufficient quantities was a problem, as was the fact that not all of China was fully monetised; this presented a particular difficulty when it came to military pay since theatres of action were often in remote regions, where coins were all but useless. Grain, meanwhile, went rotten after a time. As a result, bolts of raw silk were used regularly as currency, either as pay or, as in the case of one Buddhist monastery in Central Asia, as a fine for monks who broke the foundation's rules.[47] Silk became an international currency as well as a luxury product.

The Chinese also regulated trade by creating a formal framework for controlling merchants who came from outside territories. A remarkable collection of 35,000 texts from the garrison town of Xuanquan, not far from Dunhuang, paints a vivid picture of the everyday goings-on in a town set at the neck of the Gansu corridor. From these texts, written on bamboo and wooden tablets, we learn that visitors passing into China had to stick to designated routes, were issued with written passes and were regularly counted by officials to ensure that all who entered the country also eventually made their way home. Like a modern hotel guest folio, records were kept for each visitor, noting how much they spent on food, what their place of origin was, their title and in which direction they were headed.[48]

These measures are to be understood not as a form of suspicious surveillance, but rather as a means of being able to note accurately who was entering and leaving China, as well as what they were doing there, and above all to record the value of the goods that were bought and sold for customs purposes. The sophistication of the techniques and their early implementation reveal how the imperial courts at the capital in Chang'an (modern Xi'an) and from the first century AD at Luoyang dealt with a world that seemed to be shrinking before their eyes.[49] We think of globalisation as a uniquely modern phenomenon; yet 2,000 years ago too, it was a fact of life, one that presented opportunities, created problems and prompted technological advance.

As it happened, developments many thousands of miles away served to stimulate demand for luxury items—and the ability to pay for them. In Parthia, the descendants of Seleucus were deposed around 247 BC by one

Arsaces, a man whose background is obscure. His descendants, known as the Arsacids, consolidated their hold on power and then set about extending it across western Asia into Persia, skilfully expropriating history to fuse Greek and Persian ideas into an increasingly coherent and robust new identity. The result was a time of stability and prosperity.[50]

But it was what was happening in the Mediterranean that provided the greatest stimulus of all. A small town in an unpromising location halfway up the west coast of Italy had slowly managed to turn itself from a provincial backwater into a regional power. Taking over one coastal city-state after another, Rome came to dominate the western Mediterranean. By the middle of the first century BC, its ambitions were expanding dramatically. And attention was focused firmly on the east.

Rome had evolved into an intensely competitive state, one that glorified the military and acclaimed violence and killing. Gladiatorial games were the bedrock of public entertainment, a place where mastery over foreign peoples and over nature was brutally celebrated. Triumphal arches all over the city provided daily reminders of military victories to its bustling population. Militarism, fearlessness and the love of glory were carefully cultivated as the key characteristics of an ambitious city whose reach was stretching forever further.[51]

The backbone of Roman power was the army, honed and conditioned to demanding standards. Soldiers were expected to be able to march more than twenty miles in five hours, hauling at least fifty pounds of equipment with them at the same time. Marriage was not only frowned on but specifically prohibited in order to keep recruits bonded to each other. Corps of highly trained, fit and intense young men who had been brought up confident in their ability and assured of their destiny were the rock on which Rome was built.[52]

The conquest of Gaul (broadly the area of modern France, the Low Countries and part of western Germany) in 52 BC brought substantial spoils, enough to cause a correction in the price of gold in the Roman Empire.[53] But there were only so many other places to take on in Europe—and few of them looked promising. What made empires great were large numbers of cities, producing taxable revenues; what made them culturally spectacular were artisans and craftsmen who developed new ideas when wealthy patrons competed with each other for their services and rewarded them for their skills. It was unlikely that places like Britain would provide lucrative additions to Rome's territories: as slate letters sent home by soldiers stationed in Britain attest, this province was a byword for grim and fruitless isolation.[54]

But Rome's transition into an empire had little to do with Europe or with establishing control across a continent that was poorly supplied with the kind of resources and cities that were honeypots of consumers and taxpayers. What propelled Rome into a new era was its reorientation towards the Eastern Mediterranean and beyond. Rome's success and its glory stemmed from its seizure of Egypt in the first instance, and then from setting its anchor in the east—in Asia.

Ruled for nearly 300 years by descendants of Ptolemy, one of Alexander the Great's bodyguards, Egypt had built fabulous wealth based on the Nile, whose floodwaters produced prodigious harvests of grain. These were not only sufficient to support the local population, but provided a handsome surplus that enabled Alexandria, at the mouth of the river, to develop into the largest city in the world according to one contemporary author, who estimated the population in the first century BC to number around 300,000.[55] Grain shipments were carefully monitored, with captains having to take a royal oath each time they filled their barges, at which point they would be issued with a receipt by a representative of the royal scribe. Only then would grain be released for loading.[56]

Rome had long cast a greedy eye over Egypt. It seized its chance when Queen Cleopatra became embroiled in a messy struggle for political mastery after the assassination of Julius Caesar. After fatefully throwing in her lot with Mark Antony at the battle of Actium in 30 BC, the Egyptian ruler was soon faced with a Roman army led by Octavius, a master of political cunning, bearing down on Alexandria. Following a series of defensive decisions that combined profound negligence with gross incompetence, Cleopatra committed suicide, either as the result of a poisonous snakebite or perhaps by a self-administered toxin. Egypt fell like a ripe fruit.[57] Octavius had left Rome as a general; he returned as its supreme ruler, with a new title shortly to be bestowed by a grateful Senate: Augustus. Rome had become an empire.

The capture of Egypt transformed Rome's fortunes. Now that it controlled the vast harvests of the Nile valley, the price of grain tumbled, providing a major boost to household spending power. Interest rates plummeted, falling from around 12 to 4 per cent; this in turn quickly fuelled the familiar boom that accompanies a flood of cheap capital: a surge in property prices.[58] Disposable income increased so sharply that Augustus was able to raise the financial threshold for qualification for membership of the Senate by 40 per cent.[59] As Augustus himself was fond of boasting, he found Rome a city built in brick, but left it in marble.[60]

This surging wealth was the result of Rome's ruthless expropriation of Egypt's tax revenues and of its enormous resources. Teams of tax inspectors fanned out across Egypt to impose a new poll tax, payable by all men aged between sixteen and sixty. Exemptions were granted only in a few special cases—for example to priests, who were able to avoid having to pay, but only after their names had been recorded carefully in temple registries.[61] This was part of a system that one scholar has termed "ancient apartheid"; its aim was to maximise the flow of money back to Rome.[62]

The process of appropriating revenues was repeated elsewhere as the tentacles of Roman economic and military expansion extended further. Not long after the annexation of Egypt, assessors were sent to Judaea to conduct a census, once again so as to ensure that taxes could be calculated accurately. Assuming the same model was used as had been employed in Egypt, which required all births and deaths to be recorded as well as the names of all adult males, the arrival in the world of Jesus Christ would have been registered by an official whose interest lay less in who the infant and his parents were, and more in what the birth represented by way of additional manpower and a future taxpayer for the empire.[63]

Rome's eyes were opened by the world it encountered in the east. Asia had already acquired a reputation for lazy luxury and fine living. It was indescribably wealthy, wrote Cicero, its harvests the stuff of legend, the variety of its produce incredible, and the size of its herds and flocks simply amazing. Its exports were colossal.[64] Such was Asia's wealth that Romans opined that its inhabitants could afford to dedicate themselves to idle pleasure. Little wonder that it was in the east that Roman soldiers came of age, wrote the poet Sallust: this was where Roman soldiers learnt how to make love, to be drunk, to enjoy statues, pictures and art. This was hardly a good thing, at least as far as Sallust was concerned. Asia may have been "voluptuous and indulging," but "its pleasures soon softened the warlike spirits of the soldiers."[65] Presented in this way, the east was the antithesis of everything that stern, martial Rome stood for.

Augustus himself made a concerted effort to understand what lay beyond the new frontiers in the east. Expeditionary forces were dispatched to the kingdom of Axum in modern Ethiopia and to the Sabbaean kingdom of Yemen, while the Gulf of Aqaba was being explored even as Roman rule in Egypt was still being cemented.[66] Then, in 1 BC, Augustus ordered a detailed survey to be conducted of both sides of the Persian Gulf to report on trade in this region and to record how the sea lanes linked with the Red Sea. He also oversaw the investigation of the land routes heading deep into Central Asia through Persia. A text known as the *Stathmoi Parthikoi* ("Parthian Stations") was produced around this time; it recorded distances between key points in the east, and carefully set out the most important locations from the Euphrates up to Alexandropolis, modern Kandahar in Afghanistan, in the east.[67]

The horizons of traders expanded substantially. According to the historian Strabo, within a few years of the occupation of Egypt, 120 Roman boats were sailing for India each year from the port of Myos Hormos on the Red Sea. Commercial exchange with India did not open up so much as explode—as is clear from an extraordinarily rich archaeological record from the subcontinent. Roman amphorae, lamps, mirrors and statues of gods have been recovered from a wide range of sites, including Pattanam, Kolhapur and Coimbatore.[68] So abundant are the coin finds dating to the reign of Augustus and his successors from the west coast of India and the Laccadive islands that some historians have argued that local rulers in the east used Roman gold and silver coins for their own currency, or melted these metals down to reuse them.[69]

Tamil literature from the period tells a similar story, recording the arrival of Roman traders with excitement. One poem talks of "cool and fragrant wine" being brought in "good ships" by the Romans, while another is rhapsodic: "The beautiful large ships . . . come, bringing gold, splashing the white foam on the waters of the Periyar [river], and then return laden with pepper. Here the music of the surging sea never ceases, and the great king presents to visitors the rare products of sea and mountain."[70] Another source provides a lyrical account of the European traders who settled in India: "The sun shone over the open terraces, over the warehouses near the harbour and over the turrets with windows like eyes of deer. In different places . . . the onlooker's attention was caught by the sight of the abodes of [the westerners], whose prosperity never waned."[71] The *Stathmoi Parthikoi* reveals what goods the Romans wanted from western India, noting where merchants could acquire valuable minerals, such as tin, copper and lead, as well as topaz, and where ivory, precious gemstones and spices were readily available.[72]

Trade with ports in India was not, however, limited to products that originated in the subcontinent. As excavations at the Red Sea port of Berenike in Egypt have shown, an array of goods from as far afield as Vietnam and Java found their way towards the Mediterranean.[73] Ports on both the western and eastern coasts of India served as emporia for goods brought from all over eastern and south-eastern Asia ready to be shipped west.[74] Then there were the goods and produce of the Red Sea, a vibrant commercial zone in its own right as well as linking the Mediterranean with the Indian Ocean and beyond.[75]

Rome's well-heeled citizens were by now able to indulge the most exotic and extravagant of tastes. Well-connected commentators complained that spending bordered on the obscene and bemoaned the voguish displays of excess.[76] This is captured perfectly in Petronius' *Satyricon*, whose most famous scene is the dinner party of Trimalchio, a former slave who had gained his freedom and amassed a fortune. The satire is acidic in its portrayal of the tastes of the new super-rich. Trimalchio wanted only the best that money could buy: pheasant brought in specially from the eastern coast of the Black Sea; guinea fowl from Africa; rare and expensive fish; plumed peacock, and much more besides, presented in excess. The grotesque theatre of presenting dish after dish—live birds sewn inside a whole pig that flew out the moment the ham was carved, or silver toothpicks being given to the guests—was a remorseless parody of the vulgarity and excess of Rome's new wealth. One of the major booms of antiquity produced one of the great literary expressions of bitter jealousy towards the nouveaux riches.[77]

New wealth brought Rome and its inhabitants into contact with new worlds and new tastes. The poet Martial typifies the internationalism and expanded knowledge of this period in a poem mourning a young slave girl, comparing her to an untouched lily, to polished Indian ivory, to a Red Sea pearl, with hair finer than Spanish wool or blonde locks from the Rhine.[78] Where couples wanting to conceive beautiful children would previously have had sex surrounded by erotic images, "now," reported one horrified Jewish writer, "they bring Israelite slaves and tie them to the foot of the bed" for inspiration, and because they could afford to.[79] Not all were impressed by the new tastes: the Tiber had been overwhelmed by the waters of the Orontes, the river that flows through Syria and southern Turkey, complained Juvenal in his *Satires* later—in other words, Asian decadence had destroyed old-fashioned Roman virtues; "clear off," he wrote, "if you take a shine to a fancy prostitute wearing barbarian headgear."[80]

. . .

For some conservative observers, it was the appearance of one commodity in particular that appalled: Chinese silk.[81] The increasing volume of this fabric available in the Mediterranean caused consternation among traditionalists. Seneca for one was horrified by the popularity of the thin flowing material, declaring that silk garments could barely be called clothing given they hid neither the curves nor the decency of the ladies of Rome. The very foundation of marital relations was being undermined, he said, as men found they could see through the light fabric that clung to the female form and left little to the imagination. For Seneca, silk was simply a cipher for exoticism and eroticism. A woman could not honestly say she was not naked when she was wearing silk.[82] Others felt the same, for repeated efforts were made to prohibit men from wearing the fabric, including edicts passed by law. Some put it simply: it was disgraceful, two leading citizens agreed, that Roman men should think it acceptable to sport silken clothing from the east.[83]

Others, though, were concerned about the prevalence of silk for different reasons. Writing in the second half of the first century AD, Pliny the Elder resented the high cost of the luxury material simply to "enable the Roman lady to shimmer in public."[84] The inflated prices were a scandal, he moaned, a hundred times the real cost.[85] Huge amounts of money were being spent annually, he continued, on luxuries "for us and our women" from Asia, with as much as 100 million sesterces per year being pumped out of the Roman economy and into trade markets beyond the frontier.[86]

This astonishing sum represented nearly half the annual mint output of the empire, and more than 10 per cent of its annual budget. But, remarkably, it does not appear to have been wildly exaggerated. A recently discovered papyrus contract recording the terms of a shipment of goods between Muziris in India and a Roman port on the Red Sea is testimony to how regular large-volume business had become by the second century AD. It sets out a series of mutual obligations, explaining clearly at what point the goods were to be considered in the hands of the owner or the shipper and outlining the sanctions if payment was not effected on the specific date.[87] Long-distance business required rigour and sophistication.

Roman merchants did not only pay with coins, however. They also traded finely worked glass, silver and gold, as well as coral and topaz from the Red Sea and frankincense from Arabia in exchange for textiles, spices and dyes like indigo.[88] Whatever form it took, the outflow of capital on this scale had far-reaching consequences. One was a strengthening of local economies along the trade routes. Villages turned into towns and towns turned into cities as business flourished and communication and commercial networks extended and became ever more connected. Increasingly impressive architectural monuments were erected in places like Palmyra, on the edge of the Syrian desert, which did well as a trading centre linking east with west. Not for nothing has Palmyra been called the Venice of the sands.[89] Cities on the north–south axis likewise were transformed, with the most dazzling example at Petra, which became one of the wonders of antiquity thanks to its position on the route between the cities of Arabia and the Mediterranean. Then there were fairs that drew in traders from hundreds, if not thousands, of miles away at convenient crossroad points. Every September at Batnae near the Euphrates "the town [was] filled with rich merchants as great crowds gather for the fair to buy and sell things sent from India and China, as well as all manner of other things which are also brought there by land and sea."[90]

Such was Rome's spending power that it even determined the design of coinage deep in eastern Asia. After being pushed from the Tarim basin by the Chinese, Yuezhi nomads had managed to secure a dominant position for themselves to the east of Persia, taking over domains that had been ruled by the descendants of Alexander's generals. In time, a thriving empire was born, named after one of the leading groupings within the tribe—the Guishang, or the Kushan—which took to minting large quantities of coins modelled on those of Rome.[91]

Roman currency poured into Kushan territory through ports in northern India, like Barbaricum and above all Barygaza, where the approach and anchorage were so treacherous that pilots were sent out to guide ships into port. Negotiating the approach to both ports was extremely dangerous for those who were inexperienced or were unfamiliar with the currents.[92] Once on land, traders could find pepper and spices as well as ivory and textiles, including both finished silks and silk yarn. It was an emporium that gathered goods from all over India, Central Asia and China—and delivered extraordinary wealth to the Kushan, who controlled the oasis towns and caravan routes that linked them.[93]

The dominant position that the Kushan were able to establish meant that, although goods were imported and exported from the Mediterranean into China in growing quantities, the Chinese themselves played little role in trade with Rome via the Indian Ocean. Only when the great general Ban Chao led a series of expeditions that took troops as far as the Caspian Sea at the end of the first century AD was an envoy dispatched to bring back more information about the "tall and regularly featured" population of the powerful empire in the west. Da Qin—or the Great Qin—as the Roman Empire was called, was reported to possess abundant supplies of gold, silver and fine jewels: it was a source of many marvellous and rare objects.[94]

China's dealings with Persia became regular and intensive. Embassies were sent several times a year, notes one Chinese source, with at least ten missions heading for Persia, and even in quieter periods some five or six being dispatched west.[95] Diplomatic envoys typically accompanied large caravans bringing goods for trading, which then returned home with products that were sought after at home—including Red Sea pearls, jade, lapis lazuli and consumables such as onions, cucumbers, coriander, pomegranates, pistachios and apricots.[96] Highly desirable frankincense and myrrh, which in fact came from Yemen and Ethiopia, were known in China as Possu—that is, Persian goods.[97] As we know from one later source, the peaches of Samarkand were considered immensely valuable: "as large as goose eggs" and with a famously rich colour to them, they were known in China as the "Golden Peaches."[98]

Just as the Chinese had few direct dealings with Rome, the Mediterranean region's knowledge of the world beyond the Himalayas and the Indian Ocean was limited, with a single Roman embassy attested as reaching the Emperor Huan around 166 AD. Rome's interest in and knowledge of the Far East was fleeting; its eyes were fixed firmly on Persia.[99] This was not just a rival and a competitor but a possible target in its own right. Even as control was still being established over Egypt, authors like Virgil and Propertius were talking excitedly of Roman influence being expanded. In a poem written to eulogise Augustus and his achievements, Horace wrote not of Roman domination of the Mediterranean, but of mastery of the entire world—including conquering the Indians and the Chinese.[100] Doing so involved moving against Persia, and this became a common preoccupation of a succession of rulers. Grandiose plans were developed to push the empire's frontier as far as the mountain pass known as the Caspian Gates deep inside Persian territory: Rome needed to control the heart of the world.[101]

In fact, efforts were made to turn these dreams into reality. In 113 the Emperor Trajan led an enormous expedition east in person. Advancing rapidly through the Caucasus before swinging south to follow the course of the Euphrates, he conquered Nisibis and Batnae, and minted coins which proclaimed that Mesopotamia had been "subjected to the power of the people of Rome." With resistance melting away, the Emperor pressed on, splitting his forces into two. The great cities of the Persian Empire were taken in quick succession, with Adenystrae, Babylon, Seleucia and Ctesiphon falling into Roman hands after a brilliant campaign that lasted a matter of months. Coins were immediately issued, struck with the uncompromising legend "PERSIA CAPTA"—Persia has been conquered.[102] Trajan then marched down to Charax, modern Basra, at the mouth of the Persian Gulf, arriving just as a merchant vessel set sail for India. He looked at the boat wistfully: if only he had been as young as Alexander the Great, he mused, he would have crossed to the Indus.[103]

With blueprints drawn up to establish new provinces of Assyria and Babylonia, Rome seemed poised to start a new chapter, one where the expansion of its frontiers would take it up to the Indus valley and as far as the gateway to China. But Trajan's success proved short-lived: a fierce fightback was already under way in the cities of Mesopotamia before the Emperor suffered a cerebral oedema that killed him, while a revolt began in Judaea and spread quickly, requiring urgent attention. Nevertheless, successive rulers kept their focus firmly pinned on Persia: it was here that military expenditure was concentrated, and where the frontier, and what lay beyond, was reported with intense interest in Rome.

In sharp contrast with the empire's European provinces, emperors campaigned regularly in Asia—although not always successfully. In 260 AD, for example, the Emperor Valerian was humiliated after being taken prisoner and held in "the abject form of slavery": used as a human footstool for the Persian ruler "by bending his back to raise the king as he was about to mount his horse," his body was eventually flayed "and his skin, stripped from the flesh, was dyed with vermilion, and placed in the temple of the gods of the barbarians, that the remembrance of a victory so signal might be perpetuated and that this spectacle might always be exhibited for our ambassadors."[104] He was stuffed so all could see the folly and shame of Rome.

Ironically, it was precisely the growth and ambition of Rome that helped galvanise Persia itself. For one thing, the latter benefited greatly from the long-distance traffic between east and west, which also served to effect a shift in Persia's political and economic centre of gravity away from the north. Previously, the priority had been to be located close to the steppes in order to negotiate with the nomad tribes for livestock and horses, and to supervise the diplomatic contacts necessary to avoid unwelcome attention and demands from the fearsome peoples on the steppes. This was why oasis towns like Nisa, Abivard and Dara had become important, home to magnificent royal palaces.[105]

With central coffers boosted from tax and transit fees drawn from growing local and long-distance trade, major infrastructure projects were now embarked on. These included the transformation of Ctesiphon on the eastern bank of the Tigris in central Mesopotamia into a worthy new capital city, and also heavy investment in ports such as Characene on the Gulf to handle increasing volumes of maritime traffic, not all of which was destined for Rome: a thriving trade had built up in glazed pottery from Persia heading to both India and Sri Lanka during the first and second centuries.[106]

But the most significant effect of Rome's military attention was that it prompted a political revolution. Faced with intense pressure from its neighbour, Persia underwent a major transformation. A new ruling dynasty, the Sasanians, emerged around 220 AD, offering a strident new vision, one which required the removal of authority from provincial governors, who had become independent in all but name, and the concentration of power at the centre. A series of administrative reforms saw a tightening of control over almost every aspect of the state: accountability was prioritised, with Persian officials issued with seals to record their decisions, to allow responsibility to be tracked and to ensure the accurate reporting of information. Many thousands of seals have survived to show just how far this reorganisation went.[107]

Merchants and markets found themselves being regulated, with one source recording how producers and traders—many arranged into guilds—were allocated specific areas in bazaars. This made it easier for inspectors to ensure that quality and quantity standards were met, and above all to collect tax duties efficiently.[108] The focus on the urban environment, the location for most commercial exchange, extended to improving water-supply systems which in some cases were extended for several miles to increase available resources and provide scope for further urban growth. Countless new towns were founded, with a later Persian text that draws on contemporary material attesting to a boom in urban development throughout Central Asia, the Iranian plateau, Mesopotamia and the Near East.[109]

Large-scale irrigation programmes in Khuzistan and Iraq were undertaken as part of a deliberate attempt to boost agricultural production, which must also have had the effect of bringing down food prices.[110] Archaeological finds show that packages were inspected prior to export, while textual material attests to copies of contracts being stamped and stored at registry offices.[111] The incorporation of towns and territories that had been subject to the Kushan for the best part of two centuries back into Persia proper also allowed for an intensification of trade with the east.[112]

As Persia soared, so Rome began to teeter. The Sasanians were not the only problem, for by 300 AD the full length of the empire's eastern border that ran from the North Sea to the Black, from the Caucasus through to the southern tip of Yemen, was under pressure. The empire had been built on expansion and was protected by a well-drilled military. As territorial growth tailed off—the result of reaching the natural boundaries of the Rhine and Danube and the Taurus and Anti-Taurus ranges in eastern Asia Minor—Rome became a classic victim of its own success: it was now itself a target for those living beyond its borders.

Desperate steps were taken to try to correct a worrying imbalance between dwindling tax revenues and the burgeoning costs of defending the frontiers—to inevitable outcry. One commentator lamented that the Emperor Diocletian, who tried to deal with the fiscal deficit aggressively, created problems rather than solving them, and "in his greed and anxiety, he turned the whole world upside down."[113] A root-and-branch review of the empire's assets was conducted, the prelude to the overhaul of the tax system. Officials were dispatched to all corners, with assessors turning up unannounced to count every single vine and every single fruit tree with the aim of raising imperial revenues.[114] An empire-wide edict was issued setting the prices for staple goods as well as for luxury imports like sesame seed, cumin, horseradish, cinnamon. A fragment of this order recently discovered in Bodrum shows how far the state was trying to reach: no fewer than twenty-six types of footwear from gilded women's sandals to "purple low-rise Babylonian-style" shoes had price ceilings set on them by Rome's tax inspectors.[115]

In the event, the strain of trying to re-establish the empire wore Diocletian out, and he retired to the coast of Croatia, to turn his attention to matters that were more enjoyable than affairs of state. "I wish you would come to Salona," he wrote to one of his former colleagues, "and see the cabbages I have planted myself"; they were so impressive, he went on, that "one could never be tempted by the prospect of power ever again."[116] Where Augustus had portrayed himself as a soldier in a famous and magnificent statue found at the Prima Porta on the outskirts of Rome, Diocletian preferred to present himself as a farmer. This summed up how Rome's ambitions had changed over the course of 300 years, from contemplating expansion to India to contemplating the cultivation of prize-winning vegetables.

As the Romans looked on nervously, a mighty storm cloud was gathering. It was the Emperor Constantine who took action. The son of one of the leading men in the empire, he was ambitious and capable, with a knack for finding himself in the right place at the right time. He had a vision of what was needed for Rome that was as clear as it was startling. The empire needed strong leadership—that much was obvious to everyone. But he had a more radical plan than simply concentrating power in his own hands: to build a new city, a new pearl on the string linking the Mediterranean with the east. The location he chose, fittingly, was the point where Europe and Asia meet.

There had long been rumours of rulers of Rome contemplating moving the seat of imperial power. According to one Roman author, Julius Caesar considered making either Alexandria or the site of ancient Troy in Asia Minor the capital as they were better located to govern where Rome's interests lay.[117] At the start of the fourth century, this finally happened, with a magnificent city established at the crossroads of Europe and Asia that was a statement of where the empire's focus was fixed.

A splendid new metropolis was built on the site of the old town of Byzantion, on the banks of the Bosporus, which in time came not only to rival Rome but to surpass it. Huge palaces were built, as was a Hippodrome for chariot racing. In the centre of the city an enormous column was set up, carved from a single massive porphyry block, with a statue of the Emperor on the top looking down. The new city was called New Rome, although it quickly came to be known as the city of its founder Constantine—Constantinople. Parallel institutions were set up to mirror those of the mother city, including a senate, whose members were sneered at by some as nouveaux riches—the sons of coppersmiths, bath attendants, sausage-makers and the like.[118]

Constantinople was to become the largest and most important city in the Mediterranean, far eclipsing its peers in size, influence and importance. Although many modern scholars strongly repudiate the idea that Constantine intended the city to be a new imperial capital, the lavish resources spent on its construction tell their own story.[119] Constantinople was situated in a commanding position for other sensitive routes, not least maritime traffic in and out of the Black Sea, and also as a listening point for developments to the east and also the north—in the Balkans and towards the plains of Pannonia, where trouble was brewing.

For the vast majority of the population in antiquity, horizons were decidedly local—with trade and interaction between people being carried out over short distances. Nevertheless, the webs of communities wove into each other to create a world that was complex, where tastes and ideas were shaped by products, artistic principles and influences thousands of miles apart.

Two millennia ago, silks made by hand in China were being worn by the rich and powerful in Carthage and other cities in the Mediterranean, while pottery manufactured in southern France could be found in England and in the Persian Gulf. Spices and condiments grown in India were being used in the kitchens of Xinjiang, as they were in those of Rome. Buildings in northern Afghanistan carried inscriptions in Greek, while horses from Central Asia were being ridden proudly thousands of miles away to the east.

We can imagine the life of a gold coin two millennia ago, struck perhaps in a provincial mint and used by a young soldier as part of his pay to buy goods on the northern frontier in England and finding its way back to Rome in the coffers of an imperial official sent to collect taxes, before passing into the hands of a trader heading east, and then being used to pay for produce bought from traders who had come to sell their provisions at Barygaza. There it was admired and presented to leaders in the Hindu Kush, who marvelled at its design, shape and size and then gave it over to be copied by an engraver—himself perhaps from Rome, perhaps from Persia, or from India or China, or perhaps even someone local who had been taught the skills of striking. This was a world that was connected, complex and hungry for exchange.

It is easy to mould the past into a shape that we find convenient and accessible. But the ancient world was much more sophisticated and interlinked than we sometimes like to think. Seeing Rome as the progenitor of western Europe overlooks the fact that it consistently looked to and in many ways was shaped by influences from the east. The world of antiquity was very much a precursor of the world as we see it today—vibrant, competitive, efficient and energetic. A belt of towns formed a chain spanning Asia. The west had begun to look east, and the east had begun to look west. Together with increasing traffic connecting India with the Persian Gulf and the Red Sea, the ancient Silk Roads of antiquity were coursing with life.

Rome's eyes had been fixed on Asia from the moment it transformed itself from a republic into an empire. And so too, it turned out, had its soul. For Constantine—and the Roman Empire—had found God; and the new faith was from the east too. Surprisingly, it came not from Persia or from India, but from an unpromising province where three centuries earlier Pontius Pilate had found infamy as governor. Christianity was about to fan out in all directions.

2

The Road of Faiths

It was not only goods that flowed along the arteries that linked the Pacific, Central Asia, India, the Persian Gulf and the Mediterranean in antiquity; so did ideas. And among the most powerful ideas were those that concerned the divine. Intellectual and religious exchange had always been animated across this region; now it became more complex and more competitive. Local cults and belief systems came into contact with well-established cosmologies. It made for a rich melting pot where ideas were borrowed, refined and repackaged.

After Alexander the Great's campaigns had dragged Greek ideas east, it was not long before ideas flowed in the other direction. Buddhist concepts made rapid headway across Asia, especially after they had been championed by the Emperor Ashoka, who purportedly converted to Buddhism after reflecting on the horrific cost of the military campaigns that had created a great empire in India in the third century BC. Inscriptions from this time bear testimony to the many people now following Buddhist principles and practices as far away as Syria and perhaps beyond. The beliefs of a sect known as the Therapeutai that flourished in Alexandria in Egypt for centuries bear unmistakable similarities to Buddhism, including the use of allegorical scriptures, the devotion to enlightenment through prayer and detachment from the sense of the self in order to find inner calm.[1]

The ambiguities of the source material make it difficult to trace the spread of Buddhism with accuracy. Nevertheless, it is striking that there is an extensive contemporary literature that describes how the religion was carried out of the Indian subcontinent and introduced to new regions. Local rulers had to decide whether to tolerate its appearance, to stamp it out or to adopt and support it. One who did the latter was Menander, a Bactrian king in the second century BC, and descendant of one of Alexander the Great's men. According to a text known as the *Milindapañhā*, the ruler was persuaded to follow a new spiritual path thanks to the intercession of an inspirational monk whose intelligence, compassion and humility stood in contrast to the superficiality of the contemporary world. It was enough, apparently, to convince the ruler to seek enlightenment through Buddhist teachings.[2]

The intellectual and theological spaces of the Silk Roads were crowded, as deities and cults, priests and local rulers jostled with each other. The stakes were high. This was a time when societies were highly receptive to explanations for everything from the mundane to the supernatural, and when faith offered solutions to a multitude of problems. The struggles between different faiths were highly political. In all these religions—whether they were Indic in origin like Hinduism, Jainism and Buddhism, or those with roots in Persia such as Zoroastrianism and Manichaeism, or those from further west such as Judaism and Christianity, and, in due course, Islam—triumph on the battlefield or at the negotiating table went hand in hand with demonstrating cultural supremacy and divine benediction. The equation was as simple as it was powerful: a society protected and favoured by the right god, or gods, thrived; those promising false idols and empty promises suffered.

There were strong incentives, therefore, for rulers to invest in the right spiritual infrastructure, such as the building of lavish places of worship. This offered a lever over internal control, allowing leaders to form a mutually strengthening relationship with the priesthood who, across all the principal religions, wielded substantial moral authority and political power. This did not mean that rulers were passive, responding to doctrines laid out by an independent class (or in some cases caste). On the contrary, determined rulers could reinforce their authority and dominance by introducing new religious practices.

The Kushan Empire, which stretched from northern India to embrace most of Central Asia in the first centuries AD, offers a case in point. There, the kings patronised Buddhism, but they also forced its evolution. It was important for a ruling dynasty that was not native to the region to create a justification for their pre-eminence. To do so, ideas were blended together from a range of sources to form a lowest common denominator that would appeal to as many as possible. As a result, the Kushans sponsored the building of temples—*devakula*, or "temples of the divine family"—which developed the concept that had already become established in this region, that rulers linked heaven and earth.[3]

Menander had earlier announced on his coinage that he was not only a temporal ruler but also a saviour—something so significant that it was noted in both Greek (*soteros*) and Indic script (*tratasa*) in bilingual legends on his coins.[4] The Kushans went further, establishing a leadership cult that claimed a direct relation to the divine, and created distance between ruler and subject. An inscription found at Taxila in the Punjab records this perfectly. The ruler, it states boldly, was "Great king, king of kings and Son of God."[5] It was a phrase that has obvious echoes with the Old and the New Testaments—as does the concept of the ruler being a saviour and a gateway into the next life.[6]

In what was tantamount to a revolution in Buddhism around the first century AD, a transformation took place in the way that that faith shaped the daily life of its adherents. In their most basic, traditional form, the teachings of the Buddha were straightforward, advocating finding a path from suffering (Sanskrit: *duḥkha*) that led to a state of peace (*nirvāna*), by means of following eight "noble paths." The route to enlightenment did not involve third parties, nor did it involve the material or physical world in any meaningful way. The journey was one that was spiritual, metaphysical and individual.

This was to change dramatically as new ways of reaching a higher state of consciousness emerged. What had been an intense internal journey, devoid of outside trappings and influences, was now supplemented by advice, help and locations designed to make the path to enlightenment and Buddhism itself more compelling. Stupas or shrines ostensibly linked to the Buddha were built, becoming points of pilgrimage, while texts setting out how to behave at such sites made the ideals behind Buddhism more real and more tangible. Bringing flowers or perfumes as an offering to a shrine would help achieve salvation, advised the *Saddharmapundarīka*, often known as the *Lotus Sutra*, that dates to this period. So too would hiring musicians to "beat drums, blow horns and conches, pan-pipes and flutes, play lutes and harps, gongs, guitars and cymbals": this would enable the devotee to attain "buddhahood."[7] These were deliberate efforts to make

Buddhism more visible—and audible—and to enable it to compete better in an increasingly noisy religious environment.

Another new idea was that of endowment—specifically endowments granted to new monasteries springing up across the routes fanning out from India into Central Asia. Donating money, jewels and other gifts became common practice, and with it the concept that donors would be "carried over the oceans of sufferings" as a reward for their generosity.[8] Indeed, the *Lotus Sutra* and other texts of this period went so far as to list which precious objects were most suitable as gifts; pearls, crystal, gold, silver, lapis lazuli, coral, diamonds and emeralds were all considered highly acceptable.[9]

Large-scale irrigation projects in the valleys of what are now Tajikistan and southern Uzbekistan built around the turn of the eras show that this period saw rising affluence and prosperity as well as increasingly vibrant cultural and commercial exchange.[10] With wealthy local elites to turn to, it was not long before monastic centres became hives of activity and home to scholars who busied themselves compiling Buddhist texts, copying them and translating them into local languages, thereby making them available for wider and larger audiences. This too was part of the programme to spread the religion by making it more accessible. Commerce opened the door for faith to flow through.[11]

Around the first century AD, the spread of Buddhism from northern India along the trade routes taken by merchants, monks and travellers accelerated rapidly. To the south, in the Deccan plateau, scores of cave temples were built, with stupas dotting the landscape deep into the Indian subcontinent.[12] To the north and east, Buddhism was transmitted with growing energy by the Sogdian merchants who played a vital role in linking China with the Indus valley. These were travelling merchants from the heart of Central Asia, classic middlemen whose own close-knit networks and efficient use of credit left them ideally positioned to dominate long-distance trade.[13]

The key to their commercial success was a dependable chain of stopping points. As more Sogdians became Buddhist, stupas were built alongside their principal routes, as can be seen in the Hunza valley of northern Pakistan: scores of passing Sogdians carved their names into rocks alongside images of the Buddha in hope that their long journeys would be fruitful and safe—poignant reminders of the traveller's need for spiritual comfort when far from home.[14]

It was not just small-scale scratchings that testify to the energetic spread of Buddhism in this period. Kabul was ringed with forty monasteries, including one that a later visitor described with awe. Its beauty was comparable to that of springtime, he wrote. "The pavement was made of onyx, the walls of pure marble; the door was made from moulded gold, while the floor was solid silver; stars were represented everywhere one looked . . . in the hallway, there was a golden idol as beautiful as the moon, seated on a magnificent bejewelled throne."[15]

Soon Buddhist ideas and practices were spreading east through the Pamir mountains and into China. By the start of the fourth century AD, there were sacred Buddhist sites all over Xinjiang province in north-western China—such as the spectacular complex of caves at Qyzyl in the Tarim basin that included halls for worship, places dedicated to meditation and extensive living quarters. Before long, western China was studded with places that were transformed into sacred spaces, at Kashgar, Kucha and Turfan for example.[16] By the 460s, Buddhist thought, practices, art and imagery had become part of the mainstream in China, robustly competing with traditional Confucianism, a broad cosmology that was as much about personal ethics as about spiritual beliefs, but which had deep roots going back a millennium. This was helped by aggressive promotion from a new ruling dynasty who, as conquerors originally from the steppes, were outsiders. As with the Kushan before them, the Northern Wei had much to gain by promoting the new at the expense of the old, and championing concepts that underlined their legitimacy. Huge statues of the Buddha were erected at Pincheng and Luoyang, far into the east of the country, together with lavishly endowed monasteries and shrines. There was no mistaking the message: the Northern Wei had triumphed and they had done so because they were part of a divine cycle, not merely brute victors on the battlefield.[17]

Buddhism made sizeable inroads along the principal trading arteries to the west too. Clusters of caves dotted around the Persian Gulf, as well as large numbers of finds around Merv in modern Turkmenistan, and series of inscriptions deep inside Persia, attest to Buddhism's ability to start competing with local beliefs.[18] The rash of Buddhist loan-words in Parthian also bears witness to the intensification of the exchange of ideas in this period.[19]

The difference, however, was that the deepening of commercial exchange galvanised Persia in another direction as it experienced a renaissance that swept through the economy, politics and culture. As a distinctively Persian identity reasserted itself, Buddhists found themselves being persecuted rather than emulated. The ferocity of the attacks led to the shrines in the Gulf being abandoned, and the stupas that had presumably been set up along the land routes within Persian territory being destroyed.[20]

Religions rose and fell as they spread across Eurasia, fighting each other for audiences, loyalty and moral authority. Communication with the divine was more than a matter of seeking intervention in daily life: it became a matter of salvation or damnation. The jostling became violent. The first four centuries of the first millennium, which saw Christianity explode from a small base in Palestine to sweep through the Mediterranean and across Asia, were a maelstrom of faith wars.

The decisive moment came with the seizure of power by the Sasanian dynasty, who overthrew the ruling regime in Persia by fomenting revolt, murdering rivals and exploiting the confusion that followed military setbacks on the frontier with Rome—above all in the Caucasus.[21] After taking power in 224 AD, Ardashīr I and his successors embarked on the full-scale transformation of the state. It involved the assertion of a strident identity that drew a line under recent history and sought to accentuate links with the great Persian Empire of antiquity.[22]

This was achieved by fusing the contemporary physical and symbolic landscape with that of the past. Key sites in ancient Iran, such as Persepolis, a capital of the Achaemenid Empire, and the necropolis Naksh-i Rustām, associated with the great Persian kings like Darius and Cyrus, were appropriated for cultural propaganda; new inscriptions, monumental architecture and rock relief carvings were added which sought to elide the present regime with glorious memories of the past.[23] The coinage was overhauled: the Greek script and busts styled on Alexander the Great that had been in use for centuries were replaced by a new and distinctive royal profile on one side—facing the opposite direction—and a fire altar on the other.[24] The latter was deliberately provocative, a statement of intent about a new identity and a new attitude to religion. So far as the limited source material for the period allows us to understand, rulers of this region had for centuries shown tolerance on matters of faith, allowing a considerable degree of coexistence.[25]

The rise of a new dynasty soon brought about a stiffening of attitudes, and the teachings of Zardusht (or Zarathushtra) were unambiguously promoted at the expense of other ideas. Known to the ancient Greeks as

Zoroaster—the great Persian prophet who lived around 1000 BC if not earlier still—he taught that the universe was divided according to two principles, Ahura Mazda (Illuminating Wisdom) and its antithesis, Angra Mainyu (Hostile Spirit), which were in a constant state of conflict. It was important, therefore, to worship the former, which was responsible for good order. The division of the world into beneficent and malevolent forces extended into every aspect of life and even affected areas such as the categorisation of animals.[26] Ritual purification was a vital element of Zoroastrian worship, above all through fire. Ahura Mazda, as the creed set out, could bring "goodness from evil, light from darkness" and salvation from demons.[27]

This cosmology allowed the Sasanian rulers the opportunity to link their power with that of the golden days of ancient Persia when the great kings professed their devotion to Ahura Mazda.[28] But it also provided a powerful moral framework for a period of military and economic expansion: the emphasis on constant struggle strengthened minds for battle, while the focus on order and discipline underscored administrative reforms that became the signature of an increasingly strident, resurgent state. Zoroastrianism had a robust set of beliefs that were entirely in line with a militaristic culture of imperial renewal.[29]

The Sasanians expanded aggressively under Ardashīr I and his son Shāpūr I, bringing oasis towns, communication routes and whole regions under direct control, or forcing them into client status. Important towns such as Sistan, Merv and Balkh were taken in a series of campaigns that began in the 220s, while a significant part of the Kushan territories became vassal states, administered by Sasanian officials who took the title *kushānshāh* (ruler of the Kushans).[30] A triumphant inscription at Naksh-i Rustām sets out the scale of the achievement, noting how Shāpūr's realm had extended deep into the east, running as far as Peshawar and "up to the boundaries" of Kashgar and Tashkent.[31]

Adherents of Zoroastrianism positioned themselves close to the centre of power when the Sasanians took the throne and did much to concentrate administrative control in their hands at the expense of all other religious minorities.[32] This was now projected into the new regions controlled by the Persian rulers. Inscriptions commissioned by the chief priest, Kirdīr, in the middle of the third century AD celebrated the expansion of Zoroastrianism. The religion and its priests had come to be esteemed and honoured far and wide, while "many fires and priestly colleges" had flourished in lands that had been conquered from the Romans. A great deal of hard work was required to spread the faith, the inscription pointedly remarks, but as Kirdīr modestly put it, "I underwent much toil and trouble for the good of the *yazads* [divine powers] and the rulers, and for the good of my own soul."[33]

The promotion of Zoroastrianism was accompanied by the suppression of local cults and rival cosmologies, which were dismissed as evil doctrines. Jews, Buddhists, Hindus, Manichaeans and others were persecuted; places of worship were ransacked, with "idols destroyed, the sanctuaries of demons demolished and transformed into temples for the gods."[34] The expansion of the Persian state was accompanied by a stern enforcement of values and beliefs that were presented as both traditional and essential for political and military success. Those who offered different explanations or competing values were hunted down and in many cases killed—such as Mani, a charismatic third-century prophet whose blend of ideas, drawing on a pot-pourri of sources from east and west, had once been championed by Shāpūr I; his teachings were now condemned as subversive, intoxicating and dangerous and his followers were mercilessly hunted down.[35]

Among those singled out for harsh treatment, and explicitly mentioned by Kirdīr in his list of those targeted, were *nasraye* and *kristyone*—that is to say "Nazarenes" and "Christians." While there has been much scholarly debate about which groups are meant by these two terms, it is now accepted that the former refers to the native population of the Sasanian Empire who had become Christian, while the latter refers to the Christians who were deported east in large numbers by Shāpūr I following the occupation of Roman Syria that took local and central authorities by surprise.[36] One of the reasons why Zoroastrianism became so embedded in the consciousness and identity of third-century Persia was as a reaction to the inroads being made by Christianity, which had started to spread alarmingly along the trade routes—just as Buddhism had done in the east. The dramatic radicalisation of Zoroastrian philosophy precisely around this time was accelerated by a hostile reaction to the Christian thought and ideas brought by merchants and by prisoners resettled in Persian territory after being deported from Syria.[37]

Christianity has long been associated with the Mediterranean and western Europe. In part, this has been due to the location of the leadership of the church, with the senior figures of the Catholic, Anglican and Orthodox churches based in Rome, Canterbury and Constantinople (modern Istan-

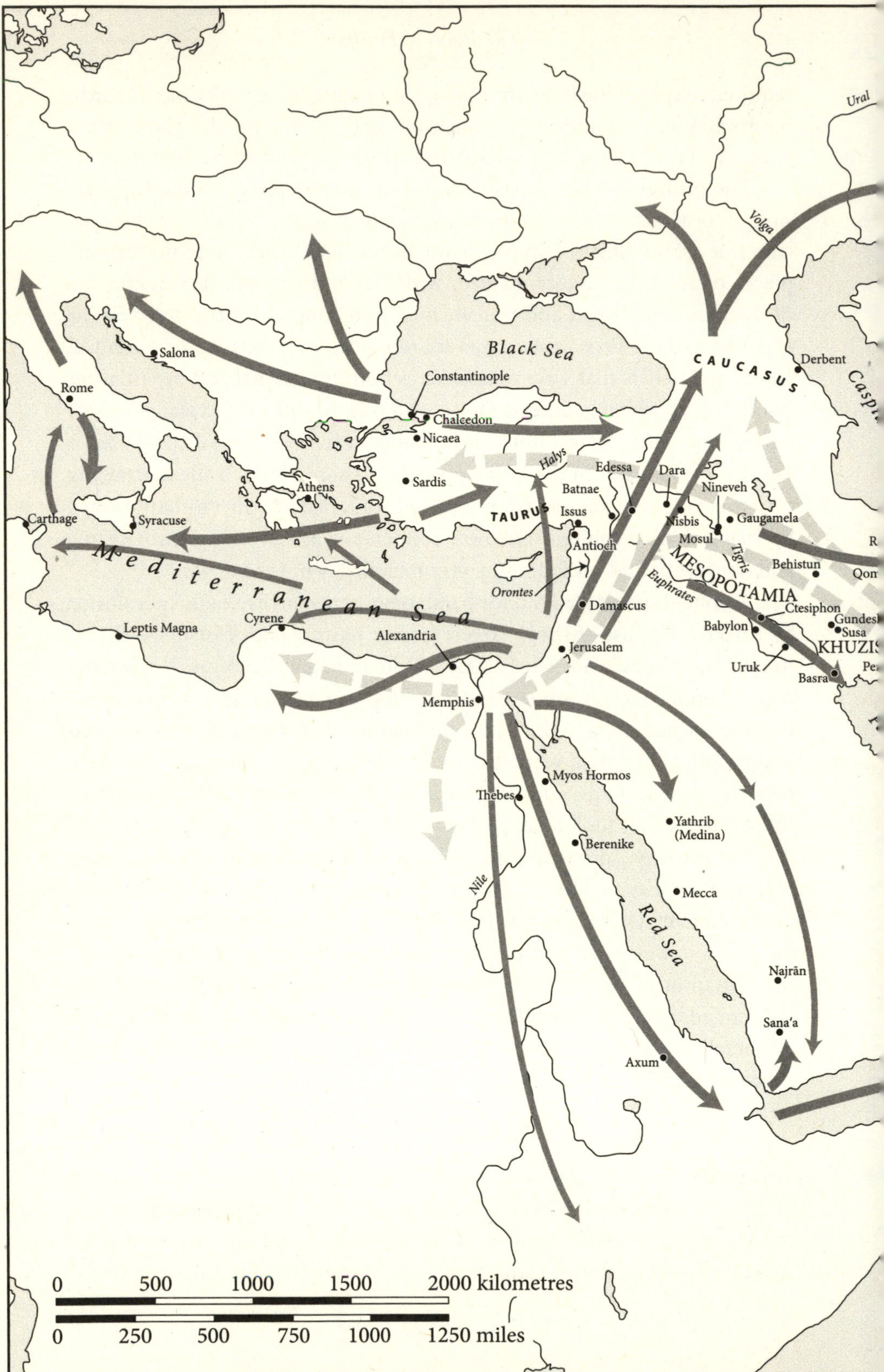

Ural
Volga
Black Sea
CAUCASUS
Derbent
Caspi
Salona
Rome
Constantinople
Chalcedon
Nicaea
Halys
Edessa
Dara
Nineveh
Sardis
Batnae
Athens
TAURUS
Issus
Nisbis
Gaugamela
Carthage
Syracuse
Mosul
Antioch
Tigris
Mediterranean Sea
MESOPOTAMIA
Behistun
Qom
Euphrates
Orontes
Damascus
Ctesiphon
Gundes
Susa
Leptis Magna
Cyrene
Babylon
Alexandria
Jerusalem
KHUZIS
Uruk
Basra
Memphis
Myos Hormos
Thebes
Yathrib
(Medina)
Berenike
Nile
Mecca
Red Sea
Najrān
Sana'a
Axum
0
500
1000
1500
2000 kilometres
0
250
500
750
1000
1250 miles

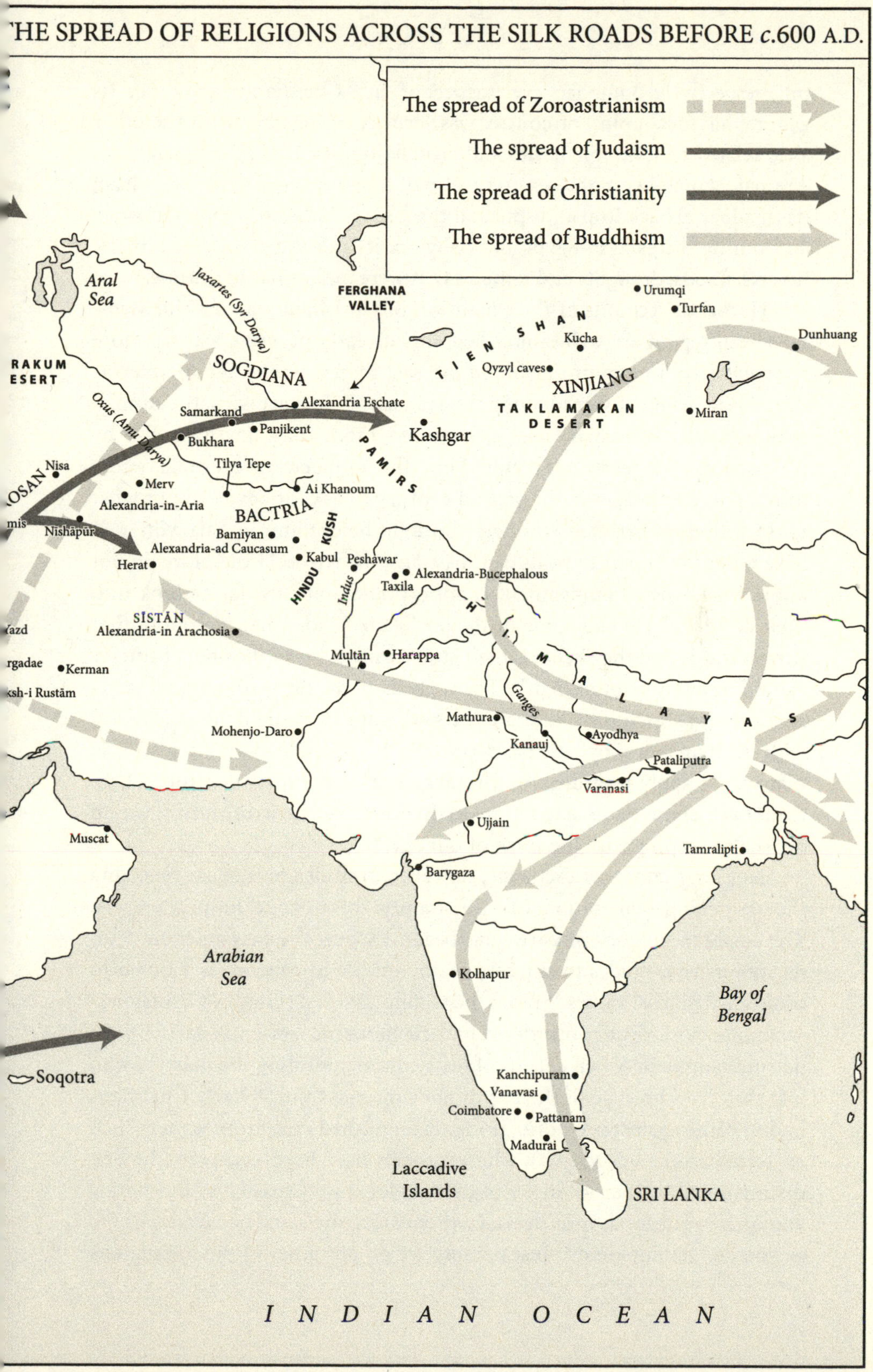
THE SPREAD OF RELIGIONS ACROSS THE SILK ROADS BEFORE c.600 A.D.
The spread of Zoroastrianism
The spread of Judaism
The spread of Christianity
The spread of Buddhism
Aral Sea
Jaxartes (Syr Darya)
FERGHANA VALLEY
RAKUM ESERT
SOGDIANA
Oxus (Amu Darya)
Alexandria Eschate
Samarkand
Panjikent
Bukhara
Kashgar
PAMIRS
Nisa
Tilya Tepe
Merv
Ai Khanoum
Alexandria-in-Aria
BACTRIA
Nishāpūr
Bamiyan
Alexandria-ad Caucasum
Kabul
HINDU KUSH
Herat
Peshawar
Indus
Taxila
Alexandria-Bucephalous
SĪSTĀN
Alexandria-in Arachosia
Yazd
Kerman
Multān
Harappa
Mohenjo-Daro
TIEN SHAN
Urumqi
Turfan
Kucha
Qyzyl caves
Dunhuang
XINJIANG
TAKLAMAKAN DESERT
Miran
HIMALAYAS
Ganges
Mathura
Kanauj
Ayodhya
Pataliputra
Varanasi
Ujjain
Tamralipti
Barygaza
Muscat
Arabian Sea
Kolhapur
Bay of Bengal
Soqotra
Kanchipuram
Vanavasi
Coimbatore
Pattanam
Madurai
Laccadive Islands
SRI LANKA
INDIAN OCEAN

bul) respectively. But in fact every aspect of early Christianity was Asian. Its geographic focal point, of course, was Jerusalem, together with the other sites related to Jesus' birth, life and crucifixion; its original language was Aramaic, a member of the Semitic group of tongues native to the Near East; its theological backdrop and spiritual canvas was Judaism, formed in Israel and during the exile in Egypt and Babylon; its stories were shaped by the deserts, floods, droughts and famines that were unfamiliar in Europe.[38]

Historical accounts of the expansion of Christianity across the Mediterranean region are well established, but its early progress was far more spectacular and more promising in the east than it was in the Mediterranean basin, where it spread along the sea lanes.[39] To start with, the Roman authorities left Christians alone, bemused more than anything else by the passion of its early adherents. Pliny the Younger, for example, wrote to the Emperor Trajan in the second century to ask for advice about what to do with the Christians who were brought before him in Asia Minor. "I have never taken part in trials of Christians," he wrote. "I therefore do not know what type of punishment is appropriate, nor how far to look into their activities." He had some of them executed, "for I had no doubt that whatever it is that they believe, their stubbornness and inflexible obstinacy should certainly be punished."[40] The reply from the Emperor advised tolerance: do not search for Christians, he said, but if they are denounced, deal with them on a case-by-case basis, "for it is not possible to set out a set rule that would apply regardless of circumstance." But on no account act on rumour or anonymous accusation; to do otherwise, he wrote loftily, would be "out of keeping with the spirit of our age."[41]

Not long after this exchange, however, attitudes hardened, reflecting the deepening penetration of Christianity throughout Roman society. The imperial military in particular began to view the new religion, with its subversive attitudes to sin, sex, death and life in general, as a threat to traditional martial values.[42] From the second century, rounds of brutal persecution saw Christians murdered in their thousands, often as part of public entertainment. A rich corpus of texts commemorating the martyrs who lost their lives because of their faith grew up as a result.[43] Early Christians had to battle against prejudice, bringing anguished cries from writers such as Tertullian (*c.* 160–225 AD), whose appeals have been compared by one distinguished scholar to Shakespeare's Shylock: we Christians "live beside you, share your food, your dress, your customs, the same necessities of life as you do," he implored.[44] Just because we do not attend Roman religious ceremonies, he wrote, does not mean that we are not human beings. "Have we different teeth, or organs of incestuous lust?"[45]

Christianity first spread east via the Jewish communities who had lived in Mesopotamia since the Babylonian exile.[46] They received reports of Jesus' life and death not in Greek translations, as almost all converts did in the west, but in Aramaic, the language of the disciples and of Jesus himself. Just as in the Mediterranean, traders were instrumental in the evangelising process in the east—with the town of Edessa, modern Urfa in south-eastern Turkey, becoming particularly prominent because of its position as a crossroads for routes running north–south and east–west.[47]

Evangelists soon reached the Caucasus, where burial practices and inscriptions in Georgia reveal the existence of a substantial population of Jews who converted.[48] Not long afterwards, there were Christian communities dotted around the Persian Gulf. Sixty tombs close to Bahrain cut into coral banks show how far the religion had reached by the start of the third century.[49] A text known as *The Book of the Laws of the Countries*, written around the same time, reports that Christians were to be found all over Persia and as far east as territory controlled by the Kushans—in other words, into what is now Afghanistan.[50]

The dissemination of the religion was encouraged by the large-scale deportations of Christians from Persia during Shāpūr I's reign in the third century. Among the exiles were high-profile figures such as Demetrius, the bishop of Antioch, who was transported to Beth Lapat, modern Gundeshāpūr in south-west Iran, where he assembled his fellow Christians around him and established a new bishopric.[51] There were some Christians of high status in Persia, such as a Roman named Candida who was a favoured concubine at the court until her refusal to abandon her faith led to her martyrdom, according to a Christian account warning of the bloodthirstiness of the Shah and those around him.[52]

These stirring stories fall into a category of literature seeking to establish the superiority of Christian customs and beliefs over traditional practices. Sources are scant, but we can get a sense of the propaganda battles being fought at the time. Unlike the other inhabitants of Persia, wrote one author, the "disciples of Christ" in Asia "do not practise the condemnable habits of these pagan peoples." This was to be welcomed, noted another writer, as a sign of how Christians improved standards in Persia and elsewhere in the east; "Persians who have become His disciples no longer marry their mothers," while those on the steppes no longer "feed on human flesh, because of Christ's word which has come to them." Such developments ought to be warmly welcomed, he wrote.[53]

It was the growing penetration and visibility of Christians in Persia in the middle of the third century that caused the Zoroastrian priesthood to react with increasing violence, echoing the response in the Roman Empire.[54] But as Kirdīr's inscription testifies, attitudes in Persia were starting to harden not just to Christianity but to other faiths too. Stamping out alternative cosmologies went hand in hand with the fervent Zoroastrianism that characterised the resurgence of Persia. A state religion was starting to emerge, one that identified Zoroastrian values as synonymous with Persian and provided what has been called "a supporting pillar of Sasanian kingship."[55]

A series of chain reactions had been set in motion, whereby competition for resources and military confrontation prompted the development of sophisticated belief systems that not only made sense of victories and success, but directly undermined those of neighbouring rivals. In the case of Persia, this meant an increasingly strident and self-confident priesthood whose role extended deep into the sphere of politics—as the inscriptions make clear.

This inevitably had consequences, especially when it was exported into border regions or newly conquered territories. Setting up the fire temples of which Kirdīr was so proud not only risked antagonising local populations but also enforced doctrine and faith by force. Zoroastrianism became synonymous with Persia. It did not take much for this religion to be seen as a tool of occupation rather than a form of spiritual liberation. It was no coincidence, then, that some began to look to Christianity precisely as an antidote to the heavy-handed promotion of beliefs from the Persian centre.

The precise circumstances of how and when rulers in the Caucasus adopted Christianity are not entirely clear. Accounts of the conversion of the Armenian King Tiridates III at the start of the fourth century were written some time later—and owe something to the desire to tell a good story as well as to the Christian bias of their authors.[56] But, according to tradition, Tiridates converted after turning into a pig and roaming naked in fields before being healed by St. Gregory, who had been thrown into a snake-infested pit for refusing to worship an Armenian goddess. Gregory healed Tiridates by causing his snout, tusks and skin to fall off before baptising the grateful monarch in the Euphrates.[57]

Tiridates was not the only important political figure to embrace Christianity in this period, for in the early fourth century Constantine, one of the most influential figures in Rome, also converted. The decisive moment came during a tempestuous civil war when Constantine took on his rival Maxentius at Milvian Bridge in central Italy in 312 AD. Shortly before the battle, the former supposedly gazed into the sky and saw "a cross-shaped light" above the sun, together with Greek words declaring "by this sign, you will conquer." The full meaning of this became clear to him after he had a dream in which an apparition of Jesus Christ explained to him that the sign of the cross would help him defeat all his rivals. This, at any rate, was how some liked to describe what had happened.[58]

Christian accounts leave little doubt about the limitless enthusiasm with which the Emperor personally oversaw the enforcement of Christianity at the expense of all other religions. We learn from one author, for example, that the new city of Constantinople was not "polluted by altars, Grecian temples or pagan sacrifices," but enriched by "splendid houses of prayer in which God promised to bless the efforts of the Emperor."[59] Another writer states that famous centres for cults were shut down by the Emperor, while oracles and divination, staple features of Roman theology, were banned. The customary sacrifice made before official business could take place was likewise outlawed, while pagan statues were pulled down and legislated against.[60] There was little room for equivocation in the story told by authors with vested interests to show Constantine as single-minded promoter of his new beliefs.

In fact, Constantine's motivations for conversion were certainly more complex than the accounts written during his lifetime or shortly afterwards like to suggest. For one thing, taking on the Christian faith adopted by large numbers in the military was shrewd politics; for another, monuments, coins and inscriptions from around the empire which depict Constantine as a staunch supporter of the cult of the Undefeated Sun (or Sol Invictus) suggest that his epiphany was perhaps more tentative than the breathless eulogies make out. Moreover, despite assertions to the contrary, the empire did not change character overnight, for leading figures in Rome, Constantinople and elsewhere continued following their traditional beliefs long after the Emperor's revelation and the enthusiastic way he set about supporting his new faith.[61]

Nevertheless, Constantine's acceptance of Christianity clearly brought about a sea change in the Roman Empire. The persecutions that had peaked during the reign of Diocletian just a decade or so earlier came to an end.

Gladiator fights, long the staple of Roman entertainment, were abolished as a result of Christian revulsion at displays that so devalued the sanctity of life. "Bloody spectacles displease us," reads an extract of a law passed in 325 and recorded in a later compilation of imperial legislation. "We [therefore] wholly forbid the existence of gladiators." Those who had previously been sent into the arena as punishment for crimes they had committed or beliefs they refused to abandon were henceforth to be sent to "serve in the mines, so that they will assume the penalty for their crimes without shedding their blood."[62]

As resources were lavished on supporting Christianity across the empire, Jerusalem was singled out for massive building works, complete with extravagant endowments. If Rome and Constantinople were administrative centres of the empire, Jerusalem was to be its spiritual heart. Parts of the city were flattened and soil dug out from beneath pagan temples was dumped as far away as possible, "stained as it was by devil worship." Excavations now revealed one holy place after another, including the cave where Jesus had been laid to rest, which was renovated and, "like our Saviour, restored to life."[63]

Constantine took charge of these works himself, directing what materials should be used in the construction of a church on the site of the Holy Sepulchre. The Emperor had been willing to delegate the choice of fabrics and the adornment of the walls to an appointee, but he wanted to be involved in the type of marble to be used, and in the selection of columns. "I should like to know your opinion," he wrote to Macarius, the bishop of Jerusalem, "whether the ceiling should be panelled or decorated in another style of some kind. If it is panelled, it might also be decorated with gold." Such choices, he went on, required his personal approval.[64]

Constantine's celebrated conversion marked the start of a new chapter in the history of the Roman Empire. Although Christianity was not made a state religion, the easing of restrictions and punishments opened the floodgates for the new faith. This was good news for Christians and Christianity in the west, but it led to disaster for Christianity in the east. Although to start with Constantine was a tactful convert, issuing coins bearing distinctly pagan images and erecting a statue of himself as Helios-Apollo in his new city, he soon became more strident.[65] Before long, he was portraying himself as the protector of Christians wherever they were—including outside the Roman Empire.

In the 330s, rumour spread that Constantine was preparing an attack on

Persia, exploiting an opening presented by a disaffected brother of the Shah who had sought sanctuary at the Roman imperial court. Persian nerves must have jangled when a letter was received from Constantine announcing that he was delighted to have learnt that "the finest provinces of Persia are filled with those men on whose behalf alone I am at present speaking; I mean the Christians." He had a specific message for the Persian ruler Shāpūr II: "I commend these persons to you for your protection . . . cherish them with your customary humanity and kindness; for by this proof of faith you will secure an immeasurable benefit both to yourself and us."[66] This might have been meant as gentle advice, but it sounded like a threat: not long beforehand, Rome had rolled its eastern frontier deep into Persian territory, and immediately set about a programme of fortification and road-building to secure these gains.[67]

When the ruler of Georgia, another Caucasian kingdom of commercial and strategic value, experienced an epiphany that was only marginally less colourful than Constantine's (the king literally saw the light after being engulfed by darkness while hunting), anxiety turned to panic.[68] With Constantine absent on the Danube frontier, Shāpūr II launched a surprise attack into the Caucasus, deposing one of the local rulers and installing his own nominee in his place. Constantine responded immediately and dramatically: he assembled an enormous army and, ordering his bishops to accompany the forthcoming expedition, arranged for a replica to be made of the Tabernacle, the structure used to house the Ark of the Covenant. He then announced that he wished to undertake a punitive attack on Persia and be baptised in the River Jordan.[69]

The scale of Constantine's ambition knew no bounds. He minted coins in advance, giving his half-nephew a new royal title: ruler of Persia.[70] Excitement spread quickly among Christians in the east, captured in a letter written by Aphrahat, head of an important monastery near Mosul: "Goodness has come to the people of God." This was the moment that he had been waiting for: Christ's kingdom on earth was about to be established once and for all. "Be certain," he concluded, "the beast will be killed at its preordained time."[71]

As the Persians prepared to mount fierce resistance, they had a huge stroke of luck: before the expedition could get going, Constantine fell ill and died. Shāpūr II proceeded to unleash hell on the local Christian population in Persia as a reprisal for Constantine's aggression. Egged on by the Zoroastrian authorities, the Shah "thirsted for the blood of the saints."[72]

Martyrs were made by the dozen: one manuscript from Edessa at the start of the fifth century records the execution of no fewer than sixteen bishops as well as fifty priests in this period.[73] Christians were now regarded as an advance guard, a fifth column that would open Persia to the Roman Empire in the west. Leading bishops were accused of making the Shah's "followers and people rebel against [his] Majesty and become slaves of the emperor who shares their faith."[74]

This bloodbath was a direct result of the enthusiastic adoption of Christianity in Rome. The persecutions unleashed by the Shah stemmed from the fact that Constantine had elided the promotion of the Roman Empire with that of Christianity. The Emperor's grand statements may have impressed and inspired men like Aphrahat, but they were immensely challenging for the leadership in Persia. Roman identity had been clear-cut before Constantine's conversion. But now the Emperor—and his successors—was willing to talk of protecting not only Rome and its citizens, but Christians in general too. It was a convenient ace to play, not least at home where the rhetoric was bound to go down well with bishops and the faithful. For those living beyond the empire's borders, however, it was potentially disastrous—as Shāpūr's victims found.

It is ironic, therefore, that while Constantine is famous for being the Emperor who laid the basis for the Christianisation of Europe, it is never noted that there was a price to pay for his embrace of a new faith: it spectacularly compromised Christianity's future in the east. The question was whether the teachings of Jesus Christ that had taken hold deep in Asia would be able to survive a determined challenge.

3

The Road to a Christian East

In due course, tensions between Rome and Persia abated, and as they did so, attitudes to religion softened. This came about because Rome was forced into retreat so firmly in the fourth century that it found itself fighting for its very life. In a series of campaigns that lasted until Shāpūr II's death in 379, Persia succeeded in taking key nodes along the trade and communication routes running towards the Mediterranean. Nisibis and Sinagra were recovered, and half of Armenia was annexed. Although this territorial rebalancing helped calm animosities, relations really improved when both Rome and Persia were faced with new challenges: disaster was looming from the steppes.

The world was entering a period of environmental change. In Europe, this was evidenced by rising sea levels and the emergence of malaria in the North Sea region, while in Asia from the start of the fourth century sharply reduced salinity in the Aral Sea, markedly different vegetation on the steppes (evident from high-resolution pollen analyses) and new patterns of glacier advances in the Tian Shan range all show fundamental shifts in global climatic change.[1]

The results were devastating, attested by a remarkable letter written by a Sogdian trader in the early fourth century and found not far from Dunhuang in western China. The merchant recounted to his fellow traders that food shortages and famine had taken a heavy toll, that such catastrophe had befallen China as to be barely describable. The Emperor had fled from the capital, setting fire to his palace as he left, while the Sogdian merchant communities were gone, wiped out by starvation and death. Do not bother trying to trade there, the author advised: "there is no profit for you to gain from it." He told of city after city being sacked. The situation was apocalyptic.[2]

The chaos created the perfect conditions for the mosaic of steppes tribes to consolidate. These peoples inhabited the belts of land linking Mongolia with the plains of central Europe, where control of the best grazing land and of reliable water supply guaranteed considerable political power. One tribe now established themselves as masters on the steppes, crushing all before them. The Sogdian trader referred to the architects of apocalypse in his letter as the *xwn*. They were the Xiongnu—better known in the west as the Huns.[3]

Between about 350 and 360 there was a huge wave of migration as tribes were shunted off their lands and driven westwards. This was most likely caused by climate change, which made life on the steppe exceptionally harsh and triggered intense competition for resources. The impact was felt from Bactria in northern Afghanistan right up to the Roman frontier on the Danube, where refugees began to appear in large numbers, begging to be allowed to resettle on imperial territory after being driven off their lands north of the Black Sea by the advancing Huns. The situation quickly became dangerously unstable. A massive Roman army sent to restore order was heavily defeated on the flat plains of Thrace in 378, with the Emperor Valens among the many casualties.[4] The defences burst open, and tribe after tribe poured through into the empire's western provinces, threatening Rome as a result. Previously, the northern lip of the Black Sea and the steppe lands stretching deep into Asia had been regarded as implacably barbarous, filled with fierce warriors and empty of civilisation or resources. It had not crossed Rome's mind that these regions could act as arteries, just like the routes linking the west with the east through Persia and through Egypt. These very regions were now about to deliver death and destruction into the very heart of Europe.

Persia was also quaking in the face of cataclysm from the steppes. Its provinces in the east buckled under the onslaught, before collapsing altogether: towns were depopulated; crucial irrigation networks fell into disrepair and broke down as raids took their toll.[5] Attacks through the Caucasus were overwhelming, and resulted in prisoners and booty being seized from the cities of Mesopotamia, Syria and Asia Minor. Then in 395 a major long-range attack devastated the cities of the Tigris and Euphrates, reaching as far as Ctesiphon, the capital, before finally being driven back.[6]

United by a common interest in repelling the barbarian hordes, Persia and Rome now formed a remarkable alliance. To keep the nomads from descending through the Caucasus, a massive fortified wall was constructed, running for nearly 125 miles between the Caspian and Black Seas, protecting the Persian interior from attack and serving as a physical barrier between the ordered world to the south and the chaos to the north. Studded with thirty forts evenly spaced along its length, the wall was also protected by a canal fifteen feet deep. It was a marvel of architectural planning and engineering, built with standardised bricks made in scores of kilns installed on site. The fortification was manned by some 30,000 troops, housed in garrisons that were set back from the wall itself.[7] The barrier was just one of several innovative steps taken by the Sasanians to defend Persia's long northern frontier with the steppe, and to protect vulnerable trading posts such as Merv, which was the first location that would be encountered by attackers coming through the Karakum desert (in what is now Turkmenistan).[8]

Rome not only agreed to make regular financial contributions to the maintenance of this Persian wall, but also, according to several contemporary sources, supplied soldiers to help defend it.[9] In a sign of how past rivalries had been set to one side, in 402 the Emperor Honorius in Constantinople appointed none other than the Shah to act as guardian to his son and heir.[10]

But by that time it was too late—as far as Rome was concerned. Displacement across the steppes north of the Black Sea had created a perfect storm that led to the empire's frontiers on the Rhine being overwhelmed. A series of raids in the late fourth century cleaved Rome's western provinces wide open, with tribal leaders gaining personal kudos from military successes as well as material gains that drew in more followers and gave fresh momentum to further attacks. As the imperial army struggled to make a stand against the attacking hordes, one wave after another crashed through the empire's defences, leading to the devastation of the province of Gaul. Things went from bad to worse when Alaric, a particularly effective and ambitious leader, marched his tribe of Visigoths down through Italy and camped outside Rome to bully the city into buying him off. As the Senate desperately tried to do so, he grew tired of being stalled, and in 410 stormed and sacked the city.[11]

Shock resonated across the Mediterranean. In Jerusalem, the news was met with disbelief. "The speaker's voice failed, and sobs interrupted his speech," wrote St. Jerome, "the city that had conquered the whole world had itself been conquered . . . who could believe it? Who could believe that Rome, built up through the ages by the conquest of the world, had fallen, that the mother of nations had become their tomb?"[12] At least the city was not torched, wrote the historian Jordanes with the weary resignation of a century's hindsight.[13]

Burning or not, Rome's empire in the west now fell apart. Soon Spain was being ravaged, attacked by tribes such as the Alans, whose homelands lay far away between the Caspian and Black Seas, and whose trade in sable skins had first been carefully charted by commentators writing in China nearly two centuries earlier.[14] Another tribal grouping, the Vandals, who had been displaced by the Huns, reached Roman North Africa by the 420s, taking control of the principal city, Carthage, as well as the vibrant and lucrative surrounding provinces that supplied most of the western half of the empire with corn.[15]

As if this were not bad enough, in the middle of the fifth century, having flushed forward a hotch-potch of tribes—Terevingian Goths, Alans, Vandals, Suevi, Gepids, Neurians, Bastarnians and others besides—the Huns themselves appeared in Europe, led by the most famous figure of late antiquity: Attila.[16] The Huns caused pure terror. They are "the seedbed of evil," wrote one Roman writer, and "exceedingly savage." Trained from youth to cope with extreme cold, hunger and thirst, they dressed in the skins of field mice that were stitched together; they would eat roots and raw flesh—which would be partially warmed by being placed between their thighs.[17] They had no interest in agriculture, noted another, and only wanted to steal from their neighbours, enslaving them in the process: they were like wolves.[18] The Huns scarred the cheeks of infant boys when they were born in order to prevent facial hair growing later in life, while they spent so long on horseback that their bodies were grotesquely deformed; they looked like animals standing on their hind legs.[19]

Although it is tempting to dismiss such comments as signs of bigotry, examinations of skeletal remains show that the Huns practised artificial cranial deformation on their young, bandaging the skull to flatten the frontal and occipital bones by applying pressure to them. This caused the head to grow in a distinctly pointed manner. It was not just the behaviour of the Huns that was terrifyingly out of the ordinary; so was the way they looked.[20]

The arrival of the Huns spelt serious danger for the eastern half of the Roman Empire, which had thus far been relatively unscathed by the upheavals that devastated much of Europe. The provinces of Asia Minor, Syria and Palestine and Egypt were still intact, as was the magnificent city of Constantinople. Taking no chances, the Emperor Theodosius II surrounded the city with formidable defences, including a huge set of Land Walls, to protect it from attack.

These walls, and the narrow strip of water separating Europe from Asia, proved to be crucial. After setting himself up just to the north of the Danube, Attila ravaged the Balkans for fifteen years, extracting heavy tribute from the government in Constantinople in return for not advancing further, and securing vast amounts of gold. Having squeezed everything he could from the imperial authorities in terms of ransoms and bribes, he advanced west; eventually his progress was checked, not by the armies of Rome, but by a coalition made up of many long-term enemies of the Huns. At the battle of the Catalaunian Plains, in what is now central France, in 451, Attila was defeated by a large force that included an astonishing array of races drawn from the peoples of the steppes. The Hun leader died not long afterwards on his wedding night—not his first. Celebrating excessively, says one contemporary, he "lay down on his back sodden with wine and sleep," suffered a brain haemorrhage and died in his sleep. "Thus drunkenness brought a shameful end to a king who had won glory in war."[21]

These days, it is voguish to talk of an age of transformation and continuities that followed the sack of Rome—rather than to describe the period as the Dark Ages. And yet, as one modern scholar argues powerfully, the impact of the rape, pillage and anarchy that marked the fifth century as the Goths, Alans, Vandals and Huns rampaged across Europe and North Africa is hard to exaggerate. Literacy levels plummeted; building in stone all but disappeared, a clear sign of collapse of wealth and ambition; long-distance trade that once took pottery from factories in Tunisia as far as Iona in Scotland collapsed, replaced by local markets dealing only with exchange of petty goods; and as measured from pollution in polar ice-caps in Greenland there was a major contraction in smelting work, with levels falling back to those of prehistoric times.[22]

Contemporaries struggled to make sense of what, to them, was the complete collapse of the world order. "Why does [God] allow us to be weaker and more miserable" than all these tribal peoples, wailed the fifth-century Christian writer Salvian; "why has he allowed us to be conquered by the barbarians? Why does he permit us to be subject to the rule of our enemies?" The answer, he concluded, was simple: men had sinned and God was punishing them.[23] Others reached the opposite conclusion. Rome had been master of the world when it was faithful to its pagan roots, argued Zosimus, the Byzantine historian (who was himself pagan); when it abandoned these and turned to a new faith, it engineered its own demise. This, he said, was not an opinion; it was a fact.[24]

Rome's collapse took the sting out of Christianity in Asia. Relations with Persia had improved in the face of their mutual interests in resisting the peoples of the steppe, and with the empire deeply enfeebled Christianity no longer looked as threatening—or perhaps even as convincing—as it had a century earlier, when Constantine was gearing up to attack Persia and liberate its Christian population. In 410, therefore, the first of several meetings took place, prompted by the Shah, Yazdagird I, to formalise the position of the Christian church in Persia and to standardise its beliefs.

As in the west, many divergent views had sprung up about what following Jesus meant precisely, about how believers should live and how they should manifest and practise their faith. As noted earlier, even Kirdīr's inscription from the third century spoke of two types of Christians, *nasraye* and *kristyone*—normally understood as differentiating between locals who had been evangelised and those who had been deported from Roman territory. Variation in practices and doctrine was a constant source of problems, perhaps not surprisingly given that in places like Rev-Ardashīr in Fars, in southern Iran, there were two churches, one conducting services in Greek, the other in Syriac. Rivalry sometimes prompted physical violence, such as in the city of Susiana (in what is now south-western Iran) where rival bishops tried to settle scores over a fist-fight.[25] Efforts by the bishop of Seleucia-Ctesiphon, one of the Persian Empire's most important cities, to bring order and unity to all Christian communities proved frustrating and ineffective.[26]

With the possibility of salvation depending on getting questions of faith right, it was important to iron out differences once and for all—something the early church fathers had been at pains to stress since the very start.[27] "I now repeat what I have said before," St. Paul reminded the Galatians; "if anyone preaches a gospel at variance with the gospel which you have received, let him be outcast!" (Gal. 1:9). It was in this context that texts were written to evangelise—literally, "to give the good news"—in order to explain who the Son of God was and what his precise message had been, and to systematise beliefs.[28]

To put an end to the debate that so troubled the early Christian church in the west, the Emperor Constantine had called a council at Nicaea in 325, where bishops from across the empire were summoned to resolve rival interpretations about the relationship between God the Father and God the Son, one of the topics that had caused the most friction, and to resolve a host of other competing theories. The council dealt with these by agreeing a structure for the church, by settling the issue of calculating the date of Easter, and by codifying a statement of faith that still holds fast in the Christian church: the creed of Nicaea. Constantine was determined to put an end to division and to underline the importance of unity.[29]

Bishops from Persia and elsewhere outside the boundaries of the Roman Empire had not been invited to attend Nicaea. Councils held in Persia in 410, and again in 420 and 424, were therefore organised to enable bishops to resolve the same issues that had been looked at by their peers in the west. The impulse to meet and discuss was supported by the Shah, described by one source as the "victorious king of kings, on whom the churches rely for peace," who like Constantine was keen to benefit from the support of the Christian communities rather than have to intervene in their squabbles."[30]

The account of what was agreed at the meetings is not entirely reliable, reflecting later power struggles between leading sees and clerics. Nevertheless, important decisions clearly were made regarding the organisation of the church. It was purportedly agreed that the archbishopric of Seleucia-Ctesiphon should act as "head and regent over us and all our brother-bishops in the whole of the [Persian] empire" (albeit against a backdrop of considerable argument and ill-feeling).[31] The important question about the mechanics of how clerical appointments were made was discussed at length, with the aim of eliminating double hierarchies in locations that contained competing Christian constituencies. Thought was given to the dates of important religious festivals, while it was also determined that the common practice of appealing to "western bishops" for guidance and intervention should be stopped, as this undermined the leadership of the church in the east.[32] Finally, the creed and canons of the Council of Nicaea were accepted, alongside agreements that had been reached at subsequent western synods in the intervening period.[33]

This should have been a seminal moment, the point where the muscle and brains of the Christian religion engaged properly, creating an institution that linked the Atlantic with the foothills of the Himalayas, with two fully functioning arms—centred on Rome and Persia, the two great empires of late antiquity—working in accord with each other. With imperial patronage in the former, and a growing acceptance by the ruler in the latter, an enviable platform had been laid that could have seen Christianity become the dominant religion not only in Europe but in Asia too. Instead, bitter infighting broke out.

Some bishops who felt undermined by the attempts to harmonise the church accused leading figures not only of not being properly educated, but of not even being properly ordained. Then there were the problems caused by an outbreak of Christian militancy, which saw a series of Zoroastrian fire temples vandalised—which in turn put the Shah in a compromising position and forced him to shift his stance away from religious tolerance towards one that championed the belief system of his aristocracy. It was a major setback. Instead of welcoming a golden age, the church found itself facing a new wave of persecution.[34]

Fiery clerical disputes were endemic in the early church. Gregory of Nazianzus, an archbishop of Constantinople in the fourth century and one of the finest early Christian scholars, recorded being shouted down by detractors. Rivals screamed at him like a giant flock of crows, he wrote. It felt like being in the middle of a huge sandstorm when they attacked him, or being savaged by animals: "they were like a swarm of wasps suddenly flying in one's face."[35]

Nevertheless, the timing of this particular breakdown in the middle of the fifth century was unfortunate. A bitter feud had been brewing for some time between two rival clerics in the west, Nestorius, the patriarch of Constantinople, and Cyril, the patriarch of Alexandria, over the question of the divine and human nature of Jesus. Debates like this were not necessarily settled by fair means. Cyril was a born politician, ruthless in his methods of winning support for his position, as an extensive schedule of bribes he paid out shows: influential figures, and their wives, were treated to luxury goods like fine carpets, chairs made of ivory, expensive tablecloths and cash.[36]

Some clerics in the east found the dispute—and the nature of its resolution—bewildering. The problem, as they saw it, lay in the sloppy translation into Greek of the Syriac term describing the incarnation—although the argument was as much about jostling for power between two leading lights in the church hierarchy, and the kudos that came from having one's doctrinal positions accepted and adopted. The clash came to a head over the status of the Virgin, who in Nestorius' opinion should be termed not *Theotokos* (the one who bears God) but *Christotokos* (the one who bears Christ)—in other words, the human nature of Jesus alone.[37]

Outflanked and outmanoeuvred by Cyril, Nestorius was deposed, a move that destabilised the church as bishops hastily changed their theological positions one way and then another. Decisions made at one council could be challenged at another, as rival factions lobbied fiercely in the background. Much discussion revolved around the question of whether Jesus Christ had two natures—divine and human—inviolably united in one person and how the two were linked. The precise relationship between Jesus and God was also a matter of intense debate, revolving around the issue of whether the former was the creation of the latter, and therefore subordinate, or a manifestation of the Almighty, and hence co-equal and co-eternal. Responses to the questions were set out forcefully at the Council of Chalcedon in 451, with the articulation of a new definition of faith which was supposed to be accepted throughout the Christian world—and was accompanied with the explicit threat that anyone who did not agree with it was to be expelled from the church.[38] The church in the east reacted furiously.

This new teaching of the western church was not just wrong, the eastern bishops argued, but verged on heresy. A reworded creed was therefore issued that set out the distinct and separate natures of Jesus, and threatened damnation for anyone who "considers or teaches others that suffering and change have attached to the divinity of our Lord."[39] The Emperor became embroiled in the debate. He closed the school in Edessa which had become the focal point of the Christian east, pumping out texts, saints' lives and advice not only in Syriac, the Aramaic dialect used in Edessa, but in a range of other languages too such as Persian and Sogdian.[40] Unlike in the Mediterranean, where Greek was the language of Christianity, in the east there was a recognition from the outset that if new audiences were to be attracted, there needed to be material available that could be understood by as many different groups as possible.

The closure of the Edessa school deepened the schism between the churches of the west and the east, not least because many scholars were expelled from imperial territory and sought refuge in Persia. Over time, this became increasingly problematic, as emperors based in Constantinople were expected to defend "orthodox" doctrine—and to crack down on teachings deemed deviant and heretical. In 532, when a peace treaty was agreed with Persia following a period of instability and conflict in the Caucasus, one of the key clauses in the agreement was that Persian officials should help track down and take into custody bishops and priests whose views were not in line with the Council of Chalcedon and whose activities were considered dangerous by the Roman authorities.[41]

Trying to soothe passions between rival religious factions was a thankless task, as the case of the Emperor Justinian shows all too well. Justinian repeatedly tried to get opposing sides to reconcile their views, summoning a major Ecumenical Council in 553 in a bid to draw a line following a period of increasingly bitter recrimination, while also personally attending more low-key meetings of leading clerics to find a way towards a solution.[42] An account written after his death shows how his efforts to find common ground were seen by some: "after filling absolutely everywhere with confusion and turmoil and collecting the wages for this, at the conclusion to his life, [he] passed over to the lowest places of punishment"—that is to say, to hell.[43] Other emperors took a different approach and, attempting to silence the cacophony and recriminations, simply forbade discussion of religious affairs.[44]

While the church in the west obsessed about rooting out variant views, the church in the east set about one of the most ambitious and far-reaching missionary programmes in history, one that in terms of scale bears comparison with later evangelism in the Americas and Africa: Christianity expanded rapidly into new regions without the iron fist of political power behind it. A rash of martyrs deep in the southern part of the Arabian peninsula shows how far the religion's tentacles were spreading, as does the fact that the King of Yemen became Christian.[45] A Greek-speaking visitor to Sri Lanka in about 550 found a robust community of Christians, overseen by clergy appointed "from Persia."[46]

Christianity even reached the nomadic peoples of the steppes, much to the surprise of officials in Constantinople who, when offered hostages as part of a peace agreement, found that some had "the symbol of the cross tattooed in black on their foreheads." Asked how this had happened, they replied that there had been a plague "and some Christians among them had suggested doing this [to bring divine protection] and from that time their country had been safe."[47]

By the middle of the sixth century there were archbishoprics deep within Asia. Cities including Basra, Mosul and Tikrit had burgeoning Christian populations. The scale of evangelism was such that Kokhe, situated close to Ctesiphon, was served by no fewer than five dependent bishoprics.[48] Cities like Merv, Gundeshāpūr and even Kashgar, the oasis town that was the entry point to China, had archbishops long before Canterbury did. These were major Christian centres many centuries before the first missionaries reached Poland or Scandinavia. Samarkand and Bukhara (in modern Uzbekistan) were also home to thriving Christian communities a thousand years before Christianity was brought to the Americas.[49] Indeed, even in the Middle Ages, there were many more Christians in Asia than there were in Europe.[50] After all, Baghdad is closer to Jerusalem than to Athens, while Teheran is nearer the Holy Land than Rome, and Samarkand is closer to it than Paris and London. Christianity's success in the east has long been forgotten.

Its expansion owed much to the tolerance and deftness of the Sasanian rulers of Persia, who were able to pursue inclusive policies at times when the aristocracy and Zoroastrian priesthood were pacified. Such was the conciliatory way that Khusraw I (531–79) dealt with foreign scholars that he became well known in contemporary Constantinople for being a "lover of literature and a profound student of philosophy," something that had one writer in Constantinople spluttering in disbelief: I find it quite impossible to think, protested the historian Agathias not long afterwards, that he can really have been so brilliant. He spoke in a rough and uncivilised tongue; how could he possibly have understood the nuances of philosophy?[51]

By the later sixth century, meetings of the church of the east were even beginning with earnest prayers for the health of the Persian ruler. And not long afterwards the Shah could be found organising the election of a new patriarch, urging all the bishops in his realm to "come quickly . . . to elect a leader and governor . . . under whose administration and leadership lie every altar and every church of our Lord Jesus Christ in the empire of the Persians."[52] The Sasanian ruler had gone from being the persecutor of Christians in Asia to being their champion.

This was at least in part a result of a growing self-confidence in Persia, fuelled by regular payments of money by the authorities in Constantinople whose military and political priorities shifted to resolving problems elsewhere. With the steppes becalmed and Rome's attention often focused on stabilising and recovering provinces in the Mediterranean that had fallen, the fifth and sixth centuries were a time of rising prosperity in Persia: religious tolerance went hand in glove with economic growth. Countless new cities were founded across Persia as the central government spent increasing tax revenues on infrastructure.[53] Massive irrigation programmes, above all in Khuzistan and Iraq, boosted agricultural production, while water-supply systems were built, or in some cases extended for several miles. An extensive bureaucratic machine ensured smooth administration from the Levant deep into Central Asia.[54] This was a period that saw major centralisation of the Sasanian state.[55]

The level of control went as far as setting out the layout of individual stalls in Persian markets and bazaars. One text records how trades were organised into regulated guilds, and notes that inspectors were on hand to ensure quality controls and assess the takings due to the treasury.[56] As wealth grew, so long-distance trade in luxury, high-value items rose too: thousands of seals used to mark packages as approved for sale or for export survive, as does a considerable corpus of written material attesting to contracts being sealed and kept at registry offices in this period.[57] Goods were carried from the Persian Gulf to the Caspian, and were taken to and from India by sea and by land. Levels of exchange with Sri Lanka and China rose sharply, as they also did with the eastern Mediterranean.[58] All the while, the Sasanian authorities retained a close interest in what was going on within their borders and beyond.

A considerable part of this long-range commerce was handled by Sogdian traders famous for their caravans, financial acumen and close family ties that enabled them to trade goods along the main arteries running across Central Asia into Xinjiang and western China. A remarkable cache of letters discovered by Auriel Stein in a watchtower near Dunhuang at the start of the twentieth century attest to trading patterns and sophisticated credit facilities, as well as to the goods and products that the Sogdians transported and sold. Among the many items they traded were gold and silver ornaments, such as hair clasps and finely crafted vessels, hemp, linen, woollen cloth, saffron, pepper and camphor; but they specialised in trading silk.[59] Sogdians were the glue that connected towns, oases and regions together. They played a major role in Chinese silk reaching the eastern Mediterranean, where it was highly prized by the Roman emperors and the elite. Likewise, they brought goods back in the other direction: coins minted in Constantinople have been found across Central Asia, including deep in China itself—as have prestige objects like a silver ewer depicting scenes from the Trojan War that was buried in the mid-sixth century alongside its powerful owner, Li Xian.[60]

As religions came into contact with each other, they inevitably borrowed from each other. Although it is difficult to trace this accurately, it is striking that the halo became a common visual symbol across Hindu, Buddhist, Zoroastrian and Christian art, as a link between the earthly and the divine, and as a marker of radiance and illumination that was important in all these faiths. A magnificent monument at Tāq-i Bustān in modern Iran depicts one ruler on horseback, surrounded by winged angels and with a ring of light around his head in a scene that would have been recognisable to followers of any of the great faiths of this region. Likewise, even poses—like the Buddhist *vitarka mudra*, formed from the right thumb and index finger of one hand touching, often with the other fingers outstretched—were adopted to illustrate connections with the divine, favoured particularly by Christian artists.[61]

Christianity flowed along trade routes, but its progress did not go unchallenged. The centre of the world had always been noisy, a place where faiths, ideas and religions borrowed from one another—but they also clashed. Competition for spiritual authority became increasingly intense. Such tension had long marked the relationship between Christianity and Judaism, where religious leaders on both sides strove to draw lines between the two: in the case of the former, intermarriage was repeatedly legislated against, while the date of Easter was deliberately moved so as not to coincide with the feast of Passover.[62] This was not far enough for some. John Chrysostom, archbishop of Constantinople at the turn of the fourth century, urged that the liturgy should be more exciting, complaining that it was difficult for Christians to compete with the theatricality of the synagogue where drums, lyres, harps and other musical instruments made for entertainment during worship—as did actors and dancers brought in to enliven proceedings.[63]

Senior Jewish figures, for their part, were no more enthusiastic about receiving new converts. "Do not have faith in a proselyte," declared one famous rabbi, Ḥiyya the Great, "until twenty-four generations have passed because the inherent evil is still within him." Converts are as irritating and difficult as scabs, noted Ḥelbo, another influential rabbi.[64] Jewish attitudes to Christianity hardened in Persia as a result of the inroads being made by the latter. This can be seen clearly from the Babylonian Talmud, the collection of texts centred on the rabbinic interpretation of Jewish law. Unlike the Palestinian Talmud, which refers to Jesus lightly and in passing, the Babylonian edition takes a violent and scathing position on Christianity, attacking doctrines, specific events and figures from the Gospels. The Virgin birth, for example, is lampooned and mocked as being as likely as a mule having offspring, while the story of the Resurrection is mercilessly ridiculed. Detailed and sophisticated counter-narratives of Jesus' life, including parodies of scenes from the New Testament and above all from the Gospel of St. John, show how threatening Christian advances had become. There was a systematic effort to assert that Jesus was a false prophet, and that his crucifixion was justifiable—in other words, deflecting blame and responsibility away from the Jews. These violent reactions were an attempt to counter the steady gains that were being made at Judaism's expense.[65]

It was important, therefore, that there were also locations where Judaism itself made progress. In the kingdom of Ḥimyar in the south-western corner of the Arabian peninsula, in what is now Saudi Arabia and Yemen, Jewish communities became increasingly prominent, as recent discoveries of synagogues such as the fourth-century structure at Qanaʾ shows.[66] Indeed, Ḥimyar adopted Judaism as the state religion—and did so enthusiastically. By the late fifth century, Christians were being regularly martyred for their beliefs, including priests, monks and bishops, after being condemned by a council of rabbis.[67]

A botched Ethiopian military expedition across the Red Sea in the early sixth century to replace the Jewish ruler with a Christian puppet resulted in vicious reprisals as steps were taken to remove all traces of Christianity from the kingdom. Churches were demolished or turned into synagogues. Hundreds of Christians were detained and executed; on one occasion, 200 who had taken sanctuary inside a church were simply burnt alive. All this was reported with glee by the king, who sent letters across Arabia rejoicing at the suffering he had inflicted.[68]

The Zoroastrian priesthood also reacted to Christianity's progress in the Sasanian Empire, especially following several high-profile conversions of members of the ruling elite. This too resulted in a series of aggressive attacks on Christian communities, including multiple martyrdoms.[69] In turn, Christians began to produce uncompromising morality tales, the most famous of which was the epic story of Qardagh, a brilliant young man who hunted like a Persian king and argued like a Greek philosopher but gave up a promising career as a provincial governor to convert. Sentenced to death, he escaped from captivity only to experience a dream telling him it was better to die for his faith than to fight. His execution, at which his father threw the first stone, was commemorated in a lengthy and beautiful narrative account whose aim was evidently to encourage others to find the confidence to become Christian.[70]

Part of the secret of Christianity's success lay in the commitment and energy of its evangelical mission. It helped, of course, that the enthusiasm was infused with a healthy dose of realism: texts from the early seventh century record clerics working hard to reconcile their ideas with those of Buddhism, if not as a short cut, then at least as a way of simplifying matters. The Holy Spirit, wrote one missionary who reached China, was entirely consistent with what the local population already believed: "All buddhas flow and flux by virtue of this very wind [that is, the Holy Spirit], while in this world, there is no place where the wind does not reach." Likewise, he went on, God has been responsible for immortality and everlasting happiness since the creation of the world. As such, "man . . . will always do honour to the name of Buddha."[71] Christianity was not just compatible with Buddhism, he was saying; broadly speaking, it *was* Buddhism.

Others tried to codify the fusion of Christian and Buddhist ideas, producing a hybrid set of "gospels" that effectively simplified the complex message and story of the former, with elements that were familiar and accessible to populations in the east in order to accelerate Christianity's progress across Asia. There was a theological logic to this dualistic approach, usually called Gnosticism, which argued that preaching in terms that had understandable cultural reference points and used accessible language was an obvious way to spread the message.[72] Little wonder, then, that Christianity found support among a broad sweep of the population: these were ideas that were deliberately made to sound familiar and easy to grasp.

Other cults, faiths and sects benefited from the same process. The teachings of Mazdak, a charismatic preacher, proved extremely popular in the late fifth and early sixth century—as we can tell from the furious and colourful criticism showered on the preacher's followers by Christian and Zoroastrian commentators alike. The attitudes and practices of Mazdak's disciples, ranging from what they ate to their supposed interest in having group sex, were electrifyingly vilified. In fact, in so far as the highly partial source material allows us to understand, Mazdak advocated an ascetic lifestyle that had obvious resonances with Buddhist attitudes to material wealth, to Zoroastrian suspicions of the physical world and to well-established Christian asceticism.[73]

In this competitive spiritual environment, it was important to defend intellectual—and physical—territory. A Chinese traveller passing through Samarkand in the sixth century noted that the local population violently opposed the law of Buddha, and chased away with "burning fire" any Buddhist who tried to take shelter.[74] On this occasion, the hostile reception had a happy ending: the visitor was eventually allowed to convene a meeting and apparently went on to persuade many to convert to Buddhism thanks to the strength of his character and of his arguments.[75]

Few understood better than the Buddhists how important it was to publicise and show off objects that supported declarations of faith. Another Chinese pilgrim who made his way to Central Asia in search of Sanskrit texts to study looked with wonder at the sacred relics venerated by the local population in Balkh. These included one of the Buddha's teeth, as well as the basin he used for washing, and a brush he used for sweeping, made of the kasha plant, but decorated with fine jewels.[76]

There were, however, more visible and more dramatic statements that were designed to win hearts and minds. Cave temples had become a well-established way of evoking and enforcing a spiritual message, lying along trade routes and eliding the idea of sanctuary and the divine on the one hand with commerce and travel on the other. The complex at Elephanta off the coast of Mumbai and the caves of Ellora in northern India provide spectacular examples. Filled with majestic and ornate carvings of deities, these were designed to showcase moral and theological superiority—in this case, the superiority of Hinduism.[77]

This had an obvious parallel with Bamiyan (in modern Afghanistan). Lying at the crossroads of routes linking India to the south, Bactria to the north and Persia to the west, Bamiyan contained a complex of 751 caves supplemented by immense figures of the Buddha.[78] Two statues, one to a height of 180 feet and another, slightly older, approximately two-thirds of the size, stood carved into vast niches in the rocks for nearly 1,500 years—until they were blown up and destroyed by the Taliban in 2001 in an act of philistinism and cultural savagery that stands comparison with the destruction of religious artefacts in Britain and northern Europe during the Reformation.[79]

When we think of the Silk Roads, it is tempting to think of the circulation always passing from east to west. In fact, there was considerable interest and exchange passing in the other direction, as an admiring seventh-century Chinese text makes plain. Syria, the author wrote, was a place that "produces fire-proof cloth, life-restoring incense, bright moon-pearls, and night-lustre gems. Brigands and robbers are unknown, but the people enjoy happiness and peace. None but illustrious laws prevail; none but the virtuous are raised to sovereign power. The land is broad and ample, and its literary productions are perspicuous and clear."[80]

And in fact, despite fierce competition and in spite of the chorus of religions fighting to make their voices heard, it was Christianity that kept chipping away at traditional beliefs, practices and value systems. In 635, missionaries in China were able to convince the Emperor to withdraw opposition to the faith and to recognise it as a legitimate religion whose message not only did not compromise imperial identity but potentially enforced it.[81]

Around the middle of the seventh century, the future seemed easy to read. Christianity was on the march across Asia, making inroads at the expense of Zoroastrianism, Judaism and Buddhism.[82] Religions had always played off each other in this region, and learnt that they had to compete for attention. The most competitive and successful, however, turned out to be a religion born in the little town of Bethlehem.[83] Given the progress that had been made over the centuries that followed the crucifixion of Jesus at the hands of Pontius Pilate, it should have been only a matter of time before the tentacles of Christianity reached the Pacific, linking the great ocean with the Atlantic in the west.

And yet, at the moment of the triumph of Christianity, chance intervened. A platform had been laid for a spiritual conquest that would not just connect towns and regions, but span continents. At that moment, however, a debilitating war broke out which undermined the existing powers and opened up opportunities to new entrants. It was like unleashing the internet in late antiquity: suddenly, a new raft of ideas, theories and trends threatened to undermine the existing order, and to take advantage of the networks that had been established over centuries. The name of the new cosmology did not reflect how revolutionary it was. Closely related to the words for safety and peace, "Islam" gave little sense of how the world was about to change. Revolution had arrived.

4

The Road to Revolution

The rise of Islam took place in a world that had seen a hundred years of turmoil, dissent and catastrophe. In 541, a century before the Prophet Muḥammad began to receive a series of divine revelations, it was news of a different threat that spread panic through the Mediterranean. It moved like lightning, so fast that by the time panic set in, it was already too late. No one was spared. The scale of death was barely imaginable. According to one contemporary who lost most of his family, one city on the Egyptian border was wiped out: seven men and one ten-year-old boy were all who remained of a once bustling population; the doors of houses hung open, with no one to guard the gold, silver and precious objects inside.[1] Cities bore the brunt of the savage attacks, with 10,000 people being killed each day in Constantinople at one point in the mid-540s.[2] It was not just the Roman Empire that suffered. Before long cities in the east were being ravaged too, as disaster spread along the communication and trade networks, devastating cities in Persian Mesopotamia and eventually reaching China.[3] Bubonic plague brought catastrophe, despair and death.

It also brought chronic economic depression: fields denuded of farmers, towns stripped of consumers and a generation scythed down in their youth naturally altered the demography of late antiquity, and caused a severe contraction of the economy.[4] In due course, this was to have an impact on the way emperors in Constantinople sought to conduct foreign policy. During the first part of the reign of Justinian (527–65), the empire had been able to achieve a series of stunning successes that saw the recovery of the provinces of North Africa and significant progress in Italy. Judicious use of force was coupled with deliberate efforts to retain the flexibility needed to deal with problems that could flare up at any time on its extended borders, including in the east. Striking this balance became increasingly difficult later during Justinian's reign as manpower shortages, inconclusive military campaigns and rising costs drained a treasury that was already depleted before the plague struck.[5]

Stagnation took hold and the public mood towards Justinian soured. Particularly fierce criticism was reserved for the way he seemed willing to buy the friendship of the empire's neighbours by paying out money and promiscuously bestowing favours. Justinian was foolish enough to think it "a stroke of good fortune to be dishing out the wealth of the Romans and flinging it to the barbarians," wrote Procopius, the scathing, and most prominent, historian of Justinian's reign. The Emperor, Procopius remorselessly went on, "lost no opportunity to lavish vast sums of money on all the barbarians," to the north, south, east and west; cash was dispatched, the author went on, to peoples who had never even been heard of before.[6]

Justinian's successors abandoned this approach and took a strident and uncompromising line with Rome's neighbours. When ambassadors from the Avars, one of the great tribes of the steppes, arrived in Constantinople shortly after Justinian's death in 565 to ask for their usual payment of tribute, they met with short shrift from the new Emperor, Justin II: "Never again shall you be loaded at the expense of this empire, and go your way without doing us any service; for from me you shall receive nothing." When they threatened consequences, the Emperor exploded: "Do you dead dogs dare to threaten the Roman realm? Learn that I will shave off those locks of yours, and then cut off your heads."[7]

A similarly aggressive stance was taken towards Persia, especially after it was reported that a powerful constellation of Türk nomads had taken the Huns' place on the Central Asian steppe and was putting pressure on their eastern frontiers. The Türks were playing an increasingly dominant role in trade, much to the annoyance of the Chinese, who portrayed them as difficult and untrustworthy—a sure sign of their rising commercial success.[8] They were led by the magnificent figure of Sizabul, who took to receiving dignitaries in an elaborate tent while reclining on a gold bed supported by four gold peacocks and with a large wagon brimming with silver conspicuously positioned near by.[9]

The Türks had extensive ambitions and dispatched envoys to Constantinople in order to propose a long-range military alliance. A joint attack, ambassadors told Justin II, would destroy Persia.[10] Eager to win glory at the expense of Constantinople's traditional rival and encouraged by the prospects, the Emperor agreed to the plan and became increasingly grandiloquent, issuing threats to the Shah and demanding the return of towns and territories ceded under previous agreements. After a poorly executed strike by the Romans had failed, a Persian counter-attack made for Dara (the site of which is now in southern Turkey), the cornerstone of the border defences. After a terrible siege lasting six months the Persians succeeded in taking the city in 574, whereupon the Emperor experienced a mental and physical breakdown.[11]

The fiasco convinced the Türks that Constantinople was an unworthy and unreliable ally, something the Türk ambassador stated point-blank in 576, angrily rejecting any chance of another attack on Persia. After putting ten fingers in his mouth, he said angrily: "As there are now ten fingers in my mouth, so you Romans have used many tongues." Rome had deceived the Türks by promising to do their best against Persia; the results had been pitiful.[12]

All the same, this reopening of hostilities with Persia marked the start of a tumultuous period that had extraordinary consequences. Two decades of fighting followed, with moments of high drama, such as when a Persian army penetrated deep into Asia Minor, before returning home. As it did so, it was ambushed, with the queen taken prisoner, along with the royal golden carriage that was decorated with precious gems and pearls. The sacred fire the Persian ruler took with him on campaign, considered to be "greater than all fires," was captured and thrown into a river, while the Zoroastrian high priest and a "multitude of the most senior people" were drowned—perhaps forcibly. The extinguishing of the sacred fire was an aggressive and provocative act, designed to belittle the religious cornerstone of Persian identity. The news was celebrated with wild enthusiasm by the Romans and their allies.[13]

As hostilities continued, religion became increasingly important. When troops revolted over a proposed reduction in pay, for example, the commanding officer paraded a sacred image of Jesus in front of the troops to impress on them that serving the Emperor meant serving God. When Shah Khusraw I died in 579 some claimed, without any foundation, "that the light of the divine Word shone splendidly around him, for he believed in Christ."[14] Stiffening attitudes led to vociferous denunciations of Zoroastrianism in Constantinople as base, false and depraved: the Persians, wrote Agathias, have acquired "deviant and degenerate habits ever since they came under the spell of the teaching of Zoroaster."[15]

Infusing militarism with a heavy dose of religiosity had implications for those on the periphery of the empire who had been courted and converted to Christianity as part of a deliberate policy to win their support and loyalty.[16] Particular effort had been made to win over the tribes of southern and western Arabia with the promise of material rewards. The bestowal of royal titles, which introduced new concepts of kinship (and kingship) that could be powerfully exploited locally, also helped convince many to throw their lot in with Constantinople.[17]

The stiffening of religious sensibilities during the confrontation with Persia therefore had consequences—because the Christianity adopted by some of the tribes was not that of the formula agreed at Chalcedon in 451, but a version or versions that held different views about the unity of Christ. Relations with the Ghassānids, Rome's long-term allies in Arabia, soured as a result of the strident messages emanating from the imperial capital.[18] Partly because of mutual religious suspicions, relations broke down at this sensitive moment—which provided the Persians with a perfect opportunity to exploit. Control was gained over the ports and markets of southern and western Arabia, as a new overland trade route was opened up connecting Persia with Mecca and ʿUkāẓ. According to the Islamic tradition, this dislocation prompted a leading figure in Mecca to approach Constantinople with a request for nomination as the phylarch, or guardian, of the city as Rome's representative, with a later, royal title of a kingship of Mecca being awarded by the Emperor to a certain ʿUthmān. A parallel process saw the appointment of a nominee to take a similar role in Yathrib—on behalf of Persia.[19]

While these tensions were crystallising in the Arabian peninsula, little progress was being made in the long-drawn-out war in its main theatre in the north. The turning point came not on the battlefield but at the Persian court at the end of the 580s, when Vahrām, a popular general who had stabilised the eastern frontier with the Türks, took matters into his own hands and revolted against the Shah, Khusraw II. The Shah fled to Constantinople where he promised the Emperor Maurice major concessions in the Caucasus and Mesopotamia—including the return of Dara—in exchange for imperial support. After Khusraw had returned home in 591, and dealt with his rival with surprisingly little ado, he set about honouring his agreement. It was, as one leading scholar has put it, a Versailles moment: too many towns, forts and important locations were handed over to the Romans, exposing the economic and administrative heartlands of Persia; the humiliation was so great that it was bound to provoke a vigorous response.[20]

The pendulum had swung both ways during intense fighting over the previous two decades. It looked to all intents and purposes as if Rome had secured a great diplomatic and political coup. Now that it had the forward bases that had previously been lacking, it finally had the chance to establish a permanent presence in the Near East. As the historian Procopius recognised, the plains of Mesopotamia that fanned out across the massive basin of the Tigris and Euphrates provided few obvious frontier points in the form of rivers, lakes or mountains.[21] This meant any gains made were vulnerable unless a giant swathe of territory could be annexed and held. Khusraw II may have regained the throne, but it came at a high price.

And yet barely a decade later the tables turned spectacularly. When Emperor Maurice was murdered by Phokas, one of his generals, in a palace coup in 602, Khusraw II seized the moment to strike and force a renegotiation. He gained confidence after a fierce attack on Dara knocked out a vital point in the Roman defensive system in northern Mesopotamia and again from Phokas' struggle to impose authority at home. When reports came that a new wave of nomad attacks was ravaging the Balkans, the Shah raised his ambitions. The traditional client-management system that was used to govern the subject peoples of northern Arabia was hastily dismantled in anticipation of a major reorganisation of the frontier that would follow Persian expansion.[22]

The Christian population was handled carefully. Bishops had learnt from experience to fear the prospect of war, since hostilities with the Romans were often accompanied by accusations of collaboration. The Shah personally presided over the election of a new patriarch in 605, inviting the senior clergy to meet and choose a new incumbent. This was a deliberate signal to provide reassurance and to show the minority population that their ruler was sympathetic to their affairs. It was an effective move, interpreted by the Christian community as a sign of benevolent protection: Khusraw was effusively thanked by the bishops, who gathered together to praise "the powerful, generous, kind and bounteous King of Kings."[23]

With the Roman Empire buckling under one internal revolt after another, Persian forces turned the screw: cities in Mesopotamia fell like dominoes, with Edessa the last capitulating in 609. Attention then turned to Syria. Antioch, the great city on the Orontes, first See of St. Peter and the major metropolis of Roman Syria, fell in 610, followed by Emesa in western Syria the following year. With the fall of Damascus in 613, another great regional centre was lost.

Things only got worse. In Constantinople, the unpopular and hubristic Phokas was murdered, his naked and dismembered remains paraded through the city's streets. The new Emperor, Heraclius, however, proved no more effective in halting the Persians, whose advances had by now acquired a devastating momentum. After defeating a Roman counter-attack in Asia Minor, the Shah's armies turned south to Jerusalem. The aim was obvious: to capture the most holy city in Christendom and, in doing so, to assert the cultural and religious triumph of Persia.

When the city fell after a short siege, in May 614, the reaction in the Roman world bordered on hysteria. The Jews were accused not just of collaborating with the Persians but of actively supporting them. According to one source, the Jews were "like evil beasts," helping the invading army—themselves compared to ferocious animals and hissing snakes. They were accused of playing an active role in massacring the local population who piously rejoiced as they died "because they were being slain for Christ's sake and shed their blood for His blood." Stories spread that churches were being pulled down, crosses trampled underfoot and icons spat on. The True Cross on which Jesus was crucified was captured and sent back to the Persian capital as a trophy of war par excellence for Khusraw. This was a truly disastrous turn of events for Rome, and one that the Emperor's propagandists immediately turned their attention to in an attempt to limit the damage.[24]

Faced with such setbacks, Heraclius considered abdicating, before deciding to take desperate measures: ambassadors were sent to Khusraw to seek peace on any terms. Through the envoys, Heraclius begged for forgiveness and blamed his predecessor, Phokas, for Rome's recent acts of aggression. Presenting himself as a submissive inferior, the Roman ruler hailed the Shah as "supreme Emperor." Khusraw listened carefully to what the envoys had to say; then he had them executed.[25]

When news filtered back, panic gripped Constantinople, enabling radical reforms to be pushed through with barely a flicker of opposition. The salaries of the empire's officials were halved, as was the pay of the military. The free distribution of bread, a long-standing political tool to win the goodwill of the capital's inhabitants, was stopped.[26] Precious metals were seized from churches in a frantic effort to boost the exchequer. In order to underline the scale of the battle ahead and atone for the sins that had led God to chastise and punish the Romans, Heraclius modified the design of the coinage. While the bust of the Emperor on the obverse remained the same, on the reverse of new coins, minted in large volumes and in new denominations, was the image of a cross set on steps: the fight against the Persians was nothing less than the fight to defend the Christian faith.[27]

In the short term, these measures achieved little. After securing Palestine, the Persians turned to the Nile delta, taking Alexandria in 619.[28] In less than two years, Egypt—the breadbasket of the Mediterranean and bedrock of the Roman agrarian economy for six centuries—fell. Next came Asia Minor, which was attacked in 622. Although the advance was checked for a time, by 626 the Persian army was camped within sight of the walls of Constantinople. As if that were not bad enough for the Romans, the Shah made an alliance with the Avar nomads who had overrun the Balkans and had marched on the city from the north. All that now separated the remnants of imperial Rome from complete annihilation was the thickness of the walls of the city of the great Constantine—Constantinople, New Rome. The end was nigh; and it seemed utterly inevitable.

Chance though was on Heraclius' side. Initial efforts to take the city failed, and subsequent assaults were beaten away with ease. The enemies' commitment began to sag, failing first among the Avars. Having struggled to pasture their horses, the nomads withdrew when tribal differences threatened to undermine their leader's authority. The Persians pulled back soon afterwards too, in part because of reports of Türk attacks in the Caucasus that required attention: impressive territorial expansion had overstretched resources, leaving newly conquered lands dangerously exposed—and the Türks knew it. Constantinople had been spared by the skin of its teeth.[29]

In an astonishing counter-attack, Heraclius, who had been leading the imperial army in Asia Minor during the siege of his capital, now tore after the retreating enemy. The Emperor first made for the Caucasus, where he met the Türk Khagan and agreed an alliance—showering him with honours and gifts, and offering him his daughter, Eudokia, as a bride to formalise ties of friendship.[30] The Emperor then threw caution to the wind and moved south, crushing a large Persian army near Nineveh (in what is now northern Iraq) in the autumn of 627, before advancing on Ctesiphon as opposition melted away.

The Persian leadership creaked under the pressure. Khusraw was murdered, while his son and successor, Kavad, appealed to Heraclius for an immediate settlement.[31] The Emperor was satisfied by the promise of territory and kudos and withdrew to Constantinople, leaving his ambassador to agree terms, which included the return of Roman territory that had been seized during the wars—and also the return of the parts of the True Cross that had been taken from Jerusalem in 614.[32] It marked a spectacular and crushing victory for the Romans.

This was not the end of it, however, for a storm was brewing which was to bring Persia to the brink of collapse. The senior general in the field, Shahrbarāz, who had masterminded the recent lightning assault on Egypt, reacted to the reversal of fortune by mounting a bid for the throne. With Persian fortunes at a low ebb and with the frontier in the east vulnerable to opportunistic attacks by Türk raiders, the case for a man of action seemed irresistible. As the coup gathered pace, the general negotiated directly with Heraclius to gain Roman support for his uprising, withdrawing from Egypt and moving on Ctesiphon with the Emperor's support.

With the situation in Persia unravelling, Heraclius celebrated with gusto the astonishing reversal of fortune to cement his popularity. He had played heavily on religion to build support and stiffen resolve during the empire's dark hours. Khusraw's attack had been explained as a direct assault on Christianity, something underlined emphatically in a piece of theatre enacted before the imperial troops, in which a letter was read out that appeared to be written in the Shah's own hand: it not only personally ridiculed Heraclius, but scoffed at the powerlessness of the Christians' God.[33] The Romans had been challenged to fight for what they believed in: this had been a war of religion.

Perhaps not surprisingly, then, Roman triumphalism produced ugly scenes. After Heraclius had led a ceremonial entry into Jerusalem in March 630 and restored the fragments of the True Cross to the Church of the Holy Sepulchre, Jews were supposedly baptised by force, as punishment for the role they were thought to have played in the fall of the city sixteen years earlier; those who fled were banned from coming within three miles of Jerusalem.[34] Eastern Christians whose beliefs were judged to be non-conformist were targeted too by imperial agents, being obliged to abandon long-standing doctrinal positions and coerced into accepting the teachings of streamlined Orthodox Christianity that now claimed to have powerful evidence that it alone truly enjoyed God's blessing.[35]

This was problematic for the church in Persia, which had not seen eye to eye with its western peer for more than a century and whose senior clergy increasingly saw themselves as the transmitters of the true faith—in contrast to the church in the west which had been systemically corrupted by deviant teachings. As the bishops of Persia put it when they met in 612, all major heresies had sprung up in the Roman Empire—unlike in Persia, where "no heresy has ever arisen."[36] So when Heraclius "restored the church to the orthodox" in Edessa and gave instructions to drive out the eastern Christians who had worshipped there in the past, it looked as though his plan was to convert all of Persia—an idea Heraclius seems to have been actively pondering since the dramatic turn of fortune. And it was to be converted into Roman, western Christianity.[37]

The resurgent, dominant religion championed by Constantinople had swept all before it. The extraordinary sequence of events had left a host of old ideas in tatters. When plague broke out in Ctesiphon, claiming Shah Kavad as a victim, it seemed obvious that Zoroastrianism was little more than wishful thinking: Christianity was the true faith, and its followers had been rewarded.[38] In this highly charged atmosphere, a new rumbling could be heard. It came from the south, from deep inside the Arabian peninsula. This region had been all but untouched by the recent fighting between the Romans and Persians, but that did not mean that it was unaffected by the monumental clashes taking place hundreds of miles away. In fact, the south-west of the heel of Arabia had long been a crucible for confrontation between the two empires, where less than a century earlier the kingdom of Ḥimyar and the cities of Mecca and Medina had thrown in their lot with Persia against a Christian coalition of forces from Constantinople and Ḥimyar's deadly Red Sea rival, Ethiopia.[39]

This was a region where beliefs had been changing, adapting and competing with each other for the best part of a century. What had been a polytheist world of multiple deities, idols and beliefs had given way to monotheism and to ideas about a single, all-powerful deity. Sanctuaries dedicated to multiple gods were becoming so marginalised that one historian has stated that on the eve of the rise of Islam traditional polytheism "was dying." In its place came Jewish and Christian concepts of a single, all-powerful God—as well as of angels, paradise, prayer and alms-giving which can be found in inscriptions that begin to proliferate across the Arabian peninsula in the late sixth and early seventh centuries.[40]

. . .

It was in this region, as war raged to the north, that a trader named Muḥammad, a member of the Banū Hāshim clan of the Quraysh tribe, retreated to a cave not far from the city of Mecca to contemplate. According to the Islamic tradition, in 610 he began to receive a series of revelations from God. Muḥammad heard a voice that commanded him to recite verses "in the name of your Lord!"[41] Panicked and confused, he left the cave, but saw a man "feet astride the horizon," and a voice that boomed at him: "O Muḥammad, thou art the prophet of God and I am Jibrīl."[42] A series of recitations followed over the coming years that were first written down around the middle of the seventh century in a single text—known as the Qur'ān.[43]

God sends apostles, Muḥammad was told by the angel Jibrīl (or Gabriel), to deliver good news or to give warnings.[44] Muḥammad had been chosen as a messenger by the Almighty. There was much darkness in the world, he was told, many things to fear, and the danger of apocalypse at every corner. Recite the divine messages, he was urged, for when you do so you "seek refuge in [Allah] from accursed Satan: no power has he over those who believe and put their trust in their Lord."[45] God is compassionate and merciful, Muḥammad was repeatedly told, but He is also severe in his punishment for those who refuse to obey him.[46]

The sources relating to the early Islamic period are complex and pose serious problems of interpretation.[47] Establishing how contemporary and later political motivations shaped the story of Muḥammad and the messages he received is not easy—and, what is more, is a matter of intense debate among modern scholars. It is difficult, for example, to understand clearly what role belief played in shaping attitudes and events, not least since distinctions were made as early as the middle of the seventh century between believers (*mu'minūn*) and those who joined them and submitted to their authority (*muslimūn*). Later writers focused closely on the role of religion and emphasised not only the power of spiritual revelation but also the solidarity of the Arabs who effected revolution—with the result that it is as unsatisfactory to talk of the conquests of the period as "Muslim" as it is to refer to them as "Arab." Moreover, identities not only shifted after this period, but during it too—and of course we are reliant on the eyes of the beholders for such labels in the first place.

Nevertheless, although even establishing a secure sequence of events can be problematic, there is a wide acceptance that Muḥammad was not the only figure in the Arabian peninsula in the early seventh century to talk about a single God, for there were other "copycat prophets" who rose to prominence in precisely the period of the Perso-Roman wars. The most notable offered messianic and prophetic visions that were strikingly similar to those of Muḥammad—promising revelations from the angel Gabriel, pointing to paths to salvation and in some cases offering holy writings to back their claims up.[48] It was a time when Christian churches and shrines were starting to appear in and around Mecca, as is clear from the archaeological record, which also bears witness to icons and cemeteries of the new converted populations. Competition for hearts, minds and souls was fierce in this region in this period.[49]

There is also growing consensus that Muḥammad was preaching to a society that was experiencing acute economic contraction as a result of the Perso-Roman Wars.[50] The confrontation and the effective militarisation of Rome and Persia had an important impact on trade originating in or passing through the Ḥijāz. With government expenditure funnelled into the army and chronic pressure on the domestic economies to support the war effort, demand for luxury items must have fallen considerably. The fact that the traditional markets, above all the cities in the Levant and in Persia, were caught up in the fighting can only have further depressed the economy of southern Arabia.[51]

Few would have felt the pinch more than the Quraysh of Mecca, whose caravans carrying gold and other valuables to Syria had been the stuff of legend. They also lost their lucrative contract to supply the Roman army with the leather needed for saddles, strapping for boots and shields, belts and more besides.[52] Their livelihood too may have been further threatened by a decline in pilgrims visiting the *haram*, an important shrine dedicated to pagan gods located in Mecca. The site was centred on a series of idols—reportedly including one "of Abraham as an old man"—but the most important of which was a red agate statue of a man with a golden right hand and with seven divinatory arrows around it.[53] As guardians of Mecca, the Quraysh did well from selling food and water to visitors and performing rituals for pilgrims. With upheaval in Syria and Mesopotamia having repercussions further beyond, and disruption in so many different aspects of daily life, it was not surprising that Muḥammad's warnings of imminent doomsday struck a powerful chord.

Muḥammad's preaching certainly fell on fertile ground. He was offering a bold and coherent explanation for traumatic levels of upheaval with immense passion and conviction. Not only were the epiphanies he had received powerful, so too were the warnings he issued. Those who followed his teaching would find that their land would be fruitful and burst with grain; those who did not would see their crops fail.[54] Spiritual salvation would bring economic rewards. There was much to gain: believers would behold nothing less than Paradise, where gardens were fed by fresh and pure water, by "rivers of wine delectable to those that drink it, and rivers of clarified honey." The faithful would be rewarded with every kind of fruit, and would receive the Lord's forgiveness at the same time.[55]

Those who rejected the divine doctrines would face not just doom and disaster but damnation: anyone who waged war on his followers would suffer terribly and receive no mercy. They were to be executed or crucified, lose limbs or be exiled: the enemies of Muḥammad were the enemies of God; truly they would suffer an awful fate.[56] This would include having skin burnt off by fire, to be replaced by fresh skin that would suffer the same fate, so the pain and torture would be never ending.[57] Those who did not believe would "abide in Hell for ever, and drink scalding water that will tear their bowels to pieces."[58]

This radical and impassioned message met with ferocious opposition from the conservative elite of Mecca, who were enraged by its criticism of traditional polytheistic practices and beliefs.[59] Muḥammad was forced to flee to Yathrib (later renamed Medina) in 622 to escape persecution; this flight, known as the *hijra*, became the seminal moment in Islamic history, year zero in the Muslim calendar. As recently discovered papyri make clear, it was the point when Muḥammad's preaching gave birth to a new religion and to a new identity.[60]

Central to this new identity was a strong idea about unity. Muḥammad actively sought to fuse the many tribes of southern Arabia into a single bloc. The Byzantines and Persians had long manipulated local rivalries and played leaders off against each other. Patronage and funding helped create a series of dependent clients and elites who were regulated and rewarded by payments from Rome and Ctesiphon. The intense war left this system in tatters. Protracted hostilities meant that some of the tribes were deprived of "the thirty pounds of gold that they normally received by way of commercial gain through trade with the Roman Empire." Worse, their requests to have their obligations fulfilled were clumsily dealt with. "The emperor can barely pay his soldiers their wages," one agent stated, "much less [you] dogs." When another envoy told the tribesmen that the prospects of future trade were now limited, he was killed and sewn up inside a camel. It was not long before the tribes took matters into their own hands. The answer was to "lay waste to the Roman land" in revenge.[61]

It was not for nothing then that the new faith was being preached in the local language. Behold, says one of the verses in the Qurʾān; here are the words from above—in Arabic.[62] The Arabs were being presented with their own religion, one that created a new identity. This was a faith designed for the local populations, whether nomad or urban, whether members of one tribe or another, and regardless of ethnic or linguistic background. The many loan-words from Greek, Aramaic, Syriac, Hebrew and Persian in the Qurʾān, the text that recorded the revelations handed down to Muḥammad, point to a polyglot milieu where emphasising similarity, rather than difference, was important.[63] Unity was a core tenet, and a major reason for Islam's imminent success. "Let there not be two religions in Arabia" were to be Muḥammad's last words, according to the investigation of one respected Islamic scholar writing in the eighth century.[64]

Muḥammad's prospects did not look promising when he was holed up in Yathrib, with his small group of early followers. Efforts to evangelise and add to the *umma*—the community of believers—were slow, and the situation was precarious as forces closed in from Mecca to attack the renegade preacher. Muḥammad and his followers turned to armed resistance, targeting caravans in a series of increasingly ambitious raids. Momentum built up quickly. Success against superior numbers and against the odds such as at the battle of Badr in 624 provided compelling evidence that Muḥammad and his men enjoyed divine protection; lucrative spoils likewise made onlookers take notice. An intense round of negotiations with leading members of the Quraysh tribe of Mecca finally resulted in an understanding being reached, since known as the treaty of al-Ḥudaybiya, which provided for a ten-year truce between Mecca and Yathrib, and lifted restrictions previously placed on Muḥammad's supporters. The number of converts now began to swell.

As the number of followers grew, so did their aspirations and ambitions. Crucial in this was the designation of a clear religious centre. The faithful had previously been told to face Jerusalem when they prayed. In 628, however, following further revelation, it was apparently announced that this instruction had been a test and should now be amended: the direction or *qibla* to face when praying was nowhere else but Mecca.[65]

Not only that, but the Kaʿba, the old focal point of the polytheistic, pagan religion in Arabia, was identified as the cornerstone for prayer and pilgrimage within the city. This was revealed as having been set up by Ishmael, the son of Abraham and the putative ancestor of twelve Arab tribes. Visitors to the city were told to process around the sacred site, chanting God's name. By doing so, they would be fulfilling the order given to Ishmael that men should be told to come from Arabia and from faraway lands, on camel and on foot, to make a pilgrimage to the place where a black stone at the heart of the monument had been brought by an angel from heaven.[66] By confirming the Ka'ba as sacred, continuity was affirmed with the past, generating a powerful sense of cultural familiarity. In addition to the spiritual benefits offered by the new faith, there were obvious advantages in establishing Mecca as a religious centre par excellence—politically, economically and culturally. It defused antagonism with the Quraysh to the point that senior members of the tribe pledged their allegiance to Muḥammad—and to Islam.

Muḥammad's genius as a leader did not end here. With barriers and opposition melting away in Arabia, expeditionary forces were dispatched to exploit opportunities opening up elsewhere that were too good to miss. The timing could not have been better either: between 628 and 632, Persia's dramatic collapse worsened as anarchy took hold. During this short period, there were no fewer than six kings who claimed royal authority; one well-informed Arab historian writing later put the number at eight—in addition to two queens.[67]

Success attracted new supporters, whose numbers grew as cities, towns and villages on Persia's southern frontier were swallowed up. These were locations that were unused to defending themselves, and folded under the first sign of pressure. Typical was the town of al-Ḥīra (located in what is now south-central Iraq), which capitulated immediately, agreeing to pay off attackers in return for guarantees of peace.[68] Utterly demoralised, senior Persian commanders likewise counselled giving money to the advancing Arab column, "on condition that they would depart."[69]

Securing greater resources was important, for it was not just the spiritual rewards on offer that won people over to Islamic teaching. Since the appearance of Muḥammad, one general is purported to have told his Sasanian counterpart, "we are no longer seeking worldly gains"; the expeditions were now about spreading the word of God.[70] Clearly, evangelical zeal was vital to the success of early Islam. But so too was the innovative way that booty and finances were shared out. Willing to sanction material gain in return for loyalty and obedience, Muḥammad declared that goods seized from non-believers were to be kept by the faithful.[71] This closely aligned economic and religious interests.[72]

Those who converted to Islam early were rewarded with a proportionately greater share of the prizes, in what was effectively a pyramid system. This was formalised in the early 630s with the creation of a *dīwān*, a formal office to oversee the distribution of booty. A share of 20 per cent was to be presented to the leader of the faithful, the Caliph, but the bulk was to be shared by his supporters and those who participated in successful attacks.[73] Early adopters benefited most from new conquests while new believers were keen to enjoy the fruits of success. The result was a highly efficient motor to drive expansion.

As the newly formed armies continued to establish political and religious authority over the nomadic tribesmen known collectively as the "desert people," or Bedouin, they made enormous inroads, bringing huge swathes of territory under their control at great speed. Although the chronology of events is difficult to re-establish with certainty, recent scholarship has convincingly shown that the expansion into Persia took place several years earlier than previously thought—at the moment Sasanian society was imploding between 628 and 632, rather than after it had done so.[74] This redating is significant, for it helps contextualise the rapid gains made in Palestine, where all the cities submitted in the mid-630s—including Jerusalem, which had only recently been recovered by the Romans.[75]

Both Rome and Persia responded to the threat too late. In the case of the latter, a crushing Muslim victory at Qādisiyyah in 636 was a huge boost for the surging Arab armies and for Islamic self-confidence. The fact that a swathe of Persian nobles fell in the course of the battle heavily compromised future resistance, and served to put an already teetering state on the canvas.[76] The Roman response was no more effective. An army under the command of the Emperor's brother Theodore was heavily defeated in 636 at the River Yarmuk, south of the Sea of Galilee, after he had seriously underestimated the size, capability and determination of the Arab force.[77]

The heart of the world now gaped open. One city after another surrendered, as the attacking forces bore down on Ctesiphon itself. After a lengthy siege, the capital eventually fell, its treasury being captured by the Arabs. Persia had been broken by the spectacular rearguard action of the Romans, but it had been swallowed up by Muḥammad's followers. Momentum was gathering fast for a disparate group of believers who had accepted their prophet's teachings, alongside opportunists and chancers who had joined them in the hope of rewards to come. With interests aligned and success following success, the only question now was how far Islam would spread.

5

The Road to Concord

Strategic genius and tactical acumen on the battlefield enabled Muḥammad and his followers to achieve a series of stunning successes. The support of the Quraysh tribe and the dominant political elite in Mecca had been crucial too, providing a platform for persuading the tribes of southern Arabia to hear and accept the message of the new faith. The opportunities that opened up with the collapse of Persia likewise came at the right moment. But two other important reasons also help explain the triumph of Islam in the early part of the seventh century: the support provided by Christians, and above all that given by Jews.

In a world where religion seems to be the cause of conflict and bloodshed, it is easy to overlook the ways in which the great faiths learnt and borrowed from each other. To the modern eye, Christianity and Islam seem to be diametrically opposed, but in the early years of their coexistence relations were not so much pacific as warmly encouraging. And if anything, the relationship between Islam and Judaism was even more striking for its mutual compatibility. The support of the Jews in the Middle East was vital for the propagation and spread of the word of Muḥammad.

Although the material for the early Islamic history is complicated, an unmistakable and striking theme can be consistently teased from the literature of this period—whether Arabic, Armenian, Syriac, Greek or Hebrew—as well as from the archaeological evidence: Muḥammad and his followers went to great lengths to assuage the fears of Jews and Christians as Muslim control expanded.

When Muḥammad was cornered in Yathrib in southern Arabia in the 620s, soliciting the help of the Jews had been one of his key strategies. This was a town—and a region—that was steeped in Judaism and Jewish history. Barely a century earlier, one fanatical Jewish ruler of Ḥimyar had overseen the systematic persecution of the Christian minority, which crystallised a broad pattern of alliances that still held firm: Persia had come in to support the Ḥimyarites against the alliance of Rome and Ethiopia. Muḥammad was eager to conciliate with the Jews of southern Arabia—starting with the elders of Yathrib.

Leading Jews in the town, later renamed Medina, pledged their support to Muḥammad in return for guarantees of mutual defence. These were laid out in a formal document that stated that their own faith and their possessions would be respected now and in the future by Muslims. It also set out a mutual understanding between Judaism and Islam: followers of both religions pledged to defend each other in the event that either was attacked by any third party; no harm would come to Jews, and no help would be given to their enemies. Muslims and Jews would co-operate with one another, extending "sincere advice and counsel."[1] It helped then that Muḥammad's revelations seemed not only conciliatory but familiar: there was much in common with the Old Testament, for example, not least the veneration for the prophets and for Abraham in particular, and there was obvious common ground for those who repudiated Jesus' status as the Messiah. It was not just that Islam was not a threat to Judaism; there were elements that seemed to go hand in glove with it.[2]

Word soon began to spread among Jewish communities that Muḥammad and his followers were allies. An extraordinary text written in North Africa in the late 630s records how news of the Arab advances was being welcomed by Jews in Palestine because it meant a loosening of the Roman—and Christian—grip on power in the region. There was heated speculation that what was going on might be a fulfilment of ancient prophecies: "they were saying that the prophet had appeared, coming with the Saracens, and that he was proclaiming the advent of the anointed one, the Christ that was to come."[3] This, some Jews concluded, was the coming of the Messiah—perfectly timed to show that Jesus Christ was a fraud and that the last days of man had arrived.[4] Not all were persuaded, however. As one learned rabbi put it, Muḥammad was a false prophet, "for the prophets do not come armed with a sword."[5]

The fact that there are other texts that say that the Arabs were welcomed by Jews as liberators from Roman rule provides important corroborating evidence about positive local reactions to the rising profile of Islam. One text about this period written a century later reports how an angel came to Rabbi Shim'on b. Yoḥai after he became disturbed by the suffering inflicted in the wake of Heraclius' recovery of Jerusalem and the forced baptism and persecution of the Jews that followed. "How do we know [the Muslims] are our salvation," he purportedly asked. "Do not be afraid," the angel reassured him, for God is "bringing about the kingdom of [the Arabs] only for the purpose of delivering you from that wicked [Rome]. In accordance with His will, He shall raise up over them a prophet. And he will conquer the land for them, and they shall come and restore it with grandeur." Muḥammad was seen as the means of fulfilling Jewish messianic hopes. These were lands that belonged to the descendants of Abraham—which meant solidarity between Arab and Jew.[6]

There were other, tactical reasons to co-operate with the advancing armies. At Hebron, for instance, Jews offered to cut a deal with the Arab commanders: "grant us security so that we would have a similar status among you," and allow us "the right to build a synagogue in front of the entrance to the cave of Machpelah" where Abraham was buried; in return, Jewish leaders stated, "we will show you where to make a gateway" in order to get past the city's formidable defences.[7]

Support from the local population was a crucial factor in the successes of the Arabs in Palestine and Syria in the early 630s, as we have seen. Recent research on the Greek, Syriac and Arabic sources has shown that, in the earliest accounts, the arrival of the attacking armies was welcomed by the Jews. This was not surprising: if we peel back the colourful later additions and venomous interpretation (such as claims that the Muslims were guilty of "satanic hypocrisy"), we read that the military commander who led the army to Jerusalem entered the Holy City in the humble dress of a pilgrim, keen to worship alongside those whose religious views were apparently seen as being if not compatible, then at least not entirely dissimilar.[8]

There were other groups in the Middle East who were not disillusioned by the rise of Islam. The region as a whole was filled with religious non-conformists. There was a plethora of Christian sects that took issue with decisions made at church councils or objected to doctrines that they deemed heretical. This was particularly true in Palestine and Sinai, where there were many Christian communities violently opposed to the conclusions reached at the Council of Chalcedon in 451 about the precise meaning of the divine nature of Jesus Christ, and who had been the subject of formal persecution as a result.[9] These Christian groups found themselves no better off following Heraclius' spectacular recovery against the Persians thanks to the assertive orthodox religious posturing that accompanied the Emperor's reconquests.

As such, some saw the successes as a means to an end, but also as being religiously sympathetic. John of Dasen, the metropolitan of Nisibis, was told by one astute Arab commander wanting to establish himself in the city that if the former provided his backing, he in turn would not just help the cleric depose the leading figure in the Christian church in the east, but install him in his place.[10] A letter sent in the 640s by a prominent cleric reports that the new rulers not only did not fight against Christians, "but even commend our religion, show honour to the priests and monasteries and saints of our Lord," and make gifts endowing religious institutions.[11]

In this context, the messages of Muḥammad and his followers earned the solidarity of local Christian populations. For one thing, Islam's stark warnings about polytheism and the worship of idols had an obvious resonance with Christians, whose own teachings mirrored these views precisely. A sense of camaraderie was also reinforced by a familiar cast of characters such as Moses, Noah, Job and Zachariah who appear in the Qur᾿ān alongside explicit statements that the God who gave Moses the scriptures, and who sent other apostles after him, was now sending another prophet to spread the word.[12]

Awareness of common ground with Christians and Jews was reinforced by the use of familiar reference points and by accentuating similarities in matters of custom and religious doctrine. God had not chosen to reveal messages only to Muḥammad: "He has already revealed the Torah and the Gospel for the guidance of mankind," reads one verse in the Qur᾿ān.[13] Remember the words of the angels told to Mary, mother of Jesus, says another verse. Echoing the Hail Mary, Islam's holy book teaches the words "God has chosen you [Mary]. He has made you pure and exalted you above womankind. Mary, be obedient to your Lord; bow down and worship with the worshippers."[14]

For Christians who were mired in arguments about the nature of Jesus and of the Trinity, perhaps most striking was the fact that Muḥammad's revelations contained a core message that was both powerful and simple: there is one God; and Muḥammad is his messenger.[15] It was easy to understand and chimed with the basis of the Christian faith that God was all-powerful, and that from time to time apostles were sent to pass on messages from above.

Christians and Jews who argued with each other about religion were crazy, records another verse in the Qur᾿ān; "have you no sense?"[16] Division was the work of Satan, Muḥammad's text warned; never allow disagreements to take hold—instead, cling together to God, and never be divided.[17] Muḥammad's message was one of conciliation. Believers who follow the Jewish faith or are Christians who live good lives "have nothing to fear or regret," says the Qur᾿ān on more than one occasion.[18] Those who believed in one God were to be honoured and respected.

There were also customs and rulings that later became associated with Islam, and which predated Muḥammad but were now adopted, apparently by the Prophet himself. For example, amputation as a punishment for theft and the passing of a death sentence for those who renounced their faith were common practices that were taken on by Muslims. Elements like almsgiving, fasting, pilgrimage and prayer became central components of Islam, compounding the sense of continuity and familiarity.[19] The similarities with Christianity and Judaism later became a sensitive topic, which was partly dealt with by the dogma that Muḥammad was illiterate. This insulated him from claims that he was familiar with the teachings of the Torah and the Bible—despite near-contemporaries commenting that he was "learned," and knew both the Old and New Testament.[20] Some have gone further still, seeking to claim that the Qur᾿ān has as its base a Christian lectionary written in an Aramaic derivative that was subsequently adapted and remoulded. This—like many claims that challenge or dismiss the Islamic tradition—has gained notoriety, though it has limited support among modern historians.[21]

That Christians and Jews were core constituencies for support during the first phase of Islamic expansion explains why one of the few verses in the Qur᾿ān that relates to contemporary events during Muḥammad's lifetime spoke in positive terms about the Romans. The Romans have been defeated, says the Qur᾿ān, referring to any one of a number of chronic setbacks during the wars with Persia before the late 620s. "But in a few years they shall themselves gain victory: such being the will of God before and after."[22] This could be guaranteed: God does not fail in his promises.[23] The message was inclusive and familiar and seemed to draw the sting out of fractious arguments that had set Christians on edge. From their perspective, Islam looked inclusive and conciliatory, and offered hope of calming tensions.

In fact, the sources are full of examples of Christians admiring what they saw among the Muslims and their armies. One text from the eighth century notes how one Christian ascetic was sent to observe the enemy and came back impressed by the experience. "I come to you from a people staying up through the night praying," he supposedly told his peers, "and remaining abstinent during the day, commanding the right and forbidding the wrong, monks by night, lions by day." This seemed entirely commendable—and served to blur the lines between Christianity and Islam. The fact that other accounts from this period talk of Christian monks adopting Muḥammad's teachings provides another sign of differences of doctrine not being entirely clear-cut.[24] The asceticism espoused by the early Muslims was also recognisable and laudable, providing a culturally familiar reference point to the Graeco-Roman world.[25]

Efforts to conciliate with the Christians were supplemented by a policy of protecting and respecting the People of the Book—that is to say, both Jews and Christians. The Qur'ān makes plain that early Muslims saw themselves not as rivals of these two faiths but as heirs to the same legacy: Muḥammad's revelations had previously been "revealed to Abraham and Ishmael, to Isaac and Jacob and the tribes"; God had entrusted the same messages to Moses and Jesus too. "We discriminate against none of them," says the Qur'ān. In other words, the prophets of Judaism and Christianity were the same as those of Islam.[26]

It is no coincidence, then, that the Qur'ān makes more than sixty references to the word *umma*, used not as an ethnic label but to mean a community of believers. On several occasions, the text notes mournfully that mankind was once a single *umma*, before differences drove people apart.[27] The implicit message was that it was God's will that differences should be put to one side. Similarities between the great monotheistic faiths are played up in the Qur'ān and in the *ḥadīth*—the collections of comments, sayings and deeds of the Prophet—while differences are consistently played down. The emphasis on treating Jews and Christians alike with respect and tolerance is unmistakable.

The sources for this period are notoriously difficult to interpret because they are complicated and contradictory, but also because many were written long after the events. However, recent advances in palaeography, the discovery of wisps of texts that were previously unknown and increasingly sophisticated ways of understanding written material are transforming long-held views of this epic period in history. Thus, while the Islamic tradition has long held that Muḥammad died in 632, recent scholarship suggests that the

Prophet may have been alive later. Multiple sources from the seventh and eighth centuries attest to a charismatic preacher figure—recently suggested as being Muḥammad himself—directing the Arab forces and spurring them onwards at the gates of Jerusalem.[28]

The extraordinary progress of Muḥammad's followers in Palestine was matched by a helpless and inept response by the authorities. Some members of the Christian clergy fought a desperate rearguard action, painting the Arabs in the worst possible light in a doomed attempt to convince the local population not to be fooled into giving their support to a message that sounded both simple and familiar. The "Saracens" are vengeful and hate God, warned the patriarch of Jerusalem, shortly after the conquest of the city. They plunder cities, ravage the countryside fields, set fire to churches and destroy monasteries. The evil they commit against Christ and against the church is appalling, as are the "foul blasphemies they pronounce about God."[29]

In fact, it appears that the Arab conquests were neither as brutal nor as shocking as the commentators make out. Across Syria and Palestine, for example, there is little evidence of violent conquest in the archaeological record.[30] Damascus, for instance, the most important city in northern Syria, surrendered quickly after terms were agreed between the local bishop and the attacking Arab commander. Even allowing for some poetic licence, the compromise was both reasonable and realistic: in exchange for allowing churches to remain open and untouched and for the Christian population to remain unmolested, the inhabitants agreed to recognise the overlordship of new masters. In practice what this meant was paying tax not to Constantinople and to the imperial authorities, but to representatives of "the prophet, the caliphs and the believers."[31]

It was a process that was replicated time and again as the Arabs began to fan out in every direction, racing down the trade and communication routes. Armies swarmed into south-western Iran, before attention turned to hunting down Yazdagird III, the last Sasanian king who had fled east. Expeditionary forces that set out against Egypt caused chaos by operating in tandem, resulting in limited and ineffective military resistance—made worse by local populations fighting against each other or being willing to negotiate terms in the face of fear and uncertainty. Alexandria, a jewel of the eastern Mediterranean, was demilitarised and forced to promise a vast tribute in exchange for assurances that churches would be left intact and the Christian population left to their own devices. News of this agreement was met with weeping and wailing in Alexandria, and even by calls that the man who had brokered it, the Patriarch Cyrus, should be stoned for his betrayal. "I have made this treaty," he declared in his defence, "in order to save you and your children." And with this, records one author writing a century or so later, "the Muslims took control of all of Egypt, south and north, and in doing so, trebled their income from taxes."[32] God was punishing Christians for their sins, wrote another author at the time.[33]

In an almost perfect model of expansion, the threat of military force led to negotiated settlements as one province after another submitted to the new authorities. To start with, overlordship in conquered territories was light and even unobtrusive. By and large, the existing majority populations were allowed to get on with their business unmolested by new masters who established garrisons and living quarters away from existing urban centres.[34] In some cases, new cities were founded for the Muslims, such as Fusṭāṭ in Egypt, Kūfa on the Euphrates, Ramla in Palestine and Ayla in modern Jordan, where the sites of mosques and governors' palaces could be chosen and built from scratch.[35]

The fact that new churches were built at the same time, in North Africa, Egypt and Palestine, suggests that a *modus vivendi* quickly established itself where religious tolerance was normative.[36] This seems to have been echoed in lands taken from the Sasanians, where at least to start with Zoroastrians were either ignored or left alone.[37] In the case of Jews and Christians, it is not impossible that this was even formalised. A complex and contentious text known as the Pact of ʿUmar purports to set out the rights that the so-called People of the Book would enjoy from their new overlords, and conversely to set out the basis for interaction with Islam: no crosses were to be marked on mosques; the Qurʾān was not to be taught to non-Muslim children, but no one was to be prevented from conversion to Islam; Muslims were to be respected at all times, and were to be given directions if they asked for help. Cohabitation of the faiths was an important hallmark of early Islamic expansion—and an important part of its success.[38]

In response, some hedged their bets, as pottery kilns from Jerash in northern Jordan show. Lamps were produced in the seventh century with a Christian inscription in Latin on one side and an Islamic invocation in Arabic on the other.[39] This was in part a pragmatic response to recent experiences, given that the Persian occupation of this region had lasted for only twenty-five years. There was no guarantee that the Arab masters were necessarily going to last either, as a seventh-century Greek text makes absolutely clear: "the body will renew itself," the author assured his readers; there was hope that the Muslim conquests might be a flash in the pan.[40]

The new regime's lightness of touch also showed itself in matters of administration. Roman coinage was used for several decades after the conquests alongside newly minted coins struck with familiar imagery and in long-established denominations; the existing legal systems were broadly left intact as well. Existing norms on a raft of social practices were adopted by the conquerors, including a number concerned with inheritance, dowries, oaths and marriage, as well as with fasting. In many cases governors and bureaucrats were left in position in former Sasanian and Roman territories.[41] Part of the reason for this was simple mathematics. The conquerors, whether Arabs or non-Arabs, true believers (*mu'minūn*) or those who had joined them and submitted to their authority (*muslimūn*), were in a chronic minority, which meant that working with the local community was not so much a choice as a necessity.

Doing so also happened because in the grand scheme of things there were larger battles to be fought following the successes in Persia, Palestine, Syria and Egypt. One was the continued struggle with the shattered remains of the Roman Empire. Constantinople itself was put under sustained pressure as the Arab leadership sought to finish the Romans off once and for all. More important even than that, however, was the battle for the soul of Islam.

In a parallel with early Christianity's internal wrangles, establishing precisely what Muḥammad had been told, how it should be recorded and spread—and to whom—became a source of major concern after his death. The struggles were ferocious: of the first four men appointed to follow the Prophet as his representative, successor or "caliph," three were assassinated. There were furious arguments about how to interpret Muḥammad's teachings, and desperate efforts to twist or appropriate his legacy. It was to try to standardise precisely what Muḥammad's message had been that the order was given, most probably in the last quarter of the seventh century, for it to be written down in a single text—the Qur'ān.[42]

The antagonism between rival factions served to harden attitudes to non-Muslims. With each group claiming to be more faithful guardians of the words of the Prophet, and therefore the will of God, it was perhaps not surprising that attention would soon turn to the *kāfir*, those who were not believers.

Muslim leaders had been tolerant and even gracious to Christians, rebuilding the church of Edessa after it was damaged by an earthquake in 679.[43] But in the late seventh century things began to change. Attention turned to proselytising, evangelising and converting the local populations to Islam—alongside an increasingly hostile attitude towards them.

One manifestation of this came during what modern commentators sometimes dub the "coin wars," as propaganda blows were traded on pieces of currency. After the Caliph began to issue coins with the legend "There is no God but God alone; Muḥammad is the messenger of God" in the early 690s, Constantinople retaliated. Coins were struck which no longer had the image of the Emperor on the front (the obverse), but put it on the reverse instead. In its place on the obverse was a dramatic new image: Jesus Christ. The intention was to reinforce Christian identity and to demonstrate that the empire enjoyed divine protection.[44]

In an extraordinary development, the Islamic world now matched the Christians like with like. Remarkably, the initial response to the issuing of coins with Jesus and the Emperor on them was to respond with an image on coins minted for a few short years of a man in the parallel role to that played by Jesus—as the protector of the lands of the faithful. Although this image is usually presumed to be that of the Caliph ʿAbd al-Malik, it is entirely possible that this is none other than Muḥammad himself. He appears in a flowing tunic, with a lustrous beard and holding a sword in a scabbard. If this is the Prophet, then it is the earliest-known image of him, and remarkably one that those who knew him during his lifetime were aware of and saw for themselves. Al-Balādhurī, writing over a century later, reports that some of Muḥammad's surviving companions in Medina who had known him well saw these coins. Another much later writer who had access to early Islamic material says much the same, noting that the Prophet's own friends were uncomfortable about the use of an image in this way. The coins did not stay in circulation long, for by the end of the 690s the currency circulating in the Islamic world was completely redesigned: all images were removed and were replaced by verses from the Qurʾān on both sides of the coin.[45]

Converting Christians was not the most important goal in the late seventh century, however, for the key battleground was between rival Muslim factions. Fierce debate broke out between those claiming to be the rightful heir to Muḥammad, during which the trump card became knowing the most about the Prophet's early life. So acute did competition become that there were serious and concerted efforts to relocate the centre of the religion away from Mecca and establish it in Jerusalem after one powerful faction emerged in the Middle East and turned against traditionalists in southern Arabia. The mosque of the Dome of the Rock, the first major Islamic sacred building, was constructed at the start of the 690s, partly with the intention of diverting attention away from Mecca.[46] As one modern commentator puts it, buildings and material culture were being used "as a weapon for ideological conflict" during a volatile period of civil war, a time when the Caliph was taking up arms against the direct descendants of the Prophet Muḥammad himself.[47]

The strife within the Muslim world explains inscriptions that were set in mosaic on both the outer and inner faces of the Dome of the Rock mosque which were aimed at mollifying Christians. Worship God, the compassionate and merciful, and honour and bless His prophet Muḥammad, they read. But they also proclaim that Jesus was the Messiah. "So believe in God and his envoys . . . bless your envoy and your servant Jesus son of Mary and peace be on him on the day of birth and on the day of death and on the day he is raised from the dead."[48] Even in the 690s, in other words, there was a blurring of religious boundaries. So close, in fact, did Islam seem that some Christian scholars thought its teachings were not so much those of a new faith as a divergent interpretation of Christianity. According to John of Damascus, one of the leading commentators of the time, Islam was a Christian heresy rather than a different religion. Muḥammad, he wrote, had come up with his ideas based on his reading of the Old and New Testaments—and on a conversation with an errant Christian monk.[49]

In spite, or perhaps because of, the relentless jostling for position and authority at the centre of the Muslim world, the peripheries continued to see astonishing expansion. Commanders who were happier in the field than fighting political and theological battles led armies ever deeper into Central Asia, the Caucasus and North Africa. In the case of the latter, the advance seemed relentless. After crossing the Straits of Gibraltar, the armies flooded through Spain and into France, where they met resistance in 732 somewhere between Poitiers and Tours, barely 200 miles from Paris. In a battle that subsequently acquired a near-mythical status as the moment the Islamic surge was halted, Charles Martel led a force that inflicted a crucial defeat. The fate of Christian Europe hung by a thread, later historians argued, and had it not been for the heroism and skill of the defenders, the continent would surely have become Muslim.[50] The truth is that, while the defeat was certainly a setback, it did not mean that new attacks would not be unleashed in the future—if, that is, there were prizes worth winning. And as far as western

Europe was concerned in this period, these prizes were few and far between: wealth and rewards lay elsewhere.

The Muslim conquests completed Europe's shunt into the shadows that had begun with the invasions of the Goths, Huns and others two centuries earlier. What remained of the Roman Empire—now little more than Constantinople and its hinterland—shrivelled and teetered on the brink of complete collapse. Trade in the Christian Mediterranean, already dwindling on the eve of the wars with Persia, foundered. Once bustling cities like Athens and Corinth contracted sharply, their populations reduced and their centres all but abandoned. Shipwrecks from the seventh century onwards, a good indicator of the volume of commercial exchange going on, disappear almost entirely. Trade that was not local simply came to an end.[51]

The contrast with the Muslim world could not have been sharper. The economic heartlands of the Roman Empire and Persia had not just been conquered but united. Egypt and Mesopotamia had been linked to form the core of a new economic and political behemoth that stretched from the Himalayas through to the Atlantic. In spite of the ideological rows, the rivalries and the occasional paroxysms of instability in the Islamic world—such as the overthrow of the existing caliphate in 750 by the ʿAbbāsid dynasty—the new empire coursed with ideas, goods and money. Indeed, this was precisely what lay behind the ʿAbbāsid revolution: it was the cities of Central Asia that paved the way for regime change. These were the hotbeds where intellectual arguments were refined and where rebellions were financed. This was where critical decisions were taken in the battle for the soul of Islam.[52]

The Muslims had taken over a world that was well ordered and studded with hundreds of cities of consumers—taxable citizens, in other words. As each fell into the hands of the caliphate, more resources and assets came under the control of the centre. Trade routes, oases, cities and natural resources were targeted and subsumed. Ports that connected trade between the Persian Gulf and China were annexed, as were the trans-Saharan trade routes that had built up, allowing Fez (in modern Morocco) to become "immensely prosperous" and home to trade that in the words of one contemporary observer produced "huge profits." The subjugation of new regions and peoples brought astonishing sums of money into the Muslim empire: one Arab historian estimated that the conquest of Sindh (in what is now Pakistan) yielded 60 million dirhams, to say nothing of the future riches to be drawn from taxes, levies and other duties.[53] In today's terms, this was worth billions of dollars.

As forces headed east, the process of extracting tribute was as lucrative and successful as it had been in Palestine, Egypt and elsewhere. The cities of Central Asia were picked off one by one, the loose links between them sealing their downfall: without an organisational structure to co-ordinate defences, each waited for its fate in turn.[54] The inhabitants of Samarkand were pressured into paying a huge sum of money for the Muslim commander to withdraw, though in time it had to surrender anyway. At least the city's governor was spared the fate of Dewashtich, ruler of Panjikent (in modern Tajikistan) who styled himself King of Sogdia; he was deceived, trapped and crucified in front of his own people. The governor of Balkh (in what is now northern Afghanistan) suffered a similar fate.[55]

The advances into Central Asia were greatly facilitated by the chaos that had started to embroil the steppe region at the same time that Persia crumbled. A devastating winter in 627–28 resulted in famine and the death of very large numbers of livestock, and precipitated a major shift in power. In the process of pushing east, the Muslim forces confronted the nomad tribes who had also benefited from the collapse of Persia. In the 730s, a crushing defeat was inflicted on the Türk nomads, whose ramifications were made more severe when Sulu, the dominant figure on the steppes, was murdered following a bad-tempered game of backgammon.[56]

As the tribal buffer disintegrated, the Muslims swept eastwards slowly but surely, taking cities, oasis towns and communication nodes, reaching the western reaches of China by the start of the eighth century.[57] In 751, the Arab conquerors were brought face to face with the Chinese, defeating them decisively in a confrontation by the Talas River in Central Asia. This brought the Muslims up to a natural boundary, beyond which there was little point expanding further—at least in the short term. In China, meanwhile, the defeat brought repercussions and upheaval, triggering a major revolt against the ruling Tang dynasty led by the Sogdian general An Lushan, which led to an extended period of unrest and instability that created a vacuum for others to exploit.[58]

Quick to do so were the Uighurs, a tribal people who had supported the Tang and benefited considerably as their former overlords withdrew to the safety of China proper to lick their wounds. To better control their growing territories, the Uighurs built permanent settlements, the most important of which, Balāsāghūn or Quz Ordu (in modern Kyrgyzstan), became the seat of the ruler, or *khagan*. It was a curious blend of city and camp, with the leader having a tent with a golden dome and throne within it. The city had twelve entry gates and was protected by walls and towers. To judge from later accounts, this was just one of many Uighur towns that sprang up from the eighth century onwards.[59]

The Uighurs quickly became the pre-eminent force on Islam's eastern frontier. In doing so, they first incorporated and then replaced the Sogdians as the leading figures in long-distance trade, especially of silk. Strings of impressive palace complexes attest to the riches generated during this period.[60] Khukh Ordung, for example, was a fortified city that was home to tent camps as well as permanent buildings that included a pavilion that the *khagan* used to receive important visitors and for religious ceremonies.[61] Faced with the rivalry of the Muslims, the Uighurs tried to retain their own identity—deciding to convert to Manichaeism, perhaps as middle ground between the Islamic world to the west and China to the east.

The Muslims' conquests had brought a vast web of trade and communication routes under their control, with the oases of Afghanistan and the Ferghana valley linked to North Africa and the Atlantic Ocean under their authority. The wealth concentrated within the centre of Asia was astonishing. Excavations in Panjikent and at Balalyk-tepe and other sites in modern Uzbekistan bear witness to patronage of the arts of the highest order—and point clearly to the money that lay behind it. Scenes from court life, as well as from Persian epic literature, were beautifully portrayed on the walls of private residences. One set of images from a palace in Samarkand shows the cosmopolitan world that the Muslims were stepping into: the local ruler is depicted receiving gifts from foreign dignitaries, who come from China, Persia, India and perhaps even Korea. Towns, provinces and palaces like these fell into the hands of the Muslim armies that were swarming along the trade routes.[62]

With this new wealth flooding into central coffers, heavy investments began to be made in places like Syria, where in the eighth century market squares and shops were built on a grand scale in the cities of Jerash, Scythopolis and Palmyra.[63] Most striking of all, however, was the construction of an enormous new city. It was to become the richest and most populous in the world, and remained so for centuries—even if some estimates made in the tenth century are over-exuberant. Basing his calculations on the number of bathhouses, the number of attendants required to maintain them and the likely distribution of baths to private houses, one author estimated the population of the city to be just under 100 million.[64] It was known as Madīnat al-Salām, or the city of peace. We know it as Baghdad.

It was the perfect symbol of the Islamic world's affluence, the heart of royal power, patronage and prestige. It marked a new centre of gravity for the successors of Muḥammad, the political and economic axis linking the Muslim lands in every direction. It provided a setting for pageantry and ostentation on a staggering scale, such as on the occasion of the marriage of Hārūn al-Rashīd, the son of the Caliph, in 781. Apart from presenting his bride with an array of pearls of unprecedented size, tunics decorated with rubies and a banquet "the likes of which had never been prepared for any woman before," the groom distributed largesse to people from all over the country. Gold bowls filled with silver and silver bowls filled with gold were taken round and shared out, as were expensive perfumes in glass vessels. Women in attendance were given purses containing gold and silver coins "and a large silver tray with scents, and a richly coloured and heavily encrusted robe of honour was bestowed on each of them. Nothing comparable had ever been seen before"—at least not in Islamic times.[65]

This was all made possible by the extraordinarily large tax revenue brought in from a vast, productive and monetised empire. When Hārūn al-Rashīd died in 809, his treasury included 4,000 turbans, 1,000 precious porcelain vessels, many kinds of perfume, vast quantities of jewels, silver and gold, 150,000 lances and the same number of shields, and thousands of pairs of boots—many of them lined with sable, mink and other kinds of fur.[66] "The least of the territories ruled by the least of my subjects provides a revenue larger than your whole dominion," the Caliph supposedly wrote to the Emperor in Constantinople in the middle of the ninth century.[67] The wealth fuelled a period of incredible prosperity and an intellectual revolution.

Private enterprise surged as levels of disposable income rose dramatically. Basra on the Persian Gulf acquired a reputation as a market where anything could be found, including silks and linen, pearls and gems as well as henna and rosewater. The market at Mosul, a city with magnificent houses and fine public baths, was an excellent place to find arrows, stirrups or saddles, according to one tenth-century commentator. On the other hand, he noted, if you wanted the finest pistachios, sesame oil, pomegranates or dates, the best place to find them was in Nīshāpūr.[68]

There was a hunger for the tastiest ingredients, the finest craftsmanship and the best produce. As tastes became more sophisticated, so did appetites for information. Even if the traditional story that Chinese prisoners captured at the battle of Talas in 751 introduced paper-making skills to the Islamic world is overly romantic, it is certainly the case that from the later part of the eighth century the availability of paper made the recording, sharing and dissemination of knowledge wider, easier and quicker. The resultant explosion of literature covered all areas of science, mathematics, geography and travel.[69]

Writers recorded that the best quinces were from Jerusalem, and the finest pastries from Egypt; Syrian figs were bursting with taste, while the umari plums of Shiraz were to die for. As more discriminating tastes could now be afforded, sternly critical reviews were no less important. Fruit from Damascus should be avoided, the same author warned, since it was tasteless (and the city's population were over-argumentative to boot). At least the city was not as bad as Jerusalem, a "golden basin filled with scorpions," where the baths were filthy, provisions overpriced and the cost of living enough to discourage even a short visit.[70] Traders and travellers brought tales back with them about places they were visiting—about what the markets there had to offer and what the peoples beyond the lands of Islam were like. The Chinese of all ages "wear silk in both winter and summer," noted one author who collated reports from abroad, with some having the finest material imaginable. This elegance did not extend to all habits: "The Chinese are unhygienic, and they do not wash their backsides with water after defecating but merely wipe themselves with Chinese paper."[71]

At least they enjoyed musical entertainment—unlike the Indian people, who regarded such spectacles as "shameful." Rulers across India eschewed alcohol too. They did not do so for religious reasons, but because of their entirely reasonable view that if drunk, "how can someone run a kingdom properly?" Though India "is the land of medicine and of philosophers," the author concludes, China "is a healthier country, with fewer diseases and better air." It was rare to see "the blind, one-eyed and the deformed," whereas "in India, there are plenty of them."[72]

Luxury items flooded in from abroad. Porcelain and stoneware from China were imported in considerable volume, and shaped local pottery trends, design and techniques—with the distinctive white glaze of Tang bowls becoming extremely popular. Advances in kiln technology helped production keep up with demand, as did developments in size: it is estimated that the largest Chinese kilns became capable of firing 12,000–15,000 pieces at a time. The increasing levels of exchange across what one leading scholar calls "the world's largest maritime trading system" can be demonstrated by the fact that a single ship, wrecked off the coast of Indonesia in the ninth century, was carrying some 70,000 ceramic items when it went down, as well as ornamental boxes, silverware, gold and lead ingots.[73] This was just one example of the profusion of ceramics, silk, tropical hardwoods and exotic animals that the sources reveal were being imported to the ʿAbbāsid world in this period.[74] Such was the quantity of merchandise flowing into the ports of the Persian Gulf that professional divers were employed to salvage jetsam around the harbours, discarded or fallen from cargo ships.[75]

There were huge fortunes to be made from supplying desirable goods. The port of Sīrāf, which handled much of the maritime traffic from the east, boasted palatial residences with eye-watering price tags to match. "I have not seen in the realm of Islam more remarkable buildings, or more handsome, wrote one author in the tenth century."[76] An array of sources attest to large-scale trade going in and out of the Gulf, as well as along the land routes that criss-crossed Central Asia.[77] Rising demand served to inspire and boost local production of ceramics and porcelain, whose buyers were presumably those who were unable to afford the very best (and most expensive) pieces from China. It was no surprise, therefore, that potters in Mesopotamia and the Persian Gulf imitated the white glaze of the imports, experimenting with alkaline, tin and eventually quartz, to develop the look of the translucent (and better-quality) porcelain made in China. In Basra and Samarra, techniques were developed using cobalt to create distinctive "blue and white wares" that centuries later would not only become popular in the Far East, but would be the hallmark of early modern Chinese pottery.[78]

In the eighth and ninth centuries, however, there could be no doubt where the main markets were. One Chinese visitor to the Arab Empire in this period marvelled at the wealth: "everything produced from the earth is there. Carts carry countless goods to markets, where everything is available and cheap: brocade, embroidered silks, pearls and other gems are displayed all over markets and street shops."[79]

Alongside increasingly sophisticated tastes came increasingly refined ideas about suitable pursuits and pastimes. Texts like *The Book of the Crown*, written in the tenth century, set out the correct etiquette for interaction between the ruler and those at the court, while recommending that nobles should hunt, practise archery, play chess and involve themselves in "other similar activities."[80] These were all borrowed directly from Sasanian ideals, but the extent of their influence can be seen in the contemporary fashions in interior decoration, with hunting scenes in particular enjoying great popularity in the private palaces of the elite.[81]

Wealthy patrons also set about funding one of the most astonishing periods of scholarship in history. Brilliant figures—many of them not Muslim—were drawn to the court at Baghdad and to centres of academic excellence across Central Asia like Bukhara, Merv, Gundishapur and Ghazni, as well as further afield in Islamic Spain and in Egypt, to work on a range of subjects including mathematics, philosophy, physics and geography.

Large numbers of texts were gathered and translated from Greek, Persian and Syriac into Arabic, ranging from manuals on horse-medicine and veterinary sciences to works of ancient Greek philosophy.[82] These were devoured by scholars who used them as the basis for future research. Education and learning became a cultural ideal. There were families like the Barmakids, originally a Buddhist family from Balkh, who gained influence and power in ninth-century Baghdad and energetically championed the translation of a wide range of texts from Sanskrit into Arabic, even setting up a paper mill to help produce copies for wider dissemination.[83]

Or there was the Bukẖtīsẖūʿ family, Christians from Gundesẖāpūr in Persia, which produced generations of intellectuals who wrote treatises on medicine and even on lovesickness—at the same time as practising as physicians, with some even serving the Caliph personally.[84] Medical texts written in this period formed the bedrock of Islamic medicine for centuries. "How is the pulse of someone who suffers from anxiety?" was Question 16 of a question-and-answer text written in medieval Egypt; the answer ("slight, weak and irregular"), noted the author, could be found in an encyclopaedia written in the tenth century.[85]

Pharmacopoeia—texts on mixing and creating medicines—listed experiments undertaken with substances like lemongrass, myrtle seeds, cumin and wine vinegar, celery seeds and spikenard.[86] Others worked on optics, with Ibn al-Haytham, a scholar who lived in Egypt, writing a ground-breaking treatise that reached conclusions not only about how vision and the brain are linked but also about differences between perception and knowledge.[87]

Or there was Abū Rayḥān al-Bīrūnī, who established that the world revolves around the sun and rotates on an axis. Or polymaths like Abū ʿAlī Ḥusayn ibn Sīnā, known in the west as Avicenna, who wrote on logic, theology, mathematics, medicine and philosophy, doing so in each case with an awe-inspiring intelligence, lucidity and honesty. "I read the *Metaphysics* of Aristotle," he wrote, "but could not comprehend its contents . . . even when I had gone back and read it forty times, and had got to the point where I had memorised it." This is a book, he added in a note that will be of comfort to students of this complex text, "which there is no way of understanding." Happening on a bookseller's stall at a market one day, however, he bought a copy of an analysis of Aristotle's work by Abū Naṣr al-Fārābī, yet another great thinker of the age. Suddenly, it all made sense. "I rejoiced at this," wrote Ibn Sīnā, "and the next day gave much in alms to the poor in gratitude to God, who is exalted."[88]

Then there were materials brought from India, including texts on science, mathematics and astrology written in Sanskrit that were pored over by brilliant men like Muḥammad ibn Mūsā al-Khwārizmī, who noted with delight the simplicity of the numerical system that allowed for the mathematical concept of zero. It provided the basis for leaps and bounds in algebra, applied mathematics, trigonometry and astronomy—the latter, in part, driven by the practical need to know in which direction Mecca lay so that prayers could be offered correctly.

Scholars took pride not only in gathering materials from all corners of the world and studying them, but also in translating them. "The works of the Indians are rendered [into Arabic], the wisdom of the Greeks is translated, and the literature of the Persians has been transferred [to us too]," wrote one author; "as a result, some works have increased in beauty." What a shame, he opined, that Arabic was such an elegant language that it was nearly impossible to translate it.[89]

This was a golden age, a time when brilliant men like al-Kindī pushed the frontiers of philosophy and of science. Brilliant women stepped forward too, like the tenth-century poet best known as Rabīʿa Balkhī, in what is now Afghanistan, and after whom the maternity hospital in Kabul is today named; or Mahsatī Ganjavī who likewise wrote eloquently in perfectly formed—and rather racy—Persian.[90]

While the Muslim world took delight in innovation, progress and new ideas, much of Christian Europe withered in the gloom, crippled by a lack of resources and a dearth of curiosity. St. Augustine had been positively hostile to the concept of investigation and research. "Men want to know for the sake of knowing," he wrote scornfully, "though the knowledge is of no value to them." Curiosity, in his words, was nothing more than a disease.[91]

This disdain for science and scholarship baffled Muslim commentators, who had great respect for Ptolemy and Euclid, for Homer and Aristotle. Some had little doubt what was to blame. Once, wrote the historian al-Masʿūdī, the ancient Greeks and the Romans had allowed the sciences to flourish; then they adopted Christianity. When they did so, they "effaced the signs of [learning], eliminated its traces and destroyed its paths."[92] Science was defeated by faith. It is almost the precise opposite of the world as we see it today: the fundamentalists were not the Muslims, but the Christians; those whose minds were open, curious and generous were based in the east—and certainly not in Europe. As one author put it, when it came to writing about non-Islamic lands, "we did not enter them [in our book] because we see no use whatsoever in describing them." They were intellectual backwaters.[93]

The picture of enlightenment and cultural sophistication was also reflected in the way that minority religions and cultures were treated. In Muslim Spain, Visigothic influences were incorporated into an architectural style that could be read by the subject population as a continuation with the immediate past—and therefore neither aggressive nor triumphalist.[94] We can also read the letters sent by Timothy, the Baghdad-based head of the church of the east in the late eighth and early ninth centuries, which describe a world where senior Christian clerics enjoyed responsive and positive personal relations with the Caliph, and where Christianity was able to maintain a base from which to dispatch evangelical missions into India, China and Tibet and on to the steppes—evidently meeting with considerable success.[95] It was a pattern mirrored in North Africa, where Christian and Jewish communities survived and perhaps even flourished long after the Muslim conquests.[96]

But it is also easy to get carried away. For one thing, despite the apparent unity conferred by the cloak of religion, there was still bitter division within the Islamic world. Three major political centres had evolved by the start of the 900s: one was centred on Córdoba and Spain; one on Egypt and the Upper Nile; and the third on Mesopotamia and (most of) the Arabian peninsula, and they fought with each other over matters of theology as well as for influence and authority. Serious schism within Islam had emerged within a generation of Muḥammad's death, with rival cases being set out to justify the correct succession from the Prophet. These quickly solidified into two competing arguments, championed by Sunnī and Shīʿa interpretations, with the latter arguing passionately that only the descendant of Ali, the Prophet's cousin and son-in-law, should rule as caliph, and the former arguing for a broader understanding.

So despite the fact that there was a notional overarching religious unity that linked the Hindu Kush with the Pyrenees through Mesopotamia and North Africa, finding consensus was another matter. Similarly, relaxed attitudes to beliefs were neither uniform nor consistent. Although there were periods of acceptance of other faiths, there were also phases of persecution and brutal proselytisation. While the first hundred years after Muḥammad's death saw limited efforts to convert local populations, soon more concerted attempts were made to encourage those living under Muslim overlordship to embrace Islam. These were not limited to religious teaching and evangelism: in the case of Bukhara in the eighth century, for example, the governor announced that all those who showed up to Friday prayer would receive the princely sum of two dirhams—an incentive that attracted the poor and persuaded them to accept the new faith, albeit on basic terms: they could not read the Qurʾān in Arabic and had to be told what to do while prayers were being said.[97]

The chain of events that began with the intense rivalry between the Roman Empire and Persia had extraordinary consequences. As the two great powers of late antiquity flexed their muscles and prepared for a final showdown, few could have predicted that it would be a faction from the far reaches of the Arabian peninsula that would rise up to supplant both. Those who had been inspired by Muḥammad truly inherited the earth, establishing perhaps the greatest empire that the world has seen, one that would introduce irrigation techniques and new crops from the Tigris and Euphrates to the Iberian peninsula, and spark nothing less than an agrarian revolution spanning thousands of miles.[98]

The Islamic conquests created a new world order, an economic giant, bolstered by self-confidence, broad-mindedness and a passionate zeal for progress. Immensely wealthy and with few natural political or even religious rivals, it was a place where order prevailed, where merchants could become rich, where intellectuals were respected and where disparate views could be discussed and debated. An unpromising start in a cave near Mecca had given birth to a cosmopolitan utopia of sorts.

It did not go unnoticed. Ambitious men born on the periphery of the Muslim *umma*, or even far beyond, were drawn like bees to honey. Prospects in the marshes of Italy, in central Europe and Scandinavia did not look too promising for young men looking to make a name (and some money) for themselves. In the nineteenth century, it was to the west and to the United States that such individuals looked for fame and fortune; a millennium earlier, they looked to the east. Better still, there was one commodity which was in plentiful supply and had a ready market for those willing to play hard and fast.

6

The Road of Furs

At its peak, Baghdad was a magnificent city to behold. With its parks, markets, mosques and bathhouses—as well as schools, hospitals and charitable foundations—it was home to mansions "lavishly gilded and decorated, and hung with beautiful tapestries and hangings of brocade and silk," their reception rooms "lightly and tastefully furnished with luxurious divans, expensive tables, exceptional Chinese vases and innumerable gold and silver trinkets." Down by the River Tigris were the palaces, kiosks and gardens which served the elite; "the scene on the river was animated by thousands of gondolas, decked with little flags, dancing like sunbeams on the water, and carrying the pleasure-seeking inhabitants of the city from one part of Baghdad to another."[1]

The vibrancy of the markets and the spending power of the court, the wealthy and the general population were magnetic. The impact of the boom extended far beyond the frontiers of the Islamic world, where the Muslim conquests created new routes that snaked in all directions, bringing goods, ideas and peoples together. For some, the extension of these networks was a cause of some anxiety. In the 840s, the Caliph al-Wāthiq sent an expedition to investigate his dream that cannibals had breached a legendary wall that popular consent held had been established by the Almighty to hold back fierce savages. It took nearly a year and a half for a reconnaissance party, led by a trusted adviser named Sallām, to report back about the state of this wall. He explained how the fortification was maintained. Guarding it was a serious business, with one family entrusted with the responsibility of conducting an inspection on a routine basis. Twice a week a hammer was struck against the wall three times in order to check it was secure. Each time, the inspectors would listen for any deviation from the norm: "if one applies one's ear to the door, one hears a muted sound like a nest of wasps," one account reports; "then everything falls silent again." The purpose was to let the savages who might bring the apocalypse with them know that the wall was guarded and that they would not be allowed to pass.[2]

The account of checking the wall is so vivid, so convincing that some historians have argued that it refers to a real expedition and to a real wall—perhaps the Jade Gate, marking the entry to China to the west of Dunhuang.[3] In fact, fear about destroyers of the world being contained behind the mountains of the east was a theme that linked the antique world with the Old and the New Testament as well as the Qur'ān.[4] Regardless of whether Sallām's journey actually did take place, terror of what lay beyond the frontiers was very real. The world was divided in two: a realm of *Iran* where order and civilisation prevailed; and one of *Turan* that was chaotic, anarchic and dangerous. As a plethora of reports from travellers and geographers who visited the steppe lands to the north make clear, those who lived outside the Muslim world were strange, and while in some respects weird and wonderful, mostly they were terrifying.

One of the most famous correspondents was Ibn Faḍlān, who was sent into the steppes in the early tenth century in response to a request by the leader of the Volga Bulghārs for learned scholars to come and explain the teachings of Islam. As Ibn Faḍlān's account makes clear, the leadership of this tribe—whose lands straddled the Volga north of the Caspian Sea where the great river intersects with the Kama—had already become Muslims, but their knowledge of its articles of faith was rudimentary. Although the Volga Bulghār leader wanted assistance in building a mosque and learning more about the revelations of Muḥammad, it quickly emerged that what he really wanted was to garner support in countering the competition posed by other tribes on the steppe.

Ibn Faḍlān was in turn bemused, amazed and horrified as he made his journey north. The life of the nomad, constantly on the move, stood in sharp contrast to the urbane, settled and sophisticated metropolitan culture of Baghdad and other cities. The G̲h̲uzz tribe were among the first peoples Ibn Faḍlān encountered. "They live in felt tents," he wrote, "pitching them first in one place and then in another." "They live in poverty, like wandering asses. They do not worship God, nor do they have any recourse to reason." He went on: "They do not wash after polluting themselves with excrement or urine . . . [and in fact] have no contact with water, especially in winter." That women did not wear a veil was the least of it. One evening they sat down with a man whose wife was present. "As we were talking, she bared her private parts and scratched while we stared at her. We covered our faces with our hands and each said: 'I seek forgiveness from God.'" Her husband simply laughed at the prudishness of the visitors.[5]

The practices and beliefs of others on the steppe were no less surprising. There were tribes who worshipped snakes, others who worshipped fish and others still who prayed to birds after becoming convinced that they had triumphed in battle thanks to the intervention of a flock of cranes. Then there were those who wore a wooden phallus round their necks that they would kiss for good luck before setting out on a journey. These were members of the Bas̱ẖgird tribe—a people of legendary savagery, who would carry the heads of their enemies around with them as trophies. They had appalling habits, including eating lice and fleas: Ibn Faḍlān saw one man find a flea in his clothes, "and having crushed it with his fingernail, he devoured it and on noticing me, said: Delicious!"[6]

Although life on the steppes was hard to fathom for visitors like Ibn Faḍlān, there was considerable interaction between the nomads and the sedentary world to the south. One sign of this was the spread of Islam through the tribes—albeit somewhat erratically. The G̱ẖuzz, for instance, professed to be Muslims and would utter suitably devout phrases "to make a good impression on the Muslims who stay with them," according to Ibn Faḍlān. But there was little substance to their faith, he noted, for "if one of them suffers an injustice or something bad happens to him, he lifts his head up to heaven and says '*bir tengri*'"—not invoking Allah, in other words, but Tengri, the supreme nomad celestial deity.[7]

In fact, religious beliefs on the steppes were complex and rarely uniform, with influences from Christianity, Islam, Judaism, Zoroastrianism and paganism jostling and blending to create composite worldviews that are difficult to disentangle.[8] Part of the spread of these shifting, adaptive spiritual views was carried out by a new type of Muslim holy men acting as a form of missionary; these mystics, known as *sufis*, roamed the steppes, sometimes naked but for a set of animal horns, tending to sick animals and impressing onlookers with their eccentric behaviour and wittering about devotion and piety. They seemed to have played a crucial role in winning converts, fusing the shaman and animist beliefs that were widespread in Central Asia with the tenets of Islam.[9]

It was not just *sufis* who had an impact. Other visitors made interventions that were decisive in spreading ideas about religion. A later account of the conversion of the Volga Bulghārs records how a passing Muslim merchant cured the tribe's ruler and his wife from serious illnesses after all other attempts to do so had failed. After making them promise to adopt his faith if he healed them, he gave them medicines, "and cured them, and they and all their people embraced Islam."[10] It was a classic conversion story: the acceptance of the leader or those close to him of a new faith was the decisive moment in large-scale adoption of a set of practices and beliefs.[11]

It is certainly true that expanding the faith into new regions became a badge of prestige for governors and local dynasties, helping them gain the attention of the Caliph as well as winning kudos within their own communities. The Sāmānids, based in Bukhara, for example, were passionate in championing Islam. One way they did so was by introducing a system of madrasas or schools, borrowing the concept from Buddhist monasteries, to teach the Qur'ān properly, while also patronising research into the *ḥadīth* tradition—sayings and actions attributed to Muḥammad. Giving money out liberally to all comers also ensured that mosques were full to bursting.[12]

However, the steppes were much more than a Wild North, a frontier zone filled with savage people with strange customs, a void into which Islam could expand and where untouched populations could be civilised. For while accounts by visitors like Ibn Faḍlān paint a picture of barbarianism, the nomadic lifestyle was in fact both regulated and ordered. Moving from place to place was not the result of aimless wandering, but rather a reflection of the realities of animal husbandry: with large herds and flocks of livestock to tend to, finding good pasture as a fact of life and doing so in a structured way was vital not just to a tribe's success but to its very survival. What looked chaotic from the outside was anything but from within.

This is perfectly captured in a remarkable text compiled in Constantinople in the tenth century which sets out how one of the principal groups that lived to the north of the Black Sea was structured to give the optimum chances of success. The Pechenegs were subdivided into eight tribes that were in turn split into a total of forty smaller units, each with clearly demarcated zones that were theirs to exploit. Moving from place to place did not mean that life in tribal societies was disordered.[13]

Although contemporary commentators, travellers, geographers and historians who took an interest in the steppe world were fascinated by the lifestyles and habits they observed, their interest was also triggered by the economic contributions made by the nomads—especially with regard to agricultural produce. The steppes supplied sedentary societies with precious services and produce. There were members of the G̱ẖuzz tribe who in Ibn Faḍlān's reckoning owned 10,000 horses and ten times as many sheep. Even if we should not set too much store by specific numbers, the scale of operations was clearly substantial.[14]

Horses were a vital part of the economy, something that is clear from the references across a range of sources about the large number of cavalry that some of the major tribes of the steppes were able to put into the field. These were reared commercially, to judge from the account of the destruction of substantial stud farms by an Arab raiding force in the eighth century and from bones found by archaeologists north of the Black Sea.[15] Farming also increasingly became an important part of the steppe economy, with crops being planted across the Lower Volga region, which included "many tilled fields and orchards."[16] Archaeological evidence from the Crimea from this period attests to farming of wheat, millet and rye on a substantial scale.[17] Hazelnuts, falcons and swords were some of the other products sold to the markets to the south.[18] So too were wax and honey; the latter was thought to provide resistance to the cold.[19] Amber was also brought to market in such quantities, not only through the steppes but from western Europe, that one leading historian has coined the term "the amber trail" to describe the routes bringing the hardened resin to keen buyers in the east.[20]

Above all else, however, was the trade in animal pelts. Furs were highly prized for the warmth and status they bestowed on their wearers.[21] One caliph in the eighth century went so far as to conduct a series of experiments to freeze a range of different furs to see which offered the best protection in extreme conditions. He filled a series of containers with water and left them overnight in ice-cold weather, according to one Arabic writer. "In the morning, he had the [flasks] brought to him. All were frozen except the one with black fox fur. He thus learned which fur was the warmest and the driest."[22]

Muslim merchants distinguished between different animal pelts, setting prices accordingly. One writer in the tenth century mentions the import from the steppes of sable, grey squirrel, ermine, mink, fox, marten, beaver and spotted hare among the varieties that were then to be sold elsewhere by traders with an eye to making good money from marking these up.[23] Indeed, in some parts of the steppe, pelts were used interchangeably with currency—with fixed exchange rates. Eighteen old squirrel skins were worth one silver coin, while a single skin was the price of "a great loaf of magnificent bread, large enough to sustain a big man." This was incomprehensible to one observer: "in any other country, a thousand loads wouldn't buy you a bean."[24] And yet there was an obvious logic to what was effectively a system of currency: having a means for exchange was important for societies that interacted with each other but lacked central treasuries that could oversee large-scale minting of coins. Skins, pelts and furs therefore served an obvious purpose in an unmonetised economy.

According to one historian, perhaps as many as half a million pelts were exported from the steppes every year. The emergence of a sprawling Islamic Empire created new channels of communication and new trade routes. The creation of a "fur road" into the steppe and forest belts to the north was the direct result of the surge in disposable wealth in the centuries following the great conquests of the seventh and eighth centuries.[25]

Not surprisingly, proximity counted for everything: being able to bring animals, pelts and other produce easily to market was crucial. The wealthiest nomadic tribes were inevitably those that were well located and able to trade actively and reliably with the sedentary world. Likewise, towns that were closest to the steppes experienced sharp upswings in their fortunes. Merv was a prime beneficiary, expanding to the point that it was described by one contemporary as the "mother of the world." Situated on the southern lip of the steppe, it was perfectly located to deal with the nomad world while also serving as a crucial point on the east–west axis running across the spine of Eurasia. In the words of one author, it was a "delightful, fine, elegant, brilliant, extensive and pleasant city."[26] Rayy, located to the west, meanwhile was known as the "gate of commerce," the "bridegroom of the earth" and the world's "most beautiful creation."[27] Or there was Balkh, which rivalled anything in the Muslim world; it could boast splendid streets, magnificent buildings, clean running water—as well as low prices for consumer goods, thanks to the bustling trade and competition in the city.[28]

Like ripples from a stone thrown into the water, those nearest to these markets felt the greatest effect. Inevitably there was a premium in being able to gain access to markets and to benefit from them. The scale of the riches at stake was such that pressures developed between tribal groupings on the steppe. Competition for the best pastureland and water sources was intensified by rivalry over access to the cities and best trade emporia. This was bound to produce one of two reactions: tensions would either escalate, resulting in violent fragmentation, or there would be consolidation within and between tribes. The choice was to fight or co-operate.

Over time, a finely balanced status quo developed, providing stability and considerable prosperity across the western steppe. Its linchpin was a part of the Türk tribal grouping that had come to dominate the area north of the Black and Caspian Seas. The Khazars, as they were known, ruled the steppes north of the Black Sea and became increasingly prominent because of the military resistance they put up during the period of the great conquests in the decades following Muḥammad's death.[29] Their effectiveness against the Muslim armies won them the support of a constellation of other tribes who united under their leadership. It also caught the attention of the Roman emperors in Constantinople who understood that there were mutual benefits to be had from striking an alliance with the dominant force on the steppes. So important were the Khazars as allies that in the early eighth century two marriage alliances were arranged between the ruling houses of Khazaria and Byzantium—the name normally given to what remained of the Roman Empire in this period.[30]

From the point of view of Constantinople, Byzantium's capital, imperial marriages with foreigners were rare; alliances with steppe nomads were all but unprecedented.[31] The development is a clear indication of how important the Khazars had become in Byzantine diplomatic and military thinking at a time when pressure on the empire's eastern frontier in Asia Minor from the Muslims was acute. The rewards and prestige given to the Khazar leader, the *khagan*, had a significant impact on Khazar society, strengthening the position of the supreme ruler and paving the way for stratification across the tribe as gifts and status were handed down through the tribe to chosen elites. It had the further effect of encouraging other tribes to become tributaries, paying tribute in return for protection and rewards. According to Ibn Faḍlān, the *khagan* had twenty-five wives, each a member of a different tribe and each the daughter of its ruler.[32] A source written in Hebrew in the ninth century likewise talks of tribes that were subject to the Khazars, with the author uncertain if there were twenty-five or twenty-eight tributaries.[33] Peoples like the Poliane, Radmichi and Severliane were among those who recognised the overlordship of the Khazars, enabling the latter to strengthen their position and become the dominant force on the western steppe in what is now Ukraine and southern Russia.[34]

Rising levels of trade and long periods of stability and peace triggered profound transformation within Khazar society. The way the leadership of the tribe functioned underwent a change, with the role of the *khagan* becoming increasingly removed from day-to-day affairs and his position evolving into a sacral kingship.[35] Lifestyles also changed. With strong demand in neighbouring regions for the produce grown, managed and produced by the Khazars and their tributaries, as well as for the fruits of long-distance commerce, settlements began to spring up that eventually developed into towns.[36]

By the early tenth century, the bustling city of Atil served as a capital, and permanent home to the *khagan*. Straddling the Lower Volga, it was home to a cosmopolitan set of inhabitants. So sophisticated was the city that there were separate courts to resolve disputes according to different customary laws, presided over by judges who would rule on disputes between Muslims, between Christians or even between pagans—while there was also a mechanism in place for how to resolve the matter if the judge was unable to reach a verdict.[37]

Atil, with its felt dwellings, warehouses and royal palace, was just one of the settlements that changed how the nomads lived.[38] Other towns grew up in Khazar territory as a result of rising commercial activity, such as Samandar, where wood buildings were characterised by their domed roofs that were presumably modelled on traditional yurts. By the early ninth century, there were sufficient numbers of Christians across Khazaria to merit the appointment not only of a bishop but of a metropolitan—effectively an archbishop—to minister to the faithful.[39] Evidently there were also substantial Muslim populations in Samandar and Atil as well as elsewhere, something that is clear from reports in the Arabic sources of large numbers of mosques built across the region.[40]

The Khazars themselves did not adopt Islam, but they did take on new religious beliefs: in the middle of the ninth century, they decided to become Jewish. Envoys from Khazaria arrived in Constantinople around 860 and asked for preachers to be sent to explain the fundamentals of Christianity.

"From time immemorial," they said, "we have known only one god [that is, Tengri], who rules over everything . . . Now the Jews are urging us to accept their religions and customs, while on the other hand the Arabs draw us to their faith, promising us peace and many gifts."[41]

A delegation was therefore dispatched with the aim of converting the Khazars. It was led by Constantine, best known by his Slavonic name Cyril and for the creation of the eponymous alphabet he devised for the Slavs—Cyrillic. A formidable scholar like his brother Methodius, Constantine stopped on his way east to spend the winter learning Hebrew and familiarising himself with the Torah in order to debate with Jewish scholars also heading to the *khagan*'s court.[42] When they arrived in the Khazar capital, the envoys took part in a highly charged series of debates against rivals who had been invited to present Islam and Judaism. Constantine's erudition carried all before him—or so it seems from the account of his life which drew heavily on his writings.[43] In fact, despite Constantine's brilliance—he was told by the *khagan* that his comments about scripture were as "sweet as honey"—the embassy did not have the desired effect, for the Khazar leader decided that Judaism was the right religion for his people.[44]

A similar version of this story was being told a century later. News of the Khazar conversion had been received by astonished Jewish communities thousands of miles west, who eagerly tried to find out more about who the Khazars were and how they came to be Jewish. There was speculation that they might be one of the lost tribes of ancient Israel. The polymath Ḥasdai b. Shaprūṭ, who was based in Córdoba in al-Andalus—that is, Muslim Spain—finally managed to make contact with the tribe. His endeavours to establish whether the Khazars were indeed Jewish or whether this was simply a tall tale put out by those wanting to win his favour had hitherto drawn a blank. When he finally received confirmation that it was indeed true that the Khazars were Jewish and, moreover, that they were wealthy and were "very powerful and maintain numerous armies," he felt compelled to bow down and adore the God of heaven. "I pray for the health of my lord the King," he wrote to the *khagan*, "of his family, and of his house, and that his throne may be established forever. Let his days and his sons' days be prolonged in the midst of Israel!"[45]

Remarkably, a copy of the *khagan*'s reply to this letter survives, with the Khazar ruler explaining his tribe's conversion to Judaism. The decision to convert, wrote the *khagan*, was the result of the great wisdom of one of his predecessors, who had brought delegations representing different faiths to

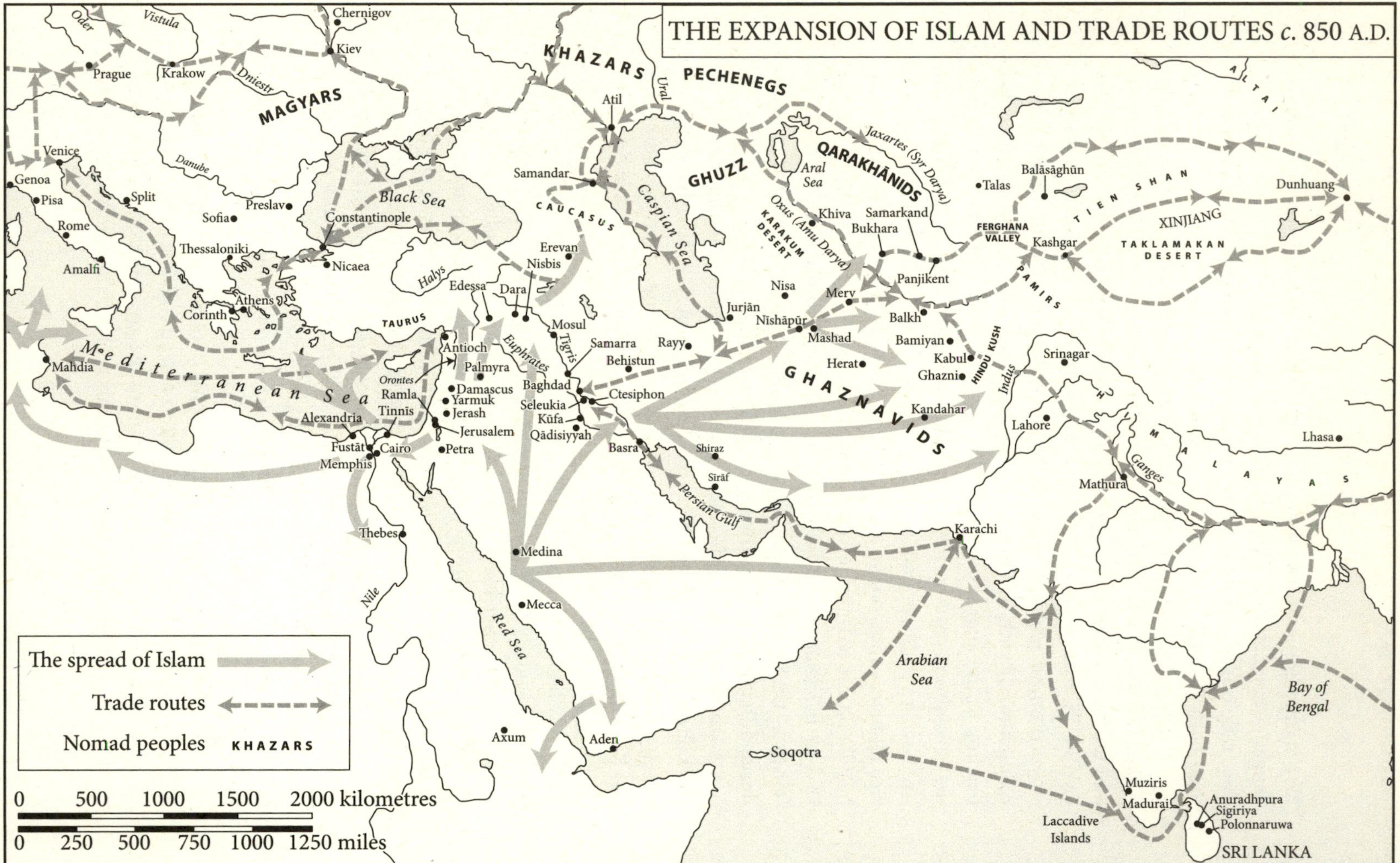

THE EXPANSION OF ISLAM AND TRADE ROUTES *c.* 850 A.D.

present the case for each. Having pondered how best to establish the facts, the ruler had asked the Christians whether Islam or Judaism was the better faith; when they replied that the former was certainly worse than the latter, he asked the Muslims whether Christianity or Judaism was preferable. When they lambasted Christianity and also replied that Judaism was the less bad of the two, the Khazar ruler announced that he had reached a conclusion: both had admitted that "the religion of the Israelites is better," he declared, so "trusting in the mercies of God and the power of the Almighty, I choose the religion of Israel, that is, the religion of Abraham." With that, he sent the delegations home, circumcised himself and then ordered his servants, his attendants and all his people to do the same.[46]

Judaism had made considerable inroads into Khazar society by the middle of the ninth century. Apart from references in Arabic sources to proselytisation by Jews in the decades before the arrival of the delegations at the *khagan*'s court and the fact that burial practices underwent a transformation during this period too, the recent discovery of a series of coins minted in Khazaria provides strong evidence that Judaism had been formally adopted as a state religion in the 830s. These coins bore a legend that provided a fine example of how faith could be packaged to appeal to disparate populations. The coins championed the greatest of the Old Testament prophets with the phrase *Mūsā rasūl allāh*: Moses is the messenger of God.[47]

This was perhaps less provocative than it sounds, since the Qur'ān after all explicitly teaches that there should be no distinction between the prophets and that the message brought by all of them should be followed.[48] Moses was accepted and revered in Islamic teaching, so praising him was in some ways uncontroversial. On the other hand, however, the evocation of Muḥammad's special status as God's messenger was a central element in the *adhān*, the call to prayer made from mosques five times a day. As such having Moses' name on the currency was a defiant statement that the Khazars had an identity of their own that was independent of the Islamic world. As with the confrontation between the Roman Empire and the Muslim world in the late seventh century, battles were fought not just between armies, but also over ideology, language and even the imagery on coins.

In fact, the exposure of Khazars to Judaism had come about through two sources. First, there were long-standing Jewish communities that had settled in the Caucasus in antiquity which must have been galvanised by the economic development of the steppe.[49] According to one tenth-century writer, many more were encouraged to emigrate to Khazaria "from Muslim and Christian cities" after it became known that the religion was not only tolerated and officially sanctioned but practised by much of the elite.[50] The correspondence between the Khazar ruler and Ḥasdai in Córdoba in the tenth century reports that rabbis were actively recruited, while schools and synagogues were built to ensure that Judaism was taught properly—with many chroniclers noting religious buildings dotted across the towns of Khazaria, as well as courts where decisions were reached after consultation with the Torah.[51]

The second trigger for the rise in interest in Judaism came from traders who were drawn in from much further away, attracted by the emergence of Khazaria as a major international trade emporium—not only between the steppe and the Islamic world, but between east and west. As numerous sources attest, Jewish merchants were highly active in long-distance trade, playing much the same role that the Sogdians had played when connecting China and Persia around the time of the rise of Islam.

Jewish merchants were highly adept linguists, fluent in "Arabic, Persian, Latin, Frankish, Andalusian and Slavic" according to one contemporary source.[52] Based in the Mediterranean, they appear to have travelled regularly to India and China, returning with musk, aloe wood, camphor, cinnamon "and other eastern products" which they traded along a chain of ports and towns that serviced markets in Mecca, Medina and Constantinople, as well as towns on the Tigris and the Euphrates.[53] They also used overland routes, heading through Central Asia to China either via Baghdad and Persia or passing through Khazar territory on their way to Balkh and east of the Oxus river.[54] One of the most important points on this axis was Rayy, just to the south of the Caspian (modern Iran), a city that handled goods coming from the Caucasus, from the east, from Khazaria and other locations on the steppe. It appears that these were first cleared through the town of Jurjān (Gorgan in northern Iran), presumably where customs duties were collected, before being taken to Rayy. "The most amazing thing," wrote one Arabic author in the tenth century, "is that this is the emporium of the world."[55]

Merchants from Scandinavia were also drawn by the opportunities on offer. When we think of the Vikings, we invariably conjure up images of attacks across the North Sea on Great Britain and Ireland, of longships with prows shaped like dragons, appearing through the fog, filled with armed men ready to rape and pillage. Or perhaps we think of the question whether the Vikings managed to reach North America centuries before the expeditions of Christopher Columbus and others. But in the Viking age the bravest and toughest men did not head west; they headed east and south. Many made fortunes and won fame not just at home but in the new lands that they conquered. The mark that they left, furthermore, was not minimal and transient, as it was in North America. In the east, they were to found a new state, named after the traders, travellers and raiders who took to the great water systems linking the Baltic with the Caspian and Black Seas. These men were known as Rus', or *rhos*, perhaps due to their distinctive red hair, or more likely thanks to their prowess with the oar. They were the fathers of Russia.[56]

It was the lure of trade and riches in the Islamic world that initially spurred Vikings to set off on the journey south. From the start of the ninth century, men from Scandinavia began to come into contact with the steppe world and also with the caliphate of Baghdad. Settlements began to spread along the Oder, the Neva, the Volga and the Dnieper rivers, with new bases springing up as markets in their own right and as trading stations for merchants bringing goods to and from the south. Staraya Ladoga, Rurikovo Gorodische, Beloozero and Novgorod (literally "new town") were new points that extended the great Eurasian trade routes into the furthest reaches of northern Europe.[57]

The longships, so celebrated in popular imagination, were adapted and made smaller by the Viking Rus' to enable them to be carried over short distances from one river or lake to another. These single-hulled boats set out in convoy on a journey that was long and dangerous. A text compiled in Constantinople in the middle of the tenth century and based on information gathered by Byzantine agents, records the treacherous conditions that had to be negotiated on the voyage south. A set of rapids on the Dniester was particularly perilous: a narrow barrage had a lethal set of rocks in the middle of it, "which stand out like islands. Against these, then, comes the water and wells up and dashes down over the other side, with a mighty and terrific din." This obstacle had been nicknamed with dry humour "Do Not Fall Asleep."[58]

As the same text notes, the Rus' were intensely vulnerable to being picked off by aggressive raiders who could see the chance for quick rewards as exhausted travellers passed through the rapids. Pecheneg nomads would lie in wait as the boats were hauled out of the water and then attack, seizing the goods and disappearing into the landscape. Guards were ordered to be on the highest state of alert against sudden assault. So relieved were the Scandinavians to get past these dangers that they would convene on an island and sacrifice cockerels or stick arrows into sacred trees as a way of giving thanks to the pagan gods.[59]

The men who made it safely to the markets around the Caspian and Black Seas needed to be robust, to say the least. "They have great stamina and endurance," noted one Muslim commentator with admiration.[60] The Rus', wrote Ibn Faḍlān, were tall "like palm trees," but more importantly they were always armed and dangerous. "Each of them carries an axe, a sword and a knife."[61]

They behaved like gangs of hardened criminals. For one thing, although they fought alongside each other against their enemies, they were deeply suspicious of each other. "They never go off alone to relieve themselves," one writer observed, "but always [go] with three companions to guard them, sword in hand, for they have little trust in each other." None would hesitate to rob a colleague, even if it meant murdering him.[62] They regularly took part in orgies, having sex in front of one another with abandon. If anyone fell ill, they were left behind. They looked the part too: "from the tips of his toes to his neck, each man is tattooed in dark green, with designs and so forth."[63] These were tough men for tough times.

They were involved in the trade of wax, amber and honey, as well as fine swords which were widely admired in the Arabic-speaking world. However, it was another line of business that was the most lucrative, the source of vast quantities of money that washed northwards, back up the river systems of Russia towards Scandinavia. This is demonstrated by the many fine silks from Syria, Byzantium and even China that have been found in graves across Sweden, Denmark, Finland and Norway. These must have represented only a tiny fraction of the textiles that were brought back that have not survived.[64]

It is the coin record, however, that speaks loudest about the scale of business conducted with faraway regions. Astonishingly rich coin finds line the great rivers heading north and have been recovered all over northern Russia, Finland, Sweden and above all in Gotland (Sweden's largest island), which show that the Viking Rus' made enormous sums from commerce with the Muslims and the fringes of the caliphate of Baghdad.[65] One leading specialist in the history of currency estimates that the amount of silver coins brought back from trading with the lands of Islam numbered in the tens and perhaps even hundreds of millions—in modern terms, it was a multi-billion-dollar industry.[66]

Rewards needed to be substantial to merit the distance and the dangers involved in travelling as far from Scandinavia as the Caspian Sea—a journey of nearly 3,000 miles. So it is perhaps not surprising that goods had to be sold in large volumes in order to generate substantial profits. There were several commodities shipped south, but the most important were slaves. There was money to be made from human trafficking.

7

The Slave Road

The Rus' were ruthless when it came to enslaving local populations and transporting them south. Renowned for "their size, their physique and their bravery," the Viking Rus' had "no cultivated fields and they live by pillaging," according to one Arabic writer.[1] It was the local population that bore the brunt. So many were captured that the very name of those taken captive—Slavs—became used for all those who had their freedom taken away: slaves.

The Rus' were careful with their prisoners: "they treat the slaves well and dress them suitably, because for them they are an article of trade," noted one contemporary.[2] Slaves were transported along the river systems—remaining chained while the rapids were negotiated.[3] Beautiful women were particularly highly prized, sold on to merchants in Khazaria and Volga Bulghāria who would then take them further south—though not before their captors had sexual intercourse with them one last time.[4]

Slavery was a vital part of Viking society and an important part of its economy—and not just in the east. Considerable literary and material evidence from the British Isles shows that one of the most common purposes of longship attacks was not the indiscriminate rape and pillage of popular imagination, but taking captives alive.[5] "Save us, O Lord," one ninth-century prayer from France implores, "from the savage Norsemen who destroy our country; they take away . . . our young, virgin boys. We beg you to save us from this evil."[6] Shackles, manacles and locks have been found along slaving routes especially in northern and eastern Europe, while new research suggests that holding pens previously thought to have been for livestock were in fact designed to corral people who were due to be sold in places like Novgorod, where the market lay at the intersection of the High Street and Slave Street.[7]

So rampant was the desire for profit from slavery that, although some Scandinavians obtained licences from local rulers to plunder new regions and take prisoners, others were more than willing to put each other in bond—"as soon as one of them catches another," recorded one well-informed cleric writing in northern Europe in the eleventh century. He would have little doubt what to do next: at the first opportunity, "he mercilessly sells him into slavery either to one of his fellows or to a barbarian."[8]

Many slaves were destined for Scandinavia. As one famous Old Norse poem, "The Lay of Rigr" ("Rígsþula"), puts it, society was divided into three simple categories: aristocracy (*jarlar*), freemen (*karlar*) and slaves (*ðrælar*).[9] But many others were sent to where good money was paid for fine specimens, and nowhere was there greater demand, nowhere was there greater spending power than the buoyant and wealthy markets in Atil that ultimately fed Baghdad and other cities in Asia, as well as elsewhere in the Muslim world, including North Africa and Spain.

The ability and willingness to pay a high price provided rich rewards and laid the basis for stimulating the economy of northern Europe. To judge from the coin finds, there was a surge in trade in the latter part of the ninth century, a time of major growth in the Baltic, southern Sweden and Denmark, with towns like Hedeby, Birka, Wolin and Lund expanding rapidly. Find-spots spread over an increasingly wide area along the rivers of Russia show a sharp intensification in levels of exchange, with a marked rise in the number of coins found that were minted in Central Asia—above all in Samarkand, Tashkent (al-Shāsh), Balkh and elsewhere along the traditional trade, transport and communication routes into what is now Afghanistan.[10]

Demand for slaves in these cash-rich locations was intense, and not just from those from the north. Huge numbers were imported from sub-Saharan Africa: one trader alone boasted of selling more than 12,000 black slaves in markets in Persia.[11] Slaves were also taken from the Turkic tribes of Central Asia, whom one author from this period notes were highly prized because of their courage and resourcefulness. When it comes to choosing "the most precious slaves," noted another commentator, the best came "from the land of the Turks. There is no equal to the Turkish slaves among all the slaves of the earth."[12]

Some idea of the likely scale of the slave trade can be deduced from a comparison with slavery in the Roman Empire, an area that has been studied in much greater detail. Recent research suggests that at the height of its power the Roman Empire required 250,000–400,000 new slaves each year to maintain the slave population.[13] The size of the market in the Arabic-speaking lands was considerably larger—assuming the demand for slaves was analogous—stretching from Spain through to Afghanistan, which would suggest that the numbers of slaves being sold may have been far greater even than those for Rome. Although the limitations of the source material are frustrating, some idea of the likely scale comes from the fact that one account talks of a caliph and his wife owning a thousand slave girls each, while another was said to own no fewer than four thousand. Slaves in the Muslim world were as ubiquitous—and silent—as they were in Rome.[14]

Rome also provides a useful comparison for the way that slaves were bought and sold. In the Roman world, there was keen competition between the wealthy for prize captives taken from beyond the empire's frontiers—curios valued for their unusual looks and as talking points. Personal preference also played a part, with one well-appointed aristocrat insisting on having matching slaves, all equally attractive and all of the same age.[15] Similar ideas prevailed with rich Muslims, as later guidebooks to help with the slave-buying process make clear. "Of all the black [slaves]," wrote one eleventh-century author, "the Nubian women are the most agreeable, tender and polite. Their bodies are slim with a smooth skin, steady and well proportioned . . . they respect their master as if they were created to serve." Women of the Beja people, whose home was in what is today Sudan, Eritrea and Egypt, "have a golden complexion, beautiful faces, delicate bodies and smooth skins; they make pleasant bed-fellows if they are taken out of their country while they are still young." A thousand years ago, money could not buy love, but it could help you get what you wanted.[16]

Other guidebooks offered equally helpful pointers. "When you set out to buy slaves, be cautious," wrote the author of another eleventh-century Persian text best known as the *Qābūs-nāma*. "The buying of men is a difficult art because many a slave appears to be good" but turns out to be quite the opposite. "Most people imagine that buying slaves is like any other form of trading," the author added; in fact, the skill of buying slaves "is a branch of philosophy."[17] Beware of yellowness of complexion—a sure sign of haemorrhoids; be careful too of men blessed with good looks, floppy hair and eyes—"a man having such qualities is either over-fond of women or prone to act as a go-between." Make sure to have a possible purchase lie down; then you should "press on both sides and watch closely" for any signs of inflammation or pain; and double-check "hidden defects," such as bad breath, deafness, stutter or hardness at the base of the teeth. Follow all these instructions (and plenty more besides), the author declared, and you will not be disappointed.[18]

Slave markets thrived across central Europe, stocked with men, women and children waiting to be trafficked to the east—and also to the court at Córdoba, where there were more than 13,000 Slavic slaves in 961.[19] By the mid-tenth century, Prague had become a major commercial centre attracting Viking Rus' and Muslim merchants to buy and sell tin, furs and people. Other towns in Bohemia likewise were good places to buy flour, barley and chickens—and slaves, all of which were very reasonably priced, according to one Jewish traveller.[20]

Slaves were often sent as gifts to Muslim rulers. At the start of the tenth century, for example, an embassy from Tuscany to Baghdad brought the ʿAbbāsid Caliph al-Muktafī a selection of high-value gifts, including swords, shields, hunting dogs and birds of prey. Among the other presents offered as a token of friendship were twenty Slavic eunuchs and twenty particularly beautiful Slavic girls. The flower of youth from one part of the world was exported to indulge those in another.[21]

The engagement with long-distance trade was so extensive that when Ibrāhīm ibn Yaʿqūb passed through Mainz, he was astonished by what he found in the markets: "it is extraordinary," he wrote, "that one should be able to find, in such far western regions, aromatics and spices that only grow in the Far East, like pepper, ginger, cloves, nard and galingale. These plants are all imported from India, where they grow in abundance." That was not all that surprised him: so too did the fact that silver dirhams were in use as currency, including coins minted in Samarkand.[22]

In fact, the impact and influence of coins from the Muslim world had been felt much further away—and would continue to be so for some time to come. Around 800, King Offa of Mercia in England, constructor of the famous dyke to protect his lands against the incursions of the Welsh, was copying the design of Islamic gold coins for his own currency. He issued coins with the legend "Offa rex" (King Offa) on one side and an imperfect copy of Arabic text on the other, even though this would have meant little to those handling coins in his kingdom.[23] A large hoard found in Cuerdale in

Lancashire and today held in the Ashmolean Museum in Oxford also contains many ʿAbbāsid coins minted in the ninth century. That the currency had reached the backwaters that were the British Isles is an indication of just how far the markets of the Islamic world had sprawled.

It was the sale of slaves that paid for the imports that began to flood into Europe in the ninth century. The spices and drugs that are increasingly visible in the sources as highly desirable luxury objects or as medical necessities were funded by large-scale human trafficking.[24] And it was not only the Viking Rus' who profited from the almost insatiable demand for slaves: merchants in Verdun made immense profits selling eunuchs, usually to Muslim buyers in Spain; Jewish traders who dealt with long-range commerce were also heavily involved in the sale of "young girls and boys" as well as eunuchs, as Arabic sources from this period suggest.[25]

Other sources likewise note the role played by Jewish merchants in bringing "slaves [and] boys and girls" from Europe, and carrying out operations to castrate young men on arrival—presumably as a form of gruesome certification procedure.[26] The slave trade promised good returns, which was one reason why it was not only European slaves that were brought east: Muslim entrepreneurs reportedly also got in on the act, raiding Slavic lands from eastern Iran—although enslaved captives pointedly "had their manhood left intact, their bodies unspoiled."[27]

Such captives were also turned into eunuchs and were highly valued. If you took Slavic twins, wrote one Arabic author in this period, and castrated one, he would certainly become more skilful and "more lively in intelligence and conversation" than his brother—who would remain ignorant, foolish and exhibit the innate simple-mindedness of the Slavs. Castration was thought to purify and improve the Slavic mind.[28] Better still, it worked, wrote the same author, though not for "the blacks," whose "natural aptitudes" were negatively affected by the operation.[29] So great was the scale of traffic of Slavic slaves that it impacted the Arabic language: the word for eunuch (*ṣiqlabī*) comes from the ethnic label referring to the Slavs (*ṣaqālibī*).

Muslim traders were highly active in the Mediterranean. Men, women and children were brought from all over northern Europe to Marseilles where there was a busy market for buying and selling slaves—often passing through subsidiary markets such as Rouen, where Irish and Flemish slaves were sold to third parties.[30] Rome was another key slave-trading centre—though some found this repugnant. In 776, Pope Hadrian I decried the sale of humans like livestock, condemning the sale of men and women to "the unspeakable race of Saracens." Some, he claimed, had boarded ships bound for the east voluntarily, "having no other hope of staying alive" because of recent famine and crushing poverty. Nevertheless, "we have never sunk to such a disgraceful act" of selling fellow Christians, he wrote, "and God forbid that we should."[31] So widespread was slavery in the Mediterranean and the Arabic world that even today regular greetings reference human trafficking. All over Italy, when they meet, people say to each other, "schiavo," from a Venetian dialect. "Ciao," as it is more commonly spelt, does not mean "hello"; it means "I am your slave."[32]

There were others who viewed the bonding of Christians into captivity and their sale to Muslim masters as indefensible. One such was Rimbert, bishop of Bremen, who used to tour the markets in Hedeby (on the borders of modern Germany and Denmark) in the late ninth century ransoming those who professed their Christian faith (but not those who did not).[33] This sensibility was not shared by all. Among those with no compunction about human trafficking were the inhabitants of an unpromising lagoon located at the northern point of the Adriatic. The wealth it accumulated from slave trading and human suffering was to lay the basis for its transformation into one of the crown jewels of the medieval Mediterranean: Venice.

The Venetians proved to be singularly successful when it came to business. A dazzling city rose up from the marshes, adorned with glorious churches and beautiful *palazzi*, built on the lucrative proceeds of prolific trading with the east. While it stands today as a glorious vision of the past, the spark for Venice's growth came from its willingness to sell future generations into captivity. Merchants became involved in the slave trade as early as the second half of the eighth century, at the very dawn of the new settlement of Venice, though it took time for the benefits and the profits to flow through in volume. That they eventually did so is indicated by a series of treaties drawn up a century later, in which the Venetians agreed to be bound by restrictions on the sale of slaves, including returning slaves to other towns in Italy who had been brought to Venice illegally for sale. These negotiations were in part a reaction to the growing success of the city, an attempt to clip Venetian wings by those threatened by its affluence.[34]

In the short term, the restrictions were circumvented by raiding parties that captured non-Christians from Bohemia and Dalmatia and sold them on at a profit.[35] In the longer term, however, normal business was resumed. Treatises from the late ninth century suggest that Venice simply paid lip-service to local rulers who were concerned that it was not just slaves that were being sold but also freemen. The Venetians were accused of willingly selling the subjects of neighbouring lands, whether Christians or not.[36]

Eventually, the slave trade began to dwindle—at least from eastern and central Europe. One reason for this was that the Viking Rus' shifted their focus from long-distance trafficking to the business of protection rackets. Attention focused on the benefits that the Khazars enjoyed from the trade that passed through towns like Atil, thanks to the levies raised on all merchandise transiting Khazar territory. The famous Persian geographical treatise *Hudūd al-'Ālam* states that the very basis of the Khazar economy lay in its tax revenues: "the well-being and wealth of the king of the Khazars are mostly from maritime duties."[37] Other Muslim commentators repeatedly note the substantial tax receipts collected by the Khazar authorities from commercial activities—which included levies charged on inhabitants of the capital.[38]

Inevitably, this caught the attention of the Viking Rus', as did the tribute paid to the *khagan* by the various subject tribes. One by one these were picked off and their loyalties (and payments) redirected to aggressive new overlords. By the second half of the ninth century, the Slavic tribes of central and southern Russia were not only paying tribute to the Scandinavians, but were being forbidden to make any further payments "to the Khazars, on the grounds that there was no reason for them to pay it." Payment was to be made to the Rus' leader instead.[39] This mirrored practices elsewhere—such as in Ireland, where protection money gradually replaced human trafficking: after being attacked year after year, records the Annals of St. Bertin, the Irish agreed to make annual contributions, in return for peace.[40]

In the east, it was not long before the increasingly heavy presence of the Rus' resulted in outright confrontation with the Khazars. After launching a series of raids on Muslim trading communities on the Caspian Sea that "spilled rivers of blood" and continued until the Viking Rus' were "gorged with loot and worn out with raiding," the Khazars themselves were attacked.[41] Atil was sacked and completely destroyed in 965. "If a leaf were left on a branch, one of the Rus' would carry it off," wrote one commentator; "not a grape, not a raisin remains [in Khazaria]."[42] The Khazars were effectively removed from the equation, and profits from trade with the Muslim world flowed in even greater volumes towards northern Europe—as the quantities of coin hoards found along the waterways of Russia show.[43]

. . .

By the end of the tenth century, the Rus' had become the dominant force on the western steppe, controlling lands that stretched from the Caspian across the north of the Black Sea as far as the Danube. One source talks of the vibrancy of the markets they now oversaw, where it was possible to buy "gold, silks, wine and various fruits from Greece, silver and horses from Hungary and Bohemia, and from Rus', furs, wax, honey, and slaves."[44] However, the authority they exerted over these lands was not absolute. Relations with the nomadic peoples were often tetchy because of the competition for resources, as the ritual execution of one prominent Rus' leader in this period by Pecheneg steppe nomads shows: the capture of the prince was gleefully celebrated, and his skull was lined with gold and kept as a victory trophy, to be used to celebrate ceremonial toasts.[45]

Nevertheless, in the course of the tenth century Rus' control of the waterways and of the steppes continued to strengthen, and the communication routes running southwards became increasingly secure. This process was accompanied by a gradual transformation of commercial, religious and political orientation. One reason for this was that after nearly 300 years of stability and affluence, the caliphate in Baghdad underwent a series of dislocations. Prosperity had served to loosen ties between the centre and outlying regions, which in turn opened possibilities for friction as local potentates built up power and came into conflict with each other. The dangers this could pose were graphically shown when Basra was sacked in 923 by Shīʿa insurgents, before Mecca was attacked seven years later and the sacred Black Stone looted from the Kaʿba.[46]

A series of unusually severe winters between the 920s and 960s made matters worse. Conditions were so bad that food shortages became increasingly regular. It was not unusual for people to be forced "to pick the grains of barley from the dung of horses and asses and eat them," wrote one author; rioting and civil disorder broke out frequently.[47] As one Armenian chronicler put it, after seven successive years of crop failure in the 950s, "many went mad," and attacked each other senselessly.[48]

Internal unrest enabled a new dynasty, the Būyids, to establish political control over much of the caliphate's core territory in Iran and Iraq, retaining the Caliph as a figurehead with greatly reduced powers. In Egypt, on the other hand, the regime was toppled entirely. In a tenth-century version of the Arab Spring, Shīʿa Muslims who had previously managed to establish an emirate in North Africa that was more or less independent of the mainstream Sunnī caliphates of Baghdad and Córdoba moved on the

Egyptian capital, Fusṭāṭ. In 969, taking advantage of the catastrophic failure of the annual Nile floods that left many dead or starving, revolution spread through North Africa.[49] The new masters were known as Fāṭimids—who as Shīʿa Muslims had very different views about legitimacy and authority, and about the true legacy left by Muḥammad. Their rise had serious implications for the unity of the Muslim world: rifts were opening up, with fundamental questions being asked about the past, present and future of Islam.

The upheaval, and the resulting decline of commercial opportunities, was one reason why the Viking Rus' increasingly turned their attention to the Dnieper and Dniester rivers feeding into the Black Sea, rather than moving along the Volga and towards the Caspian. Their attention began to turn away from the Muslim world to the Byzantine Empire and to the great city of Constantinople, fabled in Norse folklore as "Mikli-garðr" (or Miklegarth)—that is, "the great city." The Byzantines were wary of the attentions of the Rus', not least since a daring raid in 860 had taken the city's inhabitants—and its defences—completely by surprise. Who are these "fierce and savage" warriors, "ravaging the suburbs, destroying everything," wailed the patriarch of Constantinople, "thrusting their swords through everything, taking pity on nothing, sparing nothing?" Those who died first were the lucky ones, he went on; at least they were spared knowledge of the calamities that followed.[50]

Rus' access to the markets of Constantinople was tightly regulated by the authorities. One treaty from the tenth century notes that a maximum of fifty Rus' were allowed into the city at any one time, and had to enter through a given gate; their names were to be recorded and their activities in the city monitored; restrictions were set on what they could and could not buy.[51] They were recognised as dangerous men who needed to be treated carefully. Nevertheless, relations eventually began to normalise as towns like Novgorod, Chernigov and above all Kiev evolved from trading stations into fortified strongholds and permanent residences.[52] The adoption of Christianity by the Rus' ruler Vladimir in 988 was important too, both because it led to the creation of an ecclesiastical network ministered at the outset by clergy sent from Constantinople, and because of the inevitable cultural borrowings that flowed northwards from the imperial capital. These influences eventually affected everything from icons and religious artefacts to the design of churches and to the way that the Rus' dressed.[53] As the Rus' economy became more mercantile, the warrior-like society became increasingly urban and cosmopolitan.[54] Luxury items like wine, oil and silks were exported from Byzantium and sold on, with traders recording invoices and receipts on birch bark.[55]

The redirection of the gaze of the Rus' from the Muslim world towards Constantinople was the result of a pronounced shift in western Asia. For one thing, successive emperors had taken advantage of the unrest and uncertainty in the 'Abbāsid caliphate. Many of Byzantium's eastern provinces had been lost during the Muslim conquests, and this led to a fundamental reorganisation of the empire's provincial administration. In the first half of the tenth century, the tide began to turn. One by one, bases that had been used to launch assaults on imperial territory in Anatolia were picked off and recovered. Crete and Cyprus were retaken, restoring stability to the eastern Mediterranean and the Aegean, which had been at the mercy of Arab pirate raids for decades. Then in 969 the great city of Antioch, a major commercial emporium as well as a centre for textile production, was also seized.[56]

This reversal of fortunes spurred a sense of revival in the Christian world. It also represented a significant redirection of assets and revenues away from Baghdad and towards Constantinople: tax and customs revenues that had previously flowed towards the caliphate now filled the imperial treasuries. This heralded the beginning of a golden age for Byzantium, a period of artistic and intellectual renaissance among philosophers, scholars and historians, of large-scale building of churches and monasteries, and the founding of institutions such as a law school to train judges who could oversee the running of an expanded empire. Byzantium was also a prime beneficiary of the breakdown in relations between Baghdad and Egypt in the late tenth century. In the late 980s, Emperor Basil II came to terms with the newly proclaimed Fāṭimid Caliph, establishing formal trade links and promising to have his name proclaimed in the daily prayers said in the mosque in Constantinople rather than that of his 'Abbāsid rival in Baghdad.[57]

Buoyant markets in the imperial capital, fuelled by economic and demographic growth, were mirrored by introspection and uncertainty in the 'Abbasid caliphate. The result was the reorientation of trade routes from the east, with a clear shift away from the continental hinterland through Khazaria and the Caucasus to the Red Sea. The land routes that had made Merv, Rayy and Baghdad blossom were supplanted by shipping along the maritime lanes. The boost to Fusṭāṭ, Cairo and above all to Alexandria was unmistakable, with the middle classes mushrooming as these cities thrived.[58] Byzantium was well placed, and soon began to enjoy the fruits of its new relations with the Fāṭimids: from the later tenth century, as Arabic and Hebrew reports make clear, merchant ships were putting in and sailing off from Egyptian ports around the clock, heading for Constantinople.[59]

Egyptian textiles became prized across the eastern Mediterranean. Linen produced at Tinnīs was so sought after that Nāṣir-i Khusraw, one of the great Persian writers and travellers of the period, reported: "I have heard that the ruler of Byzantium once sent a message to the sultan of Egypt that he would exchange a hundred cities of his realm for Tinnīs alone."[60] The appearance of Amalfitan and Venetian merchants in Egypt from the 1030s and from Genoa three decades later reveals that others from further afield than Constantinople were alert to the opening up of new sources of goods.[61]

From the point of view of the Rus' and the new northern trade networks, the changes in the principal routes to market for spices, silks, pepper, hardwoods and other items brought from the east had little impact: there was no need to have to choose between Christian Constantinople and Muslim Baghdad. On the contrary, if anything, having two potential sources for buying and selling goods was better than having one. Silk reached Scandinavia in considerable quantities—as testified by the recovery of more than a hundred silk fragments from a remarkable ship excavated at Oseberg in Norway, and also from Viking graves where silks from the Byzantine world and Persia were buried as prestige objects alongside the men who had owned them.[62]

There were still those in the mid-eleventh century who thought that they would make their fortunes in the Islamic lands of the east, just as their forefathers had done. A rune-stone by Lake Mälar near Stockholm in Sweden set up in the middle of the eleventh century by a woman named Tóla to commemorate her son Haraldr and his brothers-in-arms provides one example. "Like men, they went a long way in the search for gold," it states; they had their successes, but then died "in the south, in Serkland," that is to say, in the land of the Saracens—the Muslims.[63] Or there is the stone set up by Gudleif in memory of his son, Slagve, who "met his end in the east in Khwarezm."[64] Texts like the saga of Yngvar the Wayfarer, Haraldr's brother, likewise commemorate ambitious escapades that took Scandinavians to adventures in the Caspian and beyond. In fact, recent research suggests that a permanent Viking colony may even have been established in the Persian Gulf in this period.[65]

But attention was increasingly focused on the Christian east and on

Byzantium. As western Europe's horizons expanded, there was rising interest in visiting the land where Jesus Christ had lived, died and risen from the dead. Pilgrimage to Jerusalem became a source of understandable kudos.[66] Exposure to the Holy City also underlined the paucity of the Christian heritage of western Europe—particularly when compared to the Byzantine Empire. Helena, the mother of the Emperor Constantine, had begun the process of bringing relics to Constantinople in the fourth century. By the eleventh century, the astonishing collections in the city were widely held to include relics such as the nails that had been used to crucify Jesus; the Crown of Thorns; the clothes over which lots had been cast; and parts of the True Cross, as well as hair of the Virgin Mary, the head of John the Baptist and much more besides.[67] By contrast, there was little of note in the reliquaries of Europe: although kings, cities and church foundations were becoming richer, they had little physical connection with the story of Jesus Christ and his disciples.

Jerusalem and Constantinople as the home and guardian of Christianity drew growing numbers of men to the Christian east, and to the imperial capital in particular—in order to trade, to take service or to simply pass through on the way to the Holy Land. Men from Scandinavia and the British Isles were welcomed into the Varangian guard, an elite corps entrusted as the bodyguard of the Emperor himself. It became a rite of passage to serve in this brigade, with men such as Haraldr Sigurðarson, later King of Norway (and better known as Harald Hardrada), serving in the brigade before heading for home.[68] The call of Constantinople echoed loudly around all of Europe in the eleventh century. Documents record that in the eleventh century it was home to men from Britain, Italy, France and Germany—as well as from Kiev, Scandinavia and Iceland. Traders from Venice, Pisa, Amalfi and Genoa set up colonies in the city in order to buy goods and export them home.[69]

The places that mattered were not in Paris or London, in Germany or Italy—but in the east. Cities that connected to the east were important—like Kherson in the Crimea or Novgorod, cities that linked to the Silk Roads running across the spine of Asia. Kiev became a linchpin of the medieval world, evidenced by the marriage ties of the ruling house in the second half of the eleventh century. Daughters of Yaroslav the Wise, who reigned as Grand Prince of Kiev until 1054, married the King of Norway, the King of Hungary, the King of Sweden and the King of France. One son married the daughter of the King of Poland, while another took as his wife a member of the imperial family of Constantinople. The marriages made in the next generation were even more impressive. Rus' princesses were married to the King of Hungary, the King of Poland and the powerful German Emperor, Henry IV. Among other illustrious matches was Gytha, the wife of Vladimir II Monomakh, the Grand Prince of Kiev: she was the daughter of Harold II, King of England, who was killed at the battle of Hastings in 1066. The ruling family in Kiev was the best-connected dynasty in Europe.

An ever growing cluster of towns and settlements fanned out in every direction across Russia, each a new pearl added to the string. Towns like Lyubech, Smolensk, Minsk and Polotsk rose as Kiev, Chernigov and Novgorod had done before them. This was precisely the same process that had already seen Venice, Genoa, Pisa and Amalfi rise in wealth and power: the key to their growth was business with the east.

The same held true for southern Italy. In one of the most striking achievements of the early Middle Ages, Norman mercenaries who had first been attracted by Apulia and Calabria in the early eleventh century managed to become a leading force in the Mediterranean. In the space of a generation, they overthrew their Byzantine paymasters and then turned their attention to overwhelming Muslim Sicily—a lucrative and strategically vital staging post that linked North Africa with Europe and controlled the Mediterranean.[70]

What had propelled the rise to power in each case was trade and access to desirable goods. And in this sense it ultimately mattered little where the dividing line was between Christianity and Islam, and whether the best markets were in Constantinople, Atil, Baghdad or Bukhara—or, by the eleventh century, in Mahdia, Alexandria or Cairo. Despite the insistence of many sources that high politics and religion mattered, for most merchants and traders such issues were complications that were better avoided altogether. In fact, the problem was not where to trade or whom to trade with, but how to pay for luxury objects that could be sold on for healthy profit. In the eighth to tenth centuries, the base commodity for sale had been slaves. But as the economies of western and eastern Europe became more robust, galvanised by huge influxes of silver coinage from the Islamic world, towns grew and their populations swelled. And as they did so, the levels of interaction intensified, which in turn led to the demand for monetisation, that is to say, trade based on coinage—rather than, for example, on furs. As this transition happened and local societies became more complex and sophisticated, stratification developed and urban middle classes emerged. Money, rather than men, began to be used as currency for trade with the east.

In a neat mirror image, the magnetic forces that drew men from Europe were being felt in the east as well. The frontiers that had been established by the Muslim conquests and the expansion into Central Asia began to dissolve in the eleventh century. The various Muslim dynasties across Central Asia had long employed men from the steppes in their armies, as had the caliphate in Baghdad—just as the emperors in Constantinople were doing at the same time with men from northern and western Europe. Dynasties like the Sāmānids had actively recruited soldiers from the Turkic tribes, usually as *ghulām*, or slave troops. But as these began to be relied on increasingly not only in rank-and-file positions but in command positions, it was not long before the moment came when senior officers began to cast an eye on taking power for themselves. Service was supposed to offer opportunities to the ambitious; it had not been supposed to deliver the keys to the kingdom too.

The results were dramatic. By the start of the eleventh century, a new empire centred in Ghazna (now in eastern Afghanistan) had been established by descendants of a Turkic slave-general which could put so large an army in the field that one contemporary compared numbers to a myriad of "locusts or ants, innumerable and immeasurable as the sand of the desert."[71] The Ghaznavids conquered lands that stretched from eastern Iran into northern India, becoming great patrons of visual arts and literature. They championed the work of outstanding writers like Firdawsī, author of the glorious *Shāhnāma*, one of the jewels of early medieval Persian poetry—even if recent research suggests that the great poet probably did not travel to the court in Afghanistan to present his work in person, as has long been presumed.[72]

The Qarakhānid Turks were other beneficiaries of the weakening centre in Baghdad, establishing control over Transoxiana by carving out a realm to the north of the Amu Darya (the great Oxus river which flows across the border of modern Uzbekistan and Turkmenistan), agreeing with the Ghaznavids that the river should mark the boundary between their respective territories.[73] Like their neighbours, the Qarakhānids championed a flourishing school of scholars. Perhaps the most famous surviving text is the *Dīwān lughāt al-turk* (The Collection of Turkish Dialects) by Maḥmūd al-Kāshgharī, which takes the centre of the world to be the Qarakhānids' capital of Balāsāghūn in Central Asia, set out in a beautiful map that tells us much about how this brilliant polymath saw the world around him.[74]

Many other fabulously rich texts were produced, works that give a flavour of the refinement—and concerns—of a vibrant and wealthy society. One text that stands out is the *Kutadgu Bilig* (The Book of Wisdom that Brings Eternal Happiness) written in the late eleventh century in Qarakhānid Turkish by Yūsuf Khāṣṣ Ḥājib. It is filled with advice that ranges from stressing how much more sensible it is for a leader to respond to problems calmly than in anger to recommendations on how a magnate should host a good banquet. Where modern books on etiquette grate with facile statements of the obvious, it is difficult not to be charmed by this author, writing a thousand years ago, urging rulers to prepare well for a good dinner party. "Have cups and serving-cloths cleaned. Purify the house and hall, and set out the furnishings. Choose food and drink that is wholesome, tasty and clean so that your guests may eat to their hearts' content." Be sure to keep glasses topped up, the advice continues, and look after any latecomers graciously and generously: no one should ever leave a feast hungry or cursing.[75]

Arriviste potentates were in need of such advice—as uncomfortable in their own skin as newly rich tycoons of today wanting the right interior design and the right food and drink on the table for when guests arrive (you cannot go wrong, assures the author of the *Kutadgu Bilig*, with water flavoured with conserve of rose). Some of the more determined, however, eschewed the idea of setting up their own court and eating fancy food, and instead set their minds on the greatest prize of all—Baghdad. From the late tenth century, the Seljuks, descendants of a leader originally from the G͟huzz tribal constellation (mainly based in modern Kazakhstan), started to build up momentum. They proved adept at switching sides at opportune moments, offering their services to local rulers in return for appropriate rewards. It was not long before this began to translate into real power. Between the late 1020s and late 1030s, the Seljuks skilfully brought one city after another under their own control, with Merv, Nīshāpūr and Balkh submitting in turn. Then, in 1040, they defeated the Ghaznavids in battle, inflicting a crushing defeat on the numerically superior enemy at Dandanakan.[76]

The meteoric rise of the Seljuks from slave soldiers to power-brokers extraordinaire was confirmed in 1055 when they entered Baghdad at the invitation of the Caliph, driving out the unpopular and ineffective Būyid dynasty. Coins were minted in the name of the leader, Ṭughrıl Beg, while the order was given to say the *ḫuṭba* in his name—that is, to invoke blessing for his rule during daily prayers. In a further mark to show the dominance of his position in Baghdad and across the caliphate, Ṭughrıl was awarded two new titles: *al-Sulṭān Rukn al-Dawla*, and *Yamīn Amīr al-Muʾminīn*—Pillar of the State, and the Right Hand of the Commander of the Faithful.[77]

This was not without irony. The names of the sons of the eponymous founder of the dynasty suggests that the Seljuks were originally Christian or perhaps even Jewish. With names like Michael, Israel, Moses and Jonah, it is likely that they were among those on the steppes who had been evangelised either by the missionaries referred to by the Patriarch Timothy, or else by merchants who had introduced Judaism to the Khazars.[78] Although the timing and circumstances of their conversion to Islam are unclear, it was evidently difficult to hang on to religious beliefs that were a minority among the Muslim masses without losing legitimacy as they advanced rapidly. Had their successes been won more slowly, the world might have started to look very different, with a state emerging in the east led by rulers that were either Christians or Jews. As it was, the Seljuks chose to convert. But it was non-Muslim upstarts from the fringes of the caliphate who found themselves guardians of Muḥammad's legacy, champions of Islam and masters of one of the most powerful empires in history.

Even before their seizure of power in the ʿAbbāsid capital, the Byzantines had become concerned by the rise of the Seljuks. Their inexorable rise had stirred other nomads on the periphery to launch increasingly daring raids deep into the Balkans, in the Caucasus and Asia Minor, startling local populations with the speed of their attacks. Their horses, noted one commentator, were "swift as eagles, with hooves as solid as rock." They pounced on cities "as insatiably as hungry wolves devouring their food."[79]

In a misguided attempt to shore up defences in the east, the Emperor Romanos IV Diogenes set out from Constantinople with a large army, meeting with disaster in 1071 at Manzikert where the Byzantine forces were caught by surprise and humiliated. In a famous battle still celebrated today as the moment of the birth of the state of Turkey, the imperial army was surrounded and crushed and the Emperor taken prisoner. The Seljuk ruler, Alp Arslan, made the Byzantine leader lie on the ground and placed his foot on his neck.[80]

In fact, the Seljuks and the regime in Baghdad were much less concerned with the Byzantine Empire than they were with the Fāṭimid caliphate in Shīʿa Egypt. The two forces quickly locked horns, wrestling over control of Jerusalem. While this was going on, relations were established with Constantinople that were not so much cordial as positively supportive, thanks to the overlap of mutual interests that both had in curtailing the bands roaming Asia Minor who were using the classic steppe strategy of raiding and seeking payments in return for peace. For the Byzantines, this threatened dislocation to the fragile provincial economy; to the Seljuks, it represented a challenge to the authority of the leader as warlords emerged with ideas above their station. For the best part of two decades, the Emperor and the Sultan co-operated, with high-level discussions going so far as to discuss a potential marriage tie to bind the two rulers together. In the 1090s, however, the balance collapsed as the Seljuk world descended into a succession crisis, leaving upstart leaders in Asia Minor to raise the stakes by creating fiefdoms for themselves that made them virtually independent of Baghdad—and serious thorns in the side of Byzantium.[81]

With one calamity following another, the Christian Byzantine Empire was rapidly brought to its knees. With few cards left to play, the Emperor took drastic action: appeals were sent to leading magnates all over Europe, including to the Pope, Urban II. Appealing to the papacy was a last-ditch attempt to stop Byzantium teetering over into the abyss, and it was not without risk: forty years earlier, an escalation in tension between the churches of Rome and Constantinople had resulted in a schism that saw patriarchs and emperors excommunicated and priests threatening each other with the burning fires of hell. While part of the argument turned on doctrine, and particularly on the question of whether the Holy Spirit proceeds from the Son as well as from the Father, at the heart of the issue was a wider competition for control of the Christian faithful. Reaching out to the Pope meant glossing over division as well as looking to rebuild relations—both of which were easier said than done.[82]

The Emperor's envoys found Pope Urban II at Piacenza in March 1095, where they "implored his lordship and all the faithful of Christ to bring assistance against the heathen for the defence of this holy church, which had now been nearly annihilated in that region by the infidels who had conquered her as far as the walls of Constantinople."[83] The Pope immediately grasped what was at stake, and took action. Making his way north of the Alps, he held a church council at Clermont where he announced that it was the duty of Christian knighthood to march to the aid of their brethren in the east. Urban then began an exhausting tour to rally support from leading magnates, above all in France, cajoling and persuading them to take part in a great expedition that would end up in the Holy City of Jerusalem. The hour of need in the east looked like it might deliver unity to the church.[84]

The call to arms lit well-set tinder. Increasing numbers of Christian pilgrims had made their way to visit the Holy Places in the decades before the Pope's appeal for help. News travelled fast in a world where there were extensive links between western Europe and Constantinople. With pilgrim routes all but closed because of the dislocation in Asia Minor and the Middle East, and alarming reports circulating about the advances being made by the Turks in Anatolia which provided graphic accounts of the sufferings of Christians in the east, many were convinced that the apocalypse was nigh. Urban's call to arms met with a massive response: in 1096, tens of thousands of men set off for Jerusalem.[85]

As the copious source material shows, most of those who set off for the east were motivated by faith and by reports of horrors and atrocities that had substance to them. But while the Crusade is chiefly remembered as a war of religion, its most important implications were worldly. The first great struggle between the powers of Europe for position, riches and prestige in faraway lands was about to begin, triggered by the realisation of the prizes on offer. Things had shifted in such a way that, suddenly, the west was about to drag itself closer to the heart of the world.

8

The Road to Heaven

On 15 July 1099, Jerusalem fell to the knights of the First Crusade. The journey east had been almost unbearably difficult. Many of those who set out never made it to the Holy City, killed in battle, dead from disease or hunger or taken into captivity. As the Crusaders at last reached Jerusalem, they shed tears of happiness and relief as they approached the city walls.[1] When the walls of the city were finally breached after a six-week siege, the attackers were primed to shed blood. As one who witnessed the carnage that followed put it, Jerusalem was soon filled with dead bodies, corpses piled up "on mounds as big as houses outside the city gates. No one has ever heard of such a slaughter."[2] "If you had been there," wrote another author a few years later, "your feet would have been stained to the ankles with the blood of the slain. What shall I say? None of them were left alive. Neither women nor children were spared."[3]

News of the capture of the Holy City spread like wildfire. The leaders of the expedition became household names overnight. One above all captured the public imagination: Bohemond, son of a Norman legend who had made a name for himself in southern Italy and Sicily, was the star of the earliest accounts of the First Crusade. Suitably handsome, with blue eyes and a smooth strong chin and sporting a distinctive short haircut, Bohemond displayed a courage and guile that were the talk of western Europe. When he returned from the east at the start of the twelfth century, he was fêted as a hero, mobbed everywhere he went, with eligible would-be brides pushed in front of him to choose from.[4]

Bohemond seemed to stand for everything about the emerging new world. From the perspective of the Latin chroniclers of the time, he was the perfect talisman for a decisive transfer of power from east to west. Christendom had been saved by the brave knights who had marched thousands of miles to Jerusalem. The Holy City had been liberated by the Christians—not the Greek Orthodox Christians of the Byzantine Empire, but those of Normandy, France and Flanders who made up the overwhelming majority of the expedition. The Muslims had been expelled from a city they had controlled for centuries. Bleak predictions of forthcoming apocalypse had been everywhere on the eve of the Crusade; these were now replaced by optimism, by strident self-confidence and ambition. In a matter of five years, expectations went from fearing the end of the world to welcoming the start of a new era—an age dominated by western Europe.[5]

New colonies were founded in Outremer—literally "overseas"—ruled over by new Christian masters. It was a graphic expansion of European power: Jerusalem, Tripoli, Tyre and Antioch were all under the control of Europeans and governed by customary laws imported from the feudal west which affected everything from the property rights of the new arrivals, to tax gathering, to the powers of the King of Jerusalem. The Middle East was being recast to function like western Europe.

Over the next two centuries, enormous effort went into holding on to the territories conquered during the First Crusade and in its aftermath. The papacy repeatedly sought to impress on the knighthood of Europe that they had an obligation to defend the Holy Land. Serving the King of Jerusalem meant serving God. This message was powerfully articulated and widely circulated, resulting in large numbers of men making their way to the east, some of whom became Templar knights—a particularly popular new order whose zealous mixture of military service, devotion and piety proved intoxicatingly glamorous.

The road to Jerusalem became a road to heaven itself. At the very outset of the First Crusade in 1095, Pope Urban II had stated that those taking the cross and joining the expedition to the Holy City would receive absolution from their sins. This evolved during the course of the campaign, when the idea developed that those who fell in battle against the infidel should be considered to be on a path to salvation. Journeying east was a journey in this life and the way to reach paradise in the next.

While accounts of the triumph of Christianity, the papacy and the knighthood resounded from pulpit to pulpit and tavern to tavern in sermon, song and verse in the Christian west, in the Muslim world the reaction was mostly one of apathy. Although there had been concerted efforts to deal with the Crusaders before the capture of Jerusalem and immediately afterwards, resistance was local and limited. Some were perplexed by this laissez-faire attitude. A judge in Baghdad supposedly stormed into the Caliph's court to decry the lack of reaction to the arrival of the armies from Europe: "How dare you slumber in the shade of complacent safety," he said to those who were present, "leading lives as frivolous as garden flowers, while your brothers in Syria have no dwelling place save the saddles of camels and the bellies of vultures?" There was unspoken acquiescence in Baghdad and Cairo, based on the feeling that perhaps Christian occupation might be better than either Shīʿa or Sunnī rivals having control of the city. Although the speech made some around the Caliph weep, most remained aloof—and did nothing.[6]

The success of the First Crusade came as no consolation to the Jews of Europe or Palestine, who had witnessed shocking violence at the hands of the supposedly noble Crusaders. In the Rhineland, women, children and the elderly had been butchered in a sudden escalation of anti-Semitism in Europe. Jews were paying the price for the refocusing of western Europe's manpower and attention towards the east.[7] The bloodlust was directly linked to the idea that the Jews were responsible for Jesus' crucifixion and that the lands of Israel should be held by the Christians of Europe. Nothing would get in the way of new connections being burrowed into the Levant.

The Crusade was hardly a triumphant story as far as the Byzantines were concerned either. Behind the military success of the Crusade and its poster boy Bohemond lay a less heroic tale—not of glorious achievements and spectacular success, but of the duplicitous betrayal of the empire. All the leaders of the expedition had met Emperor Alexios I personally as they passed through the imperial capital in 1096–97 and swore an oath, over relics of the Holy Cross, that they would hand over all the towns and territories that they conquered which had previously belonged to Byzantium.[8] As the expedition dragged on, Bohemond became obsessed with how to wriggle out of these commitments and to seize the prizes for himself—chief of which was the great city of Antioch.

He took his chance when the city was captured following a debilitating siege. In one of the most dramatic stand-offs of the age, he was confronted in the Basilica of St. Peter in Antioch and challenged to defend his refusal to hand the city over to the Byzantine Emperor as promised. As Raymond of Toulouse, the most powerful of all the Crusader leaders, solemnly reminded him: "We swore upon the Cross of the Lord, the crown of thorns and many holy relics that we would not hold without the consent of the emperor any city or castle in his dominion." Bohemond simply stated that the oaths were null and void because Alexios had not kept his side of the bargain; and with that he simply refused to carry on with the expedition.[9]

It was a mark of the brilliance of the propaganda campaign mounted in the early twelfth century which placed Bohemond squarely at the centre of the triumph of the Crusade that there was no mention of the fact that its supposed hero was nowhere near the Holy City when it fell. After a delay of nearly a year spent trying to resolve the impasse over Antioch, the Crusader army eventually set off without him. As the knights processed around Jerusalem in order to give thanks to God before starting the siege, some in bare feet to show their humility, Bohemond was hundreds of miles away, lording it over his new prize, which he had secured through sheer obstinacy and ruthlessness.[10]

The stand made by Bohemond at Antioch and in the surrounding region stemmed from the realisation that there were exceptional opportunities on offer in the eastern Mediterranean. In this sense, his seizure of the city was the next step in the magnetic process that had dragged ambitious, capable men from northern and western Europe for decades and centuries beforehand. The Crusade might be best remembered as a war of religion, but it was also a springboard for accruing serious wealth and power.

It was not only the Byzantines who were unimpressed by Bohemond's refusal to hand over Antioch and by his aggressive and malicious behaviour, which saw poisonous stories circulated around Europe about Alexios by his supporters. There were others who had been deeply unenthusiastic about the Crusade in the first place—notably Roger of Sicily, part of an older generation that had made fortunes for themselves and did not want to see their position compromised. According to one Arabic historian, Roger was dismissive of plans to attack Jerusalem and tried to dampen the spirits of those excited by the prospect of new Christian colonies in the Mediterranean. Hearing of the plan to take Jerusalem, "Roger raised his leg and then gave a loud fart. 'By the truth of my religion,' he said, 'there is more use in that than in what you have to say.'" Any advance against the Muslims would compromise his relations with leading figures in Muslim North Africa—to say nothing of the problems it would create in Sicily itself, where there was a significant Muslim population—causing friction and interrupting trade. The resulting loss of income would be compounded, he said, by revenues from agricultural land going down because exports would inevitably suffer. "If you are determined to wage holy war on the Muslims," he said, then do so. But leave Sicily well out of it.[11]

There were grounds for the disquiet expressed by the likes of Roger of Sicily. Mediterranean markets had experienced volatility in the decades before the Crusade. Constantinople's spending power had declined rapidly in the face of a major financial crisis. The price of indigo dye being sold in Alexandria, for example, collapsed by more than 30 per cent in 1094 alone, and it is reasonable to assume there was a similar impact on the trade in pepper, cinnamon and ginger—even if the sources do not say so explicitly.[12] The lucrative trade between North Africa and Europe via Palestine, which saw brazil-wood being sold at a 150 per cent profit in 1085, must likewise have experienced contraction.[13] Sudden supply and demand shocks could lead to wild swings in prices—such as the surge in the cost of wheat that followed the Norman conquest of Sicily, or the near halving of the value of flax in the Mediterranean because of over-supply in the mid-eleventh century.[14]

Such fluctuations in prices and in wealth paled when compared with the transformation of the Mediterranean triggered by the impact of the Crusade. In the tenth and eleventh centuries, wrote the North African historian Ibn Khaldūn, Muslim fleets had such complete command of the seas that Christians were not even able to float a plank in it.[15] But although the Muslims had long dominated the Mediterranean, they were about to lose control of the waves to a new set of rivals: the city-states of Italy were the latest additions to the great trading networks of the east.

In truth, Amalfi, Genoa, Pisa and Venice had begun to flex their muscles well before the 1090s. In the case of the latter, trade in slaves and other commodities led to strong links being built up with towns on the Dalmatian coast such as Zara, Trogir, Split and Dubrovnik, which served as stepping stones along the Adriatic and beyond. These trading stations represented local market places and provided safe locations where long journeys could be broken. The fact that the Italian communes had permanent colonies of merchants in Constantinople, as well as in other cities in Byzantium, reveals their growing interest in trade with the eastern Mediterranean.[16]

This fuelled economic growth back in Italy, where such great riches were being generated in Pisa in the late eleventh century that the bishop and citizens imposed limits on the height of towers built by nobles keen to show off their wealth.[17]

The Italian city-states were quick to grasp that the seizure of Jerusalem would open up exciting commercial possibilities. Even before the Crusaders had reached the Holy City, Genoa, Pisa and Venice had fleets out on the water, making for Syria and Palestine. In each case, the initiative to put to sea was either the direct result of appeals from the papacy to participate in the enterprise, or stemmed from the impulse to defend Christians from the horrific atrocities that were being reported by eyewitnesses and emissaries from Byzantium.[18] But while spiritual motivations were an important factor, it quickly became apparent that there were significant material rewards on offer as well. The Crusaders were precariously placed after the capture of Jerusalem, in dire need of provisioning and desperate to establish links back to Europe. The fleets of the city-states put them in a powerful negotiating position when it came to dealing with the new masters of the Holy Land. Their hand was strengthened further by the Crusaders' need to secure the littoral and ports such as Haifa, Jaffa, Acre and Tripoli where maritime power was essential in mounting a successful siege.

Terms were struck which gave fabulous potential benefits in return for help. As reward for taking part in the siege of Acre in 1100, for instance, the newly arrived Venetians were promised a church and market square in every city captured by the Crusaders, as well as one-third of all plunder taken from the enemy and immunity from all taxes. It was the perfect example of what one scholar has termed the classic Venetian blend of "piety and greed."[19]

When Caesarea was besieged in 1101, it was the Genoese who were ideally placed to secure an impressive haul of booty together with favourable trading terms. Their position was further enhanced three years later when Baldwin I, King of Jerusalem, awarded the Genoese a sweeping set of tax exemptions as well as other legal and commercial rights—such as being free of royal jurisdiction in cases involving capital punishment. They were also awarded a third of the city of Caesarea, a third of the city of Arsuf and a third of Acre—with a generous proportion of the latter's tax revenues. The king also committed to pay an annual retainer to Genoa, and to grant a third share of future conquests on the condition that suitable military support was given in return.[20] Agreements like this were signs of the weakness of the Crusaders' position in the east; but for the city-states they were the basis for fortunes that transformed them from regional centres into international powers.[21]

Not surprisingly, such dizzying rewards sparked intense competition between Pisa, Genoa and Venice. Amalfi, which had been slow off the mark in getting ships out to the east, was unable to compete, excluded from the Great Game that now kicked off as the other rivals contended for access, concessions, lucrative trading terms. As early as 1099, the Pisans and Venetians came to blows, with the latter sinking twenty-eight of a fifty-strong squadron of Pisan ships off Rhodes. Hostages and captured vessels were then released in a show of magnanimity because, according to a later source, Venetians carried the cross of the Lord not only stitched into their tunics (as the Crusaders were instructed to do by the Pope) but also stamped on their souls.[22]

The background to this particular fracas was that in 1092 Venice had been granted extensive trading concessions across the Byzantine Empire as part of a grand strategy by the Emperor Alexios to stimulate the economy. This saw the Venetians awarded landing pontoons in the harbour of Constantinople, and being exempted from taxes on both imports and exports.[23] The primary motivation of the Venetians seven years later, therefore, was to keep Pisa out of this market place, and in doing so to protect the highly attractive terms that they had negotiated with the Emperor. As part of the settlement with Venice, the Pisans were forced to agree that they would never again enter Byzantium "for the sake of trade, nor fight against Christians in any manner whatsoever, unless on account of devotion to the Holy Sepulchre." That, at least, was how the Venetians reported what happened.[24]

Enforcing such treaties was easier said than done, and in fact, by the early twelfth century, the Byzantine Emperor had granted Pisa its own privileges that were not dissimilar to those previously granted to Venice, if not quite as generous. Although they too were granted a quay and anchorage in the imperial capital, Pisan merchants were offered only discounted customs duties, rather than full exemption from them.[25] This was a case of trying to water down a monopoly that threatened to give the Venetians an excessive advantage over their competitors.[26]

The scramble between the city-states of Italy for trading dominance in the eastern Mediterranean was frantic and ruthless. But it was not long before Venice emerged as the clear victor. This owed much to the city's geographic position in the Adriatic, which meant a shorter sailing time to

Venice than the trip to either Pisa or Genoa; it also helped that anchorages on this route were better, making it a safer journey too, at least once the treacherous Peloponnese had been negotiated. That Venice's economy was stronger and more developed was also important, as was the fact that the city had no local competitor to bog it down—unlike Pisa and Genoa, whose intense rivalry removed both from the Levant at crucial moments as they competed over control of their coastlines and above all that of Corsica.[27]

This played to Venice's advantage when a large army of western knights was comprehensively routed in what became known as the battle of the Field of Blood in 1119, a defeat that dealt a shattering blow to Antioch's viability as an independent Crusader state.[28] With Pisa and Genoa caught up in their own squabbles, desperate appeals were sent from Antioch to the Doge in Venice, begging for help in the name of Jesus Christ. A powerful force was put together because, as one generous contemporary commentator put it, the Venetians wanted "with the help of God to extend Jerusalem and the area adjacent, all for the advantage and glory of Christendom."[29] Significantly, however, the pleas for assistance from King Baldwin II were accompanied by the promise of new and additional privileges in return.[30]

The Venetians used this opening to teach the Byzantines a lesson. The new Emperor, John II, who succeeded his father Alexios in 1118, had concluded that the domestic economy had recovered sufficiently to justify refusing to renew the concessions given to the Venetians more than two decades earlier. As a result, as the Venetian fleet made its way east towards Antioch, it laid siege to Corfu and threatened further action if the Emperor did not renew the award. A stand-off followed until the Emperor backed down and reconfirmed the privileges first granted by his father.[31]

This success was more than matched by the gains made when the Doge's ships finally reached the Holy Land. Gauging the situation shrewdly, the Venetians made a loan to the western leaders in Jerusalem to enable them to fund their own forces to launch an attack on the ports that were held by the Muslims. A hefty premium was extracted in return. Venice would receive a church, a street and a square of good size in every royal and baronial city in the kingdom of Jerusalem. An annual fee would be paid to the Venetians, secured on the substantial future tax revenues of Tyre, the leading trade emporium in the region. When that city fell following a siege in 1124, Venice's status in the region was transformed by the granting of extensive concessions that would apply throughout the kingdom of Jerusalem. From having a mere foothold, the Italian city had engineered a position of such strength that some realised it threatened to compromise the authority of the crown and immediately attempted to water down some of the terms.[32]

This was ostensibly a time of faith and intense religious conviction, a period marked by self-sacrifice in the name of Christianity. But religion had to jostle alongside realpolitik and financial concerns—and the church hierarchy knew it. When the Byzantine Emperor John II tried to assert his claim over Antioch, the Pope issued a declaration to all the faithful, telling them that anyone who helped the Byzantines would face eternal damnation.[33] This had everything to do with keeping Rome's allies happy, and little to do with theology or doctrine.

But the best example of the blending of the spiritual and material came after the loss of Edessa to the Muslims in 1144—another major reversal for the Crusaders. Calls went out across Europe for reinforcements to take part in an expedition that would become the Second Crusade. The cheerleading was led by Bernard of Clairvaux, a charismatic and energetic figure, who was realistic enough to understand that the remission of sins and the possibility of salvation through martyrdom might not persuade everyone to head east. "To those of you who are merchants, men quick to seek a bargain," he wrote in a letter that was circulated widely, "let me point out the advantages of this great opportunity. Do not miss them!"[34]

By the middle of the twelfth century, the Italian city-states were lucratively exploiting the enviable positions they had so brilliantly built in the east. With preferential access to Constantinople as well as to the main cities on the coast of both the Byzantine Empire and Palestine, Venice's stepping stones now extended right the way across the eastern Mediterranean, not only to the Levant, but before long to Egypt too. Some looked on jealously, like Caffaro, the most famous Genoese historian of the Middle Ages. Genoa "was asleep and suffering from indifference," he wrote mournfully of the 1150s; it was "like a ship sailing across the sea without a navigator."[35]

This was something of an exaggeration, revealing a little of the author's disapproval of the powerful families who dominated Genoese politics. In fact, Genoa was also thriving in this period. As well as making sure that its privileges in the Crusader states were regularly reaffirmed, the city built ties in the western Mediterranean. In 1161, a truce was agreed with the Almohad Caliph in Morocco, which provided access to markets and protection from assault. By the 1180s, trade with North Africa accounted for more than a third of Genoese commercial activity, and an extensive infrastructure of warehouses and hostels had sprung up along the littoral to support merchants and enable business to take place smoothly.[36]

Genoa, Pisa and Venice stimulated the growth of a string of other towns around them—just as Kiev had done in Russia. Cities like Naples, Perugia, Padua and Verona expanded rapidly, with new suburbs expanding so fast that city walls were repeatedly rebuilt further and further out from the centre. Although assessing population sizes is difficult in the absence of clear empirical data, there is no doubt that the twelfth century saw a major surge in urbanisation in Italy as markets boomed, middle classes formed and incomes rose.[37]

Ironically, the basis for this growth in the age of the Crusades lay in the stability and good relations between the Muslim world and the Christians, both in the Holy Land itself and elsewhere. Although there were regular clashes in the decades after the capture of Jerusalem in 1099, it was only in the late 1170s that there was a dramatic escalation of tension. On the whole, Crusaders learnt how to deal with the majority Muslim populations that came under their sway, and with those further afield. Indeed, the King of Jerusalem regularly brought his own lords to heel, preventing them from launching reckless forays on passing caravans or on neighbouring cities that might antagonise local leaders or demand a major reaction from Baghdad or Cairo.

Some new arrivals to the Holy Land found this hard to understand and were a constant source of problems as a result, as local observers recognised. Newcomers could be incredulous that trade with the "infidel" was taking place on a daily basis, and took time to realise that in practice things were not as black and white as they had been painted back in Europe. In time, prejudices wore off: westerners who had been in the east for a while "are much better than those recently arrived," wrote one Arabic author who was appalled by the crude and uncouth habits of new arrivals—as well as by their attitudes to anyone who was not Christian.[38]

There were Muslim parallels to this way of thinking too. One *fatwa*, or declaration, issued in the 1140s urged Muslims neither to travel to the west nor trade with the Christians. "If we travel to their country the price of commodities will rise, and they will gather from us huge sums of money which they will use to fight Muslims and raid their lands."[39] By and large, however, for all the fiery rhetoric on both sides, relations were remarkably calm and considered. Indeed, in western Europe, there was considerable curiosity about Islam. Even at the time of the First Crusade, it had not taken long for some to form positive opinions about the Muslim Turks. "If only the Turks had stood firm in the faith of Christ and Christendom," wrote the author of one of the most popular histories of the expedition to Jerusalem wistfully—perhaps even hinting at the previous religious background of the Seljuks before they became Muslims; "you could not find stronger or braver or more skilful soldiers."[40]

It was not long either before the scientific and intellectual achievements of the Muslim world were being actively sought out and devoured by scholars in the west, such as Adelard of Bath.[41] It was Adelard who scoured the libraries of Antioch and Damascus and brought back copies of algorithmic tables that formed the foundation for the study of mathematics in the Christian world. Travelling round this region was to have one's eyes opened. When he returned home, he "found the princes barbarous, the bishops bibulous, judges bribable, patrons unreliable, clients sycophants, promisers liars, friends envious and almost everybody full of ambition."[42] These views were formed from the sanguine recognition of the east's sophistication compared to the cultural limitations in the Christian west. Adelard's view was shared by others—such as Daniel of Morley, who moved from England to study in Paris in the latter part of the twelfth century. The austere supposed intellectuals in that city flattered to deceive, simply sitting "still as statues, pretending to show wisdom by remaining silent." Realising that there was nothing he could learn from these men, Daniel moved to Muslim Toledo "as quickly as [he] could, so that [he] could hear the wisest philosophers of the world."[43]

Ideas from the east were taken on eagerly, if unevenly. Peter the Venerable, abbot of Cluny, which was the powerhouse of theological and intellectual thought in medieval France, arranged to have the Qurʾān translated so that he and other Christian scholars might better understand it—and, admittedly, use it to reinforce pre-existing views about Islam as deviant, shameful and dangerous.[44] Nor was it only to the Muslim lands that western Europeans turned for inspiration. Texts produced in Constantinople were also translated into Latin, such as the commentaries on Aristotle's *Nicomachaean Ethics* commissioned by Anna Komnene, daughter of Alexios I, which eventually found their way to Thomas Aquinas—and thence into the mainstream of Christian philosophy.[45]

In the same way, it was not only trade with the Muslims that lay at the heart of the economic and social blossoming of Europe in the twelfth century, for Constantinople and the Byzantine Empire were a major motor in the commerce of the Christian Mediterranean—responsible for half the international trade of Venice, to judge from the surviving documents for this period.[46] Even so, and while glass, metalwork, oil, wine and salt from Byzantium were exported to markets in Italy, Germany and France, it was products being brought from further afield that were most highly prized, sought after and profitable.

The demand for silk, cotton, linen and fabrics produced in the eastern Mediterranean, in the middle of Asia or in China was enormous, as inventories, sales lists and treasuries of churches in western Europe make clear.[47] Cities in the Levant capitalised on the emerging markets—with Antioch establishing itself as a trading centre where materials could be shipped west, but also as a production centre in its own right. Textiles from the city such as "Cloth of Antioch" were marketed so successfully and became so desirable that King Henry III of England (ruled 1216–72) had "Antioch Chambers" in each of his principal residences: the Tower of London, Clarendon and Winchester Palaces, and Westminster.[48]

Spices also began to flow to Europe from the east in increasing volumes. These reached three primary hubs—Constantinople, Jerusalem and Alexandria—and were then shipped to the Italian city communes and on to markets in Germany, France, Flanders and Britain, where there were fat profits to be made on the sale of exotic goods. In some ways the desire to buy expensive luxuries from the orient was a similar process to the steppe nomads' demand for silk bolts from the Chinese court: in the medieval world, just as today, the wealthy needed to differentiate themselves by showing off their status. Although trade in expensive objects and goods involved only a small proportion of the population, they were important because they enabled differentiation—and therefore reveal social mobility and rising aspirations.

While Jerusalem had a totemic role as the centre-point of Christendom, it also had a role as an emporium in its own right, although the town of Acre outranked it as a trading centre. A list of taxes to be collected in the kingdom in the later twelfth century provides a detailed insight into what could be bought there at that time, as well as betraying the close attention of a sophisticated chancery anxious not to lose out on valuable revenues. Charges were to be applied to the sale of pepper, cinnamon, alum, varnish, nutmeg, flax, cloves, aloe wood, sugar, salt fish, incense, cardamom, ammonia, ivory and much besides.[49] The vast majority of these goods did not originate in the Holy Land but were transited there via the trade routes controlled by the Muslims—including through the ports of Egypt, which exported an impressive catalogue of spices, textiles and luxury objects according to an Arabic tax treatise of this period.[50]

Ironically, therefore, the Crusades not only served to stimulate economies and societies in western Europe; they also enriched Muslim middlemen who spotted that new markets could produce rich rewards. One of the canniest was Rāmisht of Sīrāf in the Persian Gulf, who made a fortune in the early twelfth century. His genius was to meet rising demand by acting as a middleman for goods from China and India, with one of his agents shipping goods valued at over half a million dinars in one year alone. His wealth was legendary—as was his generosity. He paid for a golden water spout to replace that made of silver at the Kaʿba in Mecca, and personally funded new fabric—Chinese cloth whose "value cannot be estimated," according to one account of this period—that was draped over the Kaʿba after the original became damaged. His good deeds led to him having the rare distinction of being buried in Mecca, where the text written on his tombstone reads: "Here lies the ship-owner Abuʾl-Qāsim Rāmisht; 'May God have mercy on him and on whoever asks for mercy for him.'"[51]

The riches at stake inevitably led to an intensification of rivalries and a new chapter in the medieval Great Game: the pursuit of primacy in the eastern Mediterranean at all costs. By the 1160s, competition between the Italian city-states was so acute that there were running battles between Venetians, Genoese and Pisans in the streets of Constantinople. Despite attempts by the Byzantine Emperor to intervene, outbreaks of violence were to become regular occurrences. This was presumably the result of increasing commercial competition and the consequence of falling prices: trading positions had to be protected, by force if necessary.

The self-interest of the city-states antagonised the capital's inhabitants, both because of the damage done to property in the city and because the flexing of western muscles was increasingly evident elsewhere. In 1171, the Byzantine Emperor responded to growing disillusion by imprisoning thousands of Venetians and ignoring pleas for redress, let alone apologising for his unilateral, unannounced actions. When Doge Vitale Michiel was unable to resolve matters after sailing to Constantinople in person, the situation in Venice became febrile. With crowds gathered hoping to hear positive news, disappointment turned to anger which then gave way to violence. Attempting to flee his own people, the Doge made for the convent of San Zaccaria; before he could get there, a mob caught up with him and lynched him.[52]

The Byzantines were no longer Venice's allies and benefactors but rivals and competitors in their own right. In 1182, the inhabitants of Constantinople attacked the citizens of the Italian city-states who were living in the imperial capital. Many were killed, including the representative of the Latin church, whose head was dragged through the city's streets behind a dog.[53] This was just the start of rising animosities between the Christians of the two halves of Europe. In 1185, Thessaloniki, one of the Byzantine Empire's most important cities, was sacked by a western force from southern Italy. The west had sunk a harpoon into the eastern Mediterranean with the First Crusade; now it was reeling its prey in.

For some, though, the tensions provided an opportunity. The star of a brilliant general named Ṣalāḥ al-Dīn al-Ayyubī had been rising in Egypt for some time. With good connections, an astute mind and no little charm, the man better known as Saladin recognised that conflict in Constantinople could work to his advantage. He moved quickly to conciliate the Byzantines, making a point of inviting the Greek patriarch of Jerusalem to visit Damascus, treating him with conspicuous generosity to demonstrate that he, rather than the Christians from the west, was the natural ally for the empire.[54]

At the end of the 1180s, the Byzantine Emperor Isaac II was sufficiently well disposed to write "to [my] brother the Sultan of Egypt, Saladin" to share intelligence reports with him, warning that rumours about the empire's intentions put out by his enemies were without foundation, and asking Saladin to consider sending military support against the westerners.[55] Anti-western sentiment had been brewing in Constantinople for decades. One writer in the middle of the twelfth century stated that men from western Europe were unreliable, rapacious and willing to sell family members in return for money. Although many so-called pilgrims claimed to be devout, wrote the daughter of one emperor, they were really motivated only by greed. They were constantly planning to capture the imperial city, damage the reputation of the empire or harm their fellow Christians.[56] It was a story that was to become expanded and cemented in Byzantine consciousness in the late twelfth century and above all after 1204.

It was a view that found an echo in the Holy Land itself, where the knights were so violent and irresponsible it was almost as though they had a death wish. Time and again in the late twelfth century, leading figures made idiotic decisions, picked fatuous fights with each other and failed to prepare for the tidal wave that was approaching them in spite of obvious warning signs. Their carrying-on bemused one Muslim visitor from Spain in this period. It is amazing to see, wrote Ibn Jubayr, that "the fires of discord burn" between Christians and Muslims when it comes to politics and fighting; but when it comes to trade, travellers "come and go without interference."[57]

Merchants could be assured of security wherever they went, regardless of their faith, and regardless of whether there was peace or war. This was the result, wrote the author, of a good working relationship, whereby mutual tax treaties ensured co-operation, as did severe punishments. Latin traders who did not respect the agreements and crossed agreed boundaries, even if only by "the length of the arms," had their throats cut out by fellow Christians anxious not to upset the Muslims or mess up long-standing commercial ties. Ibn Jubayr was both bemused and impressed. It is "one of the most pleasing and singular conventions of the [westerners]."[58]

As the court in Jerusalem turned in on itself, infighting between rival factions became endemic, creating the perfect conditions for the rise of bullish and ambitious figures who over-promised success and caused untold damage to Christian–Muslim relations. Chief among these was Reynald of Châtillon, whose recklessness almost single-handedly brought down the kingdom of Jerusalem.

A veteran of the Holy Land, Reynald recognised that pressure was mounting as Saladin's position in Egypt strengthened—especially after the latter began to bring large parts of Syria under his control, thereby surrounding the Christian kingdom. Reynald's attempts to mitigate the threat were spectacularly unsuccessful. His hot-headed decision to attack the port of Aqaba on the Red Sea provoked near-hysterical reactions among Arab commentators, who screamed that Medina and Mecca were under threat and that the apocalypse and the end of time were at hand.[59]

Such moves were not just antagonistic, but escalated the prestige and popularity that the Saladin would gain if he could deliver a crushing blow to the Crusader state. Of all the Christians in the east, wrote one contemporary Muslim writer, Reynald was "the most perfidious and wicked . . . the most eager to cause harm and to do evil, to break firm promises and serious oaths, to violate his word and to perjure himself." Saladin swore "that he would have his life."[60]

He soon had his chance. In July 1187, the knights of the Crusader kingdom of Jerusalem were caught at the Horns of Hattin where they were outmanoeuvred, outthought and outfought by Saladin in a devastating battle that left almost every western combatant dead or captured. Members of the military orders who had been taken prisoner, notably Hospitallers and Templars—firebrands who lacked the willingness to compromise when dealing with non-Christian communities—were summarily executed. Saladin sought out Reynald of Châtillon personally, and beheaded him. Whether or not Reynald was the principal architect of the Crusaders' demise is open to debate, but he made for a convenient scapegoat for the defeated Latins and the victorious Muslims alike. Whatever the truth, barely two months after the battle Jerusalem surrendered peacefully to the Muslims, its gates flung open after terms had been agreed to spare the city's inhabitants.[61]

The fall of the city was a humiliating blow for the Christian world and a major setback for Europe's connections with the east. The papacy took the news badly—Urban III apparently dropped dead on hearing of the defeat at Hattin. His successor, Gregory VIII, led the soul-searching. The Holy City had fallen, he announced to the faithful, not only because of "the sins of its inhabitants but also [because of] our own and those of the whole Christian people." The power of the Muslims was rising, he warned, and would advance unless it was checked. He urged that kings, princes, barons and cities that were arguing with each other should set aside their differences and respond to what had happened. This was a frank admission that, for all the rhetoric about the knighthood being motivated by faith and piety, the reality was that self-interest, local rivalries and squabbling were the order of the day. Jerusalem had fallen, the Pope said, because of the failure of the Christians to stand up for what they believed in. Sin and evil had overwhelmed them.[62]

This provocative and strident message had an immediate effect, and it was not long before the three most powerful men in the west began preparations to launch a retaliatory expedition. With Richard I of England, Philip II of France and the mighty Frederick Barbarossa, the German Holy Roman Emperor, vowing to recover the Holy City, it seemed reasonable to think that there was a chance not just to retake Jerusalem but to re-embed the Christian position in the Middle East. The efforts of 1189–92, however, were a fiasco. Frederick drowned crossing a river in Asia Minor, miles from the proposed theatre of combat. There were fierce arguments among the leadership about strategic objectives, with disagreements all but bringing the armies to a standstill. This was typified by the attempt of Richard "the Lionheart" to turn the expedition away from Jerusalem itself and focus instead on the occupation of Egypt—a richer and juicier prize. As it was, the campaign achieved few permanent gains, and failed to put Jerusalem under pressure. In fact, before the leaders headed for home, it was striking that their attention turned to Acre, the primary emporium in the Levant—which had no value from a biblical or religious perspective.[63]

Hardly a decade later, there was another attempt to recover the Holy Land. Venice was to be the cornerstone of the assault this time, transporting men east by ship. Initially reluctant to help, the Doge was persuaded to back the initiative after receiving commitments that the cost of constructing the fleet required to transport the massive number of troops needed for the expedition would be funded by the participants. The Venetians also insisted on shaping the direction of the forthcoming campaign, mandating that the fleet would make for Egypt rather than the ports serving Jerusalem. This decision, according to one closely involved in the planning, "was kept a closely guarded secret; to the public at large, it was announced that we were going overseas."[64]

The proposed expedition was a match made in heaven: spiritual salvation and the promise of rich rewards for those who took part. The wealth of Egypt was the stuff of legend. Its people were "devoted to luxurious living," wrote one author in this period, and were fabulously wealthy as a result of "taxes from the cities both on the coast and farther inland." These, he noted with a sigh, produced a "vast amount of annual revenue."[65]

The Venetians were acutely aware of what was at stake, for their city's traditional arteries leading east had been subject to upheaval and uncertainty. With the turbulence following Saladin's successes matched by a period of instability in Byzantium, Venice was desperate to get exposure to Alexandria and the ports at the mouth of the Nile, places where it had traditionally been under-exposed: perhaps as little as 10 per cent of Venetian trade was with Egypt before 1200.[66] The city had previously lost out to Pisa and Genoa, which both had decisive advantages over their Italian rival in volumes of trade and in the connections they had established with commerce coming through the Red Sea—rather than overland to Constantinople and to Jerusalem.[67] The prizes on offer go a long way to accounting for the risks that Venice took in agreeing to build a huge fleet, which involved suspending all other work for the best part of two years.

It soon became clear, however, that the numbers of those keen to take part were far lower than anticipated—leaving Venice dangerously out of pocket. Events now overtook the Crusaders, with policy being improvised on the go. In 1202, the fleet arrived at Zara on the Dalmatian coast, a city that had been at the centre of a long-running struggle between Venice and Hungary. As it became clear that an attack was imminent, the confused citizens hoisted banners marked with crosses over the walls, assuming that there had been a chronic misunderstanding and refusing to believe that a Christian force would attack a Christian city without provocation—and against the express orders of Pope Innocent III. The city was not spared; Venice was extracting its pound of flesh from the knights.[68]

As the Crusaders considered how to justify such actions and argued about what to do next, a golden opportunity presented itself when one of the claimants to the throne in Byzantium offered to reward the army generously if they helped him take power in Constantinople. The forces that had originally set out for Egypt under the impression that they were heading for Jerusalem found themselves by the walls of the Byzantine capital, weighing up their options. As negotiations with factions inside the city dragged on, discussion among the Crusaders turned to how to take the city, and above all how to divide it and the rest of the empire between them.[69]

Venice had already learnt to guard its interests in the Adriatic and the Mediterranean jealously; it had strengthened this position by taking direct control of Zara. Here was the chance to seize control of the biggest prize of all, and in doing so secure direct access to the east. At the end of March 1204, men began to move into position to besiege New Rome. All-out assault began in the second week in April. Ladders, battering rams and catapults that were meant to help wrest control of cities from the Muslims were instead used against what was still by far the largest Christian city in the world. Ships that had been designed and built to blockade harbours in Egypt and the Levant were used to cut off sea access to the famous Golden Horn, in full view of the great cathedral of Hagia Sophia. On the eve of the battle, bishops reassured the westerners that the war "was a righteous one and that they should certainly attack the [Byzantines]." Referring to the disputes about doctrine that surfaced with convenient regularity when there were other, more material issues at stake, the priests said that the inhabitants of Constantinople could be assaulted on the basis that they had declared that "the law of Rome counted for nothing and called all who believed in it dogs." The Byzantines, the Crusaders were told, were worse than the Jews; "they are the enemies of God."[70]

When the walls were breached, chaotic scenes followed as the westerners rampaged through the city. Whipped into a religious frenzy by the poisonous words that had been dripped into their ears, they plundered and desecrated the city's churches with particular thoroughness. They stormed the treasuries of Hagia Sophia, stealing the jewelled vessels containing the relics of saints and jesting with the spear that had pierced Jesus' side on the cross. Silver and precious-metal objects used to celebrate the Eucharist were seized. Horses and donkeys were led into the church to be loaded up with booty, some slipping on the polished marble floors that were polluted with "blood and filth." To add insult to injury, a rowdy prostitute sat in the patriarch's seat singing obscene songs. To one Byzantine eyewitness, the Crusaders were nothing other than the forerunners of the Antichrist.[71]

There is more than enough source material to indicate that such accounts were not exaggerated. One western abbot went directly to the church of the Pantokrator (Christ the Almighty), established in the twelfth century by the imperial family. "Show me the most powerful relics you have," he commanded a priest, "or you shall die immediately." He found a chest filled with church treasures, into which he "eagerly thrust both hands." When others asked him where he had been and if he had stolen anything, all he would say, with a nod and a smile, was "we have done well."[72]

Little wonder then that as one Byzantine inhabitant left the city, he threw himself to the ground, wept and reproached the walls because "they alone were unmoved, neither shedding tears nor destroyed on the ground; they remained standing, quite upright." It was as though they were mocking him: how had they not protected the city? The very soul of the city was ripped out by the rampaging troops in 1204.[73]

Constantinople's physical riches were spirited away to churches, cathedrals, monasteries and private collections all over western Europe. Sculptures of horses that had stood proudly at the Hippodrome were loaded on to ships and transported to Venice where they were mounted above the entrance to St. Mark's Cathedral; innumerable relics and precious objects were likewise transported to the city, where they remain today, admired by tourists as examples of fine Christian craftsmanship rather than war booty.[74]

As if that were not bad enough, when Enrico Dandolo, the blind old Doge who had come from Venice to witness the attack on Constantinople, died the following year, it was decided that he should be buried in Hagia Sophia. He was the first person in history to be buried in the great cathedral.[75] It was a highly symbolic statement that spoke volumes about the rise of Europe. For centuries, men had looked east to make their fortunes and realise their ambitions—whether spiritual or material. The sack and capture of the biggest and most important city in Christendom showed that the Europeans would stop at nothing to take what they wanted—and needed—to get closer to the centre of where the world's wealth and power lay.

Although they looked like men, the westerners behaved like animals, wrote one prominent Greek cleric mournfully, adding that the Byzantines were treated with abysmal cruelty as virgins were raped and innocent victims impaled. The sack of the city was so brutal that one modern scholar has written of a "lost generation" in the years that followed the Fourth Crusade as the Byzantine imperial apparatus was forced to regroup in Nicaea in Asia Minor.[76]

In the meantime, the westerners set about dividing the empire among themselves. After consulting tax registers in Constantinople, a new document entitled *Partitio terrarum imperii Romaniae*—The Partition of the Lands of the Roman Empire—was produced, setting out who would take what. This was no accidental or haphazard process; it was cold and calculated dismemberment.[77] From the very outset, men such as Bohemond had shown that the Crusades—which promised to defend Christendom, to do the Lord's work and deliver salvation to the many who took the cross—could be hijacked for other purposes. The sack of Constantinople was the obvious culmination of the desire of Europe to connect and embed itself in the east.

As the Byzantine Empire was dismantled, the Europeans led by the Italian city-states Pisa, Genoa and Venice rushed to seize strategically and economically important regions, towns and islands at each other's expense. Fleets clashed regularly off Crete and Corfu as each vied to gain control of the best bases and to obtain the best access to markets.[78] On land too, there was a scramble for territory and status that was particularly fierce in the fertile plains of Thrace, Constantinople's breadbasket.[79]

Attention soon turned again to Egypt, which in 1218 became the focus of another large-scale expedition whose aim was to fight through from the Nile delta to Jerusalem. Francis of Assisi joined the armies that sailed south in the hope of persuading the Sultan al-Kāmil to renounce Islam and become a Christian—something even the charismatic Francis was not able to achieve despite being given the opportunity to do so in person.[80] After taking Damietta in 1219, the Crusaders attempted to march on to

Cairo, which ended in a disastrous routing at the hands of the unconverted al-Kāmil that ultimately brought the expedition to an ignominious halt. As the leaders considered an offer to agree terms and argued between themselves about the right course of action to take in the face of heavy defeat, reports were received of what seemed nothing less than a miracle.

News came through that a large army was marching from deep inside Asia to help the western knights against Egypt. Crushing all opposition as they advanced, they were heading to the Crusaders' relief. The identity of the inbound relief force was immediately obvious: these were the men of Prester John, the ruler of a vast and phenomenally wealthy kingdom whose inhabitants included the Amazons, Brahmans, Lost Tribes of Israel and an array of mythical and semi-mythical creatures. Prester John ostensibly ruled over a kingdom that was not only Christian but as close to heaven on earth as possible. Letters that started to appear in the twelfth century left little doubt as to his magnificence or the glory of his realm: "I, Prester John, am the lord of lords, and I surpass all the kings of the entire world in wealth, virtue and power . . . Milk and honey flow freely in our lands; poison can do no harm, nor do any noisy frogs croak. There are no scorpions, no serpents creeping in the grass." It was rich in emeralds, diamonds, amethysts and other precious stones, as well as in pepper and elixirs that staved off all illnesses.[81] Rumours of his arrival were enough to affect decisions made in Egypt: the Crusaders simply needed to hold their nerve and victory would be assured.[82]

This proved to be an early lesson for the European experience of Asia. Unfamiliar with what to believe, the Crusaders set great store by rumours that struck a chord with reports that had circulated for decades following the defeat of the Sultan Aḥmad Sanjar in Central Asia in the 1140s. This incident had given rise to impossibly convoluted and optimistic ideas about what lay beyond the Seljuk Empire. As news first swept through the Caucasus of forces advancing like the wind, gossip quickly became fact: it was said that "magi" were heading west bearing crosses and portable tents that could be erected into churches. The liberation of Christendom seemed to be at hand.[83] One leading cleric at Damietta spelt this out in no uncertain terms, preaching that "David, king of the two Indies, was hastening to the aid of the Christians, bringing with him most ferocious peoples who will devour the sacrilegious Saracens like beasts."[84]

It soon became clear how wrong these reports were. The rumbling that could be heard from the east was not Prester John, his son "King David" or a Christian army marching to the aid of their brethren. It was the noise preceding the arrival of something altogether different. What was heading towards the Crusaders—and towards Europe—was not the road to heaven, but a path that seemed to lead straight to hell. Galloping along it were the Mongols.[85]

9

The Road to Hell

The tremors that were felt in Egypt came from the other side of the world. In the late eleventh century, the Mongols were one of many tribes living on the northern fringe of China's boundary with the steppe world, with one contemporary describing them as "living like animals, guided neither by faith nor by law, simply wandering from one place to another, like wild animals grazing."[1] According to another author, "they regarded robbery and violence, immorality and debauchery as deeds of manliness and excellence." Their appearance was similarly regarded with disgust: like the Huns of the fourth century, they wore "skins of dogs and mice."[2] These were familiar descriptions of the behaviour and manners of nomads as viewed by outside observers.

Although the Mongols seemed to be chaotic, bloodthirsty and unreliable, their rise was not the result of a lack of order, but precisely the opposite: ruthless planning, streamlined organisation and a clear set of strategic objectives were the key to establishing the largest land empire in history. The inspiration behind the Mongol transformation was a leader named Temüjin, or blacksmith. We know him by his title and nickname of "universal ruler," or perhaps, "fierce ruler": Činggis, or Genghis Khan.[3]

Genghis Khan came from a leading family within the tribal union, and his destiny had been foretold from the moment he was born "clutching in his right hand a clot of blood the size of a knucklebone"; this was interpreted as a propitious sign of glories that lay ahead.[4] Despite the fearsome reputation he acquired in the Middle Ages and which still endures, Genghis Khan built his position and power slowly, striking deals with fellow tribal leaders and choosing his allies astutely. He also chose his enemies well, and, above all, he picked the right moment to take them on. He arranged his most devoted followers around him both as a personal bodyguard and as an iron inner circle made up of warriors (*nökürs*) upon whom he could rely unquestioningly. This was a meritocratic system where ability and loyalty were more important than tribal background or shared kinship with the leader. In return for unstinting support, the leader provided goods, booty and status. Genghis Khan's genius was to be able to supply these benefits prodigiously enough to guarantee loyalty—and to do so with metronomic regularity.[5]

This was made possible by an almost constant programme of conquest. One tribe after another was brought under his sway by force or by threat, until he had established himself as the undisputed master of the Mongolian steppes by 1206. Attention then turned to the next ring of peoples, such as the Kyrgyz, the Oirat and the Uighurs situated to the west of China in Central Asia, who submitted and swore formal oaths of allegiance. The incorporation of the latter in 1211 was particularly important, as is clear from the gift to the Uighur ruler, Barchuq, of a Činggisid bride after he had declared that he was ready to become Genghis Khan's "fifth son."[6] This was partly a reflection of the importance of lands occupied by the Uighurs in the Tarim basin, but was also because the Uighur language, alphabet and what one modern historian calls the "literati" had been becoming increasingly important in Mongolia. The Uighurs' elevated cultural status was one reason for the recruitment into service en masse of their scribes and bureaucrats—including a certain "Tatar Tonga," who became tutor to Genghis Khan's sons.[7]

Attention turned to more ambitious targets. In a series of attacks starting in 1211, the Mongols forced their way into China under the rule of the Jin dynasty, sacking the capital, Zhongdu, and forcing the rulers to evacuate and relocate their capital southwards on multiple occasions, with the invaders securing substantial plunder. Expansion was even more impressive elsewhere. The timing could not have been better. Central authority in the Muslim world weakened in the course of the twelfth century as a patchwork of states of varying size, capability and stability emerged to challenge the primacy of Baghdad. As it happened, the ruler of Khwārazm had been busy picking off local rivals, with one eye on expanding eastwards into China himself. The consolidation that came as a result now simply meant that when the Mongols defeated him, as they duly did, chasing him to an island in the Caspian where he died not long afterwards, the door to Central Asia was wide open: the path had been cleared before them.[8]

Sources paint vivid pictures of the vile savagery that accompanied the attack that began on Khwārazm in 1219. The invaders, wrote one historian, "came, they sapped, they burned, they slew, they plundered and they departed."[9] I wish I had never been born, wrote another, so I would not have had to live through such traumas. At least the Muslim Antichrist will only destroy his enemies, he went on; the Mongols, on the other hand, "spared none. They killed women, men, children, ripped open the bodies of the pregnant and slaughtered the unborn."[10]

The Mongols cultivated such fears carefully, for the reality was that Genghis Khan used violence selectively and deliberately. The sack of one city was calculated to encourage others to submit peacefully and quickly; theatrically gruesome deaths were used to persuade other rulers that it was better to negotiate than to offer resistance. Nīshāpūr was one of the locations that suffered total devastation. Every living being—from women, children and the elderly to livestock and domestic animals—was butchered as the order was given that not even dogs or cats should be left alive. All the corpses were piled up in a series of enormous pyramids as gruesome warnings of the consequences of standing up to the Mongols. It was enough to convince other towns to lay down arms and negotiate: the choice was one of life or death.[11]

News travelled fast of the brutality that faced those who took the time to weigh up their options. Stories such as that of a high-ranking official who was ordered into the presence of a newly arrived Mongol warlord and had molten gold poured into his eyes and ears became widely known—as was the fact that this murder was accompanied by the announcement that this was fitting punishment for a man "whose disgraceful behaviour, barbarous acts and previous cruelties deserved the condemnation of all."[12] It was a warning to those who considered standing in the way of the Mongols. Peaceful submission was rewarded; resistance was punished brutally.

Genghis Khan's use of force was technically advanced, as well as strategically astute. To mount a lengthy siege on fortified targets was challenging and expensive because of the demands of sustaining a large mounted army whose need for pasture could quickly exhaust the surrounding region. For this reason, military technicians who could expedite a swift victory were highly valued. At Nīshāpūr in 1221, we learn of 3,000 giant crossbows being used, as well as 3,000 stone-hurling machines and 700 projectors of incendiary material. Later, the Mongols became intensely interested in the techniques that had been pioneered by western Europeans, copying designs for catapults and siege engines created for the Crusaders in the Holy Land and using them against targets in East Asia in the late thirteenth century. Control of the Silk Roads gave their masters access to information and ideas that could be replicated and deployed thousands of miles away.[13]

Curiously, given their reputation, one explanation for the astounding successes of the Mongols in early thirteenth-century China, Central Asia and beyond was that they were not always seen as oppressors. And with good reason: in the case of Khwārazm, for example, the local population had been ordered to pay a year's taxes up front to fund the construction of new fortifications around Samarkand and to pay for squadrons of archers against an imminent Mongol attack. Putting such strain on households hardly retained goodwill. In contrast, the Mongols invested lavishly in the infrastructure of some of the cities they captured. One Chinese monk who visited Samarkand soon after its capture was amazed to see how many craftsmen there were from China and how many people were being drawn in from the surrounding region and further afield to help manage the fields and orchards that had previously been neglected.[14]

It was a pattern repeated time and again: money poured into towns that were rebuilt and re-energised, with particular attention paid to championing the arts, crafts and production. Blanket images of the Mongols as barbaric destroyers are wide of the mark, and represent the misleading legacies of the histories written later which emphasised ruin and devastation above all else. This slanted view of the past provides a notable lesson in how useful it is for leaders who have a view to posterity to patronise historians who write sympathetically of their age of empire—something the Mongols conspicuously failed to do.[15]

But there could also be no mistaking how the Mongols' use of force chilled the blood of those who heard of an impending assault. As they swarmed west, hunting down those who had resisted them or fled in the hope of escape, the Mongols struck terror into hearts and minds. In 1221, armies under the command of two of Genghis Khan's sons advanced like lightning through Afghanistan and Persia, ravaging all before them. Nīshāpūr, Herat and Balkh were taken, while Merv was razed to the ground and its entire population murdered, according to one Persian historian, save for a group of 400 artisans who were brought back to the east to work at the Mongol court. The ground was stained red with the blood of the dead: a small group of survivors apparently counted the corpses and put the number of the dead at more than 1.3 million.[16] Breathless reports of similar death tolls elsewhere have convinced modern commentators to talk in terms of genocide, mass murder and the slaughter of 90 per cent of the population.[17]

While it is difficult to be precise about the scale of death inflicted in the attacks, it is worth noting that many (though not all) of the towns apparently ravaged by waves of attackers recovered quickly—suggesting that the later Persian historians whom we have to rely on may have been keen to over-emphasise the devastating effects of the Mongol attacks. But even if they magnified the suffering, there could be no doubt that the winds that blew violence from the east did so with tremendous force.

They were relentless too. No sooner had the principal cities of Central Asia been reduced than the Caucasus was plundered, before the raiders then appeared in southern Russia. They were hunting tribal rivals, the Qıpchāqs or Cumans, to teach them a lesson for daring not to submit. Genghis Khan may have died in 1227; but his heirs proved to be equally resourceful—and spectacularly successful.

In the late 1230s, after extraordinary successes in Central Asia masterminded by Ögödei, who became the Great Khan, or supreme leader, soon after his father's death, the Mongols launched one of the most stunning attacks in the history of warfare, mounting a campaign that surpassed even that of Alexander the Great in terms of speed and scale. Forces had already once before advanced from the steppes into Russian territory, appearing in "countless numbers, like locusts," according to one monk of Novgorod. "We do not know where they came from or where they disappeared to," he wrote; "only God knows because he sent them to punish us for our sins."[18] In textbook fashion, when the Mongols returned, they demanded tribute, threatening destruction to those who refused. One after another, towns were attacked, with Ryazan, Tver' and eventually Kiev comprehensively sacked. In Vladimir, the prince and his family, together with the town's bishop and other dignitaries, took sanctuary in the church of the Holy Mother of God. The Mongols set fire to the church, burning its occupants alive.[19] Churches were destroyed, wrote one of the bishop's successors, "holy vessels defiled, sacred objects trampled on the ground, and clergy were fodder for the sword."[20] It was as though wild beasts had been released to devour the flesh of the strong and to drink the blood of the nobles. It was not Prester John and salvation coming from the east, but Mongols bringing the apocalypse.

The terror the Mongols aroused was reflected in the name by which they were soon being referred to: Tatars, a reference to Tartarus—the abyss of torment in classical mythology.[21] Reports of their advance reached as far as Scotland while, according to one source, herring went unsold in ports on the east coast of Britain as merchants who normally came from the Baltic to buy it did not dare to leave home.[22] In 1241, the Mongols struck into the heart of Europe, splitting their forces into two, with one spur attacking Poland and the other heading for the plains of Hungary. Panic spread through the entire continent, especially after a large army led by the King of Poland and the Duke of Silesia was destroyed, and the head of the latter paraded on the end of a lance, together with nine sacks filled with "the ears of the dead." Mongol forces now moved west. When King Béla IV of Hungary fled to Dalmatia, taking refuge in Trogir, it was time for priests to say masses, praying for protection from evil, and to lead processions to implore the support of God. The Pope, Gregory IX, took the step of announcing that any who helped defend Hungary would receive the same indulgence as that granted to Crusaders. His offer met with little enthusiasm: the German Emperor and the Doge of Venice were more than aware of what the consequences would be if they tried to help and ended up on the losing side. If the Mongols had now chosen to continue westward, as one modern scholar puts it, "it is unlikely that they would have encountered any coordinated opposition."[23] Europe's moment of reckoning had arrived.

With a gall that is almost admirable, some contemporary historians now began to claim that the Mongols had been halted by brave resistance, or even defeated in imaginary battles that seemed to become more real as time went on. In fact, the Mongols were simply uninterested in what western Europe had to offer—at least for the time being. The priority was to admonish Béla for granting sanctuary to the Cumans and, perhaps worse, for ignoring repeated demands to hand them over: such resistance had to be punished at all costs.[24]

"I am aware that you are a rich and powerful monarch," read one letter to King Béla from the Mongol leadership, "that you have many soldiers under your command, and that you alone rule a great kingdom." In words that would be familiar to any professional racketeer, things were spelled out, bluntly. "It is difficult for you to submit to me of your own free will," it went on; "and yet it would be much better for your future prospects if you were to do so."[25] In the world of the steppes, slighting a powerful rival was almost as bad as confronting them head-on. Béla needed to be taught a lesson. He was therefore chased single-mindedly through Dalmatia, even though there were other, gaping opportunities elsewhere. The Mongols ravaged everything as they went, sacking one town so spectacularly that a local chronicler noted that nobody was left even "to piss against a wall."[26]

At that point, Béla—and Europe—were saved by a stroke of great fortune: Ögödei, the Great Khan, suddenly died. To the devout, it was obvious that their prayers had been answered. To high-ranking Mongols, it was vital to be present at and participate in the selection of the man who should take the mantle of leadership. There was no such thing as primogeniture. Rather the choice of who should succeed to the position of highest authority rested on who made their case best and loudest in person to a conclave of senior figures. The decision of whom to back could make or break commanders' lives and careers: if a patron rose to the top, the share of the rewards could be disproportionately high. This was not the moment to be chasing troublesome monarchs through the Balkans. It was time to be at home, watching the situation unfurl. And with that, the Mongols took their foot off the throat of Christian Europe.

Although it is the name of Genghis Khan that is synonymous with the great conquests of Asia and the attacks on lands far beyond, the Mongol leader died in 1227 after the initial phase of empire building in China and Central Asia had been carried out, but before the dramatic attacks on Russia and the Middle East and the invasion that brought Europe to its knees. It was his son Ögödei who oversaw the expansion that massively increased the extent of Mongol lordship, masterminding campaigns that extended into the Korean peninsula, Tibet, Pakistan and northern India—as well as in the west. It was Ögödei who deserved much of the credit for the Mongol achievement, and equally some of the responsibility for its temporary halt: for his death in 1241 provided crucial breathing space.

As the world paused to see who would take charge, streams of envoys were sent from Europe and the Caucasus across Asia to find out who these marauders were, where they had come from, what their customs were—and to come to an understanding with them. Two groups of ambassadors took letters with them demanding in the name of God that the Mongols not attack Christians, and that they consider adopting the true faith.[27] Between

1243 and 1253, four separate embassies were sent by Pope Innocent IV, while King Louis IX of France also dispatched a mission led by William of Rubruck, a monk from Flanders.[28]

The reports they produced of their travels were as graphic and alien as those produced by Muslim travellers to the steppes in the ninth and tenth centuries. The European visitors were fascinated and appalled in equal measure. Although immeasurably powerful, wrote William of Rubruck, the new masters of Asia did not live in cities, except at the capital Karakorum, where he met the Great Khan in an enormous tent that was "completely covered inside with cloth of gold."[29] These were people whose behaviour and habits were exotic and unrecognisable. They did not eat vegetables, drank fermented mare's milk and emptied their bowels without a thought for those they were talking to—and in public, no further away from where one was standing than "one could toss a bean."[30]

The account of another envoy, John of Plano Carpini, became widely known throughout Europe in this period; it painted a similar picture of squalor, decadence and unfamiliarity, a world where dogs, wolves, foxes and lice were treated as food. He also reported on rumours he had heard about creatures that lay beyond the Mongol lands—where some people had hooves and others heads of dogs.[31] John brought back ominous information about the scenes that accompanied the enthronement of the next Great Khan, Güyüg. The list of dignitaries from regions, tribes and realms that recognised Mongol overlordship conveyed something of the astonishing scale of the empire: leaders from Russia, Georgia, Armenia, the steppes, China and Korea were in attendance, as were no fewer than ten sultans and thousands of envoys from the Caliph.[32]

John was given a letter to take back to Rome by the Great Khan. All the lands in the world have been conquered by the Mongols, it said. "You should come in person," it demanded of the Pope, "with all the princes, and serve us." If you do not do so, the Great Khan warned, "I shall make you my enemy." There was an uncompromising answer meanwhile for the Pope's entreaties that the Mongol ruler become Christian: how do you know whom God absolves, and to whom he shows mercy?, the Khan wrote angrily. All the lands from the rising to the setting sun are subject to me, he went on, which did little to recommend the Pope's God. The letter was stamped with a seal that united the power of the Great Khan with that of "the eternal Tengri"—the supreme deity of traditional steppe-nomad beliefs. This was not promising at all.[33]

Nor was it reassuring that plans were being made for new attacks on central Europe, with an assault actively being considered against the north of the continent too.[34] The Mongols had a worldview that stopped nothing short of global domination: conquering Europe was simply the next logical step in the plan for the heirs of Genghis Khan to bring yet more territory under their sway.[35]

Fear of the Mongols now provoked a game of religious dominoes in Europe. The Armenian church entered into discussions with the Greek Orthodox patriarchate in order to build an alliance and gain protection in the event of a future attack. The Armenians also opened negotiations with Rome, signalling their willingness to declare that they were in agreement with the papacy's interpretation of the procession of the Holy Spirit—a topic that had caused much friction in the past.[36] The Byzantines did the same, sending a mission to Rome and proposing ending the schism which had cleaved the Christian church in two since the eleventh century, and which had deepened rather than healed as a result of the Crusades.[37] Where priests and princes in Europe had failed to reunite popes and patriarchs, the Mongols had succeeded: attacks from the east, and the very real threat that they would be repeated, had brought the church to the point of full reunion.

Just when religious harmony seemed a certainty, the sands shifted. After the Great Khan Güyüg died unexpectedly in 1248, there was a succession struggle within the Mongol leadership that took time to resolve. As this played out, the rulers of Armenia and Byzantium received assurances that no attack was imminent. According to William of Rubruck, in the case of the latter this was because the Mongol envoy who had been sent to the Byzantines was heavily bribed and as a result intervened to prevent an assault.[38] It was certainly true that the Byzantines were desperate to deflect the attention of the Mongols and did all they could to avoid attack. In the 1250s, for example, another delegation sent from Karakorum was led through difficult terrain in Asia Minor on purpose by Byzantine guides and made to watch the imperial army parade when they arrived to meet with the Emperor. These were desperate attempts to convince the Mongols that the empire was not worth attacking—or, if it was, that troops would be waiting for them.[39]

In fact the Mongols decided not to attack for different reasons: neither Anatolia nor Europe was the focus of their attention simply because there were fatter and better targets elsewhere. Expeditions were sent to what remained of China until it capitulated completely in the late thirteenth century, at which point the ruling Mongol dynasty adopted the imperial title of Yüan and founded a new city on the site of the old city of Zhongdu. This now became the Mongol capital, designed to crown the achievements of taking control of the entire region between the Pacific and the Mediterranean. The new metropolis has retained its importance ever since: Beijing.

Other major cities also received considerable attention. The new Khan, Möngke, focused the Mongol armies on the pearls of the Islamic world. One city after another fell as the attacking army surged westwards. In 1258, they reached the walls of Baghdad and, after a brief siege, wreaked devastation. They swept through the city "like hungry falcons attacking a flight of doves, or like raging wolves attacking sheep," wrote one writer not long afterwards. The city's inhabitants were dragged through the streets and alleys, like toys, "each of them becoming a plaything." The Caliph al-Mustaʿṣim was captured, rolled up in fabric and trampled to death by horses.[40] It was a highly symbolic moment that showed who held real power in the world.

Immense booty and riches were seized during these conquests. According to an account produced in the Caucasus by allies of the Mongols, the victors "sank under the weight of the gold, silver, gems and pearls, the textiles and precious garments, the plates and vases of gold and silver, for they only took these two metals, the gems, the pearls, the textiles and the garments." The seizure of fabrics was particularly significant: as with the Xiongnu at the height of their power, silk and luxury materials played a crucial role in demarcating elites within the tribal system and were highly prized as a result. The Mongols often specifically required tributes in the form of gold cloth, purple gauze, precious garments or silks; on occasion, it was stipulated that such payments should be made in the form of livestock which should be adorned with damask, gold fabric and precious jewels. "Cloths of silk and gold and cotton" were requested in such specific quantities and qualities that the leading scholar in this field has likened it to a detailed shopping list—one that was "both demanding and remarkably well informed."[41]

There was barely time to digest news of the sack of Baghdad before the Mongols appeared once again in Europe. In 1259, they advanced into Poland, sacking Kraków, before sending a delegation to Paris to demand the submission of France.[42] At the same time, a separate army swung west from Baghdad against Syria and into Palestine. This caused blind panic among the Latins living in the east, where the Christian position in the Holy Land had been reinforced by a fresh burst of Crusade energy in the middle of the thirteenth century. Although large-scale expeditions by the Holy Roman

Emperor Frederick II and then by Louis IX of France restored Jerusalem, briefly, to Christian hands, few had any illusions about how precarious the hold was over Antioch, Acre, and other remaining towns.

Until the appearance of the Mongols, the threat had seemed to come from Egypt and from a highly aggressive new regime that had seized power there. With remarkable irony, the new Egyptian overlords were men from similar stock to the Mongols themselves—nomads from the steppes. Just as the ʿAbbāsid caliphate of Baghdad had been taken over by its slave soldiers recruited from the Turkic tribes on the steppes, so the same thing happened in the caliphate of Cairo in 1250. In the case of Egypt, the new masters were known as Mamlūk, as a result of being largely descendants of slaves (*mamalik*) who had been taken from the tribal constellations north of the Black Sea and traded through the ports of the Crimea and the Caucasus to serve in the Egyptian military. Their number included Mongol tribesmen who had either been caught up in the slave traffic or as *wāfidīyah*—literally newcomers—had fled from the oppressive dominant factions in the sort of internal scuffles that were commonplace on the steppes, and sought sanctuary and service in Cairo.[43]

The Middle Ages in Europe are traditionally seen as the time of Crusades, chivalry and the growing power of the papacy, but all this was little more than a sideshow to the titanic struggles taking place further east. The tribal system had led the Mongols to the brink of global domination, having conquered almost the whole continent of Asia. Europe and North Africa yawned open; it was striking then that the Mongol leadership focused not on the former but on the latter. Put simply, Europe was not the best prize on offer. All that stood in the way of Mongol control of the Nile, of Egypt's rich agricultural output and its crucial position as a junction on the trade routes in all directions was an army commanded by men who were drawn from the very same steppes: this was not just a struggle for supremacy, it was the triumph of a political, cultural and social system. The battle for the medieval world was being fought between nomads from Central and eastern Asia.

The Christians in the Holy Land reacted to the Mongol advance with blind panic. First Antioch, one of the crown jewels under Crusader control, was surrendered, while another, Acre, reached an accommodation with the Mongols, judging them to be the lesser of two evils. Desperate appeals were dispatched to the rulers of England and France begging for military assistance. The westerners were saved by the intervention of their sworn enemy—the Mamlūks of Egypt—who moved northwards to confront the army that was ripping through Palestine.[44]

Having swept all before them for the best part of six decades, the Mongols now suffered their first serious setback, defeated at ʿAyn Jālūt in northern Palestine in September 1260. Despite the assassination of the victorious general, Sultan Quṭuz, in an internal power struggle, the Mamlūks pressed forward gleefully. As they did so, they found much of their work had been done for them: the Mongols, in breaking the resistance of the local population, had forged towns and regions into a single entity. Just as Genghis Khan had benefited from the consolidation of Central Asia before his invasion early in the thirteenth century, so did the Mongols inadvertently gift Syria and the important cities of Aleppo and Damascus to their rivals. The Mamlūks were able to walk in almost unopposed.[45]

The Christians in the Holy Land and in Europe looked on in horror, unsure what would happen next or what lay in store for them as a result. But it did not take long for attitudes to the Mongols to be entirely reshaped. It began to dawn on Christian Europe that despite the traumatic encounters they had experienced from the terrifying hordes of horsemen galloping over the northern lip of the Black Sea into the plains of Hungary, the Mongols just might be the saviours they had once been mistaken for when they had first burst into view.

In the decades after 1260, repeated missions were dispatched from Europe and the Holy Land to try to form an alliance with the Mongols against the Mamlūks. Frequent embassies travelled in the other direction too, sent by Hülegü, the dominant Mongol warlord in Asia, and his son Aqaba, whose readiness to negotiate was dictated primarily by their interest in using western seapower against Egypt and against its newly conquered territories in Palestine and Syria. Matters were complicated, however, by the first signs of proper friction among the Mongols themselves.

By the later thirteenth century, the Mongol world had become so vast—stretching from the Pacific to the Black Sea, from the steppes into northern India to the Persian Gulf, that strains and cracks began to appear. The empire divided into four main branches, which became increasingly hostile to each other. The senior line was centred in China; in Central Asia, it was the heirs of Chaghatay (a man described by one Persian writer as "a butcher and a tyrant," an accursed man who was "cruel and blood loving"—pure

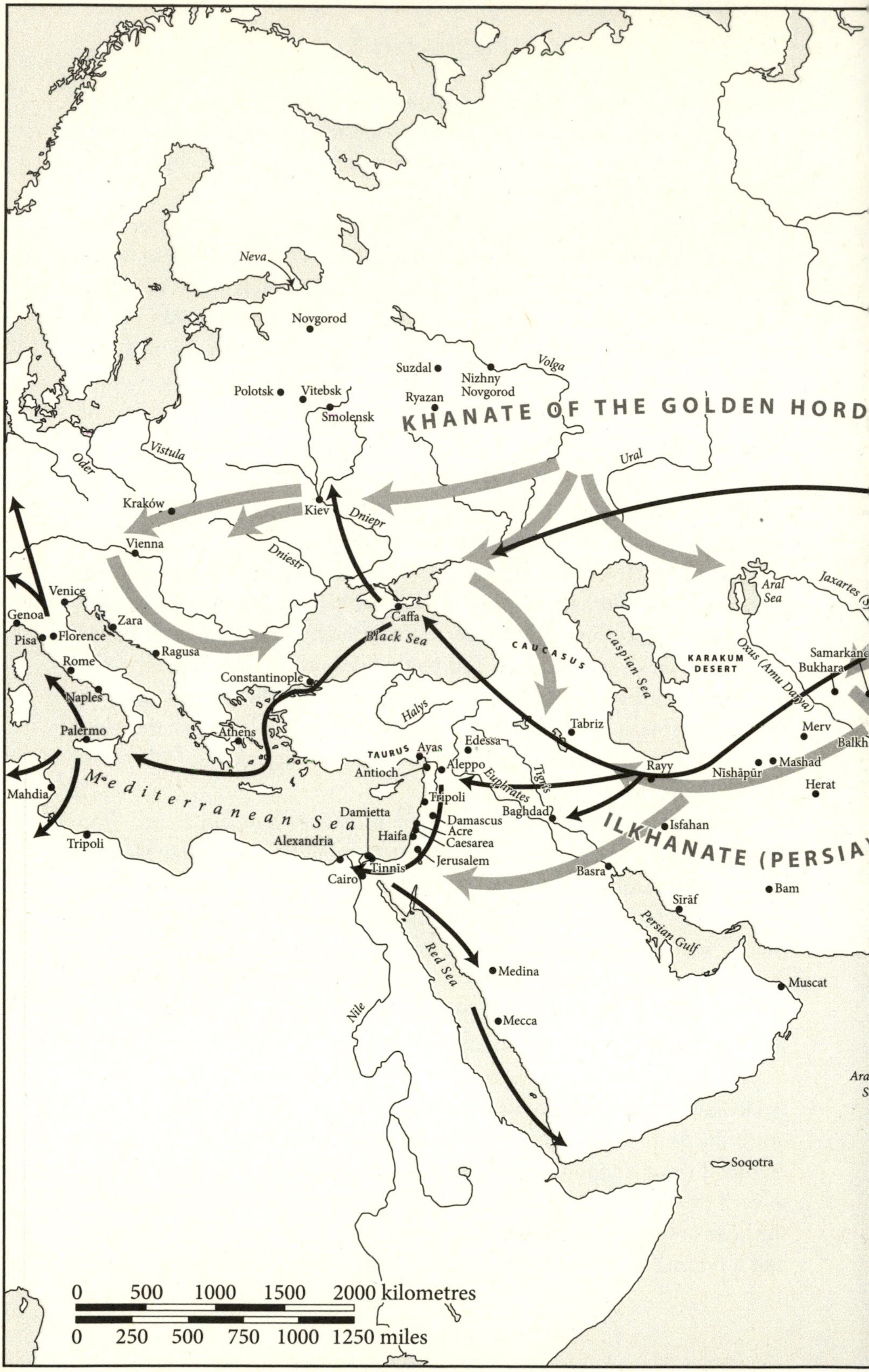

Neva
Novgorod
Suzdal
Volga
Nizhny Novgorod
Polotsk
Vitebsk
Ryazan
Smolensk
KHANATE OF THE GOLDEN HORD
Vistula
Oder
Ural
Kraków
Kiev
Dniepr
Vienna
Dniestr
Aral Sea
Jaxartes
Venice
Genoa
Zara
Caffa
Pisa
Florence
Black Sea
Ragusa
CAUCASUS
Caspian Sea
KARAKUM DESERT
Oxus (Amu Darya)
Samarkand
Bukhara
Rome
Constantinople
Naples
Halys
Palermo
Athens
Tabriz
Merv
TAURUS
Ayas
Edessa
Balkh
Antioch
Aleppo
Tigris
Rayy
Mashad
Nīshāpūr
Mahdia
Mediterranean Sea
Euphrates
Herat
Tripoli
Damietta
Baghdad
Damascus
Acre
Haifa
Caesarea
Isfahan
ILKHANATE (PERSIA
Tripoli
Alexandria
Jerusalem
Tinnis
Cairo
Basra
Bam
Sīrāf
Persian Gulf
Red Sea
Medina
Muscat
Nile
Mecca
Soqotra
0 500 1000 1500 2000 kilometres
0 250 500 750 1000 1250 miles

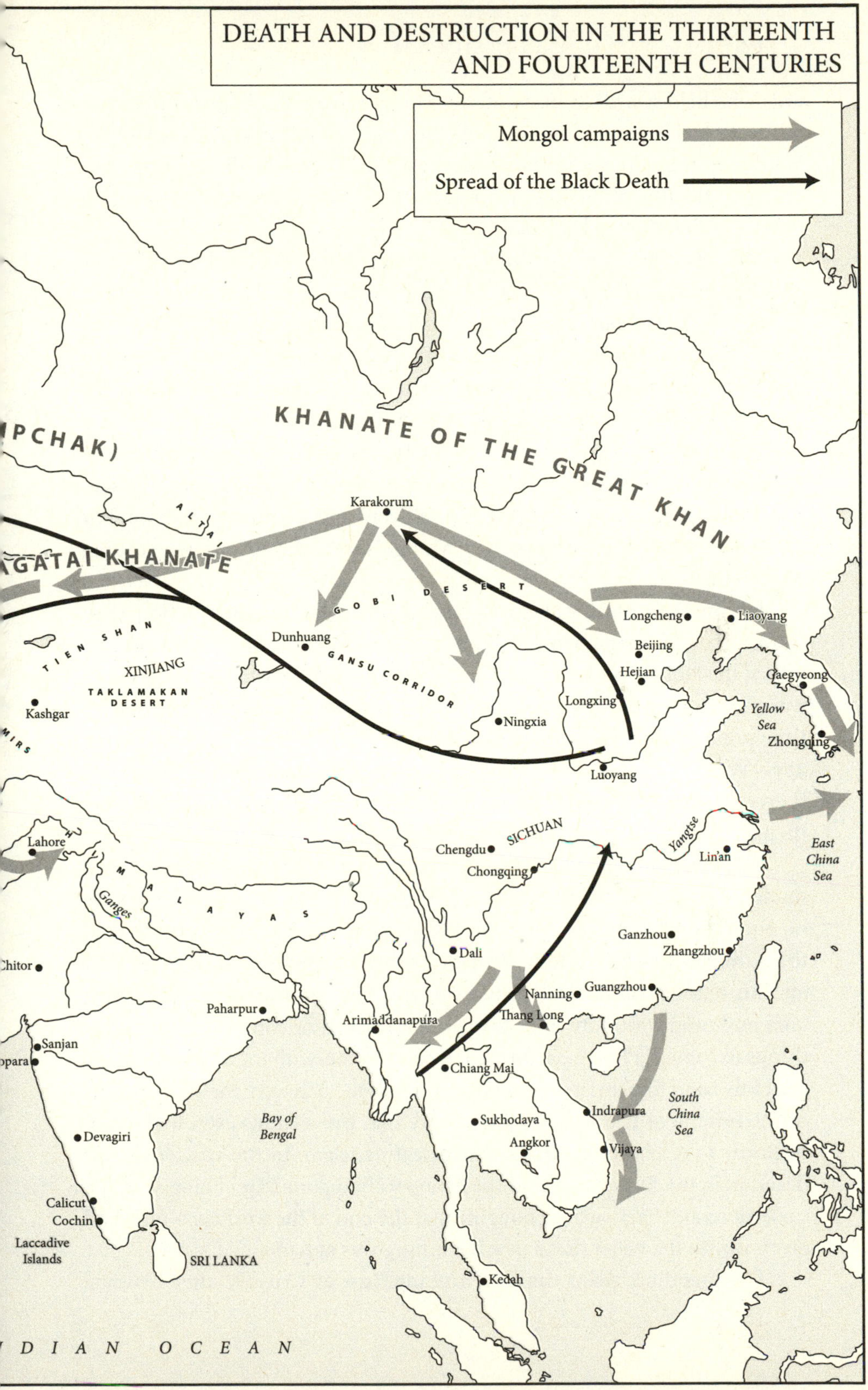
DEATH AND DESTRUCTION IN THE THIRTEENTH AND FOURTEENTH CENTURIES
Mongol campaigns
Spread of the Black Death
KHANATE OF THE GREAT KHAN
PCHAK)
GATAI KHANATE
ALTAI
Karakorum
GOBI DESERT
Dunhuang
GANSU CORRIDOR
TIEN SHAN
XINJIANG
TAKLAMAKAN DESERT
Kashgar
MIRS
Longcheng
Liaoyang
Beijing
Hejian
Longxing
Ningxia
Luoyang
Gaegyeong
Yellow Sea
Zhongqing
Lahore
HIMALAYAS
Ganges
SICHUAN
Chengdu
Chongqing
Yangtse
Lin'an
East China Sea
Ganzhou
Zhangzhou
Dali
Chitor
Paharpur
Nanning
Guangzhou
Thang Long
Arimaddanapura
Sanjan
opara
Chiang Mai
Indrapura
South China Sea
Bay of Bengal
Sukhodaya
Devagiri
Angkor
Vijaya
Calicut
Cochin
Laccadive Islands
SRI LANKA
Kedah
DIAN OCEAN

evil) who held sway.[46] In the west, the Mongols who dominated the steppes of Russia and beyond into central Europe came to be known as the Golden Horde, while in Greater Iran the rulers were known as the Īlkhānids—a reference to the title of Īl-Khān that marked them as subordinate to the main branch of the Mongol leadership.

The Mamlūks now skilfully manipulated the tribal politics of their enemy, coming to terms with Berke, the leader of the Golden Horde, whose rivalry with the Īlkhānids had already spilled into open conflict. This served to increase the chances of an agreement being reached between Christian Europe and the Īlkhānids. The closest such plans came to fruition was in the late 1280s when an embassy led by Rabban Sauma, the bishop of Uighuria in western China, was sent by the Īlkhānid leader to visit the major leaders in western Europe to finalise the terms of a military alliance. Rabban Sauma was a good choice—urbane, intelligent and a Christian to boot. For all their reputation for savagery, the Mongols were shrewd in their reading of foreigners.

No one was more excited to hear about plans for joint action than Edward I, King of England. A highly enthusiastic Crusader, Edward had visited the Holy Land in 1271 and had been horrified by what he had seen. It was bad enough, he concluded, that the Christians appeared to spend more time arguing with each other than fighting the Muslims. But what truly appalled him was the Venetians: not only were they trading with the infidel, they were supplying them with materials for making siege engines that were then used against Christian towns and forts.[47]

The king was delighted, then, to receive the bishop from the east, and made clear that his priority was to see the recovery of Jerusalem. "We have no subject of thought except upon this matter," the English monarch told the bishop, before asking him to celebrate the Eucharist for the king himself and his retinue. He treated the bishop with honour and respect, lavishing gifts and money on him after throwing a feast in celebration of the great things to come.[48] Plans were formed to collaborate, with the aim of securing the Holy Land for Christendom once and for all. Such were the expectations of the imminent triumph of Christianity that processions even took place in Rome to celebrate the imminent defeat of Islam. In the space of a few decades, in the European mind the Mongols had gone from being saviours to demons and back again. Thoughts that the end of the world was nigh had given way to the belief that a new beginning was at hand.

The grandiose plans came to nothing. Just as Crusade after Crusade had delivered less than promised, all the fine talk of an alliance that spanned thousands of miles and involved the fate of global religions did not produce any meaningful results. For Edward I, it turned out that there were problems closer to home that were more important. Rather than forming a grand alliance with the Mongols against Muslim Egypt, the English king was forced to head to Scotland to put down the rebellion of William Wallace. With other European monarchs similarly preoccupied, the Christian presence in the Holy Land finally came to an end: two centuries after the knights of the First Crusade had captured Jerusalem, the last footholds gave way. Sidon, Tyre, Beirut and Acre surrendered to the Mamlūks in 1291. It turned out that goodwill and enthusiasm alone were not enough to support, save or hold on to the locations that lay at the heart of the Christian faith.

For a while, there were false dawns. In the winter of 1299, the Mongols finally achieved what they had sought to do for more than a generation: a crushing defeat of the Mamlūk army. Their victory was so emphatic that rumours circulated round Europe that Jerusalem had been recovered by Christians in the east who had fought alongside their Mongol allies. Rumours spread that the Īlkhānid ruler had converted to Christianity and was serving as a new protector of the Holy Land. Some reports excitedly announced even better news: not content with expelling the Mamlūks from Syria and Palestine, the Mongols had apparently burst through defences and taken Egypt as well.[49] It all sounded too good to be true. A major victory had indeed been won by the Mongols on the battlefield, but the enthusiastic tales were nothing more than misunderstandings, rumours and wishful thinking. The Christian Holy Land was gone for good.[50]

The Crusades had played a vital role in shaping the medieval west. The power of the papacy had been transformed, with the Pope becoming not just an authoritative cleric but a figure with military and political capabilities of his own; the qualities and behaviour of the elite had been framed by ideas about service, devotion and knightly piety; and the idea of Christianity as the common denominator of the continent of Europe had taken root. But in the final analysis it had become clear from experience that while capturing and holding Jerusalem was wonderful in theory, in practice it was difficult, expensive and dangerous. And so, after being placed at the centre of European consciousness for two centuries, the Holy Land quietly slipped out of view. As the poet William Blake put it in the early nineteenth century, it would be infinitely preferable to build Jerusalem in an easier and more convenient location—such as "in England's green and pleasant land."[51]

The Crusades ultimately failed: attempts to colonise the most important locations in Christendom had not worked. The same could not be said, however, for the Italian city-states that succeeded where Christian knights had faltered. While devout knights had been forced out, the maritime states simply readjusted and burrowed ever deeper into Asia. There was no way they would relinquish their position. On the contrary, after the loss of the Holy Land, the issue for them was not about reducing their reach. It was about extending it.

10

The Road of Death and Destruction

Even before the fall of the cities and ports in the Levant, both Genoa and Venice had taken steps to find new routes to trade along, new points to buy and sell goods, new ways to make sure they did not lose out. With trade passing through the Holy Land increasingly strangled in the thirteenth century by the rise in military tensions, both communes established new colonies on the north coast of the Black Sea in the Crimea, in the mouth of the Sea of Azov and in Armenian Cilicia, where the town of Ayas became a new gateway for commodities and luxuries coming from the east.

There was a lot of money to be made. Differentials between the price of grain on the north and south coasts of the Black Sea provided a perfect opportunity for the city-states to exploit with their huge transport vessels that were able to transport foodstuffs in considerable volumes.[1] These ships also proved useful in moving other goods—such as people. Both the Genoese and the Venetians resumed large-scale slave trading, buying captives to sell on to Mamlūk Egypt, in defiance of attempts by the papacy to ban the trafficking of men, women and children to Muslim buyers.[2]

Old rivalries were hard to set to one side. Genoa had already shown how far it was willing to go to crush rivals, destroying the Pisan fleet almost in its entirety in 1282 and then refusing to ransom those taken prisoner. Pisa never recovered fully from the blow inflicted by its rival. Among those captured was a certain Rustichello, who spent more than a decade in prison before being joined by a fellow inmate also taken hostage during a Genoese naval victory—this time over the Venetians in the Adriatic. Striking up a friendship with him, Rustichello took to writing down his fellow prisoner's memories of his remarkable life and journeys: we have Genoa's brutality and relentless focus on the medieval struggle for power to thank for the recording of Marco Polo's travels.

The ruthless duels for commercial supremacy raged wherever Venice and Genoa came into contact: there were violent clashes in Constantinople, confrontations in the Aegean and in Cyprus, and full-blooded battles in the Adriatic. By the time Pope Boniface VIII brokered a truce in 1299, the two had fought each other to a standstill. But the energy, effort and expense devoted to reaching this position in the first place showed just how much rested on trying to make connections with Asia.

Nevertheless, it had been worth it. By 1301, the Hall of the Great Council in Venice was enlarged after it had been unanimously agreed that it was no longer big enough to hold all its powerful members, whose number had grown along with the rising wealth of the city.[3] In the case of Genoa, on the other hand, a poem written around the end of the thirteenth century extols the beauty of the city, which was "filled from head to toe with *palazzi*," and whose skyline was adorned with large numbers of towers. The source of the city's riches was the abundant supply of goods from the east—including ermine, squirrel and other furs traded on the steppes, as well as pepper, ginger, musk, spices, brocades, velvet, cloth of gold, pearls, jewels and precious stones. Genoa was rich, the author goes on, because of the network it had created, serviced by its galleys and ships: the Genoese are scattered all over the world, he boasted, creating new Genoas wherever they go. Truly, wrote the anonymous author, God had blessed the city and wanted it to flourish.[4]

One important reason for the boom in Venice and Genoa was the skill and foresight they showed in feeding their customers' desires—and those of the traders who came from other cities in Europe to buy the goods that had been brought there. With Egypt and the Holy Land proving too volatile and economically risky, the Black Sea quickly became a trading zone of the greatest importance.

But behind the rise of the Italian city-states was the fiscal sophistication and restraint of the Mongols when it came to taxing commerce. A range of sources indicate that duties on exports passing through the Black Sea ports never exceeded 3–5 per cent of the total value of the goods; this was highly competitive when compared with tolls and levies extracted on products passing through Alexandria, where sources talk of taxes of 10, 20 and even 30 per cent.[5] As any trader knows, margins count for everything. There was a strong incentive, therefore, to ship through the Black Sea—which only served to make this an even more important route to the east.

Sensitive pricing and a deliberate policy of keeping taxes low were symptomatic of the bureaucratic nous of the Mongol Empire, which gets too easily lost beneath the images of violence and wanton destruction. In fact, the Mongols' success lay not in indiscriminate brutality but in their willingness to compromise and co-operate, thanks to the relentless effort to sustain a system that renewed central control. Although later Persian historians were highly vocal in asserting that the Mongols were disengaged from the process of administering their empire, preferring to leave such mundane tasks to others, recent research has revealed just how involved they were in the detail of everyday life.[6] The great achievement of Genghis Khan and his successors was not the ransacking of popular imagination but the meticulous checks put in place that enabled one of the greatest empires in history to flourish for centuries to come. It was no coincidence, then, that Russian came to include a broad range of loan words, drawn directly from the vocabulary relating to Mongol administration—and particularly those to do with trade and communication: words for profit (*barysh*), money (*dengi*) and the treasury (*kazna*) all originated from contact with the new masters from the east. So too did the postal system in Russia, based on the Mongol method of delivering messages quickly and efficiently from one side of the empire to another through a network of relay stations.[7]

Such was the genius of the Mongols, in fact, that the platform for long-term success was established right from the very beginning. As Genghis Khan and his successors expanded their reach, they had to incorporate new peoples within a coherent system. Tribes were deliberately broken down, with loyalties refocused on attachments to military units and above all allegiance to the Mongol leadership itself. Distinguishing tribal features, such as how different peoples wore their hair, were stamped out, with standardised fashions enforced instead. As a matter of course, those who submitted or were conquered were dispersed across Mongol-controlled territory to weaken bonds of language, kinship and identity and to aid the assimilation process. New names were introduced in place of ethnic labels to underline the new way of doing things. All this in turn was reinforced by a centralised system of rewards where booty and tribute were shared out: proximity to the ruling dynasty counted for everything, in turn encouraging a broad if brutal meritocracy, where successful generals reaped rich rewards and those who failed were quickly rooted out.[8]

While tribal identities were extinguished, there was consistent and remarkable broad-mindedness when it came to the question of faith. The Mongols were relaxed and tolerant on religious matters. Ever since the time of Genghis Khan, the leader's retinue had been allowed to practise whatever beliefs they wanted. Genghis himself "viewed the Muslims with the eye of respect, so also did he hold the Christians and 'idolaters' [that is, Buddhists] in high esteem," according to one later Persian writer. As far as his descendants were concerned, each was left to their own devices and their own conscience in deciding which faith to follow. Some chose to adopt Islam, others Christianity, with "others again cleaving to the ancient canon of their fathers and forefathers and inclining to no direction."[9]

There was some truth in this, as missionaries who flocked east looking for people to convert soon found.[10] William of Rubruck was surprised to come across priests all over Asia on his journey to the Mongol court, but even more surprised to find them agreeing to bless white horses each spring as herds were gathered near Karakorum; moreover, such blessings were performed in a manner more in keeping with pagan rituals than with Christian doctrine.[11] But taking a few short cuts was evidently seen as worthwhile—a small detail in the bigger picture of winning converts. As contacts between Europe and Central Asia increased, dioceses began to spring up once again in the east, including deep in the steppes, while monasteries were founded in northern Persia, such as in Tabriz, which became home to a flourishing community of Franciscan monks.[12] That they were allowed to flourish spoke volumes about the protection they were given and the Mongols' relaxed approach to religion.

In fact, things went considerably further. At the end of the thirteenth century, John of Montecorvino was sent to the Great Khan by the Pope with a letter "inviting him to receive the Catholic faith of our Lord Jesus Christ." Although John's mission did not meet with success, he nevertheless set about converting as many people as he could, paying ransoms to free captive children whom he then schooled in Latin and Greek, writing out psalters for them by hand. In time, even the Great Khan himself would come to hear them chanting during service, enthralled by the beautiful singing and the mystery of the Eucharist. Such was John's success that a mission was sent by Pope Clement V in the early 1300s to appoint him, not to the rank of bishop but to a greater position to reflect his achievements and to spur the creation of a church hierarchy across the Mongol Empire: the archbishop of

Beijing. The failure of the Crusades did not mean the failure of Christianity in Asia.[13]

Some of this religious tolerance was clever politicking. The Īlkhānids seem to have been particularly adept at telling religious figures what they wanted to hear. Hülegü, for example, told one Armenian priest that he had been baptised when a child; the church in the west was so eager to believe this that illustrations were circulated in Europe depicting Hülegü as a Christian saint. Others, however, were told a different story. The Buddhists, for example, were assured that Hülegü followed the teachings leading to enlightenment. There were many instances of high-ranking figures in the Mongol world becoming Christian and then converting to Islam or vice versa, switching their religion as convenient. The phlegmatically faithful were masters at being all things to all people.[14]

Winning hearts and minds was crucial to the smooth expansion of the empire. This harked directly back to the approach taken by Alexander the Great when he had defeated the Persians—and would have been approved of by commentators like Tacitus, who was deeply critical of the short-sightedness of a policy of plunder and indiscriminate devastation. Instinctively, the Mongols knew how to be great empire-builders: tolerance and careful administration had to follow up on military might.

Shrewd decisions taken when it came to dealing with important potential allies paid off handsomely. In Russia, the blanket exemption of the church from all taxes and from military service was met with jubilation, just one example showing that sensitive handling could generate goodwill even after brutal conquest.[15] Likewise, devolving responsibilities was a highly effective way of reducing animosities and tensions. The case of Russia is again instructive, with one local ruler who was singled out to collect taxes and payments being given a generous cut of the proceeds. Not for nothing did Ivan I, Grand Prince of Moscow, become known as "Ivan Kalita"—or Ivan the moneybags: he was in charge of gathering levies and taxes to fill the Mongol treasuries, evidently doing well for himself in the process. The concentration of wealth and power in the hands of trusted figures like Ivan resulted in the emergence of a pre-eminent dynasty which could be relied on and which prospered at the expense of rival families. The effects were deep—and long lasting: some scholars have argued that it was the Mongols' system of government that laid the ground for Russia's transformation into a fully fledged autocracy by empowering a small handful of individuals to lord it over the population, as well as over their peers.[16]

Militarily dominant, politically astute and theologically tolerant, the

Mongols' template for success was far removed from our common perceptions of them. But, for all their efficiency, they were also lucky in their timing. In China, they came across a world that had seen population growth, economic expansion and technological developments following a sharp rise in agricultural productivity.[17] In Central Asia, they found fractured statelets riven by rivalries and ripe for consolidation. In the Middle East and Europe, they came into contact with societies that were both monetised and increasingly stratified—that is to say, able to pay tribute in cash, and whose populations had spending power and prodigious appetites for luxury products. Across the continents of Asia and Europe, Genghis Khan and his successors were not just stumbling into a world that offered rich pickings; they found themselves stepping into a golden age.[18]

Just as the Islamic conquests of the seventh century had a profound impact on the global economy as taxes, payments and cash flowed towards the centre from all corners of the world, so too did the Mongol successes of the thirteenth century reshape the monetary systems of Eurasia. In India, new rituals and pastimes were introduced from the steppe world, such as formal processions where the ruler's ornate saddle was carried ostentatiously before him.[19] In China, meanwhile, culinary habits changed to adopt flavours, ingredients and cooking styles favoured by the new overlords from the steppes. Texts like the *Yinshan zhengyao*, a dietary guidebook listing "Proper and Essential Things for the Emperor's Food and Drink," include many dishes influenced by nomad cuisine and tastes, heavily emphasising the boiling of food as the preferred means of cooking.[20] Using every piece of an animal carcass—second nature to those dealing with livestock for their living—became part of the mainstream. Kublai Khan was one who was devoted to the foods of his ancestors, reportedly serving fermented milk, horse meat, camel hump and mutton soup thickened with grain as delicacies to his court.[21] At least these sound more palatable than sheep's lung or a paste based on the fat of sheep's tail or head that appear in a fourteenth-century cooking manual.[22]

Europe also felt the cultural impact of the Mongol conquests. Striking new fashions were imported from and influenced by the emergence of the new empire. Mongol styles became modish after the first waves of panic died down. In England, 250 bands of dark-blue "Tatar" cloth were used to make the insignia for the country's oldest and grandest order of chivalry, the Knights of the Garter. At the Cheapside Tournament in 1331, the opening ceremony saw men parade dressed in fine Tatar clothing, wearing masks to look like Mongol warriors. Influences from the east even lay behind the *hennin*, the most distinctive fashion accessory of the Renaissance across Europe. The conical headgear favoured by ladies and so visible in the portraiture of the fourteenth century onwards appears to have been directly inspired by the distinctive hats worn at the Mongol court in this period.[23]

But the Mongol conquests had other, more substantial effects, for they served to transform the economies of Europe. The never-ending stream of envoys being dispatched to the court of the khans was soon accompanied by missionaries and merchants following in their footsteps. Suddenly, not only the Mongols but Asia as a whole entered into Europe's field of vision. Tales brought back by travellers were devoured by those eager to find out more about the exotic world that was suddenly coming into focus in the east.

The stories were greeted with wonder. There was an island beyond China, according to Marco Polo, where the ruler's palace had golden roofs and golden walls several inches thick. In India, the same author revealed, animal flesh was thrown into steep ravines that were filled with diamonds—but also infested with snakes—in order to attract eagles who would then fly down to retrieve the meat bringing the gems that were impressed into it up with them, to be collected later and more easily. Pepper, noted another traveller from this period, came from swamps filled with crocodiles that had to be frightened away by fire. In the accounts of contemporary travellers, the wealth of the east was legendary—and stood in sharp contrast to that of Europe.[24]

This conclusion should have been neither surprising nor new. The themes were familiar from the classical texts that were starting to be read again as society and economy developed in continental Europe, and intellectual curiosity began to return. The reports brought back by Marco Polo and others struck an obvious chord with accounts by Herodotus, Tacitus, Pliny and even the Song of Solomon of bats using their claws to guard marshes where cassia grew, of venomous flying serpents protecting aromatic trees in Arabia, or of phoenixes building nests of cinnamon and frankincense which they then filled with other spices.[25]

Naturally, the mystique of the east—and tales of the dangers involved in gathering goods that were rare and highly prized—was closely linked to expectations of the prices the goods would fetch when brought back to Europe. Goods, produce and spices that were dangerous to make or harvest would naturally be very costly.[26] In order to be better informed, handbooks and compendia started to appear around 1300 on how to travel and trade in Asia—and, above all, how to get a fair price. "In the first place, you must let your beard grow long and not shave," wrote Francesco Pegolotti, the author of the most famous guide of this period; and be sure to take a guide along for the journey—you will more than make up in savings whatever you pay extra for a good one, he advised. But the most important information he set out was what taxes were due in what locations, what the difference in weights, measures and coinage were, and what different spices looked like—and how much they were worth. In the medieval world as in the modern, the point of these guidebooks was to avoid disappointment and to reduce the chances of being taken advantage of by unscrupulous merchants.[27]

That Pegolotti himself was not from Venice or Genoa, the two powerhouses of thirteenth- and fourteenth-century Europe, but from Florence was itself revealing. There were new upstarts eager to get a piece of the action in the east—such as Lucca and Siena, whose traders could be found in Tabriz, Ayas and other trading points in the east—buying spices, silks and fabrics from China, India and Persia as well as elsewhere. The sense of new horizons opening up was nowhere better expressed than on the map that hung in the Great Council Hall of the Palazzo Pubblico in Siena: designed to be rotated by hand, the chart showed the world centred on the Tuscan town, setting out distances, transport networks and Siena's very own network of agents, contacts and intermediaries stretching deep into Asia. Even obscure towns in the centre of Italy were starting to look to the east for inspiration and profits and thinking in terms of establishing their own connections to the Silk Roads.[28]

Fundamental to European expansion was the stability that the Mongols provided across the whole of Asia. Despite the tensions and rivalries between the different branches of the tribal leadership, the rule of law was fiercely protected when it came to commercial matters. The road system in China, for example, was the envy of visitors who marvelled at the administrative measures in place to provide security for travelling merchants. "China is the safest country and best country for the traveller," wrote the fourteenth-century explorer Ibn Baṭṭūṭa; this was a place where a reporting system that apparently accounted for each outsider on a daily basis meant that "a man travels for nine months alone with great wealth and has nothing to fear."[29]

It was a view echoed by Pegolotti, who noted that the route from the

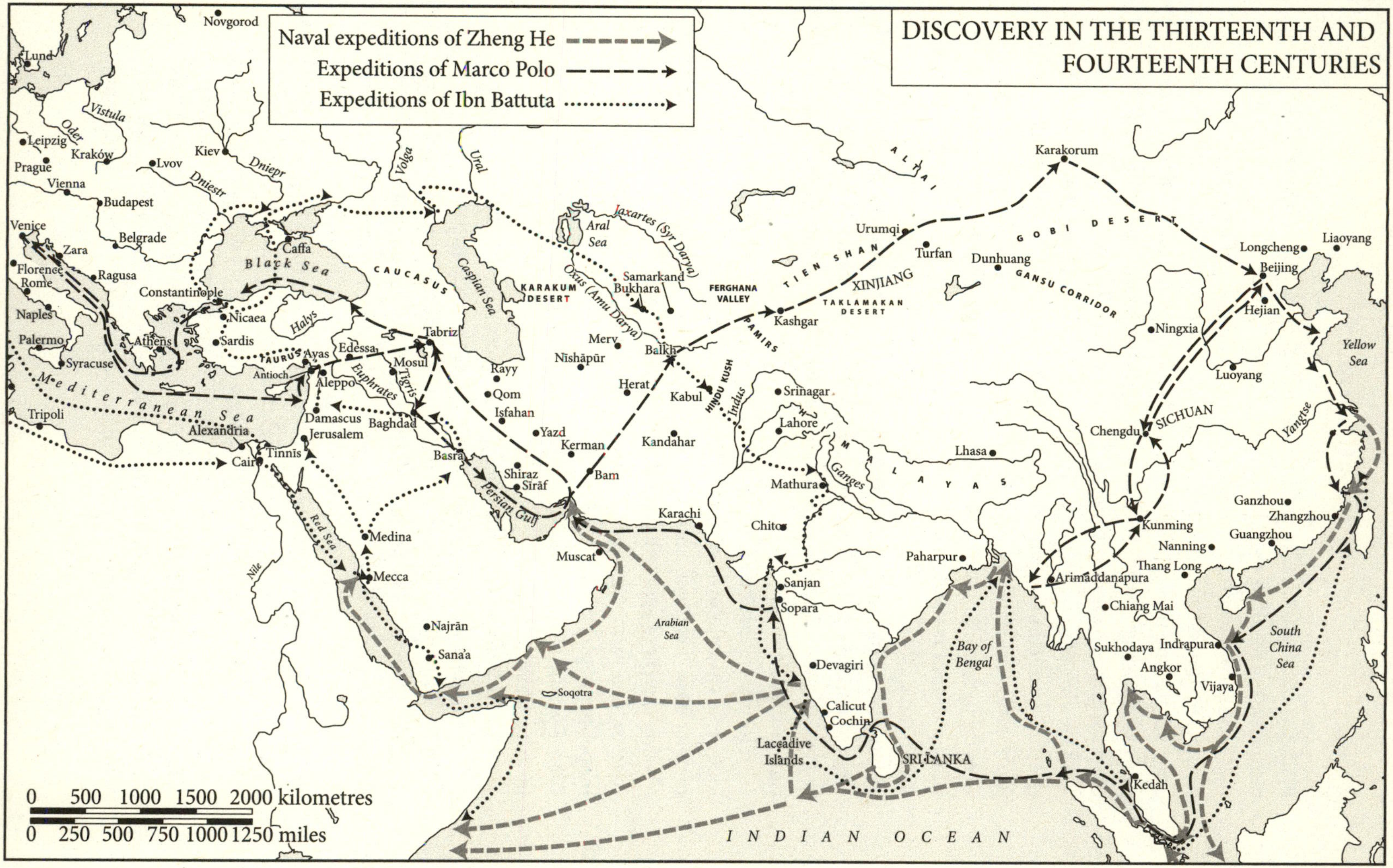
DISCOVERY IN THE THIRTEENTH AND FOURTEENTH CENTURIES
Naval expeditions of Zheng He
Expeditions of Marco Polo
Expeditions of Ibn Battuta
0 500 1000 1500 2000 kilometres
0 250 500 750 1000 1250 miles
Novgorod
Lund
Leipzig
Prague
Kraków
Vistula
Oder
Vienna
Budapest
Lvov
Kiev
Dniepr
Dniestr
Volga
Ural
Venice
Zara
Florence
Rome
Naples
Palermo
Syracuse
Ragusa
Belgrade
Constantinople
Athens
Nicaea
Sardis
Caffa
Black Sea
CAUCASUS
Halys
TAURUS
Ayas
Antioch
Aleppo
Edessa
Mosul
Tigris
Euphrates
Tabriz
Mediterranean Sea
Tripoli
Alexandria
Cairo
Tinnīs
Damascus
Jerusalem
Baghdad
Basra
Caspian Sea
KARAKUM DESERT
Aral Sea
Jaxartes (Syr Darya)
Oxus (Amu Darya)
Samarkand
Bukhara
Merv
Nīshāpūr
Balkh
Rayy
Qom
Isfahan
Yazd
Kerman
Shiraz
Sīrāf
Bam
Herat
Kabul
Kandahar
Persian Gulf
HINDU KUSH
FERGHANA VALLEY
PAMIRS
Kashgar
TIEN SHAN
XINJIANG
TAKLAMAKAN DESERT
Urumqi
Turfan
Dunhuang
GOBI DESERT
GANSU CORRIDOR
ALTAI
Karakorum
Longcheng
Liaoyang
Beijing
Hejian
Yellow Sea
Ningxia
Luoyang
SICHUAN
Chengdu
Yangtse
Kunming
Ganzhou
Zhangzhou
Guangzhou
Nanning
Thang Long
Arimaddanapura
Chiang Mai
Sukhodaya
Indrapura
Angkor
Vijaya
South China Sea
Kedah
Lhasa
HIMALAYAS
Srinagar
Lahore
Indus
Ganges
Mathura
Chitor
Karachi
Paharpur
Sanjan
Sopara
Devagiri
Calicut
Cochin
Laccadive Islands
SRI LANKA
Bay of Bengal
Arabian Sea
INDIAN OCEAN
Muscat
Soqotra
Red Sea
Nile
Medina
Mecca
Najrān
Sana'a

Black Sea as far as China "is perfectly safe, whether by day or by night." This was partly the result of traditional nomad beliefs about the hospitality that should be shown to strangers, but it was also a function of a wider view that commerce should be encouraged. In this sense, the competitive taxes levied on goods passing through the Black Sea found obvious echoes on the other side of Asia, where maritime trade passing through ports on China's Pacific coast also grew thanks to deliberate efforts to increase customs revenues.[30]

One area where this proved highly effective was in the export of fabrics, the production of which received a major boost in the thirteenth and fourteenth centuries. The textile industries in Nīshāpūr, Herat and Baghdad were deliberately built up, while the city of Tabriz alone expanded in size by a factor of four over the course of just over a hundred years, to accommodate traders as well as the craftsmen and artisans who were conspicuously well treated in the aftermath of the Mongol conquests. Although there was a near-insatiable demand for fine cloth and fabric in markets to the east, increasing quantities were exported to Europe from the late thirteenth century onwards.[31]

Horizons expanded everywhere. In China, ports like Guangzhou had long served as windows on to the world of southern Asia. Such major commercial hubs were well known to Persian traders, Arab geographers and Muslim travellers who left accounts of bustling street life in towns on the coast as well as in the interior and provided reports of a churning, cosmopolitan population. Such was the level of interaction and exchange that Persian and Arabic provided many loan words and idioms still common in modern Chinese.[32]

China's knowledge of the outside world, on the other hand, had been distinctly sketchy and limited, as a text shows that was written in the early 1200s by an imperial official in charge of foreign trade in Guangzhou in southern China, a site blessed with an outstanding natural harbour in the delta of the Pearl River. The account, designed for merchants, sailors and travellers, makes a valiant attempt to explain business practices in the Arabic-speaking world and beyond, listing goods that could be bought, and describing what Chinese traders might expect. But, like many travellers' accounts of this period, it is riddled with inaccuracies and semi-mystical beliefs. Mecca, for example, was not home to the house of the Buddha, nor a location where Buddhists came once a year on pilgrimage; there was no land where women reproduced by "exposing themselves naked to the full force of the south wind." Melons in Spain did not measure six foot in diameter, and could not feed more than twenty men; nor did sheep in Europe grow to the height of a full-grown man, to be cut open each spring in order to allow a dozen pounds of fat to be taken out before being stitched up again with no after-effects.[33]

When much of Asia became united under the Mongols, however, there was a sharp improvement in maritime trade links, particularly in places of strategic and economic significance—such as in the Persian Gulf—that were subject to extensive oversight by the new authorities, keen to encourage long-distance commercial exchange and boost revenues.[34] As a result, the cultural climate of Guangzhou during the thirteenth century became far more knowing and less provincial.

By the 1270s, the city had become the central point for China's maritime imports and exports. For every ship that set sail for Alexandria with supplies of pepper for Christian lands, reported Marco Polo in the late thirteenth century, more than a hundred put in to the Chinese port—a comment that finds a neat echo in Ibn Baṭṭūṭa's comments, written soon afterwards, that on his arrival in the city he saw a hundred ships sailing into the gulf of Guangzhou, as well as innumerable smaller vessels.[35] Commerce in the Mediterranean was large; trade in the Pacific was huge.

We do not have to rely solely on ambiguous or unreliable written sources to establish how important the city became as a commercial centre.[36] A shipwreck from the bay of Guangzhou dating to precisely this period reveals that goods were being imported from all over southern Asia and in all likelihood from the Persian Gulf and East Africa too. Pepper, frankincense, ambergris, glass and cotton made up just a part of a valuable cargo that went down off the coast of China in or soon after 1271.[37] Merchants could be found crossing the South China Sea in ever greater numbers, establishing trading posts in Sumatra, on the Malay peninsula and above all on the Malabar coast of southern India, home to the world's great supply of pepper—long established as a favoured commodity in China as well as in Europe and elsewhere in Asia.[38] By the middle of the fourteenth century, so many ships were sailing to towns like Calicut that some observers commented that all maritime transport and travel in this part of the Indian subcontinent was being undertaken in Chinese boats. An example of their typical flat-bottomed design has been recently identified wrecked off the coast of Kerala.[39]

The lubricant in this long-distance trade was silver, which took on the form of a single currency across Eurasia. One reason for this was the innovation in financial credit in China that had been introduced before Genghis Khan's time, including the introduction of bills of exchange and the use of paper money.[40] Adopted and improved by the Mongols, the effect was the liberation of enormous amounts of silver into the monetary system as new forms of credit caught on. The availability of the precious metal suddenly soared—causing a major correction in its value against gold. In parts of Europe, the value of silver plunged, losing more than half its value between 1250 and 1338.[41] In London alone, the surge in silver supply allowed the royal mint to more than quadruple output between 1278 and 1279 alone. Production rose sharply across Asia too. In the steppes as well, coin production took off as rulers of the Golden Horde began to strike coins in large quantities.[42] New regions were stimulated too. Japan, which had relied heavily on barter or on payments in products such as rice as an exchange mechanism, shifted to a monetary economy and became increasingly active in long-distance trade.[43]

The most important effect that the Mongol conquests had on the transformation of Europe, however, did not come from trade or warfare, culture or currency. It was not just ferocious warriors, goods, precious metals, ideas and fashions that flowed through the arteries connecting the world. In fact something else entirely that entered the bloodstream had an even more radical impact: disease. An outbreak of plague surged through Asia, Europe and Africa threatening to annihilate millions. The Mongols had not destroyed the world, but it seemed quite possible that the Black Death would.

As well as being home to livestock and nomads for thousands of years, the Eurasian steppe also forms one of the world's great plague basins, with a string of linked foci stretching from the Black Sea as far as Manchuria. The ecological conditions of arid and semi-arid landscape lend themselves perfectly to the spread of the bacterium *Yersinia pestis* that is transmitted from one host to another principally by fleas through blood feeding. Plague was spread most effectively and quickly by rodent hosts such as rats, although camels could also become infected and play an important role in its transmission—as research closely linked to the Soviet Union's biological-warfare programme during the Cold War period showed.[44] Although plague can be spread by consuming or handling host tissues or by inhaling infected materials, transmission to humans is most commonly effected by fleas vomiting bacilli into the bloodstream before feeding, or by bacilli in their faeces contaminating abrasions in the skin. Bacilli are then carried to the lymph nodes, such as in the armpit or the groin, multiplying rapidly to cause swellings or buboes that Boccaccio, who lived through the plague, described as growing as large as an apple, or the size of an egg "more or less."[45] Other organs are then infected in turn; haemorrhaging causes internal bleeding and the distinctive black bags of pus and blood that make the disease as visually terrifying as it is lethal.

Modern investigation into *Yersinia pestis* and plague has made clear the crucial role played by environmental factors to the enzootic cycle, where seemingly insignificant changes can transform the disease from being localized and containable to spreadable on a large scale. Small differentials in temperature and precipitation, for example, can dramatically change the reproductive cycles of fleas crucial to the development cycle of the bacterium itself, as well as the behaviour of their rodent hosts.[46] A recent study that assumed an increase of just one degree in temperature suggested that this could lead to a 50 per cent increase in plague prevalence in the great gerbil, the primary host rodent of the steppe environment.[47]

Although it is not clear precisely where the ultimate origin of the disease of the mid-fourteenth century lay, plague spread rapidly in the 1340s as the outbreak moved out of the steppes through Europe, Iran, the Middle East, Egypt and the Arabian peninsula.[48] It really took hold in 1346 when what an Italian contemporary described as "a mysterious illness that brought sudden death" began to sweep through the Golden Horde by the Black Sea. A Mongol army laying siege to the Genoese trading post of Caffa following a dispute about trade terms was annihilated by illness that killed "thousands and thousands every day," according to one commentator. Before withdrawing, however, "they ordered corpses to be placed in catapults and lobbed into the city in the hope that the intolerable stench would kill everyone inside." Rather than being overwhelmed by the smell, it was the highly contagious disease that caught hold. Unknowingly, the Mongols had turned to biological warfare to defeat their enemy.[49]

The trading routes that connected Europe to the rest of the world now became lethal highways for the transmission of the Black Death. In 1347, the disease reached Constantinople and then Genoa, Venice and the Mediterranean, brought by traders and merchants fleeing home. By the time the population of Messina in Sicily realised there was something wrong with the Genoese who had put in, arriving covered with boils, vomiting incessantly and coughing up blood before dying, it was already too late: although the Genoese galleys were expelled, the disease took hold and devastated the population.[50]

It spread rapidly northwards, reaching the cities of northern France and Bavaria by the middle of 1348. By that time, ships putting in to ports in Britain had already brought "the first pestilence . . . carried by merchants and sailors."[51] So many began to die across towns and villages in England that the Pope in "his clemency granted a plenary indulgence for confessed sins." According to one contemporary estimate, scarcely a tenth of the population survived; several sources report that so many perished that there were not enough people to bury the dead.[52]

Instead of bringing goods and valuables, ships criss-crossing the Mediterranean brought death and devastation. Infection was not only spread by contact with plague victims or by the rats which were always a feature of maritime travel; even the goods in the hold turned into lethal cargoes as fleas infested furs and food destined for mainland Europe as well as for ports in Egypt, the Levant and Cyprus, where the first victims tended to be infants and the young. Soon the disease had been transmitted along the caravan route to reach Mecca, killing scores of pilgrims and scholars and provoking serious soul searching: the Prophet Muḥammad had supposedly promised that the plague which ravaged Mesopotamia in the seventh century would never enter the holy cities of Islam.[53]

In Damascus, wrote Ibn al-Wardī, the plague "sat like a king on a throne and swayed with power, killing daily one thousand or more and decimating the population."[54] The roads between Cairo and Palestine were littered with the bodies of victims, while dogs tore at the corpses piled up against the walls of mosques in Bilbais. In the Asyut region of Upper Egypt meanwhile, the number of taxpayers fell from 6,000 before the Black Death to just 116—a fall of 98 per cent.[55]

Although such population contractions may also reflect people fleeing their homes, there can be little doubt that the death toll was enormous. "All the wisdom and ingenuity of man" was powerless to prevent the spread of disease, wrote Boccaccio, the Italian humanist scholar, in his introduction to the *Decameron*; in the space of three months, he noted, more than 100,000 lost their lives in Florence alone.[56] Venice was all but depopulated: accounts agreed that no less than three-quarters of its citizens died during the outbreak.[57]

To many, it seemed to signal the end of the world. In Ireland, one Franciscan monk concluded his account of the ravages caused by plague by leaving blank space "for continuing [my] work, in case anyone should still be alive in the future."[58] There was a sense of impending apocalypse; in France chroniclers reported that it "rained frogs, snakes, lizards, scorpions and many other similar poisonous animals." There were signs from the sky that made God's displeasure clear: enormous hailstones struck the earth, killing people by the dozen, while towns and villages burnt down after being set ablaze by thunderbolts that produced "stinking smoke."[59]

Some, like the King of England, Edward III, turned to fasting and prayer, with Edward ordering his bishops to follow suit. Arabic handbooks written around 1350 provided guides for the Muslim faithful to do much the same, advising that saying a specific prayer eleven times would help, and that chanting verses relating to the life of Muḥammad would provide protection from boils. In Rome, solemn processions were held where the penitent and fearful marched barefoot in hair-shirts, flagellating themselves to show contrition for their sins.[60]

These were among the least creative efforts to appease God's wrath. Avoid sex and "every fleshly lust with women," urged one priest in Sweden, and for that matter also do not bathe, and avoid the south wind—at least until lunch time. If this was a case of hoping for the best, then a counterpart in England was at least rather more direct: women should wear different clothes, urged one English priest, for their own sake, as well as that of everyone else. The outlandish and revealing outfits they had got used to sporting were simply asking for divine punishment. The trouble had started when "they began to wear useless little hoods, laced and buttoned so tightly at the throat that they only covered the shoulders." That was not all, for "in addition, they wore *paltoks*, extremely short garments . . . which failed to conceal their arses or their private parts." Apart from anything else, "these misshapen and tight clothes did not allow them to kneel to God or to the other saints."[61]

Wild rumours circulated in Germany that the disease was not natural, but the result of Jews poisoning wells and rivers. Vicious pogroms were carried out, with one account reporting how "all the Jews between Cologne and Austria" were rounded up and burnt alive. So bad were the outbreaks of anti-Semitism that the Pope intervened, issuing proclamations forbidding any violent action against the Jewish populations in any Christian country, and demanding that their goods and assets be left unmolested.[62] Whether this was effective or not was another matter. It was not the first time, after all, that fear of disaster, hardship and excessive religious outpourings resulted in the widespread slaughter of the Jewish minority in Germany: there had been terrible suffering in the Rhinelands at the time of the First Crusade when circumstances were not dissimilar. It was dangerous to have different beliefs at times of crisis.

Europe lost at least one-third of its population to the plague, and perhaps much more, with conservative estimates of the number of dead placed somewhere around the 25 million mark in an assumed total population of 75 million.[63] Work on more recent epidemics of plague has also demonstrated that during large outbreaks small villages and rural areas report much higher levels of death than cities. It seems that the key determinant of spreading plague is not the density of the human population (as had usually been thought) but that of rat colonies. The disease does not spread any more quickly in a packed urban environment where there are more households per infected rodent colony than in the countryside. Escaping from cities and towns for the countryside did not in fact increase one's chances of cheating death.[64] From field to farm and city to village, the Black Death created hell on earth: putrid, rotting bodies, oozing with pus, set against a background of fear, anxiety and disbelief at the scale of suffering.

The effects were crushing. "Our hopes for the future have been buried alongside our friends," wrote the Italian poet Petrarch. Plans and ambitions for further discovery of the east and for fortunes to be made were overshadowed by darker thoughts. The only consolation, Petrarch went on, was the knowledge "that we shall follow those who went before. I do not know how long we will have to wait, but I know it cannot be very long." All the riches of the Indian Ocean, the Caspian or the Black Sea, he wrote, could not make up for what had been swept away.[65]

And yet, despite the horror it caused, the plague turned out to be the catalyst for social and economic change that was so profound that far from marking the death of Europe, it served as its making. The transformation provided an important pillar in the rise—and the triumph—of the west. It did so in several phases. First was the top-to-bottom reconfiguration of how social structures functioned. Chronic depopulation in the wake of the Black Death had the effect of sharply increasing wages because of the accentuated value of labour. So many died before the plague finally began to peter out in the early 1350s that one source noted a "shortage of servants, craftsmen, and workmen, and agricultural workers and labourers." This gave considerable negotiating powers to those who had previously been at the lower end of the social and economic spectrum. Some simply "turned their noses up at employment, and could scarcely be persuaded to serve the eminent unless for triple wages."[66] This was hardly an exaggeration: empirical data shows that urban wages rose dramatically in the decades after the Black Death.[67]

The empowerment of the peasantry, of labourers and of women was matched by a weakening of the propertied classes, as landlords were forced into accepting lower rents for their holdings—deciding it was better to receive some revenue than nothing at all. Lower rents, fewer obligations and longer leases all had the effect of tilting power and benefits towards the peasantry and urban tenants. This was further enhanced by a fall in interest rates, which declined noticeably across Europe in the fourteenth and fifteenth centuries.[68]

The results were remarkable. With wealth now more evenly distributed through society, demand for luxury goods—imported or otherwise—soared as a result of more consumers being able to purchase items that had previously been unaffordable.[69] Spending patterns were affected by other demographic changes that the plague had produced, notably the shift in favour of the working young, who were best placed to take advantage of new opportunities opening up before them. Already less disposed to saving because of their close shave with death, the new up-and-coming generation, better paid than their parents and with better prospects for the future, set about spending their wealth on things they were interested in—not least of which was fashion.[70] This in turn stimulated investment in and the rapid development of a European textile industry that began to turn out fabrics in such volume that they had a major impact on the trade in Alexandria as imports fell sharply. Europe even began to export in the opposite direction too, flooding the market in the Middle East and causing a painful contraction that stood in direct contrast to the invigorated economy to the west.[71]

As recent research based on skeletal remains in graveyards in London demonstrates, the rise in wealth led to better diets and to better general health. Indeed, statistical modelling based on these results even suggests that one of the effects of the plague was a substantial improvement in life expectancy. London's post-plague population was considerably healthier than it had been before the Black Death struck—raising life expectancy sharply.[72]

Economic and social development did not occur evenly across Europe. Change took place most rapidly in the north and the north-west of the continent, partly because this region was starting from a lower economic point than the more developed south. This meant that the interests of landlord and tenant were more closely aligned and therefore more likely to end in collaboration and in solutions that suited both parties.[73] It was also significant, however, that the cities in the north did not carry the same ideological and political baggage as many of those in the Mediterranean. Centuries of regional and long-term commerce had created institutions such as guilds that controlled competition and were designed to hand monopolistic positions to defined groups of individuals. Northern Europe, by contrast, began to boom precisely because competition was not restricted—causing urbanisation and economic growth to happen at a markedly faster rate than in the south.[74]

Different behavioural profiles also emerged across different parts of Europe. In Italy, for example, women were either less tempted or were less able to enter the labour markets, and continued to marry at the same age and to have as many children as before the outbreak of plague. This contrasted sharply with the situation in the northern countries, where the demographic contraction gave women the chance to become wage-earners. One effect of this was to raise the age at which women tended to get married—which in turn had longer-term implications for family sizes. "Don't hurtle into marriage too soon," advised Anna Bijns in a poem written in the Low Countries, for "one who earns her board and clothes shouldn't scurry to suffer a man's rod . . . Though wedlock I do not decry; unyoked is best! Happy the woman without a man!"[75]

The transformations triggered by the Black Death laid foundations that were to prove crucial for the long-term rise of north-western Europe. Although the effects of the divergence between parts of Europe would take time to evolve, the systemic flexibility, the openness to competition and, perhaps most importantly of all, the sense of awareness in the north that geography counted against them and that a strong work ethic was required in order to turn a profit, all laid the basis for the later transformation of the European economies in the early modern period. As modern research is increasingly making clear, the roots of the industrial revolution of the eighteenth century lay in the industrious revolution of the post-plague world: as productivity rose, aspirations were cast upwards and levels of disposable wealth increased along with opportunities to spend it.[76]

As the bodies were finally buried and the Black Death faded to become a horrific memory (periodically brought to life by cyclical secondary outbreaks), southern Europe underwent change too. In the 1370s, the Genoese tried to take advantage of the terrible effect that plague had had on Venice, where suffering had been particularly acute, and attempted to wrest control of the Adriatic. The gamble backfired spectacularly: unable to deliver a decisive blow, Genoa found itself suddenly overstretched and vulnerable. One by one, the appendages that the city-state had added over generations linking the city to the Middle East, the Black Sea and North Africa were picked off by rivals. Genoa's loss was Venice's gain.

Freed from the attentions of its long-term competitor, Venice now soared as life returned to normal, exerting a vise-like grip over the spice trade. Pepper, ginger, nutmeg and cloves were imported in increasing quantities, above all via Alexandria. On average, Venetian ships were bringing back over 400 tons of pepper per year from Egypt, as well as shipping considerable volumes from the Levant. By the late fifteenth century, nearly 5 million pounds of spices were passing through Venice each year to be sold on at handsome profits elsewhere, where they were used in food, medicine and cosmetics.[77]

It also seems to have been the main point of entry for pigments used in paintings. Often referred to collectively as "oltremare de venecia" (Venetian goods from overseas), these included verdigris (literally, green from Greece), vermilion, fenugreek, lead-tin yellow, bone black and a gold substitute known as purpurinus or mosaic gold. The most famous and distinctive, however, was the rich blue that came from lapis lazuli, mined in Central Asia. The golden age of European art—of Fra Angelico and Piero della Francesca in the fifteenth century, and then of artists like Michelangelo, Leonardo da Vinci, Raphael and Titian—owed much to their ability to use colours drawn from pigments that were part of the extension of contacts with Asia on the one hand and rising levels of disposable wealth to pay for them on the other.[78]

Trade missions to the east were so lucrative that the republic auctioned them off in advance, guaranteeing payments while devolving market, transport and political risks to the successful bidder. As one Venetian put it proudly, galleys set off from the city in all directions—to the coast of Africa, to Beirut and Alexandria, to the Greek lands, to the south of France and to Flanders. Such wealth flowed into the city that *palazzi* shot up in value, especially in the best locations near the Rialto and St. Mark's cathedral. With land rare and expensive, new techniques were used in the construction of buildings, such as replacing spectacular but indulgent double courtyard staircases with smaller stairwells that required less space. Nevertheless, said one proud Venetian, even normal merchants' houses were lavishly appointed with gilded ceilings, marble staircases, balconies and windows fitted with the finest glass from nearby Murano. Venice was the distribution point for European, African and Asian trade par excellence—and had the trappings to show it.[79]

It was not just Venice that flourished. So too did the towns dotted along the Dalmatian coast which served as stopping points on the outbound and inbound journeys. Ragusa, modern Dubrovnik, saw extraordinary levels of prosperity in the fourteenth and fifteenth centuries. Disposable wealth quadrupled between 1300 and 1450, spiralling up so quickly that a cap on dowries was enforced to stop payments that were rising rapidly; the city was so awash with cash that steps were taken partially to abolish slavery: in times of such plenty, it seemed wrong to hold fellow humans in bondage and not to pay them for their work.[80] Like Venice, Ragusa was busy building its own trading network, developing extensive contacts with Spain, Italy, Bulgaria and even India, where a colony was established in Goa, centred on the church of St. Blaise, Ragusa's patron saint.[81]

Many parts of Asia saw a similar surge in growth and ambition. Business boomed in southern India as trade with China built up alongside that from the Persian Gulf and further afield. Guilds sprang up to ensure security and quality controls, but also to create a monopoly that obstructed the rise of local competition. These guilds concentrated money and influence in the hands of a self-selecting group who maintained a dominant position on the Malabar coast and in Sri Lanka.[82] Under this system, commercial relations were formalised to ensure transactions were done efficiently and fairly. According to an account written by the Chinese traveller Ma Huan in the early fifteenth century, prices between buyer and seller were set by a broker; all taxes and duties were calculated and had to be paid in advance before goods were released and shipped. This made for good long-term trading prospects: "the people there are very honest and trustworthy," Ma Huan added.[83]

That was the theory, at any rate. In fact, the towns on the southern coast of India did not operate in a vacuum, and competed with each other fiercely. Cochin emerged as a rival to Calicut in the fifteenth century after an aggressively competitive tax regime succeeded in attracting considerable trade. This became something of a virtuous circle, as it caught the eye of the Chinese. A series of major expeditions led by the great admiral Zheng He, a Muslim eunuch, to demonstrate China's naval power, assert its influence and gain access to long-distance trade routes deep into the Indian Ocean, the Persian Gulf and the Red Sea, paid special attention to building up ties with the ruler of Cochin.[84]

These missions were part of an increasingly ambitious set of measures taken by the Ming dynasty that replaced the Mongol Yuan rulers in the middle of the fourteenth century. Lavish funds were spent on Beijing, building an infrastructure to supply and defend the city. Considerable resources were devoted to trying to secure the steppe frontier to the north and on competing with a resurgent Korea in Manchuria, while the military presence to the south was built up with the result that regular tribute missions began to arrive from Cambodia and Siam bringing local specialities and luxury items in considerable quantities in return for the promise of peace. In 1387, for example, the kingdom of Siam sent 15,000 pounds of both pepper and sandalwood, and then two years later ten times that amount of pepper, sandalwood and incense.[85]

Widening horizons in this way, however, had its costs. Zheng He's first expedition involved some sixty large ships, several hundred smaller vessels and nearly 30,000 sailors, representing a very substantial outlay in terms of pay, equipment and the extensive gifts sent along with the admiral for use as tools of diplomacy. This and other initiatives were paid for by a sharp rise in the production of paper money, but also by increasing mining quotas—which led to a trebling of revenues from this sector in just over a decade after 1390.[86] Improvements in the agricultural economy and tax collection also produced a sharp uplift in proceeds for the central government and stimulated what one modern commentator has described as the creation of a command economy.[87]

China's fortunes were helped by developments in Central Asia, where a warlord of obscure origins rose to become the single most famous figure of the late Middle Ages: Timur's—or Tamurlaine's—achievements became celebrated in plays written in England, his savage aggression a part of modern Indian consciousness. Forging a great empire across the Mongol lands stretching from Asia Minor to the Himalayas from the 1360s onwards, Timur embarked on an ambitious programme to construct mosques and royal buildings across his realm, in cities such as Samarkand, Herat and Mashad. Carpenters, painters, weavers, tailors, gem cutters, "in short craftsmen of any kind" according to one contemporary, were deported from Damascus, when it was ransacked, to embellish cities to the east. An account by an envoy from the King of Spain to the Timurid court provides a vivid portrait of the scale of the construction, and of the level of ornamentation lavished on these new buildings. At the Aq Saray palace, near Samarkand, the gateway was "beautifully adorned with very fine work in gold and blue tiles," while the principal reception room was "panelled with gold and blue tiles, and the ceiling is entirely of gold work." Even the famed craftsmen of Paris would not have been able to produce such fine workmanship.[88] This was nothing in comparison to Samarkand itself and Timur's court, which was decorated with golden trees "with trunks as thick as might be a man's leg." Among the golden leaves were "fruits" which on closer inspection turned out to be rubies, emeralds, turquoise stones and sapphires, along with large, perfectly round pearls.[89]

Timur was not afraid to spend the money he extracted from the peoples he subjugated. He bought silks from China that were "the finest in the whole world," as well as musk, rubies, diamonds, rhubarb and other spices. Caravans of 800 camels at a time brought merchandise to Samarkand. Unlike some people—such as the inhabitants of Delhi, 100,000 of whom were executed when the city was taken—the Chinese did well from Timur.[90]

It seemed, though, that they would be the next to suffer. According to one account, Timur spent time reflecting on his early life, and concluded that he needed to atone for "acts like pillage, the taking of captives, and massacre." He decided that the best way to do so was by "mounting a holy war against the infidels, so that, in accordance with the dictum 'Good deeds wipe out bad deeds,' those sins and crimes might be forgiven." Timur suspended relations with the Ming court, and was on his way to attack China when he died in 1405.[91]

The problems did not take long to materialise. Fragmentation and rebellion broke out in the Persian provinces as Timur's heirs jostled to take control of his empire. But more structural difficulties were unleashed by a global financial crisis in the fifteenth century that affected Europe and Asia. The crisis was caused by a series of factors that resonate 600 years later: over-saturated markets, currency devaluations and a lopsided balance of payments that went awry. Even with the growing demand for silks and other luxury products, there was only so much that could be absorbed. It was not that appetites were sated or that tastes had changed, it was that the exchange mechanism went wrong: Europe in particular had little to give in return for the fabrics, ceramics and spices that were so highly prized. With China effectively producing more than it could sell abroad, there were predictable consequences when the ability to keep buying goods dried up. The result has often been described as a "bullion famine."[92] Today, we would call it a credit crunch.

In China, state officials were not well paid, which led to regular corruption scandals and extensive inefficiencies. Worse, even when correctly and fairly assessed, taxpayers could not keep up with the irrational exuberance of a government that was keen to spend on grandiose schemes on the assumption that revenues would only ever rise. They didn't. By the 1420s, some of the richest parts of China were struggling to meet their obligations.[93] The bubble had to burst, and in the first quarter of the fifteenth century, it did. The Ming emperors raced to cut costs, calling time on improvements to Beijing, suspending expensive naval expeditions and projects like the Grand Canal scheme that at its height employed tens if not hundreds of thousands, constructing a water network to connect the capital with Hangzhou.[94] In Europe, where data is more plentiful, deliberate efforts were made to deal with the contraction by debasing the coinage—although the relationship between the shortage of precious metal, hoarding and fiscal policy is a complex one.[95]

What is clear, however, is that global money supplies ran short from Korea to Japan, from Vietnam to Java, from India to the Ottoman Empire, from North Africa to continental Europe. Merchants in the Malay peninsula took matters into their own hands and struck a crude new currency out of tin, of which there was a plentiful local supply. But, put simply, the precious-metal supply that had provided a common currency linking one side of the known world with the other—albeit not always in standard unit, weight or fineness—broke down and failed: there was not enough money to go round.[96]

It is possible that these difficulties were made worse by a period of climatic change. Famine, unusual periods of drought coupled with cases of destructive flooding in China tell a powerful story of the impact that environmental factors had on economic growth. Evidence from sulphate spikes in ice-cores from the northern and southern hemispheres suggest that the fifteenth century was a period of widespread volcanic activity. This triggered global cooling, with knock-on effects across the steppe world, where intensifying competition for food and water supplies heralded a period of dislocation, especially in the 1440s. All in all, the story of this period was one of stagnation, hard times and a brute struggle for survival.[97]

The effects and ramifications were felt from the Mediterranean to the Pacific, fuelling a growing sense of unease about what was going on in the world. Although the rise of Timur's empire had not provoked widespread fear in Europe, the rise of the Ottomans certainly made many increasingly anxious. The Ottomans had swarmed across the Bosporus in the late fourteenth century, delivering crushing defeats on the Byzantines, the Bulgarians and the Serbs and establishing themselves in Thrace and the Balkans. Constantinople was left hanging by a thread, a Christian island surrounded by a sea of Muslims. Passionate pleas for military support from the royal courts of Europe went unanswered, leaving the city dangerously exposed. Finally, in 1453, the imperial capital fell, the capture of one of the greatest cities of Christendom a triumph for Islam, which was once again in the ascendant. In Rome, there were accounts of men crying and beating their chests when news came through that Constantinople had fallen, and of prayers being offered by the Pope for those trapped in the city. But Europe had done too little when it mattered; now it was too late.

The fate of Constantinople was the source of acute concern in Russia, where it was seen not so much as heralding a Muslim resurgence as marking the imminent end of the world. There were long-standing Orthodox prophecies that Jesus would come at the start of the Eighth Millennium and sit at the Last Judgement, and these seemed to be on the point of being fulfilled. The forces of evil had been unleashed and had delivered a devastating blow to the Christian world. So convinced were senior clergy that the apocalypse was at hand that a priest was sent to western Europe to find more specific information about precisely what time of day it would take place. Some decided that there was no point in calculating the dates when Easter and other moveable holy-feast days would fall in the future, on the basis that the end of time was about to arrive. Based on the Byzantine calendar that was used in Russia, the timing seemed to be crystal clear. Using the date of the Creation as 5,508 years before Christ, the world was going to end on 1 September 1492.[98]

On the other side of Europe, there were others who shared the conviction that Armageddon was fast approaching. In Spain, attention focused on Muslims and Jews, at a time of growing religious and cultural intolerance. The former found themselves expelled from Andalusia by force of arms, the latter issued with an uncompromising order to convert to Christianity, leave Spain or be executed. Desperate to liquidate their assets, a fire-sale ensued, with property scooped up by investors who picked up vineyards in exchange for pieces of cloth, as estates and fine houses were sold for a pittance.[99] What made it worse was that within a decade these bargains were to soar in value.

Many Jews chose to head for Constantinople. They were welcomed by the city's new Muslim rulers. "You call Ferdinand a wise ruler," Bāyezīd II purportedly exclaimed, greeting the arrival of Jews in the city in 1492, even though "he impoverishes his own country to enrich mine."[100] This was not simple point-scoring: in scenes which would bemuse many today but which evoke the early days of Islam, Jews were not just treated with respect but welcomed. The new settlers were given legal protection and rights, and in many cases were given assistance to start new lives in a strange country. Tolerance was a staple feature of a society that was self-assured and confident of its own identity—which was more than could be said for the Christian world where bigotry and religious fundamentalism were rapidly becoming defining features.

One example of a man who fretted over the future of the faith was Christopher Colón. Although by his own calculations there were still 155 years to go before the Second Coming, Colón was outraged that little more than lip-service was being paid to matters of religion by the "faithful," and was particularly appalled by Europe's lack of concern for Jerusalem. With a fervour bordering on obsession, he drew up plans to launch a new campaign to liberate the Holy City, while at the same time developing a second fixation about the precious metals, spices and gems that were so abundant and cheap in Asia.[101] If only it were possible to get better access to them, he concluded, they could in turn easily fund a major expedition to liberate Jerusalem.[102] The problem was that being based in the Iberian peninsula placed him at the wrong end of the Mediterranean and made his grand idea little more than a pipe dream.[103]

Maybe, just maybe, there was hope. There were, after all, the voices of astrologers and cartographers like Paolo Toscanelli in Florence, who had argued that a route to Asia could be found by sailing west from the edge of Europe. After a titanic struggle to convince others to share a vision which bordered on the reckless and foolhardy, Christopher Colón's scheme finally started to become concrete. Letters of greeting were prepared for the Great Khan—with a blank space to be filled in once his exact name was ascertained; he was to be an ally in the recovery of Jerusalem. Interpreters were recruited so that it would be possible to converse with the Mongol leader and his representatives. Specialists were hired who knew Hebrew, Chaldean (related to the Aramaic spoken by Jesus and the disciples) and Arabic, the language that was thought likely to be most useful for dealing with the Khan and his court. As one scholar notes, rising anti-Muslim sentiment in Europe meant that just as Arabic was being frowned on and prohibited by law in the Old World, it was also considered the best way to communicate when western Europe finally connected with the Far East.[104]

Three ships set sail from Palos de Frontera in southern Spain on 3 August 1492, less than a month before the end of the world was being anticipated in Russia. As he unfurled his sails and set off into the unknown, little did Colón—more familiar as Christopher Columbus—realise that he was about to do something remarkable: he was about to shift Europe's centre of gravity from east to west.

When another small fleet under the command of Vasco da Gama set out from Lisbon five years later on another long voyage of discovery, rounding the southern tip of Africa to reach the Indian Ocean, the final pieces necessary for Europe's transformation fell into place. Suddenly, the continent was no longer the terminus, the end point of a series of Silk Roads; it was about to become the centre of the world.

11

The Road of Gold

The world changed in the late fifteenth century. There was no apocalypse, no end of time, as Columbus and others feared—at least not as far as Europe was concerned. A series of long-range expeditions setting out from Spain and Portugal connected the Americas to Africa and Europe and ultimately to Asia for the first time. In the process, new trade routes were established, in some cases extending existing networks, in others replacing them. Ideas, goods and people began to move further and more quickly than at any time in human history—and in greater numbers too.

The new dawn propelled Europe to centre-stage, enveloping it in golden light and blessing it with a series of golden ages. Its rise, however, brought terrible suffering in newly discovered locations. There was a price for the magnificent cathedrals, the glorious art and the rising standards of living that blossomed from the sixteenth century onwards. It was paid by populations living across the oceans: Europeans were able not only to explore the world but to dominate it. They did so thanks to the relentless advances in military and naval technology that provided an unassailable advantage over the populations they came into contact with. The age of empire and the rise of the west were built on the capacity to inflict violence on a major scale. The Enlightenment and the Age of Reason, the progression towards democracy, civil liberty and human rights, were not the result of an unseen chain linking back to Athens in antiquity or a natural state of affairs in Europe;

they were the fruits of political, military and economic success in faraway continents.

This seemed unlikely when Columbus set sail into the unknown in 1492. Reading his logbook in the twenty-first century, excitement and fear, optimism and anxiety still spill out of it. Certain though he was of finding the Great Khan—and of the role he would play in the liberation of Jerusalem—there was, he knew, every chance that the journey would end in death and disaster. He was heading for the east, he wrote, not by the "way it is customary to go, but by the route to the West, by which route we do not know for certain that anyone previously has passed."[1]

There was, nevertheless, some precedent for this ambitious expedition. Columbus and his crews were part of a long and successful period of exploration that had seen new parts of the world open up in Africa and the eastern Atlantic to the Christian powers on the Iberian peninsula. This had been driven in part by attempts to access the gold markets of West Africa. The mineral wealth of this region was the stuff of legend, a region known to early Muslim writers simply as "the land of gold." Some contended that "gold grows in the sand as carrots do, and is picked at sunrise." Others thought the water had magical properties that made bullion grow in the darkness.[2] The output of gold was prodigious and its economic effects were huge: chemical analysis shows that Muslim Egypt's famously fine coinage was made from gold from western Africa, transported by trans-Saharan trade routes.[3]

Much of this commercial exchange was controlled from late antiquity onwards by Wangara traders.[4] Malian by origin, these tribesmen played much the same role that Sogdian merchants did in Asia, traversing difficult terrain and setting up points along the dangerous routes across the desert to enable them to trade over long distance. This commercial traffic led to the emergence of a network of oases and trading bases, and in time to the development of flourishing cities such as Djenné, Gao and Timbuktu, which became home to royal palaces and splendid mosques, protected by magnificent baked brick walls.[5]

By the early fourteenth century, Timbuktu in particular was not just an important commercial centre but a hub for scholars, musicians, artists and students who gathered around the Sankoré, Djinguereber and Sīdī Yaḥyā mosques, beacons of intellectual discourse and home to countless manuscripts collected from all over Africa.[6]

Not surprisingly, the region attracted attention from thousands of miles away. There had been gasps in Cairo when Mansa Musa—or Musa, King of Kings of the Malian Empire—"a devout and just man" whose like had not been seen before, passed through the city in the fourteenth century on his way to Mecca on pilgrimage, accompanied by an enormous retinue and carrying huge amounts of gold to give as presents. So much was spent in the markets during his visit to the city that a mini-depression is supposed to have been triggered across the Mediterranean basin and in the Middle East as the price of bullion apparently plummeted under the pressure of the huge inflow of new capital.[7]

Writers and travellers from far-distant countries made it their business carefully to note down royal lineages of the Malian kings, and to record the court ceremonies of Timbuktu. The great North African traveller Ibn Baṭṭūṭa, for example, journeyed across the Sahara to see the city and its majestic Mansa Musa for himself. The ruler would come out of the palace wearing a gold skullcap and a tunic made of the finest red cloth, behind musicians playing gold- and silver-stringed instruments. He would then sit in a lavishly decorated pavilion—topped by a golden bird the size of a falcon—to hear the day's news from across his empire. With astonishing wealth at the king's disposal, Ibn Baṭṭūṭa found it hard to hide his disappointment that Mansa Musa was not more lavish with his gifts—at least to him. "He is a miserly king," Baṭṭūṭa wrote, "not a man from whom one might hope for a rich present."[8]

Christian Europe's interest had also been piqued by tales of legendary riches that followed the gold being traded in Egypt and along the North African coast, in cities like Tunis, Ceuta and Bougie, which had been home for centuries to colonies of merchants from Pisa, Amalfi and above all Genoa, the primary conduit of African gold in the Mediterranean.[9] Despite these mercantile contacts, there was little knowledge or understanding in Europe of how gold reached the coastal cities, or of the complex networks that brought ivory, rock crystal, hides and tortoiseshell from as far away as the Limpopo up the Swahili coast and into the African interior, as well as to the Red Sea, Persian Gulf and Indian Ocean. From Europe's perspective, the Sahara was a blanket that shrouded the rest of the continent in mystery: there was no way of knowing what went on beyond the narrow, fertile coastal strip of North Africa.[10]

There certainly was an awareness, on the other hand, that land beyond the desert was home to great riches. This is something neatly captured by the famous Catalan Atlas, a map commissioned by Pedro IV of Aragon in the late fourteenth century, which depicts a dark-skinned ruler, usually assumed to be Mansa Musa, dressed in western fashion and holding a huge nugget of gold alongside a note spelling out the scale of his wealth: "so abundant is the gold found in his country," it says, "that he is the richest and most noble king in the land."[11]

For a long time, however, the pursuit of direct access to the gold and treasures of western Africa remained fruitless; the barren coastline of what is now southern Morocco and Mauritania offered small incentive and even less reward, and there seemed little point in sailing south past hundreds of miles of inhospitable and uninhabited desert into the unknown. Then, in the fifteenth century, slowly, the world began to open up.

Expeditions into the eastern Atlantic and down the African coast had led to the discovery of a series of island groups, including the Canary Islands, Madeira and the Azores. As well as raising the possibility of further discoveries, they also became lucrative oases in their own right thanks to their climate and rich soils that made them perfectly suited to crops like sugar, which was soon being exported not only to Bristol and Flanders but as far as the Black Sea. By the time Columbus set sail, Madeira alone was producing more than 3 million pounds in weight of sugar per year—albeit at the cost of what one scholar has described as early modern "ecocide," as forests were cleared and non-native animal species like rabbits and rats multiplied in such numbers that they were seen as a form of divine punishment.[12]

Although the ambitious rulers of Castile, who had slowly consolidated power in most of the Iberian peninsula, had an eye on expanding into this New World, it was the Portuguese who seized the initiative.[13] Since the thirteenth century, Portugal had been actively building trading links to connect northern and southern Europe with the markets of Africa. As early as the reign of King Dinis (ruled 1279–1325), large transport ships were regularly dispatched to "Flanders, England, Normandy, Britain and La Rochelle" as well as to "Seville and other parts" of the Mediterranean, filled with goods from Muslim North Africa and elsewhere.[14]

Now, as Portugal's ambitions began to grow, so did its might. First, Genoa was squeezed out of the gold trade; then in 1415, after years of planning, Ceuta, a Muslim city on the North African coast, was captured. This was little more than a statement of intent, for it had limited strategic or economic value. If anything, in fact, it proved counter-productive as it came at considerable expense, upset long-standing commercial ties and antagonised the local population thanks to heavy-handed gestures such as the celebration of Mass in the city's great mosque, which was converted into a Christian church.[15]

This belligerent posturing was part of a wider hostility towards Islam that was growing across the Iberian peninsula at the time. When Henry the Navigator, the son of the King of Portugal, wrote to the Pope in 1454 to request a monopoly over the navigation of the Atlantic, he said his motivation was to reach "the Indians who, it is said, worship the name of Christ, so that we can . . . persuade them to come to the aid of the Christians against the Saracens."[16]

Such sweeping ambitions were not the full story, since requests to legitimise Portuguese expansion were as much about thwarting European rivals as they were about leading a charge against the Islamic world. And in fact Portugal's lucky break came not from provoking discord with Muslim traders and disrupting traditional markets but from finding new ones. Of crucial importance were the island groups in the eastern Atlantic, which facilitated exploration, providing harbours and havens that could serve as bases for taking on provisions and fresh water and enabling ships to sail further from home with greater security.

From the middle of the fifteenth century, colonies were settled as part of a deliberate effort to extend Portugal's tentacles and establish control over the most important sea lanes. Arguim, just off the west coast of modern Mauritania, and then São Jorge da Mina on the Atlantic seashore of modern Ghana, were built as fortresses that also had extensive warehousing facilities.[17] These were designed to enable the accurate cataloguing of imports, something that was significant for the Portuguese crown which insisted that trade to Africa from the mid-fifteenth century was a royal monopoly.[18] An administrative framework was established from the very start which formally set out how each of the latest points on the expanding Portuguese maritime network should be run. When new discoveries were made, such as the Cape Verde Islands in the 1450s, there was a tried and tested template that could be applied.[19]

The Castilians did not sit idly by as this happened; they attempted to loosen the Portuguese grip on the newly founded points along the chain running south, using direct force against ships flying their rival's flag. Tensions were soothed by the Treaty of Alcáçovas in 1479, which gave Castile control of the Canary Islands on the one hand, while conceding authority over the other island groups as well as control over trade with West Africa to Portugal on the other.[20]

However, it was not high politics, papal grants or royal competition over territorial possessions that opened up Africa and transformed the fortunes of western Europe. The real breakthrough came when entrepreneurial ships' captains realised that in addition to trading oil and skins and looking for opportunities to buy gold, there were easier and better opportunities on offer. As had proved the case many times before in the history of Europe, the best money was to be had in the trafficking of people.

The African slave trade exploded in the fifteenth century: it proved highly lucrative from the outset. There was considerable demand for manpower to work on farms and plantations in Portugal—with slaves brought back in such numbers that the crown prince who sponsored the first expeditions was compared to no less a figure than Alexander the Great for having forged a new age of empire. It was not long before the houses of the wealthy were described as "being full to overflowing of male and female slaves," allowing their owners to use their capital elsewhere and become even richer.[21]

Few showed any moral repugnance at enslaving people captured in western Africa, even if some sources suggest empathy. One Portuguese chronicler records the groans, wails and tears of a group of Africans who had been captured in one raid on the west coast and brought back to Lagos in 1444. As it dawned on the captives that it was now necessary "to part fathers from sons, husbands from wives, brothers from brothers," the sorrows intensified—even for those watching: "what heart, however hard it might be, would not be pierced with piteous feeling to see that company?" noted one onlooker.[22]

Such reactions were rare, with neither buyers nor sellers sparing a thought for those who were sold. Nor did the crown, which saw slaves not only as additional manpower but also as a source of income via the *quinto*—the tax of one-fifth of the profit on revenues of trade with Africa—and for which, therefore, the greater the numbers brought back and sold the better.[23] And even the chronicler who claimed to have been moved by what he saw on the quayside in Lagos had no qualms when, two years later, he took part in a slaving raid in which a woman and her two-year-old son, spotted collecting shellfish on a beach, were captured along with a fourteen-year-old girl who struggled so furiously that it took three men to force her into

The fabrics of the Silk Roads were highly desirable, and were sometimes even used as currency. This textile from the eighth or ninth century shows the famous horses of central Asia.

© Feng Wei Photography / Getty Images

The Silk Roads present many challenges, obstacles and natural barriers. These include the Pamir mountains, where passes were heavily protected, such as at Tashkurgan's Stone Fort (*above*), near Kashgar, and the treacherous Taklamakan Desert in Xinjiang, western China (*below*).

© Feng Wei Photography / Getty Images

Pictures from History / Bridgeman Images

Women preparing newly woven silk. This image was made by the Chinese Emperor Huizong of the Song dynasty, early twelfth century.

Pictures from History / David Henley / Bridgeman Images

Ceramic sculpture of a Sogdian trader, mounted on a Bactrian camel, dating to the Tang dynasty (618–907 AD).

Lavish decorations from Sogdian palaces in Panjikent attest to the rewards of trade across Asia.

Walter Callens / Getty Images

Kaveh Kazemi / Getty Images

Inscription at Naksh-i Rustām of the chief priest, Kirdīr, trumpeting the triumph of Zoroastrianism.

Afghan School / Valley of the Buddhas, Bamyan, Afghanistan /

The Buddhas of Bamiyan, symbols of the advance of Buddhism into Central Asia. They were blown up by the Taliban in 2001.

A Sogdian translation of a Christian psalter, using Syriac script. Disseminating faith in local languages was an important factor in how they spread.

The Crucifixion, from the Rabbula Gospels, a Syriac illuminated manuscript from the sixth century.

Laurentian Library / Florence

Photo12 / UIG via Getty Images

The "Standing Caliph" coin, perhaps depicting the Prophet Muḥammad himself.

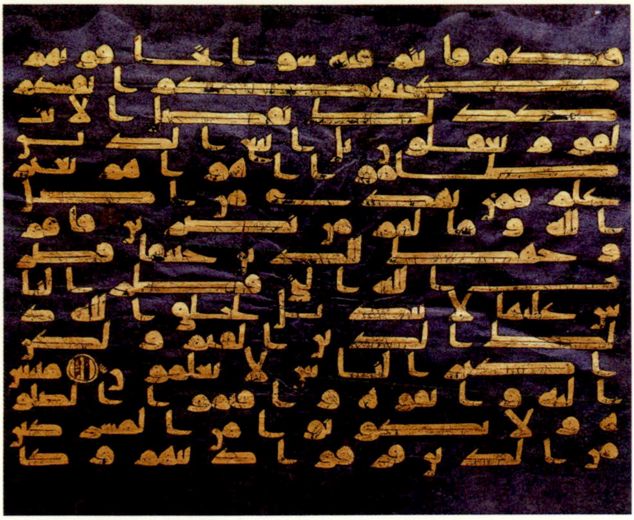

Marie-Lan Nguyen / Commons

A folio of an indigo-dyed copy of the Qur'ān, North Africa, ninth or tenth century.

Topkapı Palace Museum, Istanbul, Turkey / Bridgeman Images

The new Muslim empire brought wealth flooding back to the centre. Here the Sultan is shown surrounded by his courtiers, from a manuscript of the Persian epic poem the *Shāhnāma* by Firdawsī.

Muslim rulers were great patrons of the arts and of scholarship. Scholars in discussion at an ʿAbbāsid library, image from the *Maqāmāt* of al-Ḥarīrī.

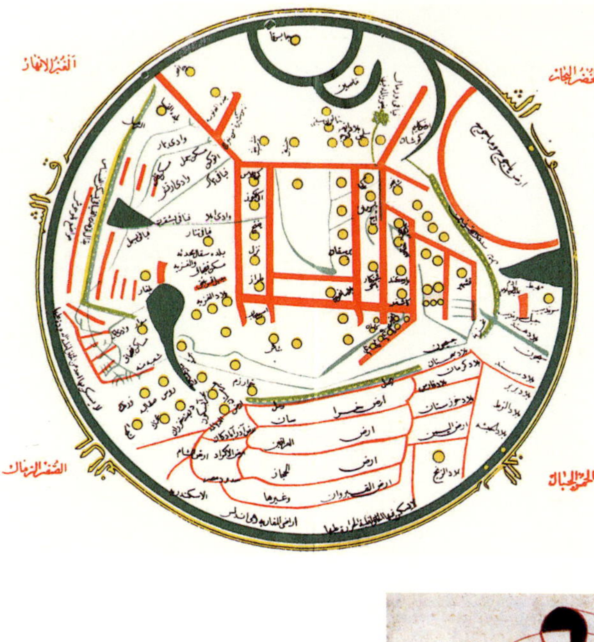

The map of Maḥmūd al-Kāshgharī, showing Balāsāghūn as the centre of the world.

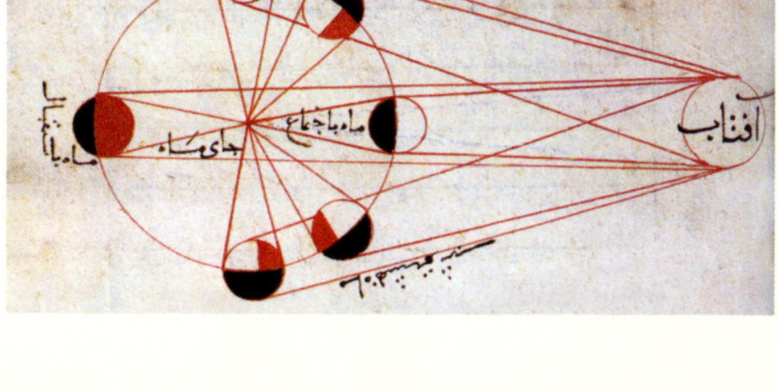

Illustration of al-Bīrūnī's explanation of the phases of the moon.

De Agostini / Getty Images

War and trade went hand in hand. The forbidding defensive walls of Bukhara.

Ben Stansall / AFP / Getty Images

Berig-Wikimedia Commons

Detail from a rune-stone from Tilinge, Sweden, commemorating the death of a Scandinavian adventurer in "Serkland"—the land of the Saracens, or Arabs.

The Vikings were heavily involved in human trafficking. Their reputation for violence played an important part in their success.

Fine Art Images / Heritage Images / Getty Images

The Mongols swept across Asia with astonishing speed. Here, Genghis Khan pursues an enemy, supported by his men.

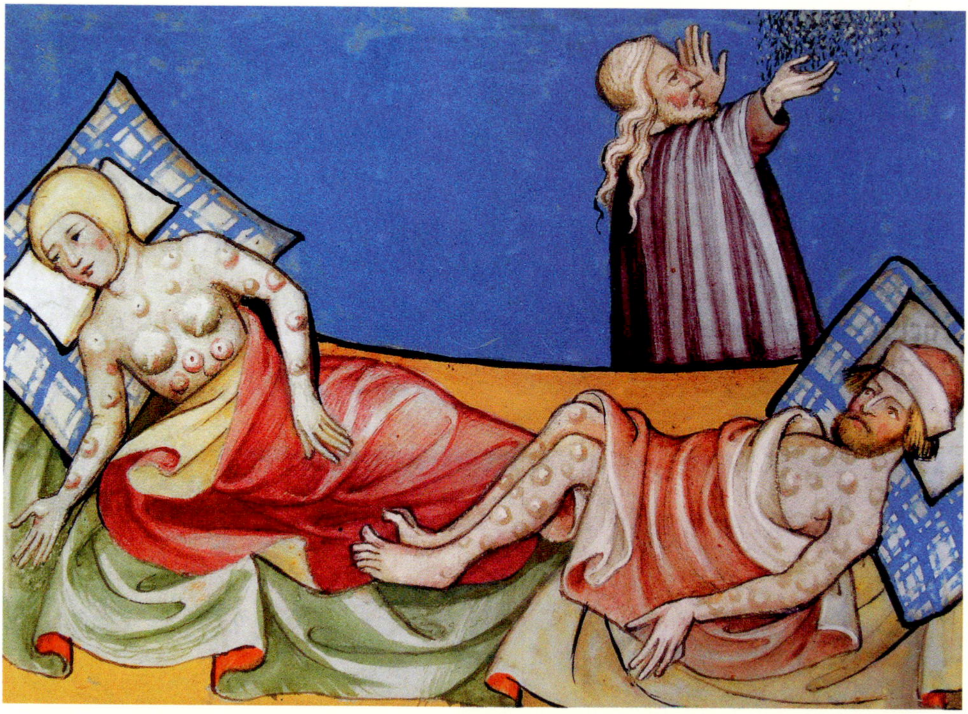

Pictures from History / Bridgeman Images

It was not just trade and conquest that flowed along the Silk Roads; so did disease. The most devastating was the Black Death, which ravaged Asia and Europe in the fourteenth century. Victims depicted in the Toggenburg Bible have the distinctive swellings that Boccaccio said could be the size of apples.

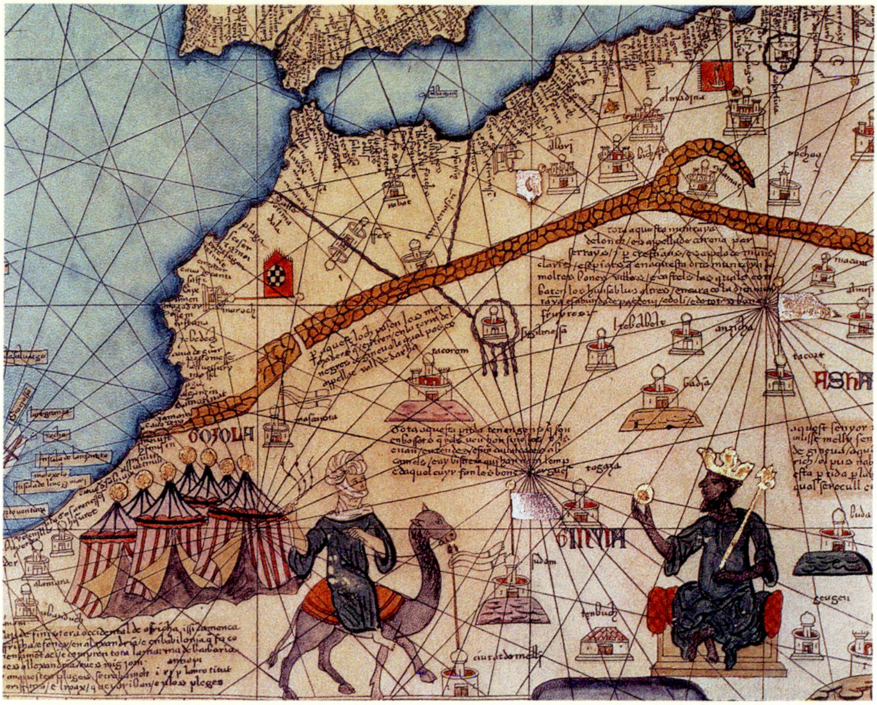

The gold of West Africa was famous across the Mediterranean. The great Malian king, Mansa Musa, "the richest and most noble" of rulers, holds a large golden nugget in this detail from the Catalan Atlas, 1375.

China became increasingly interested in the world beyond the Pacific in the fifteenth century. The Chinese admiral Zheng He explored the Indian Ocean and the coast of East Africa. This wall painting from the Chinese temple shrine, Penang, Malaysia, shows one of his ships.

Culture Club / Getty Images

Map of the Indian Ocean, Persian Gulf and Bay of Bengal by Jan Huyghen van Linschoten—the doyen of European mapmakers.

Blanton Museum of Art / University of Texas, Au

Cortés and Xicoténcatl, whose alliance brought about the demise of the Aztecs. Cortés claimed to suffer from an illness that could only be cured by gold.

Private Collection / The Stapleton Collection / Bridgeman Images

The bustling port of Calicut in south-western India, a century after Vasco da Gama's expedition. European traders who flocked to Asia could make huge profits from selling goods to the new rich back home.

Getty Images

The stunning mausoleum of Gūr-i Mīr in Samarkand, resting place of Timur and his heirs.

Getty Images

The Taj Mahal, a symbol of love—and of the sharp surge in wealth in India in the seventeenth century.

© Victoria and Albert Museum, London

The Dutch delegation being received in Udaipur by the Maharana Sangram Singh in 1711 (*detail*). Negotiating (and reconfirming) trade privileges was vital to defend European commercial interests.

Fine Art Images / Heritage Images / Getty Images

The Dutch Golden Age: Vermeer's *Girl Reading a Letter at an Open Window*—with a bowl in the foreground in the distinctive blue and white colours of Asian ceramics.

De Agostini / Getty Images

The East India Company made fortunes for many of its officers. Its spectacular failure led to a government bail-out that antagonised many in Britain's colonies. In 1773, men dressed as "Indians" tipped tea into the harbour in Boston in protest. The Boston Tea Party was a milestone on the route to the American Declaration of Independence.

Private Collection / © Look and Learn / Elgar Collection / Bridgeman Images

The assassination of Alexander Burnes in Kabul on 2 November 1841. Burnes had been a popular commentator on Central Asian affairs before his death.

Getty Images

Sir Edward Grey, British Foreign Secretary at the start of the First World War. Grey believed good relations with Russia were vital to Britain's interests in India and the Perisan Gulf.

Manoutchehr Eskandari-Qajar / Qajar (Kadjar) Dynasty Pages

Shah Moẓaffar od-Dīn, whose requests for loans created problems—and opportunities—for London and St. Petersburg.

Bundesarchiv

Herbert Backe, architect of the plan to divide the Soviet Union into "surplus" and "deficit" zones. It was envisaged that millions would starve to death as a result.

Heinrich Hoffmann / ullstein bild via Getty Images

Hitler's mountain home, "the ultimate source of decorating inspiration," according to *Homes & Gardens.* Hitler drew inspiration for German expansion east from British India—and from European settlers in America. The Volga, he said, was to be Germany's Mississippi, with the indigenous population expelled beyond this frontier.

General Photographic Agency / Getty Images

William Knox D'Arcy, a "capitalist of the highest order," who won an exclusive concession to "probe, pierce and drill at will the depths of Persian soil" for sixty years.

Keystone-France / Gamma-Keystone via Getty Images

Mohammed Mossadegh, Prime Minister of Iran who was deposed by a CIA-led plot in 1953. He was said to diffuse "a slight reek of opium."

Dmitri Kessel / The LIFE Picture Collection / Getty Images

RIGHT: The Shah of Iran, Reza Pahlavi, and his wife. "My visions were miracles that saved the country," he told one interviewer.

Associated Press

The return of Ayatollah Khomeini to Iran in 1979 was greeted with wild celebrations in Teheran. The BBC estimated that 5 million people took to the streets.

Pierre Perrin / Gamma-Rapho via Getty Images

Saddam Hussein, wearing his favoured military fatigues. He was identified by the British in the 1960s as someone with whom "it would be possible to do business."

Getty Images

Osama bin Laden. U.S. intelligence reports before 9/11 noted that there was considerable sympathy for his message in the Arabic-speaking world—though few endorsed his terrorist methods.

Edson Walker / Getty Images

The Khan Shatyr Entertainment Centre in Astana, Kazakhstan. The futuristic transparent tent houses a shopping centre, sports facilities, cinemas—and an indoor beach resort.

Heydar Aliyev International Airport in Baku, Azerbaijan. One of the state-of-the-art transport hubs being built along the New Silk Road.

Kerem Sanliman

the boat. At least, says the chronicler matter-of-factly, she "had a pleasurable presence for a Guinean."[24] Men, women and children were routinely rounded up in raids that resembled animal hunts. Some begged the crown prince for a licence to equip multiple vessels and head off in convoy. Not only did he approve, but he "at once commanded . . . banners to be made, with the Cross of the Order of Jesus Christ"—one for each ship. Human trafficking was thus in league with the crown and with God.[25]

All this new money did not impress everyone back home. One visitor from Poland in the late fifteenth century was struck by the lack of grace, elegance and sophistication of the country's inhabitants. The men of Portugal, he wrote, were "coarse, poor, lacking in good manners and ignorant despite the pretence of wisdom." As for the women, "few are beautiful; almost all look like men, though in general they have lovely black eyes." They also had magnificent posteriors, he added, "so full that I say it in all truth in the whole world nothing finer is to be seen." Nevertheless, it was only fair to note that the women were also lewd, greedy, fickle, mean and dissolute.[26]

Although the slave trade had considerable impact on the Portuguese domestic economy, the role it played in the exploration and discovery of the long African coastline in the fifteenth century was much more important. Portuguese vessels kept sailing ever southwards to seek their prey, finding time and again that the further they went, the less well-defended settlements proved to be. Curious village elders and chieftains who marched out to meet those arriving from Europe were routinely butchered on the spot, their shields and spears taken as trophies for the king or crown prince.[27]

Spurred onwards in search of rich and easy pickings, explorers pushed ever further along the African coast in the last quarter of the fifteenth century. In addition to slaving expeditions, ships bearing emissaries were dispatched by King João II of Portugal, who was keen to build close relations with powerful local rulers in order to protect his country's position against the Spanish. One such representative was none other than Christopher Columbus, who was soon using his experiences to calculate what might be required to supply, service and maintain other long-distance voyages. He also tried to use this new information on the length of the African coast to estimate what the size of the earth might be, in anticipation of an ambitious journey of his own in the future.[28]

Other explorers lived in the present. In the 1480s, Diogo Cão discovered the mouth of the River Congo, paving the way for the formal exchange of embassies with the powerful king of the region, who agreed to be baptised.

This delighted the Portuguese, who used it to burnish their credentials with the papacy in Rome, especially when the King of Kongo went to war with his enemies carrying a papal banner bearing the sign of the cross.[29] In 1488, the southern tip of the continent was reached by the explorer Bartolomeu Dias; he christened it the Cape of Storms, before returning home after a highly perilous journey.

Portugal guarded its expansion jealously, to the point that when Columbus approached João II around the end of 1484 to fund an expedition to take him westwards across the Atlantic, his proposal fell on deaf ears. Although the Portuguese king's interest was sufficiently roused to "send a caravel in secret to attempt what [Columbus] had offered to do," the fact that even Dias' dramatic discoveries were not followed up suggests that Portugal's primary concern was to consolidate its expansion in the parts of the new world it had recently come into contact with, rather than to expand further still.[30]

Things changed when Columbus finally found the sponsorship he was looking for from Ferdinand and Isabella, the rulers of Castile and Aragon, and set sail in 1492. News of his discoveries across the Atlantic drove Europe wild with excitement. New lands and islands which were part of "India beyond the Ganges had been discovered," he announced confidently in a letter sent to Ferdinand and Isabella on his way back to Spain. These new territories were "fertile to a limitless degree . . . beyond comparison with others"; spices grew there in such large quantities that it did not bear reckoning; there were "great mines of gold and other metals" waiting to be exploited, as well as extensive trade to be done "with the mainland . . . belonging to the Great Khan." Cotton, mastic, aloe wood, rhubarb, spices, slaves and "a thousand other things of value" were all to be found in abundance.[31]

The reality was that Columbus had been confused and mystified by what he found. In place of the cultured people he had been expecting to encounter, he came across local populations who went about naked and seemed, to his eyes, astonishingly primitive. While they were "very well formed, with handsome bodies and good faces," he noted, they were also credulous, delighted by the gift of red caps, beads and even broken pieces of glass and pottery. They had no idea of weapons, taking swords by the blade when shown them, cutting themselves as a result "through ignorance."[32]

In some respects, this seemed like good news: those he met "are very gentle and do not know what evil is," he observed; they are "aware that there is a God in heaven and convinced that we come from the heavens; and they very quickly say any prayer that we tell them to say and they make the sign of the cross." It was a matter of time before "a multitude of peoples" would be converted "to our Holy Faith."[33]

In fact, the letter which swaggeringly recounted his extraordinary discoveries—copies of which were disseminated so fast that versions were circulating in Basel, Paris, Antwerp and Rome almost before Columbus and his sailors had reached home waters—was a masterpiece of the dark arts, nothing more than what some historians have called "a tissue of exaggerations, misconceptions and outright lies."[34] He had not found gold mines, while plants identified as cinnamon, rhubarb and aloe were nothing of the sort. Nor was there the remotest sign of the Great Khan. The claim that there was so much treasure to be had that within seven years there would be sufficient funds to pay for 5,000 cavalry and 50,000 footsoldiers and effect the conquest of Jerusalem was nothing short of outright deception.[35]

It was a pattern that continued as Columbus made further voyages across the Atlantic. He again assured his patrons Ferdinand and Isabella that he had found gold mines, blaming illness and logistical problems for his failure to produce better hard evidence, sending parrots, cannibals and castrated males instead to try to conceal the truth. Just as he had been certain that he had been close to Japan on his first expedition, so he reported with complete confidence now that he was near the mines of Ophir, which had yielded the gold to build Solomon's Temple, after finding a few impressively large nuggets on the island of Hispaniola. Later he claimed to have discovered the gates of paradise itself when he reached what was in fact the mouth of the Orinoco.[36]

Some of Columbus' men, infuriated by the way he obsessively managed every detail of his expeditions, by how stingily he rationed provisions and by how easily he lost his temper when anyone disagreed with him, returned to Europe with information that poured cold water over the admiral's reports, which were anyway becoming frankly tiring in their implausible optimism. Crossing the Atlantic was a farce, Pedro Margarit, a Spanish explorer, and Bernardo Buyl, a missionary monk, told the rulers of Spain: there was no gold, and they had found nothing to bring back other than naked Indians, fancy birds and a few trinkets; the costs of the expeditions would never be recovered.[37] This utter failure to find treasures was perhaps one reason why attention shifted from material wealth to the erotic in these new territories.

Accounts about the newly discovered lands written in the late fifteenth and early sixteenth centuries increasingly focused on unusual sexual practices, intercourse in public and sodomy.[38]

But then fortunes changed. In 1498, while exploring the Paria peninsula in what is now northern Venezuela, Columbus came across locals wearing strings of pearls around their necks and shortly afterwards discovered a set of islands with astonishingly rich oyster beds. Explorers rushed to fill their ships with the prizes. Contemporary accounts record how sacks filled to bursting with pearls, "some as large as hazelnuts, very clear and beautiful," were shipped back to Spain, generating fortunes for the captains and crews who brought them home.[39] The sense of excitement was heightened by stories of the quantities of pearls waiting to be gathered, by their enormous sizes and above all by the reports of the prices at which they were sold by the locals—which were swiftly exaggerated as rumours swirled around Europe. One, ostensibly written by Amerigo Vespucci but either heavily embroidered or more likely a forgery, told how the Italian explorer had been able to acquire "a hundred and nineteen marks of pearls" (around sixty pounds in weight), in exchange for "nothing other than bells, mirrors, glass beads and brass leaves. One [of the natives] traded all the pearls he had for one bell."[40]

Some pearls were so large that they became famous in their own right—such as "La Peregrina" (the "Pilgrim pearl"), which remains one of the largest single pearls ever found, and the similarly named "La Pelegrina," famed for its unparalleled quality. Both held pride of place in royal and imperial treasuries across Europe for centuries, depicted in portraits of sovereigns by Velázquez, and more recently, as centrepieces of legendary modern collections, such as that of Elizabeth Taylor.

The pearl bonanza was followed by the discovery of gold and silver as the Spanish investigations of Central and southern America brought them into contact with sophisticated and complex societies such as the Aztecs and, soon afterwards, the Inca. Inevitably, exploration turned to conquest. Columbus had noted on his very first expedition that the Europeans enjoyed a major technological advantage over the people he had come into contact with. "The Indians," as he wrongly called them, "do not have arms and are all naked, and of no skill in arms, and so cowardly that a thousand would not stand against three."[41] They had watched with wonder at one banquet as Columbus showed them the accuracy of a Turkish bow, and then demonstrated the power of a small Lombard cannon and of a spingard—a heavy gun capable of piercing armour. The new arrivals might have admired the idyllic and naive characteristics of the people they encountered, but they were also proud of their instruments of death, which had evolved from centuries of near-incessant fighting against both Muslims and neighbouring Christian kingdoms in Europe.[42]

Columbus had already advised on the passivity and naivety of those he encountered on his first crossing. "They are fit to be ordered about and made to work, plant and do everything else that may be needed, and build towns and be taught our customs," he wrote.[43] From the very outset, the local populations were identified as potential slaves. Violence quickly became standard. On the island of Cuba in 1513, villagers who arrived to present the Spanish with gifts of food, fish and bread "to the limit of their larder" were massacred "without the slightest provocation," in the words of one dismayed observer. This was just one atrocity among many. "I saw . . . cruelty on a scale no living being has ever seen or expects to see," wrote the Spanish friar Bartolomé de las Casas of his experiences in the earliest days of European settlement, in a horrified report designed to inform those back home of what was happening in the New World.[44] What he saw was just the beginning, as he reported in his coruscating account of the treatment of the "Indians" in his *Historia de las Indias*.

The native populations in the Caribbean and the Americas were devastated. Within a few short decades of Columbus' first voyage, the numbers of the indigenous Taíno people fell from half a million to little more than 2,000. This was in part due to ferocious treatment at the hands of those who began to style themselves as "conquistadors"—or conquerors—such as Hernán Cortés, whose bloodthirsty expedition to explore and secure Central America resulted in the death of the Aztec ruler, Moctezuma, and the collapse of the Aztec Empire. Cortés stopped at nothing to enrich himself. "I and my companions," he told the Aztecs, "suffer from a disease of the heart that can be cured only with gold."[45] Rest assured, he purportedly promised Moctezuma, "have no fear. We love you greatly. Today our hearts are at peace."[46]

Cortés exploited the situation perfectly—although stories that his successes stemmed from the Aztecs' belief that he was the manifestation of the god Quetzalcoatl were later inventions.[47] Striking an alliance with Xicoténcatl, leader of the Tlaxcalan, who was keen to profit from the demise of the Aztecs, the Spanish set about dismantling a highly sophisticated state.[48] As became standard in other locations in the Americas, the locals were treated with contempt. The native population, wrote one commentator in the mid-sixteenth century, "are such cowards and so fearful that the sight of our men alone strikes them down with fear . . . causing them to flee like women simply because of a small number of Spaniards." In judgement, wisdom and virtue, he wrote, "they are as inferior as children are to adults." Indeed, he went on, they were more like monkeys than men—that is to say, they could hardly be considered to be human.[49]

Through a combination of ruthlessness that stands comparison with the great Mongol invasions across Asia, Cortés and his men seized the Aztec treasures, pillaging "like little beasts . . . each man utterly possessed by greed," according to an account compiled in the sixteenth century from eyewitness testimonies. Exquisite items were looted, including "necklaces of heavy gems, anklets of beautiful workmanship, wristbands, ankle rings with little golden bells and the turquoise diadem that is the insignia of the ruler, reserved only for his use." Gold was stripped from shields and mountings and melted into bars; emeralds and jade were looted. "They took everything."[50]

That alone was not enough. In one of the great atrocities of the early modern period, the nobility and priesthood of Tenochtitlán, the Aztec capital, were massacred during a religious festival. The small Spanish force went berserk, chopping off the hands of drummers before attacking the crowds with spears and swords. "The blood . . . ran like water, like slimy water; the stench of blood filled the air," as the Europeans went from door to door looking for new victims.[51]

It was not only the use of force and fortunate alliances that shattered the indigenous population. So too did the diseases that were brought from Europe.[52] The inhabitants of Tenochtitlán fell in huge numbers to highly contagious outbreaks of smallpox, to which they had no resistance and which appeared for the first time around 1520.[53] Famine followed. With mortality rates among women particularly high, agricultural production, for which they were largely responsible, collapsed. Matters were made worse because, as people fled to get away from the disease, there were fewer still to plant and harvest crops, so it was not long before the supply chain broke down completely. Fatalities from disease and hunger were catastrophic.[54]

A calamitous outbreak, perhaps of influenza, but more likely smallpox again, accounted for a large proportion of the Cakchiquel Mayan population of Guatemala in the 1520s, where the stench of the rotting corpses hung heavily in the air as dogs and vultures devoured them. Then, a few years later, another pandemic struck: this time, measles. The old populations of the New World did not stand a chance.[55]

The sea lanes to Europe now became thick with heavily laden ships from the Americas. This was a new network to rival those across Asia, in both distance and scale, and soon surpassed them in value: scarcely imaginable quantities of silver, gold, precious stones and treasures were carried across the Atlantic. Stories of the riches of the New World were heavily embroidered. One popular account in the early sixteenth century told of large nuggets of gold being washed from hillsides into rivers where they were then gathered in nets by the locals.[56]

Unlike the tales told in Columbus' first reports that flattered to deceive, precious metals really were now flowing homewards. Albrecht Dürer was stunned by the quality of the craftsmanship of Aztec treasures he saw exhibited in 1520. "Nothing I have seen in all my days rejoiced my heart so much as these things," he wrote of objects that included "a sun entirely of gold" and a silver moon, both six feet in width. He was transfixed by "the amazing artistic objects," marvelling "at the subtle ingenuity of the men in those distant lands" who had created them.[57] Boys like Pedro Cieza de León—who grew up to be a conquistador of Peru—stood on the quayside in Seville, staring in astonishment as they watched ship after ship being unloaded and treasure being taken off by the cartload.[58]

Ambitious men raced across the Atlantic to take advantage of the opportunities that the New World presented. Armed with contracts and concessions from the Spanish crown, hardened figures like Diego de Ordás, who accompanied Cortés in Mexico and later led expeditions to explore Central America and what is now Venezuela, made vast fortunes for themselves, milking the local population for tribute. This in turn created a surge in the royal coffers back in Spain, as the crown took its cut.[59]

It was not long before systematic approaches to information-gathering were being formulated at home, resulting in reliable maps being made, new finds being charted, pilots being trained and, of course, imports back home being catalogued and correctly taxed.[60] It was as if a highly tuned engine had been switched on, pumping the riches from Central and South America directly to Europe.

In addition, serendipity of timing, marriage ties, failed pregnancies and broken betrothals had produced a single heir to the kingdoms of Naples,

Sicily and Sardinia, as well as to territories sprawling across Burgundy and the Low Countries—and Spain. With seemingly unlimited funds flowing back across the Atlantic, the Spanish king Charles V was not just master of a new empire in the Americas but the dominant figure in European politics. Ambitions were recalibrated accordingly: in 1519, Charles moved to strengthen his position further, using his extraordinary financial muscle to ensure his election as Holy Roman Emperor.[61]

Charles' good fortune was disruptive for other European leaders, who found themselves outgunned, outmanoeuvred and outjostled by a ruler determined to expand his power ever further. His wealth and influence stood in sharp contrast with those of figures like Henry VIII of England, whose income was positively embarrassing compared with that of the church in his own country—to say nothing of that of his Spanish peer. Henry—a highly competitive man who in the words of the Venetian envoy to London had "an extremely fine calf to his leg," combed his hair short and straight "in the French fashion" and had a round face "so very beautiful that it would become a pretty woman"—could not have chosen a worse moment to try to shuffle his domestic arrangements.[62]

At a time when Charles V had become the puppet-master of much of Europe and of the papacy, Henry's insistence that he wanted his marriage annulled so that he could take up with Anne Boleyn—a woman who, in the words of one contemporary, was "not one of the handsomest women in the world" but was blessed with eyes that were "black and beautiful"—was reckless in the extreme given that the wife he was abandoning was none other than Charles V's own aunt, Catherine of Aragon.[63] In the upheaval that followed the Pope's refusal to sanction an annulment, the King of England was not just taking on the papacy; he was picking a fight with the richest man in the world, and a man who was the master of continents.

Spain's growing importance in Europe and its rapid extension in Central and South America were little short of miraculous. A remarkable shift in wealth, power and opportunity had resulted in Spain's transformation from a provincial backwater at the wrong end of the Mediterranean into a global power. For one Spanish chronicler, this was nothing less than "the greatest event since the Creation—other than the incarnation and the death of the one who created it."[64] For another, it was clearly God himself who had revealed "the provinces of Peru, from which such a great treasure of gold and silver had been concealed"; future generations, opined Pedro Mexía, would not believe the quantities that had been found.[65]

The discovery of the Americas was soon followed by the import of slaves, bought in the markets of Portugal. As the Portuguese knew from their experiences in the Atlantic island groups and West Africa, European settlement was expensive, was not always economically rewarding and was easier said than done: persuading families to leave their loved ones behind was hard enough, but high death rates and testing local conditions made this even more difficult. One solution had been to send orphans and convicts forcibly to places like São Tomé, in conjunction with a system of benefits and incentives, such as the provision of a "male or female slave for personal service," to create a population base on which a sustainable administrative system could be built.[66]

Within three decades of Columbus' crossing, the Spanish crown was already formally regulating the export and transport of slaves from Africa to the New World, awarding licences to Portuguese traders whose hearts and minds had been hardened by generations of human trafficking.[67] Demand was almost insatiable in a region where violence and disease reduced life expectancy. Just as had been the case when the Islamic world boomed in the eighth century, a surge in the concentration of wealth in one part of the world meant there was a sharp rise in the demand for slaves from another. Wealth and bondage went hand in hand.

It did not take long before African rulers began to protest. The King of Kongo made a series of appeals to the King of Portugal decrying the impact of slaving. He protested about young men and women—including those from noble families—being kidnapped in broad daylight to be sold to European traders who then branded them with hot irons.[68] He should stop complaining, the Portuguese sovereign replied. Kongo was a huge land that could afford to have some of its inhabitants shipped away; in any event, he went on, it benefited handsomely from trade, including that of slaves.[69]

Some Europeans, at least, were anguished by the plight of slaves and the seemingly relentless focus on extracting rewards from newly discovered lands. Although the prospect of recovering Jerusalem had slipped into the shadows, the idea of evangelisation as a Christian duty quickly emerged in its place.[70] The European settlers in South America, one senior Jesuit wrote angrily in 1559, "fail to understand" that the purpose of colonisation "was not so much to obtain gold or silver, or to people the land or to build mills, or . . . bring wealth [home] . . . as it was to glorify the Catholic faith and save souls."[71] The point was to spread God's word rather than to make money. It was a clear echo of the protests of Christian missionaries travelling along the burgeoning trade routes and settlements on the steppes of southern Russia and Central Asia centuries earlier, who likewise complained that a fixation with trade distracted from matters of higher importance.

In the case of the New World, there were good grounds for complaint about the disregard for the benefits of spiritual rewards. Gold was heading back to Spain in such volume that by the middle of the sixteenth century some were describing the era as surpassing the legendary age of Solomon. So much treasure was being shipped, Charles V was told in 1551, that "this period should more rightly be known as an *era dorada*"—a Golden Age.[72]

Not all the riches extracted from the Americas made it back to Spain. Almost as soon as fleets began to bring treasure home, sharp-eyed adventurers and pirates based in ports in France and North Africa could be found trying to cut them off and seize the spoils for themselves—either lying in wait on the final approach to the mainland or, as time went on, venturing into the Caribbean to intercept fat targets further afield.[73]

Accounts of the prizes on offer drew in opportunists from far and wide. "The reports of the great riches and glory" that could be gained off the Atlantic seaboard of North Africa, wrote one contemporary despairingly, lured men there "with the same excitement that spurred the Spanish on to the mines in the Indies."[74] These included Muslim raiders, who as well as setting about capturing inbound ships laden with produce also turned their attention to ravaging ports and towns on the coast of Spain, carting off thousands of prisoners in the process, who were ransomed or even sold on as slaves.

The raids were dressed up as being religiously motivated, although this was a heavily idealised way of seeing things. But even in the case of European piracy there were political points to be made. Attacks on Iberian vessels became a regulated industry, with licences known as *lettres de marque* being issued by Christian rivals to the King of Spain. The latter in turn promptly issued heavily incentivised pirate-hunting contracts, known as *contra-corsarios*, to bring the worst culprits to justice. Those that were successful found rich rewards from the crown, and also considerable fame—such as Pedro Menéndez de Avilés who notched up his prey in the manner of a wartime fighter pilot chalking up kills.[75]

A New World had been discovered overseas, but a new world was also being created at home, one where vibrant new ideas were encouraged, where new tastes were indulged, where intellectuals and scientists jostled and competed for patrons and funding. The rise in disposable incomes for those directly involved in the exploration of the continents and the wealth they brought back funded a cultural transfusion that transformed Europe. A swathe of rich patrons emerged in a matter of decades, keen to spend on luxury. There was an increasing desire for the rare and the exotic.

Europe's new wealth gave it swagger and confidence, and also reinforced faith in a way that the recapture of Jerusalem had been expected to do. To many, it was entirely obvious that the seemingly limitless fortune yielded from the Americas was an affirmation of God's blessings and had been "ordained by the Lord on high, who both gives and takes away kingdoms from whomever and in whatever way he wishes."[76] The dawn of a new era, a veritable Golden Age, caused the fall of Constantinople to the Turks in 1453, which had prompted wailing, breast-beating and tears in the streets of Rome, to be forgotten.

The task now was to reinvent the past. The demise of the old imperial capital presented an unmistakable opportunity for the legacy of ancient Greece and Rome to be claimed by new adoptive heirs—something that was done with gusto. In truth, France, Germany, Austria, Spain, Portugal and England had nothing to do with Athens and the world of the ancient Greeks, and were largely peripheral in the history of Rome from its earliest days to its demise. This was glossed over as artists, writers and architects went to work, borrowing themes, ideas and texts from antiquity to provide a narrative that chose selectively from the past to create a story which over time became not only increasingly plausible but standard. So although scholars have long called this period the Renaissance, this was no rebirth. Rather, it was a Naissance—a birth. For the first time in history, Europe lay at the heart of the world.

12

The Road of Silver

Even before the discovery of the Americas, trading patterns had begun to pick up after the economic shocks of the fifteenth century. Some scholars argue that this was caused by improved access to gold markets in West Africa, combined with rising output in mines in the Balkans and elsewhere in Europe, perhaps made possible by technological advances that helped unlock new supplies of precious metals. It seems, for example, that silver production rose five-fold in the decades after 1460 in Saxony, Bohemia and Hungary, as well as in Sweden.[1] Other scholars point to the fact that tax collection became more efficient in the second half of the fifteenth century. Economic contraction had forced lessons to be learnt, not the least of which was the need to control the tax base more vigilantly—something that in turn led to what has been called the "revival of monarchy," where centralisation was as important from a monetary point of view as it was socially and politically.[2]

To judge from the account of a Korean traveller, the velocity of trade seems to have increased in the late fifteenth century. In the port of Suzhou, around seventy miles from Shanghai, ships were gathering "like clouds," wrote Ch'oe P'u, waiting to take their shipments of "thin silks, gauzes, gold, silver, jewels, crafts" to new markets. The city was filled with rich merchants and boasted impressive standards of living. "The people live luxuriously," he wrote enviously, noting that "market quarters are scattered like stars" in this rich and fertile region.[3] Although this was promising, the key lay not in the harbours of the Chinese Pacific coast but thousands of miles away, in the Iberian peninsula.

The solution came in two parts. Europe's gradual economic upturn in the latter part of the fifteenth century had already stimulated consumer demand for luxury products. An immense reservoir of resources built up as the riches of the New World were shipped to Spain. In Seville, gold and silver were "stored like wheat" in the customs house, prompting the construction of a new building that could receive the astonishing volume of incoming goods so that they could be taxed correctly.[4] One observer wrote of his amazement as the haul of one fleet was unloaded: on one day alone, he saw 332 "cart loads of silver, gold and precious pearls" being brought to be formally accounted for; six weeks later, he saw another 686 loads of precious metal being brought in. There was so much, he wrote, that the "Casa [de Contratación] could not accommodate it all and it overflowed onto the patio."[5]

The huge windfall that came with Columbus' crossing of the Atlantic coincided with the spectacular success of another maritime expedition that was no less ambitious. Just as fears began to grow in Spain that Columbus' attempts to find a route to Asia had been an expensive mistake, another fleet was equipped and made ready to sail. Placed under the command of Vasco da Gama, the crews were received by the King of Portugal, Manuel I, before they left. Pointedly neglecting to mention the recent discoveries across the Atlantic, the sovereign outlined da Gama's objective: to find a "new way to India and the countries lying near to it." In doing so, he went on, "the faith of Our Lord Jesus Christ" would be proclaimed as "new kingdoms and realms" were seized from the Infidels—that is, the Muslims. But he had an eye on more immediate rewards too. Would it not be wonderful, he mused, to acquire "the riches of the East that are so celebrated by the ancient authors"? Just look, he continued, at how Venice, Genoa and Florence and the other great Italian cities had benefited from trade with the east. The Portuguese were painfully aware that they lay not just on the wrong side of the world but even at the wrong end of Europe.[6]

That all changed with da Gama's speculative expedition. Things did not look promising when his ships first reached southern Africa. The disappointment was less with the inhabitants, who dressed in skins and wore sheaths over their genitals, or with the food—the meat from seals and gazelles and the roots of herbs for chewing. It was that when samples of cinnamon, cloves, pearls, gold "and many other things" were shown to the locals, "it was clear that they had no knowledge of them whatsoever."[7]

As he rounded the Cape of Good Hope and headed north, da Gama's luck changed. At Malindi, he not only learnt of the passage east, but found an experienced pilot willing to help him deal with the monsoon winds and reach India. After a journey lasting ten months, he anchored off the port of Calicut.[8] He had succeeded where Columbus had failed; he had found a sea route to Asia.

There were already communities of traders from close to home; among the first voices he heard were those speaking in a familiar tongue. "The Devil take you!" shouted one of two Muslim merchants from Tunis who could speak Spanish and Genoese; "what brought you here?!" After exchanging pleasantries, what they said next was music to his ears: "What good fortune you have, what good fortune! There are so many rubies here, so many emeralds! You should give great thanks to God for bringing you to a land where there are such riches!"[9]

Nevertheless, the Portuguese struggled to make sense of what they saw—just as Columbus had done. Temples filled with statues of Hindu gods wearing crowns were thought to be churches adorned with images of Christian saints, while water thrown in purification rituals was interpreted as holy water being dispensed by Christian priests.[10] Stories of how St. Thomas, one of Jesus' disciples, had reached India and converted large numbers to Christianity had long circulated in Europe, prompting no end of erroneous conclusions to be drawn and brought back by da Gama—not least that there were large numbers of Christian kingdoms in the east ready to fight against Islam. Much of what was reported about what had been seen in the east turned out to be misleading or plain wrong.[11]

Negotiations with the Zamorin, the ruler of Calicut, further tested da Gama, who was forced to explain why—if the King of Portugal truly possessed incredible wealth, far in excess of "any king of these parts" as the admiral told him—he could offer no evidence of these riches. Indeed, when he produced a selection of hats and wash basins, along with some strings of coral, sugar and honey, the Zamorin's courtiers laughed out loud: not even the poorest merchant from Mecca would insult their ruler with such a pitiful selection of gifts, they said.[12]

Tension mounted. The Portuguese found their movements restricted as they were kept under the watchful eye of a large contingent of guards, "all armed with swords, two-edged battle-axes, shields, and bows and arrows." Da Gama and his men feared the worst, until, without warning, the Zamorin announced that he would allow the Portuguese to land their goods and to trade after all. They eagerly stocked up on spices and merchandise to show what they had found on their travels, and set off home. What they brought back home changed the world.

Da Gama's return after two years of epic travel led to rapturous celebration. In a ceremony in Lisbon cathedral to mark his success, Vasco was openly likened to Alexander the Great, a comparison that was eagerly adopted and repeatedly used by contemporary writers—and not just in Portugal—to describe the achievement of opening up a new and unfamiliar world in the east.[13]

That he had reached India was a major propaganda triumph for King Manuel, who immediately wrote to Ferdinand and Isabella (his parents-in-law) trumpeting the achievements, writing with undisguised delight about how his men had brought "cinnamon, cloves, ginger, nutmeg and pepper," together with other spices and flora, as well as "many fine stones of all sorts, such as rubies and others." "Doubtless," he added gleefully, "your Highnesses will hear of these things with much pleasure and satisfaction."[14] Columbus spoke of potential; da Gama had delivered results.

The rulers of Spain received some consolation. After the first expedition across the Atlantic, Ferdinand and Isabella had lobbied the Pope to grant to Spain sovereignty of all territories discovered across the Atlantic—in the same way that the papacy had done repeatedly in the course of the fifteenth century in relation to Portuguese expeditions in Africa. No fewer than four papal bulls were issued in 1493 setting out how new discoveries should be treated. After much bickering over precisely where to draw a longitudinal line, terms were eventually reached in 1494 with the signing of the Treaty of Tordesillas, which established a boundary 370 leagues beyond the Cape Verde islands. A "straight line" should be drawn, the treaty stated, "north and south, from pole to pole, on the said ocean sea, from the Arctic to the Antarctic." Everything to the west would belong to Spain, and everything to the east to Portugal.[15]

Thirty years later, the full significance of the agreement was becoming clear. By 1520, Portuguese ships had explored ever further east, travelling beyond India to reach Malacca, the Spice Islands and Guangzhou. The Spanish, meanwhile, not only realised that they had discovered two continents in the Americas, but—with the astonishing expedition of a

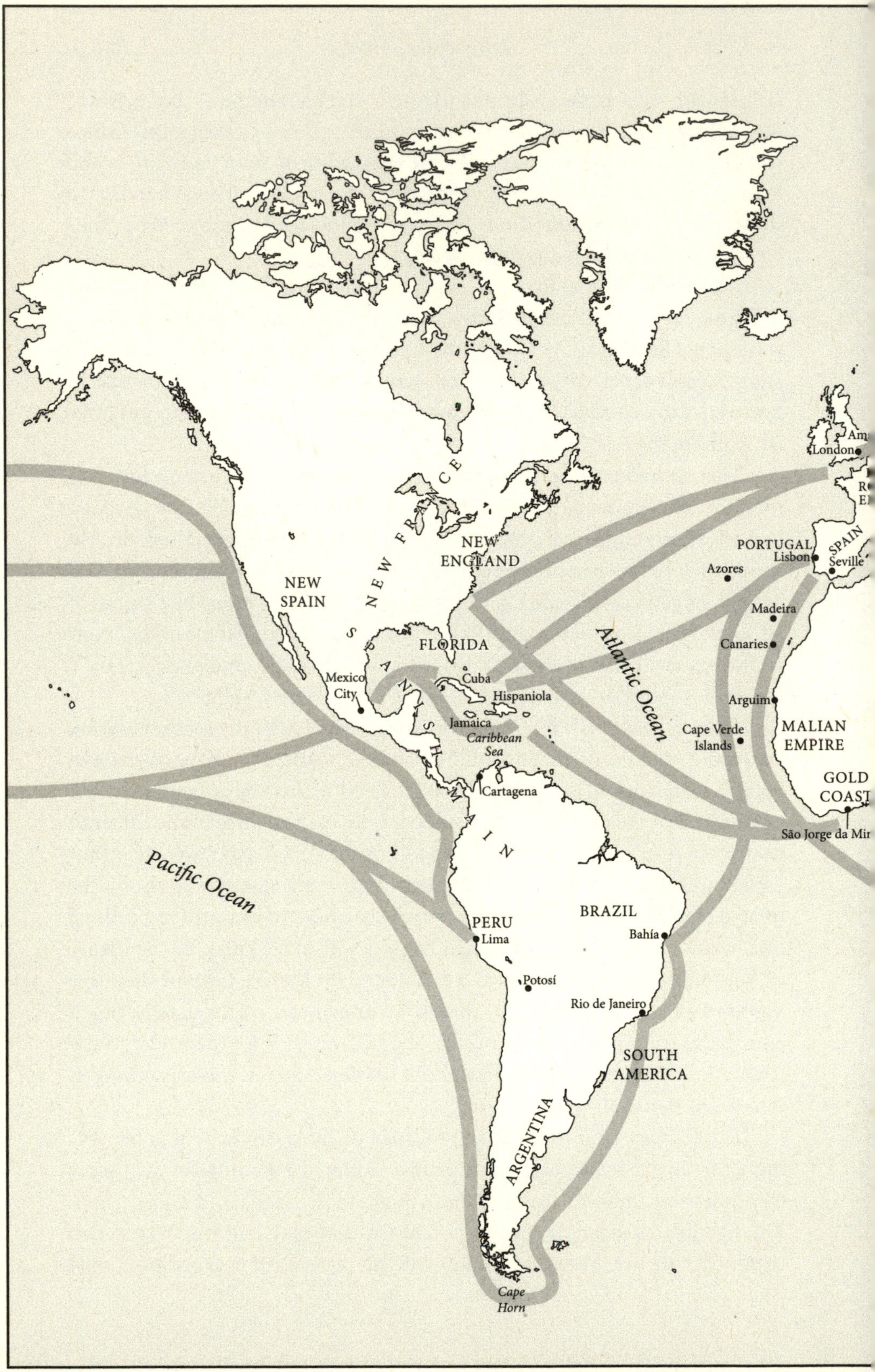

NEW FRANCE
NEW ENGLAND
NEW SPAIN
SPANISH MAIN
FLORIDA
Mexico City
Cuba
Hispaniola
Jamaica
Caribbean Sea
Cartagena
Atlantic Ocean
Pacific Ocean
PORTUGAL
Lisbon
SPAIN
Seville
London
Azores
Madeira
Canaries
Arguim
Cape Verde Islands
MALIAN EMPIRE
GOLD COAST
São Jorge da Mi
BRAZIL
PERU
Lima
Bahía
Potosí
Rio de Janeiro
SOUTH AMERICA
ARGENTINA
Cape Horn

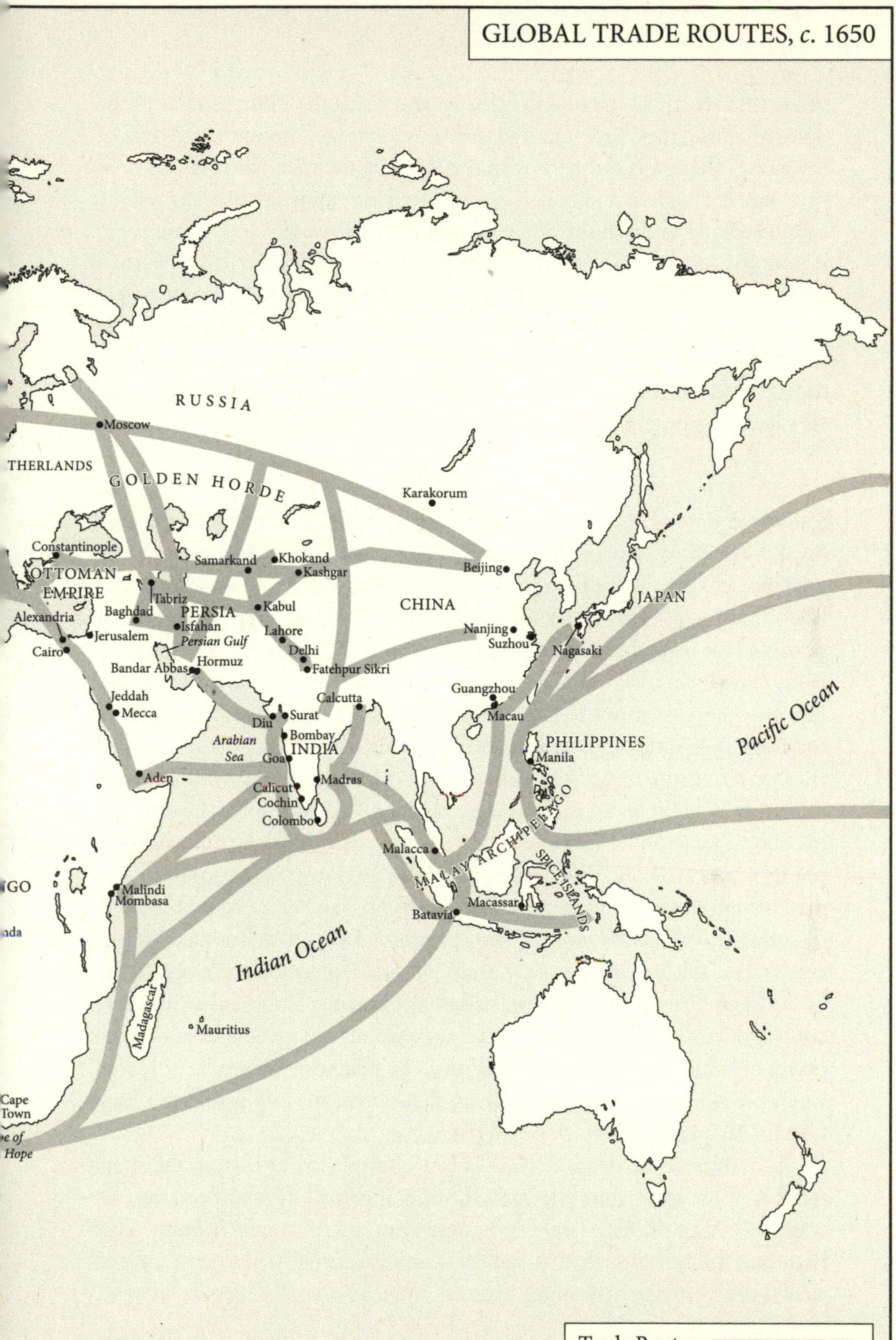

GLOBAL TRADE ROUTES, c. 1650
RUSSIA
Moscow
THERLANDS
GOLDEN HORDE
Karakorum
Constantinople
OTTOMAN EMPIRE
Samarkand
Khokand
Kashgar
Beijing
Tabriz
PERSIA
Kabul
CHINA
JAPAN
Alexandria
Baghdad
Isfahan
Lahore
Nanjing
Suzhou
Jerusalem
Persian Gulf
Delhi
Nagasaki
Cairo
Bandar Abbas
Hormuz
Fatehpur Sikri
Guangzhou
Jeddah
Mecca
Calcutta
Macau
Diu
Surat
Bombay
INDIA
PHILIPPINES
Arabian Sea
Goa
Manila
Pacific Ocean
Aden
Madras
Calicut
Cochin
Colombo
MALAY ARCHIPELAGO
Malacca
SPICE ISLANDS
GO
Malindi
Mombasa
Macassar
Batavia
nda
Indian Ocean
Madagascar
Mauritius
Cape Town
e of Hope
Trade Routes

sailor who managed to cross the Pacific and reach the Philippines and the Spice Islands—they had achieved an unprecedented circumnavigation of the globe. There was some irony in the fact that the man who led this mission was Portuguese and had taken service from a Spain that was willing to fund efforts to reach the Spice Islands from the west—and secure them not for his country of birth but for its neighbour and rival.[16] When Fernão de Magelhães, better known as Ferdinand Magellan, embarked on this epic expedition in 1519–20, Portugal and Spain went back to the negotiating table to agree a line in the Pacific to match the one that had been drawn in the Atlantic. The two Iberian neighbours divided the globe between them; they had the blessing of the papacy—and therefore of God.[17]

The rest of Europe now had to adjust to the rising fortunes of Spain and Portugal. News of da Gama's return home in 1499 was received with a mixture of shock, gloom and hysteria in Venice: one loud voice told all who would listen that the discovery of a sea route to India via southern Africa meant nothing less than the end for the city.[18] It was inevitable, said Girolamo Priuli, that Lisbon would take Venice's crown as the commercial centre of Europe: "there is no doubt," he wrote, "that the Hungarians, the Germans, the Flemish and the French, and all the people from across the mountains who used to come to Venice to buy spices with their money, will now turn to Lisbon." For Priuli, the reasons were obvious. Everyone knew, he stated in his diary, that goods reaching Venice overland went through endless checkpoints where taxes and duties had to be paid; by transporting goods by sea, the Portuguese would be able to offer goods at prices Venice could not hope to compete with. The numbers told the story: Venice was doomed.[19] Others reached similar conclusions. Guido Detti, a Florentine merchant based in Portugal in the early 1500s, was adamant that the Venetians would lose control of commercial traffic because they would not be able to match the prices of goods brought by sea to Lisbon. The people of Venice, he observed wryly, would have to go back to being fishermen; the city would fall back into the lagoons from which it had risen.[20]

Rumours of the demise of Venice were misplaced, at least in the short term. As more sober voices stressed, the opening up of a sea route to the east was not without risks. Many Portuguese vessels never made it home. Less than half the 114 ships that passed the southern tip of Africa had returned safely, the Venetian statesman Vicenzo Querini told the Senate in 1506.

"Nineteen are lost for sure, almost all of them laden with spices, and of another forty, nothing is known."[21]

Nevertheless, envoys were soon sent by Venice to Muslim Egypt to discuss ways of co-operating against the Portuguese, with suggestions of joint military operations and even, anticipating the construction of the Suez canal centuries later, contemplating whether a waterway should or could be dug through to the Red Sea to allow passage to "as many ships and galleys as one wanted."[22]

Although the Portuguese were convinced that operations directed against them in the Red Sea and off the coast of India in the early sixteenth century were the result of a grand alliance orchestrated against them by Venice, in truth the Egyptians needed little encouragement to try to impose control over their own shipping lanes. The appearance of rising numbers of Portuguese ships had been unwelcome, not least because the new arrivals were highly aggressive. On one occasion Vasco da Gama himself captured a ship filled with hundreds of Muslims returning to India after going on pilgrimage to Mecca. Ignoring the desperately generous offers of those on board to pay a ransom, he ordered the ship to be set on fire in an act so grotesque that one observer avowed, "I will remember what happened every single day of my life." Women held up their jewellery to beg for mercy from the flames or from the water, while others held up their infants to try to protect them. Da Gama watched impassively, "cruelly and without any pity" as every last passenger and crew member drowned before his eyes.[23]

Attacks on ports and strategically sensitive locations were a worrying development for Egypt. Jeddah, the port of Mecca, was attacked in 1505, while soon afterwards Muscat and Qalhāt, key points in the Persian Gulf, were sacked and their mosques burnt to the ground.[24] Worrying too was the fact that the Portuguese began to think in terms of establishing a network of bases in a chain connecting back to Lisbon. There could be nothing more important, argued the commander and explorer Francisco de Almeida in 1505, "than to have a castle at the mouth of the Red Sea, or very near to it," since this would mean that "all of those in India would rid themselves of the foolish idea that they might trade with anyone other than ourselves."[25]

In the face of such violence and posturing, squadrons were dispatched at the command of the Sultan in Cairo with orders to patrol the Red Sea and its approaches and, where appropriate, to engage in direct action.[26] Some Portuguese commanders concluded that a change in tactics was necessary. Their ships were being needlessly exposed to danger, one told the King of

Portugal. It would be better to abandon forts that had been built in provocative locations such as on the island of Soqotra at the mouth of the Red Sea and instead to foster cordial relations with Muslim Egypt.[27]

The initial burst of Portuguese exploration had been accompanied with swaggering violence and brutal intolerance. It did not take long, however, for things to settle down and for the initial swashbuckling rhetoric about the triumph of Christianity and the demise of Islam to give way to a more sanguine and realistic approach. With commercial opportunities aplenty, attitudes to Islam, Hinduism and Buddhism quickly softened—just as they had done in the Crusader states, as bluster was replaced by acknowledgement that a heavily outnumbered minority needed to establish a working relationship to ensure its survival.

This cut both ways, for rival rulers in India and in places like Macau and the Malay peninsula were more than willing to compete with each other by giving better and better trading terms to the European merchants to make sure that additional inflows of money would go to them and not to their rivals.[28] In this context, it was in everyone's interests to play down differences of faith as far as possible. Nonetheless, there were still some who harboured grandiose schemes. Afonso de Albuquerque mused that the capture of Malacca meant that "Cairo and Mecca will be ruined, and Venice will be able to obtain no spices except what merchants are able to buy in Portugal"; he therefore set about slaughtering the Muslim population of the city, which ultimately succeeded only in disrupting trade and generating hostility and profound mistrust.[29] The ruling family retreated, establishing new sultanates in Perak and Johor that provided leadership in the face of continuous competition from European powers.[30] However, in large part, and unlike in the Americas, the discovery of the route to the east generally became a story of co-operation rather than conquest. The result was a huge increase in trade from east to west.

With Europe all but buckling under the weight of the riches being extracted from the Americas, the ability to pay for luxury goods from Asia rose dramatically. Soon, the shops of Lisbon, Antwerp and other emporia in Europe were bursting with Chinese porcelain and Ming silks.[31] By far the most important imports, however, in terms of both quantity and desirability, were spices. Pepper, nutmeg, cloves, frankincense, ginger, sandalwood, cardamom and turmeric had been highly valued in food preparation in

Europe since Roman times, prized both as ingredients that transformed the taste of bland foodstuffs and for their medicinal effect.

Cinnamon, for example, was considered good for the heart, stomach and head, and was thought helpful in curing epilepsy and palsy. Nutmeg oil was recognised as a treatment for diarrhoea and vomiting as well as in fighting the common cold. Cardamom oil soothed the intestines and helped reduce flatulence.[32] In one Arabic manual written in the Mediterranean around this time, a chapter entitled "Prescriptions for increasing the dimensions of small members and for making them splendid" suggested rubbing a mixture of honey and ginger on to the private parts; the effect would be so powerful and produce such pleasure that the man's sexual partner would "object to him getting off her again."[33]

Competition to supply these newly minted markets was ferocious. Despite the alarm in Venice that followed news of Vasco da Gama's first expedition, the long-established trade routes were not replaced overnight. If anything, they thrived thanks to rising demand in Europe: then as now, consumers were not interested in how goods reached the market place; the only thing that mattered was price.

Traders watched each other jealously, recording what was being bought and for how much. The Portuguese recruited merchants such as Mathew Becudo in the Levant to spy on the size of caravans and convoys coming from Egypt and Damascus overland and by sea, and to report on the quantities of goods they were carrying. Rumours of bad crops, of ships being lost with their cargoes or of political unrest could affect prices on a day-to-day basis—making speculation a tricky business. There could be major fluctuations of supply depending on precisely when the spice fleet set sail, tilting the market heavily in favour of traders in the eastern Mediterranean who had access to better information and depended on less risky routes to market than rounding the continent of Africa.[34]

In the meantime, choosing what to invest in was a nerve-racking business. In 1560, Alessandro Magno, a young merchant from Venice, watched anxiously as the price of pepper went up in Alexandria by 10 per cent in a matter of days, prompting him to cancel his existing orders and switch his investment to cloves and ginger. It was essential to avoid being caught up in a bubble that might not just cost him his margins but lose him capital. As a middleman, his livelihood depended on being able to buy the right goods at prices his customers would be willing to pay.[35]

With millions of pounds of spices, above all pepper, reaching Europe each year, what had been an elite luxury business quickly became part of the cultural and commercial mainstream, driven by mass-market supply and demand. The potential for profit explains why the Portuguese set about building a Silk Road of their own, establishing a chain of ports and harbours linking Lisbon with the coast of Angola, Mozambique and East Africa and beyond in a sprawling set of trading stations with permanent colonies dotted from India to the Malacca Straits and the Spice Islands. They met with considerable success in doing so—to the point that within a few decades of Vasco da Gama's expedition to India, a substantial part of Portuguese state revenues came from the spice trade.[36]

Nevertheless, they faced stern challenges, not least because others were determined not to miss out on a share of the market. After taking control of Egypt in 1517 following a period of turbulence in the Near and Middle East, the Ottomans emerged as the dominant force in the eastern Mediterranean—and as a major threat to Europe. "Now that the most atrocious Turk has captured Egypt and Alexandria and the whole of the eastern Roman empire," wrote Pope Leo X, "he will covet not just Sicily and Italy but the whole world."[37]

The sense of threat was heightened by the Ottomans' military successes in the Balkans and an ominous move deeper into the centre of Europe. A clash was coming, wrote the great philosopher Erasmus in a letter to a friend in the first half of the sixteenth century, that would decide the fate of the world, "for the world cannot any longer bear to have two suns in the sky." The future, he predicted, would belong either to the Muslims or to the Christians; it could not belong to both.[38]

Erasmus was wrong—as were his peers in the Ottoman world, who were no less forthright in their predictions that "just as there is only one God in heaven [so too] there can be only one empire on earth."[39] There was no fight to the death, even though the massive army that tore into Hungary and central Europe in 1526 created waves of panic following the Turkish success against a hastily assembled western force at Mohács in southern Hungary. What did emerge, however, was an intense and long-standing rivalry, which spilled into the Indian Ocean, the Red Sea and the Persian Gulf.

Flush with confidence, the Ottomans spent heavily to strengthen their commercial position across Asia. A network of buying agents was established, while a series of castles were restored and upgraded to protect the sea lanes in the Mediterranean, Red Sea and Persian Gulf. Modernisation of the roads running inland from the Gulf through Basra to the Levant made this route so reliable, secure and fast that eventually even the Portuguese came to use it for their communications with Lisbon.[40]

This was all the more surprising given the regular use of force by the Ottomans against the Portuguese. The Ottomans launched a major attack on the Portuguese fort at Diu in north-west India in 1538, and made repeated strikes against Portuguese shipping.[41] One sea captain, Sefer, enjoyed a series of successes in the mid-sixteenth century that were so spectacular that a bounty was put on his head. The Ottomans are growing "constantly richer with spoils taken from the Portuguese," moaned one European captain, noting how Sefer's fleet was becoming ever larger; seeing how successful he had been with a small number of ships at his disposal, "how much more trouble will he give [us], and how many more riches will he send [home], when one day he has thirty?"[42] The Ottomans were proving to be formidable rivals: another Portuguese observer wrote in 1560 that every year millions of pounds of spices were reaching Alexandria (the most important of the emporia in the eastern Mediterranean for goods from the east); "it is no wonder," he moaned, "that so little comes to Lisbon."[43]

By this time, profits from the spice trade were already beginning to slow noticeably, prompting some Portuguese to turn away from spices and invest in other Asian goods and products, most notably cotton and silk. This shift became marked around the end of the sixteenth century by which time textiles were being shipped in ever increasing volumes back to Europe.[44] Some contemporary commentators suggested (and some modern scholars agree) that this was the result of high levels of corruption among Portuguese officials involved in the spice trade and the effect of poor decisions on the part of the crown, both when it came to claiming an excessively high tax on imports and when it came to setting up an inefficient distribution network in Europe. Ottoman competition had succeeded in putting the Portuguese—and margins—under intense pressure.[45]

At the heart of this rivalry in the Indian Ocean and elsewhere was the competition to secure maximum tax revenues for goods heading to cash-rich buyers in Europe. Ottoman success reaped handsome dividends. Central coffers in Constantinople swelled in the face of rising volumes of traffic passing through ports in the Red Sea, the Persian Gulf and the Mediterranean, although growing demand domestically also played a role in boosting government revenues.[46] Annual remittances grew significantly in the course of the sixteenth century, which in turn spurred social and economic change not only in the cities but in the countryside too.[47]

It was not just in Europe, then, that a Golden Age dawned. Vast building programmes were undertaken across the Ottoman world, from the Balkans to North Africa, funded by ever growing tax receipts. Many of the most spectacular projects were designed by Sinān, chief architect of Sultan Sulaymān the Magnificent (ruled 1520–66), whose soubriquet alone captures the spirit, and affluence, of the time. Sinān built more than eighty major mosques, sixty madrasas, thirty-two palaces, seventeen hospices and three hospitals, as well as many bridges, aqueducts, bathhouses and warehouses during the reigns of Sulaymān and his son Selīm II. The Selimiye mosque, built in Edirne (in modern north-west Turkey) between 1564 and 1575, was a highlight of architectural daring and engineering brilliance such that it was "worthy of the admiration of humankind," according to one contemporary account. But it was also a statement of religious ambition: "people of the world" had said it would not be possible to build a dome as large as that of the Hagia Sophia in Constantinople "in the lands of Islam." The mosque in Edirne showed that they were wrong.[48]

In Persia, there was a similar surge in spending on lavish building work and the visual arts that rivalled the cultural blossoming in Europe. A new empire had emerged under the Safavid dynasty from the splinters of the Timurid realm that had fractured after the death of Timur in the early fifteenth century. It reached a high-point during the reign of Shah ʿAbbās I (ruled 1588–1629), who oversaw an astonishingly ambitious reconstruction of Isfahan (in what is now central Iran), where old markets and gloomy streets were torn down and replaced with shops, baths and mosques constructed according to a carefully laid-out master plan for the city. Major irrigation works ensured that new Isfahan would be plentifully supplied with water—something that was essential for the Bāgh-i Naqsh-i Jahān, the "world-adorning garden," a masterpiece of horticultural design that lay at the heart of the city. The glorious Masjid-i Shāh mosque was also built, intended—as Edirne had been—to be a jewel on a par with the very best of the Islamic world. As one contemporary noted, the Shah made Isfahan "like a paradise with charming buildings, parks in which the perfume of the flowers uplifted the spirit, and streams and gardens."[49]

Books, calligraphy and the visual arts—especially miniature painting—flourished in a culture that was self-assured, intellectually curious and increasingly international. Treatises explained how to create good art, the

Qānūn al-Ṣuvar for example doing so in witty and stylish rhyming couplets. Bear in mind, the author of this work warns the reader, that it is all very well wanting to master the skill of painting, but "you must know that, to achieve mastery in this field, natural talent is a major consideration."[50]

Prosperity helped open new horizons: the Carmelite monks in Isfahan were able to present the Shah with a Persian translation of the Book of Psalms, which was gratefully accepted; and Pope Paul V sent a set of medieval illustrations from the Bible, which the Shah enjoyed so much that he commissioned Persian commentaries explaining what the scenes depicted. It was a time when Jews in the region made copies of the Torah in Persian, but using Hebrew characters—a sign of religious tolerance but also of the cultural self-confidence of Persia at this time of growth.[51]

The Ottoman and Persian empires did well from the sharp rise in transit taxes and import duties on goods coming from further east, and of course from domestic goods and products that were much in demand among the newly wealthy in Europe, from royal houses to merchant families, from court favourites to well-to-do farmers. But although the Near East did well from the cascade of gold, silver and other treasures that flowed across the Atlantic from the Americas, the chief beneficiaries were the places where most of the exports originated: India, China and Central Asia.

Europe became a clearing house for bullion that came in from spectacularly rich sources, such as the mine at Potosí, high in the Andes in what is now Bolivia, which turned out to be the single largest silver strike in history, accounting for more than half of global production for over a century.[52] New techniques for extracting the metal using a mercury-amalgam process were developed, making mining cheaper, quicker and even more profitable.[53] The discovery enabled an extraordinary acceleration in the redistribution of resources from South America, through the Iberian peninsula and on to Asia.

Precious metal was melted down and struck into coinage that was shipped east in astonishing quantities. From the mid-sixteenth century, hundreds of tons of silver were exported to Asia each year to pay for sought-after eastern goods and spices.[54] A shopping list drawn up in Florence in the 1580s shows how large appetites had become. The Grand Duke Francesco de Medici provided generous funds to Filippo Sassetti, a Florentine merchant about to set off for India, along with instructions to purchase a range of exotic goods. He duly received capes, textiles, spices, seeds and wax models of plants, a particular personal interest of the Grand Duke and his brother, Cardinal Ferdinando, as well as a range of medicines, including a remedy against poisonous snakebites.[55] Such acquisitive curiosity was typical of powerful and cultured men at this time.

Europe and the Near East sparkled with the discoveries coming from the Americas and the opening up of the sea route along the coast of Africa. But nowhere shone more brightly than India. The period following Columbus' crossing of the Atlantic corresponded to one of consolidation across a realm that had disintegrated after the death of Timur. In 1494, Bābur, one of his descendants, inherited lands in the Ferghana valley in Central Asia and set about trying to expand them, focusing his attention on Samarkand—with fleeting success. After being finally ejected from the city by Uzbek rivals, he moved south and, after years of struggle with little to show for it, he turned his attentions elsewhere. First, he made himself master of Kabul and then took control of Delhi by expelling the tyrannical Lodi dynasty whose members were wildly unpopular thanks to their regular and savage persecutions of the Hindu population.[56]

Bābur had already shown himself to be a keen builder, taking pleasure in setting out the magnificent garden of the Bāgh-i Wafa in Kabul with impressive fountains, pomegranate trees, clover meadows, orange groves and plants brought from far and wide. When the oranges turn yellow, he wrote proudly, "it is a beautiful sight—really handsomely laid out."[57] As he established himself in India, he carried on with his glorious garden designs—despite complaining about the difficulties of the terrain. He was dismayed that water supply was such a problem in the north of the Indian subcontinent; "everywhere I looked," he wrote with horror, "was so unpleasant and desolate" that it was hardly worth the effort of trying to create something special. Eventually he steeled himself, settling on a site near Agra: "although there was no really suitable place [near the city], there was nothing to do but work with the space we had." Eventually, after considerable effort and great expense, in "unpleasant and inharmonious India," splendid gardens were created.[58]

Despite Bābur's initial misgivings, the timing of his move south could not have been better. It did not take long for the new domain to turn into a mighty empire. The opening up of new trade routes and the enthusiastic purchasing ability of Europe meant that there was a sudden influx of hard currency into India. A considerable proportion of this was spent buying horses. Even in the fourteenth century, we have reports of thousands of horses being sold each year by dealers in Central Asia.[59] Horses bred on the steppes were popular, not least because they were bigger—and better fed—than those reared on the subcontinent itself, which were "by nature so small that, when a man is upon them, his feet nearly touch the ground."[60] With European silver pouring in to buy goods from the east, much was spent buying the best steeds, for reasons of prestige, for social differentiation and for ceremonial events—rather as money that has flowed more recently into oil-rich states has been spent on the best rides: Ferraris, Lamborghinis and other fine cars.

There were great profits to be made from the horse trade. It had been one of the very first things to catch the eye of the Portuguese when they reached the Persian Gulf and the Indian Ocean. Excited reports were sent home in the early sixteenth century about the demand for thoroughbred Arabian and Persian horses, and about the high prices that Indian princes were willing to pay for them. The Portuguese became so heavily involved in the lucrative business of shipping horses that it spurred technological change, with vessels like the *Nau Taforeia* being built with horse transport in mind.[61]

Most horses, however, came from Central Asia. With money flowing into India, one contemporary commentator told of eye-wateringly high margins as the inflationary pressures of a surge in demand outstripping supply kicked in.[62] Rising revenues prompted investment in building bridges, upgrading caravanserais and ensuring the security of major routes running north. The result was that the cities of Central Asia enjoyed another burst of life and splendour.[63]

The infrastructure necessary to support the horse trade was also lucrative. One quick-witted speculator invested in rest-houses along the main routes, establishing more than 1,500 in the space of fifteen years in the middle of the sixteenth century. The rising flow of money into this region is even recognised in the writing of Guru Granth Saheb, the great sacred text of Sikhism, where the mundane and the commercial sit squarely alongside the spiritual: buy goods that will last, the gurus advised their followers; and always keep accurate accounts, for these are a means of enshrining truth.[64]

There was a boom in gateway cities that were well located to hold major horse markets, including Kabul. The most important to flourish, however, was the city of Delhi, which grew rapidly thanks to its position close to the Hindu Kush. As the city's commercial importance grew, so did the position of its rulers.[65] A thriving local textile industry soon developed, producing materials that were highly prized across Asia and beyond, carefully nurtured by the Mughal authorities.[66]

It was not long before a mighty realm sprawled outwards, using its financial muscles to knock out one region after another and unite them into a single entity. Over the course of the sixteenth century, Bābur, followed by his son Humāyūn and grandson Akbar I, oversaw the dramatic territorial expansion of the Mughal Empire, which by 1600 stretched from Gujarat on the west coast of India to the Bay of Bengal, and from Lahore in the Punjab deep into central India. This was not conquest for conquest's sake. Rather, it was a case of taking advantage of a unique set of circumstances to seize control of cities and regions that offered juicy and rapidly growing income streams that reinforced and strengthened a nascent empire. As one Portuguese Jesuit noted in a letter to his Order at home, the conquest of Gujarat and Bengal, both studded with bustling cities and fat tax bases, made Akbar the master of the "gem of India."[67] Each new addition provided more power to the centre, enabling even more momentum to build up.

The Mughals brought new ideas, tastes and styles with them. Miniature painting, long favoured by the Mongols and the Timurids, was now championed by the new rulers, who brought in master practitioners from far and wide to create a thriving school of visual arts. Watching wrestling became popular, as did pigeon racing, both favoured Central Asian pastimes.[68]

Innovation in architecture and garden design was even more pronounced, with the influence of buildings and landscapes honed and perfected in Samarkand soon becoming evident across the empire. The results can be seen today. Humāyūn's magnificent tomb stands in Delhi not only as a masterpiece of Timurid design, constructed by an architect from Bukhara, but as testimony to a new era in Indian history.[69] New landscaping styles were also introduced, transforming the built environment and its relationship with its surroundings further still, heavily influenced by practices and ideas from Central Asia.[70] Lahore flourished with grand new monuments and carefully planned open spaces.[71] With huge resources at their disposal and the wind in their sails, the Mughals transformed the empire in their own image. And they did so on an extraordinary scale.

The astonishing city of Fatehpur Sikri, built in the second half of the sixteenth century as a new capital, provides an unequivocal picture of the seemingly unlimited resources and imperial aspirations of the buoyant ruling house. An exquisitely designed series of courtyards and buildings built from red sandstone blended styles and designs from Persia and Central Asia with those of India to create a splendid court where the ruler could receive visitors and leave them in no doubt of his power.[72]

The most famous monument testifying to the immense wealth that resulted from money flowing in from Europe was the mausoleum built by Shah Jahān in the early seventeenth century for his wife, Mumtāz. To mark her death, Shah Jahān distributed huge quantities of food and money to the poor. After a suitable burial plot had been selected, millions of dollars in today's terms were spent constructing a building topped with a dome, before millions more were spent adding a golden screen and cupolas decorated with enamelled work of the highest quality and vast amounts of gold. Pavilions "encircled by superb canopies" were added either side of the mausoleum, which then had gardens set out all around it. The foundation was endowed with an income from nearby markets to ensure that it would be properly maintained in the future.[73]

For many, the Taj Mahal is the most romantic monument in the world, an extraordinary demonstration of a husband's love for his wife. But it represents something else too: globalised international trade that brought such wealth to the Mughal ruler that he was able to contemplate this extraordinary gesture to his beloved spouse. His ability to complete it stemmed from the profound shifts in the world's axis, for Europe and India's glory came at the expense of the Americas.

Shah Jahān's lavish expression of sorrow at his wife's death finds a neat parallel with that articulated on the other side of the globe not long before. The Mayan Empire had also been flourishing before the arrival of the Europeans. "Then there was no sickness; they had then no aching bones; they had then no high fever; they had then no smallpox; they had then no burning chest; they had then no consumption. At that time the course of humanity was orderly. The foreigners made it otherwise when they arrived here. They brought shameful things when they came," was how one author writing not long afterwards put it.[74] Gold and silver taken from the Americas found its way to Asia; it was this redistribution of wealth that enabled the Taj Mahal to be built. Not without irony, one of the glories of India was the result of the suffering of "Indians" on the other side of the world.

Continents were now connected to each other, linked by flows of silver. It drew many to seek their fortunes in new locations: by the late sixteenth century, an English visitor to Hormuz in the Persian Gulf recorded that the city was teeming with "Frenchmen, Flemings, Almains, Hungarians, Italians, Greeks, Armenians, Nazaranies, Turks and Moors, Jews and Gentiles, Persians [and] Muscovites."[75] The call of the east was a powerful one. It was not just the thought of commercial gain that drew men in growing numbers from Europe, but also the prospect of well-paid employment. There was no shortage of opportunities for gunners, pilots, navigators, galley commanders or shipbuilders in Persia, India, the Malay peninsula and even Japan. There were chances for those seeking to start new lives for themselves: deserters, criminals and undesirables, whose skills and experience were valuable to local rulers. Those who did well were able in effect to establish themselves as independent princelings, as was the case in the Bay of Bengal and the Molucca Sea, where one fortunate Dutchman found he was able to cavort "with as many women as he pleaseth," singing and dancing "all day long, near-hand naked" while completely inebriated.[76]

In 1571, the foundation of Manila by the Spanish changed the rhythm of global trade; for a start it followed a programme of colonisation whose character was markedly less destructive for the local population than had been the case after the first Atlantic crossings.[77] Originally established as a base from which to acquire spices, the settlement quickly became a major metropolis and an important connection point between Asia and the Americas. Goods now began to move across the Pacific without passing through Europe first, as did the silver to pay for them. Manila became an emporium where a rich array of goods could be bought. Many different kinds of silk could be acquired there, according to one highly placed official in the city around 1600, as could velvets, satins, damasks and other textiles. And so too could "many bed ornaments, hangings, coverlets and tapestries," as well as tablecloths, cushions and carpets, metal basins, copper kettles and cast-iron pots. Tin, lead, saltpetre and gunpowder from China were also available—alongside "preserves made of orange, peach, pear, nutmeg and ginger," chestnuts, walnuts, horses, geese that resembled swans, talking birds and many other rarities. Had I tried to list everything for sale, continued the author, "I would never finish, nor have sufficient paper for it."[78] Manila was, in the words of one modern commentator, "the world's first global city."[79]

This naturally had important implications for other trade routes. It was no coincidence that there was a chronic contraction in the Ottoman Empire not long after the route via Manila had been established. While this owed something to domestic fiscal pressures and overspending on expensive military campaigns against the Habsburgs and Persia, the emergence of a new major crossroads for trans-continental commercial exchange thousands of miles away was also a factor in the Ottoman Empire's declining revenues.[80] The amount of silver heading from the Americas through the Philippines and on into the rest of Asia was staggering: at least as much passed this way as it did through Europe in the late sixteenth and early seventeenth centuries, causing alarm in some quarters in Spain as remittances from the New World to Europe began to fall.[81]

The silver road was strung round the world like a belt. The precious metal ended up in one place in particular: China. It did so for two reasons. First, China's size and sophistication made it a major producer of luxury goods, including the ceramics and porcelain that were so desirable in Europe that a huge counterfeit market quickly grew up. The Chinese, wrote Matteo Ricci while visiting Nanjing, "are greatly given to forging antique things, with great artifice and ingenuity," and generating large profits thanks to their skill.[82] In China, books were written advising on how to spot fakes, with Liu Dong explaining how to authenticate Xuande bronzework or Yongle porcelain.[83]

China was able to supply the export market in volume and to step up production accordingly. Dehua in Fujian province, for example, became a centre dedicated to making porcelain to suit European tastes. Silk manufacture likewise received investment so that western appetites could be catered for. This was shrewd business practice, and helped the receipts of the Ming authorities to rise sharply, with some scholars asserting that they multiplied no less than four times between 1600 and 1643.[84]

The second reason why so much money flowed into China was an imbalance in the relationship between precious metals. In China, silver's value hovered around an approximate ratio to gold of 6:1, significantly higher than in India, Persia or the Ottoman Empire; its value was almost double its pricing in Europe in the early sixteenth century. In practice, this meant that European money bought more in Chinese markets and from Chinese traders than it did elsewhere—which in turn provided a powerful incentive to buy Chinese. The opportunities for currency trading and taking advantage of these imbalances in what modern bankers call arbitrage were grasped immediately by new arrivals to the Far East—especially those who recognised that the unequal value of gold in China and Japan produced easy profits. Traders scrambled to buy and sell currencies and precious metals. Merchants operating out of Macau took cargoes of carefully chosen goods to Japan, according to one eyewitness, but were interested only in trading it for silver.[85] Some could scarcely hide their excitement at the opportunity. The value of silver in relation to gold was so high that it made the latter amazingly cheap, noted Pedro Baeza; "a profit of 75 to 70 per cent would be made," he wrote, if one precious metal exchanged for another in the east was brought to the Spanish territories in the Americas or back to Spain itself.[86]

The effects of the inflows of silver into China are complex and difficult to assess fully. Nevertheless, the flow of precious metal from the Americas had an obvious effect on Chinese culture, the arts and learning in the sixteenth and seventeenth centuries. Painters like Shen Zhou and the others who formed the Four Masters (the great contemporary artists of the Ming dynasty) obtained patronage and financial reward for their work. Artists such as Lu Zhi found demand for their talents in private commissions from a growing middle class who were interested in developing their pastimes and pleasures.[87]

This was an age of experimentation and discovery, with texts like the *Jin Ping Mei*, an erotic novel often known as "The Golden Lotus" after one of its leading characters, challenging attitudes not only to literary forms but to sex itself.[88] New wealth helped to sustain scholars like Song Yingxing, who produced an encyclopaedia covering topics from snorkelling to the use of hydraulics in irrigation, and whose work was highly regarded and widely appreciated.[89] The rising interest in Confucianism, and the esteem in which specialists like Wang Yangming were held, bears witness to the desire for explanations and solutions in a period of considerable change.[90]

Maps like the Selden map, recently rediscovered in the Bodleian Library in Oxford, likewise demonstrate the increasing Chinese interest in trade and travel in this period, offering an extensive overview of South-East Asia, complete with shipping routes. However, these are something of an exception: in this period, as before, Chinese maps typically retained a cloistered view of the world, with visual representations bounded to the north by the Great Wall and to the east by the sea. This was symptomatic of China's readiness to play a passive role at a time when the world was opening up; but it also reflected European naval superiority in East Asia where Dutch, Spanish and Portuguese vessels targeted each other—but also regularly seized Chinese junks and their cargoes too.[91] China was not keen to take part in running battles between aggressive rivals, let alone to be made to suffer as a result; in the circumstances, the inclination to become increasingly introspective, but at the same time reap the benefit of traders coming to them, seemed entirely logical.

Much of the silver that flooded into China was spent in a series of major reforms, not the least of which were the monetisation of the economy, the encouragement of free labour markets and a deliberate programme to stimulate foreign trade. Ironically, China's love of silver and the premium it placed on this particular precious metal became its Achilles heel. With such great quantities of silver reaching China, above all through Manila, it was inevitable that its value would start to fall, which over time caused price inflation. The net result was that the value of silver, and above all its value in relation to gold, was forced into line with other regions and continents. Unlike India, where the impact of the opening up of the world produced new wonders of the world, in China it was to lead to a serious economic and political crisis in the seventeenth century.[92] Globalisation was no less problematic five centuries ago than it is today.

As Adam Smith later noted in his famous book on the wealth of nations, "the discovery of America and that of a passage to the East Indies by the Cape of Good Hope, are the greatest and most important events recorded in the history of mankind."[93] The world was indeed transformed by the roads of gold and silver that opened up following Columbus' first expedition and Vasco da Gama's successful journey home from India. What Adam Smith did not say in 1776, however, is how England fitted into the equation. For if the century that followed the discoveries of the 1490s belonged to Spain and Portugal, with the fruits showered on the empires of the east, then the next 200 years would belong to countries in the north of Europe. Against all expectations, the world's centre of gravity was about to move again. This time it would belong to a Britain that was about to become Great.

13

The Road to Northern Europe

The world was transformed by the discoveries of the 1490s. No longer on the sidelines of global affairs, Europe was becoming the world's engine. Decisions made in Madrid and Lisbon now echoed and reverberated thousands of miles away, as once they had done from ʿAbbāsid Baghdad, from Luoyang in Tang dynasty China, from the Mongol capital at Karakorum or from Timur's Samarkand. All roads now led to Europe.

This left some deeply frustrated. None were more bitter than the English. It was bad enough that the treasuries of England's rivals multiplied overnight; what made it worse was the triumphal and tiring story that the gold and silver raining down on the Spanish crown was part of God's design. This was particularly painful following England's break with Rome. "How great is the power that the Divine Majesty has placed in the hands of the kings of Spain," wrote one Jesuit priest in the sixteenth century; Spain's wealth has been "ordained by the Lord on high, who both gives and takes away kingdoms from whomever and in whatsoever way he wishes."[1]

The message was that Protestant rulers should expect punishment for abandoning the true faith. With the Reformation in full swing, violence and oppression erupted across Europe between Catholics and Protestants. Rumours swirled of imminent military action against England, especially after the false dawn had passed following the death of Mary I, under whom it had seemed that the country would revert to adherence to Rome and accept papal authority. When her half-sister, Elizabeth I, took the throne in 1558, she had to walk a precarious tightrope between the competing religious demands of a vocal and powerful lobby group on the one hand and insurrection by those who were disaffected, sidelined or victimised in the atmosphere of intolerance on the other. Being all things to all men was made no easier by England's relative isolation on the fringes of Europe. By the time that Pope Pius V issued a bull in 1570 entitled *Regnans in Excelsis*, declaring Elizabeth to be "the pretended Queen of England and the servant of crime" and threatening to excommunicate any of her subjects who obeyed her laws, thoughts were turning to how to fight off an expected invasion when—rather than if—it came.[2]

Heavy investment was made in the Royal Navy to create a formidable and effective first line of defence. State-of-the-art dockyards were built, such as at Deptford and Woolwich on the Thames, where warships were designed and maintained with ever increasing efficiency, which in turn helped revolutionise the construction of commercial vessels. Ships that could hold more cargo, travel faster, stay out at sea longer and carry more crew and more powerful cannon began to be built.[3]

The doyen of shipwrights was Matthew Baker, himself the son of a master builder. He adopted mathematical and geometric principles—set out in a seminal text entitled "Fragments of Ancient English Shipwrightry"—to create a new generation of ships for Queen Elizabeth.[4] These designs were quickly adopted for commercial use, with the result that the number of English ships weighing a hundred tons or more almost tripled in the two decades after 1560. The new generation of vessels quickly gained a reputation for their speed, for handling well and for the formidable threat they presented when encountered at sea.[5]

The fruits of the build-up of England's naval forces became apparent when Spain attempted to send a huge fleet to pick up troops from the Netherlands in the summer of 1588 for a full-blown invasion of England. Outmanoeuvred and outduelled by the English, the surviving members of the Spanish Armada returned home in shame. Although most of the ships that were lost foundered on reefs and in unusually severe storms rather than at the hands of the English, few doubted that the naval investment had paid off handsomely.[6]

The capture four years later of the *Madre de Deus*, a Portuguese caravel, off the Azores as it returned from the East Indies laden with pepper, cloves, nutmeg, ebony, tapestries, silks, textiles, pearls and precious metal, made the point about seapower even more emphatically. The haul from this single ship, which was towed into Dartmouth harbour on the south coast, was reckoned to be worth half of England's regular annual imports. Its seizure prompted agonised discussions about how the booty should be shared out between the crown and those responsible for the success—something that was not made easier when high-value portable items quickly went missing.[7]

Successes like these were good for confidence and encouraged increasingly disruptive behaviour in the Atlantic and elsewhere. England began to build ties with anyone who was an enemy of Catholic rulers in Europe. In the 1590s, for example, Queen Elizabeth made a point of releasing Muslims from North Africa who had been serving as "gally-slaves" on captured Spanish ships, providing them with clothes, money "and other necessities," before sending them home safely.[8] The English, moreover, had support from the Muslims of North Africa in an attack on Cádiz in 1596—an incident that is referred to at the very start of Shakespeare's *Merchant of Venice*. Such was the alignment of interests in this period that one modern commentator talks of the English and the Moors participating in a "jihad" against Catholic Spain.[9]

As a result of England's attempt to challenge the new Spanish and Portuguese routes to the Americas and to Asia, considerable effort was devoted to forging close relations with the Ottoman Turks. At a time when most of Europe looked on with horror as Turkish forces were all but knocking on the gates of Vienna, the English backed a different horse. They were conspicuous by their absence when other Christian states assembled to form a "Holy League," a coalition that gathered to attack the Ottoman fleet at Lepanto in the Gulf of Corinth in 1571. The victory of the Holy League prompted scenes of jubilation across Europe, where poetry, music, art and monuments were created to commemorate the triumph. In England, it was met with silence.[10]

Even after this, the Sultan in Constantinople was assiduously courted with warm letters of friendship and the dispatch of gifts from the court of Queen Elizabeth—with the result that "sincere greetings and abundant salutations, rose perfumed, which emanate from pure mutual confidence and the abundance of amity" were sent back to London.[11] Among the presents dispatched from England was an organ, designed by Thomas Dallam and shipped to Constantinople in 1599. Dallam was horrified when, due to heat and humidity, "all glewinge failed," and the pipes were damaged in transit. The English ambassador took one look "and sayde that it was not worthe iid [tuppence]." The organ was resurrected after Dallam had battled round the clock to mend the damage—and impressed the Sultan, Mehmet III, so much when he played it for him that he was showered with gold and offered "tow wyfes, either tow of his Concubines or els tow virgins of the beste I could Chuse."[12]

Elizabeth's approaches to the Sultan were underpinned by the prospect of opportunities that had opened up following the Turkish advance into Europe. The Pope had long been urging Christian rulers to rally to prevent further losses, warning gravely that "if Hungary is conquered, Germany will be next, and if Dalmatia and Illyria are overrun, Italy will be invaded."[13] With England resolutely ploughing its own furrow, developing good relations with Constantinople seemed sensible foreign policy—as well as offering the prospect of developing commercial links.

In this respect, it is striking that a formal trade agreement was made which gave English merchants in the Ottoman Empire privileges more generous than those accorded to any other nation.[14] No less striking was the common language that was used in communication between Protestants and Muslims. It was no coincidence, for example, that Queen Elizabeth wrote to the Ottoman Sultan that she herself was "by the grace of the most mightie God . . . the most invincible and most mightie defender of the Christian faith against all kinde of idolatries, of all that live among the Christians, and falslie professe the name of Christ."[15] Ottoman rulers were equally alert to the opportunities to reach out to those who had split from the Catholic church, underlining similarities in how they too interpreted their faith—especially when it came to visual images: among the many errors of "the faithless one they call the Pope," wrote Sultan Murad to "members of the Lutheran sect in Flanders and Spain," was that he encouraged the worship of idols. It was much to their credit that the followers of Martin Luther, one of the architects of the Reformation, had "banished the idols and portraits and bells from churches."[16] Against all the odds, England's Protestantism looked as if it could help open doors rather than close them.[17]

Positive views of the Ottomans and of the Muslim world spread into mainstream culture in England. "Mislike me not for my complexion," says the Prince of Morocco to Portia in Shakespeare's *Merchant of Venice*, when attempting to win her hand in marriage. The king was a man, the audience was informed, who had fought bravely for the Sultan on many occasions and was a fine match for the heiress (who stands as a cipher for Queen Elizabeth herself)—and a man who was shrewd enough to realise that "all that glisters is not gold." Or there is *Othello*, where the tragic nobility of the protagonist, a "Moor" (and therefore presumably a Muslim) in Venetian service, contrasts sharply with the double standards, hypocrisy and deceit of the Christians around him. "The Moor is of a constant, loving, noble nature," the audience is told at one point—a reference to the belief that Muslims could be considered trustworthy and resolute when it came to making promises, and were therefore reliable allies.[18] Indeed, the Elizabethan era saw the emergence of Persia too as a common, and positive, cultural reference point in English literature.[19]

Coupled with positive portrayals of Muslims and their realms in England were scathing attitudes towards the Spanish. The publication of Bartolomé de las Casas' account of the conquest of the New World was therefore a godsend, especially in the context of the revolution pioneered by Johannes Gutenberg a hundred years earlier which had enabled texts to be printed in quantities that would previously have been considered unimaginable.[20] This allowed accounts like that of de las Casas, a Dominican friar, to be disseminated quickly and relatively cheaply. As with the technological advances in the early twenty-first century, it was the sudden increase in speed in the sharing of information that made the difference.

The account of de las Casas was important because the priest had grown increasingly disillusioned by the suffering of the native populations in the Americas, which he witnessed at first hand. The text, setting out the atrocities in gruesome detail, was seized upon in England, where it was translated as *A Short Account of the Destruction of the Indies* (*Brevisima relación de la destrucción de las Indias*). Widely circulated in the 1580s either in full or abridged to include the most damning passages, it presented an unequivocal portrait of the Spanish as mass murderers and of Spain as a cruel, bloodthirsty realm. The translator of the text, James Aligrodo, wrote in his introduction that "12. 15. or 20. millions of poore reasonable creatures' had been slaughtered.[21]

Stories spread quickly through Protestant Europe, noting the Spaniards' grisly treatment of those whom they believed to be their inferiors. The analogy was obvious: the Spanish were natural-born oppressors who behaved towards others with ominous cruelty; given the chance, they would persecute those closer to home in just the same way.[22] It was a conclusion that struck fear into the people of the Low Countries, which were locked in an increasingly vicious struggle with Spain in the late sixteenth century as the latter sought to assert its authority in regions where the Reformation had attracted strong support. Richard Hakluyt, the famous chronicler and advocate of British settlement in the Americas, described how Spain "governs in the Indies with all pride and tyranny," and casts innocents into slavery, who mournfully "cry with one voice," begging for freedom.[23] This was the Spanish model of empire, in other words, one of intolerance, violence and persecution. England, of course, would never behave in so shameful a manner.[24]

That was the theory. In fact, attitudes to slavery and violence were more ambiguous than such high-minded promises suggest. In the 1560s, English sailors repeatedly tried to take a share of the lucrative slave trade in West Africa, with Sir John Hawkins using investment from Queen Elizabeth herself to help generate healthy profits shipping men across the Atlantic. Having concluded that "Negroes were very good merchandise in Hispaniola and that store of Negroes might easily be had upon the coast of Guinea," Hawkins and his backers were more than willing to get in on the action. Far from refusing to deal with Spanish "tyrants" in the New World, those at the highest levels of English society did rather well out of them.[25]

Ultimately, England's posturing was framed by a keen awareness that it was in a weak position to exploit the astonishing opportunities that had been created by the great changes of the early sixteenth century. Religious dispute and unfortunate timing had turned the country into the sworn enemy of the rising global power that Spain had become, leaving it poorly placed to benefit from the flood of riches coming from the Americas or from the trade flowing into Venice through the Red Sea and the land routes from the east. Criticism of the Spanish was all very well, but it did little to hide the fact that the English were scavengers, grateful for whatever crumbs came their way. England was "swarminge at this day with valiant youths," noted the writer Richard Hakluyt, and thanks to a chronic "lack of employment" was suffering from a woeful economic position. Would it not be wonderful, he asked, to put young men to work to create a navy capable of making "this realm . . . lords of all those seas [of the world]"?[26] Talk of ruling the waves was ambitious; but there was nothing wrong with dreaming.

The English did not sit still while southern Europe boomed. Expeditions were dispatched in all directions to try to open up trade routes and build new networks of trade, transportation and communication. Few delivered encouraging results. Missions led by Martin Frobisher to explore the North-West Passage in the 1570s returned home without finding a hoped-for route to Asia—which was bad enough; what made them positively embarrassing was that the large quantities of gold brought back from what is now Canada and trumpeted as discoveries to rival those made elsewhere in the Americas turned out to be nothing of the sort. The glittering metal was marcasite, or white iron pyrite—fool's gold.[27]

There were other disasters. Attempts to reach China through the Barents Sea ended in tragedy. Sir Hugh Willoughby and his men found their vessel trapped by ice near Murmansk as winter set in. All froze to death, their bodies discovered the following year. According to the Venetian ambassador to London, they were frozen solid "in various postures, like statues," some "seated in the act of writing, pen still in hand and spoon in mouth; others opening a locker."[28]

Further efforts to establish trade links with Russia in order to access goods from the east were hampered first by the fact that the English arrived at the moment that Ivan IV was at his most terrible, and second by the limitations of Russian commerce in Asia in the sixteenth century. Although this was about to expand dramatically, routes through to the Caspian and beyond were still too insecure for merchants to pass safely; even heavily guarded caravans were liable to be picked off by bandits.[29]

Merchants were also sent to Persia on several occasions in the 1560s, in a rather desperate bid to establish commercial links there. Usually carrying documents from Queen Elizabeth promising friendship and alliance, the envoys requested privileges from the Shah "upon an honest intent, to establish trade of merchandise with your subjects, and with other strangers trafficking in your realms."[30] So anxious were the English to gain concessions that traders were under strict instructions not to talk about religion after being wrongfooted in their responses when challenged about the relative virtues of Islam and Christianity by their devout Muslim hosts. If anyone asks about the state of faith at home in future, travellers were advised, it was better "to passe over it in silence, without any declaration of it."[31] In Europe, religious posturing counted for everything as Catholics and Protestants fought ferociously with each other; beyond, it could be conveniently left to one side.

By the start of the seventeenth century, there was little to show for the attempts to emulate the success of the Spanish and the Portuguese. New trading entities had been set up to try to raise money from private funds, starting with the Company of Merchant Adventurers for the Discovery of Regions, Dominions, Islands and Places Unknown, founded in 1551. A cluster of new and separate companies with different geographic ambitions mushroomed around it. The Spanish Company, the Eastland Company, the Levant Company, the Russia Company, the Turkey Company and the East India Company were founded with royal charters that granted monopolies on commerce within a designated region or country on the basis that business overseas was risky and required substantial investment. As such, incentivising merchants by protecting future success was an innovative way of trying to build up England's trade—and with it, extending the country's political tentacles.

Despite their impressive-sounding names, royal endorsements and high hopes, the results were meagre to start with. England remained firmly on the periphery of world affairs, while Spain's position seemed to grow stronger and stronger. Precious metals gathered over centuries by the Aztecs, the Incas and others were gathered up and dispatched to Spain over the course of a few decades, along with the riches of mines that had either not previously been discovered or had been poorly exploited—such as at Potosí, which was said to produce a million pesos per year for the Spanish crown alone.[32]

Huge though Spain's finds were, however, there was only so much treasure that could be squeezed from the New World. Resources were, after all, finite—as were those oyster beds off the coast of Venezuela that were devastated following the fishing of tens of billions of oysters in just thirty years in the early sixteenth century.[33] Nevertheless, the Spanish treated the windfall as a bottomless pit, using the new-found wealth to fund a litany of grandiose schemes such as the building of the enormous palace at El Escorial, as well as financing never-ending military action against rivals all over Europe. There was a strong sense within the Spanish court that it was necessary to act as the Almighty's policeman, delivering his will on earth—by force if necessary. Spain found it all but impossible to resist military confrontation with Protestants and Muslims alike. It was a new chapter for holy war.

As the earlier Crusades had shown, holy warfare's appetite for men and money could be ruinously expensive for royal treasuries. The situation was not helped by the willingness of the Spanish crown to use debt to finance its projects, which encouraged short-term and ambitious decisions while hiding consequences that would only become clear later—especially when things went wrong. Fiscal mismanagement and incompetence were part of the picture; but ultimately Spain's inability to control military spending proved catastrophic. Incredibly, it became a serial defaulter on its debts in the second half of the sixteenth century, failing to meet its obligations no fewer than four times.[34] It was like a lottery winner that had gone from rags to riches—only to squander the prize money on luxuries that were unaffordable.

The effects of the flood of riches were felt elsewhere. As it was, there had been a price revolution across Europe as inflation took hold thanks to the money flow from the Americas, which naturally led to more and more consumers chasing a finite quantity of goods. Growing urbanisation exacerbated the problem, driving prices higher still. In Spain, the price of grain alone quintupled in the century after Columbus' discoveries.[35]

Things eventually snapped in the provinces and towns of the Low Countries, which formed part of the Spanish demesne, where anger was fanned by the way that Spain sought to solve its financial woes through heavy taxation. Northern Europe was a hive of productive urban centres, with Antwerp, Bruges, Ghent and Amsterdam emerging in the fourteenth and fifteenth centuries as important emporia for goods to and from the Mediterranean, Scandinavia, the Baltics and Russia, as well as the British Isles. Naturally, they blossomed further still following the opening up of trade from India and the Americas.[36]

These cities became magnets for merchants from far and wide, which in turn made for vibrant social and economic life and for strong civic identities. The growing populations required surrounding land to be used efficiently, prompting rapid advances not only in yield management of crops in the surrounding territory but also in irrigation techniques, such as the construction of dykes and sea walls to allow every piece of available land to be used profitably. The burgeoning size and productivity of the cities of the Low Countries and their hinterlands made them lucrative honey pots—centres which generated tax revenues, something not lost on the Spanish rulers who by luck of dynastic marriage and inheritance controlled most of this region.[37]

It was not long before individual provinces and cities were howling in dismay at the introduction of punitively high levels of taxation, coupled with brutally heavy-handed attitudes on matters of faith. The ideas of

Martin Luther, John Calvin and others who emphasised the institutional corruption of distant political rulers and the spiritual importance of the individual fell on fertile ground in these heavily urbanised areas and helped Protestantism embed deep roots in the region. Economic and religious persecution proved a powerful cocktail for fomenting revolt and eventually led to the Union of Utrecht of 1581—a declaration of independence by what became the Union of Seven Provinces, effectively the Dutch Republic. The Spanish responded with a show of force, together with an embargo on trade across the Low Countries that began in 1585. The aim was to starve the rebel provinces and cities of oxygen and force them into submission. As is so often the case when sanctions are put in place, the result was the opposite: faced with little alternative, the separatists went on the offensive. The only way to survive was to use every ounce of knowledge, skill and expertise they had to their advantage; it was time to turn the tables.[38]

In the last years of the sixteenth century, circumstances came together to provide the context for a miracle in the Low Countries. Spain's attempt to suppress the region caused large-scale emigration, as the population migrated north from the southern provinces, causing cities like Ghent, Bruges and Antwerp to suffer what one scholar has called "a catastrophic haemorrhage of inhabitants." The timing was fortuitous. The trade ban ensured that there were huge stockpiles of grain and herring, which meant that food supplies were both plentiful and cheap. Although rents rose quickly, the swelling of the population also produced a boom in house construction, and brought together an effective group of experienced merchants and other professionals who were trying to escape the pressure exerted by the Spanish.[39]

When the blockade was finally lifted in 1590, the Dutch moved quickly to clear out Spanish troops who had been sent to maintain order, taking advantage of the fact that Philip II of Spain had become embroiled in military conflict elsewhere in Europe. Suddenly free from military pressure and with a window of opportunity presenting itself, the Dutch threw themselves into international trade, seeking to build connections with the Americas, Africa and Asia.

There was a clear commercial logic to the plan of establishing their own trade routes. Bringing goods direct to the Dutch Republic would avoid two rounds of taxation: first, goods would arrive without having had duties creamed off in ports in Portugal and Spain where cargoes were typically taxed before being sent north. Second, the fact that the Dutch authorities would now collect the revenues themselves, rather than pass them back to the Iberian masters, meant that the money produced from the thriving commerce in the Low Countries would not leech out to fund imperial ambitions and reckless spending elsewhere. This would bring immediate benefits and create a virtuous circle as greater profits could be reinvested, generating even stronger cash flows—both for individual merchants and for the fledgling republic.[40]

The ambitious programme paid dividends from the outset. An expedition that set out for the east in 1597 returned home the following year in triumph, carrying cargoes that produced profits of 400 per cent. Fleets now began to fan out in all directions, funded by investors emboldened by such strong returns on their capital.[41] In 1601 alone, fourteen separate expeditions set sail for Asia, while as many as a hundred vessels a year were soon crossing the Atlantic to acquire salt from the Araya peninsula, which was vital for the domestic herring trade.[42]

The Spanish were outraged; they renewed their military action and imposed another blockade. According to the brilliant philosopher and lawyer Hugo Grotius, this simply reinforced the point that the Dutch had to take their destiny into their own hands. Rather than step back in the face of threats and pressure, the only choice was to invest yet more in commercial ventures and build a trade network as quickly as possible to help build up firepower and reinforce independence. It was a question of all or nothing.[43]

Key to Dutch success was superb shipbuilding, and above all innovations in the classic designs that had long enabled herring fleets to operate successfully in the North Sea and in shallow harbours thanks to their low draughts. From the 1550s, as the English built quicker and stronger warships, the Dutch focused their efforts on developing vessels that handled even better, could carry more cargo, required fewer crew to operate—and were therefore cheaper to run. These ships, called *fluyts*, set a new benchmark for commercial shipping.[44]

The Dutch did their homework and were well prepared when they set sail. While their European predecessors who had crossed the Atlantic and rounded the Cape of Good Hope were journeying into the unknown, the Dutch were not. They knew what they were looking for and where to find it. Authors like Jan Huyghen van Linschoten, secretary to the archbishop of Goa, who spent his time thoroughly researching trade routes, harbours, markets and local conditions across Asia, produced texts such as the *Itinerario*, which provided comprehensive blueprints that served almost as instruction manuals for those setting out for the east.[45]

Other works were also useful in preparing traders for their travels. The Dutch were world leaders when it came to cartography. Maps and sea charts prepared by the engraver Lucas Janszoon Waghenaer in the 1580s were considered indispensable throughout Europe thanks to their detail and accuracy. Attention was paid to collecting precise information and producing updated, detailed atlases of the East Indies as well as of the Caribbean; these set the standard for modern navigational aids in the early seventeenth century.[46]

Then there were texts that helped explain the vocabulary and grammar of the strange languages that Dutch traders could expect to encounter on their travels. One of the earliest of these new linguists was Fredrik de Houtman, whose Dutch–Malay dictionary and grammar was published in 1603 following his release from prison in Aceh by the Sultan of Sumatra, where he had diligently learnt the language of his captors.[47] Such vocabulary lists were avidly studied by merchants heading to Asia in the sixteenth century; they set out useful words and phrases translated from Dutch into Malayalam, Malay, Bisayan, Tagalog, Tamil and other languages.[48]

The underlying secret to Dutch success in the seventeenth century was common sense and hard work. The Dutch reckoned that the way to work was not to follow the example of England, where the chartered companies used sharp practices to limit beneficiaries to a small circle of intimates, all looking after each other's interests and using monopolistic practices to protect their positions. Instead, capital was pooled and risks shared among as wide a body of investors as possible. In due course, the conclusion was reached that despite competing ambitions and rivalries between provinces, cities and indeed individual merchants, the most efficient and powerful way to build up trade was by combining resources.[49]

In 1602, therefore, the government of the United Provinces created a single entity to conduct trade with Asia on the principle that this would be stronger and more powerful than the sum of its parts. It was a bold move, not least since it involved soothing local rivalries and convincing all involved that interests would not only be aligned but be better served this way. The creation of the Verenigde Oost-Indische Compagnie (VOC)—the East Indies Company—and not long afterwards the sister corporation for the Americas, the West-Indische Compagnie (WIC)—the West Indies

Company—was a textbook example of how to set up a world-class multinational corporation.[50]

The Dutch model proved astonishingly successful. Although some, like the merchant and founder of the WIC, Willem Usselincx, argued that the best idea was to colonise parts of the Americas that were yet to be settled, a clear plan took shape.[51] The aim was not to try to compete with other European merchants such as in Goa where Portuguese, Venetian and German traders lived side by side; it was to displace them.[52]

The aggressive approach paid off immediately. Attention turned first to the Spice Islands, where the isolated Portuguese community was expelled in 1605 as part of a systematic programme to establish control over the East Indies. Over the following decades, the Dutch kept consolidating their position, establishing a permanent headquarters in Batavia—the name a nod to the appellation given to the inhabitants of the Low Countries during the time of the Roman Empire—in what is now Jakarta.

Military force was used to take and secure a chain of points linking back to the motherland. Although the Dutch were frustrated in a few locations, such as Macau and Goa, the gains that were made in the seventeenth century were impressive indeed. Soon, it was not just the Europeans abroad who were beleaguered by the Dutch, but local rulers too whose realms were strategically sensitive or economically important. Control was established over Malacca, Colombo, Ceylon and Cochin, before the sultanate of Macassar (in modern Indonesia) was targeted in 1669. Macassar was the missing piece necessary in establishing a monopoly over the spice trade with Asia. Renamed New Rotterdam, its capture was followed by the construction of a major fort, as had been the case elsewhere—a statement of intent that such gains were not going to be surrendered lightly.[53] A map held in the state archives in The Hague depicts the veritable spider's web that was spun as the Dutch built up their position in the East Indies.[54]

The same pattern was followed elsewhere. Rivals were pushed out of West Africa as the Dutch succeeded in dominating the gold trade, and in due course became heavily involved in slave trafficking to the Americas. New strongholds were founded, such as Fort Nassau in modern Ghana. The Portuguese were pushed out of other bases, such as Elmina, on the Ghanaian coast, which passed into Dutch hands in the middle of the seventeenth century. There was considerable success in the Caribbean and the Americas too, to the point that by the 1640s the Dutch had gained a major share of trans-Atlantic shipping, and controlled the sugar trade outright.[55]

The Low Countries were transformed. Fortunes were made for those who had invested in long-distance trade early on, while those who were beneficiaries of the new rich did well too. Universities were founded at Leiden and Groningen where scholars could push the boundaries of academic disciplines thanks to the funding of generous patrons. Artists and architects flourished, revelling in the sudden interest and wealth of a freshly minted bourgeoisie. In times of extraordinary affluence, magnificent buildings started to go up in Amsterdam, which rose from the water as Venice had done centuries earlier. Areas like the Jordaan were reclaimed from the sea as canal houses went up on the Keizersgracht and near by that were feats of engineering as well as architectural wonders.

The influence of the Silk Roads began to be felt in the arts. A thriving ceramics industry blossomed in Haarlem, Amsterdam and above all in Delft, heavily influenced by the look, feel and design of items imported from the east. Chinese visual themes dominated, while the characteristic blue and white wares developed centuries earlier by potters in the Persian Gulf, which had become popular in China and in the Ottoman Empire, were adopted so widely that they became the distinctive feature of Dutch ceramics as well. Imitation was not only the sincerest form of flattery; in this case, it was also part of joining a global system of material culture that now linked the North Sea with the Indian Ocean and the Pacific.[56]

With demand increasing for objects that helped show status, the arts in general in the Netherlands flourished. Some have suggested that 3 million paintings were produced in the seventeenth century alone.[57] It was inevitable that this would stimulate new ideas and also raise standards, providing a context for painters like Frans Hals, Rembrandt and Vermeer to create works of breathtaking beauty. Given the remarkable way that the Dutch had worked together to enjoy success, it was entirely appropriate that some of the most beautiful works recorded groups, such as *The Banquet of the Guard of St. Adrian* (the Civic Guard of Haarlem) by Frans Hals, or Rembrandt's famous work *The Company of Captain Frans Banning Cocq and Lieutenant Willem van Ruytenburch Preparing to March Out*—more usually referred to as *The Night Watch*, which was commissioned for the Banqueting Hall of the Civic Guard of Amsterdam.

Individuals were eager patrons too, with the merchant Andries Bicker for example hiring Bartholomeus van der Heist to commemorate his success and newly elevated social status, or the shipbuilder Jan Rijcksen asking Rembrandt to paint a portrait of him and his wife working together on nautical designs. It was the turn of the Dutch—and of Dutch art—to experience a golden age.[58]

The Dutch were keen to show off their homeware, as in the case of Vermeer's *Young Girl Reading a Letter at an Open Window*, where a blue and white bowl features prominently in the foreground.[59] An English visitor to Amsterdam in 1640 could not hide how impressed he was by what he saw. In the Low Countries, wrote Peter Mundy, even houses of "indifferent quality" were filled with furniture and ornaments "very Costly and Curious, Full of pleasure and home contentment, as Ritche Cupboards, Cabinetts . . . Imagery, porcelain, Costly Fine cages with birds" and more besides. Even butchers and bakers, blacksmiths and cobblers had paintings and luxury trinkets in their homes.[60] "I was amazed," wrote the English diarist John Evelyn about the annual fair in Rotterdam at around the same time; it was flooded with paintings, especially with "landscapes and drolleries, as they call those clownish representations." Even common farmers had become avid art collectors.[61] These attitudes were typical of the growing numbers of English visitors to the Low Countries in this period.[62]

The Dutch Golden Age was the result of a finely executed plan. It also had the benefit of being well timed, coming at a time when much of Europe was in disarray, engaged in endless rounds of costly and inconclusive military hostility which engulfed the continent during the Thirty Years' War of 1618–48. This volatility presented opportunities, for the attention and resources that were diverted into arenas closer to home allowed the Dutch to pick off their targets on different continents one by one without facing retribution. The bloody fighting in the seventeenth century enabled the Dutch to establish a dominant position in the east at the expense of their rivals in Europe.

European warfare, however, had an even more important role: it prompted the rise of the west. Discussions about Europe in this period emphasise that the Enlightenment and the Age of Reason saw a coming of age where ideas of absolutism were replaced by notions of freedom, rights and liberty. But it was Europe's entrenched relationship with violence and militarism that allowed it to place itself at the centre of the world after the great expeditions of the 1490s.

Even before the near-simultaneous discoveries of Columbus and Vasco da Gama, competition between kingdoms in Europe had been intense. For centuries, the continent had been characterised by fierce rivalry between states that frequently erupted into open hostility and war. This in turn prompted advancements in military technology. New weapons were developed, introduced and then refined after being tested on the battlefield. Tactics evolved as commanders learnt from experience. The concept of violence was institutionalised too: European art and literature had long celebrated the life of the chivalrous knight and his capacity to use force judiciously—as an act of love and of faith, but also as an expression of justice. Stories about the Crusades, which praised nobility and heroism and hid treachery, betrayal and the breaking of sworn oaths, became intoxicatingly powerful.

Fighting, violence and bloodshed were glorified, as long as they could be considered just. This was one reason, perhaps, why religion became so important: there could be no better justification of war than its being in defence of the Almighty. From the outset, the fusion of religion and expansion were closely bound together: even the sails of Columbus' ships were marked by large crosses. As contemporary commentators constantly stressed, in regard to the Americas, but also as Europeans began to fan out over Africa, India and other parts of Asia, and then Australia as well, it was all part of God's plan for the west to inherit the earth.

In fact, Europe's distinctive character as more aggressive, more unstable and less peace-minded than other parts of the world now paid off. After all, this was why the great vessels of the Spanish and the Portuguese had proved successful in crossing the oceans and connecting continents together. The traditionally built craft that had sailed across the Indian and Arabian seas for centuries with little change to their design were no match for western vessels that could outmanoeuvre and outgun them at will. Continuous improvements in ship design that made them faster, stronger and more deadly widened the gulf ever further.[63]

The same was true of military technology. Such was the reliability and accuracy of arms used in the Americas that small numbers of conquistadors were able to dominate populations that were vastly superior numerically—and populations that were advanced and highly sophisticated, except when it came to weapons. In the Inca lands, wrote Pedro de Cieza de Léon, law and order were carefully maintained, with great care taken "to see that justice was meted out and that nobody ventured to commit a felony or theft."[64] Data was collected annually across the Inca Empire to make sure taxes were calculated correctly and fairly paid, with births and deaths recorded centrally and kept up to date. The elite had to work the land themselves for a set number of days each year and did so "to set an example, for everybody was to know that there should be nobody so rich that . . . he might disdain or affront the poor."[65]

These were not the savages described by triumphalists in Europe; in fact they seemed positively enlightened in comparison to the highly stratified societies that had emerged throughout most of the continent, where the gap between the powerful and the weak was cemented in an aristocratic patrimony that protected the social position of the powerful. Although Europeans might have thought they were discovering primitive civilisations and that this was why they could dominate them, the truth was that it was the relentless advances in weapons, warfare and tactics that laid the basis for the success of the west.

One reason why the domination of Africa, Asia and the Americas was possible was the centuries of European practice in building fortifications that were all but impregnable. Castle-building had been the staple of European society since the Middle Ages, with thousands of spectacular strongholds springing up across the continent. Their purpose, of course, was to withstand heavy and determined attack; their extraordinary number was testimony to the fear and regularity of assault. Europeans were world leaders in building fortresses and in storming them. It was striking how the European insistence on constructing imposing sites that could be secured from the inside was a source of bemusement to locals. No other traders had built forts in the past, noted the Nawab of Bengal in the 1700s, so why on earth did the Europeans insist on doing so now?[66]

The great irony, then, was that although Europe experienced a glorious Golden Age, producing flourishing art and literature and leaps of scientific endeavour, it was forged by violence. Not only that, but the discovery of new worlds served to make European society more unstable. With more to fight over and ever greater resources available, stakes were raised, sharpening tensions as the battle for supremacy intensified.

The centuries that followed the emergence of Europe as a global power were accompanied by relentless consolidation and covetousness. In 1500, there were around 500 political units in Europe; in 1900, there were twenty-five. The strong devoured the weak.[67] Competition and military conflict were endemic to Europe. In this sense, later horrors in the twentieth century had their roots in the deep past. The struggle to dominate neighbours and rivals spurred improvements in weapons technology, mechanisation and logistics, which ultimately allowed arenas of warfare to be expanded substantially and enabled the numbers killed to rise from the hundreds to the millions. In time, persecution could be perpetrated on a massive scale. It was not for nothing that world war and the worst genocide in history had their origins and execution in Europe; these were the latest chapters in a long-running story of brutality and violence.

Thus, while focus normally falls on the investment in art and the impact of new wealth on culture in the sixteenth and seventeenth centuries, it is perhaps more instructive to look to the parallel advances in weapon-making in this period. Just as paintings were produced in enormous quantities for a hungry audience, so too were guns. By the 1690s, some 600,000 flintlocks were being sold by the entrepreneur Maximilien Titon in central France alone; some contemporaries thought it was impossible even to estimate how many workers were employed in the handgun industry in Saint-Etienne because they were so numerous. Between 1600 and 1750, the rate of successful fire of handguns multiplied by a factor of ten. Technological advances—including the inventions of ramrods, paper cartridges and bayonets—made guns cheaper, better, quicker and more deadly.[68]

Similarly, although the names of scientists like Galileo Galilei, Isaac Newton and Leonhard Euler have become famous to generations of schoolchildren, it can be all too easy to forget that some of their most important work was on the trajectory of projectiles and understanding the causes of deviation to enable artillery to be more accurate.[69] These distinguished scientists helped make weapons more powerful and ever more reliable; military and technological advances went hand in hand with the Age of Enlightenment.

It was not that aggression did not exist in other societies. As numerous examples across other continents would show, any conquest could bring death and suffering on a large scale. But periods of explosive expansion across Asia and North Africa, such as in the extraordinary first decades of the spread of Islam or during the time of the Mongol conquests, were followed by long periods of stability, peace and prosperity. The frequency and rhythm of warfare was different in Europe to other parts of the world: no sooner would one conflict be resolved than another would flare up. Competition was brutal and relentless. In that sense, seminal works like Thomas Hobbes' *Leviathan* were quintessential texts that explained the rise of the west. Only a European author could have concluded that the natural state of man was to be in a constant state of violence; and only a European author would have been right.[70]

Moreover, the thirst for military confrontation lay behind other developments that were closely related to warfare, such as those in finance. Governments in Europe were hungry for capital to fund armies, leading to the establishment of debt markets where money could be raised against future tax revenues. Betting on success could produce handsome profits and unlock titles and other social benefits for canny investors whose investment in government debts could naturally be presented as patriotism: investing in state finances was a way of getting ahead, as well as becoming rich. London and Amsterdam became global centres of finance, specialising in sovereign debt, but also in increasingly complex stock-market listings.[71]

One reason for the rise to prominence of London and Amsterdam was the socio-economic acceleration of northern Europe. The latest research suggests that the population almost doubled in England and the Low Countries between 1500 and 1800. Most of this growth was felt in densely populated areas where the number of large towns rose by nearly three times.[72] The process was particularly acute in the Low Countries: in the middle of the seventeenth century, as many as half the residents of Amsterdam are thought to have moved to the city from elsewhere.[73] States with more urban centres had a considerable advantage over those with large rural populations. It was less time-consuming, easier and more efficient to gather taxes from cities, not least since the velocity of commercial exchange was so much greater than in the countryside. Densely populated areas also produced more reliable income streams and were less risky to lend to. England and the Dutch Republic could borrow more at better rates than their commercial and political competitors.[74] Then, as now, to make money in finance it was not enough to be smart; you had to be in the right place. And increasingly, that meant London or Amsterdam.

This marked the start of the death-knell for Italy and the Adriatic. Already on the back foot thanks to new routes to market which brought goods directly to the richest consumers, the city-states with their deeply entrenched rivalries stood no chance against clusters of towns able and willing to combine their resources. Such large sums were raised to fund expansion that it became standard to spend more than half of state revenues simply servicing national debts.[75] It was expensive to be locked in a constant fight against neighbours and constantly striving to gain a political, commercial and cultural edge over them. Europe became a continent running at two speeds: Old Europe in the east and the south which had dominated for centuries and which now sagged and stagnated; and New Europe, in the north-west, which boomed.[76]

Some saw the writing on the wall before others. As early as 1600, the British ambassador to Venice was able to write that "in the matter of trade, the decay is so manifest that all men conclude within twenty yeares space" the city would all but collapse. Venice had once dominated trade with the east, but was no longer able to compete. Scores of mighty ships "of above 1000 tun apeece" used to bring goods back home or head out to reload; now "not one is to be seene."[77] It was not long before the city began to reinvent itself, transforming from a commercial powerhouse to a centre of lascivious living, a hedonist's delight. Although the authorities tried to put an end to the wearing of bigger and better jewels, to increasingly ostentatious parties and pleasure-seeking thrills, the city's reinvention was in many ways understandable: what other choices did it have?[78]

In the place of international commerce and high politics, Venice, Florence and Rome became stops on a tourist trail for the new rich. Although first referred to as the Grand Tour in 1670, such expeditions began a century earlier, when a trip to Italy was first recognised as presenting an opportunity to buy high-quality antiquities as well as more voguish art, whose prices leapt as the numbers of visitors rose.[79] It was a rite of passage, not just for the individuals who took part but for culture as a whole: the fruits of southern Europe were being devoured by the north. As the continent's centre of gravity shifted, so did the jewels of ancient and contemporary culture. Three of the finest collections of ancient sculptures in the world, held at the British Museum, the Fitzwilliam Museum in Cambridge and the Ashmolean Museum in Oxford, were gathered by culturally curious travellers who were blessed with deep pockets.[80]

They brought back ideas about architecture, monumental tomb design and sculpture; it was not long before the poetry, art, music, garden design, medicine and science of classical antiquity were being extensively borrowed from, as England and the Low Countries set about modelling the glory of the present on that of the past.[81] Roman citizens would have stood agape at the idea that small landowners and petty officials from what had once been a leafy if out-of-the-way province of the empire were commissioning busts portraying themselves not just as the heirs to the Romans but as emperors.[82] Soon they would be doing more: Britannia was about to rule.

14

The Road to Empire

The shift in power to the north of Europe left some unable to compete and keep up. In the Ottoman world, for instance, the number of cities with populations of more than 10,000 remained broadly the same between 1500 and 1800. There was no pressure to intensify agricultural production to service growing demand—which meant that the economy remained sluggish and static. Tax collection was also inefficient, partly a result of tax farming, which incentivised individuals to make quick gains at the expense of the state's long-term income.[1]

Ottoman bureaucrats had proved to be highly skilled administrators, adept at centralising resources and managing the distribution of the population to ensure that harvests and supplies ended up where they were most needed. As the empire swallowed up more territory in the fifteenth and sixteenth centuries, this had worked efficiently and smoothly. When the momentum of expansion slowed, however, the fragility of the system became apparent, under pressure from the cost of sustaining military action on two fronts—in Europe in the west and with Safavid Persia in the east—but also as a result of climatic change that had a particularly severe impact on the Ottoman world.[2]

The social structures in the Muslim world, which developed along very different lines to those in western Europe, also proved to be an important factor. Islamic societies generally distributed wealth more evenly than their

Christian counterparts, largely thanks to very detailed instructions set out in the Qur'ān about legacies—including principles that were positively enlightened by the standards of the day when it came to the share women could and should expect from the estates of their father or husband. A Muslim woman could expect to be much better looked after than her European peer; but this came at the expense of allowing large-scale wealth to remain within the same family for a long period of time.[3] This in turn meant that the gap between rich and poor was never as acute as it became in Europe because money was redistributed and recirculated more widely. These values to some extent inhibited growth: as a general rule, teaching and stipulations about legacies meant that families found it hard to accumulate capital over successive generations because inheritance was progressive and egalitarian; in Europe, primogeniture concentrated resources in the hands of one child, and paved the way for great fortunes to be built up.[4]

For some, the fact that Europe—or rather north-western Europe—had never had it so good was a cause of anxiety. Calvinist priests in the Low Countries preached with terrifying conviction about money being the root of evil and about the perils of indulging in luxury.[5] Similar sentiments could be found in England, where men such as Thomas Mun, a particularly angry commentator of the early seventeenth century, bemoaned the "misspending of . . . time in idleness and pleasure," warning that material wealth would bring poverty of knowledge and "general leprosie" of body and soul.[6]

Of course, the benefits of growth were not shared evenly. Rising rents were good for landlords, but less good for tenants; exposure to larger markets meant that there was considerable price pressure as domestic production of wool, textiles and other goods was exposed to more competition.[7] The fall in moral standards that came with economic and social upheaval was enough to encourage some to take drastic action. The time had come to establish new pastures, concluded the more conservative, to find a place where it would be possible to practise a simple lifestyle that prioritised religious devotion and spiritual purity—a place for a fresh start, and a return to basics.

The Puritans who settled New England did so in protest against the changes that had accompanied Europe's rise and against the affluence that followed. They were reacting to the strange stream of new ideas and goods that made the world seem a very different place—where Chinese porcelain was appearing on household dining tables, where marriage of people with different skin colour to Europeans was giving rise to questions about identity and race, and where attitudes about the body were prompting what one scholar has recently termed the "first sexual revolution."[8]

To escape, the answer was to head across the Atlantic. The destination of choice was not the Caribbean, where many had gone to turn the land into sugar plantations using slave labour, but the virgin lands of New England where emigrants could lead an idealised existence of devout simplicity. The only difficulty, of course, was the native population, who "delight to tormente men in the most bloodie manner that may be; fleaing some alive with the shells of fishes, cutting of the members and joynts of others by peacemeale and broiling on the coles, eat the collops of their flesh in their sight whilst they live, with other cruelties horrible to be related."[9] But even this lot were worth risking; it would still be better than the world they had left behind. It is easy to forget that the feast of Thanksgiving, first celebrated by Pilgrim Fathers to mark their safe arrival in a land of plenty, was also a commemoration of a campaign against globalisation: it was not only hailing the discovery of a new Eden, but triumphantly rejecting the paradise at home that had been destroyed.[10]

For those of a different bent, who were not interested in building a bastion of austerity and religious conservatism, but wanted to discover the new, to benefit from and share in the attractions and tantalising delights that were on offer in the world, there was an alternative: go east and head for Asia. Building a platform to enable England to make connections with Asia in a structured and organised way was a slow and often frustrating process. The East India Company (EIC), which was granted a royal monopoly on trade with all lands east of the Cape of Good Hope in 1600, managed to displace the Portuguese from Bandar Abbas in the Persian Gulf and Surat in north-west India through force, thereby establishing footholds that hinted at future opportunities. Nevertheless, competing against the all-powerful Dutch East India Company (VOC) was a challenge.[11] Volumes of trade back to England did begin to grow; but the supremacy of the Dutch was such that in the middle of the seventeenth century, they were shipping around three times as much by value as the English.[12]

The relationship between the English and the Dutch was a complicated one. For one thing, the Low Countries provided customers and credit for English goods, so while there was commercial rivalry between the EIC and the VOC, their successes were not mutually exclusive. For another, the Spanish provided a common enemy and grounds for military and political co-operation between the two staunchly Protestant states. Some leading

English figures took great heart from major Dutch naval successes against Spain in the English Channel in 1639 and not long afterwards at Itamaracá off the coast of Brazil, with the result that the pompous Oliver St. John, leading one of the many delegations sent to The Hague to cement ties, even made the radical proposal that the two countries should "enter into a more intimate alliance and nearer union"—in other words, that they should merge into one.[13]

The unpredictability of the European powers was such that, barely a year after proposing a confederation, England and the Dutch were at war. The *casus belli* was the passing of the Navigation Act shortly after the St. John delegation's return home, when Parliament enacted a law requiring that all cargoes bound for England be carried into English ports by English ships. Although there was unquestionably a commercial motivation behind this legislation, namely to drive revenues towards an economy that had been ravaged by domestic fighting, it was also significant that there was a growing, vocal and apocalyptic lobby in England that insisted that the Dutch were motivated only by profits, were too materialistic and lacked religious conviction.[14]

The Act was an indication of England's sharpening aspirations. Just as rhetoric about the Spanish a century earlier became increasingly poisonous, so too did criticisms of the Dutch, especially when intense fighting broke out at sea as the Dutch sought to keep the shipping lanes open to their own ports through the Channel and the North Sea. This provoked nothing less than a maritime revolution in England. The navy had been well funded even during Tudor times; now, however, it was systematically overhauled. In the course of the second half of the seventeenth century, considerable resources were lavished on a large-scale shipbuilding programme. Expenditure on the navy rose so sharply that it soon consumed nearly a fifth of the entire national budget.[15] The process was overseen by Samuel Pepys, whose very personal diaries give little sense of the military and geopolitical shift that was taking place—or of the scale of the change running through shipyards up and down the country.[16]

Pepys gathered the most up-to-date manuals by Dutch specialists—including that of Nicolaes Witsen, the master theorist of shipbuilding—and set about applying rigour and discipline to everything from setting up schools that taught the "art of navigation" to commissioning written doctrines that set out the latest techniques for an ambitious and well-funded new generation of designers.[17]

The maritime revolution was based on three separate observations. The first was that specialised, heavy vessels were more effective than light cruisers. Success hung on being able to deliver concentrated firepower—and being able to resist it. Ship design was modified accordingly, with the emphasis on large, powerful ships that were like floating castles. The second observation was that experience could teach better lessons. Encounters with the Dutch fleets in the 1650s and 1660s resulted in devastating losses, both in terms of ships lost or captured and in terms of senior officers and captains lost in battle: in 1666, nearly 10 per cent of the navy's senior commanders were killed in a single engagement. As a result of such bruising encounters, naval tactics were systematically re-evaluated. Training manuals such as *Fighting Instructions* by Admiral Blake, one of the great naval leaders of the age, were disseminated and digested. Sharing knowledge and learning from the past was crucial in making the navy the best in the world: between 1660 and 1815, combat fatalities among English (British) captains fell by an astonishing 98 per cent.[18]

The third and no less important observation was how the navy functioned as an institution. In order to become a lieutenant, it became necessary to spend three years at sea and to pass an exam conducted by superior officers. Subsequent promotions were based strictly on ability rather than on patronage, which meant not only that the ablest rose to the top, but that they did so with the endorsement of their peers. The incentivising transparency of this meritocratic system was further enhanced by a system that rewarded those who had served for longest in the most important capacities. It was broadly identical to the organisation put in place in the earliest days of Islam and which had proved so effective during the Muslim conquests. In England now too, spoils were shared according to a pre-set allocation, with officers and sailors rewarded in proportion to seniority and length of service. This made promotion highly desirable and lucrative, which again served to propel the most able to the top, especially as the process was overseen by the Admiralty board, whose aim was to filter out favouritism and partiality. These were optimum labour contracts, in other words, designed to reward and incentivise performance; furthermore, they were fair.[19]

It was not long before the reforms brought rewards. Heavy investment in the navy extended England's reach substantially, giving it the chance to take advantage of any European rivalries, outbreaks of war or other openings in the Caribbean and elsewhere that presented themselves.[20] It also dovetailed with the long and slow process of trying to build up a stronger trading position in Asia, where the fruits of hard work were finally ripening. As well as Surat, the East India Company established an important centre in the south-east of the subcontinent at Madrasapatnam (now Madras), where in the first half of the seventeenth century a concession was negotiated with the local ruler to trade free of customs. As modern corporations would quickly recognise, generous tax breaks were a major boon, enabling long-distance rivals to be undercut—and, in due course, locals too. And as modern corporations would also recognise, as settlements became larger and more successful, the Company was perfectly placed to renegotiate better and better terms. Over the course of seventy years, Madras was transformed into a thriving metropolis. The pattern was replicated in other locations, most notably in Bombay and Calcutta, the jewel of Bengal, and the fortunes of the East India Company rose steadily upwards.[21]

As was the case with the VOC in Holland, the lines between England's government and the EIC were blurred. Both companies had the right to behave as a quasi-branch of the state—granted the right to mint coins, form alliances and not just maintain armed forces but also use them. Taking service with these highly commercialised organisations, which benefited from both government protection and very powerful investors, made for an attractive career path. Men were drawn from all over England and indeed from other parts of the world too—including the bastion of conservatism that was New England. There were rich rewards for the ambitious and the quick-witted who rose through the ranks of the Company.[22]

Typical was a man born in Massachusetts in 1649, who moved with his family back to England as a small boy before entering the service of the East India Company. Initially holding the lowly position of writer, he eventually rose through the ranks to become governor of Madras itself. He did well for himself there—too well, in fact, for he was removed from his position after five years, with rumours swirling about how much he had gained personally during his tenure. That he returned home with five tons of spices, large quantities of diamonds and innumerable precious objects suggests that the accusations were well founded—as does his own epitaph in Wrexham in North Wales where he was buried: "Born in America, in Europe bred, in Africa travell'd and in Asia wed . . . Much good, some ill, he did; so hope all's even and that his soul throu' mercy's gone to Heaven." He spent his money liberally back in England, though he did not forget the land of his birth:

towards the end of his life, he gave a generous sum to the Collegiate School of Connecticut, which recognised his gift by renaming itself after a benefactor who might make further donations in the future: Elihu Yale.[23]

Yale had been in the right place at the right time. In the 1680s, the Qing court in China lifted its restrictions on foreign trade, leading to a surge in exports of tea, porcelain and Chinese sugar. As a result, ports like Madras and Bombay were not only important trade centres in their own right, but became staging posts in a new and vibrant global trading network.[24] The late seventeenth century marked the start of a new era of contacts between Europe and China. These were not confined to commerce. The mathematician Gottfried Leibniz, who developed the binary system, was able to hone his ideas thanks to texts about Chinese arithmetic theories sent to him by a Jesuit friend who had gone to live in Beijing towards the end of the seventeenth century. Those who were in a position to take advantage of the new commercial or intellectual connections that were being made could do very well for themselves.[25]

By the time of his endowment, Yale himself was sensitive to the way that the east and India in particular were being increasingly seen as a short cut to great wealth. "You must not be impatient in your progress nor make haste for riches," he wrote to his godson, Elihu Nicks; "my fortune cost me near 30 years' patience."[26] As one of the first wave of Englishmen to fill his boots, it was a bit rich to be giving such stern advice to the next generation. And as it happened, the prospects of becoming unfeasibly rich in Asia were just about to get even better. The Golden Age was dawning in England.

That an island in the North Atlantic came to dominate international affairs, to be the heart of an empire that controlled a quarter of the globe and had influence far beyond, would have astonished historians and empire-builders of the past. Britain was an inhospitable place, wrote one of the great historians of late antiquity, where the air was so poisonous in some places that it could kill if the wind changed direction.[27] It was inhabited by Britons—whose name, speculated one author not long afterwards, came from the Latin *brutus*, that is, irrational or stupid.[28] Separated from the rest of Europe by the Channel, it was distant, isolated and peripheral. These weaknesses now became formidable strengths—and underpinned the rise of one of the greatest empires in history.

There were many reasons for Britain's ultimate success. Scholars have noted, for example, that levels of social and economic inequality were lower than in other countries in Europe, and that the bottom tiers of the population had noticeably higher levels of calorie consumption than their continental peers.[29] Recent research has also emphasised that changes in lifestyle played a role, as work rates and efficiency rose sharply thanks to the rewards on offer from the growing economy. Britain's surging success also owed much to the fact that it was home to so many innovators.[30] Fertility levels, which appear to have been lower in Britain than in most other European countries, also had an important correlation with per capita incomes, as resources and assets passed into fewer hands than on the continent.[31]

But the trump card that proved unbeatable was that of geography. England—or Britain after the union with Scotland in 1707—had a natural barrier protecting it from its rivals: the sea. This was helpful in terms of dealing with military threat, but it was a godsend when it came to government expenditure. With no land frontiers to defend, Britain's military expenditure was a fraction of its continental rivals.' It has been estimated that, while England's armed forces were approximately the same size as those of France in 1550, by 1700 the French had almost three times more men in service. These needed equipment and pay, meaning spending was proportionately far greater in France than in England; revenues were also proportionately lower in France as soldiers and sailors—each a potential generator of taxable income and indirect taxes through consumption—were removed from fields, factories and other employment to serve their country.[32]

It was as though Britain was vaccinated from the contagious problems of Europe that saw seemingly never-ending warfare as states on the mainland squabbled and fought in almost every possible permutation in the seventeenth and eighteenth centuries. The British learnt to intervene judiciously, taking advantage of circumstances that were in their favour, but staying out of it when the dice were loaded against them. It was also becoming clear that what happened in Europe could determine one's fate on the other side of the world. Intense arguments about who would inherit the throne of Austria could have consequences that led to fighting and exchanges of territory in European colonies all over the world: the issue of the legitimacy of Maria-Theresa's succession in the 1740s provoked outbreaks of fighting from the Americas to the Indian subcontinent that lasted nearly a decade. The result when matters were finally settled in 1748 was that Cap Breton in Canada and Madras in India changed hands between the French and the British.

. . .

This was just one example of how competition between European powers had effects on the other side of the world. Towns in India were handed to the French by the Dutch at the end of the 1690s as a result of the settlement of the Nine Years' War in Europe; islands in the Caribbean changed hands between Britain and France as part of peace settlements two decades later after further intense fighting in Europe; while huge swathes of North America were swapped between the British and French when disputes over the Spanish throne were settled.

Marriages could also deliver vast territories, strategic bridgeheads or great cities—such as Bombay, handed over to England as part of the dowry of Catherine of Braganza when she married King Charles II in the 1660s. It was an act of generosity that, as the city's Portuguese governor accurately predicted, spelt the end of Portugal's power in India.[33] Activities in bedchambers in Europe, hushed mutterings in palace corridors in its capital cities concerning potential brides or assumed slights by flighty rulers who were quick to have their egos piqued had implications and ramifications thousands of miles away.

On one level, such intrigues were of little concern to those in the east, who cared little if the Dutch, British, French or others held the upper hand. In fact if anything, the rivalries in Europe seemed merely to generate increasingly lavish benefits. Throughout the seventeenth century, rival delegations could be found heading to the Mughal Emperor, to the rulers of China and of Japan to curry favour and have new trading concessions granted or old ones reconfirmed. This elevated the importance of intermediaries—such as Muqarrab Khan, a port official in Gujarat, who oiled the wheels with the Emperor Jahāngīr in the early seventeenth century—who did well for themselves as a result.[34] In Khan's case, the goods he bought in 1610, made up of "Arabian horses," slaves from Africa and other luxuries, took more than two months simply to clear customs.[35]

The British in Asia operated, as one historian has put it, on the principle that "everything and everyone had a price."[36] This provoked extravagant gift-giving—but also protest from some who condemned the covetousness of those who were courted. The Mughal Emperor Jahāngīr, for example, had a particular soft spot for being given "overgrown elephants"—and perhaps dodos too—as gifts, and was said to have a heart "so insatiable, as that it never knows when it hath enough; being like a bottomless purse, that can never be fill'd, for the more it hath, the more it covets."[37]

Dutch envoys brought coaches, suits of armour, jewels, fabrics and even spectacles to Beijing in the 1660s in a bid to win favour following the loss of their position in Taiwan shortly beforehand.[38] An account of another extravagant Dutch delegation, this time to Lahore in 1711, shows the tremendous effort that went in to flattering and winning valuable contacts, as do glorious images made of their reception in Udaipur as the embassy made its way north. Laquerware from Japan, elephants from Ceylon and horses from Persia were taken as gifts, as were spices from the Dutch colonies, alongside European goods: cannon, telescopes, sextants and microscopes. Nothing was left to chance, even though on this occasion circumstances contrived to leave the envoy's request to renew trade concessions unresolved.[39]

It took a long time for the fuller implications of the shifting sands in Europe to work their way through to the east. To all intents and purposes, the more merchants arriving to trade and the bigger the ships they came in the better: this meant more gifts, more rewards and greater volumes of trade. As it was, Mughal emperors such as Akbar, Shah Jahān and Awrangzīb (ruled 1658–1707) were partial to having themselves weighed on their birthdays, with gems, precious metals and other treasures being repeatedly loaded on to the scales until they were balanced—hardly the best incentive to maintain a trim waistline.[40]

Then there were the bribes payable to middlemen who demanded money to "escort" travellers and merchants to their destination, much to the frustration of some who felt that the principle, as well as the amount, was annoying. English merchants who had their goods impounded at Rajmahal in 1654 felt there was no option other than to bribe the governor and his officials—just as the Dutch always had to do.[41] Complaints about lack of fairness could reach the Mughal emperors, who sometimes punished those who had lined their pockets too well: apparently, one judge accused of not being impartial was made to stand in front of the ruler and be bitten by a cobra; on another occasion, gatekeepers were whipped after a musician complained that he would have to hand over a portion of a stipend awarded to him by the Emperor on his way out of the palace.[42]

Funds coming in to India continued to fuel the artistic, architectural and cultural blossoming that had accompanied the enormous injections of capital since the early sixteenth century. Increasing sums percolated into Central Asia, partly as a result of tribute paid by rulers like Awrangzīb to secure peaceful relations to the north, but also as a result of horse-buying on a massive scale from breeders whose herds grazed on the steppes. As many as 100,000 horses were being bought in the markets of northern India each year—and at sky-high mark-ups if some sources are to be believed.[43] Even greater numbers of livestock were also sold to merchants from India, as well as from Persia, China and increasingly Russia, leading to further wealth flowing into the region. Cities such as Khokand (in modern Uzbekistan) flourished, with accounts talking rapturously of the quality of the rhubarb, tea, porcelain and silk that could be bought at cheap prices and in considerable quantities.[44]

Despite the rise of European trade, the networks crossing the spine of Asia were still very much alive and kicking. This is shown by the records of the VOC that note that tens of thousands of camel-loads of textiles were being sent each year from India to Persia via the old routes through Central Asia. English, French, Indian and Russian sources likewise provide information about continued overland trade and give some idea of its scale in the seventeenth and eighteenth centuries: travellers in Central Asia talk consistently about large volumes of goods being sold in markets, about enormous numbers of horses being reared and brought to places like Kabul, an "excellent trading centre" where caravans converged from all over Asia to buy and sell a wide range of textiles, aromatic roots, refined sugars and other luxuries.[45] Increasingly important in this continental trade were the minorities who helped lubricate commercial exchange, thanks to shared customs, family ties and the ability to create credit networks that worked over long distances. In the past, the Sogdians had played this role. Now it was Jews and above all Armenians who did so.[46]

Under the surface, powerful currents were swirling unseen. European attitudes to Asia were hardening, shifting from seeing the east as a wonderland filled with exotic plants and treasures to a place where the locals were as limp and useless as in the New World. Robert Orme's attitudes were typical of the eighteenth century. The first official historian of the East India Company, Orme penned an essay whose title "On the effeminacy of the inhabitants of Indostan" reveals much about how contemporary thinking had toughened. A bullish sense of entitlement was rising fast.[47] Attitudes towards Asia were changing from excitement about profits to be made to thoughts of brute exploitation.

This outlook was captured perfectly in the "nabob," the term given to East India Company officials who did absurdly well for themselves in Asia. They behaved like hoodlums and loan sharks, lending money locally at exorbitant rates of interest, using Company resources for their own benefit and creaming outrageous profits off transactions for themselves. It was the Wild East—a prelude to similar scenes in the west of North America a century later. Go to India, the memoirist William Hickey's father told him, and "cut off half a dozen rich fellow's heads . . . and so return a nabob." Serving the EIC in India was a one-way ticket to fortune.[48]

The path was not without hardship or danger, for conditions in the subcontinent were not easy, and disease could put a swift end to ambitions. As far as the evidence allows us to ascertain, although mortality levels dropped thanks to improvements in sanitation and hygiene, as well as in medicine and healthcare, the numbers of those sent home or deemed unfit for service rose steadily.[49] Experiences could be traumatic, as the merchant sailor Thomas Bowrey and his friends found out when they paid sixpence for a pint of "Bangha," an infusion of cannabis, in India in the late seventeenth century: one "sat himself down upon the floor and wept bitterly all afternoon"; another, "terrified with fear . . . put his head in a great jar and continued in that posture for four hours or more"; "four or five lay upon the carpets highly complimenting each other in high terms," while another "was quarrelsome and fought with one of the wooden pillars of the porch until he had little skin upon the knuckles of the fingers."[50] It took time to get used to other parts of the world.

On the other hand, rewards were astounding—so much so that it became commonplace for playwrights, the press and politicians to mock the newly rich. There were howls of contempt about the boom in tutors being hired to teach gentlemanly pursuits like fencing and dancing, about the nervousness in choosing the right tailor, about knowing the right things to talk about at dinner.[51]

Hypocrisy was everywhere. It was grotesque, William Pitt the Elder told fellow MPs in the late eighteenth century, that "the importers of foreign gold have forced their way into Parliament by such a torrent of private corruption, as no private hereditary fortune could resist."[52] There was no need, he felt, to note that his own grandfather had brought back one of the world's great gemstones, the Pitt diamond, from his spell in India and used the wealth he had accumulated during his spell as governor of Madras to buy a country estate—and the parliamentary seat that came with it.[53] Others were also outspoken. It was awful, a furious Edmund Burke told an inquiry in the House of Commons not long afterwards, that "nabobs" were destroying society—by throwing their wealth around, becoming MPs and marrying the daughters of the gentry.[54] Getting angry about such matters had little effect, however: after all, who would not want an ambitious and rich young buck for a son-in-law, or a generous spouse for a husband?

The key to unlocking these great fortunes lay in the transition of the

East India Company from a mercantile operation ferrying goods from one continent to another into an occupying power. The shift into both drug-dealing and racketeering was seamless. Opium was grown in increasing volumes on plantations in India to fund purchases of silk, porcelain and above all tea from China. Imports of the latter soared, with official figures that chart a rise from 142,000 pounds of tea bought in 1711 to 15 million pounds eighty years later—figures which conceal further shipments that must have been smuggled to avoid tax. In a neat mirror image, rising addiction to luxury goods in the west was effectively being traded for—and soon matched by—rising addiction to drugs in China.[55]

Making money in other dubious ways was no less lucrative. Although protection had been offered to local rulers in India in the eighteenth century on an increasingly regular and large scale, the decisive moment came in 1757 when an expedition led by Robert Clive was sent to Calcutta to intervene following an attack on the city by the Nawab of Bengal. Clive was soon being offered enormous sums to provide support for rival local candidates wanting to assume power. In no time, he found he was granted control of the *diwani*—the tax take of the region—and was able to help himself to the revenues of one of the most populated and economically vibrant parts of Asia, home to a textile industry that was responsible for more than half of all Britain's imports from the east. Almost overnight, he became one of the richest men in the world.[56]

A House of Commons Select Committee that was set up in 1773 to look at the aftermath of the conquest of Bengal revealed the staggering sums taken from the Bengali purse. Over £2 million—tens of billions in today's terms—had been distributed as "presents," almost all of it finding its way into the pockets of EIC employees locally.[57] The outrage was compounded by disgraceful and shocking scenes in Bengal itself. By 1770, the price of grain had been driven higher and higher, with catastrophic results as famine kicked in. The death toll was estimated in the millions; even the governor-general declared that a third of the population had died. Europeans had thought only of enriching themselves as the local population starved to death.[58]

The situation was entirely avoidable. The suffering of the many had been sacrificed for personal gain. To howls of derision, Clive simply answered—like the chief executive of a distressed bank—that his priorities had been to protect the interests of shareholders, not those of the local population; he deserved no criticism, surely, for doing his job.[59] Things were to get worse. The loss of manpower in Bengal devastated local productivity. As revenues collapsed, costs suddenly rose sharply causing panic that the golden goose had laid its last egg. This prompted a run on the shares of the EIC and pushed the Company to the brink of bankruptcy.[60] Far from its directors being superhuman administrators and wealth-creators, it turned out that the practices and culture of the Company had brought the intercontinental financial system to its knees.

After desperate consultation, the government in London concluded that the EIC was too big to fail and agreed a bail-out. To fund this, however, cash had to be raised. Eyes turned to the colonies in North America, where taxes were substantially lower than in Britain itself. When Lord North's government passed the Tea Act in 1773, it thought it had found an elegant solution to pay for the EIC rescue, while also bringing at least part of the tax regime of the American colonies closer into line with Britain's. It provoked fury among settlers across the Atlantic.

Leaflets and pamphlets were widely distributed in Pennsylvania that described the East India Company as an institution "well versed in Tyranny, Plunder, Oppression, and Bloodshed." It was a symbol of all that was wrong with Britain itself, where the highest levels of society were in thrall to the greedy, self-serving interest groups enriching themselves at the expense of the common people.[61] Ships carrying tea were turned back as a united front among colonists refused to bow before the demands of a government that did not allow them representation in the political process. When three vessels put in to Boston harbour, there was a tense stand-off between the locals and the authorities. On the night of 16 December, a small group of men dressed as "Indians" boarded the boats and tipped the tea into the harbour; they would rather it went to the bottom of the sea than be forced to pay taxes to London.[62]

Seen from an American perspective, the chain of events that led to the Declaration of Independence of the United States had a very American context. But from a wider vantage point the causes can be traced back to the tentacles of British power extending ever further in search of new opportunities, and from the efficacy of the Silk Road that had caused disequilibrium by pumping back too much too quickly. London was trying to balance competing demands on opposite sides of the world, and attempting to use revenues generated by taxes in one location to fund expenditure in another, leading to disillusionment, dissatisfaction—and revolt. The pursuit of profits had been relentless, which in turn had spurred a growing sense of self-confidence and arrogance. The East India Company, Clive told inquisitors on the eve of its collapse, was an imperial power in all but name. It ruled over countries that were "rich, populous, fruitful," and was "in possession . . . of twenty millions of subjects."[63] As those in the American colonies recognised, there was ultimately little difference between being a subject in one territory controlled from Britain rather than another. If Bengalis could starve to death, why not those living in the colonies, whose rights seemed no better or greater? It was time to go it alone.

The American War of Independence provoked much soul-searching in Britain as to how it should treat the regions where it had built up trading positions that were not just commercially lucrative but had real political clout too. The effective conquest of Bengal marked a signal moment in so far as it changed Britain from being a country that supported colonies of its own émigrés to becoming a domain that ruled other peoples. It was a steep learning curve to make sense of what this meant and how to balance the desires of the centre of the empire with the needs of its extremities. Britain found itself administering peoples who had laws and customs of their own, and having to work out what to borrow from new communities, what to lend—and how to build a platform that was workable and sustainable. An empire was being born.

Its genesis marked the end of a chapter. The passing of most of India into British hands ensured that the overland trade routes were starved of oxygen, as buying and spending power, assets and attention were decisively diverted to Europe. The decline in the importance of cavalry in the face of yet more improvements in military technology and tactics, particularly relating to firepower and heavy artillery, also played a role in depressing the volumes passing along the roads that had criss-crossed Asia for millennia. Central Asia, like southern Europe before it, began to fade.

The loss of thirteen colonies in North America was a humiliating setback for Britain and underlined how important it was to keep British possessions secure. And in that sense, the appointment of Lord Cornwallis as governor-general of India was an eye-opener: it was Cornwallis who had played a prominent role in the debacle across the Atlantic and who had surrendered Yorktown to George Washington. Perhaps the idea was that painful lessons had been learnt, and those who had learnt them were best placed to make sure that the same thing did not happen again elsewhere. Britain might have lost the United States, but it would never lose India.

15

The Road to Crisis

The disaster in America was a great shock for Britain, a setback which suggested that the empire could be vulnerable. The British had managed to build up a dominant position—directly, as well as through the East India Company—that brought prosperity, influence and power. It fiercely protected its stepping stones—the oases that linked together to connect back to London—and was jealously vigilant against any attempts to dislodge or weaken its grip on the channels of communication from the Sea of Java to the Caribbean, from Canada to the Indian Ocean.

Although the nineteenth century is normally seen as the high water mark of empire, a time when Britain's position continued to strengthen, there were signs that the opposite was the case—that its grip was beginning to loosen, prompting desperate rearguard action that often had disastrous strategic, military and diplomatic consequences. The realities of trying to retain and hold on to territories scattered across the globe led to dangerous games of brinkmanship being played with local and global rivals, with increasingly high stakes. By 1914, these rose to the point that the fate of the empire itself was gambled on the outcome of war in Europe: it was not a series of unfortunate events and chronic misunderstandings in the corridors of power in London, Berlin, Vienna, Paris and St. Petersburg that brought empires to their knees, but tensions over the control of Asia that had been simmering for decades. It was not Germany's spectre that lay behind the First World War; so too did that of Russia—and above all the shadow that it cast on the east. And it was Britain's desperate attempt to prevent this shadow growing that played an important note in bringing the world to war.

The threat that Russia posed to Britain grew like a cancer in the century before the assassination of Franz Ferdinand, as Russia transformed itself from a ramshackle, archaic kingdom with an agrarian economy into a reformed and ambitious empire. This set alarm bells ringing in London with increasing regularity and at increasing volume as it became clear that Russian growth and expansion had not just brought its interests into competition with those of Britain but threatened to overwhelm them.

The first sign of problems came in the early 1800s. For many decades, Russia had been rolling back its frontiers to incorporate new territories and new populations on the steppes in Central Asia, which were made up of a mosaic of tribal populations to its south and east, like the Kyrgyz, the Kazakhs and the Oirats. To start with, this was done with a reasonably soft touch. Although Marx was deeply critical of the imperialist process of creating "new Russians," it was undertaken with considerable sensitivity.[1] In many cases local leaders were not just richly rewarded but were also allowed to remain in power; their positions within their territories were endorsed and formally recognised by St. Petersburg. Concessions such as sweeping tax breaks, land grants and exemptions from military service likewise made Russian overlordship easier to tolerate.[2]

Territorial expansion fuelled economic growth that began to accelerate across the nineteenth century. For one thing, the previous heavy expenditure on defences against raids and attacks from the steppes was reduced, freeing funds to be used elsewhere and in other ways.[3] For another, rich rewards were garnered from gaining access to the wonderfully fertile land of the steppe belt that stretched across the top of the Black Sea and extended far into the east.

Russians had previously been forced to cultivate less attractive terrain for their crops, resulting in grain yields that were among the lowest in Europe and which exposed the population to the threat of famine. One British visitor in the early eighteenth century noted that the Kalmyk, a grouping of the Oirat tribe who had made the Lower Volga and the northern fringes of the Caspian their home, were able to put out 100,000 well-armed, able-bodied men. But with the fear of attack all but constant, agriculture did not fully develop. "A few hundred acres" of the fertile land of this region, wrote the same traveller, "would be of great value in England, tho' here it is waste and uncultivated."[4] Trade suffered, as did the development of towns, which remained modest in size—and in number: only a very small part of the population was urbanised before 1800.[5]

As this began to change, Russia's ambitions and horizons began to expand. In the early nineteenth century, imperial troops attacked the Ottoman Empire, securing major concessions, including control of Bessarabia, the region bound by the Dniester and Prut rivers, as well as considerable territories by the Caspian Sea. This was followed soon afterwards by an attack to the south of the Caucasus that inflicted a series of embarrassing defeats on Persia.

The balance of power in the Caucasus was tilting decisively. These were regions, provinces and khanates that had been either independent or Persian clients for centuries. Redrawing this map represented a major shift in the region, and an unequivocal sign of Russia's growing ambition along its southern frontier. It did not take the British long to understand the significance of this—especially once news was received that a French mission had been sent to Persia to compromise Britain's position in the east. Revolution in France in 1789 had produced similar results to the Black Death, with large-scale suffering giving way to a new age of determination and resurgence.

By the end of the eighteenth century, Napoleon was plotting not only to conquer Egypt but to dislodge the British from India. He was purported to have written to the powerful Tipu Sultan of Mysore to tell him of the numerous and invincible French forces that would soon "deliver you from the iron shackles of England."[6] Certainly, the lure of India loomed large in the minds of French strategic thinkers at the time.[7] It continued to do so, as is clear from the dispatch of one of Napoleon's trusted generals, the Comte de Gardane, to Persia in 1807, with orders to agree an alliance with the Shah, but also to make detailed maps to prepare for a major French campaign in the Indian subcontinent.[8]

The British reacted immediately, dispatching a senior official, Sir Gore Ouseley, to counter French overtures to the Shah along with a suitably impressive delegation that would "impress the Native at large with the permanence of our connection."[9] A great deal of work now went into impressing the Shah and his court, even though behind closed doors few tried to hide their disdain for local customs. Particular scorn was reserved for the seemingly incessant demand for lavish presents. Ouseley was dismayed to learn that a ring he had presented to the Persian ruler, along with a letter from King George III, was deemed too small and not valuable enough. "The meanness and covetousness of these people," he wrote indignantly, "are quite disgusting."[10] It was an attitude shared by another British officer visiting Teheran around the same time. The Persians are obsessed, he wrote, with the formalities of giving gifts and presents—to the extent that a long book could be written about "the rules of sitting down and standing up."[11]

In public, things were rather different. Ouseley—a fluent Persian-speaker—made sure when he arrived that he was received further away from the capital than the French ambassador, understanding that this reflected higher status on him and on his mission, and took care to arrange a meeting with the Shah sooner than his rival, noting with pleasure that his chair was positioned closer to the throne than normal.[12] The effort to win goodwill extended to the dispatch of British military advisers, in the form of two Royal Artillery officers, two NCOs and ten gunners, who trained Persian soldiers, advised on frontier defences and even led surprise attacks on the Russian position at Sultanabad, where the garrison's surrender in early 1812 was a propaganda coup.

Things changed when Napoleon attacked Russia in June of the same year. With the French bearing down on Moscow, the British saw the benefits of distancing themselves from Persia and siding with the Russians—"our good friends" as Ouseley called them in a report sent to the Foreign Secretary which also noted the wider implications of the French attack on Russia. This was for the best, Ouseley concluded, for there is a "very perverse trait in the Persian character which renders them insensible of, and ungrateful for, all favours conferred upon them"; the friendships he had worked so hard to win could be sacrificed easily and without much regret, since Persians were the "most selfish egotists in the world."[13]

Britain's prioritisation of its relations with Russia led to disappointment in Persia, where it was felt that previously reliable allies had changed course unexpectedly. This turned to bitter recrimination after a surprise attack through the Caucasus by Russian forces, emboldened by the repulse of Napoleon in 1812. To many, the fact that Ouseley—who had made such efforts to cultivate the Shah—drafted the humiliating Treaty of Gulistan in 1813 following the Russo-Persian War which awarded most of the western flank of the Caspian, including Dagestan, Mingrelia, Abkhazia, Derbent and Baku, to Russia, seemed nothing less than an act of betrayal.

That the terms of the treaty heavily favoured Russia provoked disgust among the Persians, who interpreted it as a sign of profound untrustworthiness and self-interest. I am extremely disappointed about Britain's conduct, wrote the Persian ambassador to Lord Castlereagh, the Foreign Secretary. "I depended on the great friendship of England," and on the "strong promises" that had been given regarding support for Persia. "I am disappointed totally" by the way things had turned out, the ambassador went on, warning that "if things remain as they are now left, they are not at all for the honour of England."[14] As a result of Napoleon's attack, Russia had become a useful ally; the sacrifice of ties with Persia was the price that had to be paid.

Russia's increasing importance at an international level was not limited to Europe or to the Near East, for its tentacles stretched further still. In contrast to how we now look at the world, in the first half of the nineteenth century Russia's eastern frontier was not in Asia at all, but somewhere else altogether: in North America. Colonies had first been established across the Bering Sea in what is now Alaska, with communities then founded on the west coast of Canada and beyond, as far south as Fort Ross in Sonoma County, California, in the early 1800s. These were no transient merchants, but permanent settlers who invested in building harbours, storage facilities and even schools. Young local boys of "Creole origin" on the Pacific seaboard of North America were schooled in the Russian language and taught the Russian curriculum, and some were sent to study in St. Petersburg, in some cases to enrol in the prestigious Academy of Medicine.[15] In a curious coincidence of timing, imperial envoys from the Tsar were arriving in San Francisco Bay to discuss provisioning with the Spanish governor at almost exactly the same time that Sir Gore Ouseley was sounding out the Russians as allies following Napoleon's invasion of 1812.[16]

The problem was that, as Russia's boundaries began to expand at greater pace, so did its confidence. Attitudes to those beyond the frontiers began to harden. Increasingly, the peoples of South and Central Asia came to be seen as barbarous and in need of enlightenment—and were treated accordingly. This had disastrous consequences, most notably in Chechnya, where shocking violence was meted out to the local population in the 1820s by Aleksei Ermolov, a headstrong and bloody-minded general. This not only paved the way for the emergence of a charismatic leader, the Imam Shamil, to lead an effective resistance movement; it also poisoned relations between this region and Russia for generations.[17]

Stock images of the Caucasus and the steppe world as places of violence and lawlessness caught hold, typified by poems such as *The Prisoner of the Caucasus* by Alexander Pushkin, and *Lullaby* by Mikhail Lermontov, which features a bloodthirsty Chechen creeping along a river bank, armed with a dagger, wanting to murder a child.[18] Where Russia was bordered in the west by "the most sophisticated enlightenment," one leading political radical told an audience in Kiev, in the east it was faced with profound ignorance. It was a duty, therefore, "to share our insight with our semi-barbaric neighbours."[19]

Not everybody was so certain. For decades to come, Russian intellectuals argued about which way the empire should look: to the *salons* and refinement of the west; or to the east, to Siberia and Central Asia. There was a range of answers. For the philosopher Pyotr Chaadaev, Russians belonged "to none of the great families of mankind; we are neither of the West nor of the East."[20] But to others the virgin territories of the east offered opportunities, a chance for Russia to have its own India.[21] The great powers of Europe stopped being viewed as paragons to be emulated and became rivals whose ascendancy should be challenged.

The composer Mikhail Glinka turned to early Rus' history and the Khazars for inspiration for his opera *Ruslan and Ludmila*, while Alexander Borodin looked east, writing the symphonic poem *In the Steppes of Central Asia*, which evokes caravans and long-distance trade across the steppes, and *Polovtsian Dances*, inspired by the rhythms of the nomadic lifestyle.[22] Interest in "orientalism," whether evident in theme, harmony or instrumentation, was a constant feature of Russian classical music of the nineteenth century.[23]

Dostoevskii put forward with passion his case that Russia ought not only to engage with the east but to embrace it. In a famous essay entitled "What is Asia to Us?," he argued in the late nineteenth century that Russia had to free itself from the shackles of European imperialism. In Europe, he wrote, we are hangers-on and slaves; in Asia, "we go as masters."[24]

Views like these were born of continuing success abroad. Further gains were made in the Caucasus in the 1820s after a Persian attack went badly wrong. Still smarting from the terms of the Gulistan treaty and emboldened by the animosity of the local populations to General Ermolov, whose hanging of women and children in public squares disgusted onlookers, Shah Fatḥ ʿAlī ordered a move against Russian positions in 1826.[25] The response was devastating: after Ermolov had been sacked from his post, the Tsar's troops streamed south through the mountain passes of the Caucasus, knocked out the Persian armies and forced a settlement in 1828 that was far worse than that imposed fifteen years earlier: yet more territory was ceded to Russia, along with an enormous cash payment. Such was the humiliation that the weakened Shah had to ask the Tsar formally to agree to support the succession of his heir, Prince ʿAbbās Mīrzā, after his death, for fear that he would otherwise not be able to take the throne, let alone hold power.

It was not long before violent riots erupted in Teheran. Crowds targeted the Russian embassy, storming the building in February 1829. The minister in the city, the thirty-six-year-old playwright Alexander Griboyedov, author of the gloriously satirical *Woe from Wit*, who had taken an uncompromising line in dealing with Persia, was murdered and his body, still in uniform, dragged through the streets of the city by a mob.[26] The Shah acted immediately to prevent a full-blooded invasion. He dispatched a favoured grandson to make an apology to the Tsar, together with poets to extol him as the "Suleiman of our times," and more importantly sent one of the world's greatest gemstones as a gift. The Shah diamond, weighing nearly ninety carats, had once hung above the throne of the emperors of India, surrounded by rubies and emeralds. It was now sent to St. Petersburg as the ultimate peace offering. It did the trick: the whole affair, declared Tsar Nicholas I, should now be forgotten.[27]

Tensions rose in London. At the start of the nineteenth century, a British mission had been sent to Persia in order to counter the threat and megalomania of Napoleon. Now Britain found itself facing a challenge from a different and unexpected rival: it was not France that was the threat any more, but Russia—and what is more, its reach seemed to be extending every day in every direction. Some had seen it coming. British policy meant that "Persia was delivered, bound hand and foot, to the Court of St. Petersburg," noted Sir Harford Jones, who served as ambassador to Teheran. Others were more forthright. As far as policy in Asia is concerned, wrote Lord Ellenborough, a senior figure in the Duke of Wellington's Cabinet in the 1820s, Britain's role was simple: "to limit the power of Russia."[28]

It was worrying indeed, then, that the events that had played out in Persia had strengthened the Tsar's hand, making him protector of the Shah and his regime. When serious uprisings broke out against Russian rule on the Kazakh steppes in 1836–37, interrupting trade with Central Asia and India, Russia encouraged the new Persian Shah Muḥammad to move on Herat in western Afghanistan in the hope of opening up a new, alternative trade route through to the east. Military and logistical support was also provided to the Persian forces, to help them achieve their objectives.[29] The British were caught cold—and panicked.

Lord Palmerston, the Foreign Secretary, was alarmed by this turn of events. "Russia and Persia are playing tricks in Affghanistan [*sic*]," he wrote in the spring of 1838—although he remained optimistic that things would soon be satisfactorily resolved.[30] Within a few weeks, however, he had become genuinely concerned. The jewel in the British Empire's crown suddenly looked vulnerable. Russia's actions had brought it "a little too near to our door in India," he wrote to one confidant. A month later, he was warning others that the barrier between Europe and India had been taken away, "laying the road open for invasion up to our very gate."[31] The situation looked bleak indeed.

The emergency dispatch of a force to occupy the island of Kharg in the Gulf was enough to deflect the Shah's attentions and call off the siege of Herat. But the steps taken next were a disaster. Anxious to build up a reliable leader who would help bolster the security of its position in Central Asia, Britain intervened in the messy affairs of Afghanistan. After it had been reported that the country's ruler, Dost Muḥammad, had received envoys from Russia proposing co-operation, the British took the decision to support his rival, Shah Shuja, with the intention of establishing him in his place. In return, Shuja agreed to the garrisoning of British troops in Kabul and to approve the recent annexation of Peshawar by Britain's collaborator, the powerful and influential Maharajah of Punjab.

To start with, things went like clockwork, as Quetta, Kandahar, Ghazni and Kabul—the key points controlling access on the east–west and north–south axes—were brought under control with minimum fuss. But not for the first time, and certainly not for the last, outside intervention created a lightning rod for the disparate and normally divided interests within Afghanistan. Tribal, ethnic and linguistic differences were set to one side as local support for Dost Muḥammad snowballed at the expense of the self-serving and unpopular patsy Shah Shuja—especially after directives had been issued that seemed to favour the British at the expense of the local population. Mosques across the country began refusing to read out the *ḫuṭba*, the acclamation honouring the ruler, in the name of Shuja.[32] It was not long before Kabul itself became increasingly unsafe for anyone British or suspected of having pro-British sympathies.

In November 1841, Alexander Burnes, a Scotsman whose extensive travel across this region was well known in Britain thanks to his celebrated publications and his ceaseless self-promotion, was ambushed and assassinated in the capital.[33] Not long afterwards, the decision was made to withdraw to India. In January 1842, in one of the most humiliating and notorious episodes in British military history, the evacuating column under the command of Major-General Elphinstone was attacked on its way to Jalalabad through the mountain passes and annihilated in the winter snow. Legend had it that only one man reached the town alive—Dr. William Brydon, whose well-placed copy of *Blackwood* magazine saved his life: he had rolled it up and put it inside his hat in an attempt to keep his head warm; it took most of the blow from a sword that would otherwise surely have killed him.[34]

Britain's attempts to forestall Russian progress elsewhere were no more successful. Missions to build bridges with the Emir of Bukhara and gain influence to the north of Afghanistan backfired spectacularly. The quaintly unsophisticated picture painted of this region by Alexander Burnes and others gave a false sense that the British would be welcomed with open arms. Nothing could be further from the case. The fiercely independent Central Asian khanates of Khiva, Bukhara and Khokand had no interest whatsoever in becoming involved in what one typically self-regarding would-be British power broker naively referred to as "the great game."[35] Two British officers, Colonel Charles Stoddart and Arthur Conolly, who arrived in the early 1840s to offer solutions to the problems of Anglo-Russian relations in Central Asia, were decapitated in front of a large crowd of enthusiastic onlookers.[36]

A third figure to reach Bukhara was a colourful individual named Joseph Wolff. Son of a German rabbi, Wolff converted to Christianity; he was expelled from theological college in Rome, before studying theology at Cambridge University under the direction of an anti-Semite whose views were so provocative that he was pelted with rotten eggs by students in the streets of Cambridge.[37] Setting out as a missionary, he initially headed east in search of the lost tribes of Israel. Eventually, he made for Bukhara to find the missing envoys, of whom nothing had been heard. The emir might have guessed that an eccentric was on his way after receiving a letter in advance, announcing that "I, Joseph Wolff, am the well-known Darveesh of the Christians." Be aware, he went on, that "I am about to enter Bokhara" to investigate reports that Conolly and Stoddart had been put to death, a rumour that "I, knowing the hospitality of the inhabitants of Bokhara, did not believe." He was lucky not to share their fate after being imprisoned and told to await his death. He was eventually released and allowed to go free; but it had been a close-run thing.[38]

Ironically, Bukhara and Central Asia more generally held little interest for Russia from a strategic point of view. Basic ethnographies published in this period, such as Alexei Levshin's writing on the Kazakhs, which became popular in St. Petersburg, revealed an increasing curiosity about these people who could neither read nor write, but among whom "the rudiments of music and poetry" could be detected, in spite of their apparent ignorance and roughness.[39] As Burnes' writing pointed out, Russia's aims in the region were decidedly modest: the two priorities were to encourage trade and to stop the sale of Russians into slavery. The problem was that this was not the message that sank in from Burnes' work; what really hit home back in Britain was his alarmist report that "the court of St. Petersburg have long cherished designs in this quarter of Asia."[40]

This dovetailed with growing British anxiety in other quarters. The consul-general in Baghdad, Henry Rawlinson, lobbied tirelessly, warning all who would listen that unless Russia's rise was checked the British Empire would be gravely threatened in India. There were two options: Britain should either extend the empire into Mesopotamia to build a proper buffer protecting the approach from the west; or a major force should be sent from India to attack the Russians in the Caucasus.[41] Rawlinson took it upon himself to support local anti-Russian insurgencies wherever he could find them: he funnelled arms and money to Imam Shamil, whose power base in Chechnya was a constant thorn in Russia's side in the mid-nineteenth century.[42] The support he provided helped establish a long tradition of Chechen terrorism against Russia.

Inevitably, then, Britain seized the chance to cut Russia down to size as soon as the opportunity presented itself. A series of scuffles about the treatment of Christians in the Ottoman Empire was quickly and deliberately escalated until a substantial British force was dispatched to the Black Sea in 1854, where it was joined by the French who were anxious about protecting their extensive business interests in Constantinople, Aleppo and Damascus. The aim was simple: Russia was to be taught a lesson.[43]

As Lord Palmerston put it while hostilities were raging, "the main and real object of the war was to curb the aggressive ambition of Russia." The obscure war that was being fought in the Crimea, in the Sea of Azov and with flash outbreaks elsewhere—in the Caucasus and by the Danube, for example—had a prize at stake that was far more significant than it seemed at face value. Indeed, the charismatic and respected British Foreign Secretary himself went so far as to present a formal plan to his colleagues in the government for the dismemberment of Russia: the way to control Russia, and by implication to protect British interests in India, was to hand control of the Crimea and the entire Caucasus region to the Ottomans.[44] Although this extravagant scheme did not get off the ground, it is a powerful indication of what a major issue Russia's expansion had become in the British official mind.

Some were appalled by the Anglo-French invasion. Writing furiously and voluminously about the war as it progressed, Karl Marx found fertile material with which to develop ideas about the ruinous impact of imperialism that he had first set out in *The Communist Manifesto* a few years earlier. Marx documented increases in military and naval expenditure in detail and provided running commentaries in the *New York Tribune* in which he fiercely attacked the hypocrisy of those who had dragged the west to war. He could hardly contain his glee when Lord Aberdeen was forced to stand down as Prime Minister in the face of widespread disillusionment at the heavy casualties sustained in Russia. As prices rose in London, sparking protests at home, it seemed obvious to Marx that Britain's imperialist policies were being dictated by a small elite and came at the expense of the masses. Communism was not born of the Crimean War, but it was certainly sharpened by it.[45]

So was the unification movement in Italy. After Russia's nose had been bloodied—at the expense of many French and British troops, including those who took part in the infamous charge of the Light Brigade—settlement terms were finally discussed in Paris. One of those at the negotiating table was Count Cavour, Prime Minister of Sardinia, who owed his place to the decision of Vittorio Emanuele, the island's king, to send a force of auxiliaries to the Black Sea in support of France. He used his moment in the spotlight shrewdly, calling for a united, independent Italy, a rallying cry that was viewed sympathetically by the allies and helped galvanise supporters back home.[46] Five years later, the King of Sardinia had become King of Italy, a new country forged of disparate cities and regions. The imposing Altare della Patria monument that stands in the centre of Rome and which was built three decades later, in the words of Primo Levi, in order to make Rome feel Italian and to make Italy feel Roman, marked the culmination of developments that had been given momentum by the fight over land and influence thousands of miles to the east.[47]

For Russia, the terms imposed at the peace talks of Paris in 1856 were nothing short of disastrous. Britain and France collaborated to tie a noose around their rival's neck: stripped of hard-won gains in the Caucasus, Russia suffered the ignominy of being deprived of military access to the Black Sea, which was declared neutral and closed to all warships. Likewise, the coastline was to be demilitarised, free from fortifications and stores of armaments.[48]

The aim was to humiliate Russia and to strangle its ambitions. It had the opposite effect—this was a Versailles moment, where the settlement was counter-productive and had dangerous consequences. Quite apart from the fact that the settlement was so punitive and restrictive that the Russians immediately tried to slip its shackles, it also prompted a period of change and reform. The Crimean War had revealed that the Tsar's army was no match for allied troops, who were more experienced and better trained. After some hard-hitting reports had been prepared for the Tsar, Alexander II, which set out the shortcomings of the Russian army in merciless detail, a root-and-branch overhaul of the military was carried out.[49]

Dramatic steps were taken: conscription was reduced from twenty-five years' service to fifteen, lowering the average age of the army at a stroke, while bulk orders of up-to-date equipment were issued to replace antiquated and inefficient matériel.[50] But the most striking change came from far-reaching social reform. Although a severe banking crisis in the late 1850s also played a role, it was defeat in the Crimea and shame at the terms that followed that prompted the Tsar to abolish serfdom, a system under which a significant part of the population was tied to the land and indentured to wealthy landlords. Within five years, serfdom had been swept away, ending centuries of slavery in Russia.[51] This was not before time, according to some contemporaries.[52] It presaged a surge towards modernisation and economic liberalism that propelled growth at a phenomenal rate in the second half of the nineteenth century: iron production rose five-fold between 1870 and 1890, while the impressive expansion of the railway network served, as one modern scholar has put it, to "emancipate Russia from the limitations imposed by her geography"—in other words, by linking the vast country together.[53] Far from bottling Russia up, the British helped let the genie out of the bottle.

The intensification of Russian aspirations could be felt even as the ink was drying on the treaty signed in Paris. One of the Tsar's delegates at the peace talks, a military attaché named Nikolai Ignat'ev, was so enraged by the treatment of Russia, and by the restrictions of Russian control over its own littoral on the Black Sea in particular, that he made arrangements with Prince Gorchakov, former classmate and confidant of Alexander Pushkin, to lead a mission into Central Asia. The aim was unequivocal: "the investigation [of this region] and the promotion of friendly ties will raise Russia's influence—and lower that of Great Britain."[54]

Ignat'ev lobbied intensively for expeditions to be sent to Persia and Afghanistan, and for envoys to visit the khanates of Khiva and Bukhara. The aim, he said bluntly, was to find a route to India via either of the two great rivers that flow from the Aral Sea—the Syr Darya or the Amu Darya. It would be ideal, he argued, if Russia could build an alliance with the peoples bordering India and also work up their hostility to Britain: this was the way to set Russia on the front foot—and not just in Asia.[55]

The missions led by Ignat'ev and others paid dividends. In the fifteen years that followed the end of the Crimean War, Russia brought hundreds of thousands of square miles under its control without having to resort to force. Well-led expeditions, coupled with shrewdly applied diplomatic pressure on China, allowed "immense strides" to be made in the Far East "in the short space of ten years," as one seasoned observer noted in a report for the Foreign Office in London in 1861.[56]

Not long afterwards, yet more of the southern steppe fell into Russia's lap, along with the oasis cities straddling the heart of Asia. By the late 1860s, Tashkent, Samarkand and Bukhara, as well as much of the prosperous Fergana valley, had become "protectorates" or vassals of St. Petersburg, a prelude to full annexation and incorporation within the empire. Russia was building its own massive trade and communication network, which now connected Vladivostok in the east to the frontier with Prussia in the west, and the ports of the White Sea in the north to the Caucasus and Central Asia in the south.

The story was not unremittingly positive. Although a much needed programme of modernisation had been embarked on after the debacle of the Crimean War, Russia's sinews strained as it grew. Generating cash to help fund the empire's transformation was a constant problem, one that led to the embarrassing decision to divest it of Alaska for geopolitical and financial reasons.[57] Nevertheless, as concerns grew about what change in Russia meant for Britain's empire, thoughts in London turned to devising ways to stem the tide; or failing that, to divert Russia's attention elsewhere.

16

The Road to War

In the late nineteenth century, Russian confidence, bullishness even, was rising fast. It was not long before attention turned to having the Black Sea clauses of the Treaty of Paris rescinded. One after another, chanceries across Europe were quietly canvassed for support for revising the treaty in general and removing the relevant clauses in particular. Most presented little opposition. There was one exception: London. In the winter of 1870, a copy of the circular outlining a proposal to drop the clauses that had been presented to the British Cabinet was leaked to the press in St. Petersburg, along with the news that it had been flatly rejected in London. Prince Gorchakov's efforts to force the matter went down well in Russia; they were met with howls of fury in the British press.[1]

The line taken by the *Spectator* was typical of the shocked indignation. Russia's attempt to renegotiate was diabolical, it declared; a "more daring and open defiance of European law, of international morality and of British policy than the Russian note was never uttered to the world."[2] The proposal to drop the clauses convinced some that war was imminent and that Britain had no choice but to use force to maintain the restrictions on Russia. This reaction was monstrous, wrote John Stuart Mill in a letter to *The Times*; the moves might be provocative, but they should not lead to military conflict. Even Queen Victoria agreed, sending a telegram to her Foreign Secretary, Lord Granville: "Could any hint be given to the leading journals," she wrote, "to refrain from rousing the war spirit here?"[3]

The high levels of anxiety were triggered not so much by concerns about the Black Sea as by the general worry about Russia flexing increasingly strong muscles. With military action an unrealistic possibility and faced with a poor hand of cards, Britain had little choice but to concede—prompting acerbic exchanges between the Prime Minister, William Gladstone, and the charismatic Benjamin Disraeli in the House of Commons. Russia got what it wanted, namely the freedom to do as it chose along the littoral and to station warships in the ports of the Crimea and elsewhere on the northern shore of the Black Sea. This was met with euphoria in St. Petersburg, according to one British eyewitness, and was presented as a "triumph" for Russia. Tsar Alexander II, who was "said to be personally overjoyed," ordered the "Te Deum" to be sung in the chapel of the Winter Palace, before praying at the Cathedral of Saints Peter and Paul "for some time with signs of deep emotion."[4]

Britain had been powerless to translate its economic power into diplomatic and political success. New approaches were soon adopted. One of the topics that came up for discussion was that of the title of the British ruler. Given the size and distribution of the dominions, regions, peoples and places that were subject to the British sovereign, it was proposed that the monarch should be upgraded from a royal to an imperial title. This cosmetic change provoked fierce debate in the Houses of Parliament, with traditionalists appalled by the idea of changing ranks, titles and names that had held good for centuries. Kings had supreme authority over subordinate rulers, Lord Granville told the House of Lords; there was no reason or justification for upgrading the sovereign's title. "My Lords," he declared, "in regard of the dignity of Her Majesty herself, no name can appeal to the imagination so forcibly as that of Victoria, Queen of Great Britain and Ireland." This was how the monarch should be known.[5]

The problem was Russia and the Tsar. Apart from harking back to imperial Rome (the word Tsar is a simple contraction of "Caesar)," the Tsar's formal title in all its glory when used in official correspondence and on formal occasions made reference to an elaborate and lengthy list of the territories that he lorded over. In the mid-1870s, Disraeli—by now Prime Minister—stressed to Parliament that a higher title than queen would help give confidence to the population of India, already concerned about the Russian advance into Central Asia. Queen Victoria agreed with the principle, writing to Disraeli to say that "attacking Russia from India is the right way," and that an upgraded title might help focus the loyalty of her subjects in India.[6]

Some MPs were unconvinced of the need to compete in this way. Surely we British, "who have ruled India for a hundred years," said one parliamentarian, are not so unsure of ourselves that we need to alter the title of the queen, solely "in order that our sovereign may be placed on terms of equality with the Emperor of Russia?"[7] Others, however, stressed the dramatic change in the situation in the east, defiantly proclaiming that "the British hold over Hindoostan is intended to endure," and that therefore "no part of that territory must be ceded." That Russia's frontiers were now only a few days' march from those of Her Majesty's dominions in India was a cause for alarm.[8] After heated debate in Parliament, the Bill was passed in 1876 proclaiming that Victoria was not only a queen, as she had been crowned nearly four decades earlier, but an empress too. She liked it: at Christmas she sent Disraeli a card signed "Victoria, Regina et Imperatrix"—Victoria, Queen and Empress.[9]

Seemingly superficial steps like this were accompanied by more practical measures in an increasingly tense environment as the British constantly fretted about losing ground to their rivals. Both Britain and Russia became obsessed with setting up networks to spy on each other, to win over the local population and to cultivate those with influence. Colonel Maclean of the Punjab Cavalry and the Indian Political Service was one of those deputed to monitor events in the borderlands between Persia, India and Afghanistan in the 1880s. He established groups of merchants and operators of local telegraph exchanges and incentivised them to pass on information about what was going on in the region. Maclean homed in on Muslim clerics, providing them with gifts of shawls, carpets, cigars and even diamond rings in order to impress the local population with the benefits of co-operating with Britain. Maclean justified these bribes as a way of channelling support to influential friends. In fact they served to strengthen religious authority across a fractious region that was the focus of intense competition from outside.[10]

From the British point of view, there was real concern about Russia's intentions and capabilities and about the threat that its expansion in Central Asia posed to the defences of India. Talk in London turned to military confrontation with Russia, with Disraeli advising the Queen to be ready to authorise British troops to be sent "to the Persian Gulf, and [that] the Empress of India should order her armies to clear Central Asia of the Muscovites and drive them into the Caspian."[11] So nervy were the authorities that the viceroy, Lord Lytton, ordered not one but two invasions of Afghanistan in 1878–80, installing a puppet ruler on the throne in Kabul. Persia was assiduously courted and persuaded to sign the Herat Convention in which

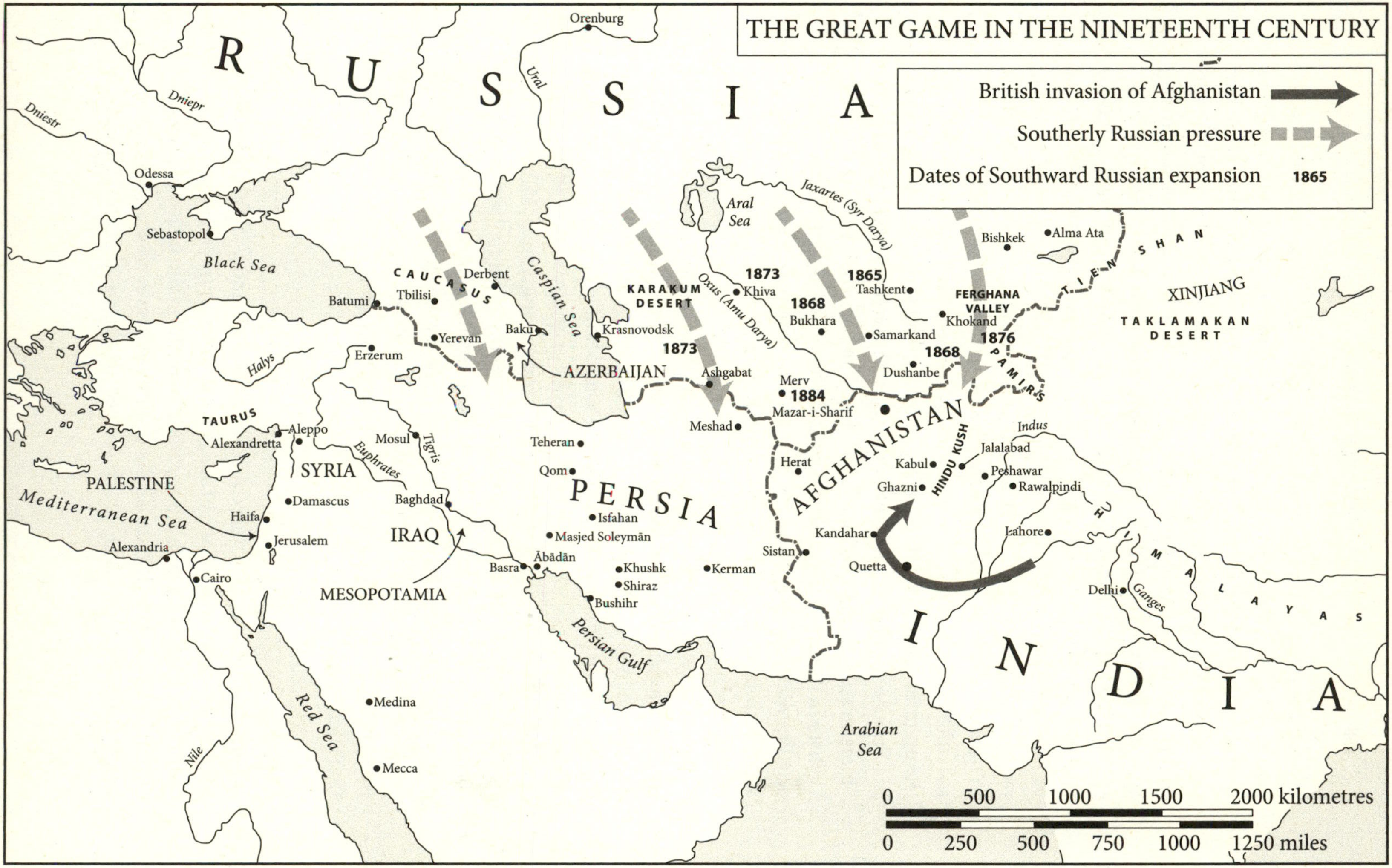
THE GREAT GAME IN THE NINETEENTH CENTURY
British invasion of Afghanistan
Southerly Russian pressure
Dates of Southward Russian expansion
1865
RUSSIA
Orenburg
Ural
Dniepr
Dniestr
Odessa
Sebastopol
Black Sea
CAUCASUS
Tbilisi
Derbent
Batumi
Yerevan
Baku
Caspian Sea
Krasnovodsk
KARAKUM DESERT
AZERBAIJAN
Erzerum
Halys
Aral Sea
Jaxartes (Syr Darya)
Oxus (Amu Darya)
1873
Khiva
1873
Ashgabat
1868
Bukhara
1865
Tashkent
Samarkand
FERGHANA VALLEY
Khokand
1876
1868
Dushanbe
PAMIRS
Bishkek
Alma Ata
TIEN SHAN
XINJIANG
TAKLAMAKAN DESERT
Merv
1884
Mazar-i-Sharif
Meshad
AFGHANISTAN
HINDU KUSH
Indus
Jalalabad
Kabul
Peshawar
Rawalpindi
Ghazni
Herat
Kandahar
Quetta
Sistan
Lahore
Delhi
Ganges
HIMALAYAS
INDIA
TAURUS
Aleppo
Alexandretta
Mosul
Tigris
Euphrates
SYRIA
PALESTINE
Mediterranean Sea
Damascus
Haifa
Jerusalem
Alexandria
Cairo
Baghdad
IRAQ
MESOPOTAMIA
Teheran
Qom
PERSIA
Isfahan
Masjed Soleymān
Ābādān
Basra
Khushk
Kerman
Shiraz
Bushihr
Persian Gulf
Red Sea
Nile
Medina
Mecca
Arabian Sea
0 500 1000 1500 2000 kilometres
0 250 500 750 1000 1250 miles

it committed to protect Central Asia against Russian advance. This was no easy task, as Persia had its own interests in this region and was nursing bruises following the recent and unhelpful British intervention that had favoured Afghanistan at its expense.[12] In the meantime, steps were taken to build up contacts beyond Kandahar in order to have better early-warning systems for any Russian initiative, military or otherwise.[13]

Considerable energy was expended by senior officers in assessing how to deal with a possible Russian invasion of the Raj. From the late 1870s, a series of reports were prepared that looked at the question from a broad strategic perspective: it was recognised that disagreements and tensions with Russia in other theatres could and probably would have an impact in the east. One memorandum looked at "the measures which should be adopted in India in the event of England joining Turkey in the War against Russia"—following the Russian invasion of the Balkans in 1877. Another, written in 1883, asked, "Is an invasion of India by Russia Possible?," and another not long after that, "What are Russia's Vulnerable Points and How have Recent Events Affected our Frontier Policy in India?" A sign of how seriously these were taken is clear from the appointment of their author, the hawkish General Sir Frederick (later Lord) Roberts, as commander-in-chief of India in 1885.[14]

Not everyone shared this bleak view of the situation in Asia, even after a set of invasion plans prepared by General Alexei Kuropatkin had been acquired by the British in 1886.[15] Henry Brackenbury, director of military intelligence, felt that the Russian threat was being exaggerated, in terms of Russia's willingness to attack and in terms of the readiness of the Tsar's army to do so.[16] George Curzon, then a promising young MP and prize fellow of All Souls, but within a decade viceroy of India, was even more dismissive. He saw no master plan or grand strategy behind Russia's interests in the east. Far from being "consistent or remorseless or profound," he wrote in 1889, "I believe it to be a hand-to-mouth policy, a policy of waiting upon events, of profiting by the blunders of others, and as often of committing such herself."[17]

It was certainly true that there was much bluster and wishful thinking in Russian attitudes to the big picture in Central Asia, and regarding India in particular. There were hotheads within the military who talked of grandiose schemes of replacing Britain as the dominant power in the subcontinent, while steps were also taken which seemed to suggest that Russia's interest was far from passive: for example, officers were sent on courses to teach them Hindi, in preparation for imminent intervention in India. There was encouragement too, such as from Maharajah Duleep Singh of Punjab, who wrote to Tsar Alexander III promising to "deliver some 250,000,000 of my countrymen from the cruel yoke of the British rule," and claiming to speak for "most of the powerful princes of India"—seemingly an open invitation for Russia to expand its frontiers further south.[18]

In practice, however, things were not quite so simple. For one thing, Russia was already struggling with the thorny issue of how to incorporate the vast new regions that had recently been brought within the imperial orbit. Officials sent to Turkestan grappled with land registries that were complex and often contradictory, and their attempts to streamline local taxes and laws met with inevitable opposition.[19] Then there were the gloomy realities engendered by public opinion, which gave rise to what the Council of Ministers in St. Petersburg called the "fanatical mood on our eastern borderlands" resulting from the influence of Islam in almost every aspect of the day-to-day life of the "new Russians" who were now part of the Tsar's empire.[20] The worry about insurrection and rebellion in these freshly added territories was so great that mandatory military service was waived in these regions, and financial demands were kept deliberately low. Russian peasants, as one leading intellectual noted acidly, did not enjoy such generous treatment.[21]

Complications also arose from views about the local populations. Russian critics drew attention to Britain's deeply prejudiced attitudes, observing that British soldiers treated traders in the bazaars in Tashkent "as something nearer animals than men"; on one occasion, the wife of a British captain apparently refused to let the Maharajah of Kashmir escort her into dinner, claiming he was a "dirty Hindu." For all their criticisms, however, Russian attitudes were no more enlightened: tsarist officers may have complained to each other about how the British treated the locals, but there was little evidence to show that they truly saw things differently. "All Hindus without exception," wrote one nineteenth-century Russian visitor to India, "devote all their skill and all their soul to the most horrible usury. Woe betide the unhappy native who is seduced by their deceitful promises!"[22]

Nevertheless there was a frisson of excitement about the new worlds Russia was coming into contact with, as the Minister of the Interior, Pyotr Valuev, articulated in his diary in 1865. "Tashkent has been taken by General Cherniaev," he wrote. "Nobody knows why or for what purpose . . . [but]

there is something erotic in all that we are doing on the far frontiers of our empire." The extension of the borders was marvellous, he wrote. First Russia reached the River Amur, then the Ussuri. And now Tashkent.[23]

And yet, despite the teething problems, Russia's influence and involvement in the east continued to expand at accelerating speed as it developed its own Silk Roads. The construction of the Trans-Siberian Railway, and the connection with the Chinese Eastern Railway, led to an immediate boom in trade, with volumes nearly trebling between 1895 and 1914.[24] This was supported by new entities like the Russo-Chinese Bank, set up to finance economic expansion in the Far East.[25] As the Russian Prime Minister, Pyotr Stolypin, told the Duma, the Russian parliament, in 1908, Russia's east was a region pregnant with prospects and resources. "Our distant and inhospitable frontier territory is rich in gold, wood, furs and immense spaces suitable for agriculture." Although sparsely populated now, he warned, these spaces would not remain empty for long. Russia needed to seize the opportunities currently open to it.[26]

This was hardly reassuring from Britain's point of view, given how jealously its position in the Far East had been guarded. Opening up markets in China in particular had proved difficult. In 1793, for example, the first British mission had been dealt with loftily by the Qianlong court after asking for the right to establish a trading community. China's connections penetrated deep into "every country under Heaven." As such, the British request was hardly unexpected, noted a letter from the Emperor that was brought back to King George III. "As your Ambassador can see for himself," the author went on dismissively, "we possess all things. I set no value on objects strange or ingenious, and have no use for your country's manufactures."[27]

In fact, this was bluster—for in due course terms were agreed. The aggressive response was rather based on the acute awareness that Britain's tentacles were extending ever further, and that attack was the best form of defence.[28] As it happened, initial Chinese suspicions were not far off the mark, for once trading privileges were given, Britain had little hesitation in using force to preserve and extend its position. Central to the commercial expansion was the sale of opium, despite fierce protests by the Chinese, whose outrage at the devastating effects of drug addiction was shrugged off by the British authorities.[29] The opium trade had expanded in a major way following the Treaty of Nanking in 1842, which opened up access to ports where the trade had been restricted previously, while also ceding Hong Kong to the British; further concessions were granted after British and French forces marched on Beijing in 1860, looting and burning the Old Summer Palace.[30]

Some saw this as a seminal moment that marked yet another chapter in the triumph of the west. "Thus it has been the destiny of England," ran one report in the British press, "to break down a government fabric which has so long mystified the European world, and to uncover to its own subjects its hollowness and its evils." Another commentator was equally blunt. The "mysterious and exclusive barbarism" of the Chinese Empire, he wrote, had been dismantled by "the force of active and intrusive Western Civilisation."[31]

As Britain sought to counter the continuing emergence of Russia in the Far East, the decision was taken in 1885 to occupy the islands of Komondo off the southern coast of the Korean peninsula—"as a base," the Cabinet was told, "for the blockade of the Russian force in the Pacific" and also "as an advanced station to support operations against Vladivostock."[32] This was a move aimed at protecting Britain's strategic position, and above all its trade with China—if necessary with a pre-emptive strike. In 1894, before the railways had opened up new possibilities, more than 80 per cent of all customs revenue collected in China was paid by Britain and by British companies—whose ships also carried more than four-fifths of China's total trade. It was obvious that Russia's rise, and that of the new land routes that would bring produce to Europe, would come at Britain's expense.

It was in this context of increasing rivalry and tension that it became known at the end of the 1890s that Russia had begun to take steps to woo Persia. This raised the prospect of an alliance that might pose a threat to the north-western approach to India. In London, it had previously been conceded, albeit after much deliberation, that pressure on the subcontinent from Russia via Afghanistan through the Hindu Kush was likely to be limited. For strategists armed with pencils and maps, plotting a route from Central Asia through this geographically challenging region looked easy; but it was recognised that, while a surprise small-scale assault could not be discounted, the reality was that the terrain minimised a major military effort through mountain passes that were well known for being treacherous and extremely difficult to penetrate.

The approach through Persia was another matter. Russia had become increasingly active on its southern flank, occupying Merv in 1884 in a move that caught British officials and agents by surprise—they first learnt about it from newspaper reports—and wooing the leadership in Teheran. With Russia's frontier now less than 200 miles from Herat, the road to Kandahar and therefore India was wide open. More worrying still was that the expansion had been followed up with infrastructure projects to connect new regions to the Russian heartlands. In 1880, construction started on the Trans-Caspian Railway, with a line soon connecting through to Samarkand and Tashkent, and by 1899 a spur connected Merv to Kushk, within striking distance of Herat.[33] These railway lines were not just symbolic: they were arteries that would allow provisions, weapons and soldiers to be delivered to the British Empire's back door. As Field Marshal Lord Roberts emphasised to the officers of the Eastern Command not long afterwards, it was regrettable that the railways had been extended so far. Now, however, a line had been established "over which Russia could not be allowed to cross." If it did, he stated, it would be "considered a *casus belli*"—that is, grounds for war.[34]

The railway lines also represented an economic threat. In 1900, the British embassy in St. Petersburg forwarded to London a summary of a pamphlet that had been written by a Russian officer advocating the extension of track into Persia and Afghanistan. It was likely, the officer admitted, that the British would not react well to the new transport system, but this was no surprise: after all, a railway connection that spanned Asia would "place the whole trade of India and Eastern Asia with Russia, and Europe in [Russian] hands."[35] This was something of an exaggeration, as one senior diplomat observed in reply to this report. "The strategical considerations put forward by the author are of no great value," wrote Charles Hardinge, because it would be madness for Russia to make a move on this region given Britain's control of the Persian Gulf.[36]

Nevertheless, at a time when British anxieties were already heightened, such murmurs about Russia's commercial reach extending in this direction provided yet another cause for concern. As it was, phantoms and plots were being seen at every corner, and dutifully recorded by anxious British diplomats. Awkward questions were asked about why the presence of a certain Dr. Paschooski in Bushihr had not been spotted more quickly, together with updates on whether his claims to be treating plague victims were really true; the visit of a Russian nobleman, identified as "Prince Dabija," was likewise viewed with extreme suspicion, and the fact that he seemed to be "very reticent about his movements and intentions" duly noted and passed on.[37] In London, Russia moved to the top of the agenda of Cabinet meetings, drew the attention of the Prime Minister himself and became one of the Foreign Office's top priorities.

In the short term, Persia was the arena where competition was most intense. The rulers of Persia had grown fat on generous soft loans provided by those seeking to build good relations with a nation that was blessed with an enviable strategic location as the fulcrum between east and west. Britain had carefully satisfied the prodigal whims and financial appetites of Persia's rulers in the late nineteenth century until, in 1898, the extravagantly moustachioed Shah, Moẓaffar od-Dīn, dropped a bombshell, rejecting a proposed new loan of £2 million. A high-ranking official was immediately dispatched to find out more, but was stonewalled. Lord Salisbury, the British Prime Minister, followed the situation personally, issuing instructions to the Treasury to soften the conditions and increase the quantum of the proposed facility. Rumours about what was going on behind the scenes began to circulate: finally, it emerged that Russia was offering to lend a much higher amount than Britain was willing to lend, and on much better terms.[38]

This was smart manoeuvring by St. Petersburg. Tax revenues in Russia were rising sharply while foreign investment was also beginning to flood in from outside. Slowly but surely, a middle class was starting to emerge—men like Lopakhin in Chekhov's *Cherry Orchard*, who a generation earlier would have been tied to the land, were taking advantage of social change, new domestic markets and new export opportunities to make fortunes for themselves. Economic historians like to highlight growth by noting sharp rises in urbanisation, in pig-iron production and in the amount of new railway track being laid down. But one need look only as far as the literature, art, dance and music of this period, the blossoming of Tolstoy, Kandinskii, Diaghilev, Tchaikovskii and many many others, to get a sense of what was happening: culturally and economically, Russia was booming.

Increasingly buoyant, it was inevitable that Russia would make overtures to Persia by feeding its insatiable hunger for cash, which stemmed in part from the structural inefficiencies of the administration and in part from the expensive tastes of its ruling classes. After Sir Mortimer Durand, the British minister in Teheran, had reported back with information gathered from Austrian sources in Constantinople in early 1900 that revealed that the Tsar's government was willing to lend money and effectively outbid Britain, all hell broke loose in London.[39] Committees were set up to look at extending the railway from Quetta to Sistan and to build a network of telegraph lines—"to save southern Persia," as Lord Curzon wrote, "from falling into [Russia's] grasp."[40]

Radical proposals were suggested to counter Russia's perceived advance, including undertaking major irrigation works in the Sistan region as a way of cultivating the land and building ties locally. There was even talk of the British seeking a lease of land in Helmand province, so that routes through to India could be protected effectively.[41] By now it was thought to be a question of when, and not if, Russia would attack. As Lord Curzon put it in 1901, "we wanted buffer states between ourselves and Russia." One by one, each of these had been "crushed out of existence." China, Turkestan, Afghanistan and now Persia had been lifted off the board. The buffer, he added, has been "reduced to the thinness of a wafer."[42]

Lord Salisbury was desperate, urging his Foreign Secretary, Lord Lansdowne, to find a way to lend money to Persia. "The situation seems . . . hopeless," the Prime Minister wrote in October 1901. The Treasury was reluctant to improve its offer, alarmed by how quickly the Shah and his entourage worked their way through substantial sums. Options were running out. "If the money is not found," the Prime Minister wrote, "Russia will establish a practical protectorate [in Persia] and we can only by force save the Gulf Ports from falling into it."[43]

Fear of just that happening had surfaced the previous year when it was reported that Russia was preparing to take control of the port of Bandar Abbas, a strategically vital location controlling the Straits of Hormuz—the narrowest point in the Persian Gulf. As one alarmed peer told the House of Lords, "the presence of a naval arsenal in the Persian Gulf in the hands of a great Power would be a menace not only to our trade with India and China, but also to that of Australasia."[44] As British warships were ordered to take counter-measures in the event of any move by the Russians, Lord Lansdowne was adamant: "We should regard the establishment of a naval base, or of a fortified port, in the Persian Gulf by any other Power as a very grave menace to British interests." The consequences, he said, would be serious. He meant war.[45]

Russian ghosts were everywhere. Anxious Foreign Office officials pored over a stream of reports on the activities of tsarist officers, engineers and surveyors in Persia that was flooding back to London.[46] The significance of a new Russian-backed trading company operating between Odessa on the Black Sea and Bushihr on the southern coast of Persia was earnestly discussed in Parliament, while MPs were alarmed by confident reports that shadowy figures who claimed to be spotting "birds, butterflies and other animalculae" were in fact Russian agents distributing rifles to tribesmen in contentious border regions and stirring up discontent.[47] The situation attracted the attention of King Edward VII, who wrote to the Foreign Secretary in 1901 stating his concern that "Russian influence seems daily preponderating in Persia to the detriment of England," and urging him to tell the Shah that failure to stand up to the Russians would not be tolerated.[48] It counted for little that the British minister in Teheran, Sir Cecil Spring-Rice, reported that the Shah swore blind that he "does not intend to take up position in Persia which would facilitate the invasion of India."[49]

Anxiety mounted at a time when there was an acute sense of imperial overstretch. Confrontation with the Boers in southern Africa and the Yihetuan uprising (better known as the Boxer Rebellion) in China drove home the idea that Britain was at risk of being overwhelmed overseas—further exacerbating fears of Russian advance. A doom-laden report presented to the Cabinet in London at the end of 1901 stated that the Russians would be able to deliver 200,000 men into Central Asia, and more than half that number uncomfortably close to the Indian border, once the railway line was extended from Orenburg to Tashkent.[50] This came hot on the heels of a report from Batumi in Georgia that the Russians were about to transfer 20,000 men to Central Asia—a false alarm, as it turned out.[51] The problem was that from Britain's point of view the options seemed limited: the cost of reinforcing the frontier was ruinous—calculated a few years later to be no less than £20 million, plus a rolling annual cost.[52]

Violent scenes on the streets of St. Petersburg in 1905 and the catastrophic defeat of the Tsar's navy in the Russo-Japanese War provided small comfort to those who thought it was only a matter of time before Russia broke its shackles. Britain could ill afford to resist what was openly referred to as the "menacing advance of Russia"; other solutions were needed to stop a bad situation from becoming worse. Perhaps, one paper prepared by military intelligence suggested, it was time to agree terms with Germany to concentrate Russian minds?[53]

In London, talk turned to the possibility of a British military intervention in Mesopotamia, part of the now constant preoccupation with shoring up Britain's presence across the Middle East. The Committee for Imperial Defence reviewed the possibility of occupying Basra, while there was excited discussion about dismembering Asiatic Turkey to gain access to the rich fields of the Euphrates. Then there were proposals in 1906 for a railway line to be built from the Persian Gulf to Mosul, which among other benefits would allow British troops to be delivered to Russia's soft underbelly in the

Caucasus.[54] One by one these were dismissed, on the grounds of practicality and cost: as Sir Edward Grey, the new Foreign Secretary warned, the cost of an invasion—and of securing and defending new frontiers—would run into the millions.[55]

Grey had another idea. Britain's position in the east was limited and dangerously exposed. What was needed was the reorientation of Russia's focus away from this region altogether. In a bold statement given to *The Times* just a month before his appointment at the end of 1905, he made it clear that there would be much to gain if an understanding could be reached about "our Asiatic possessions." No British government, he said, would "make it its business to thwart or obstruct Russia's policy in Europe." It was "urgently desirable," therefore, "that Russia's position and influence" should be expanded in Europe—and diverted, in other words, from Asia.[56]

The timing could not have been better. France was becoming increasingly agitated about the burgeoning economic growth of Germany, its neighbour and bitter rival. Memories of the Franco-Prussian War of 1870–71, which had led to the siege of Paris and a Prussian victory parade through the centre of the city following the agreement of an armistice, were still fresh in the mind. The speed of that invasion had been a great shock, prompting fears that another lightning strike might catch France unawares again—especially since one of the effects of the attack had been the unification of Germany into an empire, proclaimed in the Palace of Versailles itself.

This was bad enough. The French were deeply alarmed by the surging rise in German industry in the two decades after 1870 as coal production doubled and metal production trebled.[57] The upswing in the economy led to greater and greater investment in an already impressive military machine on both land and sea. French diplomats worked furiously behind the scenes in the early 1890s to conclude a military convention and then a full-blown alliance with Russia, the primary purpose of which was self-defence: both countries agreed to attack Germany in the event that the latter or its allies mobilised their armies—and indeed both gave formal undertakings to act against Britain in the event that London moved against either.[58]

The British desire to reorientate Russian attention to its western border was therefore music to French ears. The first phase of a realignment between London and Paris took place in 1904, when an Entente Cordiale was signed following detailed discussions of mutual interests around the world. Not surprisingly, the role of Russia was central to these negotiations. In 1907, the moment came when the circle of alliances was completed. Formal agreement was reached with Russia across the heart of the world, with a fixed line demarcating spheres of influence in Persia alongside terms to restrict Russian involvement in Afghanistan to a minimum.[59] The way to relieve India "from apprehension and strain," Edward Grey argued, was to forge a more positive understanding with Russia. This would ensure that "Russia does not get hold of the parts of Persia which are dangerous to us."[60] As he confided in 1912, he had long had misgivings about the traditional policy of simultaneously trying to push and contain Russia, noting that "for years, I have held that this was a mistaken policy."[61] Seeking an alliance, in other words, was a much more elegant and productive way to move forward.

Senior diplomats recognised, however, that rapprochement with Russia came at a price: Germany. As Sir Charles Hardinge, permanent undersecretary at the Foreign Office in London, stressed in 1908, "it is far more essential for us to have a good understanding with Russia in Asia and the Near East, than for us to be on good terms with Germany."[62] It was a message he was at pains to repeat, even after he had been posted to India as viceroy two years later. "We are practically impotent," he wrote, if Russia were to escalate in Persia. It was therefore worth doing everything possible to balance the situation in Europe: "it is far more disadvantageous to have an unfriendly France and unfriendly Russia than an unfriendly Germany."[63] Britain's relations with Russia were "being subjected to severe strain" as a result of tensions in Persia, agreed Sir Arthur Nicolson, ambassador to St. Petersburg. "I think," he went on, "that it is absolutely essential that we should at all costs maintain to the full our understanding with Russia."[64]

Keeping Russia happy at all costs became the driving thrust of British policy after the alliance had been signed. In 1907, Sir Edward Grey told the Russian ambassador to London that Britain might consider being more flexible on the issue of the Bosporus—if the Russians agreed to establish "permanent good relations."[65] This was enough to prompt a shuffling of the European house of cards, as St. Petersburg embarked on a round of diplomatic horse-trading that included gaining Austrian support on the issue of the Bosporus Straits in exchange for acquiescence over the annexation of Bosnia—a deal that was to have spectacular consequences.[66]

In 1910, Sir Edward Grey wrote again of the need to sacrifice relations with Berlin if necessary: "we cannot enter into a political understanding with Germany which would separate us from Russia and France."[67] The single-mindedness of this approach was keenly felt in St. Petersburg, which recognised the frantic courting by the British—and the opportunities it presented. "It seems to me," mused the Russian Foreign Minister Sergei Sazonov towards the end of 1910, that "the London cabinet looks upon the Anglo-Russian Convention of 1907 as being important for the Asiatic interest of England." That being the case, he went on, it seemed that Britain could be pushed to make valuable concessions "in order to keep a Convention alive which is of such importance to them."[68] It was an astute observation.

As Russian forces began in 1910 to make new forays into Mongolia, Tibet and Chinese Turkestan, British observers could barely hide their alarm.[69] The extension of Russia's reach emphatically underlined just how weak Britain's position was. Things could hardly have looked worse, as Grey's downbeat assessment in the spring of 1914 made clear. It was the same story in Afghanistan, Tibet, Mongolia and Persia: "all along the line we want something, and we have nothing to give." In Persia, there remained "nothing to concede" to Russia, he noted, while there was no leverage in Afghanistan either. Worse, "the Russians are willing to occupy Persia, and we are not."[70] Britain was spent—at least in Asia. It was time, surely, for the endgame. The question was where and when that would come.

As the reality of the difficulties facing them sank in, British officials did not lose sight of the fact that they also had to contend with the ultimate nightmare scenario, one that could easily make a fragile position even worse: an alliance between Russia and Germany. These fears had stalked British policymakers for some time. Indeed, an important element of the Anglo-Russian alliance of 1907 had been to co-operate and find a status quo that was mutually beneficial in Asia. To maintain the fine balance, Sir Arthur Nicolson stressed to Grey, it was essential to "deter Russia from moving towards Berlin."[71]

The sense of mounting panic was made worse by the continuing growth of German capabilities—and ambitions. Berlin's buoyant economy and the rise in its military spending were sources of concern. Some senior figures in the British Foreign Office had no doubt at all that Germany's aim was to "obtain the preponderance on the continent of Europe," and that this would lead to military confrontation. After all, all empires faced challenges from rivals, Sir Edward Grey was reminded; "personally," said Nicolson, "I am convinced that, sooner or later, we shall have to repeat the same struggle with Germany." It was vital, therefore, to keep France and Russia happy.[72]

Germany's potential to destabilise a finely balanced equilibrium in Europe, and therefore beyond, meant that there was something of a perfect storm brewing. Fears that "Russia should emerge on the side of the Central Powers' Alliance [that is, Germany, Austro-Hungary and Italy]" became acute. Dislodging relations between Britain, Russia and France and "smashing . . . the Triple Entente" was perceived to be the overriding goal of Berlin.[73] "We are sincerely afraid," admitted Grey during a later round of anxiety, of the possibility that Russia could be tempted to leave the Triple Entente.[74]

The fears were not without some basis. The German ambassador to Persia, for example, recognised that while there was "little to be gained" in that country, useful concessions elsewhere could be wrung from St. Petersburg if Russian interests in Persia were perceived as being at stake.[75] This is what lay behind a meeting between the Kaiser and Tsar Nicholas II at Potsdam in the winter of 1910, accompanied by high-level discussions between the respective Foreign Ministers, which simply seemed to confirm fears that the "European groupings," as Sir Arthur Nicolson called them, might be rearranged—to Britain's detriment.[76]

Suspicion of Germany and its actions (real or imagined) had been burnt into the psyche of British diplomats well before the alliance of 1907. Three years earlier, Sir Francis Bertie received a letter from one of the assistant clerks at the Foreign Office shortly before Bertie's appointment as ambassador to Paris, which told him how important it was that the mission in France should be led by "someone there with his eyes open and above all to German designs." In reply, Bertie wrote that it was quite right to breathe distrust about Germany: "she has never done anything for us but bleed us. She is false and grasping and our real enemy commercially and politically."[77]

Ironically of course, the sense of German menace was itself underpinned by the vulnerability felt by this middle European nation as it faced the possibility of being caught in the middle of a Franco-Russia alliance which talked of military co-operation and joint attack in the event of provocation. It was not long before festering paranoia about being trapped on two flanks led the German High Command to consider its own options. In the aftermath of the Franco-Russian alliance of 1904, the Chief of the General Staff of the German army, Count Alfred von Schlieffen, came up with a plan that drew heavily on the experiences of 1870 when the French had been torn to shreds, and posited a scenario in which the Kaiser's army might neutralise France before swinging east to deal with Russia. The plan was ambitious militarily and logistically: it would require a million railwaymen, 30,000 locomotives, 65,000 passenger cars and 700,000 goods wagons, that would shift 3 million soldiers as well as 86,000 horses and mountains of ammunition over a seventeen-day period.[78]

This blueprint was mirrored by similar planning at the time by the Russian army, which by the summer of 1910 had devised Plan 19, a set of detailed steps to be taken in the event of a German attack that involved falling back on a chain of fortresses along a north–south line running from Kovno to Brest, and preparing for a counter-attack. Two variants were developed to this proposal in 1912, known as Plans 19A and G, the latter of which involved a swift counter-attack in the event of Germany commencing hostilities, and whose aim was blunt: "the transfer of the war into [enemy] territory"—that is to say, into Germany and the Austro-Hungarian Empire.[79]

The German High Command, as well as the Kaiser, were acutely aware of the pressure ratcheting up from outside, and of the sense of being pushed into a corner. The public outcry over a proposal to build a railway line from Berlin to Baghdad bemused the Kaiser: surely, he reasoned, the laying down of track thousands of miles away would be an issue only if there were a war between his country and England. And in the event that that happened, he went on, would it be realistic to think that we would want our soldiers stationed so far away from home?[80]

Or there was the reaction to Germany's response to the deployment of French troops in Morocco in 1911, in contravention of a previous agreement between Berlin and Paris. On that occasion, the dispatch of a German cruiser, *Panther*, in an attempt to strong-arm the French into a settlement, backfired badly. Not only was Germany given an embarrassing public lesson that its political reach was severely limited, but to make matters worse Berlin saw a heavy fall in the stock market: in the wake of the Morocco crisis in September 1911, shares crashed by more than 30 per cent, causing the Reichsbank to lose more than a fifth of its reserves in a single month. Even if this financial disaster was not engineered by the French, as many Germans believed, it was certainly true that the former had exploited the situation, withdrawing short-term funds in an act that undoubtedly played a role in creating a liquidity crisis.[81]

Considerable effort went into opening up new channels and building new connections and alliances. Much attention was paid to the Near and Middle East, with German banks expanding heavily into Egypt, Sudan and the Ottoman Empire, while a programme of establishing posts in Arabic, Persian and related studies was not only generously endowed but was followed by the Kaiser himself. The increasing links between the Islamic and

German-speaking worlds caught the imaginations of the young, as well as of academics, soldiers, diplomats and politicians. One young man in the early years of the twentieth century wrote wistfully that when he looked out at the beautiful buildings of Vienna and at the Ringstraße—the road surrounding the city—he could not help but experience a "magical effect." Yet Adolf Hitler did not feel he was back in the Holy Roman Empire, or in classical antiquity, just two obvious choices of a romanticised past; he felt as though he was in a scene from *A Thousand and One Nights*.[82]

A dangerous siege mentality was building up in Germany, alongside an acute sense that Berlin had powerful enemies and was at their mercy. Helmuth von Moltke, Schlieffen's successor as Chief of the General Staff, as well as other senior officers became convinced that war was inevitable and that the sooner conflict came the better; postponing confrontation, he argued, would be to Germany's disadvantage. It was better to start a war and engage with the enemy, Moltke said in the spring of 1914, "while we still stand a chance of victory."[83]

Why was there such hatred of us, wrote Robert Musil in Berlin in September 1914; where did the envy come from that "was no fault of our own?"[84] He was right to note the rising tension in Europe, which was being stoked in popular culture. Books about German spies and German plans to take over Europe became enormously popular. *The Invasion of 1910*, written by William LeQueux, sold more than a million copies and was translated into twenty-seven languages; then there was *When William Came: A Story of London under the Hohenzollern*, by Saki, another bestseller that came out on the eve of the war, which sees the hero return from Asia to find Britain defeated and occupied by the Germans.[85]

It was almost a self-fulfilling prophecy therefore that the Germans should look to find ways to minimise risks or to be able to counter them. It was entirely understandable, for example, that assurances and agreements should be sought from Russia—though this fact alone further alarmed Britain.[86] Likewise, the recommendations for the German army made by General Colmar von der Goltz, who had spent more than a decade reforming the Ottoman army (where he was known as "Goltz Pasha)," were all about trying to provide some manoeuvrability in a military crisis. While Turkish support could be useful against Russia, Goltz told his colleagues, it could be "of the highest value" against Britain in the Near East.[87]

. . .

The problem was that the attention that Germany paid to the Ottoman world put too much pressure on Russia's nerves. Officials in St. Petersburg were deeply sensitive about the Straits—and edgy about the prospect of a new player muscling in on what they perceived to be their turf. Talk had turned to occupying Constantinople on numerous occasions around the turn of the century; by the end of 1912, plans began to be developed to have Russian forces take control of the city—in theory only on a temporary basis during a round of warfare in the Balkans.[88] Nevertheless, the Russians were antagonised too by the apparent indifference of their allies, the British and the French, to the situation that saw increasing German control of the Ottoman military which included the secondment of a commanding officer of the Ottoman fleet. There was particular anguish about the imminent delivery to the Turks of two British-built dreadnoughts: these state-of-the-art battleships would give the Ottomans a decisive and calamitous advantage over Russian naval forces, wailed the Tsar's Naval Minister in 1914, and result in a "crushing, near six-fold superiority" over the Russian Black Sea fleet.[89]

The threat this posed was not just military but economic. More than a third of all Russian exports passed through the Dardanelles before the First World War, including nearly 90 per cent of cereals that were loaded at ports like Odessa and Sevastopol in the Crimea. As such, pleas to London to block, suspend or cancel the delivery of warships became an unhelpful trigger in a game of bluff and double-bluff between the great powers on the eve of war.[90] Some were in no doubt about how high the stakes were. "Our entire position in the Near East" is at risk, the Russian ambassador to Constantinople told St. Petersburg; "the unassailable right which we have acquired through centuries of immeasurable sacrifices and the shedding of Russian blood" was in serious danger.[91]

In this context, Italy's attack on Libya in 1911 and the Balkan Wars of 1912–13 that followed simply set off a chain reaction, as the Ottoman Empire's outlying provinces were picked off by opportunistic local and international rivals at moments of weakness. With the Ottoman regime teetering on the brink of collapse, ambitions and rivalries in Europe sharpened dramatically. For their part, the Germans began to think seriously about expanding into the east and establishing a protectorate to create a "German Orient."[92] While this sounded like expansionism, there was an important defensive streak to such thought too which chimed with growing aggressive sentiments that ran deep through the German High Command.[93] Germany, like Britain, was coming to expect the worst; and in the Germans' case, that meant stopping the Russians from taking control of the best parts of an Ottoman Empire that was widely thought to be rotting, while for the Russians it meant realising long-held dreams and securing a long-term future whose significance could not be overstated.

That Britain represented a threat to Germany—and vice versa—was, however, something of a red herring. Although modern historians talk insistently about the desire of the former to contain the latter, the jigsaw of competition across Europe was complex and multi-faceted. Certainly, it was far more complex than the simplistic story of a great rivalry between two nations that only burst into life as the First World War took shape and played out. By 1918, the real causes of the conflict had become obscured, as a distorting emphasis was placed on the naval race that saw expenditure on shipbuilding spiral upwards; on aggressive attitudes behind the scenes demanding war; and on the blind bloodlust of the Kaiser and his generals as they sought to provoke a war in continental Europe.

The reality of the story was very different. Although the days that followed the assassination of Franz Ferdinand saw a series of misunderstandings, discussions, ultimata and permutations that would be all but impossible to recreate, the seeds of war grew out of changes and developments located many thousands of miles away. Russia's rising ambition and the progress it was making in Persia, Central Asia and the Far East put pressure on Britain's position overseas, resulting in the fossilisation of alliances in Europe. All that stood in the way of further erosion of the enviable platform that Britain had built over the previous centuries was a series of mutual guarantees designed above all to keep Russia, the master-in-waiting, tied up.

Nevertheless, while storm clouds had been gathering, there seemed little immediate danger in the first months of 1914. "I have not seen such calm waters," wrote Arthur Nicolson in May, "since I have been at the Foreign Office."[94] Indeed, it promised to be a vintage year. Employees at the Ford Motor Co. in the United States were celebrating the doubling of their wages in January, the result of rising sales and innovative attempts to encourage an increase in production. Doctors were contemplating the consequences of the first successful non-direct blood transfusion, carried out in Brussels following pioneering work on the use of sodium citrate as an anticoagulant. In St. Petersburg, what kept most people worried in the early summer were the forest fires whose thick black smoke made the heavy summer air even more oppressive than usual. In Germany, inhabitants of

Fürth in northern Bavaria were in ecstasy after the town's team won a thrilling match against the mighty VfB Leipzig, defeating the odds by scoring a winning goal in extra time to become national football champions for the first time—making a hero of their coach, the Englishman William Townley. Even nature was being kind, according to the English poet Alice Meynell: the start of the summer of 1914 was idyllic, with a bumper harvest to look forward to; moon after moon was "heavenly sweet" as "the silken harvest climbed the down."[95]

In Britain, there was no sense of impending doom nor of imminent confrontation with Germany. The academics of Oxford University were preparing to celebrate German culture and intellect. There was already a large portrait of Kaiser Wilhelm II hanging in the Examination Schools that had been given as a gift following the German ruler's award of an honorary Doctorate of Civil Law in 1907.[96] But towards the end of June 1914, scarcely a month before the outbreak of hostilities, the leading lights of the city gathered to watch a procession of distinguished German figures receive honorary degrees. Among those applauded as they walked to the Sheldonian Theatre in their colourful gowns were the Duke of Saxe-Coburg-Gotha, the composer Richard Strauss, and Ludwig Mitteis, a rather pedestrian expert on Roman law, while honorary doctorates were conferred on the Duke of Württemberg and Prince Lichnowsky, German ambassador to London.[97]

Three days later Gavrilo Princip, a young idealist who was not yet twenty, discharged two bullets from a pistol at a passing car on the streets of Sarajevo. The first did not hit its target, instead striking in the stomach and mortally wounding the Archduchess Sophie, who was sitting in the back of the car with her husband. The second did: it killed Franz Ferdinand, heir to the throne of the Austro-Hungarian Empire. And with that, the world changed.[98]

Modern historians often focus on the "July crisis" of the weeks that followed and on the missed opportunities for peace, or on the way many had long feared and anticipated the outbreak of hostilities: recent scholarship has emphasised that the atmosphere as the world slipped towards war was one not of gung-ho bravado but of anxiety and misunderstanding. It was a nightmare scenario. As one leading historian has so aptly put it, "the protagonists of 1914 were sleepwalkers, watchful but unseeing, haunted by dreams, yet blind to the reality of the horror" they were about to unleash.[99]

By the time Sir Edward Grey realised that "the lamps are going out all over Europe," it was already too late.[100]

In the days after the assassination, it was fear of Russia that led to war. In Germany's case, it was the widespread apprehension about its neighbour to the east that was crucial. The Kaiser was repeatedly told by his generals that the threat posed by Russia would get stronger as its economy continued to surge forward.[101] This was echoed in St. Petersburg, where senior officials had formed the view that war was inevitable and that it was better for military confrontation to begin sooner rather than later.[102] The French too were anxious, having concluded long before that the best course they could take was to urge constant and consistent moderation in St. Petersburg, as well as in London. They would support Russia come what may.[103]

In Britain's case, it was the fear of what would happen if Russia cast its lot elsewhere that drove policy. As it was, by the start of 1914 there was already talk at the Foreign Office of realigning Britain with Germany in order to bring Russia in check.[104] With stand-off turning into crisis, diplomats, generals and politicians now tried to work out what would happen next. By the end of July, the diplomat George Clerk was writing anxiously from Constantinople to advise that Britain needed to do whatever was necessary to accommodate Russia. Otherwise, he said, we would be faced with consequences "where our very existence as an Empire will be at stake."[105]

Although some tried to pour cold water on such alarmist claims, the British ambassador to St. Petersburg, who had only recently cautioned that Russia was so powerful "that we must retain her friendship at almost any cost," now sent a telegram that was unequivocal.[106] Britain's position, he said, was "a perilous one," for the moment of truth had arrived: the choice now had to be made between supporting Russia "or renouncing her friendship. If we fail her now," he advised, "that friendly co-operation with her in Asia that is of such vital importance to us" would come to an end.[107]

There was no middle ground, as the Russian Foreign Minister made clear towards the end of July: while less than two weeks earlier he had been pledging that Russia "was free from all aggressive aims and in no way dreaming of any forcible acquisitions," now he was talking about the consequences if allies failed to stand side by side at the moment of reckoning. If Britain remained neutral now, he warned, it "would be tantamount to suicide."[108] This was a thinly veiled threat about British interests in Persia, if not in Asia as a whole.

As the "July crisis" escalated, British officials talked publicly about peace conferences, mediation and the defence of the sovereignty of Belgium. But the die was cast. Britain's fate—and that of its empire—was pinned on the decisions that were made in Russia. The two were rivals masquerading as allies; while neither was seeking to alienate and antagonise the other, it was obvious that the pendulum of power had swung away from London towards St. Petersburg. No one knew this better than the German Chancellor, Theobald von Bethmann-Hollweg, a well-connected career politician, who had been having sleepless nights for some time, praying for divine protection. Now, as he sat "on the terrace under a starry sky" ten days after the Sarajevo assassination, as the gears of war slowly locked into place, he turned to his secretary and said: "the future belongs to Russia."[109]

Just what this future involved was not clear in 1914. Russia's strength could easily flatter to deceive, for it was still in the early phases of social, economic and political metamorphosis. A scare in 1905 had almost plunged the country into full-scale revolution as demands for reform were largely ignored by a deeply conservative establishment. Then there was the heavy dependence on foreign capital, where outside funding was responsible for almost half of all new capital investments between 1890 and 1914—money that came in on the assumption of peace and of stable political conditions.[110]

Large-scale transformation took time, and was rarely painless. Had Russia stayed calm and chosen a less confrontational way to stand by its Serbian ally, its destiny—and with it that of Europe and Asia, if not North America too—would have been very different. As it was, 1914 brought the showdown that Queen Victoria had anticipated decades earlier: everything, she had said, boiled down to "a question of Russian or British supremacy in the world."[111] Britain could not afford to let Russia down.

And so, like a nightmarish game of chess where all possible moves are bad ones, the world went to war. As the initial euphoria and jingoism gave way to tragedy and horror on an unimaginable scale, a narrative developed that reshaped the past, and cast the confrontation in terms of a struggle between Germany and the Allies, a debate which has centred on the relative culpability of the former and the heroism of the latter.

The story that became embedded in public consciousness was that of German aggression and of the just war fought by the Allies. Explanations were needed for why a generation of bright young men with their futures ahead of them had been cast aside. Answers were needed to explain the sacrifice of brilliant figures like Patrick Shaw Stewart, a scholar whose superlative achievements at school, at university and in business had astonished his contemporaries as well as his correspondent, Lady Diana Manners, to whom he sent letters rich with erotic quotations in Latin and Greek.[112] Or to explain why working-class men who joined up alongside their friends to fight in specially constituted Pals Battalions were mown down in the opening hours of the catastrophic Somme offensive in 1916.[113] Or why there were war memorials across the country bearing the names of the men who had given their lives for their country—able to record the names of the fallen but not the silence that descended on villages and towns because of their absence.

It was not surprising, therefore, that a powerful narrative emerged that glorified the soldiers, celebrated their bravery and paid tribute to the sacrifices they had made. Winston Churchill wrote after the war that the British army was the finest force that had ever been assembled. Each man was "inspired not only by love of country but by a widespread conviction that human freedom was challenged by military and Imperial tyranny." The fight had been noble and just. "If two lives or ten lives were required by their commanders to kill one German, no word of complaint ever rose from the fighting troops . . . No slaughter however desolating prevented them from returning to the charge," declared Churchill. The fallen were "martyrs not less than soldiers [and] fulfilled the high purpose of duty with which they were imbued."[114]

Many at the time, however, did not see it this way. Some, like Edwin Campion Vaughan, a young lieutenant who had enlisted full of hope, could not understand the scale of suffering or its purpose. After seeing his company wiped out and facing the prospect of writing a casualty report, Campion Vaughan recorded, "I sat on the floor and drank whisky after whisky as I gazed into a black and empty future."[115] The stunning corpus of poetry produced during the war likewise paints a very different picture of how the conflict was viewed at the time. And so too do the number of courts martial that took place during the war, which hardly suggest a unanimity of resolve: more than 300,000 offences were dealt with by military courts—to say nothing of more minor matters of indiscipline that were dealt with in other ways.[116]

It was striking too that the locus of the conflict became anchored in the trenches of Flanders and among the horrors of the Somme. War had broken out far away from the networks that linked the empires of Europe with territories across the globe, away from the pressure points that had built up in Persia and in Central Asia and at the gateways to both India and the Far East which were of such great concern to British policymakers and politicians in the late nineteenth and early twentieth centuries. And yet the impending confrontation had been coming for decades. Britain looked on as Russia strained to show its support for Serbia, just as Grey had predicted. "A strong Slav feeling has arisen in Russia," he noted only a few years earlier, referring to the increasing call in the Balkans for Russia to play a greater role in the region as a protector of Slavic identity. "Bloodshed between Austria and Servia [*sic*] would certainly raise this to a dangerous height."[117] Here was the tinder that could set the world on fire.

In the circumstances, therefore, as Russia began to prepare to make a statement to the rest of the world, Britain had to stand full square behind its ally and rival—even if many found this confusing. When war broke out, Rupert Brooke—soon to find fame as a war poet—could barely contain his anger. "Everything's just the wrong way round," he wrote. "I want Germany to smash Russia to fragments, and then France to break Germany . . . Russia means the end of Europe and of any decency."[118] He had no doubts who Britain's real enemy was.

Conversely, the start of hostilities in turn meant sharpening animosities towards Germany—not only in 1914, but in the way that the war unfolded and when peace was settled four gruesome years later. The "hoary colleges of Oxford look down / On careless boys at play," wrote one war poet, "but when the bugles sounded—War! / They put their games away." The "shaven lawns" of the university were given up in exchange for "a bloody sod": "They gave their merry youth away / For country and for God."[119] The celebration of British ties with Germany and the honorary degrees given to its most famous sons quickly became a bitter memory that was best forgotten.

It was not surprising then that blame for the war should be affixed squarely on Germany, both in principle and in fact. Enshrined in the Treaty of Versailles was a clause that was categorical in assigning blame for the war: "The Allied and Associated Governments affirm and Germany accepts the responsibility of Germany and her allies for causing all the loss and damage to which the Allied and Associated Governments and their nationals have been subjected as a consequence of the war imposed upon them by the aggression of Germany and her allies."[120] The aim was to lay the grounds for redress and reparations to be paid; instead, it all but guaranteed a reaction—providing fertile ground to be exploited by a skilled demagogue who could unite national sentiment around the core of a strong Germany rising from the ashes.

The victors were such in name and in hope only. Over the course of four years, Britain went from being the world's largest creditor to being its largest debtor; France's economy was left in ruins after funding a war effort that put immense strains on the workforce and the country's financial and natural resources. In the words of one scholar, Russia meanwhile "entered the war to protect the empire [but] concluded with imperial destruction."[121]

The collapse of the European powers opened up the world for others. To cover the shortfalls in agricultural production and to pay for weapons and munitions, the Allies took on huge commitments, commissioning institutions such as J. P. Morgan & Co. to ensure a constant supply of goods and materials.[122] The supply of credit resulted in a redistribution of wealth every bit as dramatic as that which followed the discovery of the Americas four centuries earlier: money flowed out of Europe to the United States in a flood of bullion and promissory notes. The war bankrupted the Old World and enriched the New. The attempt to recoup losses from Germany (set at an eye-watering and impossibly high level equivalent to hundreds of billions of dollars at today's prices) was a desperate and futile attempt to prevent the inevitable: the Great War saw the treasuries of the participants ransacked as they tried to destroy each other, destroying themselves in the process.[123]

As the two bullets left the chamber of Princip's Browning revolver, Europe was a continent of empires. Italy, France, Austro-Hungary, Germany, Russia, Ottoman Turkey, Britain, Portugal, the Netherlands, even tiny Belgium, only formed in 1831, controlled vast territories across the world. At the moment of impact, the process of turning them back into local powers began. Within a matter of years, gone were the emperors who had sailed on each other's yachts and appointed each other to grand chivalric orders; gone were some colonies and dominions overseas—and others were starting to go in an inexorable progression to independence.

In the course of four years, perhaps 10 million were dead from fighting, and half the same again from disease and famine. Over $200 billion had been spent by the Allies and the Central Powers fighting each other. European economies were shattered by the unparalleled expenditures that were exacerbated by falling productivity. Countries engaged in the fighting posted deficits and clocked up debts at a furious pace—debts they could not afford.[124] The great empires that had dominated the world for four centuries did not slip away overnight. But it was the beginning of the end. Dusk was beginning to descend. The veil of shadows from behind which western Europe had emerged a few centuries earlier was starting to fall once again. The experience of war had been shattering; it made control of the Silk Roads and its riches more important than ever.

17

The Road of Black Gold

Few of William Knox D'Arcy's classmates at London's prestigious Westminster School can have thought that he would go on to have a prominent role in reshaping the world—especially when he did not arrive back for the start of term in September 1866. William's father had been caught up in some unsavoury business in Devon that led to him being declared bankrupt and deciding to move with his family to start a new life in the quiet town of Rockhampton in Queensland, Australia.

His teenage son got on with his studies quietly and diligently enough, qualifying as a lawyer and in due course setting up his own practice. He made a comfortable living and became an upstanding member of the local community, serving on the committee of the Rockhampton Jockey Club and indulging a love for shooting whenever time permitted.

In 1882, William had a stroke of fortune. Three brothers named Morgan had been looking to exploit what they thought was a potentially large gold find at Ironstone Mountain, just over twenty miles away from Rockhampton. In search of investment to help them establish a mining operation, they turned to the local bank manager, who in turn pointed them in the direction of William Knox D'Arcy. Intrigued by the possibility of a good return on his capital, Knox D'Arcy formed a syndicate with the bank manager and another mutual friend, and invested in the Morgan brothers' scheme.

As with all mining operations at their outset, a cool head was needed as an alarming amount of cash was swallowed up in the search for a jackpot. The Morgan brothers soon lost their nerve, rattled by the rate at which their funds were being expended, and sold their interest to the three partners. They sold at just the wrong moment. The gold deposits at what had been renamed Mount Morgan turned out to be among the richest in history. Shares that had been sold in the business shot up 2,000-fold in value, while over a ten-year period the return on the investment was 200,000 per cent. Knox D'Arcy, who controlled more shares than his partners and over a third of the business, went from being a small-town lawyer in Australia to one of the richest men in the world.[1]

It was not long before he packed up in Australia and headed for England in triumph. He bought a magnificent town house at 42 Grosvenor Square and a suitably grand estate at Stanmore Hall, just outside London, which he had remodelled and decorated with the finest furnishings money could buy, hiring Morris & Co., the firm set up by William Morris, to take care of the interiors. He commissioned a set of tapestries from Edward Burne-Jones that took four years to weave, such was their quality. Entirely appropriately, they celebrated the quest for the Holy Grail—a suitable cipher for the discovery of incalculable treasure.[2]

Knox D'Arcy knew how to live the good life, renting a fine shooting estate in Norfolk and taking a box by the finishing post at the Epsom races. Two drawings in the National Portrait Gallery capture his character perfectly. One has him sitting back contentedly, with a jovial smile on his face, his generous girth testimony to his enjoyment of fine food and excellent wines; the other has him leaning forward as if to share stories of his business adventures with a friend, champagne glass in front of him, cigarette in hand.[3]

His success and extraordinary wealth made him an obvious man to seek out for those who, like the Morgan brothers, needed investors. One such was Antoine Kitabgi, a well-connected official in the Persian administration who was put in touch with Knox D'Arcy towards the end of 1900 by Sir Henry Drummond-Wolff, former British envoy in Teheran. Despite being a Catholic from a Georgian background, Kitabgi had done well for himself in Persia, rising to become director-general of Persian Customs and a man with fingers in many pies. He had been involved in several attempts to draw in investment from abroad to stimulate the economy, negotiating or attempting to negotiate concessions for outsiders to take positions in the banking sector and in the production and distribution of tobacco.[4]

These efforts were not entirely motivated by altruism or patriotism, for men like Kitabgi realised that they could parlay their connections into lucrative rewards if and when deals were agreed. Their line of business was opening doors in return for money. This was a source of deep irritation in London, Paris, St. Petersburg and Berlin, where diplomats, politicians and businessmen found the Persian way of operating opaque, if not downright corrupt. Efforts to modernise the country had made little progress, while the old tradition of relying on foreigners to run the armed forces or take key administrative roles resulted in frustration all round.[5] Every time Persia took one step forward, it seemed to take another back.

It was all very well criticising the ruling elite, but they had long been trained to behave in this way. The Shah and those around him were like over-indulged children who had been taught that if they held out long enough, they would be rewarded by the great powers, who were terrified that they would lose position in this strategically crucial region if they did not cough up. When Shah Moẓaffar od-Dīn was not invested with the Order of the Garter during his visit to England in 1902 and refused to accept any lesser honour, he left the country making it clear he was "very unhappy"; this prompted senior diplomats to set about convincing the reluctant King Edward VII, in whose gift membership of the order lay, to invest the Shah after his return home. Even then there were mishaps with this "terrible subject" when it was discovered that the Shah did not possess knee-breeches, which were deemed essential to the investiture—until one resourceful diplomat discovered a precedent where a previous recipient had received the honour wearing trousers. "What a nightmare that Garter episode was," grumbled the Foreign Secretary Lord Lansdowne afterwards.[6]

And in fact, while the bribery that went hand in hand with getting anything done in Persia seemed vulgar, in many ways the Persians who scuttled back and forth through the corridors of power and the great financial centres of Europe in the late nineteenth and early twentieth century were not dissimilar to the Sogdian traders of antiquity who travelled over long distances to do business, or the Armenians and Jews who played the same role in the early modern period. The difference was that where the Sogdians had to take goods with them to sell, their later peers were selling their services and their contacts. These had been commoditised precisely because there were handsome rewards to be made. Had there been no takers, doubtless things would have been rather different. As it was, Persia's location between east and west, linking the Gulf and India with the tip of Arabia, the

Horn of Africa and access to the Suez Canal, meant that it was courted at no matter what cost—albeit through gritted teeth.

When Kitabgi approached Drummond-Wolff and was put in touch with Knox D'Arcy, who was described as "a capitalist of the highest order," he had his eye not on Persia's tobacco or banking sector but on its mineral wealth. And Knox D'Arcy was the perfect person to talk to. He had struck gold once before in Australia; Kitabgi offered him the chance to do so again; this time it was black gold that was at stake.[7]

The existence of substantial oil deposits in Persia was hardly a secret. Byzantine authors in late antiquity wrote regularly of the destructive power of "Median fire," a substance made from petroleum most likely taken from surface seepages in northern Persia comparable to the inflammable "Greek fire" that the Byzantines made from outflows in the Black Sea region.[8]

The first systematic geological surveys in the 1850s had pointed to the likelihood of substantial resources below the surface and led to a series of concessions being given to investors, lured by the prospect of making their fortunes at a time when the world seemed to be disgorging its treasures to lucky prospectors, from California Gold Country to the Witwatersrand basin in southern Africa.[9] Baron Paul Julius de Reuter, founder of the eponymous news agency, was one who moved in on Persia. In 1872, de Reuter gained "the exclusive and definite privilege" to extract whatever he could from "the mines of coal, iron, copper, lead and petroleum" across the whole of the country, as well as options on the construction of roads, public works and other infrastructure projects.[10]

For one reason or another, these came to nothing. There was fierce local opposition to the grant of licences, with populist figures like Sayyid Jamāl al-Dīn al-Afghānī deploring the fact that "the reins of the government [were being] handed to the enemy of Islam." As one of the most vocal critics wrote, "the realms of Islam will be soon under the control of foreigners, who will rule therein as they please and do as they will."[11] There was also international pressure to contend with, which led to the original de Reuter concession being declared null and void barely a year after it had been agreed.[12]

Although de Reuter agreed a second concession in 1889 that gave him the rights to all Persia's mineral resources other than precious metal—in return for substantial "gifts" of money to the Shah and his key officials as well as an agreed royalty payment on future profits—this lapsed when efforts to find oil that could be exploited in commercially viable quantities failed within the designated ten-year time frame. Life had not been made any easier by what one leading British businessman described as "the backward state of the country, and the absence of communication and transport," made worse by the "direct hostility, opposition and outrage from high officials of the Persian Government."[13] Nor was there any sympathy in London. There were risks to doing business in this part of the world, one internal minute noted; anyone who expected things to work as they did in Europe was extremely foolish. "It is their own fault" if expectations were left disappointed, it stated coldly.[14]

Knox D'Arcy was, nevertheless, intrigued by the proposition put to him by Kitabgi. He studied the findings of the French geologists who had been surveying the country for the best part of a decade and took soundings from Dr. Boverton Redwood, one of Britain's leading experts on petroleum and author of handbooks on oil production and on the safe storage, transportation, distribution and use of petroleum and its products.[15] There was no need to do all this research, Kitabgi meanwhile assured Drummond-Wolff, asserting that "we are in the presence of a source of riches [that are] incalculable."[16]

Knox D'Arcy was interested enough by what he read and heard to strike a deal with those whose help would be needed to win a concession from the Shah, namely Edouard Cotte, who had served as de Reuter's agent and was therefore a familiar face in Persian circles, and Kitabgi himself—while Drummond-Wolff was also promised a reward further down the line should the project be successful. Knox D'Arcy then approached the Foreign Office to get its blessing for the project, and duly sent his representative Alfred Marriott to Teheran to commence negotiations with a formal letter of introduction.

While the letter itself had little intrinsic value, requesting simply that the bearer be offered whatever assistance he may require, in a world where signals could easily be misread the signature of the Foreign Secretary was a powerful tool, suggesting that the British government stood behind Knox D'Arcy's initiative.[17] Marriott looked at the Persian court with wonder. The throne, he wrote in his journal, was "entirely encrusted with diamonds, sapphires and emeralds, and there are jewelled birds (<u>not</u> peacocks) standing on the sides"; at least, he was able to report, the Shah was an "exceedingly good shot."[18]

In fact, the real work was done by Kitabgi, who according to one report managed to secure "in a very thorough manner the support of all the Shah's principal Ministers and courtiers, not even forgetting the personal servant who brings His Majesty his pipe and morning coffee"—a euphemism for greasing their palms. Things were going well, Knox D'Arcy was told; it seemed likely that a petroleum concession would "be granted by the Persian government."[19]

The process of getting an agreement in writing was tortuous. Unseen obstacles appeared from nowhere, prompting cables back to London to ask for advice from Knox D'Arcy—and for authorisation to fork out still more. "I hope you will approve this as to refuse would be to lose the affair," Marriott urged. "Don't scruple if you can propose anything for facilitating affairs on my part," came the reply.[20] Knox D'Arcy meant that he was happy to be liberal with his money, and was willing to do whatever it took to get what he wanted. It was impossible to tell when new demands were made or promises given as to who the real beneficiaries were; there were rumours that the Russians had got wind of the negotiations, which were supposedly being conducted in secret, and false trails were laid to put them off the scent.[21]

And then, almost without warning, word came through (while Marriott was at a dinner party in Teheran) that the Shah had signed the agreement. In return for £20,000, with the same amount in shares to be paid on the formation of the company, plus an annual royalty of 16 per cent on net profits, Knox D'Arcy, described in the formalities as a man "of independent means residing in London at No. 42 Grosvenor Square," was granted sweeping rights. He was awarded "a special and exclusive privilege to search for, obtain, exploit, develop, render suitable for trade, carry away and sell natural gas, petroleum, asphalt and ozokerite throughout the whole extent of the Persian Empire for a term of 60 years." In addition, he received the exclusive right of laying pipelines, establishing storage facilities, refineries, stations and pump services.[22]

A royal proclamation that followed announced that Knox D'Arcy and "all his heirs and assigns and friends" had been granted "full powers and unlimited liberty for a period of sixty years to probe, pierce and drill at their will the depths of Persian Soil," and entreated "all officials of this blessed kingdom" to help a man who enjoyed "the favour of our splendid court."[23] He had been handed the keys to the kingdom; the question was whether he could now find the lock.

Experienced observers in Teheran were not convinced. Even if "petroleum is discovered, as their agents believe will be the case," noted Sir Arthur Hardinge, Britain's representative to Persia, major challenges lay ahead. It was worth remembering, he went on, that "the soil of Persia, whether it contains oil or not, has been strewn of late years with wrecks of so many hopeful schemes of commercial and political regeneration that it would be rash to predict the future of this latest venture."[24]

Perhaps the Shah too was gambling that little would come of the affair and that he could simply help himself to upfront payments as he had done in the past. It was certainly true that the economic situation in Persia at this time was dire: the government was facing a major budgetary shortfall, producing a precarious and worrying deficit, with the result that it was worth cutting corners to get money from Knox D'Arcy's deep pockets. This was also a time of intense anxiety within the British Foreign Office, which paid much less attention to the newly awarded concession than it did to the overtures Teheran was making both to London and, worryingly, to St. Petersburg in the years before the First World War.

The Russians reacted badly to news of the Knox concession. As it was, they had almost managed to derail the award when the Shah received a personal telegram from the Tsar urging him not to proceed.[25] Knox D'Arcy had been sufficiently worried that Russian noses would be put out of joint by the agreement that he had directed that rights in the northern provinces be specifically excluded so as "to give no umbrage" to Persia's powerful northern neighbour. From London's point of view, the worry was that Russia would over-compensate for losing out by being more accommodating to the Shah and his officials than ever.[26] As Britain's representative in Teheran warned Lord Lansdowne, the award of a concession might be "fraught with political and economic results" if oil was found in any meaningful quantity.[27] There was no disguising the truth that pressure was ratcheting up in the rivalry for influence and resources in the Gulf region.

In the short term things blew over, largely because Knox D'Arcy's project seemed doomed to failure. Work was slow thanks to the difficult climate, the large number of religious festivals and the regular and dispiriting mechanical failure of the rigs and drills. There was open hostility too in the form of complaints about pay, about working practices and about the small number of locals who were employed, while there was also no end of trouble with local tribes wanting to be bought off.[28] Knox D'Arcy grew nervous about the lack of progress and how much of his money was being spent. "Delay serious," he cabled his drilling team less than a year after the concession was agreed; "pray expedite."[29] A week later, he sent another dispatch: "have you free access to wells?" he asked his chief engineer in despair. Logbooks reveal large quantities of pipes, tubes, shovels, steel and anvils being shipped from Britain, alongside rifles, pistols and ammunition. Wage slips from 1901–2 also show funds being spent in ever increasing quantities. It must have felt to Knox D'Arcy that he was burying his money in the sand.[30]

If he was anxious, then so too were his bankers at Lloyds, who became increasingly perturbed about the size of the overdraft of a man they had assumed had limitless funds at his disposal.[31] What made it worse was that there was little to show for the hard work and high costs: Knox D'Arcy needed to convince other investors to buy shares in the business and thereby take pressure off his personal cash flows and provide the capital to take things forward. His teams were producing promising signs of oil; what he needed was a major strike.

As he grew increasingly desperate, Knox D'Arcy sounded out potential investors or even buyers for his concession, travelling to Cannes to meet with Baron Alphonse de Rothschild, whose family already had extensive interests in the oil business in Baku. This set off alarm bells in London. In particular, it caught the attention of the British navy: Sir John Fisher, First Lord of the Admiralty, had become evangelical in his belief that the future of naval warfare and of mastery of the seas lay in switching from coal to oil. "Oil fuel," he wrote to a friend in 1901, "will absolutely revolutionise naval strategy. It's a case of 'Wake up England!'"[32] Despite the failure to deliver a knock-out discovery, all the evidence suggested that Persia had the potential to be a major source of oil. If this could be secured for the exclusive use of the Royal Navy, then so much the better. But it was essential that control of such resources should not be surrendered into foreign hands.

The Admiralty stepped in to broker an agreement between Knox D'Arcy and a Scottish oil company that had met with considerable success in Burma. After offering a contract to the latter in 1905 to supply the navy with 50,000 tons of oil per annum, the directors of the Burmah Oil Company were persuaded to take a major stake in what was renamed the Concessions Syndicate. They did so not out of patriotic duty but because it was a sensible diversification strategy, and because their track record also enabled them to raise more capital. Although this allowed Knox D'Arcy to breathe a sigh of relief, writing that the terms he had achieved "were better than I could have obtained from any other company," there was still no guarantee of success—as the ever sceptical British diplomatic representative in Teheran noted drily in his reports home. Finding oil was one problem; handling persistent attempts at blackmail was another.[33]

True enough, the new partnership had little to show for its efforts over the next three years. Wells that were drilled failed to bear fruit, while expenditure ate away at the finances of shareholders. By the spring of 1908, the directors of the Burmah Oil Company were openly talking about pulling out of Persia altogether. On 14 May 1908, they sent word to George Reynolds, leader of operations in the field and a man described by one of those who worked with him as single-minded, determined and made of "solid British oak," to prepare to abandon operations. He was instructed to drill two wells that had been established at Masjed Soleymān to a depth of 1,600 feet. If no oil were found, he should "abandon operations, close down and bring back as much of the plant as is possible," and ship it to Burma where it would prove more useful.[34]

As the letter made its way through the post houses of Europe and the Levant and on to Persia, Reynolds carried on with his job, unaware of how close he was to being shut down. His team kept drilling, forcing a way through rock so hard that it forced the drill bit loose. The bit was lost in the hole for several days; as the clock was ticking down, it was finally recovered and reattached. On 28 May, at four in the morning, they hit the motherlode, striking oil and sending black gold shooting high into the air. It was a huge find.[35]

Arnold Wilson, a British army lieutenant who was in charge of the security of the site, sent a coded cable back home with the news. It simply said: "See Psalm 104, verse 15 second sentence."[36] The verse entreated the good Lord to bring forth from the earth oil to make faces shine with happiness. The discovery, he told his father, promised fabulous rewards for Britain—and hopefully, he added, for the engineers "who have persevered so long, in spite of their top-hatted directors . . . in this inhospitable climate."[37]

Investors who piled into the Anglo-Persian Oil Company, the vehicle that controlled the rights to the concession, after shares were offered in 1909 reckoned that the first well at Masjed Soleymān was just the tip of the iceberg and there would be high rewards in the future. Naturally, it would take time and money to build up the infrastructure necessary to allow oil to be exported, as well as to drill new wells and find new fields. Nor was it easy running things smoothly on the ground, where Arnold Wilson complained he had to spend time bridging the cultural gap between the British "who cannot say what they mean and Persians who do not always mean what they say." The British, he declared, saw a contract as an agreement that would stand up in court; the Persians simply saw it as an expression of intentions.[38]

Nevertheless, a pipeline was soon built to connect the first field to the island of Ābādān in the Shaṭṭ al-ʿArab, which had been chosen as the location for a refinery and export centre. It took Persia's oil to the Gulf, where it could then be loaded on to ships and brought back to Europe to be sold at a time when the continent's energy needs were rising sharply. The pipeline itself was highly symbolic, for it marked the first strand in what was to become a web of pipelines criss-crossing Asia that gave new form and life to the old Silk Roads.

Problems were brewing. The discovery of oil made the piece of paper signed by the Shah in 1901 one of the most important documents of the twentieth century. For while it laid the basis for a multi-billion-dollar business to grow—the Anglo-Persian Oil Company eventually became British Petroleum—it also paved the way for political turmoil. That the terms of the agreement handed control of Persia's crown jewels to foreign investors led to a deep and festering hatred of the outside world, which in turn led to nationalism and, ultimately, to a more profound suspicion and rejection of the west best epitomised in modern Islamic fundamentalism. The desire to win control of oil would be the cause of many problems in the future.

On a human level, Knox D'Arcy's concession is an amazing tale of business acumen and triumph against the odds; but its global significance is on a par with Columbus' trans-Atlantic discovery of 1492. Then too, immense treasures and riches had been expropriated by the conquistadors and shipped back to Europe. The same thing happened again. One reason for this was the close interest paid by Admiral Fisher and the Royal Navy, who monitored the situation in Persia closely. When Anglo-Persian experienced cash-flow problems in 1912, Fisher was quick to step in, concerned that the business might be acquired by producers like Royal Dutch/Shell, which had built up a substantial production and distribution network from an initial base in the Dutch East Indies. Fisher went to see the First Lord of the Admiralty, a rising political star, to impress on him the importance of converting the engines of naval battleships from coal-burning to oil. Oil is the future, he declared; it could be stored in large quantities and was cheap. Most important, however, was that it enabled ships to move faster. Naval warfare "is pure common sense," he said. "The first of all necessities is SPEED, so as to be able to fight—*When* you like, *Where* you like and *How* you like." It would allow British ships to outmanoeuvre enemy ships and give them a decisive edge in battle.[39] Listening to Fisher, Winston Churchill understood what this meant.

Switching to oil would mean that the power and efficiency of the Royal Navy would be raised to "a definitely higher level; better ships, better crews, higher economies, more intense forms of war power." It meant, as Churchill noted, nothing less than that the mastery of the seas was at stake.[40] At a time when pressure was rising in international affairs and confrontation looked increasingly likely in some form or other, whether in Europe or elsewhere, considerable thought went into how this advantage could be established and pressed home. In the summer of 1913, Churchill presented a paper to the Cabinet entitled "Oil Fuel Supply for His Majesty's Navy." The solution, he argued, was to buy fuel forward from a range of producers, and even to consider taking "a controlling interest in trustworthy sources of supply." The discussion that followed did not lead to a definite conclusion, other than an agreement that the "Admiralty ought to secure its oil supplies . . . from the widest possible area and the most numerous sources of supply."[41]

Less than a month later, things had changed. The Prime Minister now believed, along with his ministers, in the "vital necessity" of oil in the future. He therefore told King George V in his regular round-up of noteworthy developments that the government was going to take a controlling stake in Anglo-Persian, in order to secure "trustworthy sources of supply."[42]

Churchill was vocal in championing his cause. Securing oil supplies was not just about the navy; it was about safeguarding Britain's future. Although he saw that coal underpinned the empire's success, it was oil on which much depended. "If we cannot get oil," he told Parliament in July 1913, "we cannot get corn, we cannot get cotton and we cannot get a thousand and one commodities necessary for the preservation of the economic energies of Great Britain." Reserves should be built up in case of war; but the open market could also not be trusted—because it was becoming "an open mockery" thanks to the efforts of speculators.[43]

Anglo-Persian therefore seemed to offer the solution to many problems. Its concession was "thoroughly sound" and, with sufficient funds behind it, could probably be "developed to a gigantic extent," according to Admiral Sir Edmond Slade, formerly director of naval intelligence and head of the task force in charge of running the rule over the company. Control of the company, with the guaranteed oil supply this would entail, would be a godsend for the navy. The key, concluded Slade, was taking a majority stake "at a very reasonable cost."[44]

Negotiations with Anglo-Persian moved quickly enough that by the summer of 1914 the British government was in a position to buy a 51 per cent stake—and, with it, operational control of the business. Churchill's eloquence in the House of Commons saw a large majority vote in favour. And so it was that British policymakers, planners and military could take comfort in the knowledge that they had access to oil resources that could prove vital in any military conflict in the future. Eleven days later, Franz Ferdinand was shot dead in Sarajevo.

In the flurry of activity that surrounded the build-up to war, it was easy to overlook the importance of the steps Britain had taken to safeguard its energy needs. This was partly because few realised just what deals had been done behind the scenes. For in addition to buying a majority stake in Anglo-Persian, the British government had also agreed terms in secret for a twenty-year supply of oil for the Admiralty. This meant that Royal Navy ships that put to sea in the summer of 1914 did so with the benefit that they could bank on being refuelled should confrontation with Germany drag on. Conversion to oil made British vessels faster and better than their rivals; but the most important advantage was that they could stay out at sea. Not for nothing did Lord Curzon give a speech in London in November 1918, less than two weeks after the armistice had been agreed, in which he told fellow diners that "the Allied cause had floated to victory upon a wave of oil." A leading French senator agreed jubilantly. Germany had paid too much attention to iron and coal, he said, and not enough to oil. Oil was the blood of the earth, he said, and it was the blood of victory.[45]

There was some truth in this. For while the attention of military historians focuses on the killing fields of Flanders, what happened in the centre of Asia was of major significance to the outcome of the Great War—and even more important to the period that followed. As the first shots were being fired in Belgium and northern France, the Ottomans were pondering what role they should play in the escalating confrontation in Europe. While the Sultan was adamant that the empire should stay out of the war, other loud voices argued that cementing traditionally close links with Germany into an alliance was the best course of action. As the great powers of Europe were busy issuing ultimata and declaring war on each other, Enver Pasha, the mercurial Ottoman Minister of War, contacted the commander of the army headquarters in Baghdad to warn him of what might lie ahead. "War with England is now within the realm of possibilities," he wrote. If hostilities broke out, he went on, Arab leaders should be roused to support the Ottoman military effort in a holy war. The Muslim population of Persia should be roused to revolution against "Russian and English rule."[46]

In this context, it was not surprising that within weeks of the start of the war, a British division was dispatched from Bombay to secure Ābādān, the pipelines and the oilfields. When this had been done, the strategically sensitive town of Basra was occupied in November 1914, whereupon the town's inhabitants were told by Sir Percy Cox during a flag-raising ceremony that "no remnant of the Turkish administration remains in this place. In place thereof, the British flag has been established, under which you will enjoy the benefits of liberty and justice, both in regard to your religious and secular affairs."[47] The customs and beliefs of the locals mattered little; what was important was protecting access to the natural resources of the region.

Aware that their hold over the Gulf region was tenuous, the British made overtures to leading figures in the Arab world, including Ḥusayn, Sharīf of Mecca, who was offered a tempting deal: if Ḥusayn "and the Arabs in general" were to provide support against the Turks, then Britain "will guarantee the independence, rights and privileges of the Sharifate against all external foreign aggression, in particular that of the Ottomans." That was not all, for another, even juicier incentive was offered up too. Perhaps the time had come when "an Arab of true race will assume the Caliphate at Mecca or Medina." Ḥusayn, guardian of the holy city of Mecca and a member of the Quraysh, and descendant of Hāshim, the great-grandfather of the Prophet Muḥammad himself, was being offered an empire in return for his support.[48]

The British did not really mean this, and nor could they really deliver it. However, from the start of 1915, as things took a turn for the worse, they were prepared to string Ḥusayn along. This was partly because a swift triumph in Europe had not materialised. But it also stemmed from the fact that the Ottomans were finally beginning to counter-attack against the British position in the Persian Gulf—and also, worryingly, in Egypt too, threatening the Suez canal, the artery that enabled ships from the east to reach Europe weeks faster than if they had to circumnavigate Africa. To divert Ottoman resources and attention, the British decided to land troops in the eastern Mediterranean and open a new front. In the circumstances, cutting deals with anyone who might take the pressure off the Allied forces seemed an obvious thing to do; and it was easy to over-promise rewards that might only be paid far in the future.

Similar calculations were being made in London about the rise of Russian power. Although the horrors of war quickly became apparent, there were some influential figures in Britain who were concerned that the war would end too soon. The former Prime Minister Arthur Balfour was anxious that a rapid defeat of Germany would make Russia more dangerous still by fuelling the ambitions of the latter to the extent that India might be at risk. There was another worry: Balfour had also heard rumours that a well-connected lobby in St. Petersburg was trying to come to terms with Germany; this, he reckoned, would be as disastrous for Britain as losing the war.[49]

Concerns about Russia meant that ensuring its loyalty was of paramount importance. The prospect of control of Constantinople and the Dardanelles was the perfect bait to retain the bonds that united the Allies and to draw the tsarist government's attention towards an acutely sensitive topic. Mighty though Russia was, its Achilles heel was its lack of warm-water ports other than in the Black Sea, which was connected to the Mediterranean first by the Bosporus and second by the Dardanelles, the narrow stretches of water separating Europe from Asia at either end of the Sea of Marmara. These channels served as a lifeline, connecting the grainfields of southern Russia with export markets abroad. Closure of the Dardanelles, leaving wheat to rot in the storehouses, had inflicted devastating damage on the economy during the Balkan Wars of 1912–13 and had led to talk of war being declared on the Ottomans who controlled them.[50]

The Russians were delighted, therefore, when the British raised the question of the future of Constantinople and the Dardanelles at the end of 1914. This was "the richest prize of the entire war," Britain's ambassador announced to the Tsar's officials. Control was to be handed to Russia once the war was over, though Constantinople ought to remain a free port "for goods in transit to and from non-Russian territory," alongside the concession that "there shall be commercial freedom for merchants ships passing through the Straits."[51]

Although there was little sign of a breakthrough on the western front, with both sides suffering extraordinarily heavy losses and with years of bloodshed still in prospect, the Allies were already sitting down to carve up the lands and interests of their rivals. There is no little irony in this considering the charges of imperialism that were laid against Germany and its partners after the armistice. Just months after the war had started, the Allies were already thinking of feasting on the carcasses of their defeated enemies.

In this sense, there was more at stake than dangling the carrots of Constantinople and the Dardanelles before the Russians, for at the start of 1915 a commission under the chairmanship of Sir Maurice de Bunsen was set up to report on proposals for the future of the Ottoman Empire after victory had been assured. Part of the trick was dividing things up in a way that suited those who were allies at present but rivals in the past, and potentially in the future too. Nothing should be done, wrote Sir Edward Grey, to arouse suspicions that Britain had designs on Syria. "It would mean a break with France," he wrote, "if we put forward any claims in Syria and Lebanon"—a region that had seen substantial investment by French businesses in the eighteenth and nineteenth centuries.[52]

In order, therefore, to show solidarity with Russia and to avoid confrontation with France over its sphere of influence in Syria, it was decided to land a large force made up of troops from Britain, Australia and New Zealand not, as had originally been planned, at Alexandretta (now in south-eastern Turkey) but on the Gallipoli peninsula at the mouth of the Dardanelles Straits that guarded access to Constantinople.[53] It was a landing site that proved to be singularly ill suited to hosting a major offensive, and a death trap for many of those who tried to fight their way on to land, uphill against well-fortified Turkish positions. The disastrous campaign that followed had at its origins the struggle to establish control over the communication and trade networks linking Europe with the Near East and Asia.[54]

The future of Constantinople and the Dardanelles had been set out; now that of the Middle East needed to be resolved. In a series of meetings in the second half of 1915 and at the start of 1916, Sir Mark Sykes, an overconfident MP who had the ear of Lord Kitchener, the Secretary of State for War, and François Georges-Picot, an uppity French diplomat, divvied up the region. A line was agreed by the two men, which stretched from Acre (in the far north of what is now Israel) north-eastwards as far as the frontier with Persia. The French would be left to their own devices in Syria and Lebanon, the British to theirs—in Mesopotamia, Palestine and Suez.

Dividing up the spoils in this way was dangerous, not least since conflicting messages about the future of the region were being transmitted elsewhere. There was Ḥusayn, who was still being offered independence for the Arabs and the restitution of a caliphate, with him at the head; there were the peoples of "Arabia, Armenia, Mesopotamia, Syria and Palestine," who the British Prime Minister was busy stating publicly should be "entitled to a recognition of their separate national conditions," seemingly a promise of sovereignty and independence.[55] Then there was the United States, which had received repeated assurances from the British and French that they were fighting "not for selfish interests but, above all, to safeguard the independence of peoples, right and humanity." Both Britain and France passionately claimed to have noble aims at heart and were striving to set free "the populations subject to the bloody tyranny of the Turks," according to *The Times* of London.[56] "It was all bad," wrote Edward House, President Wilson's foreign policy adviser, when he found out about the secret agreement from the British Foreign Secretary. The French and the British "are making [the Middle East] a breeding place for future war."[57] He was not wrong about that.

At the root of the problem was that Britain knew what was at stake thanks to the natural resources that had been found in Persia, and which Mesopotamia also seemed likely to possess. Indeed, a concession for the oil of the latter was approved (though not formally ratified) on the day of Franz Ferdinand's assassination in 1914. It was given to a consortium led by the Turkish Petroleum Company, in which Anglo-Persian was the majority shareholder, with minority stakes given to Royal Dutch/Shell and Deutsche Bank and a sliver to Calouste Gulbenkian, the deal-maker extraordinaire who had put the agreement together.[58] Whatever was being promised or committed to the peoples and nations of the Middle East, the truth was that behind the scenes the shape and the future of the region was being dreamed up by officials, politicians and businessmen who had one thing in mind: securing control over oil and the pipelines that would pump it to ports to be loaded on to tankers.

The Germans realised what was going on. In a briefing paper that found its way into British hands, it was contended that Britain had two overriding strategic goals. First was to retain control of the Suez canal, because of its unique strategic and commercial value; second was to hold on to the oilfields in Persia and the Middle East.[59] This was a shrewd assessment. Britain's sprawling trans-continental empire covered nearly a quarter of the globe. Despite the many different climates, ecosystems and resources it encompassed, there was one obvious lack: oil.

With no meaningful deposits to speak of in any of its territories, the war offered Britain the chance to put that right. "The only big potential supply," wrote Sir Maurice Hankey, bookish Secretary to the War Cabinet, "is the Persian and Mesopotamian supply." As a result, establishing "control of these oil supplies becomes a first-class war aim."[60] There was nothing to

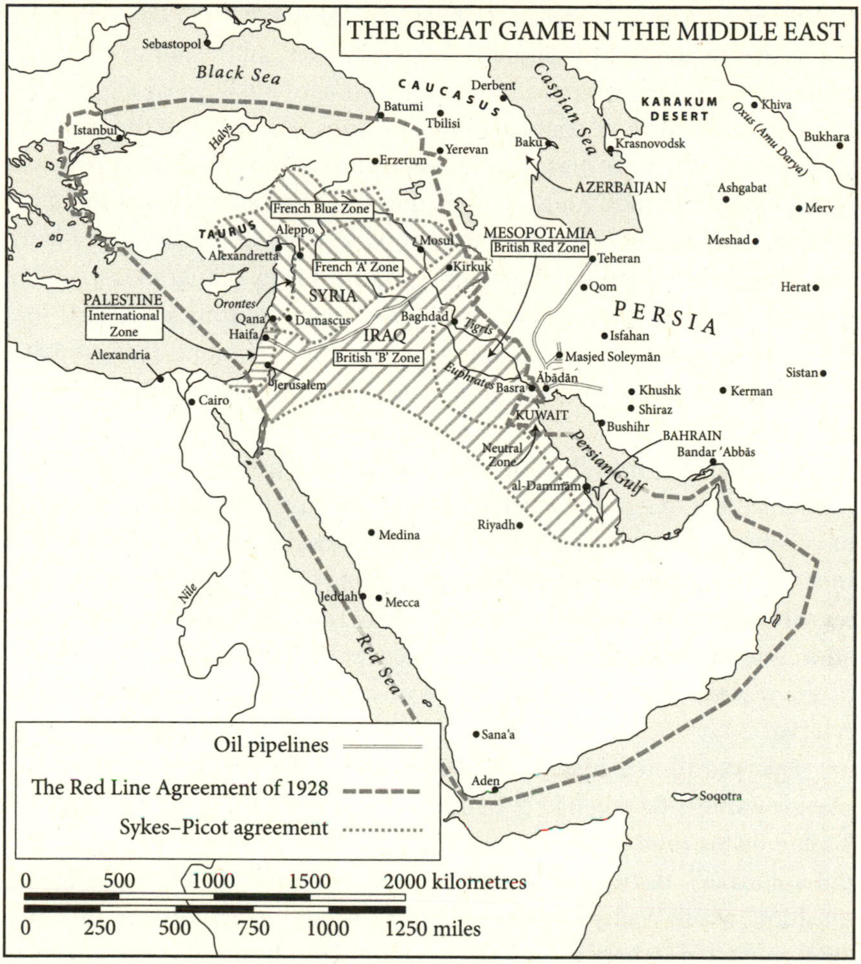

be gained in this region from a military perspective, Hankey stressed when he wrote to the Prime Minister, David Lloyd George, the same day; but Britain should act decisively if it was "to secure the valuable oil wells" in Mesopotamia.[61]

Few needed convincing. Before the war ended, the British Foreign Secretary was talking in uncompromising terms about how the future looked to him. There were doubtless questions ahead concerning the dismemberment of their rivals' empires. "I do not care," he told senior figures, "under what system we keep the oil, whether it is by perpetual lease or whatever it may be, but I am quite clear it is all-important for us that this oil should be available."[62]

There were good reasons for such determination—and for the anxieties that underpinned it. At the start of 1915, the Admiralty had been consuming 80,000 tons of oil per month. Two years later, as a result of the larger number of ships in service and the proliferation of oil-burning engines, the amount had more than doubled to 190,000 tons. The needs of the army had spiralled up even more dramatically, as the fleet of 100 vehicles in use in 1914 swelled to tens of thousands. By 1916, the strain had all but exhausted Britain's oil reserves: stocks of petrol that stood at 36 million gallons on 1 January plummeted to 19 million gallons six months later, falling to 12.5 million just four weeks after that.[63] When a government committee looked into likely requirements for the coming twelve months, it found that estimates indicated that there would be barely half the amount available to satisfy likely demand.[64]

Although the introduction of petrol rationing with immediate effect did something to stabilise stock levels, continued concerns about problems of supply led to the First Sea Lord ordering Royal Navy vessels to spend as much time in harbour as possible in the spring of 1917, while cruising speed was limited to twenty knots when out at sea. The precariousness of the situation was underlined by projections prepared in June 1917 that by the end of the year the Admiralty would have no more than six weeks' supplies in reserve.[65]

This was all made worse by Germany's development of effective submarine warfare. Britain had been importing oil in large quantities from the United States (and at increasingly high prices), but many of the tankers did not make it through. The Germans had managed to sink "so many fuel oil ships," wrote Walter Page, the U.S. ambassador to London, in 1917, that "this country may very soon be in a perilous condition."[66] A revolution in technology that enabled engines to run more quickly and more effectively had accompanied the rapid mechanisation of warfare after 1914. Both were driven by the ferocious land-war in Europe. But in turn the rise in consumption meant that the question of access to oil, which had already been a serious concern before the outbreak of hostilities, became a major—if not the decisive—factor in British international policy.

Some British policymakers had high hopes of what lay ahead. One experienced administrator, Percy Cox, who had served in eastern Persia and knew the country well, suggested in 1917 that Britain had the chance to gain such a tight grip on the Persian Gulf that the Russians, the French, the Japanese, the Germans and the Turks could be excluded permanently.[67] As a result, although the collapse of Russia into revolution in 1917 and the peace settlement with Germany soon after the Bolshevik seizure of power was worrying as far as the war in Europe was concerned, it brought a silver lining elsewhere. Under autocratic rule, Lord Balfour told the Prime Minister in the summer of 1918, Russia had been "a danger to her neighbours; and to none of her neighbours so much as ourselves."[68] Its implosion was good news for Britain's position in the east. There arose a real opportunity to cement control over the whole region that stretched between Suez and India, thereby securing both.

18

The Road to Compromise

In Persia, the British were intent on installing a reliable strongman who would serve their interests well. A senior figure at the court soon caught their eye: Prince Farman-Farma was known to hold extensive investments on the London stock exchange and his considerable fortune was therefore closely linked to the continued success of the British Empire. Intensive lobbying was undertaken to get him appointed Prime Minister, with the British representative in Teheran having an audience with the Shah on Christmas Eve in 1915 to make clear how favourably Farman-Farma's appointment would be viewed in London. "A change of Prime Minister was inevitable in the near future," the Shah was told, especially given all the "hostile elements" in the government in Teheran. The Shah was easily convinced: "he quite agreed and urged that it should be done at once. He promised to urge FF to accept office immediately."[1] Farman-Farma was duly appointed a few days later.

In Mesopotamia, the lack of a local figurehead to collaborate with made things more difficult. The British had taken matters into their own hands, sending troops from Basra to occupy Baghdad in the spring of 1917. Little thought was given to what would happen next, as Lord (formerly Sir Charles) Hardinge wrote from London to Gertrude Bell, the brilliant, mercurial scholar and traveller who knew this region as well as anyone. "It really would not matter," he suggested, "if we choose three of the fattest men from

Baghdad or three of the men with the longest beards who would be put up as the emblems of Arab rule." The British just needed any leader on whom they could effectively impress the benefits of co-operation with the occupying force; naturally, this would involve bribing them handsomely.[2]

There were, however, other serious problems to face—more significant than teasing out the future political set-up of this region. Leading voices in Britain were already advocating the revision of the Sykes–Picot agreement, even as the ink was drying. This was caused not by any qualms about the overt imperialism of the secret deal, but rather by a report prepared by Admiral Slade, previously director of the intelligence division at the Admiralty, who had been responsible for assessing the Persian oilfields in 1913 and had shortly afterwards been appointed a director of the Anglo-Persian Oil Company. Slade stressed that "under no possible circumstances can we be disturbed in our enjoyment" of the Persian oilfields, and that that was true of other parts of the region too. There were indications, he added, of the presence of significant quantities of oil in "Mesopotamia, Koweit, Bahrein and in Arabia." He strongly recommended that the lines be redrawn to ensure that as much as possible of these territories fell within the British-controlled zone. "It is important to secure control of all the oil rights in these areas so that no other Power can exploit them for their [own] benefit."[3] The Foreign Office watched nervously, gathering articles in European newspapers that demanded Germany's "indispensable requirement of the freedom of the sea in Persian Gulf" as an indication that the sooner Britain secured its position, the better.[4]

By the end of 1918, just weeks after the end of the war, Britain managed to get what it wanted: the Prime Minister, David Lloyd George, convinced Prime Minister Clemenceau of France to amend the agreement and cede control of Mosul and the surrounding area. This was done partly by playing on the fear that Britain might stand in the way of France establishing a protectorate over Syria, but also by hinting that British support on the issue of Alsace-Lorraine in the settlement negotiations which were due to begin shortly was by no means certain. "What do you want?" Clemenceau asked Lloyd George bluntly in London. "I want Mosul," the British Prime Minister replied. "You shall have it. Anything else?" "Yes," came the reply, "I want Jerusalem too." The reply was the same: "You shall have it." Clemenceau was "right as a die and never went back on his word," recalled one senior civil servant who had the ear of Lloyd George.[5]

The British had also identified Palestine as a target owing to its location as a buffer against any threat to the Suez canal, which served as one of the empire's most vital arteries and over which control had been established in 1888. Just as British troops had moved on Baghdad, therefore, so they advanced on Palestine from the south and, improbably, from the east with T. E. Lawrence emerging from the desert to take Aqaba in the summer of 1917. A few months later, Jerusalem fell too, despite fierce counter-attacks from the Ottoman Seventh and Eighth Armies, led by General Erich von Falkenhayn, who had served as Chief of the General Staff of the German army earlier in the war. The British General Edmund Allenby entered the city on foot as a mark of respect, having captured the city in what the British Prime Minister called "a Christmas present for the British people."[6]

Palestine was important for another reason. Concerns had been growing about the rising levels of Jewish immigration to Britain, with the numbers arriving from Russia alone rising by a factor of five between 1880 and 1920. At the turn of the twentieth century, there had been discussions about offering land in East Africa to encourage Jewish émigrés to settle there, but by the time of the war attention had shifted to Palestine. In 1917, a letter from the Foreign Secretary, Arthur Balfour, to Lord Rothschild was leaked to *The Times* that spoke of "His Majesty's Government [viewing] with favour the establishment in Palestine of a national home for the Jewish people."[7] Known as the Balfour Declaration, the idea of designating territories for Jews to settle was what Balfour later described to the House of Lords as "a partial solution to the great and abiding Jewish problem."[8]

Although the championing of a homeland for European Jews has understandably attracted attention, Britain also had its eye on Palestine for its position in relation to the oilfields and as a terminus for a pipeline linking to the Mediterranean. This would save a journey of a thousand miles, planners later noted, and would give Britain "virtual control over the output of what may well prove to be one of the richest oil fields in the world."[9] It was imperative, therefore, that Britain had a strong presence in Palestine, that it had control over Haifa, with its good, deep harbour, which made it the ideal place for loading oil on to British tankers, and that the pipeline ran to this port—rather than to the north, and French-controlled Syria.

As Britain's strategic thinking went at the time, Haifa would provide a perfect terminus for oil piped from Mesopotamia. So it proved. By 1940, more than 4 million tons of oil was flowing along the pipeline that was built after the war, enough to supply the entire Mediterranean fleet. It was, as *Time* magazine called it, the "carotid artery of the British empire."[10] The world's largest empire was receiving massive transfusions of the black blood of oil, pumped directly from the heart of the world.

By the start of 1918, then, thoughts had long since turned to the shape of the post-war world and how the spoils of victory would be divided. The problem was that there was a difference between deals struck among clubbable politicians, testy diplomats and planners armed with maps and pencils in European capital cities, and the reality on the ground. It was all very well planning for a carve-up of territories where the interests of Britain and France would be expanded and protected, but things became rather more complicated when practicalities intruded.

For example, in the summer of 1918, the British General Lionel Dunsterville was ordered to advance from north-western Persia to the Caspian, while other senior officers were sent to monitor the Caucasus, with the aim of ensuring that the Turks did not seize control of the oilfields of Azerbaijan, take the region south of the Caspian or gain control of the Trans-Caspian Railway that led to the Afghan border. This was classic overstretch, an all but impossible mission—and one that sure enough ended in disaster. Advancing Turkish forces surrounded Baku, trapping Dunsterville inside for six weeks before allowing him to withdraw. Horrific scenes of bloodshed then followed as locals settled scores after the city had surrendered.[11]

Panic enveloped officials in the India Office in London, who frantically sought authorisation to send agents into Central Asia to keep track of what was going on there in the wake of Turkish resurgence and turmoil in Russia, where rioting and demonstrations in the Samarkand district, the Fergana valley and Tashkent played a role in revolution breaking out across the whole empire.[12] "All effective control over native population of Turkestan has been removed," wrote the Secretary of State to the viceroy, Lord Chelmsford, at the start of 1918, "owing to the collapse of central government in Russia and complete breakdown in discipline in the Russian army."[13]

In response to warnings that anti-British sentiments among the Muslim population of the region were running high, envoys were dispatched to monitor the situation and oversee the spread of anglophile propaganda. Officers were sent to Kashgar and Meshed to assess the mood, while there were tortuous discussions about whether to send armed forces into Afghanistan and Tashkent, or to approve more grandiose schemes such as encouraging the Emir of Afghanistan to expand westwards and occupy the

Murghab valley as far as Merv.[14] New ideas, new identities and new aspirations were springing up across Ukraine, the Caucasus and Central Asia after the Russian Revolution, as demands for self-expression if not self-determination grew louder and louder.

Complications arose when those who had seized power in Russia found their dreams of international revolution thwarted in Europe and so turned their attention to Asia. Trotsky, fizzing with enthusiasm as usual, took up with gusto the theme of cultivating the revolutionary project in the east. "The path to India might well be much easier to travel in the current circumstances and what is more, quicker than the one leading to a Soviet in Hungary," he wrote in a memorandum that was circulated to his peers in 1919. "The route to Paris and London is through the cities of Afghanistan, the Punjab and Bengal."[15]

Delegates from "the enslaved popular masses of Persia, Armenia and Turkey," as well as from those of Mesopotamia, Syria, Arabia and beyond, were summoned to a conference in Baku in 1920, where one of the principal Bolshevik demagogues did not mince his words. "We are now faced with the task of kindling a real holy war" against the west, he told listeners. The time had come, he said, to "educate the masses of the East to hate and to want to fight against the rich." That meant fighting against the wealthy "Russian, Jewish, German, French . . . and organizing a true people's holy war, in the first place against British imperialism."[16] The hour had arrived, that is, for a showdown between east and west.

The message went down well. Apart from the cheering delegates, there were those who took action—intellectuals, such as Muḥammad Barakatullāh who wrote on the elision of "Bolshevism and the Islamic Nations," urged the advance of socialism throughout Muslim Asia. Newspapers, universities and military schools were set up across Central Asia to cater for and further radicalise the local populations.[17]

Showing a surprising degree of flexibility, the Soviets were prepared to compromise with any who might help their cause. For example, the Bolshevik leadership had few qualms about making overtures to the ruler of Afghanistan, King Amanullah, after he sought to distance himself from British influence and launched an attack on the British in India to the west of the Khyber. Although the military confrontation was a fiasco, the Bolshevik regime delighted in finding an ally in the east and sent an offer of assistance, along with assurances that the liberation of the east from imperialism was a fundamental part of the revolutionary programme—assurances that were unlikely to be entirely comforting to a ruling monarch.

Russian audacity and opportunism provoked shrill calls of alarm in Britain, with *The Times* reporting on the "Bolshevist menace to India: Afghan stepping stone." British troops were moved north into Afghanistan, among them a young corporal named Charles Kavanagh whose recently discovered diary paints a vivid picture of what he saw—and finds many echoes in the more recent experiences of western servicemen in the same region. Ambushes and attacks by insurgents were a daily hazard, he wrote. Afghan men were not afraid to dress as women in gowns that hid their faces as well as their rifles. Avoid offering your hand to shake that of a local you do not know, he wrote: "they will seize it with their left hand, and stab you with their right."[18]

Different visions of the future were being offered in the aftermath of the Great War. On the one hand, there was the impulse towards self-determination, championed at least to start with by the Bolsheviks. "Organise your lives as you choose, and without any obstacles," Lenin declared. "You have the right to do so. Know that your rights, like those of all the peoples of Russia, are protected by the full power of the revolution and its agencies."[19] This extended to progressive views about gender equality: women were given the vote in the Kyrgyz, Turkmen, Ukrainian and Azerbaijani Soviet republics—before they were given the vote in the United Kingdom. Posters put up in Tashkent in 1920, written in Uzbek, displayed a figure in front of four ghostly veiled figures urging the emancipation of Muslim women: "Women! Take part in elections to the Soviet!"[20]

This early post-Revolutionary progressivism contrasted sharply with the imperialist attitudes of western powers and their resolve to retain control of assets and resources deemed vital to national interests. None were as active or as aggressive as the British, who were above all determined to hang on to control of oil supplies. In so far as it had troops in the field, Britain had a head start, enabling the landscape to be shaped in a way that suited its needs. In the case of Mesopotamia, this was done by forging a new country that was given the name of Iraq. It was a hotch-potch made up of three former Ottoman provinces that were profoundly different in history, religion and geography: Basra looked southwards towards India and the Gulf; Baghdad was closely linked with Persia; Mosul naturally connected to Turkey and Syria.[21] The amalgam satisfied no one except London.

The country was a rickety construction at best. The British helped install the erstwhile ally Faisal—the heir of the Sharīf of Mecca—as sovereign, in part as a reward for his co-operation during the war, in part in sympathy for his having been drummed out of Syria where he had originally been promised the throne, and in part because of the lack of any other obvious candidate. The fact that he was a Sunnī Muslim where the local population was predominantly Shīʿa was thought to be something that could be smoothed over with the introduction of the new trappings of a nation, such as guard-changing ceremonials, a new flag (designed by Gertrude Bell) and a treaty that recognized Iraqi "national sovereignty," but obliged the king and his government to be directed by Britain "on all important matters," including foreign relations and defence. Subsequent annexes gave Britain the right to make appointments to the judiciary and to impose financial advisers to administer the country's economy.[22] This devolved imperial rule was cheaper from a financial point of view than full colonial occupation at a time when Britain itself was facing up to huge national debts built up during the war—but it was cheaper politically too. More than 2,000 British soldiers had been killed in rioting and civil unrest in Mesopotamia in 1920.[23]

Concerted efforts were made to impose a similar grip on Persia. In 1919, an agreement was signed that would install British advisers to run both the treasury and the armed forces, as well as overseeing infrastructure projects. This went down badly in Persia and elsewhere. With Britain holding a controlling interest in the Anglo-Persian Oil Company, the Russians and the French were already concerned that Britain's hold over Persia was too strong. The bribes (or "commissions)" paid to get the agreement signed meanwhile produced howls of protest in Persia—not least against the Shah himself. "God condemn to everlasting shame / He who betrayed the land of Sassan," wrote one well-known poet at the time, citing Persia's deep and glorious past; "tell the zealous Artaxerxes The Long-armed / The enemy annexed your kingdom to England."[24] Such critics ended up in prison.[25]

The Foreign Commissar of the fledgling Soviet Union also reacted furiously: Britain "is trying to lasso the Persian people into total slavery." It was shameful, he declared in a statement, that the country's rulers had "sold you to the English robbers."[26] The reaction in Paris was little different. Caught unprepared by the battle for oil, and having surrendered Mosul seemingly for nothing, the French had been pressing to have their own advisers take up positions in Teheran to further their own national interests. This was given short shrift by Lord Curzon, who could barely hide his outrage at being asked if he would sanction such an appointment. Persia, he told Paul Cambon, the French ambassador to London, was "only saved from complete insolvency by the aid of Great Britain." France should mind its own business.[27]

The reaction in France was furious and bitter. Funding was given to place anti-British propaganda in the press in Persia, while excoriating articles at home took aim at the Anglo-Persian agreement—and at the Shah. This half-centimetre-tall midget, said *Le Figaro* in a piece that was widely cited in Teheran, "had sold his country for one centime."[28] The French had been on the winning side in the war, but they had been outmanoeuvred by their ally.

In fact, the British were nonplussed by the Shah's demands for money, which were as constant as they had been before the war began. This had been a problem too with Prince Farman-Farma, whose spell as Prime Minister had not proved as successful as the British had hoped. Reports back to London talked of his "disinclination to work honestly" and his "rapacity"; this was "fast making his continuance of office impossible."[29] A more reliable figure was needed.

Cometh the hour, cometh the man. Reza Khan was "a powerfully built, well set up, big boned man, well above average height," Sir Percy Loraine, Britain's representative to Teheran, reported approvingly in 1922. Khan gets straight to the point, the report went on, "and does not waste time in exchanging the delicately phrased but perfectly futile compliments so dear to the Persian heart." Although he was clearly both "ignorant and uneducated," Loraine was impressed: "in speaking with him, I had rather the impression of an unemployed brain than of an empty one." This was music to the ears of the Foreign Office. "Sir P. Loraine's estimate of Reza Khan is decidedly encouraging," one official back in London noted on the report. "While he is [not] free from the vices of his compatriots, his heart seems to be in the right place." His racial origins were also positively received: "that he is half Caucasian [through his mother] is in his favour," read another minute. In short, he was exactly the sort of man the British thought they could do business with.[30]

He seemed to be "a strong and fearless man who had his country's good at heart," according to Sir Edmund Ironside, commander of a British force sent to secure northern Persia amid growing concerns about Russian designs around the Caspian Sea. Just how much support the British gave Reza Khan and what role they played in allowing him to become the power behind the throne—and eventually, in 1925, to install himself as shah—has been hotly debated. At the time, however, many following events closely had little doubt about Britain's role as king-maker.[31] The American representative in Teheran, John Caldwell, remarked that Reza was so close to the British that he was "practically a spy."[32]

It was not surprising that the Americans were also paying close attention to this part of the world. A report circulated by the Planning Section of the U.S. Naval Forces in Europe in 1918 spoke of the need for the United States to prepare for commercial rivalry with Britain. "Four great powers have arisen in the world to compete with Great Britain for commercial supremacy," it opined. Spain, Holland, France and Germany had all been seen off by Britain. The United States was the "fifth commercial power, the greatest one yet . . . Historical precedent warns us to watch closely" what Britain was up to.[33] The importance of the oilfields meant that careful attention had to be paid to this part of this world.

This was especially true given the growing concerns in the United States about its own oil supplies. Just as Britain had worried about lack of resources before the war, there was mounting anxiety in America about possible shortages immediately after it. Rising consumption patterns were a cause for alarm, as were estimates about proven oil reserves. These would run out in nine years and three months, according to the director of the U.S. Geological Survey. The lack of "necessary supply at home and abroad" represented a major problem, admitted President Wilson.[34]

For this reason, the State Department encouraged Standard Oil, one of the biggest American producers, to look into what it referred to as "the possibility of entering into an agreement with the Persian Government for development of oil resources in north Persia," in the region not covered by Anglo-Persian's concession.[35] U.S. interest prompted an ecstatic response in Teheran: Britain and Russia had interfered in Persia long enough, said reports in the local press, constantly compromising the country's independence. The United States, the emerging new empire, was the perfect white knight. "If the Americans, with their flourishing wealth, establish economic relations with our country," one Persian newspaper article declared hopefully, "we are sure our resources will not remain sterile and we will no longer be so much afflicted by poverty."[36] Such great expectations were widely shared across the country: telegrams flooded into the capital welcoming the prospect of U.S. investment. The startled American mission in Teheran observed that these were signed by "the foremost mullahs, notables, some government officials and merchants."[37]

The British reacted angrily, telling the State Department in no uncertain terms that American interest in Persia's oil was not just unwelcome but illegal. Although the region in question had not been conceded to Anglo-Persian, the British declared that it was subject to a separate agreement previously reached between Persia and Russia that had not been correctly terminated. As such, exploration rights could not be sold to the Americans—or to anyone else. These were weasel words, and ultimately proved fruitless as the Persians went ahead regardless, granting Standard Oil a fifty-year concession.[38]

Not for the first time, the American experience proved to be a false dawn. It had been hoped in Persia that U.S. involvement and investment would offer a real alternative to British clout in the region. However, practicalities dictated that any operator needed to cut a deal with Anglo-Persian to gain access to its pipeline infrastructure. What is more, once discussions got going, hope gave way to more disappointment for the Persians. The Americans were "more British than the British," noted the Persian representative in Washington—which he did not mean as a compliment. It turns out, fumed one editorial in a Teheran newspaper, that the United States and Britain were one and the same: both were "worshippers of gold and stranglers of the weak," obsessed with furthering their own interests and "trying to divide [the] precious jewel" of national oil resources and take them from "the hands of the childish politicians of Persia."[39]

The story had familiar echoes of the discovery of the Americas 400 years earlier. While local populations had not been decimated in the same way as those encountered by the Spanish, the process was effectively the same: the expropriation of treasures by the nations of the west meant that riches flowed out of one continent to another, with minimal benefit to the inhabitants of those lands. There were other parallels with what had happened following Columbus' sailing across the Atlantic. Just as Spain and Portugal had divided the world between them with the treaties of Tordesillas in 1494 and Zaragoza three decades later, so too did the western powers now split the resources of the world lying between the Mediterranean and Central Asia.

Territories ringed on maps in coloured pencil formed the basis of an accord between the British and the French known as the "Red Line Agreement," which divided the oil assets of the region between Anglo-Persian on the one hand and the Turkish Petroleum Company (of which Anglo-Persian—and thus the British government—were major shareholders) on the other, with a formal agreement not to compete in each other's territories. This was important for France, which had its eye on securing a strong position in the Levant because of the long history of trading ties and substantial French commercial investments going back many decades. Just as the Iberian powers had done, France and Britain shared out control of valuable assets like spoils which had been claimed as of right. It felt like a new age of empire.

The problem was that this new era of empire was almost immediately beset with the traumatic realisation that the world was changing—and changing fast. It was all very well having elaborate plans and trying to assert Britain's control over the oil and the pipeline networks, but this came at a price. With Britain's national debt soaring, painful and difficult discussions took place about the cost of maintaining troops in the numbers needed to run an empire effectively. The overwhelming cost, wrote Lord Curzon, "is one that can no longer be sustained." It was a conclusion duly taken on board by Winston Churchill, by now Colonial Secretary, who recognised that "everything that happens in the Middle East is secondary to the reduction of expense."[40]

This mismatch between ambition and ability was a recipe for disaster—a predicament made worse by the obduracy of senior diplomats. The British minister in Teheran, for example, lorded it over the Persians, whom he described contemptuously as "smelly" and "shifty brutes." In Baghdad, meanwhile, London's representative had houses knocked down in order "to extend the gardens of Britain's embassy"—something one observer remarked wryly which "undoubtedly improved what was already a beautiful residence" but which was "less than universally popular with the Iraqis."[41] There was a lofty sense of entitlement in all this, the sense that the present and future of these countries lay unassailably in the hands of the British. Rulership was in the gift of policymakers in London, who had little concern for the interests of local populations and focused instead on Britain's strategic and economic priorities. In the 1920s alone, the British were either directly responsible for or played a supporting role in installing or deposing rulers in Iraq, Persia and Afghanistan, while also becoming involved in the question of the title used by the King of Egypt following independence in 1922.[42]

Inevitably, this bred festering problems that over time became poisonous. Gertrude Bell had been right to predict, as early as 1919, that "a horrible muddle" was being made of the Near East, and that the scenario was like "a nightmare in which you foresee all the horrible things which are going to happen and can't stretch out your hand to prevent them."[43] Britain was playing a dangerous game in choosing who to support and when—and where—to intervene.

Broken promises and disappointed peoples lay scattered across the region from the Levant eastwards. Commitments to support, help and protect the interests of local populations gave way to the promotion and protection of Britain's commercial and strategic interests—even if that meant splitting up territories along new and artificial boundaries, or abandoning communities like the Christian Assyrians of Iraq who found themselves in a uniquely vulnerable position following the carve-up of the Middle East at the end of the First World War.[44]

The broader results in Iraq were a disaster. A new feudalism took root as local magnates were handed large tracts of former Ottoman state land in return for their support for the British mandate—curtailing social mobility, widening inequality and fanning dissatisfaction as rural communities lost their land rights and their means of living. In Kut province in eastern Iraq, two families were able, over the course of three decades, to acquire more than half a million acres between them.[45] The scenario was much the same in Persia, where the wealth generated by oil revenues was concentrated in the hands of the Shah and those around him. In this sense, it was precisely the knowledge that the British government was the majority shareholder of Anglo-Persian—which by the 1920s was responsible for nearly half the country's revenues—that prompted increasingly determined anti-British sentiments and a rising tide of nationalism.

This was also a sign of the times, as reactions against colonialism were gaining an almost unstoppable momentum across the empire. In 1929 in India, the Lahore session of the Indian National Congress set out a "Declaration of Independence" (Purna Swaraj). "The British Government in India has not only deprived the Indian people of their freedom but has based itself on the exploitation of the masses," it stated. India has been ruined, and "must forthwith sever the British connection and attain . . . complete independence." The time had come for civil disobedience.[46]

It was all but inevitable that this cocktail of disenchantment, disgust and disenfranchisement would catch on elsewhere. But the growing frustration in the Middle East also stemmed in part from the realisation that the benefits promised by the oil finds had proved so elusive. The western oil corporations that controlled the concessions were dextrous and highly creative when it came to making royalty payments. Just as in the modern world, a web of subsidiary companies was set up with the aim of using inter-company loans to create losses that could be used to reduce or even eliminate altogether the apparent trading profits of the operating companies—and therefore manipulate downwards the royalties due under the concession agreement. This was grist to the mill. Angry reports ran in the newspapers that spoke of "foreigners [being allowed] to drain the country of her oil resources and deliberately reducing the revenue of Persia by granting illegal and unnecessary exemption from customs duty." At least things were not as bad in Persia as they were in neighbouring Iraq, which was a colony in all but name.[47]

To try to head off the rising tide of local anger, the directors of Anglo-Persian went on a charm offensive: they promised a host of new benefits, ranging from educational opportunities to helping upgrade the railways, to considering making royalty payments more generous. It was plain wrong, high-ranking Persians complained, that the Persian government held no shares in the business. "The Persians," one observer recorded, "felt that an industry had been developed on their soil in which they had no real share"; they insisted that this was not a question of money, since "no financial reward would dispel this feeling" of alienation.[48] Anglo-Persian's chairman, the urbane Sir John Cadman, urged calm, suggesting to his opposite number at the negotiating table that it was in no one's interests for the press to create the "erroneous and painful impression" that the business was not a fair and equitable one.[49] This was all very well, he was told; what was in everyone's interests was that there should be a partnership. As it stood, it was little more than outright exploitation.[50]

Drawn-out discussions about if and how to renegotiate the Knox D'Arcy concession came to nothing. Eventually, the Persians snapped. Even before 1929, the discovery of oil in Mexico and Venezuela (the work in the latter led by George Reynolds, who had struck the all-important well at Masjed Soleymān) led to a major correction downwards in oil prices. After Wall Street had crashed, prompting a dramatic fall-off in demand, the Persians took matters into their own hands. Finally, in November 1932, following a sharp decline of royalty payments and continuing financial chicanery whereby detailed figures were deliberately withheld from Teheran, the Shah declared that the Knox D'Arcy concession was cancelled with immediate effect.

This was disgraceful, complained British diplomats. "If we do not make ourselves felt at the outset," advised one senior official, "we shall have far worse trouble with the Persians later."[51] The declaration was a "flagrant" offence, said another.[52] In the eyes of the British, the contract agreed three decades earlier should stand, no matter what. It was true that considerable financial risks had been taken to open up the oil business in the first place, and that it had required hefty investment to create an infrastructure that enabled resources to be exploited. Nevertheless, the riches that were unlocked as a result were huge. The clamour to share these more evenly was simply ignored; in the manner of the great banking scandals of the early twenty-first century, Anglo-Persian and the interests that sat behind it were too big to fail.

In this case, however, the process of equalising the situation and putting things right was a quick one—largely because Persia had the potent negotiating tool of being able to harass, prevent and hinder production to force a renegotiation. In the spring of 1933, a new deal was hammered out. The Persian delegation met with oil executives at the Beau Rivage hotel in Geneva and explained that they were familiar with the terms of a recent agreement about oil in Iraq, demanding that these at least be matched. The initial proposal—which included Anglo-Persian ceding 25 per cent of the shares, a guaranteed annual income, profit share and board representation—was dismissed by Sir John Cadman as preposterous and impossible.[53]

Although the discussions that followed were perfectly cordial, it soon became clear that efforts to avoid a major renegotiation would fail. By April 1933, a new deal had been struck. More attention would be paid to the "Persianisation" of the oil business—that is, hiring and training more locals to be involved in the business at all levels, from management down to more lowly positions. The region covered by concession was dramatically reduced to a quarter of its original size, albeit the sweetest bite of the cherry; a fixed royalty fee was agreed that removed the screen of currency and oil-price fluctuations; a minimum annual payment was guaranteed, regardless of production levels or market prices achieved; the Persian government would also share in the wider benefits of Anglo-Persian, receiving a share of the profits that the company made in its other jurisdictions. Cadman did not comment when the Persian negotiators told him he should see the new agreement as a "personal triumph for [himself] and his colleagues." His notes disclose his reaction: "I felt that we had been pretty well plucked."[54]

The Persians, and others who were watching, saw a different moral in the story. The lesson was that, for all the bluster, the west's bargaining position was a weak one. Those with the resources could ultimately force the hand of those who held the concession, and make them come to the table. The west could complain as bitterly as it liked, but it turned out that possession truly was nine-tenths of the law.

This became one of the key themes of the second half of the twentieth century. New connections were rising that straddled the spine of Asia. A web was being spun not of towns and oases but of pipelines that linked oilwells to the Persian Gulf and, by the 1930s, to the Mediterranean. Resources and wealth were pumped along these lines to ports like Haifa and Ābādān—a site that became home to what was for more than fifty years the world's biggest refinery.

Control of this network was everything, as the British recognised even before the First World War broke out. To the optimist, things still looked rosy. After all, despite the renegotiation of concessions in 1933, strong links had been built up with this part of the world, and there was still much to be gained from co-operating with those whose resources were of such enormous importance; and Britain, surely, was in a better position than anyone else.

The reality, however, was that the tide had already turned. The power and influence of the west was in decline—and seemed certain to diminish further. There was a price to pay for constant interference in local affairs; there was a price to pay for remodelling the gardens of the embassy; and there was a price to pay for never quite playing with a straight bat. That price was reservation, misgivings and mistrust.

The two very different outlooks were perfectly captured at a dinner in Baghdad in 1920, just as the shape of the new Near and Middle East was becoming clear. One of those attending was the dynamic and fiercely intelligent Gertrude Bell, who had been recruited at an early stage in the First World War to work for British intelligence, and was an astute observer of Arab politics. Rest assured, she told Jaʿfar alʿ-Askarī, soon to be appointed Prime Minister of the new country of Iraq, that "complete independence is what we [the British] ultimately wish to give." "My lady," he replied, "complete independence is never given—always taken."[55] The challenge for countries like Iraq and Persia was to free themselves of outside interference, and to be able to decide their own futures. The challenge for Britain was how to prevent them from doing so. It was a conflict waiting to happen. First, though, there was another disaster that was about to take place, again driven by control of resources. This time it was not oil but wheat that lay at the heart of impending catastrophe.

19

The Wheat Road

The British magazine *Homes & Gardens* has long prided itself on being at the cutting edge of interior design. "Mixing beautiful features with gorgeous real-life homes and gardens, expert advice and practical information," the magazine declares in its recent marketing strapline, is "the ultimate source of decorating inspiration." Its November 1938 issue gushed with praise about a mountain bolt-hole rich in Alpine chic. "The colour scheme throughout this bright, airy chalet is light jade green," wrote the correspondent, enlivened by the passion for cut flowers displayed by the owner—who as it happened was also the property's "decorator, designer and furnisher, as well as architect." His watercolour sketches hung in the guest bedrooms, alongside old engravings. A "droll raconteur," the owner loved being surrounded by a range of "brilliant foreigners, especially painters, musicians and singers," and would often bring in "local talent" to play pieces by Mozart or Brahms for after-dinner entertainment. The article's author was very impressed by Adolf Hitler.[1]

Nine months later, on 21 August 1939, an eagerly awaited call came through to the telephone exchange which *Homes & Gardens* reported was next to his modern office and which allowed "the Führer" to be in contact with "his friends or Ministers." During supper, a message was passed to Hitler. According to one who was present, "he scanned it, stared into space for a moment, flushed deeply, then banged on the table so hard that the glasses rattled." He turned to his guests and said excitedly, "I have them! I have them!"[2] He sat down to eat, no doubt faced with the usual "imposing array of vegetarian dishes, savoury and rich, pleasing to the eye as well as to the palate," admired by the *Homes & Gardens* journalist a year earlier, and prepared by Hitler's personal chef, Arthur Kannenberg—who often came out of the kitchen in the evenings to play his accordion.[3]

After the meal, Hitler called his dinner guests together, and told them that the paper he was holding contained the text of a reply that he had been waiting for from Moscow. Stalin, the undisputed master of the Soviet Union, had agreed to sign a treaty of non-aggression with Germany. "I hope," the teletype read, "that [this] will bring about a decided turn for the better in relations between our two countries."[4] Two nights later, after the news had been announced, Hitler and his entourage stood on the terrace, looking into the valley below. "The final act of *Götterdämmerung* could not have been more effectively staged," noted the leading Nazi, Albert Speer.[5]

Ironically, the extraordinary agreement was prompted by British and French foreign policy. Both countries had been trying desperately to find ways to contain the German Chancellor after becoming alarmed by his high-stakes political poker in the 1930s—with little success. So little, in fact, that Mussolini confided in his Foreign Minister Count Ciano that Britain's politicians and diplomats were not made of the same stuff as "the Francis Drakes" and the other "magnificent adventurers who created the empire"; in fact, they are "the tired sons of a long line of rich men, and they will lose their empire."[6]

Following Germany's occupation of Czechoslovakia, a tougher line was taken. In the afternoon of 31 March 1939, the Prime Minister Neville Chamberlain rose in the House of Commons. "In the event of any action which clearly threatened Polish independence," he said solemnly, "His Majesty's Government would feel themselves bound at once to lend the Polish Government all support in their power. They have given the Polish Government an assurance to this effect. I may add that the French Government have authorised me to make it plain that they stand in the same position in this matter as do His Majesty's Government."[7]

Rather than guaranteeing Poland's security, this sealed its fate. Although the Prime Minister told the House of Commons that the Foreign Secretary had met with the Soviet ambassador, Ivan Maiskii, the same morning in an attempt to smooth things over, the assurances offered to Poland set in motion a chain of events that led straight to the wheatfields of Ukraine and southern Russia. The struggle was to spell death for millions.[8]

The aim had been to lock Germany into stalemate, using the threat of war to deter any move against its neighbour to the east. In fact, as Hitler quickly understood, he had been dealt an ace—albeit one that required astonishing gall to play: here was a chance to make a deal with the Communist Soviet Union. Although the USSR was a bitter rival to Nazi Germany in many respects, suddenly there was common ground where the interference of Britain and others had provided an opening. Stalin too realised how the cards fell. He had also been given an opportunity—one that he likewise required astonishing gall to take advantage of: reaching terms with Hitler.

The idea of an alliance between the two states seemed beyond the realms of plausibility or reality. Since Hitler had been voted to power in 1933, relations between Germany and the USSR had deteriorated sharply, with vitriolic media campaigns in both countries portraying the other as demonic, ruthless and dangerous. Trade had all but collapsed: while nearly 50 per cent of all imports to the Soviet Union had come from Germany in 1932, six years later the figure had fallen to below 5 per cent.[9] But with the guarantees extended to Poland, the two countries finally had something in common: a wish to destroy the state that was sandwiched between them.[10]

In the spring of 1939, there was a flurry of diplomatic activity. The Soviet chargé d'affaires in Berlin and the leading German expert on eastern Europe met to set out grounds for improving relations, and to look for areas of possible co-operation, including the resumption of trade. These talks accelerated quickly, taken forward in Moscow by discussions between the German ambassador and Vyacheslav Molotov, the new Commissar of Foreign Affairs, whose predecessor, Maxim Litvinov, had been dismissed because of his Jewish background—an obstacle when dealing with the anti-Semitic German regime. Litvinov, "the eminent Jew," wrote Winston Churchill, "the target of German antagonism, was flung aside like a broken tool . . . bundled off the world stage to obscurity, a pittance and police supervision."[11]

By the summer, things had moved forward to the point that Joachim von Ribbentrop, the German Foreign Minister, was able to send messages to Moscow that explained that just because National Socialism and Communism were very different, there was "no reason for enmity between our two countries." If there was an appetite to discuss matters, he suggested, then further rapprochement was possible. At the heart of the matter was Poland: could a deal be done in which Poland would be dismembered and divided up between them?[12]

The question was taken up by Stalin personally. Poland had been a bête noire since the Revolution. For one thing, the peace agreements at Versailles had awarded the Poles a swathe of territory that had been Russian before 1914; for another, Poland had taken military action that had threatened the very success of the Bolshevik seizure of power in the years after 1917. Fear of Polish spies was a regular and common feature in the Soviet purges of the 1930s that saw millions arrested and many hundreds of thousands executed. Barely two years before negotiating with Germany, Stalin had personally signed orders demanding the "liquidation of the network of spies of the Polish Military Organisation," which led to tens of thousands more being arrested, of whom more than four-fifths were then shot.[13] His response to the German question about co-operation, not least over Poland, was positive and encouraging.

It was followed up immediately. Two days after Stalin's reply, two Focke-Wulf Condor planes touched down in Moscow to be met by a Soviet guard of honour and two sets of flags fluttering in the wind. Half bore the image of the hammer and sickle, the tools of the urban proletariat and the peasantry, unmistakable symbol of Communism; the others were flags of the Third Reich, designed by Hitler himself—as he explained in *Mein Kampf*: "In red, we can see the social idea of the [National Socialist] movement, in white the nationalist idea, and in the *swastika* the mission of the struggle for the triumph of the *Aryan* man."[14] In one of the most extraordinary and unexpected sights of the twentieth century, the flags representing Communism and Fascism flew side by side as the Germans disembarked from the planes. The delegation was headed by Ribbentrop, the German Foreign Minister, described by one former teacher as "the most stupid in the class, full of vanity and very pushy" and now trusted to broker an agreement between bitter rivals.[15]

After being driven to the Kremlin to meet with Stalin and Molotov, Ribbentrop expressed his hope for good relations. "Germany asks for nothing from Russia—only peace and trade," he said. Stalin gave a typically direct reply. "For many years now, we have been pouring buckets of shit over each other's heads, and our propaganda boys could not do enough in that direction. Now all of a sudden, are we to make our peoples believe all is forgotten and forgiven? Things do not work so fast."[16]

In fact, they did. Within a few hours, the outline of a deal had been put together, with an agreed text to be made public together with a secret annexe delineating spheres of influence in the Baltics and in Poland, and effectively providing each side with carte blanche to move in and do as they pleased up to the defined line. Satisfied, Stalin called for vodka in the small hours of the morning to celebrate a toast. "I know how much the German *Volk* love their Führer," he said using the German word. "I would like to drink his health." Further rounds of toasts followed, with Molotov scarcely able to contain his joy. "It was our great comrade Stalin who began this coup of political relations," he beamed. "I drink to his health."[17]

Stalin's euphoria continued at his dacha just outside Moscow the next day where he joined senior members of the Politburo in a duck shoot. Of course it is all a game of bluff, he said, "a game to see who can fool whom. I know what Hitler's up to. He thinks he's outsmarted me, but actually it's I who's tricked him."[18] Hitler, of course, thought precisely the same thing. When a note was passed to him at around midnight in his Alpine idyll, reporting that the final agreement had been signed, his reaction—like Stalin's—was that of a gambler convinced that he is on a hot streak: "we've won," he declared triumphantly.[19]

The Soviet leader came to terms with Germany to buy time. Stalin had no illusions about Hitler or about the long-term threat he posed. Indeed, at the 17th Party Congress of the Communist Party in 1934, sections from *Mein Kampf* were recited to illustrate the dangers posed by Germany and its Chancellor. Stalin himself had read Hitler's infamous work, underlining passages that set out the need for Germany to expand its territories into the east.[20] The Soviet Union, however, needed to recover after a period of chronic turmoil. Catastrophic famine, the result of short-sighted and bloody-minded policy, had led to the deaths of millions from starvation and illness in the early 1930s. The suffering was horrific, and on a colossal scale. One boy who was eight years old at the time later recalled looking at a girl in his classroom in Khar'kov, who had put her head on her desk and closed her eyes during a lesson, seemingly fast asleep; in fact, she had died of starvation. They would bury her, he knew, "just as they buried people yesterday and the day before yesterday and every day."[21]

In the years that followed, Soviet society devoured itself. Seniority within the Communist party offered no protection, as Stalin moved in on his closest rivals and former colleagues. In a spectacular series of show trials, held in Moscow, men who had become household names, not just in the Soviet Union but internationally, were sensationally accused of being counter-revolutionaries, tried and sentenced to death. Men like Grigorii Zinoviev, Lev Kamenev, Nikolai Bukharin and Karl Radek, heroes of the

1917 Revolution, were among many sent to their deaths, denounced in venomous language as Fascist dogs, terrorists, degenerates and vermin by the chief prosecutor Andrei Vyshinskii. In a travesty of intellectual and cultural history, Vyshinskii was then honoured for his poisonous attacks when the Institute of Government and Law of the Soviet Academy of Sciences was rechristened to bear his name.[22]

Attention then turned to the army. The High Command was not so much decimated as annihilated, ravaged by a perverted and ruthless logic: it stood to reason that if junior officers were guilty of sedition, then their seniors were guilty either of complicity or of negligence. So one confession, beaten from a broken man, served to unleash cascades of arrests. The aim, one secret police officer later testified, was to prove the existence of a "military conspiracy within the Red Army that implicated as many participants as possible."[23]

Of the 101 members of the supreme military leadership, all but ten were arrested; of the ninety-one detained, all but nine were shot. These included three of the five marshals of the Soviet Union and two of its admirals, as well as the entire senior air force personnel, every head of every military district, and almost every divisional commander. The Red Army was brought to its knees.[24] In the circumstances Stalin needed breathing space to rebuild. The German approach was a godsend.

Hitler, on the other hand, was playing for higher stakes. He was desperate to gain access to resources that were essential if Germany was to build a position of strength and power in the long term. The problem was that Germany was poorly located geographically to gain access to the Atlantic and to trade with the Americas, Africa and Asia; Hitler therefore set his sights on the east. Behind his decision to reconcile with the Soviet Union was the idea that this would give him access to his very own Silk Road.

After the pact had been signed, therefore, Hitler summoned his generals to his Alpine chalet so that he could address them on what had been agreed and what he planned. Leaning on the grand piano, he talked at length about himself. The German people were lucky to have him, he declared, a man in whom they had total confidence. But now, he went on, it was time to seize the moment. "We have nothing to lose," he said to his senior officers; Germany can survive for only a few years in its current economic condition; "we have no other choice," he told the generals.[25]

An alliance with the Soviet Union would not only allow the recovery of lands taken away by the Treaty of Versailles; it would guarantee Germany's future. Everything hinged on Germany's success—and it was vital to remember this at all times. "Close your hearts to pity," he said. "Act brutally. Eighty million people must obtain what is their right. Their existence must be made secure."[26] He was talking about the invasion of Poland, but also about the new dawn that would result from the rapprochement with the Soviet Union. For Hitler, coming to terms with Stalin did more than offer the chance to raise the stakes further in his game of political brinkmanship; it offered the prospect of resources. Although he had talked often about *Lebensraum*, or living space, for the German people since he first rose to prominence, what was at stake, he told his generals, were concrete prizes: grain, cattle, coal, lead and zinc. Germany, at last, could be free.[27]

Not all those listening were convinced. Hitler said that the war would take six weeks; it would take more like six years, muttered General von Reichenau.[28] Nor was General Liebmann impressed. The speech, he said, was boastful, brash and "downright repulsive." Hitler was a man who had lost all sense of responsibility. Yet—as the leading modern authority on Nazi Germany notes—no one spoke out against him.[29]

Hitler was convinced that he had found a way to protect Germany's future. One particular area of weakness was the inadequacy of domestic agriculture. As recent research suggests, this was a sector that had suffered during the 1930s as the German war machine began to be assembled, consuming resources, time and money. In fact, new legislation actually served to reduce the amount of investment in agriculture in this period.[30] Germany remained heavily dependent on imports because home production did not provide enough for self-sufficiency.[31] Talking to a senior diplomat in Danzig in August 1939, Hitler brought up the topic of the impossible strain that had been placed on Germany during the First World War—one of his long-term recurring themes. Now, however, he claimed to have the answer. We need Ukraine, "so that no one is able to starve us again as they did in the last war."[32]

Ukraine, or rather the fruits of its rich fertile soil, was delivered to him with the signing of the non-aggression pact in 1939. The months that followed Ribbentrop's visit to the Russian capital saw Nazi and Soviet officials shuttling back and forth between Moscow and Berlin. The Germans were confident that the opening could be translated into an agreement, especially with regard to "all territorial problems from the Black to the Baltic Seas," as

Ribbentrop told Molotov in August 1939.[33] More delicate discussions centred on trade terms and above all on volumes and prices for Soviet wheat, oil and other materials needed to sustain Germany's invasion of Poland and its aftermath. Stalin was fuelling Hitler's war.[34]

The alliance gave Hitler the confidence and the promise of resources that enabled him to attack Poland, safe in the knowledge that his position in the east would be secure following his agreement with Stalin ("I can guarantee on my word of honour that the Soviet Union will not betray its partner," said the Russian leader when the agreement was signed).[35] As one of the more astute senior officers realised, though, agreeing to dismantle Poland made Germany more vulnerable—not less—by dragging the Soviet frontier dramatically westwards; it would be better, noted Franz Halder, to remain on good terms with Russia and focus on the British positions in the Middle East and the Mediterranean.[36]

On 1 September 1939, barely a week after the historic agreement, German troops poured over the frontier, scything their way through Polish defences. Alongside the seizure of territory as the advance closed on Warsaw was the aim of decapitating the Polish elite. As Hitler saw it, "only a nation whose upper levels are destroyed can be pushed into the ranks of slavery." As such, officers and leading figures were targeted—by those who knew what they were looking for: fifteen of the twenty-five commanders of the squads instructed to seek out and annihilate "the upper levels of society" had doctorates, mostly in law or philosophy.[37]

The realignment of Germany and the Soviet Union and the attack on Poland caught Britain and France cold. Although war was declared, neither country provided much meaningful military or logistical support to the Poles. The Royal Air Force did undertake some limited bombing operations, but by far the most common payloads carried by aircraft that flew over German territory were not incendiary devices but leaflets whose aims were rather hopeful, if not downright naive. "There is good reason to believe that the German authorities feared the effect of our propaganda," read the minutes of the very first item on the Cabinet meeting agenda in early September 1939. The fact that "our aircraft were able to fly with impunity all over the North-West of Germany" was bound to have "a depressing effect on the morale of the German people." Dropping more leaflets in the future might be very effective, it was agreed.[38]

In the meantime, panicked appraisals flooded back to London from

India and Central Asia—for the agreement signed by Molotov and Ribbentrop did not just provide a channel of essential supplies for Germany and pave the way for war in Europe. The minister in Kabul, Sir Kerr Fraser-Tytler, warned that there was much speculation locally about whether Britain would provide military support in the event of a Soviet invasion of Afghanistan.[39] These concerns were shared by the India Office, where the Secretary of State released an alarmist document for the War Cabinet in London that painted a near hopeless picture of Indian defences, especially its anti-aircraft resources, which apparently amounted to nothing more than a single battery consisting of eight three-inch guns.[40]

Although London was sceptical about the danger in Central Asia in the immediate short term, it was recognised that Germany's alliance with the Soviet Union did pose a threat to British interests in the east. By the spring of 1940, careful consideration was being given to what seemed to be an inevitable showdown. As a report to the War Cabinet by the Chiefs of Staff entitled "The Military Implications of Hostilities with Russia in 1940" explained, it was "unlikely that the Soviet Government would lose any time in taking action against India and Afghanistan," a development that would create "the maximum diversion of Allied strength."[41] As another report set out with chilling lucidity, there were a great many ways in which German co-operation with Moscow could be deeply detrimental to the Allies: Britain's oil interests in Iran and Iraq were potentially vulnerable and might be lost, and worse, could pass to the enemy.[42]

There was substance to these concerns. The Germans had been highly active across the Middle East and Central Asia in the 1930s, with Lufthansa establishing an extensive network of commercial flights across the region, and companies like Siemens and the Todt organisation making serious inroads into the industrial sectors in Iraq, Iran and Afghanistan. Innumerable roads and bridges had been designed by German engineers, and built or their construction supervised by German technicians. Telecommunication infrastructure had been installed by companies like Telefunken, who found their expertise in great demand.[43] These ties led to Germany being seen positively across the whole region—something that was enhanced by perceptions of Hitler in the Islamic world as a leader who was decisive and stood up for what he believed in. This message was reinforced by the nest of agents controlled by the Abwehr, German military intelligence, who had been actively building contacts and gathering support across the region between the eastern Mediterranean and the Himalayas.[44]

Indeed, by January 1940, there were active discussions within the German High Command about how the Soviets should be encouraged to intervene in Central Asia and India. Plans were circulated by General Jodl, one of the Wehrmacht's most respected senior officers, regarding a joint Germano-Soviet push into the Middle East. This would "require relatively little" effort, but would at the same time "create a trouble-spot threatening to England."[45] A separate, audacious plan to restore to the Afghan throne King Amanullah, who had taken up residence in Berlin after being deposed, was likewise carefully developed.[46] Then there were efforts to foment trouble in strategically sensitive regions. The Faqīr of Ipi, a 1930s version of Osama bin Laden—an ascetic preacher, mystical but bloodthirsty, religiously conservative yet socially revolutionary—was identified as a perfect partner to destabilise the North-West Frontier and divert British attention and resources. One problem was finding him: he was highly elusive and had given the British the slip countless times. Another was to find him unobtrusively: one mission ended in disaster when two German agents whom the Abwehr thought would be less conspicuous if disguised as leprosy experts were killed and wounded in an ambush set by the Afghan army. When contact was finally made with him, the Faqīr's demands in return for help against the British bordered on the absurd.[47]

German bridge-building elsewhere across the region had been no less energetic. Many in Iran and Iraq were taken with Hitler's dynamism and his rhetoric. There was a natural overlap, for example, between the deep anti-Semitism of the Nazi regime and that of some leading Islamic scholars. The Grand Mufti of Jerusalem, Muḥammad al-Ḥusaynī, had welcomed the rise of a man he later referred to as "al-ḥajj Muḥammad Hitler." The German leader's anti-Semitic views were grist to the mill of a man happy to call for the death of Jews, whom he referred to as "scum and germs."[48]

Admiration for Germany across the region went much further. Some scholars have pointed out the similarities between the ideology that Hitler imposed on Germany in the 1930s and a similar programme adopted in Persia of "purification" of the Persian language and customs, and a conscious effort to hark back—as the Nazis did—to a semi-mythical golden age. Indeed, the decision to change the name of Persia formally to Iran was supposedly the result of Teheran's diplomats in Berlin impressing on the Shah the importance of the idea of "Aryanism"—and the shared etymological and pseudo-historical heritage that Iran's new identity could easily reference.[49]

The foundation of the Ba'ath ("renaissance") party in Iraq likewise owed much to Nazi propaganda and to the idea of rebirth.[50] And then there was the telling exchange between Hitler and the envoy of the Saudi king. "We view the Arabs with the warmest sympathy for three reasons," Hitler told the envoy in 1939. "First, we do not pursue any territorial aspirations in Arab lands. Second, we have the same enemies. And third, we both fight against the Jews. I will not rest until the very last of them has left Germany."[51]

Not surprisingly, therefore, one plan after another was developed in London and Paris to try to contain the Germans and the Soviets. The Chief of the French General Staff, Claude Gamelin, asked for plans to be drawn up to build up a stronghold, ideally in the Balkans, that could put pressure on Germany from the rear if need be.[52] The idea was taken seriously, endorsed by the French Prime Minister, the porcine Edouard Daladier, before falling out of favour. It was replaced by an audacious plan to launch an attack on Scandinavia that was designed to cut German supplies of Swedish iron ore—which received enthusiastic backing from Winston Churchill, now First Lord of the Admiralty. "Nothing would be more deadly . . . than to stop for three or even six months this import," wrote Churchill. Britain "should violate Norwegian neutrality" and mine Norway's coastal waters. Taking these steps would threaten Germany's "war-making capacity and . . . the life of the country."[53]

Crippling Germany's supply chain was at the centre of all the discussions. Eventually, in the spring of 1940, attention turned to Baku. The head of the French Air Force, General Vuillemin, championed a plan by which Allied forces could use bases in the Middle East to strike at facilities, primarily in Soviet Azerbaijan. Squadrons operating from British bases in Iraq and from French bases in Syria could, it was claimed, reduce oil production in the Caucasus by half over the course of two to three months. According to the first draft of the plan, this would have "decisive repercussions on Russia and Germany." Subsequent versions promised even rosier projections: fewer attack groups would deliver similar gains but over a quicker time frame.[54]

The results of a bombardment of the Caucasus would be dramatic, British strategists agreed: there would be an immediate disruption of "the industrial and agricultural economies of Russia which would be incrementally paralysed and prevented from working. It will eliminate all the hopes that Germany had of rationally organising Russian production for its benefit and will, from this viewpoint, have a decisive influence on the outcome of the war." French and British planners became convinced that destroying

Russian oil facilities was the best way to remove the threat posed by Germany.[55]

Such plans for joint action were scuppered when Hitler launched a lightning attack on France. To many, the German assault looked like a work of tactical genius, catching the defenders by surprise through a series of dazzling operations, meticulously planned in advance and expertly executed by an army that was battle-hardened and had extensive experience of occupying foreign lands. In fact, as recent research shows, the success in France owed a great deal to chance. More than once, Hitler lost his nerve, instructing troops to hold position, only to find that orders did not reach group commanders until after they had moved miles ahead of where they should have stopped. Heinz Guderian, a dashing Prussian-born tank commander, was even relieved of his position for insubordination after he kept on advancing—even though the order to hold his position had probably never reached him. During this period, Hitler himself became so fearful that his forces were being caught in a non-existent trap that he came close to a nervous breakdown.[56] The rapid advance was the ill-deserved prize for a gambler who had beaten the odds.

The age of empire for western Europe had come to an end with the First World War. Now, rather than slowly fading away, Germany was about to deliver a body blow. As the Royal Air Force prepared to take to the skies for the Battle of Britain, loud voices trumpeted the end of an era. The German minister in Kabul was busy predicting that by the end of the summer Hitler would be in London. In preparation for the British Empire's final collapse, concrete proposals were put to leading figures in the Afghan government: if the country abandoned the neutral stance it had adopted at the start of the war, Germany promised to cede a large chunk of north-western India as well as the port of Karachi when these fell into its lap. It was a tempting offer. Even the British envoy in Kabul recognised that the British ship "looked like sinking," and taking the chance that it "might stay afloat" needed courage and faith. Taking steps like cutting freight costs for Afghan cotton crops to make sure the local economy did not collapse was the smallest of token gestures—and a sign of how limited Britain's options were. At this crucial moment, the Afghans held firm—or at least they wavered, not throwing their lot in with Germany straight away.[57]

By the summer of 1940, Britain and its empire were hanging on for dear life. The stroke of a pen in the small hours in Moscow the previous summer sealing an agreement between Nazi Germany and Communist Soviet Union had made the world look very different, very quickly. The future lay with a new series of connections that would link Berlin through the Soviet Union deep into Asia and the Indian subcontinent, one that would re-route trade and resources away from western Europe to its centre.

This reorientation, however, depended on continued and consistent support from the Soviet Union. Although goods and materials flowed through to Germany in the months that followed the invasion of Poland, they did not always do so smoothly. Negotiations were tense, particularly when it came to wheat and oil—two resources that were in particular demand. Stalin oversaw matters personally, deciding whether the Germans should be allowed to take delivery of a requested consignment of 800,000 tons of oil or only a much smaller amount, and on what terms. Discussing individual shipments was fraught and time consuming, and a source of near-constant anxiety for German planners.[58]

Not surprisingly, the German Foreign Office recognised how fragile the state of affairs was and produced reports underlining the dangers of over-dependence on Moscow. If for whatever reason something went wrong—change of leadership, obstinacy or simple commercial disagreement—Germany would be exposed. This was the single biggest threat to Hitler's astonishing run of military success in Europe.[59]

It was this sense of unease and uncertainty that led to the decision that was to cost the lives of millions of German soldiers, millions of Russians—and millions of Jews: the invasion of the Soviet Union. In typical fashion, when Hitler announced his latest venture at the end of July 1940, he dressed it up in terms of an ideological battle. It was time to seize the chance, he told General Jodl, to eliminate Bolshevism.[60] In fact, what was at stake were raw materials, and above all, food.

Over the course of the second half of 1940 and early 1941, it was not just the military who were set to work on the logistics of an invasion, but economic planners too. They were led by Herbert Backe, an agricultural specialist who had joined the Nazi party in the early 1920s and rose steadily through the ranks, becoming a protégé of Richard Darré, Reichsminister of Food and Agriculture. Backe's slavish devotion to the Nazi cause, coupled with his expertise in farming, led to his becoming increasingly influential in the reforms of the 1930s that regulated prices and set limits on both import and export markets.[61]

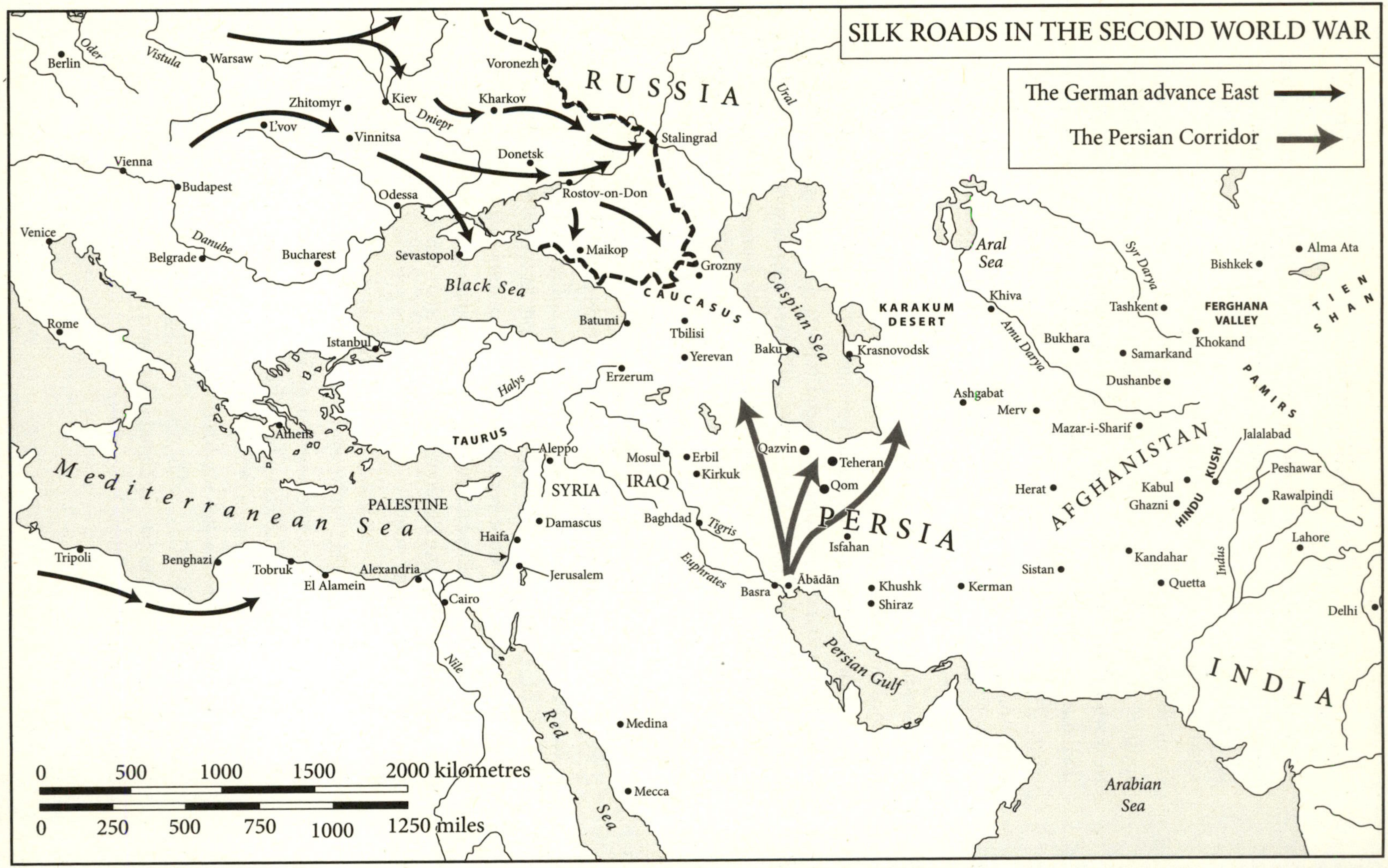
SILK ROADS IN THE SECOND WORLD WAR
The German advance East
The Persian Corridor
RUSSIA
Berlin
Oder
Vistula
Warsaw
Voronezh
Kiev
Dniepr
Zhitomyr
L'vov
Vinnitsa
Kharkov
Stalingrad
Ural
Donetsk
Vienna
Budapest
Odessa
Rostov-on-Don
Venice
Danube
Belgrade
Bucharest
Sevastopol
Maikop
Grozny
Black Sea
CAUCASUS
Caspian Sea
Aral Sea
Syr Darya
Amu Darya
Rome
Istanbul
Batumi
Tbilisi
Yerevan
Baku
Krasnovodsk
KARAKUM DESERT
Khiva
Bukhara
Tashkent
Samarkand
Khokand
FERGHANA VALLEY
Bishkek
Alma Ata
TIEN SHAN
PAMIRS
Dushanbe
Halys
Erzerum
Ashgabat
Merv
Mazar-i-Sharif
Athens
TAURUS
Aleppo
Mosul
Erbil
Kirkuk
Qazvin
Teheran
Qom
Jalalabad
Peshawar
Rawalpindi
Mediterranean Sea
PALESTINE
SYRIA
IRAQ
Damascus
Baghdad
Tigris
PERSIA
Isfahan
Herat
AFGHANISTAN
Kabul
Ghazni
HINDU KUSH
Lahore
Tripoli
Benghazi
Tobruk
El Alamein
Alexandria
Haifa
Jerusalem
Euphrates
Basra
Ābādān
Khushk
Shiraz
Kerman
Sistan
Kandahar
Quetta
Indus
Delhi
Cairo
Nile
Persian Gulf
INDIA
Red Sea
Medina
Mecca
Arabian Sea
0
500
1000
1500
2000 kilometres
0
250
500
750
1000
1250 miles

Backe was obsessed with the idea that Russia might be the solution to Germany's problems. As the Russian Empire had expanded, the steppes had been slowly transformed from a home to nomadic pastoralists to a perfect breadbasket, field upon field of cereals stretching out across flat plains as far as the eye could see. The soil was extraordinarily fertile, especially in the areas where the earth was dark from the richness of its minerals. Scientific expeditions sent to explore the region by the Russian Academy of Sciences waxed lyrical about the belt that stretched from the Black Sea deep into Central Asia, reporting excitedly that conditions were ideally suited to highly productive large-scale arable farming.[62]

Agriculture in southern Russia and Ukraine had grown at ferocious speed before the 1917 Revolution, boosted by growing domestic demand, rising exports and scientific research into the best-quality wheat and how to maximise yields from lands that had been grazed for millennia by nomads and their livestock.[63] No one knew the potential of the steppes, which had expanded production so quickly in the late nineteenth and early twentieth centuries, better than Herbert Backe: his area of expertise, and the topic of his doctoral dissertation, was Russian grain.[64] A small, wiry man who wore glasses and dressed smartly, Backe led teams that produced successive drafts of what the aims and objectives of an invasion should be. As he stressed to Hitler, Ukraine was the key: control of the rich agricultural plains that ran across the north of the Black Sea and on past the Caspian would "liberate us from every economic pressure."[65] Germany would be "invincible" if it could take the parts of the Soviet Union that held "immense riches."[66] Gone would be the dependence on the USSR's goodwill and its whimsical leadership; the effects of the British blockade of the Mediterranean and the North Sea would be massively reduced. This was the chance to provide Germany with access to all the resources it needed.

This is exactly how Hitler came to talk about what was at stake after the attack eventually got under way in the summer of 1941. As German troops moved east with astonishing speed in the first days of the invasion, the Führer could barely contain his excitement. Germany would never leave these newly conquered lands, he asserted gleefully; they would become "our India," "our very own Garden of Eden."[67]

Joseph Goebbels, Reichsminister of Propaganda, also had little doubt that the attack was all about resources, especially wheat and other grains. In an article written in 1942, he declared in his characteristic deadpan and callous manner that the war had been started for "grain and bread, for a well-stocked breakfast, lunch and dinner table." This, and nothing more, was

Germany's war aim, he went on: the capture of "the vast fields of the east [which] sway with golden wheat, enough—more than enough—to nourish our people and all of Europe."[68]

There was an urgent reality behind comments like these, for Germany found itself running increasingly short of food and supplies—with shipments of Soviet grain failing to reduce chronic problems of supply. In February 1941, for example, German radio was broadcasting that there were food shortages across Europe as a result of trade blockades by the British that had previously been described as nothing less than "mental derangement"—or "dementia Britannica," as announcers referred to it.[69] By the summer of 1941, Goebbels was recording in his diary that shops in Berlin had bare shelves; finding vegetables for sale was a rarity. This caused unstable prices and fuelled a thriving black market, which increased the anxieties of a population that, while not yet restless, was starting to ask precisely what the benefits of German expansion had been—a development which made Hitler's propaganda chief decidedly nervous.[70] As one local official put it, the "overworked and exhausted men and women" in his part of Germany "do not see why the war must be carried on still further into Asia and Africa." Happier days were now a distant memory.[71]

The solution had been provided by Backe and his cohort of analysts. Backe himself had been at pains to note the deteriorating food situation within Germany in his annual report on supplies at the end of 1940. Indeed, in a meeting held by state secretaries in January 1941 with Hermann Göring in his capacity as co-ordinator of a Four Year Plan, he had gone so far as to warn that it would not be long before meat would have to be rationed, a step that had been repeatedly vetoed for fear of losing support not just for the war but for the Nazis.[72]

Backe's proposal was radical. While the Soviet Union was vast and varied in terms of geography and climate, it could be divided by a crude line. To the south, covering Ukraine, southern Russia and the Caucasus, were fields and resources that formed a "surplus" zone. To the north, that is central and northern Russia, Belarus and the Baltics, there was a "deficit" zone. As Backe saw it, those on one side of the line produced food; those on the other side just consumed it. The answer to Germany's problems was to concentrate on taking the former—and to ignore the latter. The "surplus" zone should be captured, and its produce diverted to Germany. The "deficit" zone was to be cut off; if and how it survived was of little concern. Its loss was to be Germany's gain.

. . .

The reality of what this meant was spelt out at a meeting that took place in Berlin just weeks before the launch of Operation Barbarossa, the codename given to the invasion of the Soviet Union. On 2 May, planners discussed the priorities and expected results of the attack: the German armies should strip what they could from the land to feed themselves as the advance progressed; the promised land was expected to start producing from the outset. The Wehrmacht was to be supplied from Russia from the moment German soldiers crossed the frontier.

The effect on those living in the "deficit" zone was also noted at the meeting. They were to be cut off at a stroke. In one of the most chilling documents in history, the minutes simply state: "as a result, *x* million people will doubtlessly starve, if that which is necessary for us is extracted from the land."[73] These deaths were the price to pay for Germany being able to feed itself. These millions were collateral damage, necessary victims for German success and survival.

The meeting went on to consider other logistical matters to ensure things went smoothly. The main arteries that linked the agricultural plains to the transport infrastructure were to be secured to enable materials to be shipped back to Germany. Careful consideration was given to what the agricultural leaders who would supervise collection of the harvest and future planting should wear: greyish silver arm stripes on their civilian clothing. As one leading scholar puts it, the meeting was a case of the mundane being mixed with the murderous.[74]

In the three weeks that followed, a concerted effort was made to quantify the numbers of likely casualties, to put a value to the "*x* million" whose deaths were forecast in the "deficit" zone. On 23 May, a twenty-page report was issued that was essentially an updated form of the conclusions that had already been reached. The "surplus" region of the Soviet Union was to be detached, its grain and other agricultural produce gathered and diverted to Germany. As discussed at the previous meeting in Berlin, the local population would suffer the consequences. These were now spelt out, with the previous, open estimate of likely deaths given definition. "Many tens of millions of people in this territory will become superfluous and will die or must emigrate to Siberia," read this report. "Attempts to rescue the population there from death through starvation . . . can only be at the expense of the provisioning of Europe. They prevent the possibility of Germany holding out till the end of the war."[75] The attack did not just concern victory in the war. It was literally a matter of life and death.

Although a list of attendees at the 2 May meeting does not survive, Backe's fingerprints are all over the agenda and the conclusions. He was highly regarded by Hitler, more so than those senior to him, and as Backe's wife wrote in her diary, the German leader sought his advice above all others during briefings to plan the invasion. Then there was the revised introduction to his dissertation that was finally published in the summer of 1941. Russia had failed to use its resources properly, he wrote; if Germany seized them, it would surely use them more efficiently.[76]

But most telling of all was a short note he wrote on 1 June 1941, three weeks before the invasion. The Russians, he wrote, needed no sympathy for what they were about to experience. "The Russian has already endured poverty, hunger and frugality for centuries . . . Do not attempt to apply the German standard of living as [your yardstick] and to alter the Russian way of life." The Russian stomach, he went on, "is stretchable." Pity for those who are to starve, therefore, would be misplaced.[77] The clarity of his thought impressed others, as Goebbels observed in his diary while preparations for the attack on the USSR gathered pace. Backe, he wrote, "dominates his department in a masterly manner. With him, everything that is possible to get done, gets done."[78]

The momentousness of what lay ahead was not lost on those involved. There will be food shortages in the winter of 1941, Goebbels predicted in his diary, so severe that other famines will look insignificant by comparison. That is not our problem, he added, with the obvious inference that it would be Russians and not Germans who would suffer.[79] Assuming that the Germans were listening as carefully to Soviet radio broadcasts as the British were, Goebbels would have taken heart from the news less than three days before the invasion began that "in central Russia, the fields look like green carpets; in the south-east, the wheat is ripening." The harvest was just starting, and it looked like a bumper crop.[80]

As preparations for the attack reached their final stages, the rank and file of the army, as well as the senior officers, had what was at stake seared into their minds. According to Franz Halder, a Bavarian career soldier who had risen inexorably through the ranks of the Wehrmacht, Hitler was typically forthright and categorical. This is a fight to the finish, he told his generals in March 1941. Force must be used in Russia "in its most brutal form." This was to be a "war of extermination." "Troop commanders must know the issues at stake." As far as the Soviet Union was concerned, Hitler said, "severity today means lenience in the future."[81]

This was all set out more fully in May 1941, by which time official *Guidelines for the Behaviour of Troops in Russia* had been prepared and were being circulated to those taking part in the invasion. These listed the threats that were to be expected from "agitators," "partisans," "saboteurs" and Jews, making clear to German soldiers that they were to trust no one and show no mercy.[82] Orders were also issued describing how the conquered territories were to be controlled. Collective punishment was to be used in the event of insurrection or resistance. Those suspected of working against German interests were to be tried on the spot and shot if found guilty, regardless of whether they were soldiers or civilians.[83]

Finally, a series of directives was issued, among them the so-called Commissar Order that gave graphic warnings of what to expect: the enemy would be likely to behave in a manner that contravened the principles of international law and of humanity. Commissars—shorthand for the Soviet political elite—fought in ways that could only be described as "barbaric and Asiatic." They were to be shown no mercy.[84]

20

The Road to Genocide

In the build-up to the German invasion of the Soviet Union, the message to the officers and the troops was consistent and remorseless: everything rested on taking the wheatfields of the south. Soldiers were told that they should imagine food eaten by Soviet citizens had been torn from the mouths of German children.[1] Senior commanders told their men that the very future of Germany rested on their success. As Colonel-General Erich Hoepner told his Panzer Group in an operational order immediately before Barbarossa began, Russia had to be crushed—and crushed "with unprecedented severity. Every military action must in conception and execution be led by the iron will mercilessly and totally to annihilate the enemy."[2] Contempt for the Slavs, hatred of Bolshevism and anti-Semitism ran through the veins of the officer corps. These now blended, as one leading historian puts it, "as the ideological yeast whose fermentation now easily converted the generals into accessories to mass murder."[3]

Hitler, while urging the implementation of horror, daydreamed about the future: the Crimea would be like the Riviera for Germans, he reflected; how wonderful it would be to link the peninsula in the Black Sea to the motherland with a motorway so that every German could visit in their People's Car (or Volkswagen). He took to wishing whimsically he was younger so that he could see how it would all turn out; it was a shame, he thought, that he would miss out on a time of intense excitement in decades to come.[4]

Himmler likewise contemplated a rosy view where "pearls of settlements" (*Siedlungsperlen*) would exist, peopled by colonisers, and ringed by villages that were home to German farmers, reaping the crops from the rich black earth.[5]

Hitler and those closest to him had two templates for expanding Germany's resource base. First was the British Empire. Germany would stamp itself on enormous new territories in the east, just as Britain had done in the Indian subcontinent. A small population of German colonisers would rule Russia, just as a few British ruled in the Raj. European civilisation would triumph over a culture that was simply inferior. The British in India were constantly cited by the Nazi leadership as a model of how large-scale domination could be accomplished by few people.[6]

But there was another model that Hitler regularly referred to as well, with which he saw parallels and to which he looked for inspiration: the United States. Germany needed to do what the European settlers in the New World had done to the native Americans, Hitler told Alfred Rosenberg, the newly appointed Reichsminister for the Occupied Eastern Territories: the local population had to be driven back—or exterminated. The Volga, he proclaimed, would be Germany's Mississippi, that is to say, a frontier between the civilised world and the chaos beyond. The peoples who had settled the Great Plains in America in the nineteenth century, he said, would surely flock to settle in the east. Germans, Dutch, Scandinavians and also, he predicted confidently, Americans themselves would find their futures and their rewards in a new land of opportunity.[7] A new world order was going to emerge thanks to the fields of Ukraine and southern Russia that stretched far into the east. It was the end of the American dream, Hitler declared: "Europe—and no longer America—will be the land of unlimited possibilities."[8]

His excitement was not just based on prospects held by the belt of land above the Black and Caspian Seas, for signs everywhere pointed to a dramatic shift in Germany's favour. One part of the German pincer was travelling towards the heart of the world from the north, while the other was coming from the south through North Africa and the Middle East. A succession of lightning victories in the deserts of North Africa in 1941 had brought Rommel and the Afrika Korps within striking distance of Egypt and thus close to taking control of the critical Suez canal, just as Barbarossa got under way. The collapse of France, meanwhile, had opened up possibilities for the Luftwaffe to use the airbases that the French had established in

Syria and the Levant after the First World War settlements, to extend Germany's reach further still.

The fate of the world hung by the most slender of threads. The key question, it seemed, turned on the timing of the invasion of the Soviet Union and whether Stalin could be taken by surprise. It was crucial to launch the attack after the harvest had been sown but before it was collected, so that German troops could benefit as they advanced into Russia. Negotiations with Moscow in 1940 had already led to shipments from the Soviet Union to Germany of a million tons of grain, nearly the same amount of petroleum and considerable quantities of iron ore and manganese. Once delivery had been taken of a further enormous consignment in May 1941, the moment was nigh.[9]

Alarmed by German troops massing in the east in the early summer of 1941, Marshal Timoshenko, Commissar of Defence, and General Georgi Zhukov confronted Stalin with a proposal to launch a pre-emptive attack, followed by an advance that would lead to an assault on Warsaw, northern Poland and part of Prussia. According to two closely matching accounts, Stalin dismissed the plan out of hand. "Have you gone mad?" he apparently asked angrily. "Do you want to provoke the Germans?" Then he turned to Timoshenko: "Look everyone . . . Timoshenko is healthy and he has a large head; but his brain is evidently tiny." Then the threat: "If you provoke the Germans on the border, if you move forces without our permission, then bear in mind that heads will roll." With that, he turned, walked out and slammed the door behind him.[10]

It was not that Stalin did not believe Hitler would attack, just that he thought he would not dare to do so yet. In fact, the reason why Stalin had personally overseen trade with the Nazi administration had been to keep a close eye on the Germans while the Soviet army was rapidly rebuilt and modernised. He was so confident he still held all the cards that even when intelligence reports were received from agents in Berlin, Rome and even Tokyo—in addition to warnings and signs from embassies in Moscow—that an attack was imminent, he simply dismissed them.[11] His scathing attitude was perfectly summed up by his reaction to a report from a spy within the German air force headquarters just five days before the invasion was launched. "You can tell your 'source' . . . to go fuck his mother," he scrawled. "This is not a 'source,'" he wrote, "it's someone spreading disinformation."[12]

Not all of those around Stalin were as blasé as the Soviet leader. German troop movements in early June led some to argue that the Red Army should be moved into defensive positions. "We have a non-aggression pact with Germany," Stalin replied incredulously. "Germany is tied up with war in the West and I am sure that Hitler will not dare to create a second front by attacking the Soviet Union. Hitler is not such a fool and realises that the Soviet Union is not Poland or France, and not even England."[13]

By 21 June, it was obvious that something serious was afoot. Sweden's ambassador to Moscow, Vilhelm Assarsson, thought there were two options: either he was about to have a front-row seat at an epic confrontation between the "Third Reich and the Soviet Empire" with extraordinarily wide-ranging consequences, or the Germans were about to issue a set of demands regarding "the Ukraine and the Baku oilwells." If the latter, he mused, he might just be witnessing "the greatest case of blackmail in world history."[14]

Hours later, it became clear it was not a game of bluff. At 3:45 a.m. on 22 June 1941, Stalin was woken by a phone call from General Zhukov who told him that the frontiers had been breached in all sectors and that the Soviet Union was under attack. At first, Stalin refused to believe what was happening, concluding that it was a gambit by Hitler, aimed at strong-arming a settlement of some kind, probably regarding trade. Only slowly did it dawn on him that this was a fight to the death. Numb from shock, he slumped into a catatonic state, leaving it to Molotov to make public announcements. "An act of treachery, unprecedented in the history of civilised nations, has taken place," Molotov announced gravely, as he took to the airwaves. But have no doubts: "the enemy will be crushed and victory will be ours." There was no mention of the fact that the Soviet Union had been dancing with the devil and now the time had come to pay up.[15]

The German advance was relentless and devastating—even though the invading force was neither as well prepared nor as well equipped as has often been presumed.[16] In a matter of days, Minsk had fallen and 400,000 Soviet soldiers were encircled and trapped. Brest-Litovsk was cut off, its defenders quickly deprived of supplies but not always of hope: as one young soldier scratched into a wall on 20 July 1941, "I am dying, but do not surrender. Farewell motherland."[17]

By this time, Stalin had begun to understand the magnitude of what was happening. On 3 July, he gave a radio speech that talked of the German invasion as a matter of "life and death for the peoples of the USSR."

He informed listeners that the invaders wanted to restore "tsarism" and the "rule of landlords." Closer to the mark was his claim that the attackers intended to obtain "slaves" for German princes and barons.[18] This was more or less correct—as long as princes and barons meant Nazi party officials and German industrialists: it would not be long before forced labour became commonplace for captured Soviet soldiers and the local population. In due course, more than 13 million people were used to build roads, to farm fields or to work in factories both for the Nazi regime directly and for private German companies—many of which remain in business today. Slavery had returned to Europe.[19]

Over the summer of 1941, the Germans seemed all but unstoppable. By September, Kiev fell after a siege that saw more than half a million Soviet soldiers captured. A few weeks later, the three battle groups that acted as spears plunging into the heart of Russia had reached Kalinin, Tula and Borodino—where Napoleon's invasion had faltered in 1812. Still the Germans continued to cut through the defences. By October, Moscow was teetering. Such was the anxiety that plans were made to evacuate the leadership to Kuibyshev, old Samarra, more than 600 miles to the east of Moscow on a bend of the Volga as it flows towards the Caspian. Lenin's body was removed from Red Square and put into storage. Preparations were made for Stalin to leave the city, only for the Russian leader to change his mind at the last minute and decide to stay: according to some reports, his train's engine was running and his bodyguards were on the platform ready to go.[20]

By November, Rostov-on-Don had fallen, the final point before the Caucasus. At the end of the month, the 3rd and 4th Panzergruppe were within twenty miles of Moscow. On 1 December, a reconnaissance unit of motorcyclists was just five miles from the capital.[21] Hitler was euphoric. The plan to decapitate the Soviet Union by knocking out Leningrad and Moscow in the north had been central to securing the "surplus" zone in the south in the long term, and the plan seemed to be on track. Two months after the attack had started, as the Russian lines were being rolled back, he spoke with excitement about the future. "The Ukraine, and then the Volga basin, will one day be the granaries of Europe. We shall reap much more than what actually grows from the soil," he said in August 1941. "If one day Sweden declines to supply us with any more iron," he went on, "that's alright. We'll get it from Russia."[22]

In the meantime, construction and technical teams moved eastwards behind the army. In September 1941, a convoy of the newly created

Sonderkommando R (Special Command Russia) set out from Berlin for Ukraine, with the aim of establishing a workable infrastructure in newly conquered territories. Made up of field kitchens, mobile offices, repair shops and police transmitters in more than a hundred vehicles, its job was to enable what one historian has called "the most radical colonisation campaign in the history of European conquest and empire building."[23]

When they reached Odessa, on the Black Sea, the officers in charge—a motley collection of under-achievers, draft-dodgers and misfits—set about occupying the finest residences for their headquarters and busied themselves with establishing the sorts of institutions that bore the unequivocal statement of long-term plans: libraries, record collections, lecture halls and cinemas to show triumphalist German films.[24]

The invasion seemed to have been an unmitigated success. Almost the entire area earmarked for sending resources back to Germany had been conquered in less than six months. Leningrad and Moscow had not yet fallen, but it seemed a matter of time before both surrendered. Elsewhere too the signs seemed promising. Although an uprising in Iraq had been put down by a hastily assembled British force that requisitioned buses from the streets of Haifa and drove east to suppress the revolt, there seemed to be grounds for thinking that Germany's new friends in the oil-rich lands south of the Caspian Sea would soon come good.[25]

By the time of the invasion of the Soviet Union, Hitler had already given his formal blessing to the idea of Arab independence, and had written to the Grand Mufti of Jerusalem to express solidarity, praising the Arabs as an ancient civilisation and as one that had common enemies with Germany in the British and the Jews.[26] The cultivation of ties in the Muslim world went so far that one German academic penned a sycophantic eulogy that among other things praised Saudi Arabia as "The Third Reich in Wahhabi style."[27]

From Britain's point of view, then, things looked desperate. Disaster had been avoided in Iraq by a hair's breadth, noted General Wavell, commander-in-chief in India, and it was vital that steps were taken to protect Iran, where it was touch and go whether German influence might be extended. "It is essential to the defence of India," he wrote to Prime Minister Winston Churchill in the summer of 1941, "that Germans should be cleared out of Iran now. Failure to do so will lead to a repetition of events which in Iraq were only just countered in time."[28]

Wavell was right to be concerned about Iran, where German propaganda had been relentless since the start of the war. In the summer of 1941, reported one American correspondent, bookstalls in Teheran were covered with copies of the magazine *Signal*, one of Goebbels' mouthpieces, while cinemas showing films like *Sieg im Westen* (Victory in the West) that celebrated German victories in France and western Europe in epic style were packed.[29]

Hitler's attack on the Soviet Union was also rapturously received in Iran. According to some reports, crowds gathered in Sepah Square in central Teheran to cheer news of the fall to the Wehrmacht of one Soviet city after another.[30] The problem was that "Iranians generally are delighted at the German attack on their ancient enemy Russia," as Sir Reader Bullard, the British ambassador, informed London in the days following the invasion.[31]

Pro-German sympathies were widespread in the army and in the bazaar, declared the distinguished Persian scholar Ann Lambton, after being asked for her views on the developing situation. Feelings ran particularly high among "younger officials [who] tend to be pro-German and to hope for a German victory."[32] The British military attaché held much the same opinion, contrasting the positive local impression of Germany with the negative views about Britain. "There is as yet only a small number [of people] who would be at all likely to support the British cause if the Germans were to reach Persia, whereas it may be anticipated that the Germans would find considerable active support."[33] This view was shared by the German ambassador in Teheran, Erwin Ettel, who reported to Berlin that a British attack would face "resolute military resistance," and would result in the Shah appealing formally for help from Germany.[34]

The anxiety that Iran might throw its lot in with Hitler was exacerbated by the knowledge that resistance was crumbling as the Germans advanced east. Such was their progress that General Auchinleck, until recently commander-in-chief, India and now appointed to head Middle East Command, was briefed that Hitler's troops would reach the Caucasus by the middle of August 1941.[35] From Britain's point of view, this was a disaster. The Germans were in desperate need of oil. If they took control of the supplies in Baku and the Caucasus, that would be bad enough. What was worse, noted Leopold Amery, Secretary of State for India, was that they would then be "pretty close" to the oilfields in Iran and Iraq and would doubtless make "every kind of mischief."[36] In other words, not only did it look as though Germany could find a solution for its Achilles heel of not having reliable access to oil to fuel its ships, planes, tanks and other vehicles, but it might compromise Britain's ability to sustain the war effort. It was vital, General Auchinleck concluded, to develop a plan—named Operation Countenance—to defend the belt stretching from Palestine to Basra and to the Iranian oilfields.[37]

Iran's importance was magnified by its strategic location. Although Stalin had previously cut a deal with Hitler in 1939, the German invasion of the Soviet Union two years later had turned the latter into an unlikely ally for the British and their friends. It was announced in Washington, therefore, that "the Government of the United States has decided to give all economic assistance practicable for the purpose of strengthening the Soviet Union in its struggle against armed aggression."[38] This was coupled with private assurances given to Stalin by the American ambassador in Moscow that the U.S. was determined "'all out' to beat Hitler" and was prepared to do whatever it took to make this happen.[39]

The problem was how to get armaments and matériel to the Soviet Union. Shipping to ports in the Arctic Circle was logistically difficult and, in the middle of winter, treacherous. The lack of suitable harbours, other than Vladivostok in the east, meanwhile, was no less problematic, not least because of Japan's dominance in this part of the Pacific. The solution was obvious: to take control of Iran. This would prevent local German agents and sympathisers gaining a foothold at a crucial moment, would better enable the protection of natural resources the Allies could ill afford to lose and would provide the best chance of co-ordinating efforts to hinder and halt the relentless drive east of the Wehrmacht.

While this suited the Allies' war ends, it also promised longer-term rewards for the British and the Soviets respectively; occupying the country would give each what they had long coveted in terms of political influence, economic resources and strategic value. Exciting opportunities had been thrown up by Hitler's decision to turn on his former ally in Moscow.

In August 1941, Iran was invaded by British troops, with Soviet forces moving in at the same time. Differences were put to one side in order to promote mutual interests in a region of profound strategic and economic importance. There was much celebration when British and Soviet troops met at Qazvin, in the north of the country, where they swapped stories and cigarettes. The foreign correspondents who met up with the Soviet army soon found themselves being treated to vodka and toasting the alliance by drinking to the health of Stalin, then Churchill, then Molotov, then Roosevelt, and then the same again in the same order. "At the end of thirty toasts in neat vodka," wrote one American journalist who was present, "half the correspondents were under the table. The Russians continued drinking."[40]

When the Shah dithered over issuing an ultimatum to expel German citizens with immediate effect, the British began to broadcast reports over the radio on the new BBC Persian Radio Service that (falsely) accused the Shah of removing the crown jewels from the capital, of using forced labour in his own business interests and of using Teheran's water supply to irrigate his private gardens—criticisms that already circulated widely according to Reader Bullard in his memoirs.[41]

The Shah prevaricated in the face of British demands, complaining to President Roosevelt about "acts of aggression" and decrying the threat to "international justice and the right of peoples to liberty." This was all very well, replied the President, but the Shah should bear in mind that "it is certain that movements of conquest by Germany will continue and will extend beyond Europe to Asia, Africa and even the Americas." Persia, in other words, was dicing with disaster by contemplating good relations with Hitler.[42] In the end, the British took matters into their own hands and forced the abdication of Reza Khan, who was by now considered a liability, and his replacement by his son, Mohammed Reza, an immaculately turned-out playboy with a love for French crime novels, fast cars and even faster women.[43]

To many Iranians, such outside interference was intolerable. In November 1941, mobs were gathering to shout "Long Live Hitler!" and "Down with the Russians and the British!," to show their disgust for how the fate of the country was being decided by soldiers who were seen as an occupying force.[44] This was not Iran's war; the disputes and military conflict of the Second World War had nothing to do with inhabitants of towns like Teheran and Isfahan, who looked on agog as their country was caught up in the struggle between European powers. These views counted for nothing.

With the situation in Iran brought forcefully under control, steps were also taken against French installations in Syria following the fall of France due to fears that they could be used against Britain and its allies in the Middle East. A hastily deployed Hurricane squadron was sent from RAF Habbaniyah, one of the airfields the British retained in Iraq after the end of the First World War, to strafe the bases of the Vichy French. Among those flying in the raids in the second half of 1941 was a young fighter pilot who later recalled coming in low to catch a Sunday-morning cocktail party of

French airmen and "a bunch of girls in brightly coloured dresses" in full swing. Glasses, bottles and high heels flew everywhere as the British fighters attacked and all took cover. It was "wonderfully comical," wrote the pilot of one of the Hurricanes—a certain Roald Dahl.[45]

The news coming into Berlin around this time seemed unremittingly good. With the Soviet Union in dire straits, and breakthroughs seemingly imminent in Persia, Iraq and Syria, there was every reason to think that Germany was on the brink of a series of conquests to compare with those of the great armies of Islam in the seventh century or the Mongol forces of Genghis Khan and his heirs. Success was within touching distance.

The reality, however, was rather different. Dramatic as the German advances appeared, both in the Soviet Union and elsewhere, they were beset by problems. For one thing, battlefield losses during the advance east greatly exceeded the number of reserves being sent out to replace them. Although spectacular victories led to huge numbers of prisoners being taken, these were often achieved at great cost. According to General Halder's own estimates, the Wehrmacht lost over 10 per cent of its men in the first two months of fighting after the start of the invasion—or more than 400,000 soldiers. By the middle of September, this had risen to more than 500,000 men, dead or wounded.[46]

The galloping surge forward also put an almost unbearable strain on supply lines. Lack of clean water was an issue almost from the outset, which in turn led to outbreaks of cholera and dysentery. Even before the end of August, it was becoming clear to the more astute that the picture was not as rosy as it seemed: shortages of basic materials like razor blades, toothpaste, toothbrushes, writing paper, needles and thread were notable from the first days of the invasion.[47] Endless rain in the late summer soaked men and equipment alike. "There is no chance at all to dry the blankets, boots and clothes properly," wrote one soldier home.[48] News of conditions reached Goebbels, who remarked in his diary that nerves of steel were needed to overcome the difficulties. In due course, he wrote, the current hardships "will seem like fond memories."[49]

Prospects in the Near East and in Central Asia likewise flattered to deceive. For all the optimism earlier in the year, Germany had little to show for the popular enthusiasm that supposedly promised to link North Africa to Syria, Iraq to Afghanistan. The prospect of establishing a meaningful presence, let alone taking control, seemed to be an illusion rather than something of substance.

And so, in spite of extraordinary territorial gains, the German High Command set about trying to shore up morale just as Moscow was teetering. At the start of October 1941 Field Marshal von Reichenau, commander of the part of Army Group South that had advanced into the "surplus" zone, issued an order to try to inject some grit back into his soldiers. Each man, he stated solemnly, was a "standard-bearer of a national ideal, and the avenger of all the bestialities perpetrated on the German peoples."[50] This was all well and good; but as men stuffed newspapers into their boots to fight off the cold, it was hard to see what effect strong words could have on a force whose members froze to death if wounded and whose skin stuck to the icy butts of their rifles.[51] As biting winter took hold, such that bread had to be chopped with axes, Hitler told the Danish Foreign Minister with disdain: "If the German people are no longer strong enough and ready to sacrifice their own blood . . . they should perish."[52] Chemical stimulants—like Pervitin, a metamphetamine that was distributed in large quantities to troops serving on the bitterly cold eastern front—were more helpful than pep talks in giving succour.[53]

Serious supply problems also characterised the invasion. It had been estimated that the battle group closing in on Moscow would need twenty-seven deliveries of fuel by train each day; in November, it received three—in the course of the whole month.[54] American economists monitoring the war focused on precisely this issue in reports entitled "The German Military and Economic Position" and "The German Supply Problem on the Eastern Front." They calculated that each 125 miles of advance would require an additional 35,000 freight cars, or a reduction of 10,000 tons in daily deliveries to the front line. The speed of the advance was proving to be a major problem.[55]

Keeping the front line supplied from the rear was bad enough. But there was a more pressing issue. The guiding principle behind the invasion had been the amputation of the rich lands of Ukraine and of southern Russia—the so-called surplus zone. Even when grain shipments were being delivered from the Soviet Union before the invasion started, the effects of the war on food supplies and diets were far more marked in Germany than they had been, for example, in Great Britain. Rather than being boosted by gains in the east, daily calorie consumption, already reduced by the end of 1940, began to plummet further.[56] In fact, the amounts of grain shipped back to Germany after Operation Barbarossa got under way were much lower than had been imported from the Soviet Union in 1939–41.[57]

German radio broadcasts attempted to boost morale—and provide assurances. Germany used to have plentiful reserves of grain, one news report stated in November 1941; "now in wartime, we have to do without this kind of luxury." But there was good news, the bulletin went on. There was no need to fear the shortages and problems of the First World War. Unlike the period between 1914 and 1918, "the German people can rely on their food control authorities."[58]

This was fighting talk, for in fact it was becoming clear that the idea of taking control of an apparently bottomless pool of resources in the east had been an illusion. The army that had been instructed to feed itself from the land was unable to do so, barely surviving and resorting to rustling livestock. Far from boosting the agricultural situation at home, meanwhile, the promised lands on which Hitler and those around him had set their hopes turned out to be a drain. The Soviets' scorched-earth policies robbed the land of much of its wealth. Meanwhile within the Wehrmacht confused and contradictory military priorities—there was constant tension over whether men, tanks, resources and fuel should be diverted to the centre, to the north or to the south—sowed seeds that would prove deadly. American estimates made in the spring of 1942 about likely crop yields in the conquered territories of the Soviet Union's south painted a pessimistic picture of the likely harvest in Ukraine and southern Russia. At most, the report suggested, two-thirds of pre-invasion yields were possible. Even that would be doing well.[59]

For all the territorial gains achieved, therefore, the campaign in the east had failed to deliver not only what had been promised but what was needed. Just two days after the invasion of the Soviet Union, Backe had presented his projections regarding wheat requirements as part of a four-year economic plan. Germany was facing a deficit of 2.5 million tons per year. The Wehrmacht needed to resolve this—and to secure millions of tons of oil-bearing seeds, and millions of head of cattle and pigs—for Germany to eat.[60] This was one reason why Hitler instructed his generals to "raze Moscow and Leningrad to the ground": he wanted to "prevent people remaining there whom we would then have to feed in the winter."[61]

Having predicted that millions would die from food shortages and famine, the Germans now began to identify those who should suffer. First in line were Russian prisoners. There is no need to feed them, wrote Göring dismissively; it is not as though we are bound by any international obligations.[62] On 16 September 1941, he gave the order to withdraw food supplies from "non-working" prisoners of war—that is, those who were too weak or too injured to act as slave labour. A month later, after rations for "working" captives had already been reduced, they were lowered once again.[63] The effect was devastating: by February 1942, some 2 million (of a total of 3.3 million) Soviet prisoners were dead, mostly as a result of starvation.[64]

To quicken the process further still, new techniques were devised to eliminate the number of mouths that needed feeding. Prisoners of war were gathered by the hundred so that the effects of pesticides that had been used to fumigate Polish army barracks could be tested on them. Experiments were also carried out on the impact of carbon monoxide poisoning, using vans that had pipes connected to their own exhausts. These tests—which took place in the autumn of 1941—were conducted in locations that were soon to gain notoriety for using the same techniques on a massive scale: Auschwitz and Sachsenhausen.[65]

The mass murders that began just weeks after the start of the invasion were a sickening response to the failure of the German attack and the abject inadequacies of the economic and strategic plans. The great granaries of Ukraine and southern Russia had not generated what had been expected of them. And there was an immediate price to pay: not the deportation or emigration of the local population, as Hitler had mentioned in conversation. With too many people and not enough food, there were two obvious targets who had been demonised in all walks of German life, in the media and in popular consciousness: Russians and Jews.

The portrayal of the Slavs as racially inferior, erratic, with a capacity for suffering and violence had been consistently developed before the war. Although the vitriol had been toned down after the Molotov–Ribbentrop agreement was signed in 1939, it started up again after the invasion. As has been forcefully argued, this played directly into the genocide of Russians that started in the late summer of 1941.[66]

Anti-Semitism was even more heavily ingrained in Germany before the war. According to the deposed Kaiser, the Weimar Republic had been "prepared by the Jews, made by the Jews and maintained by Jewish pay." Jews were like mosquitoes, he wrote in 1925, "a nuisance that humankind must get rid of some way or other . . . I believe the best thing would be gas!"[67] Such attitudes were not unusual. Events like the *Kristallnacht*, which saw co-ordinated violence against Jews on the night of 9–10 November 1938, were culminations of poisonous rhetoric that routinely dismissed the Jewish population as "a parasite [that] feeds on the flesh and productivity and work of other nations."[68]

Rising fears of what such talk—and action—would bring had already prompted some to consider making new alliances. In the mid-1930s, David Ben-Gurion, later the first Prime Minister of Israel, tried to reach an agreement with leading Arabs in Palestine to enable greater levels of Jewish emigration. This came to nothing, with a mission led by a supposed Arab moderate being sent to Berlin to agree terms on how the Nazi regime would instead support Arab plans to undermine British interests in the Middle East.[69]

Before the end of the first month of the war, in September 1939, a plan had been agreed to resettle all Jews in Poland. To start with, at least, the plan seems to have been to gather the population en masse to facilitate their removal from German territory by forcible emigration. Indeed, elaborate plans were developed in the late 1930s to deport German Jews to Madagascar, a hare-brained scheme seemingly based on the popular (but misguided) conviction of many late nineteenth- and early twentieth-century geographers and anthropologists that the native Malagasy population of this island in the south-west Indian Ocean traced their origins to the Jews.[70]

There had been discussions in Nazi Germany about deporting Jews elsewhere too. In fact, and perversely, Hitler had been championing the creation of a Jewish state in Palestine for the best part of two decades. In the spring of 1938, he spoke in support of a policy of emigration of German Jews to the Middle East and the formation of a new state to be their home.[71] Indeed, in the late 1930s, a high-level mission, led by Adolf Eichmann, had even been sent to meet with Zionist agents in Palestine to discuss how an accommodation could be reached that would solve what was often called "the Jewish question" once and for all. With considerable irony, Eichmann—who was later executed in Israel for crimes against humanity—found himself discussing how to boost emigration of Jews from Germany to Palestine, something which seemed in the interests both of the anti-Semitic Nazi leadership and of the leadership of the Jewish community in and around Jerusalem.[72]

Although the discussions did not result in agreement, the Germans continued to be seen as potentially useful partners—even after the start of the war. In the autumn of 1940, Avraham Stern, the creator of a movement called the Lehi, which became known to the authorities in Palestine as the

Stern Gang and whose members included the future Prime Minister Yitzhak Shamir as well as other founding fathers of modern Israel, sent a message to a senior German diplomat in Beirut with a radical proposal. "Common interests could exist," it began, between Germany and the "true national aspirations of the Jewish people," whom Stern (and others) purported to represent. If "aspirations of the Israeli freedom movement are recognised," it went on, Stern offered to "actively take part in the war on the German side." If the Jews could be liberated through the creation of a state, Hitler would surely benefit: apart from "strengthen[ing the] future German position of power in the Middle East," it would also "extraordinarily strengthen the moral basis" of the Third Reich "in the eyes of all humanity."[73]

This was bluster. In fact, Stern was being pragmatic—even though the hopes he placed in allying with Germany were not shared by all within his own organisation. "All we want of the Germans," he said shortly afterwards to explain his stance, is to bring Jewish recruits to Palestine. In doing so, "the war against the British to liberate the homeland will begin here. The Jews will attain a state, and the Germans will, incidentally, be rid of an important British base in the Middle East, and also solve the Jewish question in Europe . . ." It seemed logical—and horrific: leading Jewish figures were actively proposing collaboration with the greatest anti-Semite of all time, negotiating with the perpetrators of the Holocaust hardly twelve months before genocide began.[74]

As far as Hitler was concerned, where Jews were deported to was unimportant, such was the power of his anti-Semitism. Palestine was just one location among many that were considered, with locations deep inside Russia also discussed seriously. "It does not matter where one sends the Jews," Hitler told the Croatian military commander Slavko Kvaternik in 1941. Either Siberia or Madagascar would do.[75]

Faced with chronic problems in Russia, this casual attitude now hardened into something more formal and more ruthless as it dawned on Nazi planners that the fact that Jews had been gathered in camps meant that mass murder could be accomplished with little difficulty.[76] Faced with a drain on resources that were already scarce, it was a short jump for a systemically anti-Semitic regime to start to look to murder on a massive scale. Jews were already in camps in Poland; they were a ready and easy target at a time when the Nazi leadership were realising that there were millions of mouths too many to feed.

"There is a danger this winter," wrote Adolf Eichmann as early as the middle of July 1941, "that the Jews can no longer all be fed. It is to be seriously considered whether the most humane solution might not be to finish off those Jews not capable of labour by some sort of fast-working preparation."[77] The elderly, the infirm, women and children and those "not capable of labour" were dismissed as expendable: they were the first step in replacing the "*x* million" whose deaths had been so carefully forecast before the invasion of the Soviet Union.

So began a chain of events whose scale and horror were unprecedented, the shipment of human beings like livestock to holding pens where they could be divided into those who would work as slave labour and those whose lives were deemed to be the price to pay for the survival of others: southern Russia, Ukraine and the western steppe became the cause of genocide. The failure of the land to generate wheat in the anticipated quantities was a direct cause of the Holocaust.

In Paris, where the police had been carrying out secret registrations of Jewish and non-Jewish foreigners since the late 1930s, the process of deportation was simply a question of rattling through the card index that was handed to the German occupiers and then sending guards to detain entire families for transportation to camps in the east, mainly in Poland.[78] The registration of Jews in other occupied countries, such as the Netherlands, as part of the broad programme of institutionalised Nazi anti-Semitism also made the process of deporting those now identified as surplus to requirements distressingly easy.[79] Having attacked the Soviet Union with thoughts of surplus zones, thoughts now revolved around surplus populations—and how to deal with them.

As the hopes of what the invasion would bring were thwarted, the Nazi elite concluded that there was one solution for Germany's problems. In a grotesque mirroring of the meeting that had taken place in Berlin on 2 May 1941, another meeting took place less than eight months later in Wannsee, a leafy suburb of Berlin. Once again, the question revolved around the issue of the deaths of unquantifiable millions. The name given to the conclusions reached on the frosty morning of 20 January 1942 sends shivers down the spine. In the eyes of its makers, the genocide of the Jews was simply a response to a problem. The Holocaust was the "Final Solution."[80]

Before long, tanks, aircraft, armaments and supplies were on their way to Moscow from London and Washington as the fightback against Germany began to gather pace. These were networks, trade routes and communication channels that had functioned since the days of antiquity through the so-called Persian Corridor, stretching inland from the Gulf ports of Ābādān, Basra, Bushihr and others, through the interior to Teheran via Arak and Qom, and eventually through the Caucasus to reach the Soviet Union. Routes were also opened up through the Russian Far East across into Central Asia.[81]

Russia's old commercial connections with Great Britain were again activated, despite the challenges involved: Arctic convoys taking provisions and resources to Murmansk and northern Russia had been treacherous enough in the eighteenth and nineteenth centuries. Doing so within range of U-boats and heavily armoured battleships like *Tirpitz* and *Bismarck*, which treated the North Sea coast of Norway as their stamping ground, required tremendous resilience and bravery. Sometimes, less than half the number of ships that set out made it to their destination and back—and many of the servicemen who travelled this route were not given medals for their service or their bravery for decades after the end of the war.[82]

Slowly but surely the tide turned as German forces were squeezed out of the centre of the world. For a moment, it had looked as though Hitler's gamble would pay off: already master of Europe in all but name, his effort to open up Central Asia from the north and from the south seemed to be working when his troops reached the banks of the Volga. But, one by one, the gains slipped away as the German army was relentlessly and brutally driven back to Berlin.

Hitler plunged into despair as the realisation of what was happening dawned on him. A classified British report revealed that in a speech given on 26 April 1942, despite the apparent successes in the east, the German leader was betraying clear signs of paranoia and fatalism, together with growing evidence of what was termed a Messiah complex.[83] From a psychological perspective, Hitler was an astonishing risk-taker, a man who fitted the profile of a compulsive gambler.[84] His luck was finally starting to run out.

The tide began to turn during the summer of 1942. Rommel had been halted at El Alamein, putting paid to the plans of Muḥammad al-Ḥusaynī, who had told the inhabitants of Cairo to prepare lists of homes and workplaces of Jewish residents so they could be rounded up and exterminated in gas vans developed by a fanatical German officer who had been stationed locally.[85]

The entry of the United States into the war also took time to make a difference. Shocked into action by the Japanese attack on Pearl Harbor, the Americans geared up for war on two fronts. By the middle of 1942, victory at the epic battle of Midway enabled the United States to move on to the offensive in the Pacific, while major troop deployments from the start of the following year in North Africa, Sicily and southern Italy and later elsewhere in Europe too promised to turn the course of the war.[86]

Then there was the situation at Stalingrad. In the spring of 1942, Hitler had approved a proposal codenamed Operation Blue that involved German forces swinging through southern Russia to secure the oilfields in the Caucasus that had become central to the Third Reich's war planning. The offensive was ambitious and risky—and victory depended on it, as senior generals and Hitler himself realised: "if I do not get to the oil of Maikop and Grozny," the German leader declared, "then I must end the war."[87]

Stalingrad represented a major problem. It was not essential to capture the city, despite the prestige associated with its name. Although it was an important industrial centre, its significance lay in its strategic location on a bend in the Volga: neutralising Stalingrad was vital to protect the gains the Germans envisaged making in the Caucasus. By the autumn of 1942, it was clear that things had gone badly wrong. The German offensive had begun late, and soon ran into trouble. Manpower, ordnance and increasingly precious fuel—resources Berlin could ill afford to spare—were expended in huge quantities at Stalingrad, which was bad enough. Worse was the fact that attention was diverted away from the campaign's primary strategic goal: oil. Some within Hitler's inner circle, such as Albert Speer, had understood what delays would mean. Germany had to win the war "by the end of October, before the Russian winter begins, or we have lost it once and for all."[88]

While there was still much to do in terms of planning how to uproot German troops from the east and the west, and how to co-ordinate the pincers that would close in on Berlin, by the end of 1942 the thoughts of the new Allies—Britain, the USA and the Soviet Union—were turning to the future. When the leaders of the three countries met at Teheran in 1943, at Yalta in the spring of 1945 and finally at Potsdam a few months later, it was clear that the effort, expense and trauma of another massive confrontation had exhausted western Europe.

It was already obvious that old empires had to be wound down; it was simply a matter of how best to manage this process. In a sign of the pervasive moral fatigue, the question at hand was how to make the least bad decision—and even that was not done successfully. In October 1944, Churchill returned home from a visit to Moscow "refreshed and fortified," he told Stalin, thanks to the "Russian hospitality which is renowned, excel[ing] itself." Minutes record the performance of Rachmaninov's Third Piano Concerto, the opportunities for some "light shopping" alongside a host of conclusions reached during the meetings. They do not record the discussions about the fate of post-war Europe, which were excised from the official reports.[89]

The territorial integrity of Poland that the House of Commons had sworn to protect in 1939 was surrendered, its borders crudely altered when Winston Churchill decided the moment was "apt for business" and used a blue pencil to mark a map that moved a third of the country into German territory and gifted a third to the Soviet Union; he also proposed divisions across scores of other countries in central and eastern Europe that might be mutually satisfactory—such as a 90:10 split in Rumania in favour of the USSR's influence over that of Britain, and the opposite in the case of Greece; in Bulgaria, Hungary and Yugoslavia, a 50:50 division would apply. Even Churchill recognised that the "offhand manner" in which the fates of "millions of people" had been decided might be considered "rather cynical." The price of keeping Stalin sweet involved the sacrifice of the freedom of half of the continent of Europe. "Let us burn the paper," Churchill told the Soviet supremo; "No," replied Stalin, "you keep it."[90]

Churchill realised the true situation too late. In his famous speech at Fulton, Missouri in 1946 that warned of an Iron Curtain falling across Europe, he observed that "all the capitals of the ancient states of Central and Eastern Europe, Warsaw, Berlin, Prague, Vienna, Budapest, Belgrade, Bucharest and Sofia," now lay within the sphere of the Soviet Union.[91] All but Vienna and half of Berlin would stay there. The Second World War had been fought to stop the dark shadow of tyranny falling across Europe; in the end, nothing could, or would, be done to stop the Iron Curtain descending.

And so Europe was cleaved in two at the end of the Second World War. The western half had fought bravely and heroically; and for decades afterwards congratulated itself on its achievement in taking on the evil of Nazism, without paying the price of recognising its role in its genesis. Nor could it spare much thought for the part of the continent that had been surrendered in a new set of post-war settlements. The defeat of Germany had resulted in chronic war fatigue, the exhaustion of the economies of Britain and France and the collapse of those of Holland, Belgium, Italy and the

Scandinavian countries. Coupled with the dislocation was the fear not only of an arms race that was likely to involve extensive research into nuclear weapons, but of direct confrontation. With Soviet troops in Europe enjoying a 4:1 numerical superiority over those of the other Allies, supported by advantages in tank deployment, there were real fears that further hostilities might break out following the German surrender. As a result, Churchill ordered contingency plans to be drawn up that were based on a hypothesis that Hitler's defeat simply marked the end of a chapter, rather than an end point in itself. The name given to these plans concealed the reason why they had been prepared in the first place: Operation Unthinkable was eminently thinkable in the minds of British planners.[92]

The need to prepare for contingencies was firmly based in the reality of a fast-changing situation as Germany crumbled. Stalin had taken up an increasingly uncompromising position, no doubt driven by the sense of betrayal arising out of his catastrophic alliance with Hitler in 1939, but also as a result of the astonishing price that the Soviet Union had had to pay—above all at Stalingrad and Leningrad—to survive the German onslaught.[93] From Moscow's point of view it became important to build a system of buffer zones and client states, as well as to create and reinforce the fear that direct action could be taken if the Soviet Union felt threatened. In the circumstances, crippling countries to the west by targeting and even removing their industrial bases was a logical step to take—as was providing financial and logistical support for nascent Communist parties. As history shows, attack is often the best form of defence.[94]

One result of this was that Hitler's oppression was deemed worse than that of Stalin. The narrative of the war as a triumph over tyranny was selective, singling out one political enemy while glossing over the faults and failings of recent friends. Many in central and eastern Europe would beg to differ with this story of the triumph of democracy, pointing out the price that was paid over subsequent decades by those who found themselves on the wrong side of an arbitrary line. Western Europe had its history to protect, however, and that meant emphasising successes—and keeping quiet about mistakes and about decisions that could be explained as realpolitik.

This was typified by the European Union being awarded the Nobel Peace Prize in 2012: how wonderful that Europe, which had been responsible for almost continuous warfare not just in its own continent but across the world for centuries, had managed to avoid conflict for several decades. In late antiquity, the equivalent would have been giving the prize to Rome a century after its sack by the Goths, or perhaps to the Crusaders after the loss of Acre for toning down anti-Muslim rhetoric in the Christian world. The silence of the guns, perhaps, owed more to the reality that there was nothing left to fight for than to the foresight of a succession of supposedly brilliant peace-makers in the late twentieth and early twenty-first centuries, or to the wonders of an unwieldy international organisation of European states whose accounts have not been signed off by its own auditors for years.

A new world had started to emerge in 1914 as the sun began to set on western Europe. The process accelerated with the hostilities of 1939–45, and continued after they had finally ended. The question now was who would control the great trading networks of Eurasia. And there was good reason to ponder this carefully, for it had turned out that there was more to the fertile earth and golden sands of the heart of the world and to the waters of the Caspian Sea than met the eye.

21

The Road of Cold Warfare

Before the Second World War had drawn to a close, the fight to control the heart of Asia was well under way. In a grandly named "Tripartite Treaty" signed in January 1942, Britain and the Soviet Union solemnly undertook "to safeguard the Iranian people against the privations and difficulties arising as a result of the present war," and to ensure that they received enough food and clothing. In fact, as the treaty went on to make clear, the issue had little to do with the security of Iran—and everything to do with commandeering its infrastructure: the treaty therefore declared that Britain and the Soviet Union would be able to use the country's roads, rivers, pipelines, airfields and telegraph stations as they pleased.[1] This was not an occupation, stated the treaty; it was a case of help being given to an ally. Fine words—but rather creative ones.

Ostensibly, the treaty was designed to prevent German expansion into Iran and to enable resources to be brought through the Gulf to help the Allies. Some, however, reckoned that the British also had an eye on the long term. The American minister in Teheran, Louis G. Dreyfus, for example, sent regular cables back to Washington commenting on the increasingly aggressive demands made of the Shah and on the accusations that there was a fifth column in Iran working against British interests. "I am convinced," he wrote in August 1941, "that the British are using [the situation] as a pretext for the eventual occupation of Iran and are deliberately exaggerating [the] potency" of the current circumstances.[2]

Britain's aims of maintaining—and strengthening—its position in Iran were not made more attainable by the way its officials and troops treated the local population. A full decade before the war, one journalist had written a withering critique of Britain's behaviour, arguing that Iranians were treated as badly "as the East India Company was said to have treated the Indians two hundred years ago."[3] Animosities were intensified by the way British officers insisted that Iranian officers should salute their counterparts when they passed them—without this being reciprocated. There were widespread complaints that the British behave as "the Sahibs, the White Men, and treat [the Iranians] like a colonised people." This was in sharp contrast to Soviet officers who kept to themselves, rarely went out and did not demand salutes—at least according to one German intelligence officer stationed in the region.[4]

The attitudes of Sir Reader Bullard, the British ambassador at this delicate time, were typical. Food shortages and inflation during the latter part of the war had nothing to do with the failures of the occupying forces, or with the logistical difficulties of maintaining the Persian Corridor to take weapons and other goods north from the Gulf. The fault, wrote Bullard, lay with the Iranians themselves: "the Persian now has a double pleasure in stealing, raising prices to famine level, and so on; he always blames the British."[5] Remarking on "the low opinion that I have formed of the Iranians," he flippantly added in one of his missives to London that "most Persians will surely become blowflies in their next incarnation."[6] Dispatches such as these caught the attention of Winston Churchill. "However natural Sir Reader Bullard's contempt for all Persians," wrote the Prime Minister, it "is detrimental to his efficiency and our interests."[7]

What made things worse was that such deeply ingrained views of entitlement and superiority were out of kilter with the realities of the situation—where it was increasingly clear that the dominant position built by the British was at risk. Ugly scenes broke out in Teheran in 1944 when the Russians discovered that negotiations were under way to grant a concession in the north of Iran to an American consortium of oil producers. Flames were fanned by the Tudeh party, a collection of left-wing militants whose message of reform, redistribution of wealth and modernism was given considerable support from Moscow. Such was the Soviet Union's commitment to derailing discussions that at the height of these tensions Russian troops took to the streets alongside thousands of demonstrators, ostensibly to guard the protesters. To many, it looked uncomfortably as though force would be used to enable the Soviets to get their way and have the agreement cancelled. This was emphasised by the thuggish Sergei Kavtaradze, Assistant Foreign Commissar, whom Stalin had sent to Teheran to warn that there would be consequences for angering the Soviet Union.[8]

In a denouement that dripped with high drama, it was left to Mohammed Mossadegh, a canny, articulate and consummate politician who had the knack of capturing the zeitgeist. He was a man, wrote one British official, who looks "rather like a cab horse and is slightly deaf so that he listens with a strained but otherwise expressionless look on his face. He conducts conversations at a distance of about six inches at which range he diffuses a slight reek of opium. His remarks tend to prolixity and he gives the impression of being impervious to argument."[9] Mossadegh was a "Persian of the old school," according to a profile in the *Observer* that was added to Foreign Office files, "polite, prodigal of bows and handclaspings."[10] In fact, as it proved, the British seriously underestimated him.

Mossadegh began to expound a vision, first set out in parliament at the end of 1944, that Iran could not and should not allow itself to be manipulated and terrorised by outside powers. The Knox D'Arcy concession and the way that Anglo-Iranian (previously Anglo-Persian) behaved provided object lessons in what happened if leadership was not robust enough. Time and again, he said, Iran had been taken advantage of and used as a pawn by rival interests that brought little benefit to the country's people. It was simply wrong that choices should be made as to whom Iran should do business with: "let us negotiate with every state," he declared, which "wishes to buy oil, and get to work to liberate the country."[11]

Mossadegh was saying what many people had long felt—that it was invidious that the fruits lying under the soil brought limited benefits for Iran. It was hard to argue with the logic. In 1942, for example, the British government received £6.6 million in tax receipts from Anglo-Iranian's activities; Iran received barely 60 per cent of this figure as a royalty payment. In 1945, the difference was even more stark. Where the exchequer in London benefited to the tune of £16 million in taxes from the business, Teheran took £6 million—in other words, only just over a third.[12] It was not just about the money; as one well-informed British observer noted, the problem was that "no material benefits could compensate for personal degradation and loss of dignity."[13]

Such insight was unusual, as the author went on to admit. Laurence Elwell-Sutton had studied Arabic at the School of Oriental and African

Studies before working for Anglo-Iranian in Iran before the Second World War. A gifted linguist who developed a passion for Persian culture, Elwell-Sutton was flabbergasted by the clumsy way Anglo-Iranian employees treated the local population. "Too few Europeans took the trouble to find out" about Persians, finding it easier to "look on the 'natives' . . . as dirty savages with peculiar habits that were of no interest to anybody, except perhaps anthropologists." This "racial antipathy" was bound to end in disaster; "unless it goes," he concluded, "this company will."[14]

In the circumstances, it was not hard to see how momentum built behind reformers like Mossadegh. The age of European empire had long since started to erode—as had been evident in Iraq when Gertrude Bell was reminded that independence was not in Britain's gift to give. It was inevitable in Iran, and elsewhere, that there would be growing demand for countries subjected to domination and heavy influence from abroad to take control of their own destinies—and a pattern quickly emerged and accelerated as the war went on. As it did so, Britain became an empire literally in retreat as its Silk Roads collapsed.

Tidal waves of military pressure in Asia had caused a series of Dunkirks in the east—cases of shambolic retreat that served as poignant markers of the end of Britain's golden era. Hundreds of thousands fled from Burma as Japanese forces fanned out across South-East Asia, seeking to take advantage of British and French preoccupations with problems closer to home to expand into regions that had long been of strategic and economic interest to Tokyo. Germany's allies in the east were quick to realise that an opportunity had presented itself that enabled Japan to advance its own imperial credentials over a wide region. As the Japanese forces pushed forward, many suffered as a result. Some 80,000 died of starvation and disease. Scenes in the Malay peninsula were equally dramatic as thousands fell back on Penang and Singapore—with the lucky ones making it out before the city fell. One unmarried woman who was evacuated just in time wrote a few weeks later that the chaos of the British withdrawal was "a thing which I am sure will never be forgotten or forgiven" by those who witnessed or took part in it.[15]

The recoil continued as hostilities in Europe and the Pacific came to an end. The decision to pull out of India altogether came after three decades of concessions and promises that had raised expectations about self-governance, autonomy and ultimately independence. By the end of the war, British authority was fading fast and threatened to spiral out of control as months of disturbances, anti-imperial demonstrations and strikes set in that brought cities across the north of the subcontinent to a standstill. Initial plans to make a "phased withdrawal" from India which also sought to provide protection for the Muslim minorities were rejected by London as too costly and too lengthy.[16] Instead, the announcement was made in early 1947 that Britain would withdraw within sixteen months, creating panic as a result. It was a disastrous decision, as Winston Churchill, voted out of office after the war, told the House of Commons. "Will it not be a terrible disgrace to our name and record if . . . we allow one fifth of the population of the globe . . . to fall into chaos and into carnage?"[17]

When these warnings were not heeded, pandemonium broke loose in the subcontinent. Communities that had been stable for so long erupted with violence as families that had lived in towns and villages for centuries embarked on one of the largest mass migrations in human history. At least 11 million people moved across the new borders of the Punjab and Bengal.[18] The British in the meantime drew up detailed evacuation plans to try to limit the number of their own nationals likely to be caught up in the fighting.[19] This concern did not extend to the local population.

It was a similar story elsewhere as Britain stumbled from one crisis to another. In a bid to preserve the balance of the delicate situation in Palestine, so as to retain control of the refinery and port of Haifa, keep Suez secure and maintain friendly relations with leading figures in the Arabic world, active steps were taken to try to curb Jewish emigration from Europe. After plans had been drawn up by British intelligence to sabotage ships bringing refugees to Palestine—and pin blame on an apparently powerful but nonexistent Arab terrorist organisation—the British took more direct action.[20]

The low point came in the summer of 1947, after ships on their way to load Jewish émigrés in French ports had been harassed. One vessel carrying more than 4,000 Jews, including pregnant women, children and many elderly, was rammed by British destroyers as it made its way east—even though the decision had already been taken to refuse entry to the passengers when they reached Palestine.[21] Treating those who had survived concentration camps or lost family in the Holocaust in this way was a public relations disaster: it was clear that Britain would stop at nothing to maintain its interests abroad—and think nothing of others in the process.

The clumsiness was apparent in dealings with ʿAbdullāh, the ruler of

Transjordan, who was now lavished with attention and promised British military support, set out in secret agreements, for his regime after it became independent in 1946. He took advantage of this promise to embark on a plan to extend his frontiers to include all of Palestine once the British withdrew—obtaining a green light, albeit qualified, from London.[22] "It seems the obvious thing to do," his Prime Minister was supposedly told by Ernest Bevin, the Foreign Secretary; "but do not go and invade the areas allotted to the Jews."[23] Whatever steer was given, the chaos that descended on yet another part of the world where Britain was pulling back was compelling evidence of the malign effects of imperial European power. The Arab–Israeli War of 1948 may not have been the result of policy being conducted through nods, nudges and winks, but it did represent a void opening up as a result of the changing of the guard.[24]

Things were little better in Iraq, where there was turmoil after the Prime Minister, Ṣāliḥ Jabr, agreed terms with Britain in 1948 that extended the latter's use of airbases in the country for a further twenty-five years. News of the agreement led to strikes, riots and eventually Jabr's resignation as he was hounded from office by an angry mob.[25] Animosity towards Britain had been stoked by a range of issues, including the occupation of Baghdad during the Second World War and the perceived failure of the British to support the Arabs in Palestine, especially when set against the attempts of London to retain a permanent military foothold in Iraq. This was all made worse by rampant inflation and food shortages that followed poor harvests—with the result that one astute observer recognised that the "internal situation in Iraq was dangerous."[26] Britain therefore took steps to help the "Iraqi Prime Minister . . . resist popular agitation by giving him concessions." This included offering to share the airbase at Habbaniyah; the Iraqis should be happy with this "first-class example of co-operation," policymakers in London asserted. Britain would "not be prepared to make [this offer] to any other state"—and the Iraqis should be very grateful for being allowed to feel "superior to other states in the Middle East."[27]

Compounding all this was the fact that, as was the case with other countries, Iraq had little to show for the oil that was pumped from its soil. In 1950, some 90 per cent of the population were still illiterate. Worse, Britain was held responsible for exerting too strong a grip on the country: when it came to borrowing funds to build and extend the railway network, for example, Britain demanded Iraq's reserves as security. This raised the prospect that the oilfields would be taken over in the event of default—much as had happened with Suez in the nineteenth century when control of the vitally important canal and of its finances was seized by the British.[28] Britain found itself in a lose–lose situation: it had spent all its political capital and was trusted by no one. Such was the suspicion that even agencies like the Middle East Anti-Locust Unit (MEALU), which had enjoyed considerable success after being established during the war, were wound down—removing technical expertise that was helpful both in dealing with damaging swarms and in protecting the food supply.[29] The states of the Middle East were flexing their muscles and turning against the west.

In the meantime, the Soviet Union was also resurgent. A new narrative had emerged in the USSR following the defeat of Germany—one where Stalin's role in the genesis of the war as Hitler's ally was quietly forgotten, and replaced with a story of triumph and of destiny being fulfilled.[30] The Revolution of 1917 had failed to deliver the global transformation anticipated by Marx and his disciples; thirty years later, however, it seemed that the time had come for Communism to sweep across the world and dominate Asia just as Islam had done in the seventh century. It had already begun to diffuse through China, where the promises of equality, of justice and above all of land reform brought support for the Communist party and enabled it to drive government forces back and eventually off the mainland altogether.

Similar patterns were starting to be seen elsewhere, as left-wing parties began to attract increasing support in Europe and in the United States. Many were persuaded by an ideal that promised a harmony in sharp contrast to the horrors of a war that had culminated in two atomic bombs being dropped on Hiroshima and Nagasaki—including some who had worked on the nuclear programme—and were disillusioned by the fact that two titanic struggles between European nations in little more than three decades had wrought devastating results across the world.

Stalin fanned these flames astutely in a speech that was widely reported around the world in the spring of 1946. The Second World War had been inevitable, he declared, "because of the emergence of global economic and political factors that were implicit in the concept of modern monopolistic capitalism."[31] The speech was a statement of intent: capitalism had dominated the world for too long, and was responsible for the suffering, mass murder and horrors of the wars of the twentieth century. Communism was a logical reaction to a political system that had proved itself to be flawed and dangerous. It was a new system that accentuated similarities rather than differences, that replaced hierarchies with equality. It was not just an attractive vision, in other words, but a viable alternative.

Not long before, Churchill had gambled the future of the countries lying west of the Soviet Union's borders. "Poor Neville Chamberlain believed he could trust Hitler," Churchill told a junior member of his staff immediately after the negotiations at Yalta about what the post-war world would look like. "He was wrong. But I don't think I'm wrong about Stalin."[32] Chamberlain had indeed been wrong; but so too was Churchill—as he soon recognised. Nobody knows, he said on 5 March 1946 in his speech in Fulton, Missouri, "what Soviet Russia . . . intends to do in the immediate future." However, the fact that its philosophy was expansive and evangelical, he noted, meant that it represented a threat to the west. "From Stettin in the Baltic to Trieste in the Adriatic, an Iron Curtain has descended across the continent."[33]

The fate of the centre of the world hung in the balance. Iran was the fulcrum. U.S. strategists were convinced that the Soviets wanted complete domination of Iran because of its oil, but also because of its naval bases and its location in the middle of a web of international air routes. The Iranian government had awarded the concession for the oil in the north of the country to the United States only thanks to assurances from the American ambassador that the United States would, if necessary, provide military support in the event of Soviet forces entering the country following fierce opposition from Moscow to the agreement.[34]

In the summer of 1946, tensions rose as strike action took hold across Iran. With rumour and counter-rumour swirling through the streets of Teheran, the country's immediate future seemed to be at stake. Despite its strong desire to keep hold of its assets, it was painfully clear that Britain could do little to influence events where it mattered. Intelligence reports painted a gloomy picture of imminent military action by Moscow against Iran and Iraq, reporting detailed invasion plans which included information on the likely focal point of the "powerful Soviet cavalry and motorised forces" in the event of an attack. The Soviet General Staff were reported to have reached bullish conclusions about occupying Mosul and were ready to set up a "popular Iranian Government" once the Shah had been overthrown. Reprisals would then be taken, according to the British, against the previous regime whose leading figures would be branded as "traitors and collaborators." Soviet paratroopers were ready to be dropped close to Teheran to lead an assault that would quickly be over.[35]

A sense of real alarm gripped Washington. The Americans had been watching Iran closely since December 1942, when the first of 20,000 U.S. troops arrived in Khoramshahr in the Gulf to set to work on improving

Iran's transportation system. In order to oversee the logistics, a large American camp was built in Teheran itself, which became the headquarters of the U.S. Persian Gulf Command as a whole.[36] The British and the Soviets were putting their own interests first in Iran, and as a result were constantly undermining the war effort and the state of Iran at the same time. Iran was being pulled dangerously in every direction, General Patrick Hurley reported to President Roosevelt.[37]

The Americans who were deployed to Iran to support and monitor supply lines during the war initially experienced something of a culture shock. The Iranian army, found Major-General Clarence Ridley, was poorly trained, under-resourced and essentially useless. If it was to hold its own with hostile neighbours, heavy investment would be needed to train a new generation of officers and to buy good equipment. This was music to the new Shah's ears, as he was desperate to make his mark on Iran by a programme of modernisation. The problem, as his (American) budget adviser told him bluntly, was that it was not possible to build an army along the lines of those in the west: if funds were diverted to military expenditure, he was told, "there would be little if anything for agriculture, education or public health."[38]

Under-prepared, disorganised and weak, Iran seemed to have little chance of seeing off the Soviet Union at a time when Stalin's posturing and behaviour were a matter of profound concern in the United States. Some who heard Stalin's speech concluded that this was nothing other than the "declaration of World War III."[39] George Kennan, chargé d'affaires at the U.S. embassy in Moscow who had witnessed Stalin's purges at first hand, drew a similar conclusion, warning in early 1946 of a major global struggle ahead. "At the bottom of the Kremlin's neurotic view of world affairs," he wrote, is the "traditional and instinctive Russian sense of insecurity." The Soviet Union, he concluded, was "a political force committed fanatically" to engage in competition with the United States to the point that its aim was to ensure that "the internal harmony of our state be disrupted, our traditional way of life be destroyed [and] the international authority of our state be broken."[40]

Iran's political and strategic importance now propelled it to the forefront of U.S. foreign policy. Systematic efforts were made to help bolster the country. In 1949, the Voice of America radio station began broadcasting in Farsi to the local population, with the first programme featuring President Truman commenting on "the historic bond of friendship" between Iran and the United States, and promising assistance to help create a "prosperous and . . . peaceful world" that was free from oppression.[41] By the time war broke out in the Korean peninsula a year later, more direct help was being offered. As a State Department briefing put it, while the declining economy had "not yet reached catastrophic conditions," if strong support was not now given there was a risk of "the complete disintegration of the country and its absorption immediately or eventually into the Soviet bloc."[42] Truman himself needed no convincing. "If we stand by," he observed, "[the Soviets will] move into Iran and they'll take over the whole Middle East."[43]

Radio broadcasts became increasingly pointed as Iranians were told that "free nations must stand together," that "U.S. security is bound up with the security of other nations," and that the "strength of the free world" was continuing to grow. This went hand in hand with reports which emphasised the threat posed by the Soviet Union to world peace, which stated that "the aim of communist leaders is the universal suppression of human freedom" and which even went so far as to claim that "Soviet teachers make their homes in broken-down freight cars which had been condemned as unfit to transport cattle" and lacked heat, basic sanitary facilities and clean water.[44]

Financial aid began to pour into the country, rising nearly five times over the course of three years from $11.8 million in 1950 to $52.5 million in 1953. The aim was to encourage economic development in Iran, to stabilise its political culture and to lay the basis for reform, but also to provide military and technical assistance for its self-defence. These were the first stages in the building of an American client state in the Middle East.[45]

The motivation for doing so was based in part on the realisation that Britain was no longer able to prop up regimes in the way that it had done in the past, and in part on a frank recognition that Soviet expansionism required a response. Nevertheless, this was not the only reason for the close attention paid to Iran. In 1943, for example, during the major conference held by Allied leaders in Teheran, neither Winston Churchill nor President Roosevelt had bothered even to meet with the Shah. Put simply, both thought it would have been a waste of time to do so.[46] Likewise, the following year, Saudi Arabia was dismissed by the United States as a country of limited consequence, whose requests for economic help could be easily swatted away by President Roosevelt as being "a little far afield for us"; Roosevelt added that it would be better for Saudi concerns and requests to be directed to Britain than to the United States.[47] By the time the war ended, things were very different, with Saudi Arabia alone being considered to be "more important to American diplomacy than almost any other small nation."[48] The reason for this was oil.

During the war, a gritty oilman named Everette Lee DeGolyer, who had made his money in the American petroleum industry after studying geology in Oklahoma, visited the Middle East to assess the region's existing oilfields and to advise on the long-term potential and significance of the resources of the region in its own right, and in relation to those of the Gulf of Mexico, Venezuela and the United States itself. His report, even though laced with conservative estimates and caveats, was astounding. "The center of gravity of world oil production is shifting from the Gulf-Caribbean area to the Middle East—to the Persian Gulf area—and is likely to continue to shift until it is firmly established in the area."[49] One of those who travelled with him put it more bluntly when reporting back to the State Department: "The oil in this region is the greatest single prize in all history."[50]

This was not lost on the British, who reacted jealously to the prospect of the United States paying greater attention to the region as a whole. The Americans should be told to stay out of the Middle East and away from the strong position Britain had built, Churchill was told by a leading industrialist; "oil is the single greatest post-war asset remaining to us. We should refuse to divide our last asset with the Americans."[51] This was articulated forcefully by Lord Halifax, the British ambassador to Washington, who took umbrage at the way officials at the State Department had tried to deflect him. British policymakers were also concerned about what was going on, fearing that "the United States is intending to divest us of our oil assets in the Middle East."[52] The Prime Minister himself got directly involved, sending a telegram to President Roosevelt stating, "I have been watching with some misgivings" how the negotiations had been going on; "you may be sure I should only wish to arrive at what is fair and just between our two countries."[53]

This meant reaching agreement over how to divide this crucial part of the world between Britain and the United States. A meeting between Halifax and President Roosevelt resolved the problem: as far as the U.S. was concerned, the "oil in Persia was [British and] . . . we both had a share in Iraq and Kuwait and . . . Bahrein and Saudi Arabia were American."[54] It was like the agreements reached by Spain and Portugal in the late fifteenth and early sixteenth century, or the discussions held between the Allied leaders during and immediately after the Second World War, that divided the world neatly in two.

The Americans and the British set about dealing with this division in very different ways. From the U.S. perspective, the key issue was that the price of oil had doubled between 1945 and 1948—while the number of cars in the United States alone went up by more than 50 per cent and the value of motor-vehicle factory sales rose by seven times.[55] In response, initially, the United States took an approach to the situation that was reasoned to the point of enlightened: it was inevitable that countries that found themselves blessed with natural resources and being courted from all sides would seek to maximise their own positions. As such, it was sensible to renegotiate the terms of oil concessions—and to do so gracefully rather than under duress.

There were already rumblings and threats of nationalisation, which reflected the new world order. For one thing, new deals that were being made with oil-rich countries were increasingly generous and competitive—such as that struck with J. Paul Getty for a concession in the Neutral Zone between Saudi Arabia and Kuwait which paid almost double the royalties per barrel compared to what was being paid in other parts of the Middle East, and which created rivalry and antagonism in countries that had locked in to agreements at an earlier stage. This not only made them hotbeds for dissent over the way the resources were being expropriated, and prompted demands for nationalisation; it also made them vulnerable to Communist rhetoric and to overtures from Moscow.

A remarkable shift in revenues followed as the United States softened its trading positions and renegotiated a raft of deals. In 1949, for example, the U.S. Treasury collected $43 million in taxes from Aramco, a consortium of western oil companies, while Saudi Arabia received $39 million in revenues. Two years later, after changing the system of tax credits whereby businesses could offset their expenses, the business was paying $6 million in the United States but $110 million to the Saudis.[56] There was a domino effect as other concessions in Saudi, as well as in Kuwait, Iraq and elsewhere, reset their terms in favour of local rulers and governments.

Some historians have spoken of this moment of reworking the flows of currency as being as momentous as the transfer of power from London for India and Pakistan.[57] But its impact was most similar to the discovery of the Americas and the redistribution of global wealth that followed. Western corporations that controlled concessions and whose distribution was largely concentrated on Europe and the United States began to funnel cash to the Middle East and, in doing so, started a shift in the world's centre of gravity. The spider's web of pipelines that criss-crossed the region and connected east with west marked a new chapter in the history of this region. This time, it was not spices or silks, slaves or silver that traversed the globe, but oil.

The British, however, who had failed to read the signs as clearly as their American counterparts, had other ideas. In Iran, Anglo-Iranian was a lightning rod for criticism. It was not hard to see why, given the huge imbalance in the amounts paid to the British exchequer compared with royalties disbursed to Iran.[58] Although other countries in the region could also complain about the lack of benefits that were exchanged for their black gold, the scale of the unevenness in Iran made the situation look particularly bad. In 1950, although Ābādān was home to the refinery that was by now the largest in the world, the town itself had as much electricity as a single London street. Barely a tenth of the 25,000 children of school age were able to attend classes, such was the dearth of schools.[59]

As elsewhere, Britain was caught on the horns of a dilemma from which there was no escape: renegotiating the terms of the oil concession would be all but impossible, as the astute and well-connected U.S. Secretary of State Dean Acheson observed. Anglo-Iranian was majority-owned by the British government and as such was seen as a direct extension of Britain and its foreign policy—not without reason. Like the East India Company, there were blurred lines between the interests of the business and those of the British government; and as with the EIC, Anglo-Iranian was so powerful that it too was effectively a "state within a state," while its power "was in the end that of Britain."[60] If Anglo-Iranian caved in and gave Iran a better deal, concluded Acheson, then it would "destroy the last vestige of confidence in British power and in the pound." Within months, he predicted, Britain would have no overseas assets left at all.[61]

London's heavy reliance on the company's revenues made the situation precarious, as Acheson recognised. "Britain stands on the verge of bankruptcy," he wrote in a cable; without her "important overseas interests and the invisible items in her balance of payments . . . she cannot survive." This was why the British were using all the tricks of the diplomatic trade, issuing shrill reports that constantly emphasised the imminent threat of a Soviet invasion. Acheson, for one, was having none of it. "The cardinal purpose of

British policy is not to prevent Iran going commie," despite Britain's claims to the contrary; "the cardinal point is to preserve what they believe to be the last remaining bastion of Brit solvency."[62]

Things turned nasty, then, when new terms were offered to Iraq in 1950 but were conspicuously withheld from Iran at the same time. The fact that the Iraqi Oil Company was part-owned by Anglo-Iranian rubbed salt in the wounds, and provoked a furious reaction in Iran. Nationalist politicians sprang up to proclaim the iniquity of Anglo-Iranian's virtual monopoly, spicing their criticisms with comments that were intended to ruffle feathers. All corruption in Iran was the direct result of Anglo-Iranian, stated a member of the Majlis.[63] If nothing was done, it would soon come about that "women's chadors will be ripped from their heads," claimed one demagogue.[64] It would be better, said another, for the entire oil industry of Iran to be destroyed by an atomic bomb than to allow Anglo-Iranian to exploit the people and the country.[65] Mossadegh put it less bluntly. If he became Prime Minister, he purportedly said, he would "have no intention of coming to terms with the British." Instead, he went on, he would "seal the oil wells with mud."[66]

Anti-British rhetoric had been bubbling for a generation; now, it entered mainstream consciousness: Britain was the architect of all Iran's problems and could not be trusted. It considered only its own interests and was imperialist in the worst sense of the word. The elision of Iranian identity with anti-western sentiment took root. There were to be profound long-term implications.

Mossadegh seized the moment with both hands. Enough was enough, he declared. The time had come to ensure the prosperity of the Iranian nation and to "secure world peace." The radical proposal was put forward at the end of 1950 that the proceeds should not be shared with Anglo-Iranian or with anyone else, but rather "that the oil industry of Iran be declared as nationalised throughout all regions of the country, without exception."[67] Ayatollah Kashani, a populist cleric who had only recently returned from exile and was already a well-known and vocal critic of the west, gave his wholehearted support to this call to action, urging his supporters to use every method they could to deliver change. Within days, the Prime Minister, ʿAlī Razmārā, was assassinated; shortly afterwards, so too was the Minister of Education. Iran flirted with anarchy.

Britain's worst fears were realised when Mossadegh himself was chosen as the new Prime Minister by the Majlis in the spring of 1951. He at once passed a law nationalising Anglo-Iranian with immediate effect. This was a disaster, as both the press in London and the British Cabinet realised. It was important, declared the Defence Minister, "to show that our tail [can]not be twisted interminably." If Iran was "allowed to get away with it," he went on, "the next thing could be an attempt to nationalise the Suez canal."[68] Plans were drawn up to drop paratroopers into Iran to secure the refinery at Ābādān if necessary. These were the death throes of a great empire in retreat, desperately thrashing to hold on to its former glories.

Mossadegh turned the screw, giving British employees of Anglo-Iranian a week to pack and to get out of Iran in September 1951. To top it off, Ayatollah Kashani declared a national day of "hatred against the British government." Britain had become a byword for all that was wrong in Iran, one that united a wide spectrum of political beliefs. "You don't know how crafty [the British] are," Mossadegh told one high-ranking American envoy. "You don't know how evil they are. You do not know how they sully everything they touch."[69] This sort of rhetoric made him wildly popular at home; it also made him famous abroad: in 1952, he was on the cover of *Time* magazine as its Man of the Year.[70]

Britain's heavy-handed attempt to force the situation did not help. Faced with losing control not only of Anglo-Iranian but of the income it brought, the British government went into crisis mode, organising an embargo on all Iranian oil. The aim was to hurt Mossadegh and force him to capitulate. Starving Iran of funds would soon have the desired effect, opined Sir William Fraser, the British ambassador in Teheran: "when [the Iranians] need money, they will come crawling to us on their bellies." Comments like these that appeared in the mainstream press were hardly likely to help Britain's cause in the court of public opinion.[71]

Instead they simply strengthened resolve in Iran, to the point that by the end of 1952 the British were no longer so confident that the tactic of using sanctions would pay off. An approach was therefore made to the recently established Central Intelligence Agency to support a plan "of joint political action to remove [Iran's] Prime Minister Mossadegh"—in other words, to stage a coup. Not for the last time, regime change in this part of the world seemed the answer to the problem.

Officials in the United States responded favourably to British overtures. Operatives in the field in the Middle East had already been given free rein to explore creative solutions to problems with local rulers who were either not well enough disposed to the United States or seemed eager to flirt with the Soviet Union. A group of young gung-ho agents from privileged east coast backgrounds had already been involved in a putsch that saw the overthrow of the leadership in Syria in 1949, and in the removal of the corpulent, corrupt and unreliable King of Egypt, Farouk, in an operation unofficially known as "Project FF" (or Project Fat Fucker) three years later.[72]

The zeal of men like Miles Copeland and two of the grandsons of President Theodore Roosevelt—Archie and Kermit (Kim)—was reminiscent of that of the British agents in Central Asia a century earlier who felt they could shape the world, or even that of more modern counterparts who felt that passing secrets to the Soviet Union would likewise have positive effects. After the fall of the government in Syria, for example, the young Americans went off to tour "Crusader castles and off-the-beaten-path places," admiring the architecture and atmosphere of Aleppo on the way.[73] Decisions were made on the hoof. "What's the difference," Copeland asked the dour polymath Archie Roosevelt, "between my fabricating reports and your letting your agents do it? At least mine make sense."[74] The way these men in the field played hard and fast was picked up on in the U.S. with one senior intelligence officer admonishing them by saying that "irresponsible freewheeling will not be tolerated in the future."[75] Nevertheless, when it came to the question of Iran, their opinions were in high demand.

Things began to move after a routine meeting in Washington at the end of 1952 when British officials airing their anxieties about the economic impact of nationalisation struck a chord with American concerns about the possible future path of Iran. The CIA station in Teheran was anxious about Mossadegh and advised Washington separately that the U.S. should "prefer a successor government" in Iran. Planners quickly concluded that the Shah had to be brought into the plot to provide unity and calm and so that the removal of the Prime Minister could be "made to appear legal or quasi-legal."[76]

Persuading the Shah was easier said than done. A nervous and vain man, he panicked when first told of the plan, codenamed Operation Ajax. The involvement of the British in particular worried him, according to one of the American architects of the plan, who noted that he had "a pathological fear of the 'hidden hand' of the British," and feared that the operation was a trap. He required cajoling, bullying and warning: key words were dropped into BBC broadcasts from London to reassure him that the operation had been sanctioned at the very highest level; a radio speech in which President Eisenhower explicitly promised U.S. support for Iran also helped convince him; meanwhile he was told in person that if he did not lend his support Iran would become Communist—"a second Korea," as Kim Roosevelt put it.[77]

In order to ensure that "public opinion . . . be fanned to fever pitch" as a prelude to removing Mossadegh, funds were sent from Washington to cultivate key individuals and turn them against the Prime Minister. Roosevelt cultivated leading members of the Majlis, almost certainly by bribing them (the aim, he wrote euphemistically, was to "persuade" them to withdraw their support of Mossadegh).[78]

Money was spent liberally elsewhere. According to one eyewitness, the flood of American currency into Teheran was so great that the value of the dollar relative to the rial fell by nearly 40 per cent during the summer of 1953. Some of these funds were spent paying for crowds to march on the streets of the capital, organised by the CIA's two main local operatives. There were other notable recipients too—above all mullahs like Ayatollah Kashani, whose interests were judged to be mutually compatible with the aims of the plotters.[79] Muslim scholars had concluded that the precepts and anti-religiosity of Communism made the doctrine anathema to the teaching of Islam. As such, there was an obvious overlap for the CIA to strike deals with clerics, who were emphatically warned of the dangers of a Communist Iran.[80]

After British and American planners had converged on Beirut in June 1953, a plan was devised that was approved personally by Winston Churchill, the British Prime Minister, at the start of July and then by President Eisenhower a few days later. Ideas were then refined by intelligence agents for the best way of communicating to what they referred to as "rather long-winded and often illogical Persians" that regime change was wanted by the west, and should take place smoothly and without mishap.[81]

In the event, things went spectacularly wrong. Covers were blown and timings went awry as the situation descended into chaos. Spooked, the Shah flew out of the country without finding time to put on his socks. When he stopped in Baghdad on his way to Rome, he met with the U.S. ambassador to Iraq, who took the opportunity to make a proposal: "I suggested for his prestige in Iran [that] he never indicate that any foreigner had had a part in recent events." This had nothing to do with the Shah's prestige, and everything to do with keeping options open and, above all, preserving the U.S.'s clean reputation. The Shah, "worn [out] from three sleepless nights [and] puzzled by the turn of events," could hardly think straight. Nevertheless, reported the relieved ambassador back to Washington, "he agreed."[82]

As the Shah made his way to exile in Italy, Iranian radio broadcasts disseminated vicious reports, while the press denounced him as a whore, a looter and a thief.[83] The trauma was not lost on his young wife Soraya (many whispered she was younger than the reputed nineteen when she married): she recalled strolling down the Via Veneto in a red and white polka-dot dress, discussing the spiteful politics of Teheran and listening to her husband mournfully contemplate buying a small plot of land to start a new life—perhaps in the United States.[84]

Mistakes and misadventures worthy of a theatrical farce followed the Shah's flight. Rumours abounded in the streets that Mossadegh was seeking to claim the throne for himself, and the tide turned. And then, in a matter of days—and against all the odds—the Shah was on his way home, stopping in Baghdad briefly to put on the uniform of the commander-in-chief of the air force. Returning in splendour and glory, he presented himself not as a coward who had fled in fear, but as a hero coming back to take control of the situation. Mossadegh was arrested, tried and sentenced to solitary confinement; this was followed by a lengthy period of exile until his death in 1967.[85]

Mossadegh paid a heavy price for articulating a vision for the Middle East in which the influence of the west was not just watered down but removed altogether. His misgivings about Anglo-Iranian had developed into a view of the west as a whole that was both negative and damaging. This made him a troublemaker of the first order in Iran, and enough for British and American policymakers to formulate plans to remove him from the stage altogether. His loud protestations came at a time when others too were becoming vocal critics of western control of the networks linking east and west; in Egypt, rising animosity saw anti-British rioting and demands for the evacuation of British troops based at Suez. A report to the Joint Chiefs of Staff by a U.S. State Department visitor to Cairo was unequivocal about the situation. "The British are detested," he wrote. "The hatred against them is general and intense. It is shared by everyone in the country." An urgent solution was needed.[86]

Times were changing. And in this sense Mossadegh was the most articulate of those setting out the vision of a new era, one that involved the recoil of the west from the centre of Asia. Although the precise circumstances of his demise were kept hidden for decades by the intelligence agencies, who stayed alert to the "damaging consequences" declassification of material would bring, few had any illusions that the removal of Mossadegh had been orchestrated by western powers for their own ends.[87] As such, Mossadegh was the spiritual father of a great many heirs across this region. For while the methods, aims and ambitions of a group as diverse as Ayatollah Khomeini, Saddam Hussein, Osama bin Laden and the Taliban varied widely, all were united by a core tenet that the west was duplicitous and malign and that liberation for local populations meant liberation from outside influences. There were different ways of attempting to achieve this; but as the case of Mossadegh showed, those who presented a problem for the west were liable to face the consequences.

Psychologically, then, the coup was a pivotal moment. The Shah drew all the wrong conclusions, and convinced himself that the people of Iran adored him. In fact, there was ambivalence at best for the Shah, whose cavalry officer father had taken the throne only thirty years earlier. His flight to Rome demonstrated a worrying lack of backbone. His conviction that he was the man to modernise the country depended on his ability to read the prevailing political winds and to stand independently of western, above all American, intervention. This was a lot to ask of a vain man whose roving eye and love of the finer things in life provided ammunition for his rivals and left little time for good judgement.

More than anything, though, the CIA-backed coup of 1953 marked a watershed for America's role in the Middle East. Here was a "second chance" to save Iran, reasoned John Foster Dulles, the new Secretary of State, a chance to make sure it did not slip out of the west's orbit.[88] Given that a "democratic independent Iran [did not appear] to be possible in the circumstances," the U.S. ambassador to Teheran told the Shah, there were two choices: a free "undemocratic independent Iran" or a "permanently . . . undemocratic independent Iran, behind the iron curtain."[89] It was the direct antithesis of the loud and public message that the west was advocating in its struggle with Communism about freedom and about democracy.

It was the point where the United States stepped into the breach; it was the point where the United States came into serious contact with the region criss-crossed for centuries by the Silk Roads—and set about trying to control it. But there were dangers ahead. Posturing about democracy on the one hand while being prepared to sanction and even orchestrate regime change on the other made for uncomfortable bedfellows. It could be dangerous to play both sides—not least because in due course there would inevitably be a breakdown in trust and a collapse of credibility. As Britain's star continued to fade, much depended on what lessons America would learn from what had happened in 1953.

22

The American Silk Road

By taking the lead in the Middle East, the United States was stepping into a new world—one where there were obvious tensions between the goal of promoting national interests on the one hand and supporting unsavoury regimes and rulers on the other. Within weeks of Mossadegh being toppled, the State Department set about lining up American oil companies to take over Anglo-Iranian's oilwells and infrastructure. Few were keen to do so, preferring to steer well clear of the uncertainties that seemed likely to follow the Shah's return: the fact that the latter was contemplating having his former Prime Minister executed as a means of calming the situation was hardly a promising sign.

It did not help that oil production elsewhere was rising, or that there were new opportunities that promised to be the foundation of great fortunes, which were indeed to prove far greater than that made by Knox D'Arcy. Weeks before Mossadegh's fall, a company controlled by J. Paul Getty made a huge strike—described as "somewhere between colossal and history-making"—in the Neutral Zone between Saudi Arabia and Kuwait. By comparison, becoming involved in the poisonous politics of Teheran was understandably unattractive to a corporation. For the U.S. government, on the other hand, it was not just a priority but a necessity: Iran had all but stopped exporting oil during the crisis of the early 1950s. If it did not resume production soon, the country's economy would crumple, which would likely open the door to subversive factions that might tip the country towards the Soviet Union. The drying up of supplies and the rising prices would also have an unwelcome impact on Europe as it tried to rebuild in the post-war period. The State Department therefore began a sustained campaign to encourage the major U.S. producers to form a consortium to take over Anglo-Iranian's interests, intimating darkly that their concessions in Kuwait, Iraq and Saudi would be in jeopardy if no action were taken.

The U.S. government now played ringmaster as it cajoled American corporations to co-operate. As one senior oil executive put it, "from a strictly commercial point of view, our Company has no particular interest" in getting involved in the Iranian oil industry; "but we are very conscious of the large national security interests involved. We are therefore prepared to make all reasonable efforts" to help. We would never have got entangled in Iran, said another oilman, if the government "hadn't really beat us on the head."[1]

The efforts to step into Anglo-Iranian's position and to keep Iran stable were complicated by the fact that the very oil companies being asked to act as a tool of U.S. foreign policy were being prosecuted for breaking antitrust laws by the Department of Justice. Just as the message of preaching democracy had been revealed to be a flexible one, so too did that of ensuring that American laws were upheld: formal undertakings were therefore given by the Attorney-General at the request of the National Security Council that "the enforcement of the Antitrust laws of the United States against the [oil companies forming the consortium] may be deemed secondary to the national security interest." In the spring of 1954, therefore, the oil companies received formal guarantees of immunity from prosecution. So important was control over Iran that the U.S. government was prepared to put its own legal code to one side.[2]

Encouraging the participation of American oil companies was just one part of a wider plan to prop up Iran and keep it out of the grasp of the Soviet Union. Concerted efforts went into social development projects, particularly in the countryside. Around three-quarters of the population were peasants, owning no land and with minimal incomes. They were trapped in a world where landowners were opposed to agrarian reform, and where options were limited: typical rates of credit on offer to small farmers ranged from 30 to 75 per cent—levels that were all but guaranteed to strangle social mobility.[3]

Substantial funds were invested to address some of these issues. Microfinance schemes for small farm-holders were set up by the Ford Foundation, the largest philanthropic organisation in America. Support for the creation of co-operatives enabled them to go from inefficient trading of their cotton harvests at local markets to selling them at considerably better prices to brokers in Europe. Pressure was heaped on the Shah and his ministers to engage properly with the concept of rural development, albeit with limited effect and to the despair of those trying to convince senior politicians that failure to engage with illiteracy and inequality in the countryside would have long-term consequences.[4]

Direct aid from the U.S. government rose sharply too, rising from an annual average of $27 million in the years before the removal of Mossadegh to a figure nearly five times higher in the years that followed.[5] The U.S. also provided grants and loans to help bankroll a massive dam on the Karaj river, around forty miles north-east of Teheran, that was intended substantially to upgrade the electricity and water supply to the capital city—as well as to serve as a symbol of Iran's modernisation and progress.[6]

Efforts like these were part of a systematic approach to strengthening other parts of the region. Although Iran's oil wealth made it particularly significant to the west, neighbouring countries were also rising in importance because of their position along the Soviet Union's southern flank at a time when the Cold War was beginning to heat up.

The result was the construction of a belt of states between the Mediterranean and the Himalayas with pro-western governments that received considerable economic, political and military support from the United States. This slab of countries—christened the Northern Tier by the austere Secretary of State John Foster Dulles—served three aims: to act as a bulwark against the expansion of Soviet interests; to keep the resource-rich Gulf secure and continuing to pump oil to the west that would stimulate the recovery of Europe while at the same time providing revenues that were important for local stability; and to provide a series of listening posts and military bases in case tensions with the Soviet bloc spilled into open conflict.

In 1949, for example, a report prepared for the Joint Chiefs of Staff on South Asia noted that Pakistan "might be required as a base for air operations against [the] central USSR and as a staging area for forces engaged in the defense or recapture of Middle East oil areas"—while also pointing out that it was an obvious outpost from which to conduct covert operations against the Soviet Union.[7] It was vital therefore to provide assistance to Pakistan, as well as to other countries in the Northern Tier, or there was a chance that the region as a whole would take a neutral line with the west, "or, at worst . . . might fall into the Soviet orbit."[8]

These anxieties shaped United States and western policy for much of Asia in the decade after the Second World War. In 1955, the swathe of countries running from Turkey in the west through Iraq and Iran to Pakistan in the east were tied together in a single agreement that replaced a web of alliances with each other or with Britain—and became signatories of what was soon known as the Baghdad Pact. Although the stated aim of the treaty was "the maintenance of peace and security in the Middle East" under which mutual guarantees were exchanged, the reality was that it was designed to enable the west to influence a region that was of vital strategic and economic importance.[9]

Despite the careful consideration that had been given to ensuring that local governments would act favourably, mistakes in Washington created opportunities for the Soviets. At the end of 1954, for example, a discreet approach by the Afghan leadership to the United States requesting assistance and arms was dismissed by the State Department. Instead of asking for arms, Prince Naim, brother of the Prime Minister, was told, Afghanistan should focus on matters closer to home—such as resolving border disputes with Pakistan. The clumsy response, intended to show support for a regime in Karachi that had recently been described by one military attaché as of "strategic worldwide importance," backfired immediately.[10]

The news had barely reached Kabul before the Soviets stepped in to say they were willing to provide military hardware and development funds—an offer that was quickly accepted. An initial grant of $100 million was followed by further awards that enabled bridges to be built, telecommunications to be modernised and the road system expanded, including the highway between Kandahar and Herat. Money and expertise from Moscow were also responsible for constructing the 1.7-mile Salang Tunnel along a major road leading north to connect with Soviet Central Asia. This route, a symbol of Soviet–Afghan friendship, was the primary supply artery during the 1980s following the invasion of Afghanistan. Ironically, it also proved to be a vital part of the supply route bringing U.S. and Allied convoys into the country in the early twenty-first century: a highway built to strengthen Afghanistan against the west became central to the efforts of the latter to build the former in its own image.[11]

Being outmanoeuvred so emphatically was a sobering experience—especially when the same thing happened again a few months later, this time with more dramatic results. At the end of 1955, the revolutionary Gamal abdel Nasser, who had played an instrumental role in the coup three years earlier that toppled Egypt's King Farouk with CIA support, also approached Moscow for arms. Caught by surprise, the United States responded by offering to help fund a project to build a huge dam at Aswan in conjunction with Britain and the World Bank—a mirror project of the Karaj dam in Iran. There were high-level discussions between London and Washington about how else to mollify Nasser, resulting in the promise of arms and pressure being applied to Israel to agree a treaty with Egypt, in the hope of improving the increasingly tetchy relations between the two countries.[12]

Nasser had been riled by the Baghdad Pact, which he saw as an impediment to Arab unity and a western tool to preserve influence across the heart of Asia. Had the money and support been forthcoming, he might perhaps have been pacified—at least in the short term. As it was, the funding promises were withdrawn following concerns from U.S. congressmen that construction of a dam would lead to a surge in cotton production and a drop in prices that would affect American farmers.[13] This self-interest proved fatal; it was the final straw.

An expert in political brinkmanship, Nasser—described by the British Prime Minister Anthony Eden as being determined "to become the Napoleon of the Arabs"—now escalated the situation.[14] He pointedly responded to the British Foreign Secretary's pompous comment in the spring of 1956 that the Suez canal was "an integral part of the Middle East oil complex" and vital to Britain's interests with the retort that if that was the case, then Egypt should share in the profits of the canal—just as oil-producing states shared in oil revenues.[15] He realised all too well that the west would stop at nothing to retain its assets, but calculated that nationalising the canal would provide leverage which would in the long run only benefit Egypt.

As American planners set about calculating the possible impact of the closure of the canal on oil prices, leading figures in Britain slumped into a fog of doom and gloom. "The truth is that we are caught in a terrible dilemma," wrote Harold Macmillan, the highly regarded and well-connected Chancellor of the Exchequer. "If we take strong action against Egypt and as a result the canal is closed, the pipelines to the Levant are cut, the Persian gulf revolts and oil production is stopped—then the United Kingdom and Western Europe have 'had it'."[16] If nothing was done, on the other hand, Nasser would win hands down, and there would be catastrophic consequences elsewhere: all the countries of the Middle East would simply follow his lead and nationalise their oil industries.

Nasser was taking up where Mossadegh had left off. Western diplomats, politicians and intelligence operatives began to think about applying a similar solution to the problem of a leader whose policies were opposed to western interests. It did not take long before the British were looking at "ways and means of bringing down the regime."[17] As one senior diplomat in London put it, "we may have to get rid of Nasser"; the Prime Minister, Anthony Eden, did not just want to remove him; he wanted Nasser dead.[18] After rounds of diplomatic shuttling had come to nothing, Britain and France concluded that a sustained demonstration of power was needed to impress leaders across the Middle East that direct action would be taken against anyone who dared stand up against western aims.

At the end of October 1956, military action began against Egypt, with British and French forces moving to secure the canal zone, while their Israeli allies launched a strike deep into the Sinai peninsula to help secure Suez and maximise pressure on Nasser. The invasion soon turned into a fiasco. The Suez canal was closed after the Egyptians had scuttled ships, barges and maintenance vessels in and near navigation channels, while the movable rail bridge at El Fridan north of Ismaila was dropped into the water. The effect of the estimated forty-nine obstructions went beyond a shut-down of the canal; it produced what one report from this time called "a serious dislocation of normal commodity movements." Shipments of petroleum to western Europe were sharply reduced.

Further consequences were to be expected, concluded the CIA: the prices of "many basic commodities in world commerce" would be bound to rise, and there was likely to be "considerable unemployment in the countries of the Free World" whose economies were dependent on shipments coming through Suez. The impact would be felt on the Soviet Union too, whose vessels trading with the Far East faced a 7,000-mile diversion round Africa to reach their home ports in the Black Sea because of the closure of Suez. The Americans watched carefully as Moscow diverted essential cargo on to trans-Asian railway routes, whose importance rose quickly.[19]

Although more than aware of the rising tensions over Egypt, the Eisenhower administration was taken by surprise at the outbreak of military action, having not been consulted on the invasion plans. The President was incandescent, delivering a stinging rebuke to the British Prime Minister in person. The use of force in the canal zone was a propaganda disaster for the self-proclaimed guardians of the "free world," coming just as Soviet tanks rolled through the streets of Budapest to put down a popular uprising in Hungary. Ultimately, though, the action in Suez forced a different issue: it marked the moment when the United States had to choose between the western powers whose mantle it had inherited in the twentieth century and the oil-rich world of the Middle East. It chose the latter.

It was essential, reasoned President Eisenhower, that "the Arabs [not get] sore at all of us." If they did, oil supplies from the Middle East might collapse altogether, both because of the canal's closure and because production might be stopped or embargoes introduced in countries in a region naturally sympathetic to Egypt when it was being so brazenly bullied. As one senior British diplomat had already conceded, any reduction of supply would have its own devastating consequences. "If Middle East oil is denied to [Britain] for a year or two, our gold reserves will disappear. If our gold reserves disappear the sterling area disintegrates. If the sterling area disintegrates and we have no reserves . . . I doubt whether we shall be able to pay for the bare minimum necessary for our defence. And a country that cannot provide for its defence is finished."[20] This was very much a worst-case scenario, laced with doom. Even so, as Eisenhower himself recognised privately, it was hard to be "indifferent to the fuel and financial plight of Western Europe." Nevertheless, as he wrote to Lord Ismay, the first secretary-general of the mutual defence alliance NATO (North Atlantic Treaty Organisation), it was vital not to "antagonize the Arab world."[21]

In practice, this meant forcing Britain and France into a corner. Although a plan was drawn up in Washington to ship oil from the United States to western Europe, it was intentionally not put into practice in order to bring matters in Egypt to a conclusion. With confidence in the British economy collapsing and sterling's value plummeting, London was forced to turn to the International Monetary Fund for financial assistance. In barely four decades, Britain had gone from world mastery to holding out its cap and begging for help. It was bad enough, then, that the appeal to the IMF was flatly turned down; it was positively humiliating that the troops that had been sent to Egypt to fight for one of western Europe's most precious jewels were now withdrawn without having accomplished their mission. Their recall home, in the glare of the world's media, was a telling sign of how the world had changed: India had been abandoned; the oilfields of Iran had been prised from Britain's grasp; now so too had the Suez canal. The resignation of the Prime Minister, Anthony Eden, at the start of 1957 simply served as another paragraph in the final chapter of the death of an empire.[22]

The United States, on the other hand, was acutely aware of its newfound responsibilities as a superpower when it came to the countries lying across the spine of Asia. It had to tread a careful line—as the fall-out after Suez demonstrated clearly. British prestige and influence had slumped spectacularly, raising the prospect that the southern flank acting as a bulwark to the Soviet Union might "completely collapse through Communist penetration and success in the Middle East," as President Eisenhower put it at the end of 1956.[23]

Moreover, the fiasco over the aborted military action had served to rouse anti-western sentiments across the Middle East as a whole, with nationalist demagogues taking heart from Nasser's success in holding his nerve and overcoming European military pressure. As the Egyptian leader's status rose exponentially across the region, ideas of Arab nationalism began to emerge, and with it, a growing sense that the unification of all Arabs into a single entity would create a single voice that would balance that of the west on the one hand and that of the Soviet bloc on the other.

Astute observers had predicted just such an eventuality even before Nasser's masterclass in political brinkmanship. The U.S. ambassador to Teheran, Loy Henderson, who understood the region better than any other American, had concluded that nationalist voices would become increasingly vocal and powerful. "It seems almost inevitable," he wrote in 1953, "that at some time in the future . . . the Middle Eastern countries . . . will come together and decide upon unified policies."[24] Nasser was the figurehead that this movement had been waiting for.

This prompted a significant change in posture from the United States, articulated in what became known as the Eisenhower doctrine. Keenly aware that the Soviet Union was looking opportunistically at the Middle East, the President told Congress that it was essential that "the existing vacuum" in the Middle East should "be filled by the United States before it is filled by Russia." This was not just important for U.S. interests, he went on; it was vital "to the peace of the world."[25] Congress was therefore asked to approve an ambitious budget to fund economic and military aid across the region, as well as for the authority to defend any country threatened by armed aggression. While one key purpose was to pre-empt the Soviet Union, it was also intended as an alternative to Nasser's vision—one that was attractive to countries which could see the benefits of receiving substantial disbursements of money from Washington.[26]

This attempt to reposition did not convince everyone. The Israelis were unimpressed by American attempts to improve relations with the Arabs and had little truck with assurances that they too would feel the benefits of the raised profile and role played by the United States.[27] These misgivings were understandable given the anger swirling around Israel, especially in Saudi Arabia and Iraq in the wake of the botched intervention in Suez. It did not help, of course, that Israeli troops had taken part alongside British and French soldiers; but what was more important was that the country was fast becoming a totemic symbol of outside interference by the west in the affairs of the region—and as a prime beneficiary of it. As a result, increasingly aggressive noises were being made about U.S. support for Israel being incompatible with assistance for Arabs.

Israel was now a focal point for Arab nationalists to rally around. Just as the Crusaders had found in the Holy Land hundreds of years earlier, the mere existence of a state supposedly made up of outsiders was a cause for disparate Arab interests to be set to one side. As the Crusaders had found too, Israelis assumed the ambiguous and unenviable role of a target that united many enemies into one.

Anti-Israeli rhetoric featured strongly as politicians in Syria threw their lot in with Nasser and the vision he was articulating for a united Arab world. At the start of 1958, a formal merger with Egypt created a new state, the United Arab Republic, a prelude to future consolidation. Washington watched anxiously as the situation unfurled. Ambassador Henderson had warned that the emergence of a single voice might bring difficulties—"disastrous effects," as he called them. The United States wrestled with the implications and the State Department buzzed with debate, much of it highly pessimistic. A paper produced by the Bureau of Near Eastern, South Asian and African Affairs observed anxiously that Nasser's radical nationalism threatened to engulf the region, noting that American "assets" across the Middle East had been reduced or neutralised as a result of the Egyptian leader's success with Suez and his step forward with Syria.[28] Nasser's progress would inevitably pave the way for Communism, concluded John Foster Dulles, Secretary of State and elder brother of Allen Dulles, head of the CIA. It was time to take decisive action and put up "sandbags around positions we must protect."[29]

The mood worsened when what looked unmistakably like the start of a chain reaction swept eastwards across Asia. First to go was Iraq. The unification of Egypt and Syria prompted much discussion among the well-educated elite in Baghdad, for whom the attractions of pan-Arabism seemed increasingly tempting as a third way between the attentions of Washington and Moscow. But things turned poisonous in the capital in the summer of 1958, sparked by a dangerous rise in pro-Nasser sympathies and rising anti-western sentiments laced with aggressive rhetoric about Israel. On 14 July, a group of high-ranking Iraqi army officers led by Abdul Karim Qasim—a man nicknamed "the snake charmer" by contemporaries who attended a military course with him in Britain two decades earlier—staged a coup.[30]

Marching on the palace at breakfast time, the plotters rounded up leading members of the royal family, including King Faisal II, in the palace courtyard and executed them. The body of Crown Prince Abd al-Ilha, a thoughtful and rather serious man, was dragged "into the street like . . . a dog," torn apart and then burnt by an angry mob. The next day, the Iraqi Prime Minister, Nuri al-Said, a veteran politician who had witnessed the transformation of the Middle East at first hand, was tracked down as he tried to flee, dressed as a woman, and shot dead. His body was mutilated and gleefully paraded through Baghdad.[31]

These events seemed to herald a near-certain expansion of the Soviet Union's interests. Iran, the Russian supremo Nikita Khrushchev told President John F. Kennedy at a summit in 1961, would soon drop like a rotten fruit into Soviet hands—a prospect that seemed likely given that even the head of the Iranian secret police was known to be plotting against the Shah. After Moscow's State Security Committee (better known as the KGB) had failed with one assassination attempt, attention was turned to preparing landing sites and munitions dumps across Iran—presumably in anticipation of the decision to escalate efforts to foment a popular uprising and bring down the monarchy.[32]

Things looked little better in Iraq, where a senior U.S. policymaker wrote that the country "almost surely will drift into what amounts to a Communist takeover."[33] One result of this was western realignment with Nasser, who began to be viewed as the "lesser of two evils." The United States was at pains to build bridges with the mercurial Egyptian leader, who himself recognised that Arab nationalism could be compromised by what he reportedly referred to as the growing "Communist penetration of the Middle East."[34] Common cause between Washington and Cairo was underscored by the decision of the new leadership in Iraq to plot a course of its own and steer away from pan-Arabism and from Nasser; this simply raised concerns still further about the spectre of the Soviet Union.[35]

Plans for dealing with Baghdad were drawn up, with a committee appointed in the U.S. to look at "overt or covert means" of avoiding "a Communist takeover in Iraq." Limitations in the source material make it difficult to know how much involvement, if any, the CIA had in an attempted coup to remove Qasim, the nationalist Prime Minister who had deposed the Iraqi monarchy, that was staged towards the end of 1959. One of those involved, who grazed his shin during the confusion, later used his participation to near-mythical effect to show his resolve and personal bravery. His name was Saddam Hussein.[36]

Whether the plotters enjoyed U.S. support on this occasion is not certain, although records show that the American intelligence community was aware of the failed putsch before it took place.[37] The fact that elaborate plans were developed to remove key figures from positions of authority—such as an unnamed Iraqi colonel who was to be sent a monogrammed handkerchief contaminated with an incapacitating agent—also shows that active steps were being taken to try to ensure that Baghdad did not slip into Moscow's orbit.[38] It was perhaps no coincidence that when Qasim was finally deposed in 1963, his overthrow came as no surprise to American observers who later stated that this had been "forecast in exact detail by CIA agents."[39]

This deep engagement with the situation in Iraq was primarily driven by the desire to keep the Soviet Union out of the countries to its south. Building connections across the belt that spanned the Silk Roads was partly a matter of political prestige, where the United States could not afford to be seen to be losing out to a rival that offered a sharply contrasting vision for the world. But there were other reasons for the intensity of this sustained interest.

In 1955, Moscow decided to locate a major testing site for long-range missiles at Tyuratam, in what is now Kazakhstan, after concluding that the steppes provided a perfect environment in which to establish a chain of guidance antennae that would allow launches to be monitored without obstruction during flight, while also being sufficiently isolated as to pose no threat to existing urban centres. The resulting centre, later named the Baikonur Kosmodrome, became the primary location for the development and testing of ballistic missiles.[40] Even before the centre was established, the Soviets had launched the R5, which had a range of over 600 miles and was capable of carrying a nuclear warhead. In 1957, its successor—the R7, better known by its NATO codename SS6 "Sapwood"—came into production with a range of 5,000 miles, dramatically raising the threat posed by the Soviet Union to the west.[41]

The launch of Sputnik, the world's first satellite, the following year, along with the introduction of a fleet of Tupolev Tu-95 "Bear" and Myasishchev 3M "Bison" long-range strategic bombers, focused the minds of American military planners further still: it was vital that the United States should be able to monitor missile tests, keeping an eye open for developments in ballistic capabilities as well as possible hostile launches.[42] The Cold War often prompts thought of the Berlin Wall and eastern Europe as the principal arena for confrontation between the superpowers. But it was the swathe of territory within the Soviet Union's underbelly where the real game of Cold War chess was played out.

The strategic value to the United States of the countries along the USSR's southern flank had long been recognised. Now they became vitally important. Airbases, listening stations and communication networks in Pakistan became a crucial part of U.S. defence strategy. By the time the Soviet missile capability reached the intercontinental stage, Peshawar Air Station in the north of the country was providing vital intelligence-gathering services. It served as a departure point for U-2 spy-plane operations that undertook reconnaissance missions over Baikonur as well as over other major military installations, including the plutonium-processing plant at Chelyabinsk. It was from Peshawar that Gary Powers took off on the ill-fated mission that saw him shot down in Soviet airspace near Sverdlovsk in 1960 in one of the most gripping incidents of the Cold War.[43]

There was no small irony then that American political and military objectives, which were central to the defence of the free world and the democratic way of life, led to very different results. The U.S. position in this part of the world was built on a series of strongmen, with undemocratic instincts and unsavoury methods of staying in power. In the case of Pakistan, the United States were happy to deal with General Ayub Khan after he had led a coup in 1958 which he cannily billed as a "revolution away from Communism" in an effort to gain American support. He was able to impose martial law without incurring the opprobrium of his western backers, justifying his actions as being "harsh only to those who have been destroying Pakistan's moral fiber."[44] Lip-service was paid to the restoration of a "workable constitutional government," though few had any illusions that military dictatorship was likely to be long-lasting—especially after Ayub stated that it would be "some decades" before educational standards had been raised sufficiently to trust the population to vote for their leaders.[45] The United States was more than happy to provide weapons in large quantities to this dubious ally: Sidewinder missiles, jet fighters and B-57 tactical bombers were just some of the hardware sold with the approval of President Eisenhower.[46]

This had the effect of further building up the status and power of the armed forces in Pakistan, where upwards of 65 per cent of the national budget was spent on the military. It seemed the necessary price to pay to keep friends in power in this part of the world. Laying the basis for social reform was risky and time-consuming compared to the immediate gains to be made from relying on strongmen and the elites that surrounded them. But the result was the stifling of democracy and the laying down of deep-rooted problems that would fester over time.

The leadership of Afghanistan was courted equally assiduously, with the Prime Minister, Daoud Khan, for example, invited for a two-week visit to the United States at the end of the 1950s. The desire to make an impression was such that when he landed he was greeted on the tarmac by both Vice-President Nixon and Secretary of State John Foster Dulles before being cordially received by President Eisenhower, who was at pains to warn the Afghan Premier of the threat Communism posed to the Muslim countries of Asia. The United States had already begun a series of ambitious development projects in Afghanistan, such as a major irrigation scheme in the Helmand valley and a bold effort to improve the education system. It now gave further commitments in order to counter-balance substantial Soviet investments, loans and infrastructure projects that were already in operation.[47]

The problem, of course, was that it did not take long for leaders in the countries concerned to realise that they could play the two superpowers off against each other—and extract increasingly large benefits from both as a result. Indeed, when President Eisenhower visited Kabul in person at the end of the 1950s, he was asked point-blank to match the aid that was being given to his country by Moscow.[48] Refusal had consequences, but so did acquiescence.

American planners became highly agitated meanwhile about what was seen as a distinct wobble in Iran at the end of the 1950s, when Shah Reza

Pahlavi demonstrated a willingness to improve relations with Moscow following a damaging campaign of radio propaganda funded by the Soviet Union, which relentlessly played on the image of the Iranian ruler as a puppet of the west and urged the workers to rise up and overthrow his despotic regime.[49] It was enough to make the Shah consider abandoning what he called Iran's "totally antagonistic" relations with the USSR, and open up more conciliatory channels of communication and co-operation.[50]

This set off alarm bells in Washington, where strategists took an uncompromising view of Iran's pivotal importance on the Soviet Union's southern flank. By the start of the 1960s, as one report put it, the country's "strategic location between the USSR and the Persian Gulf and its great oil reserves make it critically important to the United States that Iran's friendship, independence and territorial integrity be maintained."[51] Considerable energy and resources went into supporting Iran's economy and its military and to reinforcing the Shah's control over the country.

It was considered so important to keep the Shah happy that a blind eye was turned to intolerance, and to large-scale corruption and the inevitable economic stagnation this helped to cause. Nothing was said and done about persecution of religious minorities, such as the Baha'i, who were singled out for brutal treatment in the 1950s.[52] There was precious little to show, meanwhile, for the steep increase in Iran's oil revenues, which had multiplied more than seven-fold between 1954 and 1960. The Shah's relatives and the group informally referred to in Iran as "the 1,000 families" established an iron grip on imports, making fortunes for themselves as they did so. Soft loans given by Washington simply served to line the pockets of the few at the expense of the poor, who found it difficult to keep up with the soaring cost of living—especially following a bad harvest in 1959–60.[53]

It did not help that some U.S. projects that were designed to stimulate the agrarian economy were spectacular failures. Attempts to replace traditional seeds with modern hybrids were a disaster, with the new strains proving unsuitable for the terrain and lacking resistance to disease and insect devastation. A scheme designed to help both Iranian and American poultry farmers by introducing U.S. chicks to Iran had calamitous results too, with the unavailability of suitable feed and the lack of vaccination having consequences that were all too predictable. The embarrassing failure to understand how the water table in Iran worked led to wells that drained underground reservoirs and destroyed the viability of many farms across the country.[54]

Counter-productive schemes such as these were hardly positive examples of the benefits of closer co-operation with the west and with the United States in particular. They also provided fertile ground for critics to exploit. None was more adept at doing so than a Shī'a scholar, Ruhollah Moosavi Khomeini, who caught the mood of a population that was increasingly disgruntled by low wages, the lack of economic progress and the conspicuous absence of social justice. "Your Excellency, Mr. Shah, let me give you a piece of advice," the ayatollah declared in one particularly fiery speech in the early 1960s. "You miserable wretch, isn't it time for you to think and reflect a little, and ponder where all this is leading you? . . . Mr. Shah, do you want me to say that you don't believe in Islam, and kick you out of Iran?"[55] It was enough to get him arrested, upon which riots broke out in the centre of Teheran, with crowds chanting "Khomeini or death." As CIA intelligence reports noted, even government employees joined demonstrations against the regime.[56]

Rather than heeding the warnings, the Shah responded by antagonising his critics still further. The clergy of Iran, he announced with an astonishing lack of tact on a visit to the holy city of Qom, were "ignorant and withered men whose minds have not been stirred in centuries."[57] Instead of offering concessions or instigating whole-hearted reforms, energy was focused on tightening controls. Khomeini was forced into exile, settling for more than a decade in Najaf in neighbouring Iraq, where his passionate denunciations of the Shah and his regime were not just welcomed but positively encouraged.[58]

Substantial resources were also spent building up the Savak, the Iranian secret police force, which quickly developed a fearsome reputation. Imprisonment without trial, torture and execution were used on a large scale to deal with critics of the Shah and those close to him; in a few rare cases, fortunate opponents whose high profile kept them visible—like Khomeini—were placed under house arrest and exiled to remove them from the scene.[59] The use of such tactics in the Soviet Union was the subject of vocal criticism by the United States, denounced as the antithesis of democracy and a tool of totalitarianism; in Iran, it was passed over in silence.

To maintain the support of the Shah and cement his position, funds continued to pour into Iran from Washington, building a 1,500-mile highway system linking the Persian Gulf with the Caspian, helping the construction of a major deep-water port at Bandar Abbas, allowing the power grid to be expanded and upgraded, and even providing capital to set up prestige projects, such as the creation of a national airline. Throughout the process, most western policymakers ignored the realities on the ground, choosing to see only what they wanted to see. To many U.S. observers, Iran seemed to be an unmitigated triumph. The economy of "one of the United States' staunchest friends in the Middle East was surging forward," stated a report prepared for President Johnson in 1968. Iran's GNP was rising so quickly that it was "one of the notable success stories" of recent times. The same conclusion was reached even more emphatically four years later. Following the end of the Second World War, the American embassy in Teheran noted, the United States had been forced to take a gamble on Iran and shape the country after its own image. "That gamble has paid off handsomely—probably more so than in any other developing country which has benefited from similar U.S. investment." Iran was on track, the report confidently predicted, to become "the most prosperous country in Asia after Japan"—and on a par with many countries in Europe.[60]

Those who were more sceptical were in a distinct minority. One such was the young academic William Polk, who had been called in by the Kennedy administration to advise on foreign affairs. There would be violence and even revolution if the Shah did not reform the political process, he warned; when that unrest broke out, it would only be a matter of time before the security forces would refuse to fire on protesters. Opposition to the Shah was now uniting under "the powerful Islamic institution of Iran."[61]

Polk was exactly right. At the time, however, it seemed more important to continue shoring up an ally against Communism than to press him to loosen his grip on power. And the Shah developed increasingly grandiose plans that made matters even worse. Vast amounts were invested in the military, with Iran's military spending rising from $293 million in 1963 to $7.3 billion less than fifteen years later. As a result, the country's air force and army became among the largest in the world.[62] Iran funded this extraordinary escalation thanks in part to military aid and soft loans from the United States (which profited in turn because much of the hardware was bought from American defence contractors). However, Iran also benefited from the continuing rise in oil revenues—and from the mechanism that had been set up by the world's leading producers to act as a cartel, and in doing so maximise returns.

The creation of the Organisation of Petroleum Exporting Countries (OPEC) in 1960 was designed to co-ordinate the release of oil supplies on the open market. The aim was to allow the founder members—Iraq, Iran,

Saudi Arabia, Kuwait and Venezuela—to combine their interests and boost their incomes by controlling supply, and therefore controlling prices.[63] It was the logical next step for resource-rich countries which had an eye on wresting power away from the western corporations while receiving political and financial backing from western governments.

OPEC effectively marked a deliberate attempt to curtail the influence of the west, whose interests in providing cheap and plentiful fuel for its domestic markets were distinctly different to those of the countries that were rich in deposits of oil and gas, and who were keen for the revenues they brought in to be as high as possible. Unlikely as it seems, therefore, OPEC was the spiritual protégé of an already unlikely cast of characters made up of defiant leaders like Mossadegh, the populist demagogue Nasser, the hardliner Qasim and increasingly anti-western figures in Iran typified by the Ayatollah Khomeini. All were linked by their concerted attempts to detach their states from overpowering outside attention. OPEC was not a political movement; but aligning a range of countries and enabling them to talk and act with a single voice was a key step in the process of transferring political power away from Europe and the United States to local governments.

The sheer abundance of oil in Iran, Iraq, Kuwait and Saudi combined with rising global demand meant that the mid-twentieth century was marked by a fundamental rebalancing of power. The extent of this began to become clear in 1967 when Israel caught Nasser by surprise as he massed troops on the border in preparation of an attack. Saudi Arabia, Iraq and Kuwait, supported by Algeria and Libya, two countries in North Africa where production was taking off, suspended shipments to Britain and the United States as a result of their perceived friendliness to Israel. With refineries being shut down and pipelines closed, a nightmare scenario loomed large, with the prospect of substantial shortfalls, sharp price rises and a threat to the global economy.

As it happened, the impact was minimal—because Nasser's planned assault failed before it began, and got worse as he was defeated decisively on the battle field; above all though, it was the fact that failure was quick as well as spectacular that was important: the "six-day war" was over almost as soon as it began, and Nasser and dreams of Arab nationalism were delivered a reality check. The Israeli military, backed by western technology and political support, proved to be a formidable adversary. Neither the west nor its supposed puppet state in the Middle East was ready to suffer a decisive blow just yet.[64]

For two centuries, the great powers of Europe had struggled and fought each other for control of the region and of the markets that linked the Mediterranean with India and China. The twentieth century saw the recoil of western Europe's position, and the passing of the baton on to the United States. In some ways, it was entirely appropriate that it was a nation forged from the competition between Britain, France and Spain that took up the mantle of trying to maintain control over the heart of the world. It would prove to be a tough challenge—not least since a new Great Game was about to begin.

23

The Road of Superpower Rivalry

The war of 1967 was a warning shot, a case of muscles being flexed. It was a sign of things to come. Retaining power and influence in the heart of the world was to become increasingly difficult for the west. For Britain, it became impossible. In 1968, the Prime Minister, Harold Wilson, announced that Britain would withdraw from all its defence commitments east of Suez, including from the Persian Gulf.[1] It was now up to the United States, itself a vestige and heir of the great age of European empire, to take on the mantle of retaining influence in the Middle East.

A complicated background of intense pressure from all sides meant that this was not easy to achieve. In Iraq in 1961, for example, large areas that were part of the concession granted three decades earlier to the consortium of western producers that made up the Iraq Petroleum Company were nationalised on the basis that they had been left unexploited. Attitudes in Baghdad stiffened further after Prime Minister Qasim had been ousted and then executed in front of television cameras "for the whole world to see." The new hardline regime declared that it was leading "the broader struggle to free the Arab nation from the domination of Western imperialism and exploitation by oil monopolists," and raised transit fees on the Banias pipeline overnight.[2]

The Soviets watched on with glee. The changes in the Middle East and the rising tide of anti-western sentiment had been followed carefully in Moscow. Since the Arab–Israeli War of 1967, one CIA report noted, the USSR "has followed a consistent course . . . seeking, as opportunities arose, to extend its political and military influence into a region of traditional Russian concern."[3] The Soviet Union now looked to exploit openings enthusiastically, setting about building its own network of relations stretching from the Mediterranean to the Hindu Kush, from the Caspian to the Persian Gulf.

This was partly the result of political brinkmanship between the two superpowers. Small successes were magnified into major propaganda victories, as was clear from the case of Soviet financial and technical support for the Rumaila oilfield in Iraq. The newspaper *Izvestiya* was ecstatic in its coverage, trumpeting a new benchmark in the positive co-operation between "Arab and socialist nations," pointedly remarking on how keen the USSR was to develop "a national oil industry for the Arabs." In contrast, the paper went on, western "plans to control the oil of the Arabs are falling apart."[4]

The 1960s was a period when there was a distinct ramping up of the horizons of the superpowers—and not only in the centre of Asia. In the early 1960s, the Soviet Union's support for revolutionary Cuba, which included a planned programme to station nuclear warheads on the island, almost resulted in war. Following a tense showdown at sea, Soviet ships were finally recalled rather than break through a perimeter set up by U.S. Navy vessels. Confrontation that had flared up in the Far East in the Korean peninsula at the end of the Second World War broke out again, this time in Vietnam with effects spilling into Cambodia and Laos, where the United States became embroiled in an ugly and costly war that appeared to many Americans to be a battle between the forces of the free world and those of totalitarian Communism. The full-blooded commitment of substantial numbers of ground troops did not convince others, and rising disillusionment with Vietnam became a rallying point for the emerging counter-culture movement.

As the situation in South-East Asia worsened, there was a flurry of activity as Moscow sought to take advantage of the growing disenchantment with the United States, which was so strong that Ayatollah Khomeini could declare in 1964: "Let the American President know that in the eyes of the Iranian people he is the most repellent member of the human race."[5] This disenchantment was not limited to opposition figures, clerics and populist demagogues. The President of neighbouring Iraq was prepared to refer to British and American oilmen as "bloodsuckers," while mainstream newspapers in Baghdad started to describe the west as imperialist, Zionist or even imperialistic-Zionist.[6]

Despite the hostility of such statements and the fertile ground they fell on, attitudes to the west were not all negative. In truth, the issue was not that the United States and to a lesser extent Britain were reviled for their supposed interference in the affairs of the countries sprawling from the Mediterranean eastwards and for being willing to line the pockets of a corrupt elite. Rather, the rhetoric masked the imperatives of a new reality where a region that had become peripheral over the course of several centuries was re-emerging as a result of the natural resources lying in its soil, the plentiful supply of customers willing to pay for them and rising demand. This fuelled ambitions, and in particular the demand not to be circumscribed by outside interests and influences. It was ironic, then, that a new battleground now emerged where the superpowers jostled for position as part of a new Great Game, seeking to exploit each other's weaknesses.

Iraq, Syria and Afghanistan were delighted to be awarded soft loans to buy Soviet weapons and to have highly qualified advisers and technicians dispatched from Moscow to build installations that might prove useful to their wider strategic ambitions. These included the deep-water port at Umm Qasr on the Persian Gulf, but also six military airfields in Iraq, which U.S. intelligence quickly realised could be used "to support a Soviet naval presence in the Indian Ocean."[7]

This was part of Moscow's attempt to build its own series of contacts and alliances to rival that of the Americans. Not surprisingly, then, Soviet policies were identical to those that had been pursued by Washington since the Second World War, whereby the U.S. established a number of locations that allowed them to keep one eye on the security of the Persian Gulf and Indian Ocean and another on either monitoring Soviet activities or creating forward attack bases. This was now replicated by the USSR. Soviet warships were redeployed to the Indian Ocean at the end of the 1960s to support new revolutionary regimes that had taken power in Sudan, Yemen and Somalia following years of careful cultivation by Moscow. This gave the Soviets an enviable series of footholds in Aden, Mogadishu and Berbera.[8] The USSR therefore acquired the capability to throttle access to the Suez canal, something that U.S. policy planners had feared for years.[9]

The CIA watched carefully as the Soviets systematically assisted the fishing, agricultural and other industries across the Indian Ocean area, including East Africa and the Gulf. This included training fishermen, developing harbour facilities and the sale or rental of fishing vessels at highly competitive prices. Such gestures of goodwill were reciprocated with free port access in Iraq, Mauritius and Somalia, as well as in Aden and Sana'a.[10]

The Soviets also devoted considerable efforts to cultivating Iraq and India. In the case of the latter, the USSR supplied armaments that accounted for more than three-quarters of all New Delhi's military procurement imported from abroad in the 1960s—in quantities that rose throughout the following decade.[11] Sales included some of Moscow's most sophisticated weaponry, including Atoll and Styx missiles, MiG-27 and MiG-29 fighters, and state-of-the-art destroyers, while India was also favoured with a licence to produce military aircraft that had been denied to the Chinese.[12]

Looking to the left and the right came naturally to peoples in this part of the world, and it continued to prove rewarding. In Afghanistan, a word was coined for the practice of seeking support from both superpowers: literally meaning "without sides," *bi-tarafi* became a tenet of a foreign policy that sought to balance the contributions made by the USSR with those of the United States. As one shrewd observer put it in a classic account published in 1973, Afghan army officers who had been sent on formal training programmes in the Soviet Union and the United States that were designed to build ties and develop relationships with future leaders would compare notes when they returned home. One thing in particular stood out for officers who had been talent-spotted: "neither the USA nor the USSR turned out to be the paradises painted by their respective propaganda." Rather than evangelising new converts, then, the overwhelming response of those sent abroad was to return home convinced that Afghanistan should remain independent.[13]

Similar impulses were at work in Iran where the Shah was telling anyone who would listen that he was his country's saviour. "My visions were miracles that saved the country," he told one interviewer. "My reign has saved the country, and it has done so because God was on my side." When asked why no one dared even to mention his name on the streets of Teheran, he did not seem to consider that this might be because of the terrifying apparatus of the police state that kept him in power. "I should suppose," he said, that they do not talk about the Shah "from exaggerated respect."[14]

If this was a case of self-delusion, then so too was the posturing about Communists. "Communism is against the law," the Shah told his interviewer defiantly. "It follows that a Communist is not a political prisoner but a common criminal . . . they're people we must eliminate." In almost the next breath, however, he declared proudly that Iran enjoyed "good diplomatic and trade relations with the Soviet Union."[15] This said everything about the delicate balance across the spine of Asia that had to be sought during the Cold War. The Shah had learnt from experience that antagonising his powerful neighbour to the north could have serious repercussions. It was in his interests, therefore, to take support from the United States and the west while at the same time sweetening relations with Moscow. As a result, he was perfectly happy to enter into a series of agreements to buy rocket-propelled grenade launchers, anti-aircraft guns and heavy artillery from the USSR, and to allow Soviet technicians to help expand the major steelwork plant in Isfahan.

But while this was entirely understandable realpolitik, it demonstrated the difficulties of the position which the countries of this region found themselves in. Any alignment with one of the superpowers prompted a response from the other; any attempt to keep at a distance could have disastrous consequences and could easily create openings for opposition figures. In 1968, yet another coup in Iraq gave the Soviet Union the chance to strengthen ties that it had worked hard to develop over the previous decade. These now bore fruit with a fifteen-year Treaty of Friendship and Co-operation, signed in 1972, which was seen in London as being as good as a formal "alliance with the Soviet Union."[16]

Washington's anxiety that the USSR's tentacles were spreading ever further was reinforced by events elsewhere in Asia. In 1971, Moscow signed a twenty-five-year treaty of peace, friendship and co-operation with India, and agreed to provide economic, technological and military support. Things looked ominous in Afghanistan where a coup propelled Muḥammad Dāwud to power in 1973 alongside a cadre of left-wing supporters. A number of high-profile Islamist leaders were either pushed out by or fled from the new regime. They found a welcome home in Pakistan, especially in the so-called tribal regions around Quetta, where they were actively supported by the government of Zulfiqar Ali Bhutto, who saw them as a tool to help destabilise the new government in Afghanistan—and as an easy way to burnish his own religious credentials at home.

The sense of turbulence and of an emerging new world order was palpable as the peoples of the belt between the Mediterranean and the Himalayas strove to take their futures into their own hands. The real moment when Iraq became independent, Saddam Hussein used to say later, was when it nationalised its oil industry—and took control of its own destiny in 1972. Gone were the days when westerners would turn up and lord it over the local population. The time of "foreign domination and alien exploitation," he declared, "was at an end."[17]

Oil was the fuel behind much of this movement to escape from the overbearing influence of outside powers, setting off a chain reaction that had profound long-term implications. The catalyst for a new round of change was a coup led by an ambitious young Libyan army officer who had been described as "cheerful, hard-working and conscientious" by the British army course instructor who supervised his training in the UK.[18] Muʿammar Gaddafi was certainly resourceful. At the start of 1970, shortly after seizing power, he demanded a dramatic rise in the revenues of Libyan oil—which at that time was responsible for 30 per cent of Europe's total supply. "Brothers," he had proclaimed to his countrymen, "the revolution cannot let the Libyan people be poor while they own colossal oil wealth. There are people living in huts and tents while the foreigner lives in palaces." Other countries put men on the moon, Gaddafi went on; the Libyans are exploited to the extent that they have no electricity or water.[19]

The oil companies screamed with outrage at the new regime's insistence on being paid a fair price for the oil; but they soon complied after it had been made clear that nationalisation was not an option—but that it might be. The fact that the Libyan leader could force a renegotiation was not lost on others: within weeks, OPEC was pushing to raise the contribution made to its members by western oil companies, threatening to reduce production to force agreement. It was, in the words of one Shell executive, the moment when the "avalanche" began.[20]

The results were spectacular. The price of oil quadrupled over the course of three years, putting immense strain on the economies of Europe and the U.S., where demand and consumption levels galloped ever onwards. In the meantime, the oil-producing countries were flooded by unprecedented inflows of cash. The countries in the centre of Asia and the Persian Gulf had seen their returns steadily improve almost as soon as the Knox D'Arcy concession struck oil as agreements were slowly but surely renegotiated in the decades that followed with better and better terms. But what happened in the 1970s was a shift of seismic proportions. In 1972–73 alone, Iran's oil revenues rose eight-fold. In the space of a decade, government revenues rose thirty-fold.[21] In neighbouring Iraq, the rise was no less spectacular, going up fifty times between 1972 and 1980 from $575 million to $26 billion.[22]

It was all very well complaining about the "extent of dependence by western industrial countries upon oil as a source of energy," as one senior

American official did in a report prepared for the State Department in 1973.[23] But there was an inevitability about the transfer of power—and money—to the countries straddling the spine of Asia; and there was an inevitability too about the strengthening sinews of the Islamic world that followed as ambitions were magnified.

The most dramatic expression of these came with a renewed effort to dislodge the totemic symbol of outside influence in the Middle East as a whole: Israel. In October 1973, Syrian and Egyptian forces launched Operation Badr, named after the battle that had opened the way to securing control of the holy city of Mecca in the time of the Prophet Muḥammad.[24] The assault caught not only Israeli defences by surprise, but the superpowers as well. Hours before the attack began, a CIA report confidently stated that "we relate low probability to the possibility of the initiation of a military operation against Israel by the two armies"—despite the knowledge that Egyptian and Syrian troops were gathering near the border; they were doing so either as part of a training exercise, the report concluded, or "in fear [of] offensive steps [that might be taken] by Israel."[25] Although some have argued that the KGB appeared to have been better informed of the plans, the expulsion of Soviet observers en masse from Egypt a year earlier shows how strong the desire was to settle scores locally—rather than as part of the wider struggle for Cold War supremacy.[26] In fact, the USSR had been actively trying to calm tensions in the Middle East and seeking "military relaxation" in the region.[27]

The impact of the conflict shook the globe. In the U.S., the military-alert level was raised to DEFCON 3, indicating that the risk of a nuclear launch was considered to be imminent—and higher than at any point since the Cuban missile crisis of 1962. In the Soviet Union, the focus was on containing the situation. Pressure was put on Egypt's President Sadat behind the scenes to agree a ceasefire, while the Soviet Foreign Minister, Andrei Gromyko—a consummate political survivor—personally pressed President Nixon and his newly appointed Secretary of State, Henry Kissinger, to act jointly to prevent a "real conflagration" that might easily lead to war spreading.[28]

The real significance of the Yom Kippur War, so named because the attack began on the Jewish holy day, lay not in the attempts by Washington and Moscow to work together, nor even in the spectacular results which saw one of the great military reversals in history as Israel went from being within hours of extinction to shattering the invading forces and advancing on Damascus and Cairo. In fact, what was remarkable was the way the Arabic-speaking world acted together—as a caliphate in all but name. The ringleaders were the Saudis, the masters of Mecca, who not only talked openly about using oil as a weapon but actually did so. Production was cut back, which, combined with political uncertainty, led to price rises: costs per barrel tripled almost overnight.

As queues formed round petrol stations in the United States, Secretary of State Henry Kissinger complained about "political blackmail" that threatened the stability of the developed world. The shock was enough to prompt talk of developing new strategies that would reduce or even remove altogether dependence on Middle Eastern oil. On 7 November 1973 President Nixon gave a nationwide prime-time address on TV to announce a series of measures to address the uncomfortable fact that "in recent years, our energy demands have begun to exceed available supplies." As a result, the President opined solemnly, power plants were to be converted from the use of oil to the use of coal, "our most abundant resource." Fuel for aircraft was to be restricted with immediate effect; all vehicles owned by the federal government were to be prevented from travelling faster than 50mph, "except in emergencies." "To be sure that there is enough oil to go around for the entire winter," Nixon went on, "it will be essential for all of us to live and work in lower temperatures. We must ask everyone to lower the thermostat in your home by at least 6 degrees so that we can achieve a national daytime average of 68 degrees." If it is any consolation, the President added, "my doctor tells me . . . that you really are more healthy" living at this temperature.[29]

"Now, some of you may wonder," he went on, "whether we are turning back the clock to another age. Gas rationing, oil shortages, reduced speed limits—they all sound like a way of life we left behind with Glenn Miller and the war of the forties. Well, in fact, part of our current problem also stems from war—the war in the Middle East." What was needed in addition, Nixon announced, was "a national goal," an ambitious plan to enable the U.S. to meet its "own energy needs without depending on any foreign energy source." Christened "Project Independence," the proposal was to be inspired by "the spirit of Apollo" (a reference to the space programme) and the Manhattan Project that had given the west nuclear weapons—and the ability to destroy the world. The United States was a superpower; but it was also intensely aware of its weaknesses. It was time to find alternatives and thereby decrease dependence on—and the importance of—Middle Eastern oil.[30]

The volte face produced some unexpected side-effects. The general reduction of highway speed limits to 55mph, a step intended to slow consumption, led not only to a fall in consumption of over 150,000 oil barrels per day, but also to a major reduction in the number of traffic accidents nationwide. In December 1973 alone, statistics from the National Highway Traffic Safety Administration suggested a fall in fatality levels of more than 15 per cent as a direct result of lower speed limits.[31] Studies conducted in Utah, Illinois, Kentucky, California and elsewhere demonstrated clearly the positive effect that lowering speed limits had on saving lives.[32]

The importance of reducing energy usage prompted American architects to start designing buildings that placed greater emphasis on renewable energy sources.[33] It marked a watershed moment too in the development of the electrically powered car, encouraging extensive research into the stability and efficiency of a series of competing systems, including aqueous electrolyte, solid-state and molten-salt batteries which laid the basis for the hybrid cars that reached the mass market decades later.[34] Energy became a high-profile political issue, with the governor of Georgia—and soon to be presidential candidate—Jimmy Carter vocal in his calls for a "comprehensive long-range national energy policy."[35] Congress agreed to invest heavily in solar power, while increasingly sympathetic attitudes emerged towards the nuclear industry, which was perceived as technologically reliable and as an obvious solution to energy problems.[36]

Rising prices now justified prospecting for oil in areas where oil production had previously been commercially unviable or prohibitively expensive—such as the North Sea and the Gulf of Mexico. Offshore platforms led to rapid technological advances in drilling in deep-water locations, and to investment in infrastructure, pipelines, rigs and manpower.

But none of these were immediate solutions. They all required research and investment and above all time. Turning down the air-conditioning in federal buildings, allowing "appropriate relaxation of [government] employee dress standards" and greater use of car-sharing, as President Nixon ordered in a memorandum in June 1973, were all very well, but such measures were unlikely to resolve the problem.[37] In the meantime, the oil producers in the Middle East made hay. With uncertainty about supply spooking the market and the Muslim nations of OPEC using oil as what the King of Saudi Arabia called a "weapon in a battle," prices raced almost out of control. In the last six months of 1973, the posted price rose from $2.90 per barrel to $11.65.[38]

Even when the Yom Kippur War came to an end after three weeks of bitter fighting, things never went back to normal. Indeed, the redistribution of capital from the west simply accelerated: the collective revenues of the oil-producing countries rose from $23 billion in 1972 to $140 billion just five years later.[39] Cities boomed, transformed by cash that funded the building of roads, schools, hospitals and, in the case of Baghdad, a new airport, monumental architecture and even a stadium designed by Le Corbusier. So great was the change that one Japanese architectural journal likened the transformation of the Iraqi capital to that of Paris in the late nineteenth century under the direction of Baron Haussmann.[40] Naturally, this provided those in power with valuable political capital: regimes across the Persian Gulf could make grandiose statements that linked the new affluence with their personal power.

It was no coincidence, therefore, that as the streams of cash flowing into the heart of the world turned into a torrent, the ruling classes became increasingly demagogic in their outlook. The funds at their disposal were so great that, although they could be used to provide bread and circuses in the traditional method of autocratic control, there was simply too much to lose by giving others a share of the power. There was a marked slowdown in the development of pluralistic democracy and instead a tightening of control by small groups of individuals—whether related by blood to the ruler and the ruling family as in the Arabian peninsula and in Iran, or espousing common political causes as in Iraq and Syria. Dynastic rule became the norm at a time when the industrialised world was actively breaking down barriers to improve social mobility and loudly trumpeting the merits of liberal democracy.

The redistribution of capital to the oil-rich countries—most of which were located in or around the Persian Gulf—came at the expense of a chronic slump in the economies of the developed world that buckled under the weight of depression and stagnation as the coffers of OPEC states swelled. The Middle East was awash with money, just as Britain had been in its heyday in the eighteenth century when nabobs spent cash with abandon. The 1970s were a decade of opulence, when Iran Air placed orders for Concordes, and when the imports of luxury goods like stereos and televisions soared with the number of viewers rising from just over 2 million in 1970 to 15 million just four years later.[41] Lavish spending knew no boundaries.

As had been the case when early medieval Europe had been hungry for fine fabrics, spices and luxuries from the east, the question was whether there were other ways to pay for the highly prized necessities. A millennium earlier, slaves had been shipped to the Muslim countries to help fund the purchases heading in the other direction. Now too there was a darker side to being able to afford the black gold: the sale of arms and the sale of nuclear technology.

National governments lobbied aggressively to sell weapons through state-owned businesses, or by supporting corporations that were major employers and taxpayers. The Middle East as a whole accounted for more than 50 per cent of global arms imports in the mid-1970s. In Iran alone, defence expenditure multiplied nearly ten-fold in six years to 1978, with U.S. businesses taking orders worth almost $20 billion in the same period; total military expenditure in this period has been estimated at more than $54 billion—eventually rising to nearly 16 per cent of GNP.[42]

The Shah needed little convincing when it came to buying weapons. He was a man obsessed by planes, missiles and artillery, who on one occasion turned to the British ambassador to Iran to ask, "What is the sprocket horsepower of the Chieftain tank?"—a question the diplomat struggled to answer.[43] All-comers were keen to get a piece of the action, from the Soviet Union to the French, from the East Germans to the British. Armed with seemingly limitless resources, it was a question of which surface-to-air missile systems would be bought, which anti-tank devices would sell, which fighter planes would be acquired—and which middleman to trust to get deals done in a world that seemed difficult for the outsider to navigate successfully.

In Iraq, spending on military hardware reached nearly 40 per cent of the national budget, rising by more than six times between 1975 and 1980. Few worried about the consequences of what quickly developed into a regional arms race between Iran and Iraq, or whether the ever increasing resources spent on the weapons would dangerously raise the profile of the military in both countries. On the contrary, as long as there was demand—and the ability to pay—no hurdles were put in the way of countries across the Middle East and Persian Gulf acquiring large stockpiles of weapons. The more Chieftain tanks ordered by Iran, Mirage jets by Israel, MiG-21 and MiG-23 fighters by Syria, Soviet T-72 tanks by Iraq and U.S. F-5 jets by Saudi Arabia, the better for the economies of Britain, France, the USSR and the USA.[44]

The same approach was taken with the issue of nuclear power. In the early twenty-first century, the very notion of states like Iran developing any form of nuclear capability became the subject of international condemnation and disbelief. The question of nuclear power has become inextricably linked with the proliferation of weapons of mass destruction. Iraq's nuclear potential—and the inability of inspectors from the International Atomic Energy Agency to examine facilities, laboratories and centrifuges thought, reported or known to be in the country—were a fundamental part of the justification for the invasion in 2003 that toppled Saddam Hussein.

Analogous question marks over Iran's apparent determination to develop nuclear capability and its ability to process radioactive materials have provoked similar impulses. "We can't let politics and mythology cloud reality," Secretary of State John Kerry said in the winter of 2013. "[President Obama] has been willing and made it clear that he is prepared to use force with respect to Iran's weapons, and he has deployed the forces and the weapons necessary to achieve that goal if it has to be achieved."[45] The very idea of wanting to develop nuclear energy has been seen as a danger to regional and global security. The Iranians, said Vice-President Dick Cheney in 2005, "are already sitting on an awful lot of oil and gas. Nobody can figure [out] why they need nuclear [power] as well to generate energy." "For a major oil producer such as Iran," agreed Henry Kissinger, "nuclear energy is a wasteful use of resources."[46]

Decades earlier, both men saw things very differently—as did successive White House administrations in the post-war period. In fact, the acquisition of nuclear resources had been actively encouraged by the United States in a programme whose name and aims today seem almost comical: Atoms for Peace. Conceived by the Eisenhower administration, this was a plan designed to allow the United States to participate in "an international atomic pool," and ultimately involved friendly governments being given access to 40,000 kilograms of Uranium-235 for non-military research.[47]

For three decades, sharing nuclear technology, components and materials was a fundamental part of U.S. foreign policy—a straight incentive for co-operation and support against the Soviet bloc. With the USSR becoming a force to be reckoned with in Asia and the Persian Gulf, the United States felt keenly the need to reinforce its support for the Shah, who seemed to be the only reliable leader in the region—even though there were others who did not think the same way: one prominent Saudi warned the U.S. ambassador to Riyadh that the Shah was "a megalomaniac [and] highly unstable." If Washington did not understand this, he added, "there must be something wrong with [American] powers of observation."[48]

Although there were some sceptics who cautioned against giving the Iranian ruler "everything he wants," the extension of Soviet power in the region convinced others—notably Kissinger—that support for the Shah should be reinforced. When the latter visited Washington in the mid-1970s, therefore, the memorandum Kissinger prepared for the President drew attention to the importance of visible U.S. support for the Shah, referring to him as "a man of extraordinary ability and knowledge," though such praise glossed over the chronic levels of corruption and inefficiency being reached in Iran.[49]

So eager was the United States to provide support for plans to destabilise neighbouring Iraq that it helped foment trouble with the Kurds. This had a tragic outcome, after a rebellion went badly wrong and heavy reprisals were taken against the Kurdish minority in the north of the country. Having encouraged revolt, the U.S. now stood back and watched as Iran made overtures and soon reached a settlement with Iraq over long-standing territorial boundary issues, sacrificing the Kurds in the process.[50] "Even in the context of covert action, ours was a cynical enterprise," concluded the Pike Committee that looked into clandestine American diplomacy in the 1970s.[51] Perhaps not surprisingly, having declared that there was insufficient space in the first volume of his memoirs to discuss this event, Kissinger did not make good on his promise to deal with it in his second.[52]

In other respects, the Shah was also planning for the future. He realised that the oil bonanza of the early 1970s would not last for ever and that oil reserves would eventually be depleted—which would leave Iran's own energy needs uncertain. Notwithstanding thermostats being turned down in the United States, demand for oil continued to rise, leaving Iran—and other oil-rich countries—with deep pockets to prepare for the long term. Nuclear power, concluded a report specially commissioned by the Shah, was "the most economic source of power" that would secure Iran's needs. Based on the twin assumptions that oil prices would only rise and that the costs of building and maintaining nuclear power stations would reduce, developing the nuclear industry seemed an obvious step to take—especially since this prestigious project would show how modernised Iran had become.[53] The Shah took personal charge, instructing Dr. Akbar Etemad of the new Atomic Energy Organization of Iran to report to him directly.[54]

The first port of call was the Americans. In 1974, an initial agreement was reached by which the United States agreed to sell two reactors, as well as enriched uranium, to Iran. The scope of the arrangement was expanded further in 1975, when a $15 billion trade deal was agreed between the two countries, which included provision for Iran to purchase eight reactors from the United States at a fixed price of $6.4 billion.[55] The following year, President Ford approved a deal that allowed Iran to buy and operate a U.S.-built system that included a reprocessing facility that could extract plutonium from nuclear reactor fuel, and therefore enable Teheran to operate a "nuclear fuel cycle." President Ford's Chief of Staff had no hesitation in approving this sale: in the 1970s, Dick Cheney did not find it difficult to "figure out" what Iran's motivations were.

The Shah's acquisitions from the United States were part of an ambitious and much wider plan that drew in technology, expertise and raw materials from other western countries. Work began on two pressurised water reactors near Bushihr on the Gulf in 1975 after contracts had been signed with West Germany's Kraftwerk Union AG, with the latter also committing to provide an initial fuel load and reloadings as necessary for ten years. Further letters of intent were signed with Kraftwerk as well as with Brown Boveri and with Framatome of France for a further eight reactors, including terms for Iran to be supplied with enriched uranium. Stand-alone agreements were also reached for uranium to be reprocessed in France, returned to Teheran for enrichment and then either reused domestically—or resold to a third party of Iran's choosing.[56]

Even though Iran was a signatory of the Nuclear Non-Proliferation Treaty of 1968, there was regular chatter in the intelligence community about the development of a clandestine nuclear weapons programme—hardly a surprise given that on occasion the Shah would declare that Iran would develop weapons capability "without a doubt, and sooner than one would think."[57] One CIA report written in 1974 assessing proliferation generally concluded that while Iran was at an early stage of development, it was likely that the Shah would achieve this goal in the mid-1980s—"if he is alive."[58]

Other countries too were looking to invest in nuclear facilities with civilian uses, while at the same time developing weapons capability. In the 1970s, Iraq spent aggressively under the direction of Saddam Hussein with the specific aim of building a nuclear bomb.[59] Saddam was ambitious, setting a "production target of six bombs a year" according to Dr. Khidir Hamza, who was placed in charge of the programme in the 1980s. Development on this scale would have given Iraq a larger arsenal than China within two decades.

No expense was spared. Iraqi scientists and engineers were sent abroad in their droves for training, above all to France and Italy, while at home everything possible was done to use the civilian programme to obtain the technologies, skills and infrastructure required to create a nuclear arsenal.[60]

The Iraqis were determined in their approach. Having already acquired a two-megawatt research reactor from the Soviet Union that went critical in 1967, attention turned to obtaining a gas graphite reactor and a reprocessing facility for the plutonium that would be produced as a result. When requests to France were rebuffed, feelers went out to Canada in the hope of buying a reactor similar to the one that had enabled India to test a nuclear device in 1974. This prompted the French to recommence negotiations, resulting in an agreement to build an Osiris research reactor and a smaller research reactor, both of which would be powered by weapons-grade uranium. Further materials essential for dual use were bought from Italy, including hot cells as well as a separation and handling facility capable of extracting plutonium from irradiated uranium, with a capacity of producing eight kilograms a year.[61]

Few had doubts that there was more to this than met the eye and that energy was not the only motivation. The Israelis in particular monitored developments with considerable concern, gathering detailed intelligence about the militarisation of their neighbours—focusing on the Tammuz facility near Baghdad at al-Tuwaitha, better known as the Osirak plant. Israel also invested heavily in its own nuclear weapons programme, as well as in a missile system modified from French designs that could deliver warheads with a range of just over 200 miles.[62] By the time of the Yom Kippur War of 1973, it was thought that Israel had built up an arsenal of thirteen nuclear devices.[63]

The west turned a blind eye as and when needed. In Iraq, for example, the British concluded in the early 1970s that "although repressive and singularly unattractive, the present Government seems to be well in control." It was a regime that was stable and, as such, one the British could do business with.[64] Likewise, Pakistan's activity—building facilities deep underground in the 1970s to enable covert testing and ultimately a successful detonation—went unchecked. Five horizontal tunnels were dug deep into a mountain in the Ras Koh range in Balochistan, each designed to withstand a twenty-kiloton detonation.[65] As Pakistani scientists noted ruefully, "the Western world was sure that an underdeveloped country like Pakistan could never master this technology," and yet at the same time western countries made "hectic and persistent efforts to sell everything to us . . . they literally begged us to buy their equipment."[66] As it was, it was not hard to see how stern talk about proliferation from countries like the United States, Britain and France, which refused to be subject to the inspections and rules of the International Atomic Energy Agency, grated with those that did and had to conduct their research in secret; but the real hypocrisy, in the cold light of day, lay in the enthusiasm with which the developed world rushed to earn hard cash or gain access to cheap oil.

There were half-hearted attempts to curtail the spread of nuclear materials. In 1976, Kissinger suggested that Pakistan should wind down its reprocessing project and rely instead on a U.S.-supplied facility being built in Iran that was part of a scheme devised by none other than Dick Cheney, for the plant in Iran to serve as a hub for energy needs across the region. When the President of Pakistan turned down this offer, the United States threatened to cut off the country's aid package.[67]

Even Kissinger began to reconsider the wisdom of enabling foreign governments to have access to the technologies and designs underpinning nuclear power. "I am frankly getting tired of the Iran deal [to build nuclear reactors]," he said at a State Department meeting in 1976, despite the central role he had played in brokering it. "I have endorsed it, but in any region you look at, it is a fraud . . . we are the only country which is fanatical and unrealistic enough to do things which are contrary to our national interests."[68]

Sentiments like these hinted at a growing sense in Washington that the United States was boxed in and was faced with limited options. This was articulated clearly by members of the National Security Council in the late 1970s, who later stated that "The United States had no visible strategic alternative to the close relationship with Iran," having burnt policy bridges elsewhere.[69] Although criticism of the Shah's regime, and particularly the brutal methods of the Savak, rose in the western media, the U.S. government continued to give loud and consistent support. President Carter flew in to Teheran on New Year's Eve in 1977 and was guest of honour at a dinner to mark the end of the year. "Iran," said the President, "is an island of stability in one of the more troubled areas of the world." This was because of the "great leadership of the Shah." The success of the country owed much to "Your Majesty and your leadership and to the respect and admiration and the love which your people give you."[70]

This was not so much rose-tinted glasses as a denial of reality, for storm clouds were gathering and plain for all to see. In Iran, demographic growth, rapid urbanisation and lavish overspending by a repressive regime produced a toxic cocktail. Endemic corruption did not help—with hundreds of millions of dollars taken in "commission" by the royal family and those close to the ruling regime, just for each reactor.[71] By the late 1970s, the situation in Teheran was poisonous as crowds took to the streets in growing numbers to protest about the lack of social justice—and about the rising cost of living on the back of plunging oil prices as global supplies began to exceed demand.

Growing dissent played into the hands of Ayatollah Khomeini, by now exiled in Paris after being removed from Iraq as part of the deal struck with the Shah in 1975. Khomeini—whose elder son was probably murdered by the Savak in 1977—seized control of the situation, providing a vision that at once diagnosed the ills in Iran and promised to cure them. He was a brilliant communicator, able to capture the mood just as Mossadegh had done three decades earlier. In a move that appealed to left-wing revolutionaries, Islamic hardliners and almost all those who were outside the golden loop of gilded rewards, Khomeini declared that the time had come for the Shah to step aside. The beneficiaries of good leadership should be the Iranian public and Islam—and not the Shah.

To allay fears that Iran would become a religious state, Khomeini promised that clerics, preachers and zealots would not rule the country directly, but would provide guidance. He set out four tenets that underpinned the future: the use of Islamic law; the eradication of corruption; the striking out of unjust laws; and the end of foreign intervention in Iran's affairs. It was not a catchy manifesto—but it was an effective one that spoke to multiple constituencies and encapsulated the problems and difficulties not only of Iran but of the Islamic world as a whole. The argument that wealth was being diverted into the hands of the few at the expense of the many was not just powerful but incontrovertible. In the 1970s, more than 40 per cent of the country's population were undernourished, according to World Health Organisation targets; inequality was rife, with the rich getting richer, and the position of the poor showing little improvement, if any.[72] It was up to the Iranian people to demonstrate, Khomeini declared; appeal to the soldiers "even if they fire on you and kill you." Let tens of thousands of us die as brothers. But show "that blood is more powerful than the sword."[73]

As the situation became more and more tense, the Shah—on whom so much hope had been pinned by the United States—went to Teheran airport, where he gave a brief statement to say "I am feeling tired and need a rest," before flying out of the country for the last time.[74] Whether he could have prevented what happened next is a matter of speculation. What is clearer is how some European leaders reacted to the situation. In what President Carter called "one of the worst days of my diplomatic life," Chancellor Schmidt became "personally abusive" during discussions about the Middle East, alleging that "American interference in [this region] . . . had caused problems with oil all over the world."[75]

The United States had pursued a policy of complete denial and read the runes far too late. At the start of 1979, Washington sent General Robert Huyser, commander-in-chief of U.S. European command, to Teheran to demonstrate American support for the Shah and specifically to impress on the army that the United States continued to back the regime. It did not take Huyser long to realise that the writing was on the wall—and that his life was potentially in danger. He saw enough to realise that the days of the Shah were over, and that Khomeini was unstoppable.[76]

American policy lay in tatters. Time, effort and resources had been poured into Iran as well as into neighbouring countries since the Second World War. Leaders had been courted and indulged, while those who refused to play along had been deposed or replaced. The methods used to control the interlocking parts of Asia had failed spectacularly. The western nations, to quote Sir Anthony Parsons, British ambassador to Teheran at the time, "were looking down the right telescope . . . but [we were] focused at the wrong target."[77] Worse, anti-American rhetoric now united almost all the countries of this region. Syria and Iraq looked towards the USSR; India was closer to Moscow than it was to Washington, while Pakistan was willing to take U.S. support as and when it suited. Iran was a crucial piece in the puzzle, and now it too looked in danger of falling. It seemed like the end of an era, as Khomeini noted in a speech late in 1979: "All the problems of the east stem from those foreigners from the west, and from America at the moment," he said. "All our problems come from America."[78]

The fall of the Shah prompted panic in Washington—and hope in Moscow. The collapse of Iran seemed to be a turning point that offered opportunities. It was almost comical how badly the west had misjudged the situation not only in Iran but elsewhere too—such as in Afghanistan, where the U.S. embassy in Kabul reported in 1978 that relations were excellent.[79] Indeed, to optimistic American eyes, Afghanistan looked like a major success story, just as Iran had done: the number of schools had multiplied ten-fold since 1950, with many more students turning to technical disciplines like medicine, law and science; women's education also blossomed, as the number of girls passing through primary education rose sharply. Rumours circulated that President Dāwud, who had seized power in 1973, had been recruited by the CIA and that the progressive agendas he pursued were ideas planted by the Americans. Although the gossip was not true, the fact that it required investigation by diplomats in Washington and in Moscow shows just how intense were the pressures for the two superpowers to compete—and to play the latest version of the Great Game in Asia.[80]

How things settled down after a short period of turbulence was now crucial. To all intents and purposes, it looked as though the United States was badly out of position. The bet it had placed on the Shah and on Iran looked lost; there were others across the old Silk Roads that were open to offers. With Iran going through revolution and Iraq seemingly wedded to a Soviet suitor, the United States had to think carefully what its next move might be. It proved to be a disaster.

24

The Road to Catastrophe

The revolution in Iran brought the American house of cards across the region as a whole tumbling down. The signs pointing to instability had been there for some time. The corruption of the Shah's regime, combined with economic stagnation, political paralysis and police brutality made for a poisonous combination—one that played into the hands of outspoken critics whose promises of reform fell on fertile ground.

Those who were worried about how things were moving in Iran were all the more jittery because of the signs that the USSR was actively plotting to take advantage of the situation. Soviet activity continued even after the KGB had lost its main asset in Iran, General Ahmad Mogharebi, regarded by Moscow as "Russia's best agent" with contacts across all sections of the elite in Iran. He was arrested in September 1977 by the Savak, which had become suspicious of his regular meetings with his KGB handlers.[1] This served to spur an intensification of activity by the Soviets.

There was speculation that unusually large volumes of trading in Iranian rials on the Swiss currency markets in early 1978 were the result of Soviet agents being ordered to finance supporters in Iran; the noticeably high quality of *Navid*, the newsletter distributed by the left-wing Tudeh party, convinced some that it was being printed not just with Soviet help, but in the Soviet embassy in Teheran. New camps set up outside the country to train Iranian dissidents (among others) in guerrilla warfare and Marxist doctrine were an ominous sign that Moscow was preparing to fill any void in the event of the fall of the Shah.[2] This was part of a wider engagement with a region that seemed about to go through a period of change. Additional support was therefore also given to President Assad in Syria, even though the KGB considered him "a petit-bourgeois chauvinist egomaniac."[3]

Some who were watching the situation unfold closely were convinced that doom lay around the corner. By the end of 1978, William Sullivan, the U.S. ambassador in Teheran, dispatched a cable to Washington entitled "Thinking the Unthinkable," urging that contingency plans had to be put in place immediately. This was ignored—as was Sullivan's recommendation that "we attempt to structure a *modus vivendi* between the military and religious [leaders]" at the first opportunity. He meant that the United States should try to open channels of communication with Khomeini, before he took power rather than afterwards.[4] Loud voices in the White House, however, continued in the belief that the United States could control the situation, maintaining support for the Shah and backing a proposal made at the end of January 1979 by the Prime Minister, Shapur Bakhtiar, that Ayatollah Khomeini should be arrested if he flew into Iran.[5]

The blinkered futility of this thinking became apparent within a matter of days. On 1 February 1979, Ayatollah Khomeini touched down in Teheran fourteen years after being forced into exile. Enormous crowds gathered to greet him at the airport, following him as he made his way first to the Cemetery of Martyrs, twelve miles south of Teheran, where some 250,000 supporters were waiting. "I will strike with my fists at the mouths of this government," he roared defiantly. "From now on it is I who will name the government." Reporting this speech, the BBC estimated that 5 million people lined the streets as he made his way into the capital.[6]

Things moved quickly as Khomeini's supporters took control of the country. On 11 February, the U.S. embassy went into lock-down, as Ambassador Sullivan cabled home: "Army surrenders. Khomeini wins. Destroying all classified." Sensitive material was still being shredded three days later when militants stormed the embassy compound—although order was soon restored by Khomeini's lieutenants.[7] On 16 February, Ambassador Sullivan met with Mahdī Bāzargān, the newly appointed Prime Minister, and told him that the United States had no interest in intervening in Iran's domestic affairs.[8] Less than a week later, the United States formally recognised the new government—which, following a national referendum, declared on 1 April that the country was to be known as the "Islamic Republic of Iran."

A second referendum held at the end of the year endorsed a new constitution, which stated that henceforward "all civil, penal, financial, economic, administrative, cultural, military, political and other laws and regulations in the country [are] to be based on 'Islamic' criteria."[9]

The United States had bet heavily on Iran and on the Shah for decades. It now had to pay a heavy price for its gamble going wrong. The revolution sent shockwaves round the world, causing oil prices almost to triple. The effect on the oil-hungry economies of the developed world was disastrous as inflation threatened to gallop out of control. As panic set in, there were fears of the crisis spilling over: by the end of June alarming numbers of service stations across the United States remained closed due to a lack of supply. President Carter's approval ratings fell to the all but unknown level of 28 per cent—around the same level as Nixon at the nadir of the Watergate scandal.[10] With the President's re-election campaign about to get into gear, it seemed that regime change in Teheran might be a significant factor in the forthcoming presidential election.

It was not just the rising price of oil that threatened to derail the western economies. So too did the mass cancellation of orders and the immediate nationalisation of the industry. British Petroleum (BP), the heir of the original Knox D'Arcy concession, was forced into a major reorganisation (and share sale) after oilfields that accounted for 40 per cent of its global production disappeared at a stroke. Then there were the contracts to build steel mills, upgrade airport terminals and develop ports that were scrapped overnight, and the arms contracts that were annulled and torn up. In 1979, Khomeini cancelled $9 billion of purchases from the United States, which left manufacturers with a painful hole in their accounts and sizeable amounts of stock to try to sell into other markets less keen to militarise than the Shah had been.[11]

As it was, Iran's turgid economy meant that the nuclear programme had already been slowed down before the Revolution; after it, it was cancelled altogether. The cost of the loss of business to companies like Creusot-Loire, Westinghouse Electric Corporation and Kraftwerk Union—based in France, the United States and West Germany respectively—was in the region of $330 billion.[12] Some were admirably stoic in the face of adversity. "We must never forget how well we did out of the Shah's regime," wrote the diplomat Sir Anthony Parsons, veteran of the Middle East and British ambassador to Teheran at the time of Khomeini's return. "British business and industry made an enormous amount of money out of Iran."[13] He did not say as much, but it was clear that the good times had come to an end; it was better to celebrate what the past had yielded than to bemoan what the future would withhold.

For the United States, however, the stakes went beyond the economic and political fall-out at home. It was some consolation that Khomeini and his fellow clerics had little time for the atheist politics of the Soviet Union, and little sympathy with—or affinity for—left-wing groups in Iran.[14] But even though the fall of the Shah did not lead to the USSR gaining ground, the United States was nevertheless pushed decisively on to the defensive; a series of footholds that had previously been secure became precarious or lost altogether.

After Khomeini had taken power, he immediately shut down the U.S. intelligence facilities located in Iran that served as early-warning systems for Soviet nuclear attacks, and as listening posts monitoring missile-launch tests in Central Asia. This deprived the United States of a vital means of gathering information on its rival at a time when doing so had assumed an added importance in the wake of intensive talks between the USA and USSR to limit the number of strategic ballistic missile launchers at existing levels. The closure of stations that played an important role in the verification process therefore threatened to compromise the series of strategic arms agreements that had taken years to negotiate, as well as to derail ongoing highly sensitive discussions.

It would take at least five years, the Director of the CIA, Admiral Stansfield Turner, told the Senate intelligence committee in early 1979, to restore the capability for monitoring Soviet missile tests and developments.[15] A "real gap" had emerged in U.S. intelligence collection as a result of events in Iran, noted Robert Gates, the CIA's national intelligence officer for the USSR (and later Director of the agency, as well as Secretary of Defense). "Exceptionally sensitive" efforts were therefore made to build new alliances elsewhere that would fill the void. These included high-level discussions with the Chinese leadership about building replacement facilities in western China, which led to a secret visit by Admiral Turner and Gates to Beijing in the winter of 1980–81, a trip that was only revealed to have taken place many years later (albeit with precious little detail).[16] Sites were built at Qitai and Korla in Xinjiang by the Office of Sigint (Signals Intelligence) Operations, with the new facilities operated by the Technical Department of the General Staff of the People's Liberation Army of China working closely with U.S. advisers and technicians.[17] Close co-operation between United States and Chinese military and intelligence was a by-product of the fall of the Shah.

The Iranian Revolution meanwhile may not have helped the USSR politically, but it certainly did militarily. Despite the efforts in the American embassy in Teheran to shred important documents, the speed and strength of the wave of change that had transformed the country led to some damaging losses. The Shah had bought a fleet of F-14 Tomcat fighter aircraft, along with a state-of-the-art Phoenix air-to-air missile system, Hawk surface-to-air missiles and a range of hi-tech anti-tank weapons. The Soviets were able to acquire invaluable close-up visual images, and in some cases instruction manuals for this military hardware as well. This was not just an embarrassing loss; it had potentially serious implications for U.S. national security as well as for that of America's allies.[18]

The sense of a familiar world rapidly collapsing now swept through Washington—for it was not just Iran where things suddenly looked very different. The United States had been keeping a watchful eye on the situation in Afghanistan, whose strategic importance rose further in the wake of Khomeini's Revolution. In the spring of 1979, for example, a CIA team conducted a survey to assess the country as a possible replacement location for the intelligence sites lost in Iran.[19] The problem was that the situation in Afghanistan was fast moving, and looked increasingly likely to mirror events in Iran.

The turbulence had begun when the chess-loving King Zahir Shah was deposed by his nephew Muḥammad Dāwud, who installed himself as President in his place in 1973. Then five years later Dāwud himself was ousted. His downfall did not come as a great surprise, given the increasing brutality of his regime, which saw political prisoners being routinely executed without trial, lying face down in the grounds of the notorious and chronically overcrowded Pul-i Charkhi prison just outside Kabul.[20]

The Communist hardliners who took Dāwud's place proved to be equally ruthless—and relentlessly progressive as they set out an ambitious agenda to modernise the country. It was time, they declared, to improve literacy levels dramatically, to break the "feudal" structure of the tribal system, to end ethnic discrimination, and to deliver rights for women, including educational equality, job security and access to healthcare.[21] Efforts to introduce comprehensive changes provoked a furious response that was especially strong among Muslim clerics; just as it did in the early twenty-first century, attempts to reform succeeded only in uniting traditionalists, landlords, tribal leaders and mullahs who made common cause to protect their own interests.

Opposition quickly became vocal and dangerous. The first major uprising took place in March 1979 in Herat, in the west of the country, where those proclaiming national independence, a return to tradition and the rejection of outside influence took heart from events across the border in Iran. Rioters turned on any and every target—including Soviet residents in the city, who were butchered by a rampaging mob.[22] Unrest soon spread to other cities, including Jalalabad, where Afghan military units refused to oppose the resistance, and instead turned on and killed their Soviet advisers.[23]

The USSR responded to these events cautiously, with the ageing Politburo concluding that support should be given to the troublesome and trigger-happy Afghan leadership, some of whom had long-standing personal connections with the Soviet Union, to help them face down the unrest that had spread to Kabul too. A series of measures were taken to boost the regime, led by the President, Nur Muḥammad Taraki, who was well regarded by Moscow and was thought of by some as "Afghanistan's Maxim Gorky" for his writings on "scientific socialist themes"—high praise indeed.[24] Generous shipments of grain and food were dispatched across the border, while interest payments for outstanding loans were waived. To help swell government coffers, the Soviets also offered to pay more than double what they had paid for Afghan gas for the previous decade.[25] Although requests for chemical weapons and poison gas were turned down, Moscow did provide military support, dispatching 140 artillery pieces, 48,000 guns and nearly 1,000 grenade launchers.[26]

This was all noted in Washington, where the implications of the "gradual but unmistakable" rise in Soviet involvement in Afghanistan were carefully considered. If the USSR were to provide direct military assistance to Taraki and send in troops, observed one high-level report, there would be consequences not only in Afghanistan itself but across the spine of Asia in Iran, Pakistan and China—indeed beyond.[27] The uncertainty of what would happen next was made clear with the murder of the U.S. ambassador to Kabul in February 1979. Just days after Khomeini had returned home, Ambassador Adolph Dubs's armoured vehicle was car-jacked in broad daylight on the streets of the Afghan capital, at what appeared to be a police checkpoint. He was taken to the Kabul Hotel (now the luxury Kabul Serena Hotel), where he was held hostage for a few hours before being killed during a botched rescue operation.[28]

Although it was unclear who had been behind the ambassador's kidnapping or what the motives were, it was enough to encourage the U.S. to engage more directly with what was going on in the country. Aid to Afghanistan was immediately cut, and support given to the anti-Communists and others who opposed the new government.[29] It marked the start of a long period during which the United States willingly and actively sought to cooperate with the Islamists, whose interests in resisting the left-wing agenda were naturally aligned with those of the United States. It took decades for the price of this deal to become apparent.

Behind this new approach were fears that Afghanistan might fall to the Soviets, who by the second half of 1979 appeared to be preparing for military intervention. The question of the USSR's intentions rose to the top of the agenda in U.S. intelligence briefings and became the subject of a rash of position papers outlining the latest developments—although this did not mean there was any insight into what was going on.[30] One report presented to the National Security Council with the title "What Are the Soviets Doing in Afghanistan?" provided a response that could not be faulted for its candour: "Simply, we don't know."[31] While unpicking Moscow's thinking was difficult, it was obvious that the fall of the Shah meant that the United States had lost its principal ally in the region; it looked worryingly as if a domino effect was about to make the position even worse.

The Soviets were worried about precisely the same thing. Events in Iran had produced no benefit, and in fact were assessed by Moscow as being detrimental to the USSR's interests as Khomeini's seizure of power had reduced opportunities, rather than opened them up. Contingency plans were therefore drawn up by the Soviet military for a major deployment in the event that it became necessary to reinforce what General Secretary Leonid Brezhnev called "the Government of the friendly nation of Afghanistan." The United States monitored troop movements to the north of both the Iranian and Afghan borders, recording the dispatch of a unit of Spetsnaz special forces to Kabul, alongside a battalion of paratroopers that the CIA concluded had been deployed to secure Bagram airbase, the main entry point for Soviet supplies.[32]

At this critical stage, however, the future of Afghanistan suddenly came into play. In September 1979, a power struggle saw the removal of Nur Muḥammad Taraki by Hafizullah Amin, a man who was as ambitious as he was hard to read. He had been explicitly written off as a viable leader in editorials that had appeared in *Pravda*, the official mouthpiece that reflected the thinking of the Politburo in the USSR.[33] He was now denounced in Moscow as an enemy of the revolution, a man who sought to manipulate tribal rivalries for his own ends, and "a spy for American imperialism."[34] The Soviets were also concerned about rumours that Amin had been recruited by the CIA—gossip that had been spread energetically by his enemies in Afghanistan too.[35] Records of Politburo meetings show that the leadership in Moscow was intensely worried about the reorientation of Amin towards the United States, and about the latter's eagerness to support a friendly government in Kabul.[36]

The Soviets were becoming more and more concerned about the situation. Amin's frequent meetings with the acting head of the U.S. mission in Afghanistan before his putsch seemed to indicate that Washington was repositioning itself after the catastrophic failure of its policies in Iran. When Amin became increasingly aggressive in his dealings with the Soviets in Kabul while making a series of overtures to the United States immediately after taking power, the call came for action.[37]

If the USSR did not stand firm and support its allies now, the logic went, it would lose out not only in Afghanistan but in the region as a whole. General Valentin Varennikov later recalled that senior officers "were concerned that if the United States were pushed out of Iran, they would relocate their bases to Pakistan and seize Afghanistan."[38] Developments elsewhere also concerned the Soviet leadership and gave the impression that the USSR was being pushed firmly onto the back foot. The Politburo discussed the way Washington and Beijing had improved relations in the late 1970s, noting that here too Moscow was falling behind.[39]

The United States was trying to create a "new Great Ottoman Empire" spanning Central Asia, senior Communist party officials told Brezhnev in December 1979; these fears were magnified by the absence of a comprehensive air-defence system across the USSR's southern frontier. This meant that America could point a dagger at the heart of the Soviet Union.[40] As Brezhnev put it soon afterwards in an interview in *Pravda*, Afghanistan's instability represented a "very major threat to the security of the Soviet state."[41] The sense of having to do something was palpable.

Two days after the meeting between Brezhnev and leading officials, the order was given to devise an invasion plan based on an initial deployment of 75,000–80,000 troops. The Chief of the General Staff, General Nikolai Ogarkov, a hard-headed officer of the old school, reacted angrily. An engineer by training, Ogarkov argued that this force would be far too small to hold communication routes successfully and secure key points across the country.[42] He was overruled by the Defence Minister, Dmitri Ustinov, a consummate political survivor prone to making ostentatious statements about the brilliance of the Soviet armed forces, whose fighting ability, he said, meant it could achieve "the accomplishment of any tasks set by the party and the people."[43]

Whether he actually believed this is one thing; what mattered now was that he and his generation of Second World War veterans, whose grasp on the changing world around them was fading fast, were sure that the Americans were planning to supplant the USSR. Ustinov is reported to have asked late in 1979: "If [they can] do all these preparations under our noses, why should we hunker down, play cautious and lose Afghanistan?"[44] At a Politburo meeting on 12 December, Ustinov, alongside a clutch of grey old men like Leonid Brezhnev, Andrei Gromyko, Yuri Andropov and Konstantin Chernenko, gave the go-ahead for a full-blown deployment of troops in Afghanistan.[45] It had not been a simple decision to take, Brezhnev was quoted as saying in *Pravda* a few weeks later.[46]

A fortnight after the meeting, on Christmas Eve 1979, Soviet forces began to stream over the border as part of Operation Storm 333. This was not an invasion, Ustinov declared to army commanders leading troops across the border, in a line that was to be repeated again and again by Soviet diplomats and politicians over the course of the next decade; rather, it was an attempt to restore stability at a time when the "political and military situation in the Middle East" was in turmoil, and after requests by the government in Kabul "to provide international help to the friendly Afghan people."[47]

From Washington's point of view, the timing could not have been worse. For all the Soviet fears about U.S. expansion into Afghanistan, the full extent of American weakness across the region was becoming painfully clear. After flying out of Teheran at the start of 1979, the Shah had moved from one country to another in search of a permanent home. By the autumn, President Carter was being encouraged by senior members of his administration to allow a dying man who had been a staunch friend to the United States into the country to receive medical treatment. As this was being discussed, Khomeini's new Foreign Minister told the President's advisers point-blank that "you are opening Pandora's box with this."[48] White House records show that Carter was aware of how high the stakes were if he allowed the Shah entry to the United States. "What are you guys going to advise me to do if [the Iranians] overrun our embassy and take our people hostage?" the President asked. He did not receive a reply.[49]

On 4 November, two weeks after the Shah had checked into the Cornell Medical Center in New York, militant Iranian students overwhelmed the security guards at the U.S. embassy in Teheran and seized control of the embassy compound, taking around sixty diplomatic staff hostage. Although the initial aim seems to have been to make a short, sharp protest about the decision to admit the Shah to the United States, things escalated rapidly.[50] On 5 November, Ayatollah Khomeini commented on the situation at the embassy. He did not mince his words, let alone appeal for calm. The embassies of Teheran, he declared, were breeding grounds for "underground plots [that] are being hatched" to bring down the Islamic Republic of Iran. The chief orchestrator of these plots, he went on, was "the great Satan America." With that, he called on the United States to hand over "the traitor" so that he could face justice.[51]

Initial U.S. efforts to defuse the situation ranged from the inept to the shambolic. One envoy, carrying a personal appeal from the President to Khomeini, was flatly denied an audience with the ayatollah and was unable to deliver his letter; it emerged that another envoy had been authorised to open discussions with the Palestinian Liberation Organization (PLO), whose members had been behind terror attacks such as the massacre at the Munich Olympic Games and whose primary aim was the establishment of a Palestinian state at the expense of Israel. Even more embarrassing than the disclosure that the United States was trying to use the PLO as a conduit to reach the Iranians was the news that the Iranians themselves refused to let the PLO play a mediating role in the crisis.[52]

President Carter then resolved to take more decisive action that would not only unlock the hostage situation but would also serve as a statement of intent that although the Shah had fallen, the United States was a force to be reckoned with in the centre of Asia. On 12 November 1979, in an attempt to put Khomeini's regime under financial pressure, he announced an embargo on Iranian oil. "No one," he declared as he announced the ban on imports, "should underestimate the resolve of the American government and the American people."[53] Two days later, the President went further still, issuing an executive order to freeze $12 billion of Iran's assets. This decisive action played well domestically, with Carter experiencing what was described as the largest increase in presidential popularity since the Gallup poll was invented.[54]

The sabre-rattling had little effect, however. The oil embargo was dismissed by Teheran as irrelevant. "The world needs oil," said Ayatollah Khomeini in a speech a week after Carter's announcement. "The world does not need America. Other countries will turn to those of us who have oil, and not to you."[55] The embargo was anyway not easy to enforce from a logistical point of view given that Iranian oil often passed through third parties and could still reach the U.S. That the boycott put pressure on supply inevitably threatened to drive oil prices higher—which played into the hands of the Iranian regime by boosting its revenues.[56]

The seizure of assets spooked many in the Arab-speaking world, who were concerned about the precedent set by U.S. action. The stand-off exacerbated political disagreements with countries such as Saudi Arabia, which did not see eye to eye with Washington over policy in the Middle East, particularly in relation to Israel.[57] As a CIA report prepared a few weeks after the introduction of the embargo concluded, "our current economic pressures are unlikely to have any positive effect; [in fact] their impact may be negative."[58]

Moreover, many western countries were reluctant to be drawn into the escalation of a crisis with Teheran. "It soon became apparent," Carter wrote, "that even our closest allies in Europe were not going to expose themselves to potential oil boycotts or endanger their diplomatic arrangements for the sake of American hostages." The only way to concentrate minds was to make "the direct threat of further moves by the United States."[59] Carter's Secretary of Defense, Cyrus Vance, was therefore sent on a tour of western Europe with the message that if sanctions were not imposed on Iran, the United States would take unilateral action, including mining the Persian Gulf if necessary.[60] This would naturally have an impact on oil prices—and therefore on developed economies. In order to put pressure on Teheran, Washington had to threaten its own supporters.

It was against this tense backdrop of desperate, counter-productive and badly thought through measures to force a settlement in Iran that news was received that Soviet columns were marching south into Afghanistan. U.S. policymakers were taken completely by surprise. Four days before the invasion, President Carter and his advisers had been contemplating plans to seize Iran's offshore islands, and to look at military and covert operations to overthrow Khomeini. An ominous situation had turned critical.[61]

Already facing a disastrous hostage situation, the United States was now forced to contemplate a major extension of Soviet power in this region. Moreover, Washington's views mirrored those of Moscow—namely that a move on Afghanistan was likely to be a prelude for the further expansion of one superpower at the expense of the other. Soviet sights were likely to be set next on Iran, where trouble was bound to be stirred up by agitators, as one intelligence report suggested in early 1980. The President should therefore start considering the circumstances under which "we [would] be prepared to put U.S. forces into Iran."[62]

Carter ramped up the rhetoric in his State of the Union address on 23 January 1980. The Soviet invasion of Afghanistan meant that a region of "great strategic importance" was now under threat, he said; Moscow's move had eliminated a buffer, and brought it within striking distance not only of an area that "contains more than two-thirds of the world's exportable oil" but also of the crucial Straits of Hormuz "through which most of the world's oil must flow." He therefore articulated a carefully worded threat. "Let our position be absolutely clear," he said; "an attempt by any outside force to gain control of the Persian Gulf region will be regarded as an assault on the vital interests of the United States of America, and such an assault will be repelled by any means necessary, including military force." This was a defiant statement that perfectly encapsulated attitudes to the oil of the Middle East and to the position first built up by the British and then inherited by the United States: any attempt to change the status quo would meet with a ferocious challenge. This was imperial policy in all but name.[63]

Carter's bombastic words, however, contrasted with what was happening on the ground. Discussions with the Iranians about releasing the hostages had been continuing in the background, but were becoming ever more farcical. Not only were talks being held between representatives of Teheran and a presidential aide who wore a wig, false moustache and glasses to some meetings; but, as these discussions were going on, Ayatollah Khomeini kept giving speeches about the "world-devouring USA" and about how the "great Satan" should be taught a lesson.[64]

Eventually, in April 1980, President Carter resolved to bring matters to a conclusion and authorised Operation Eagle Claw, a covert mission to rescue the hostages from Teheran. The result was a fiasco to make schoolboys blush. Eight helicopters dispatched from the nuclear-powered aircraft carrier USS *Nimitz* were supposed to rendezvous with a ground team at a location near Tabas in central Iran, where they would be led by Colonel Charlie Beckwith and a new unit of crack troops, christened Delta Force. The operation proved to be stillborn: one helicopter turned back because of weather conditions; another developed a cracked rotor and was abandoned intact, while yet another was discovered to have a damaged hydraulics system. Beckwith concluded that the mission was no longer viable and obtained permission from the President to abort. As the helicopters returned to the *Nimitz*, one flew too close to a C-130 refuelling aircraft, resulting in an explosion that brought down both—and killed eight American servicemen.[65]

It was a propaganda disaster. Khomeini, not surprisingly, portrayed it as an act of divine intervention.[66] Others looked on with bemusement at the ineptitude of the failed mission. The fact that the United States had been unable to secure the release of the hostages through negotiation or by force spoke volumes about how the world was changing. Even before the failure of the rescue mission, some of the President's advisers had felt there was a need to act decisively so as not to look impotent. "We need to do something," Zbigniew Brzezinski—the President's National Security Advisor—said, "to reassure the Egyptians, the Saudis and others on the Arabian peninsula that the US is prepared to assert its power." And that meant establishing "a visible military presence in the area now."[67]

The United States was not alone, however, in trying to find a response to the tumultuous events that would enable it to protect its interests and reputation. On 22 September, Iraq began a surprise attack on Iran, bombing Iranian airfields and launching a three-pronged ground invasion that targeted the province of Khūzestān and the cities of Ābādān and Khurramshahr. There were no doubts in Iranian minds about who lay behind these attacks. "The hands of America," thundered Khomeini, had "emerged from Saddam's sleeve."[68] The attack, claimed President Bani-Sadr, was the result of an American–Iraqi–Israeli master plan whose aims were variously described as attempts to depose the Islamic government, to reinstate the Shah or to force the disintegration of Iran into five republics. Either way, he alleged, Washington had provided the Iraqis with the blueprint for the invasion.[69]

Although the idea that the United States was behind the attack has been championed by some commentators and repeated by many others, there is little hard evidence to show that this was the case. On the contrary, the sources—which include millions of pages of documents, audio recordings and transcripts recovered from the presidential palace in Baghdad in 2003—point firmly to the fact that Saddam had acted alone, choosing an opportune moment to strike at a volatile neighbour with whom he had a score to settle after coming out on the wrong side of territorial settlements five years earlier.[70] These documents show an aggressive escalation in information-gathering by Iraqi intelligence in the months prior to the attack as thoughts in Baghdad turned to a surprise invasion.[71]

Saddam was also driven by a heavy dose of insecurity and a strong streak of megalomania. He was obsessed with Israel and with the powerlessness of the Arabs to defeat a country that was "an extension of the United States of America and the English," while at the same time complaining that any aggressive action taken against Israel by the Arabs would result in the west deciding to retaliate against Iraq. If we attack Israel, he warned his senior officers, the Americans would "throw an atomic bomb at us." The "first target" of western action, he noted, "will be Baghdad, not Damascus or Amman."[72] Somehow, in Saddam's mind, it seemed to make sense: attacking Israel would leave Iraq facing annihilation; therefore an attack on Iran should receive precedence.

The coupling of Israel and Iran could be found in the grandstanding rhetoric used by both Saddam and senior figures in the Iraqi leadership that referred excitedly to Iraq assuming the mantle of leadership for Arabs everywhere. The attack on Iran in 1980 was presented as an example of reclaiming land that had been "extorted" during the territorial settlement of 1975. This would give encouragement to others, declared Saddam to his high-ranking officials, and galvanise "all the people" whose lands have been taken from them to rise up and claim what was theirs by right too—a message intended above all for the Palestinians.[73] Saddam convinced himself that invading Iran would help the cause of the Arabs elsewhere. Driven by such perverse logic, it was little wonder that the Israeli Prime Minister, Menachem Begin, took to describing Iraq as "the most irresponsible of all Arab regimes, with the possible exception of Kaddafi."[74]

Saddam had also been ruffled by the Revolution in Iran, muttering that the removal of the Shah and the rise of Ayatollah Khomeini was "completely an American decision." The unrest was the start of a master plan, he declared, that would use Muslim clerics "to scare the Gulf people so that [the Americans] can have a presence and arrange the situation in the region" however they saw fit.[75] Such paranoia was blended with moments of genuine insight, such as when the Iraqi leader immediately grasped the significance of the Soviet move into Afghanistan—and what this meant for Iraq. Would the USSR do the same thing in the future to get its way in Baghdad, he asked; would puppet governments be set up in Iraq too, under the guise of providing help? "Is this," he asked Moscow, how you will treat your other "friends in the future"?[76]

His misgivings only grew as the USSR worked to capitalise on anti-American sentiment in Iran and set about courting Khomeini and those close to him.[77] Saddam realised that this too was potentially damaging and that Iraq might be jettisoned by Moscow in favour of its neighbour. "Soviet penetration of the region . . . should be checked," he told diplomats from Jordan in 1980.[78] Feeling increasingly isolated, he was prepared to turn away from his Soviet backers, who had stood square behind his rise to power in the 1970s. His disillusion was one reason why the Soviets were not told of the forthcoming attack until the day before it was launched—which resulted in a frosty response from Moscow.[79] By then, according to Iraqi intelligence reports, the fact that Iran was suffering from a "choking economic crisis" and was in no fit state to "defend [itself] on a large scale," represented too good an opportunity to miss.[80]

The fall of the Shah had set an extraordinary chain of events in motion. By the end of 1980, the whole of the centre of Asia was in a state of flux. The futures of Iran, Iraq and Afghanistan lay in the balance, resting on choices made by their leaders and on the intervention of outside forces. Guessing which way things would go in each of these countries let alone in the region as a whole was nigh on impossible. For the United States, the answer was to try to muddle through by playing all sides. The results were disastrous: while it was true that the seeds of anti-American sentiment had been planted earlier in the twentieth century, it was by no means inevitable that these would grow into full-blooded hatred. But U.S. policy decisions over the last two decades of the century would serve to poison attitudes across the region lying between the Mediterranean and the Himalayas.

For sure, the United States had a hard hand to play at the start of the 1980s. To start with, the Iraqi assault seemed a blessing for U.S. policy-makers, who saw in Saddam Hussein's aggression an opportunity to open discussions with Teheran. President Carter's National Security Advisor Brzezinski "made no secret of the fact that the Iraqi attack was a potentially positive development that would put pressure on Iran to release the hostages," according to a senior adviser involved in the crisis meetings that took place in this period.[81] The pressure on Khomeini's regime was amplified by the knowledge that, in order to respond to the attack, it desperately needed spare parts for military hardware that had previously been purchased from the United States. The Iranians were told that Washington might be minded to provide the relevant materials—whose value ran into the hundreds of millions of dollars—if the hostages were released. Teheran simply ignored the approach, which had the personal approval of the U.S. President.[82] Not for the first time, Iran was a step ahead: its agents had proved resourceful, buying much needed spares from elsewhere, including Vietnam, which had large stocks of U.S. equipment captured during the war.[83]

Iran was also supplied in large volume by Israel, which took the view that Saddam Hussein had to be stopped at all costs. The willingness of the Iranians and the Israelis to do business with each other was in many ways surprising, especially given the derogatory way that Khomeini in particular regularly talked about Jews and about Israel. "Islam and the Islamic people met their first saboteur in the Jewish people who are at the source of all anti-Islamic libels and intrigues," he wrote in 1970.[84] Iran and Israel were now cast as unlikely bedfellows thanks to Saddam Hussein's intervention in the Gulf.

This was one reason why Khomeini's rhetoric towards minorities and to other religions softened in the early 1980s, by which point he was referring to Judaism as "an honourable religion that had arisen among the common folk"—although he distinguished this from Zionism, which in his eyes at least was a political (and exploitative) movement that was in its essence opposed to religion. This change in posture towards religions was so extensive that the Islamic Republic of Iran even issued postage stamps with a silhouette of Jesus Christ and a verse from the Qur'ān written in Armenian.[85]

It was not just in the matter of arms sales that Israel and Iran co-operated, but in military operations too. One specific target of mutual interest was Iraq's Osirak nuclear reactor. According to one intelligence officer, a mission to attack the facility had been discussed by Iranian and Israeli representatives during clandestine talks in Paris even before Saddam's attack started.[86] Just over a week after Iraq's assault on Iran was launched, the reactor was the subject of a daring raid by four Iranian F-4 Phantom jets that targeted the research laboratories and the control building. Eight months later, in June 1981, Israeli fighter pilots went one better, badly damaging the reactor at a time when it was widely feared it was about to become critical.[87]

The Iraqi attack on Iran had been intended to deliver a short and sweet victory. To start with, even despite the assault on Osirak, things looked promising from Baghdad's point of view. As time went on, however, the tables began to turn on Iraq. The USSR punished Saddam for his unilateral action by withholding weapons supplies and suspending the shipment of arms, leaving the Iraqi leader frustrated and short of options. In a frank admission that the war was not going as well as expected, he regularly gathered his confidants around him to moan, articulating one far-fetched international conspiracy after another to explain the setbacks. But the bottom line was that the Iraqis were increasingly finding themselves outfought and outgunned. On one occasion in mid-1981, Saddam asked his generals almost forlornly: "Let us try to buy weapons now from the black market. Can we achieve that the same way the Iranians can?"[88]

Iran was indeed proving resourceful, resurgent—and increasingly ambitious. By the summer of 1982, Iranian troops had not just managed to force the Iraqis out of territories they had captured, but had penetrated across the border themselves. A special intelligence report prepared by the National Security Agency in the United States in June of that year painted an unequivocal picture: "Iraq has essentially lost the war with Iran . . . There is little the Iraqis can do alone or in combination with other Arabs, to reverse the military situation."[89] With the wind in their sails, the Iranians were now seeking to spread the idea of Islamic revolution to other countries. Funding and logistical support was given to radical Shīʿite forces in Lebanon and to organisations like Hezbollah (Party of God), while efforts were made to foment riots in Mecca and to sponsor a coup in Bahrain. "I think the Iranians pose a major threat without any question to the countries of the Middle East," the Secretary of Defense, Caspar Weinberger, was quoted as saying in July 1982; "they are a country run by a bunch of madmen."[90]

Ironically, therefore, the increasing difficulties facing Saddam Hussein's Iraq were a godsend for the United States. Although the embassy hostages were finally released from Teheran after being held hostage for more than a year following a deal struck behind the scenes, the end of the stalemate had not marked an improvement in U.S. relations with Iran. In contrast, the Soviets continued to court Khomeini—as the CIA noted with alarm. Momentum seemed to be behind the USSR, especially given its apparent success in Afghanistan where troops had occupied the cities and secured the major communication routes and seemed, from the outside at least, to be in command of the situation. Diplomatic pressure on the Soviet Union, which included a boycott of the 1980 Moscow Olympics, failed to deliver any tangible results. From Washington's point of view, there was little to be hopeful about—until it dawned on policymakers that there was an obvious move to make: to back Saddam.

As Secretary of State George Shultz later put it, if Iraq continued to retreat, the country could easily collapse—which would have been "a strategic disaster for the United States."[91] In addition to causing turmoil across the Persian Gulf and the Middle East as a whole, this would result in strengthening Teheran's hand when it came to the international oil markets. Slowly but surely, a new policy emerged. The United States decided to bet big on Iraq; this was the square of the board where Washington's chances of being able to influence what was going on in the centre of Asia were strongest. Helping Saddam was a way of remaining engaged, as well as countering the advance of both Iran and the Soviet Union.

Support took several forms. After removing Iraq from the list of state sponsors of terrorism, the United States acted to help prop up the economy, extending financial credit to support the agricultural sector and allowing Saddam to buy first non-military equipment and then "dual-use" technology, such as heavy trucks that could be used to transport equipment to the front lines. Western governments in Europe were encouraged to sell weapons to Baghdad, while U.S. diplomats worked flat out to convince other regional powers, such as Kuwait and Saudi Arabia, to help finance Iraq's military expenditure. Intelligence gathered by U.S. agents began to be passed to Baghdad, often via King Hussein of Jordan, a trusted intermediary.[92] The U.S. administration under President Reagan also helped boost Iraq's oil exports—and as a result its revenues—by encouraging and facilitating an expansion of pipelines to Saudi Arabia and Jordan to counter the problems of shipping through the Persian Gulf caused by the war with Iran. This was intended to "redress the Iran–Iraq oil export imbalance"—in other words, to level the playing field.[93]

In addition, active steps were taken from the end of 1983 to cut down sales of weapons and spares to Iran in a bid to stem battlefield advances in an initiative christened Operation Staunch. U.S. diplomats were instructed to request host nations to "consider stopping any traffic in military equipment of whatever origin that may exist between your country and Iran," until a ceasefire had been agreed in the Gulf. Diplomats should emphasise that the fighting was "threatening to all our interests"; it was imperative, the order stated, to "diminish Iran's ability to prolong the war."[94]

This measure was also intended to earn the trust of the Iraqis and of Saddam, who remained deeply suspicious of the United States and its motives, even after all these steps had been taken.[95] When President Reagan sent his ambassador-at-large, Donald Rumsfeld, to Baghdad at the end of 1983, therefore, one of the latter's explicit aims was to "initiate a dialogue and establish a personal rapport" with Saddam Hussein. As Rumsfeld's briefing notes put it, he was to reassure the Iraqi leader that the United States "would regard any major reversal of Iraq's fortunes as a strategic defeat for the West."[96] Rumsfeld's mission was judged to have been a notable success, both by the Americans and by the Iraqis. It was, furthermore, "a very good development" in the opinion of the Saudis, who were equally concerned about Khomeini's export of Shīʿa Islam across the Middle East.[97]

So important was the alignment with Iraq that Washington was prepared to play down the use of chemical weapons by Saddam, which, as one report stated, was an "almost daily" occurrence.[98] Efforts to deter the Iraqis from this should be made—but in private, so as to "avoid unpleasantly surprising Iraq through public positions."[99] It was noted too that criticism of the use of chemical weapons (strictly banned by the Geneva Protocol of 1925) would hand a propaganda victory to Iran, and do nothing to calm tensions. The U.S. sought to prevent shipments of chemicals used to manufacture mustard gas, and lobbied hard to put pressure on the Iraqis not to use chemicals on the battlefield—especially after Iran took the matter to the United Nations in October 1983.[100]

However, even when it became apparent that poison gas had been used against Iran in the course of the Badr offensive of 1985, nothing critical was said in public—other than bland statements that the United States itself was strongly opposed to the use of chemical weapons.[101] As such, however, it was highly embarrassing that Iraq's production capability, as one senior American officer pointed out, was "primarily [derived] from Western firms, including possibly a U.S. foreign subsidiary." It did not take much to realise that this raised uncomfortable questions about complicity in Saddam's acquisition and use of chemical weapons.[102]

In time, even the low-key public comments and private entreaties to high-ranking Iraqi officials about chemical weapons were dropped. In the mid-1980s, when United Nations reports concluded that Iraq was using chemicals against its own civilians, the United States responded with silence. Condemnation of Saddam's brutal and sustained moves against the Kurdish population of Iraq was conspicuous by its absence. It was simply noted in American military reports that "chemical agents" were being used extensively against civilian targets. Iraq was more important to the United States than the principles of international law—and more important than the victims.[103]

Similarly, little was said or done to curtail the nuclear programme in Pakistan thanks to the country's heightened strategic value following the Soviet invasion of Afghanistan. Across the globe, human rights came a distant second behind U.S. interests. The lessons of pre-Revolutionary Iran had not been learnt: the United States certainly did not seek to endorse bad behaviour, but it was inevitable that there was reputational damage and a price to pay for supporting dictators and those prepared to mistreat their own populations or intent on provoking their neighbours.[104]

A case in point was the help given to insurgents in Afghanistan who opposed the Soviet invasion and who became known collectively in the western press as the "Mujahidin"—literally those engaging in jihad. In fact, they were a motley collection, made up of nationalists, former army officers, religious fanatics, tribal leaders, opportunists and mercenaries. They were also, on occasion, rivals who competed with each other for recruits and for money and weapons, including the thousands of semi-automatic rifles and RPG-7 (rocket-propelled grenade launchers) that were supplied by the CIA from early 1980, mostly via Pakistan.

Despite its organisational incoherence, resistance to the Soviet military juggernaut proved nagging, constant and demoralising. Terrorist attacks became a staple feature of life in major cities and along the Salang highway and the route running south from Uzbekistan to Herat and Kandahar, the main arteries that pumped troops and equipment into Afghanistan from the USSR. Reports sent back to Moscow remarked on the worrying rise in the number of hostile incidents, as well as the difficulty of identifying perpetrators: insurgents had been instructed, one memo stated, to blend in with the local population so they could not be detected.[105]

The growing success of the Afghan rebels was impressive. In 1983, for example, a raid led by one commander, Jalaluddin Haqqani, succeeded in capturing two T-55 tanks, along with hardware that included anti-aircraft guns, rocket launchers and howitzers which he protected in a nest of tunnels near Khost, close to the Pakistani border. They were now used in strikes on convoys passing along exposed highways, providing invaluable propaganda tools that convinced the local population that the nose of the mighty USSR could be bloodied.[106]

Triumphs like these demoralised Soviet troops, who reacted brutally. Some wrote of the "thirst for blood" and the unquenchable desire for revenge after seeing colleagues and comrades killed and injured. Reprisals were horrific, with children killed, women raped and every civilian suspected of being a Mujahid. This created a vicious circle, in which more and more Afghans were drawn into supporting the rebels.[107] It was sobering, as one commentator has written, for Soviet commanders to realise that the sledgehammer of the Red Army was unable to crack the nut of an elusive, uncoordinated enemy.[108]

The strength of the insurgency impressed the United States, for which containing the Soviet expansion in Afghanistan was no longer the objective. By early 1985, talk had turned to defeating the USSR and driving the Soviets out of the country altogether.[109] In March, President Reagan signed National Security Decision Directive 166 stating that the "ultimate goal of [U.S.] policy is the removal of Soviet forces from Afghanistan"; in order to do so, it went on, it was necessary "to improve the military effectiveness of the Afghan resistance."[110] What this meant soon became clear: a dramatic escalation in the amount of arms being provided to the insurgents. The decision prompted a lengthy debate about whether this should include Stinger missiles—fearsome portable launchers capable of taking down aircraft at a range of three miles and with a considerably greater accuracy than other weapons then available.[111]

The beneficiaries of the new policy were men like Jalaluddin Haqqani, whose achievements against the Soviets and whose religious devotion convinced the U.S. Congressman Charlie Wilson—later the subject of the glowing Hollywood blockbuster *Charlie Wilson's War* (2007)—to describe him as "goodness personified." Given access to more and better hardware, Jalaluddin was able to build up his own position in southern Afghanistan, his hardline views reinforced by military success made possible by the flood of American weapons after 1985. This did not mean he felt any loyalty to the United States. In fact, he was to become a thorn in its side: after 9/11, he was named the third most wanted man in Afghanistan.[112]

The United States supported around fifty such commanders, paying retainers of $20,000–$100,000 per month depending on results and status. There was a surge of money from Saudi Arabia too in support of the Mujahidin, the result of Saudi sympathy for the rhetoric of Islamic militancy employed by the resistance, and a desire to help persecuted Muslims. Men of Saudi extraction who followed their conscience to fight in Afghanistan were highly regarded. Men like Osama bin Laden—well connected, articulate and personally impressive—were perfectly placed to act as conduits for large sums of money given by Saudi benefactors; inevitably, their access to these resources in turn built them into important figures within the Mujahidin movement itself.[113] The significance of this too was only to become apparent later.

Chinese support for the resistance also had long-term implications. China had declared its opposition to the Soviet invasion at the outset, seeing an expansionist policy with uncomfortable consequences. The USSR's move in 1979 was a "threat to peace and security in Asia and the whole world," according to one Chinese daily newspaper at the time; Afghanistan was not the real goal for the Soviets, who intended to use the country simply as a "stepping stone for a southward thrust towards Pakistan and the whole subcontinent."[114]

Those resisting the Soviet army were also actively courted by Beijing and provided with weapons in volumes that increased steadily in the 1980s. Indeed, when U.S. troops captured Taliban and al-Qaida bases at Tora Bora in 2001, they discovered large stockpiles of Chinese rocket-propelled grenade launchers and multi-barrelled missile launchers, along with mines and rifles that had been sent to Afghanistan two decades earlier. In steps that it too has come to regret, China also encouraged, recruited and trained Uighur Muslims in Xinjiang, before helping them make contact with and join the Mujahidin.[115] The radicalisation of western China has proved problematic ever since.

Heavy patronage helped the resistance to the Red Army swell, and the Soviets found themselves being ground down and sustaining serious losses of hardware, manpower—and money. In August 1986, an estimated 40,000 tons of ammunition, worth around $250 million, was blown up in an arms dump outside Kabul. Then there was the success of the U.S. Stinger missiles which brought down three MI-24 gunship helicopters near Jalalabad in 1986 and proved so effective that they changed the way air cover was used in Afghanistan: Soviet pilots were forced to modify their landing patterns, while missions were increasingly flown at night, to reduce the chances of being shot down.[116]

In the mid-1980s, prospects were starting to look rosy from Washington's point of view. Considerable effort had gone into cultivating Saddam Hussein and building trust with Iraq; the situation in Afghanistan was improving as the Soviet forces were driven on to the defensive—and eventually, by the start of 1989, out of the country altogether. To all intents and purposes, the United States had not only managed to see off Moscow's attempts to extend its influence and authority in the centre of Asia, but had managed to build new networks of its own, adapting as and when it had been forced to do so. It was a shame, one intelligence document written in the spring of 1985 stated, that given "Iran's historic, geostrategic importance" relations between Washington and Teheran were so poor.[117] Indeed, a year earlier,

Iran had been officially designated a "State Sponsor of Terrorism," which meant that there was a blanket ban on arms-related exports and sales, strict controls of dual-use technology and equipment, and a raft of financial and economic restrictions.

It was unfortunate indeed, noted another report written around the same time, that the United States had "no cards to play" in its dealings with Iran; perhaps it was worth considering a "bolder—and perhaps riskier policy," suggested the author.[118] There was much to gain—for both sides. With Khomeini now old and ailing, Washington was keen to identify the next generation of leaders who would rise to positions of power. According to some reports, there was a "moderate faction" in Iranian politics that was eager to reach out to the United States and bring about a rapprochement; engaging with these moderates would help build ties that could prove valuable in the future. There were hopes too that Iran could help secure the release of western hostages who had been taken by militant Hezbollah terrorists in Lebanon in the early 1980s.[119]

From the perspective of Iran too there were attractions in a more constructive approach. The developing situation in Afghanistan, where Iranian and American interests dovetailed neatly, was a promising start, a sign that co-operation was not only possible but could be fruitful. Moreover, Iran was keen to move forward to improve relations for other reasons. Not least of these was the more than 2 million refugees who had spilled over the border since 1980. Their influx into the country was not easy to absorb, which meant that the leadership in Teheran was perhaps more willing to cultivate friendships that might reduce volatility across the region.[120] Meanwhile, Iran was finding it difficult to source military hardware at a time of continued heavy fighting with Iraq. Despite the tide turning in its favour and despite extensive arms purchases on the black market, securing weapons and spares from the United States was more and more appealing.[121] Tentative overtures to open channels of communication were made.

Initial meetings were tetchy, difficult and uncomfortable. Determined to win over the Iranians, the Americans presented what was later revealed as being both "real and deceptive intelligence" about Soviet intentions towards Iran, focusing above all on the USSR's putative territorial designs on parts of the country in an effort to impress on Iran that aligning with the United States had obvious benefits.[122] As discussions progressed, however, so too did the information flow about matters that were of particular interest to the United States—such as about the combat-worthiness of Soviet equipment. The Americans always followed such matters attentively, and indeed paid $5,000 to acquire an AK-74 assault rifle captured in Afghanistan soon after it had been introduced by the Soviet army.[123] The Americans listened closely to Afghan fighters in assessing the merits, limitations and vulnerabilities of the T-72 tank and the MI-24 "Krokodil" assault helicopter; they learnt of the extensive use of napalm and other poison gases by the Soviets; and they also heard how the Spetsnaz special forces in operation across the country were singularly effective, probably as a result of the better training they received compared with regular Red Army soldiers.[124] This provided a valuable primer two decades later.

There was a natural elision of interests between Iran and the United States. The statements by Iranian negotiators that "Soviet ideology is directly opposed to Iran's" paralleled American attitudes towards Communism, which could be expressed equally emphatically. That the USSR was giving substantial military support to Iraq at this time was also crucial. "The Soviets," one senior figure said during the discussions, "are killing Iranian soldiers."[125] In the space of a few short years, Iran and the United States may not have gone from being the worst of enemies to the best of friends, but they were increasingly willing to put differences behind them and work towards a common goal. This attempt to plot a path through the middle of the rivalries between great powers was classic policy that would have been instantly recognisable to previous generations of Iranian diplomats and leaders.

Keen to cement the relationship, the United States began shipping weapons to Iran in contravention of its own embargo and despite pressuring foreign governments not to sell arms to Teheran. Some were opposed to this development, including Secretary of State George Shultz, who remarked that the initiative might lead to an Iranian victory, and "a fresh burst of energy for anti-Americanism throughout the region."[126] There were others who were already arguing that it served U.S. interests for Iran and Iraq to exhaust each other. Richard Murphy, one of Shultz's deputies, stated at congressional hearings the previous year that "a victory by either [Iran or Iraq] is neither militarily achievable nor strategically desirable"—sentiments that were echoed in comments by senior White House officials.[127]

The first consignment of 100 tube-launched, optical-tracked, wire-guided missile systems (TOWs) was sent in the summer of 1985. The arms were shipped via an intermediary eager to build up links with Teheran: Israel.[128] The amicable relationship seems surprising from the standpoint of the early twenty-first century when Iranian leaders routinely call for Israel to be "wiped off the map." But in the mid-1980s ties were so close that the Israeli Prime Minister Yitzhak Rabin was able to declare: "Israel is Iran's best friend, and we do not intend to change our position."[129]

Israel's willingness to participate in the U.S. arms programme owed much to its desire to keep Iraq in a position where it was forced to focus its attention firmly on its eastern neighbour—rather than contemplate action elsewhere. Nevertheless, there were considerable sensitivities relating to the arrangement with Iran. The U.S. proposal involved Israel shipping American ordnance and equipment to Teheran, before being compensated by Washington. As a result, the Israeli government asked for—and received—confirmation that the scheme had been cleared at the highest level in the United States. In fact, it had the direct and personal approval of President Reagan himself.[130]

Between the summer of 1985 and the autumn of 1986, Iran received several major shipments from the United States, including more than 2,000 TOW missiles, eighteen Hawk anti-aircraft missiles and two consignments of spares for the Hawk systems.[131] Not all were delivered through Israel, for it was not long before deliveries were made directly, though in the process the waters were muddied still further when the proceeds of the sales were used to provide funds for the Contras in Nicaragua. Ever since the Cuban missile crisis Washington had been spooked by the threat of Communism on the United States' doorstep and was keen to fund dynamic groups capable of acting as effective bulwarks against left-wing rhetoric and politics—and would pass over their shortcomings in silence. The Contras, who were in fact a loose grouping of rebels often locked in fierce conflict with each other, were a major beneficiary of American anti-Communist doctrine—and foreign policy blindness. In a mirror image of how U.S. private and public actions differed in the Middle East, aid was being passed to opposition forces in Central America despite legislation that specifically forbade the U.S. government from doing so.[132]

Matters came to a head at the end of 1986, when a series of leaks revealed what had been going on. The scandal threatened to bring down the President. On 13 November, President Reagan took to the airwaves to make a primetime nationwide address about "an extremely sensitive and profoundly important matter of foreign policy." It was a make-or-break moment, which required all his considerable charm to pull off. The President wanted to avoid apologising or sounding defensive; what was needed was an explanation. His comments encapsulated perfectly the significance of the countries of this region—and of America's need to have influence at all costs.

"Iran," he told transfixed viewers, "encompasses some of the most critical geography in the world. It lies between the Soviet Union and access to the warm waters of the Indian Ocean. Geography explains why the Soviet Union has sent an army into Afghanistan to dominate that country and, if they could, Iran and Pakistan. Iran's geography gives it a critical position from which adversaries could interfere with oil flows from the Arab States that border the Persian Gulf. Apart from geography, Iran's oil deposits are important to the long-term health of the world's economy." This justified "the transfer of small amounts of defensive weapons and spare parts," he said. Without specifying precisely what had been sent to Teheran, he stated that "these modest deliveries, taken together, could easily fit into a single cargo plane." All he had been trying to do was to bring about "an honourable end to the bloody six-year war" between Iran and Iraq, "to eliminate state-sponsored terrorism" and "to effect the safe return of all hostages."[133]

This performance did little to avert spectacular fall-out in Washington as it became known that the United States had been selling arms to Iran in what looked like a direct trade for the return of American hostages. Things became even more toxic when it emerged that those closely involved with the Iran–Contra initiative had been shredding documents that bore witness to covert and illegal actions being authorised by the President himself. Reagan appeared before a commission appointed to look into the affair, where he pleaded that his memory was not good enough to recall whether or not he had authorised the arms sales to Iran. In March 1987, he made another televised address, this time to express his anger about "activities undertaken without my knowledge"—a statement that played fast and loose with the truth, as Reagan himself now noted. "A few months ago, I told the American people I did not trade arms for hostages. My heart and best intentions still tell me that's true, but the facts and the evidence tell me otherwise."[134]

These embarrassing revelations had consequences that ran deep through the Reagan administration, where a slate of senior figures were subsequently indicted on charges ranging from conspiracy to perjury to withholding evidence. They included Caspar Weinberger, Secretary of Defense; Robert McFarlane, National Security Advisor, as well as his successor, John Poindexter; Elliott Abrams, Assistant Secretary of State for Inter-American Affairs; and a host of senior CIA officers, including Clair George, Deputy Director of Operations. The illustrious roll-call showed how far the United

States had been prepared to go in order to secure its position in the heart of the world.[135]

So too did the fact that the charges turned out to be nothing more than window-dressing: all the leading figures later received presidential pardons from President George H. W. Bush, or had their convictions overturned on Christmas Eve 1992. "The common denominator of their motivations—whether their actions were right or wrong—" read the citation, "was patriotism." The impact on their personal finances, careers and families, the President went on, was "grossly disproportionate to any misdeeds or errors of judgment they may have committed."[136] Several of those pardoned had already been convicted on charges ranging from perjury to withholding information from Congress, while Weinberger's trial had been due to start two weeks later. It was a classic case of justice being elastic, and of the ends justifying the means. The ramifications went far beyond the Washington Beltway.

Saddam Hussein was apoplectic when news broke about U.S. dealings with Iran—at a time when Iraq believed it was being supported by Washington against its neighbour and bitter rival. In a series of meetings held immediately after Reagan's first televised address in November 1986 to discuss what the President had said, Saddam ranted about how the arms sales represented a disgraceful "stab in the back" and how the behaviour of the United States set a new low for "bad and immoral behaviour."[137] The United States was determined to "shed more [Iraqi] blood," he concluded, as others agreed that only the tip of the iceberg had been uncovered. It was inevitable, commented one senior figure a few weeks later, that the United States would continue to conspire against Iraq; this was typical of imperialist powers, concurred Deputy Prime Minister Tariq Aziz.[138] The anger and sense of betrayal were tangible. "Don't trust the Americans—the Americans are liars—don't trust the Americans," one voice can be heard imploring on audio tapes recovered from Baghdad more than twenty years later.[139]

The Irangate scandal cost jobs in Washington, but it played a decisive role in the development of a siege mentality in Iraq in the mid-1980s. Let down by the United States, Saddam and his officials now saw conspiracies everywhere. The Iraqi leader started talking about fifth columnists and cutting their throats if he found them; other Arab countries whose relations with Iran or the United States seemed too close for comfort were suddenly regarded with deep suspicion. As a later high-level U.S. report concluded, Saddam became convinced after Irangate that "Washington could not be trusted and that it was out to get him personally."[140]

The belief that the United States was willing to double-deal and double-cross was hardly unfounded. The Americans had been prepared to make friends with the Shah; now they were trying to cement ties with the regime of the Ayatollah Khomeini. Substantial military and economic support was given to an unsavoury group of characters in Afghanistan solely on the basis of long-standing U.S. rivalry with the USSR. Saddam himself had been brought in from the cold when it suited policymakers in Washington—but then sacrificed when it no longer suited them. Putting American interests first was not in itself the problem; the issue was that conducting imperial-style foreign policy requires a more careful touch—as well as more thorough thinking about the long-term consequences. In each case, in the late twentieth-century struggle for control of the countries of the Silk Roads, the U.S. was cutting deals and making agreements on the hoof, solving today's problems without worrying about tomorrow's—and in some cases laying the basis for much more difficult issues. The goal of driving the Soviets out of Afghanistan had been achieved; but little thought had been given to what might happen next.

The stark reality of the world that the United States had created was all too obvious in Iraq in the late 1980s and 1990. Embarrassed American officials did their best after the debacle of Irangate to "regain credibility with the Arab states," as the Secretary of Defense put it.[141] In the case of Iraq, this meant awarding extraordinarily large credit facilities, developing initiatives to build up trade—which included loosening restrictions on dual-use and other hi-tech exports—and funding Iraq's stuttering agricultural sector. These were all steps taken to try to rebuild trust with Saddam.[142] In fact, they were understood quite differently in Baghdad: although the Iraqi leader accepted the deals he was offered, he thought this was part of another trap—perhaps a prelude to a military attack, perhaps part of an attempt to ratchet pressure upwards at a time when settling debts built up during the Iran–Iraq War was becoming a problem.

The Iraqis, declared the U.S. ambassador to Baghdad, were "quite convinced that the United States . . . was targeting Iraq. They complained about it all the time . . . And I think it was genuinely believed by Saddam Hussein."[143] At the end of 1989, rumours began to spread through the Iraqi leadership that the United States was plotting a coup against Saddam Hussein.

Tariq Aziz told the U.S. Secretary of State, James Baker, point-blank that Iraq had evidence that the United States was scheming to overthrow Saddam.[144] The siege mentality had developed into paranoia so acute that, no matter what step the Americans took, it was liable to be misinterpreted.

It was not hard to understand Iraq's misgivings—especially when loan guarantees that had been promised by Washington were abruptly cancelled in July 1990 after White House attempts to funnel financial support to Baghdad had been derailed by Congress. Worse, in addition to withdrawing $700 million of funding, sanctions were imposed as punishment for Iraq's past use of poison gas. From Saddam's point of view, this was a case of history repeating itself: the United States promising one thing and then doing another—and doing so in an underhand way.[145]

By this time, Iraqi forces were gathering in the south of the country. "Normally this would be none of our business," said the U.S. ambassador to Baghdad, April Glaspie, when she met with Saddam Hussein on 25 July 1990. In what is one of the most damning documents of the late twentieth century, a leaked transcript of the U.S. ambassador's meeting with the Iraqi leader reveals that she told Saddam she had "direct instructions from President Bush to improve our relations with Iraq," noting with admiration Saddam's "extraordinary efforts to rebuild your country." Nevertheless, Glaspie told the Iraqi leader, "We know you need funds."

Iraq was going through difficult times, admitted Saddam, who was "cordial, reasonable and even warm during the meeting," according to a separate memorandum that has also subsequently been made public.[146] Angular gas drilling, long-standing border disputes and the depressed price of oil all presented problems for the economy, he said—as did debts run up in the war with Iran. There was one potential solution, he said. Taking control of the Shaṭṭ al-ʿArab waterway, a region over which Iraq was involved in a long-running dispute with Kuwait, would help resolve some of the current problems. "What is the United States' opinion on this?" he asked.

"We have no opinion on your Arab–Arab conflicts, such as your dispute with Kuwait," replied the ambassador. She went on to clarify what this meant: "Secretary [of State James] Baker has directed me to emphasize the instruction, first given to Iraq in the 1960's, that the Kuwait issue is not associated with America."[147] Saddam had asked for a green light from the United States, and he had been given one. The following week, he invaded Kuwait.

The consequences proved catastrophic. Over the course of the next three decades, global affairs would be dominated by events in countries running across the spine of Asia. The struggle for control and influence in these countries produced wars, insurrections and international terrorism—but also opportunities and prospects, not just in Iran, Iraq and Afghanistan, but also in a belt of countries stretching east from the Black Sea, from Syria to Ukraine, Kazakhstan to Kyrgyzstan, Turkmenistan to Azerbaijan, and from Russia to China too. The story of the world has always been centred on these countries. But since the time of the invasion of Kuwait, everything has been about the emergence of the New Silk Road.

25

The Road to Tragedy

The invasion of Kuwait in 1990 triggered an extraordinary sequence of events that has defined the late twentieth and early twenty-first centuries. Saddam had once struck the British as a "presentable young man" with an "engaging smile" and none of the "superficial affability" of many of his colleagues; he liked to talk "without beating about the bush." He was a man, the British ambassador to Baghdad concluded in the late 1960s, "with whom, if only one could see more of him, it would be possible to do business."[1] Seen by the French as an "Arab de Gaulle," a man whose "nationalism and socialism" had been warmly admired by President Jacques Chirac, Saddam was someone the United States had also been willing to bet on in the early 1980s in a bid to improve what Donald Rumsfeld called "U.S. posture in the region."[2]

The attack on Kuwait, Saddam Hussein told his closest advisers in December 1990, was a form of self-defence in the wake of the Irangate scandal and the revelations of double-dealing by the United States.[3] This was not how the rest of the world saw things. Economic sanctions were quickly applied following the invasion, as the United Nations demanded an immediate Iraqi withdrawal. When Baghdad simply ignored the mounting diplomatic pressure, plans were drawn up to resolve matters decisively. On 15 January 1991, President George H. W. Bush authorised the use of military action "pursuant to my responsibilities and authority under the Constitution as President and Commander-in-Chief, and under the laws and treaties of the United States." The opening sentence of National Directive 54, which approved the use of force by "U.S. air, sea and land conventional military forces, in coordination with the forces of our coalition partners," conspicuously did not mention Iraqi aggression, violation of the sovereign territory of Kuwait or international law. Instead, in a statement that set the tone for American foreign policy over the next three decades, the President stated the following: "Access to Persian Gulf oil and the security of key friendly states in the area are vital to U.S. national security."[4] Saddam Hussein's invasion of Kuwait was a direct challenge to American power and interests.

An ambitious assault followed, with troops drawn from a broad coalition of countries led by General Norman Schwarzkopf—whose father had helped secure Iran for the Allies during the Second World War and had played a role not only in Operation Ajax, which deposed Mossadegh, but also in forming the Savak, the Iranian intelligence service that terrorised its own population from 1957 to 1979. Allied airstrikes targeted key defence, communication and weapons facilities, as land forces advanced into southern Iraq and Kuwait in Operation Desert Storm. The expedition was spectacular, but it was also rapid. Six weeks after the start of operations in January 1991, President Bush declared a ceasefire, noting in a television address on 28 February that "Kuwait is liberated. Iraq's army is defeated. Our military objectives are met. Kuwait is once more in the hands of the Kuwaitis, in control of their destiny." This is "not a time of euphoria, certainly not a time to gloat," he went on. "We must now look beyond victory and war."[5]

Bush's approval ratings soared, rising above the stratospheric levels reached by President Truman on the day of the German surrender in 1945.[6] Part of the reason for this was that the aims of the war had been clearly defined and quickly achieved, with mercifully few lives lost by coalition forces. The United States had excluded the goal of toppling Saddam himself, unless the latter used "chemical, biological or nuclear weapons," sponsored terrorist attacks or destroyed Kuwaiti oilfields—in which case, President Bush had said, "it shall become the specific objective of the United States to replace the current leadership of Iraq."[7]

The decision to end military action at the earliest opportunity was widely admired across the Arabic-speaking world and beyond—despite the fact that Iraqi forces did sabotage many Kuwaiti oilwells and set them ablaze. This was ignored, partly because it was felt that moving on the Iraqi capital would have been unacceptable "mission creep," wrote the President in a book co-authored with his National Security Advisor Brent Scowcroft in the late 1990s. Apart from antagonising allies in the Arab world and elsewhere, it was recognised that extending the ground war into Iraq and "trying to eliminate Saddam" would have come at too high a price.[8]

"We made the decision not to go to Baghdad," agreed Dick Cheney, Secretary of Defense, in a speech at the Discovery Institute in 1992, "because that was never part of our objective. It wasn't what the [United States] signed up for, it wasn't what Congress signed up for, it wasn't what the coalition was put together to do." Besides, he went on, the U.S. did not want to "get bogged down in the problems of trying to take over and govern Iraq." Removing Saddam would have been difficult, "and the question in my mind," he conceded, "is how many additional American casualties is Saddam worth? And the answer is not very damned many."[9]

Seeking to contain Saddam Hussein rather than overthrow him was the public position. Privately, it was a different story. In May 1991, just a few weeks after the ceasefire had been called, President Bush approved a plan to "create the conditions for the removal of Saddam Hussein from power." In order to effect this, he set aside a substantial sum for covert operations: $100 million.[10] Ever since the 1920s, the United States had been actively involved in propping up regimes that suited its wider strategic interests. Washington was now showing once again that it was willing to consider regime change in order to impose its vision on this part of the world.

The muscular ambition of the United States at this time was partly fired by the profound geopolitical changes witnessed in the early 1990s. The Berlin Wall had come down not long before the invasion of Kuwait, and in the months after the defeat of Iraq the Soviet Union collapsed in on itself. On Christmas Day 1991, President Mikhail Gorbachev resigned as President of the Soviet Union and announced the dissolution of the USSR into fifteen independent states. The world was seeing "changes of almost biblical proportions," President Bush told Congress a few weeks later. "By the grace of God, America [has] won the Cold War."[11]

In Russia itself, transition sparked a furious battle for control that ended in a constitutional crisis and the deposition of the old guard after army tanks had shelled the White House in Moscow, the seat of the Russian government, in 1993. This was also a period of major transition in China, as the reforms introduced by Deng Xiaoping and others following the death of Mao Zedong in 1976 began to take effect—transforming the country from an isolated, regional power into one with escalating economic, military and political ambitions.[12] The oppressive politics of apartheid were also winding down at long last in South Africa. The drums of freedom, peace and prosperity seemed to be beating loudly and triumphantly.

The world had once been divided into two, President Bush told a joint session of the Senate and the House of Representatives. There was now "one sole and preeminent power: the United States of America."[13] The west had triumphed. Cutting a few moral corners in Iraq was warranted when the overriding evangelical purpose was to accelerate the spread of the hallmark and gift of the American Empire: democracy.

Over the course of the decade that followed the invasion of Kuwait, therefore, the United States pursued a policy that was both ambiguous and ambitious. It repeated the mantra of liberating countries like Iraq and fostering the concept and practice of democracy; but it also jealously, and at times brutally, sought to protect and promote its interests in this rapidly changing world, almost no matter what the price. In Iraq, UN Resolution 687, passed in the aftermath of the Gulf War, included measures related to Kuwaiti sovereignty, but also applied sanctions to "the sale or supply . . . of commodities or products other than medicine and health supplies," with "foodstuffs" likewise excluded.[14] These measures were intended to force disarmament, including the termination of biological and chemical weapons programmes, and to force agreement on recognition of the sovereignty of Kuwait. With blanket restrictions on Iraqi exports and on financial transactions, the impact was devastating—especially on the poor. Initial estimates in the *Lancet* suggested that 500,000 children alone died from malnutrition and disease as a direct result of these policies in five years.[15] In 1996, Leslie Stahl interviewed Madeleine Albright, U.S. Ambassador to the United Nations, on the TV programme *60 Minutes* and stated that more children had died in Iraq as a result of sanctions than in Hiroshima in 1945. "I think it is a very hard choice," Albright replied; nevertheless, she went on, "we think the price is worth it."[16]

Sanctions were not the only steps taken against Iraq following the ceasefire. No-fly zones were imposed to the north of the 36th parallel and to the south of the 32nd (later extended to the 33rd) parallel soon after the ceasefire was agreed—patrolled by nearly 200,000 armed overwatch sorties flown by United States, French and British warplanes in the 1990s.[17] These no-fly zones, which between them covered more than half of Iraqi territory, were ostensibly established to protect the Kurdish minority in the north and the Shīʿite population in the south. That they were imposed unilaterally, without a mandate from the UN Security Council, showed that the west was willing to interfere in another country's internal affairs and take matters into its own hands when it suited it.[18]

This was demonstrated again in 1998, when President Clinton signed into law the Iraq Liberation Act which made it the formal "policy of the United States to support efforts to remove the regime headed by Saddam Hussein from power in Iraq and to promote the emergence of a democratic government to replace that regime."[19] Clinton also announced that $8 million was being made available for "the Iraqi democratic opposition," with the express aim of enabling the dissonant voices opposed to Saddam to "unify [and to] work together more effectively."[20]

The attempts by the United States and its allies to get what they wanted were not limited to Iraq. President Clinton made overtures to the Iranian leadership, for example, in an attempt to open dialogue and improve relations that had spiralled downwards in the aftermath of the Irangate scandal and following the catastrophic shooting down of an Iranian passenger jet in 1988 by the USS *Vincennes*. Although the full extent of the reprisals taken by Teheran is still unclear, multiple evidence trails suggest an extensive series of terrorist attacks were made against U.S. targets—possibly including the downing of Pan Am 103 over Lockerbie in December 1988, and also the bombing of a U.S. base near Dhahran in Saudi Arabia in 1996.[21]

After Iranian involvement in the latter had been strongly suggested by a U.S. investigation, President Clinton protested to President Khatami in a letter delivered by an intermediary in the late 1990s. The Iranians responded aggressively, dismissing American claims of Iranian complicity in the deaths of nineteen servicemen as "inaccurate and unacceptable." Moreover, it was disingenuous, the response asserted, for the United States to claim outrage over terrorist attacks given that it had done nothing at all to "prosecute or extradite the readily identifiable American citizens responsible for the downing of [the] Iranian civilian airliner" a decade earlier. Nevertheless, Teheran did offer hope for the future. The President should rest assured, the reply stated, that Iran had "no hostile intentions towards Americans." Indeed, "the Iranian people not only harbour no enmity but [also] have respect for the great American people."[22]

This step forward was echoed in Afghanistan, where channels of communication were opened with the hardline Taliban regime after the Supreme Leader, Mullah Omar, made contact through an intermediary in 1996. Once again, the early signs were promising. "The Taliban think highly of the US," one senior Taliban leader said, according to a confidential report of the first meeting that was prepared by the U.S. embassy in Kabul; moreover, support provided by Washington "during the jihad against the Soviets" had not been forgotten. Above all, "the Taliban want good relations with the United States."[23] This conciliatory message gave grounds for optimism, as did the fact that the United States had contacts and old friends locally who might prove useful in the future. One such was the warlord Jalaluddin Haqqani, a long-term CIA asset since the Soviet invasion, whose (relatively) liberal attitudes towards social policy and women's rights were noted in a memo that highlighted his growing importance within the Taliban.[24]

The United States was primarily concerned about Afghanistan's role as a hotbed for militants and terrorists. The Taliban had gained control of Kabul in the course of 1996, sparking growing alarm in neighbouring countries about possible regional instability, the rise of religious fundamentalism and the prospect of Russia becoming drawn into a region from which it had only just stepped back following the collapse of the USSR.

These concerns were set out at a high-level meeting with senior Taliban figures in Kandahar in October 1996. American officials were given assurances that militant training camps had been closed and that access would be provided to allow inspections to prove this was the case. Taliban officials, who included Mullah Ghous, the de facto Afghan Foreign Minister, responded encouragingly when asked about Osama bin Laden, whose activities had been of mounting concern to U.S. intelligence. The CIA linked bin Laden to attacks on U.S. soldiers in Somalia in 1992, to the bombing of New York's World Trade Center in 1993 and to the creation of "a network of al-Qaida recruitment centres and guest houses in Egypt, Saudi Arabia and Pakistan." As one intelligence report put it, he was "one of the most significant financial sponsors of Islamic extremist activities in the world."[25]

"It would be useful," American officials told Afghan representatives, "if the Taliban could tell us where he is located and ensure that he cannot carry out [terrorist] attacks." The Afghan officials replied that bin Laden was "with us as a guest, as a refugee," and as such there was an obligation to "treat a guest with respect and hospitality" in keeping with Pashto culture. "The Taliban," they said, "would not allow anyone to use [our] territory for terrorist activities." In any event, bin Laden had "promised he would not commit [terrorist attacks]" while living in Afghanistan, and furthermore had complied when the Taliban had become suspicious of him living in caves south of Jalalabad near Tora Bora and had told him "to move out [and] live in an ordinary house."[26]

Although this was superficially reassuring, it was not as emphatic as the Americans wanted, prompting a change of tack. "This man is poison," the U.S. officials told the Taliban emissaries emphatically. "All countries, even as big and powerful as the US, need friends. [And] Afghanistan especially needs friends." This was a warning shot: the implication was that there would be consequences if bin Laden was involved in any further terrorist attack. The reply by Mullah Rabbani, a high-ranking figure in the Taliban leadership, was clear, repeating what had been said before. His response was quoted in full in a cable that was sent back to Washington and copied to U.S. missions in Islamabad, Karachi, Lahore, Riyadh and Jeddah: "in this part of the world there is a law that when someone seeks refuge, he should be granted asylum, but if there are people who carry out terrorist activities, then you can point these out; we have our senses and will not permit anyone to carry out these filthy activities."[27]

These assurances were never fully tested. Nor were they taken at face value. By the spring of 1998, the CIA was working on a capture plan that involved gaining the support and co-operation of "the tribals" in Afghanistan for what was described by planners as a "perfect operation." By May, "planning for the [Osama bin Laden] rendition is going very well," according to a heavily redacted CIA report; a scheme had been developed that was "detailed, thoughtful, realistic," although it was not without risks. Whether the plan would get approval was another matter: as one involved put it, "odds the op will get the green light [are] 50–50." Senior army officers took a less optimistic view. The commander of Delta Force was reported as being "uncomfortable" with details of the scheme, while the commander of Joint Special Operations thought that the CIA plan was "out of [its] league." Although there was a "final graded rehearsal of the operation"—which went well—the plug was pulled.[28]

Before any definitive attempt to deal with bin Laden could take place, events took a decisive turn. On 7 August 1998, al-Qaida carried out simultaneous bombings of the U.S. embassies in Nairobi and Dar-es-Salaam, the largest cities in Kenya and Tanzania respectively, killing 224 people and injuring thousands more. The finger of suspicion pointed immediately at bin Laden.

Within two weeks, the U.S. took action, launching seventy-eight cruise missiles against four suspected al-Qaida bases in Afghanistan. "Our target was terror," President Clinton said in a televised address on 20 August. "Our mission was clear: to strike at the network of radical groups associated with and funded by Osama bin Laden, perhaps the preeminent organiser and financier of international terrorism in the world today." Clinton—at that point in the midst of a sex scandal relating to the intern Monica Lewinsky that threatened to bring down his presidency and had required a separate television address three days earlier—did not consult with the Taliban prior to trying to eliminate the plot's mastermind. In an attempt to pre-empt criticism, he said in his announcement that "I want the world to understand that our actions were not aimed against Islam." On the contrary, continued the beleaguered President, Islam is "a great religion."[29]

It was bad enough that the attempts to deal with Osama bin Laden proved unsuccessful. But they also antagonised the Taliban, which immediately expressed outrage at the attack on Afghan territory and against a guest who had not been proven guilty of involvement in the attacks in East Africa. Mullah Omar declared that the Taliban would "never hand over bin Laden to anyone and would protect him with our blood at all costs."[30] As one U.S. intelligence assessment explained, there was considerable sympathy for bin Laden and his extremism in the Arab world, where the message of "injustice and victimisation" of Muslim peoples went hand in glove with the popular belief that "US policies prop up corrupt regimes . . . and are designed to divide, weaken and exploit the Arab world." Few endorse bin Laden's terrorism, the report concluded, but "many share at least some of his political sentiments."[31]

These were views held by Mullah Omar himself, who in a remarkable telephone call to the State Department in Washington three days after the missile strikes stated that the "strikes would prove counter-productive and arouse anti-American feelings in the Islamic world." In the course of this recently declassified telephone call, the only known direct contact between the Afghan Supreme Leader and U.S. officials, Mullah Omar remarked on the "current domestic difficulties" being experienced by President Clinton—a reference to the Lewinsky affair. With this in mind, and in order to "rebuild US popularity in the Islamic world" following the disastrous unilateral attack, said Mullah Omar, "Congress should force President Clinton to resign."[32]

The U.S. strikes were denounced meanwhile as an attack on the "entire Afghan people" by a senior Taliban spokesman, Wakīl Ahmed Muttawakkil. Large anti-American demonstrations took place in Kandahar and Jalalabad following the assault, according to Ahmed, who discussed the attacks with U.S. officials not long afterwards. "If [the Taliban] could have retaliated with similar strikes against Washington," he stated, "it would have [done so]."[33] Like Saddam Hussein when he found out that the United States had been selling arms to Iran while claiming to support Iraq, it was the sense of betrayal and double-dealing that was damaging: the United States gave friendly messages on the one hand and then acted brutally on the other.

Wakīl Ahmed expressed his outrage over the flimsiness of the evidence that had been presented by the Americans after the U.S. military strikes. The Taliban leadership had always been clear that if bin Laden were found to be conducting terrorist activities from Afghan soil, action would be taken against him.[34] Indeed, Mullah Omar asked the State Department for substantiation almost immediately.[35] Some believed that the charges were trumped up, the Taliban official said, while others pointed out that bin Laden "had once been a trained guerrilla supported by the United States." What had been presented by the Americans amounted to nothing more than "some papers" which hardly constituted proof; a video cassette handed to the Taliban that was assumed to "contain something new" about bin Laden was simply embarrassing—it was worthless as a piece of evidence.

The attack was disgraceful, Ahmed said, resulting in the deaths of innocent Afghans and a violation of Afghan sovereignty. If the Americans really wanted a solution to the bin Laden problem, he concluded, they should talk to the Saudis; if they did so, matters would be solved in "minutes not hours."[36] Ironically, the same assessment had already been reached separately by the United States, as a flurry of diplomatic cables, research papers and recommendations about winning support in Riyadh show.[37]

The repercussions of the U.S. strikes were disastrous. As a major U.S. intelligence study of the al-Qaida threat written a year later put it, apart from the fact that the attempt to eliminate bin Laden had failed, the attack served to establish him across much of the Arabic-speaking world as well as elsewhere as "an underdog standing firm in the face of bullying aggression." There were real dangers in the growing perception of "American cultural arrogance"; it was troubling too, the report warned, that the U.S.

attack "was morally questionable" and mirrored aspects of bin Laden's own bombings, where innocent casualties suffered because of a political agenda deemed to justify the use of force. As a result, "the retaliatory cruise missile strikes . . . may ultimately prove to have done more harm than good." The United States should also be aware, the report prophetically added, that the airstrikes were likely to "provoke a new round of terrorist bombing plots."[38]

Even before that happened, the failed intervention brought unwelcome results. Views within the Taliban leadership about the outside world hardened as suspicions about the duplicity of the west took firm root. A siege mentality developed that served to accelerate the development of increasingly hardline religious views as well as a rising interest in exporting its brand of radical Islam on a worldwide basis—although one contemporary CIA report judged that it was highly unlikely that this could be done effectively.[39]

Nevertheless, U.S. pressure served to make staunchly conservative voices become increasingly fundamentalist. Those like Mullah Rabbani, deputy leader and head of the Kabul Shūrā (Council), who feared that failing to expel bin Laden would deepen Afghanistan's international isolation, were outmanoeuvred by Mullah Omar, whose hardline policy not to co-operate with or capitulate before outsiders prevailed. As a result, the Taliban moved closer to bin Laden's aggressive proposals for freeing Muslims from the grasp of the west and reinstating a fantasy pre-medieval world.[40]

This was precisely the aim of the 9/11 attacks. An intelligence report written in 1999 had already noted how bin Laden had a "large and inflated ego [and saw] himself as a player on a very large and very old historical stage e.g., he sees himself resisting the latest Crusaders."[41] It was highly revealing, then, that every single audio and video tape he released after the attack on the Twin Towers mentioned the Crusades or the Crusaders as reference points. Revolutionaries often choose to evoke an idealised past, but few look back a thousand years for inspiration and justification for terrorist acts.

In the months leading up to 9/11, intelligence pointed to the rising threat of al-Qaida. A memo "For the President only" with the ominous title "Bin Ladin [*sic*] Determined to Strike in US" and dated 6 August 2001 reported the FBI's conclusion that information gathered from "approximately 70 full field investigations" ongoing throughout the United States "indicated patterns of suspicious activity in this country consistent with preparations for hijackings or other types of attacks."[42] The United States had been nervous enough in the interim to keep the door open to the regime in Kabul, offering reassurance that "the United States was not against the Taliban, per se [and] was not out to destroy the Taliban." The problem was bin Laden. If he could be dealt with, U.S. diplomats in the region advised, "we would have a different kind of relationship."[43]

He was not dealt with. At 8:24 in the morning of 11 September 2001, it became clear that something was very wrong. Air traffic control had been trying to contact American Airlines flight 11 from Boston to Los Angeles for eleven minutes since instructing the pilots to climb to 35,000 feet. When a response came, it was unexpected: "We have some planes. Just stay quiet, and you'll be okay. We are returning to the airport."[44] At 8:46 a.m. Eastern Time, the Boeing 767 was flown into the North Tower of the World Trade Center. In the next hour and seventeen minutes, three other passenger jets that had been hijacked came down: United 175 impacted the South Tower of the World Trade Center; American 77 was flown into the Pentagon; and United 93 crashed near Shanksville, Pennsylvania.[45]

Two thousand nine hundred and seventy-seven people died on 9/11, along with nineteen terrorists. The psychological impact of the attacks, which saw the collapse of both of the Twin Towers and the Pentagon building damaged, was intense. Terrorist acts committed against embassy buildings or American troops abroad were shocking enough, but a co-ordinated attack against mainland targets was devastating. The haunting and terrifying footage of planes being deliberately flown into buildings, and the scenes of disaster, chaos and tragedy that occurred in the aftermath demanded an immediate and epic response. "The search is underway for those who are behind these evil acts," President George W. Bush said in a televised address on the evening of the attacks. "I've directed the full resources of our intelligence and law enforcement communities to find those responsible and bring them to justice. We will make no distinction," he warned, "between the terrorists who committed these acts and those who harbour them."[46]

Expressions of support flooded in from all corners of the globe—including from such unlikely quarters as Libya, Syria and Iran, whose President expressed "deep regret and sympathy for the victims," adding that "it is an international duty to try to undermine terrorism."[47] It was immediately obvious that bin Laden was behind the attacks—although the Taliban ambassador to Pakistan claimed that the former did not have the resources necessary to execute such "a well-organised plan."[48] Wakīl Ahmed Muttawakil told the Qatari broadcaster al-Jazeera the day after the attacks that the Taliban "denounce this terrorist attack, whoever is behind it."[49]

Within hours of the attacks, strategies were being drawn up to deal with bin Laden. An action plan issued on the morning of 13 September set out the importance of engaging Iran and contacting the authorities in Turkmenistan, Uzbekistan, Kyrgyzstan, Kazakhstan and China—Afghanistan's neighbours and near neighbours. A plan was set out to "[r]e-energize" them within the week that followed, with a view to preparing them for forthcoming military action against the Taliban.[50] The first step of the response to 9/11 was to line up the countries of the Silk Roads.

One of Afghanistan's neighbours was given particular attention. Pakistan had sympathies and close ties with the Taliban that went back one if not two generations. The terrorist attacks now required a straight choice for Islamabad, the head of Pakistan's Intelligence Service was told, between "black and white . . . with no grey." The country either had to "stand with the United States in the fight against terrorism or stand against us."[51]

As the pieces were moved into position for an assault on Afghanistan, the Taliban were given a final, ominous warning—to be delivered in person either by the President of Pakistan or by his security chief. "It is in your interest and in the interest of your survival to hand over all al-Qaida leaders, to close the terrorists' camps and allow the US access to terrorist facilities." The response would be "devastating" if "any person or group connected in any way to Afghanistan" was involved in terrorist attacks on the United States. "Every pillar of the Taliban regime," the curt message said, "will be destroyed."[52] The ultimatum was emphatic and clear: surrender bin Laden, or suffer the consequences.

For all the efforts to track down bin Laden and destroy the capability of al-Qaida, there was more at stake than a manhunt. In fact, attention in Washington quickly turned to the bigger picture: controlling the centre of Asia decisively and properly. Influential voices argued that what was needed was a full reshaping of the countries of this region, one where U.S. interests and security would be radically improved.

For decades, the United States had diced with the devil. For decades, the heart of Asia had been seen as singularly important—so much so that after the Second World War it became routine to refer explicitly to this region as being directly relevant to the national security of the United States. Its location between east and west made it strategically crucial in relation to superpower rivalry, while the natural resources—oil and gas above all—made what happened in the countries of the Persian Gulf and their immediate neighbours really matter to U.S. national security.

By 30 September 2001, three weeks after the atrocities of 9/11, the Secretary of Defense, Donald Rumsfeld, offered the President his "strategic thoughts" about what the United States could and should seek to achieve in the near future as part of its "war aim." "Some air strikes against al-Qaida and Taliban targets are planned to begin soon," he noted, marking the start of what he referred to as a "war." It was important, he wrote, to "persuade or compel States to stop supporting terrorism." What he proposed next, however, was dramatic and astonishingly ambitious. "If the war does not significantly change the world's political map, the US will not achieve its aim." What this meant was then spelled out clearly. "The [United States government] should envision a goal along these lines: New regimes in Afghanistan and another key State (or two)."[53] He did not need to specify which states he was talking about: Iran and Iraq.

The 9/11 attacks transformed the way the United States engaged with the world as a whole. America's future depended on securing the spine of Asia, running from Iraq's western frontier with Syria and Turkey to the Hindu Kush. The vision was set out emphatically by President Bush at the end of January 2002. By then, the Taliban had been dealt with decisively, pushed out of the major cities, including Kabul, within weeks of the start of Operation Enduring Freedom, which involved extensive air attacks and a major deployment of ground forces. Although bin Laden was still at large, the President laid out in his State of the Union address why the United States had to set its sights on more ambitious goals. Many regimes that had previously been hostile to American interests "have been pretty quiet since September 11, but we know their true nature." North Korea, a rogue state par excellence, was one. But the real focus was on the threat posed by two others: Iran and Iraq. These, along with the regime in Pyongyang, "constitute an axis of evil, arming to threaten the peace of the world." Dismantling this axis was crucial. "Our war on terror is well begun, but it is only begun."[54]

The determination to take control was overwhelming. Deposing existing regimes deemed destabilising and dangerous became paramount in the strategic thinking of the United States and its allies. Priority was given to getting rid of clear and present dangers, with little thought to what would, could or should happen next. Fixing short-term problems was more important than the long-term scenario. This was explicit in the plans made against Afghanistan in the autumn of 2001. "The [U.S. government] should not agonise over post-Taliban arrangements," suggested a paper issued after the air campaign had already started. Defeating al-Qaida and the Taliban was key; what happened afterwards could be worried about later.[55]

The same short-termism was evident in the case of Iraq, where the sharp focus on removing Saddam Hussein from power was set against a lack of planning for how the country would look in the future. The desire to get rid of Saddam had been on the agenda since the first days of the Bush administration, with the new Secretary of State, Colin Powell, asking for clarification about "[U.S.] regime change policy in Iraq" less than seventy-two hours after George Bush's inauguration—and months before 9/11.[56] In the aftermath of the terrorist attacks, attention turned almost immediately to Saddam Hussein. At a time when U.S. troops seemed to be taking inexorable control of Afghanistan, the Department of Defense was working hard to prepare for a major move on Iraq. The question was simple, as planning notes for a meeting between Rumsfeld and General Tommy Franks, Chief of Central Command make clear: "how [to] start?"[57]

Three possible triggers were envisaged—all of which could justify military action. Perhaps Saddam "moves against the Kurds in [the] north?," wondered Donald Rumsfeld in November 2001; maybe a "connection to Sept 11 attack or to anthrax attacks" (following mailings to several media outlets and to two U.S. senators in September 2001); or what if there was a "dispute over WMD inspections?" This seemed a promising line—as revealed by the comment that follows: "start now thinking about inspection demands."[58]

Over the course of 2002 and at the start of 2003, pressure was ramped up on Iraq, with the issue of chemical and biological weapons and that of weapons of mass destruction taking centre stage. The United States pursued this with an almost evangelical zeal. In the absence of "incontrovertible evidence" of a link between 9/11 and Baghdad, one report noted, only Tony Blair could be relied on to support war, albeit "at substantial political cost," while another underlined the fact that "many, if not most, countries allied with or friendly towards the United States—especially in Europe—harbour grave doubts about . . . an all-out attack on Iraq." Work therefore went into establishing a legal framework for full-scale war in anticipation of the likelihood that the United Nations would not give a clear mandate for action.[59]

Particular emphasis was given to building up the case that Iraq was not just determined to make weapons of mass destruction but was doing so covertly—and obstructing inspectors from the International Atomic Energy Agency (IAEA) at the same time. In some cases, this created problems with the monitors themselves, who found their positions overstated, compromised or even at risk altogether. In the spring of 2002, for example, José Bustani, the Brazilian director-general of the Organisation for the Prohibition of Chemical Weapons, was ousted following a special closed session—this was the first time the head of a major international organisation had been forced from their position.[60] Information gathered from one-off and often unreliable sources was given prominence, and speculation was presented as fact, the result of a single-minded determination to make the case against Iraq and Saddam appear watertight. "Every statement I make today," Colin Powell told the UN on 5 February 2003, "is backed up by sources, solid sources. These are not assertions. What we're giving you are facts and conclusions based on solid intelligence."[61]

They were nothing of the sort. Barely a week earlier, a report by the IAEA had concluded that "we have to date found no evidence that Iraq has revived its nuclear weapons programme since the programme in the 1990s," and it added that "further verification activities [would] be necessary."[62] This chimed with an update released the same day, 27 January 2003, by Hans Blix, head of the United Nations Monitoring, Verification and Inspection Commission (UNMOVIC), who stated that although inspectors occasionally faced incidents of harassment, "Iraq has on the whole cooperated rather well so far" with the demands of inspectors.[63]

As it later emerged, there was no link between Saddam Hussein and al-Qaida's attacks of 2001. Indeed, the millions of pages recovered from Baghdad following the invasion that began on 19 March 2003 have revealed conspicuously few references to terrorism at all. Rather, documents relating to the Iraqi Intelligence Service suggest that considerable care was taken to rein in those like Abu Abbas, leader of the Palestinian Liberation Front which undertook some spectacular attacks in the 1980s, and made clear that no attacks should be made on American targets under any circumstances—other than in the event of a U.S. attack on Iraq.[64]

Likewise, as we now know, the supposedly extensive and elaborate nuclear weapons programme, which was so vividly real in the minds of those who saw Iraq as a threat to regional and world peace, had little basis in fact. Trailers that Colin Powell described as mobile biological weapons facilities "hidden in large groves of palm trees and . . . moved every one to four weeks to avoid detection" turned out to be weather balloons—just as the Iraqis had said they were.[65]

The determination to get rid of Saddam Hussein at any cost went hand in hand with chronically poor planning for the aftermath. Blueprints and books produced before and as the invasion got under way set out the idyllic future that lay ahead for Iraq after liberation. The oil of Iraq, one major study claimed optimistically, was "a tremendous asset." It had the potential to "benefit every last citizen of the country, regardless of ethnicity or religious affiliation."[66] The naive assumption that wealth would be shared happily and fairly says much about the unrealistic expectations of what the consequences of the invasion would be. Yet the motif of spontaneous resolution was omnipresent. "Iraq, unlike Afghanistan, is a rather wealthy country," the White House spokesman, Ari Fleischer, stated in a briefing in February 2003. It has "tremendous resources that belong to the Iraqi people. And so . . . Iraq [should easily] be able to shoulder much of the burden for their own reconstruction." This was echoed almost precisely by Paul Wolfowitz, Donald Rumsfeld's deputy, in a hearing with the House Appropriations Committee eight days after the invasion began in March 2003. There was no need to worry, he insisted, "we're dealing with a country that can really finance its own reconstruction, and relatively soon." Oil revenues, he breezily predicted, would bring in $50 billion to $100 billion over the next "two or three years."[67]

The idea that removing Saddam would turn Iraq into a land of milk and honey was wishful thinking on an epic scale. When troops went into Afghanistan, policy planners noted solemnly that the United States "should not commit to any post-Taliban military involvement since the US will be heavily engaged in the anti-terrorism effort worldwide."[68] Expectations in Iraq were similar: 270,000 troops would be needed for an invasion of the country, according to plans drawn up by U.S. Central Command; but three and a half years later there would be no need for more than 5,000 ground troops. This all looked plausible when presented on PowerPoint slides to those who saw what they wanted to see.[69] These were light wars, in other words, ones that would be resolved quickly and enable a new balance to be established across a pivotal region of Asia.

In both cases, however, the wars proved lengthy and expensive. Iraq was all but engulfed in civil war following the fall of Baghdad and the major insurgency that followed, while in Afghanistan reaction to the intervention was as resourceful and determined as it had been against the Soviet Union in the 1980s, with Pakistan again providing crucial support for the hardline resistance fighters. Many thousands of servicemen gave their lives, while more than 150,000 U.S. veterans are listed as suffering from wounds and injuries that rank them as being at least 70 per cent disabled.[70] This comes on top of the hundreds of thousands of Afghan and Iraqi civilians killed or wounded in military action or—by virtue of being in the wrong place at the wrong time in cross-fire, drone strikes or car bombings—as "collateral damage."[71]

Financial costs galloped upwards at an astonishing pace. One recent survey estimates the cost of engagement in Iraq and Afghanistan as being as high as $6 trillion—or $75,000 for every American household once long-term medical care and disability compensation is taken into account. This represents around 20 per cent of the rise in U.S. national debt between 2001 and 2012.[72]

That the effect of the interventions has been more limited than hoped only makes things worse. By 2011, President Obama had all but given up on Afghanistan, according to his former Secretary of Defense, Robert Gates, who realised how bleak the situation was in a meeting in the White House in March 2011. "As I sat there, I thought: The President doesn't trust his commander [General Petraeus], can't stand [Afghan President] Karzai, doesn't believe in his own strategy and doesn't consider the war to be his. For him, it's all about getting out."[73] It is a description angrily echoed by President Karzai, who had been built up, supported and, in the view of many, enriched by the west. "As a nation," he told the author William Dalrymple, Afghanistan has suffered enormously because of U.S. policy; the Americans "did not fight against terrorism where it was, where it still is. They continued damaging Afghanistan and its people." There was no other way to put it, he said: "This is a betrayal."[74]

In Iraq, meanwhile, there is little to show for the loss of life, the vast cost and the dashed hopes for the future. Ten years after the fall of Saddam Hussein, the country could be found at the lower end of the indices that track the transition to healthy democracy. On human rights, press freedom, minority rights, corruption and freedom of speech, Iraq ranks no higher than it did under Saddam Hussein, and in some cases it is lower. The country has been crippled by uncertainty and unrest, with minority populations subjected to catastrophic upheaval and grotesque violence. Prospects for the future look bleak.

Then, of course, there is the reputational damage to the west in general and to the United States in particular. "We should avoid as much as possible creating images of Americans killing Moslems," Donald Rumsfeld advised President Bush two weeks after 9/11.[75] This apparent sensitivity was quickly replaced by images of inmates being held without trial in the deliberate limbo of Guantánamo Bay—a location specifically chosen on the basis that inmates could be denied the protection allowed by the U.S. Constitution. Inquiries into the run-up to the Iraq War in the United States and the United Kingdom found that evidence had been misrepresented, manipulated and moulded to support decisions that had already been reached behind closed doors. Efforts to control the media in Iraq post-Saddam, where the concept of freedom would be trumpeted by journalists using "approved US Government information" to underline "hopes for a prosperous democratic future," evoked memories of Soviet-style commissars sanctioning stories based not on reality but on a dream.[76]

On top of that come extra-judicial renditions, torture on an institutional scale and drone strikes against figures deemed—but not necessarily proven—to be threats. It says a great deal about the sophistication and pluralism of the west that these issues can be debated in public, and that many are horrified by the hypocrisy of the message of the primacy of democracy on the one hand and the practice of imperial power on the other. So appalled were some that they decided to leak classified information that laid bare just how policy was created: pragmatically, on the hoof and often with little thought about international law and justice. None of this showed the west in a good light—something felt keenly by the intelligence agencies themselves, which have fought to keep reports of the nature and extent of torture classified, even in the face of direct challenges from the U.S. Senate itself.

While attention has been focused on efforts to influence and shape Iraq and Afghanistan, it is important not to overlook the attempts to bring about change in Iran. These have included sanctions, enforced dynamically by Washington, which have arguably been counter-productive. As in Iraq in the 1990s, it is clear that the effect is strongest and most pronounced on the poor, the weak and the disenfranchised—making their bad lot even worse. Restricting Iranian oil exports of course has an impact on the standard of living not only of Iranian citizens but also of people living on the other side of the world. In a global energy market, the price per unit of gas, electricity and fuel affects farmers in Minnesota, taxi drivers in Madrid, girls studying in sub-Saharan Africa and coffee growers in Vietnam. We are all directly affected by the power politics going on thousands of miles away. It is easy to forget that, in the developing world, cents can make the difference between life and death; the enforcement of embargoes can mean silent suffocation for those whose voices cannot be heard—mothers in the slums of Mumbai, basket weavers in the suburbs of Mombasa or women trying to oppose illegal mining activities in South America. And all so that Iran is forced to disavow a nuclear programme built on U.S. technology sold to a despotic, intolerant and corrupt regime in the 1970s.

As it is, apart from the diplomatic and economic pressure put on Teheran, the United States has consistently made it clear that it would consider using force against Iran to impose an end to the enrichment programme. In the final stages of the last Bush administration, Dick Cheney claimed that he had pushed hard for strikes against Iranian nuclear facilities, even though reactors such as Bushihr are now heavily protected by sophisticated Russian Tor surface-to-air missile systems. "I was probably a bigger advocate of military action than many of my colleagues," he said in 2009.[77] Others warned him that pre-emptive strikes would make the situation across the region worse, not better. He has returned to the idea repeatedly. Negotiations will fail unless there is a threat of military action, he said in 2013, for example. "I have trouble seeing how we're going to achieve our objective short of that," he told ABC News.[78]

The theme that the west needs to threaten—and be willing to use—force to get what it wants has become a mantra in Washington. "Iran will have to prove that its programme is really peaceful," Secretary of State John Kerry said in November 2013. Iran should bear in mind, he warned, that "the president . . . has said specifically that he has not taken [the] threat [of military action] off the table." It is a message that he has articulated repeatedly. "The military option that is available to the United States is ready," Kerry said in an interview with the Saudi-owned al-Arabiya channel in January 2014. If necessary, he added, the United States would "do what it would have to do."[79] "As I have made clear time and again during the course of my presidency," President Obama stressed, "I will not hesitate to use force when it is necessary to defend the United States and its interests."[80]

Despite issuing threats designed to bring Iran to the negotiating table, the United States appears to have been taking action behind the scenes to achieve what it wants anyway. While there were several potential sources for the Stuxnet virus that attacked the centrifuges at the Natanz nuclear facility in Iran and then other reactors across the country, multiple indicators suggest that the highly sophisticated and aggressive cyber strategies targeting the nuclear programme could be traced back to the United States—and directly to the White House.[81] Cyber-terrorism is acceptable, it seems, as long as it is in the hands of western intelligence agencies. Like the threat to use force against Iran, protecting a global order that suits western interests is simply a new chapter in the attempt to maintain position in the ancient crossroads of civilisation. The stakes are too high to do otherwise.

Conclusion

The New Silk Road

In many ways, the late twentieth and early twenty-first centuries have represented something of a disaster for the United States and Europe as they have played out their doomed struggle to retain their position in the vital territories that link east with west. What has been striking throughout the events of recent decades is the west's lack of perspective about global history—about the bigger picture, the wider themes and the larger patterns playing out in the region. In the minds of policy planners, politicians, diplomats and generals, the problems of Afghanistan, Iran and Iraq seemed distinct, separate and only loosely linked to each other.

And yet taking a step back provides valuable perspective as well as remarkable insight, enabling us to see a broad region that is in turmoil. In Turkey, a battle is raging for the soul of the country, with internet providers and social media being shut down on a whim by a government divided about where the future lies. The dilemma is replicated in Ukraine, where different national visions have torn the country apart. Syria too is going through a traumatic experience of profound change, as forces of conservatism and liberalism battle each other at huge cost. The Caucasus has been through a period of transition too, with multiple issues of identity and nationalism bubbling up, most notably in Chechnya and Georgia. Then of course, there is the region further east, where the "Tulip Revolution" in Kyrgyzstan in 2005 was the prelude to a long period of political instability, and Xinjiang in western China where the Uighur population have become increasingly unsettled and hostile, with terrorist attacks now such a threat that the authorities have decreed that growing a long beard is a mark of suspicious intentions, and have begun a formal programme, known as Project Beauty, to prevent women from wearing the veil.

There is more going on, then, than the clumsy interventions of the west in Iraq and Afghanistan and the use of pressure in Ukraine, Iran and elsewhere. From east to west, the Silk Roads are rising up once more. It is easy to feel confused and disturbed by dislocation and violence in the Islamic world, by religious fundamentalism, by clashes between Russia and its neighbours or by China's struggle with extremism in its western provinces. What we are witnessing, however, are the birthing pains of a region that once dominated the intellectual, cultural and economic landscape and which is now re-emerging. We are seeing the signs of the world's centre of gravity shifting—back to where it lay for millennia.

There are obvious reasons why this is happening. Most important, of course, are the natural resources of this region. Monopolising the resources of Persia, Mesopotamia and the Gulf was a priority during the First World War, and efforts to secure the greatest prize in history have dominated the attitudes of the western world to this region ever since. If anything, there is now even more to play for than there was when the scale of Knox D'Arcy's finds first became apparent: the combined proved crude reserves under the Caspian Sea alone are nearly twice those of the entire United States.[1] From Kurdistan, where newly discovered oil reservoirs such as the Taq Taq field, whose production has risen from 2,000 to 250,000 barrels per day since 2007—worth hundreds of millions of dollars per month—to the huge Karachaganak reserve on the border between Kazakhstan and Russia which contains an estimated 42 trillion cubic feet of natural gas, as well as liquefied gas and crude oil, the countries of this region are groaning under its natural resources.

Then there is the Donbas basin that straddles Ukraine's eastern frontier with Russia, which has long been famed for coal deposits estimated to have extractable reserves of around 10 billion tons. This too is an area of rising significance because of further mineral wealth. Recent geology-based assessments by the U.S. Geological Service have suggested the presence of 1.4 billion barrels of oil and 2.4 trillion cubic feet of natural gas, as well as considerable estimated volumes of natural gas liquids.[2] Alongside this sit the natural gas supplies of Turkmenistan. With no less than 700 trillion cubic feet of natural gas estimated to be below the ground, the country controls the fourth largest supplies in the world. And then there are the mines of Uzbekistan and Kyrgyzstan that form part of the Tian Shan belt, second only to the Witwatersrand basin in South Africa for the size of its gold deposits. Or there are beryllium, dysprosium and other "rare earths" found in Kazakhstan that are vital for the manufacture of mobile phones, laptops and rechargeable batteries, as well as the uranium and plutonium that are essential for nuclear energy—and nuclear warheads.

Even the earth itself is rich and valuable. Once, it was the horses of Central Asia that were a highly prized commodity, coveted in the imperial court in China and in the markets of Delhi, as famous to the chroniclers of Kiev as those of Constantinople and Beijing. Today, large parts of the grazing land of the steppes have been transformed to become the astonishingly productive grainfields of southern Russia and Ukraine: indeed, so fertile and sought after is the trademark *chernozem* (literally "dark earth") that one NGO has found that close to a billion dollars' worth of this soil is dug up and sold annually in Ukraine alone.[3]

The impact of instability, unrest or war in this region is not just felt in the price of oil at petrol pumps across the world; it affects the price of the technology we use and even that of the bread we eat. In the summer of 2010, for example, weather conditions produced a poor harvest in Russia, with yields well below domestic demand. As soon as the likely deficit became clear, an immediate ban was placed on the international export of cereals, effective with ten days' warning. The impact on global cereal prices was instant: they rose 15 per cent in just two days.[4] Turmoil in Ukraine at the start of 2014 had a similar impact, forcing the price of wheat sharply upwards because of fears about its effect on agricultural production in the world's third largest wheat exporter.

The cultivation of other crops in this part of the world follows similar principles. Once, Central Asia was famous for Babur's orange trees and, later, for the tulips that were so highly prized in capital cities across western Europe in the seventeenth century that canal houses in Amsterdam were exchanged for single bulbs. Today it is the poppy that is fought over: its cultivation, above all in Afghanistan, underpins worldwide consumption patterns for heroin, and determines its price—and of course impacts the costs that result from treatment for drug addiction and rehabilitation care as well as the price for trying to police organised crime.[5]

This is a part of the world that may seem strange and unfamiliar to the west, and even alien to the point of bizarre. In Turkmenistan, a giant golden statue of the President that revolves to face the direction of the sun was erected in 1998, while four years later the months were renamed, with April (previously "Aprel") changed to "Gurbansoltan" after the then leader's late mother. Or there is neighbouring Kazakhstan, where the President, Nursultan Nazarbayev, was re-elected in 2011 after winning an impressive 96 per cent of the vote, and leaked diplomatic cables reveal that pop stars like Elton John and Nelly Furtado have performed private concerts for the President's family after receiving offers that were too good to refuse.[6] In Tajikistan, after briefly holding the record for the world's tallest flagpole, attention has now turned to building Central Asia's largest theatre, to sit alongside the region's largest library, biggest museum and most voluminous tea house.[7]

Meanwhile, in Azerbaijan, over on the western side of the Caspian Sea, President Aliyev—whose family was compared by U.S. diplomats to "the Corleones of *Godfather* fame"—had to make do with an only marginally less convincing 86 per cent of the vote in recent elections. Here, we learn that the ruler's son reportedly owns a portfolio of villas and apartments in Dubai worth a cool $45 million—or 10,000 years of the average Azeri income; not bad for an eleven-year-old.[8] Or there is Iran to the south, where one recent President is on record denying the Holocaust and accusing "western powers and despots" of developing HIV "so that they could sell their drugs and medical equipment to the poor countries."[9]

It is a region characterised in western minds as backward, despotic and violent. For too long, Secretary of State Hillary Clinton said in 2011, the centre of Asia has been "torn apart by conflict and division," a place where trade and co-operation have been stifled by "bureaucratic barriers and other impediments to the flow of goods and people"; the only way to a "better future for the people who live there," she concluded, was to try to create lasting stability and security. Only then will it be possible "to attract more private investment" that, in her view at least, is essential for social and economic development.[10]

For all their apparent "otherness," however, these lands have always been of pivotal importance in global history in one way or another, linking east and west, serving as a melting-pot where ideas, customs and languages have jostled with each other from antiquity to today. And today the Silk Roads are rising again—unobserved and overlooked by many. Economists have

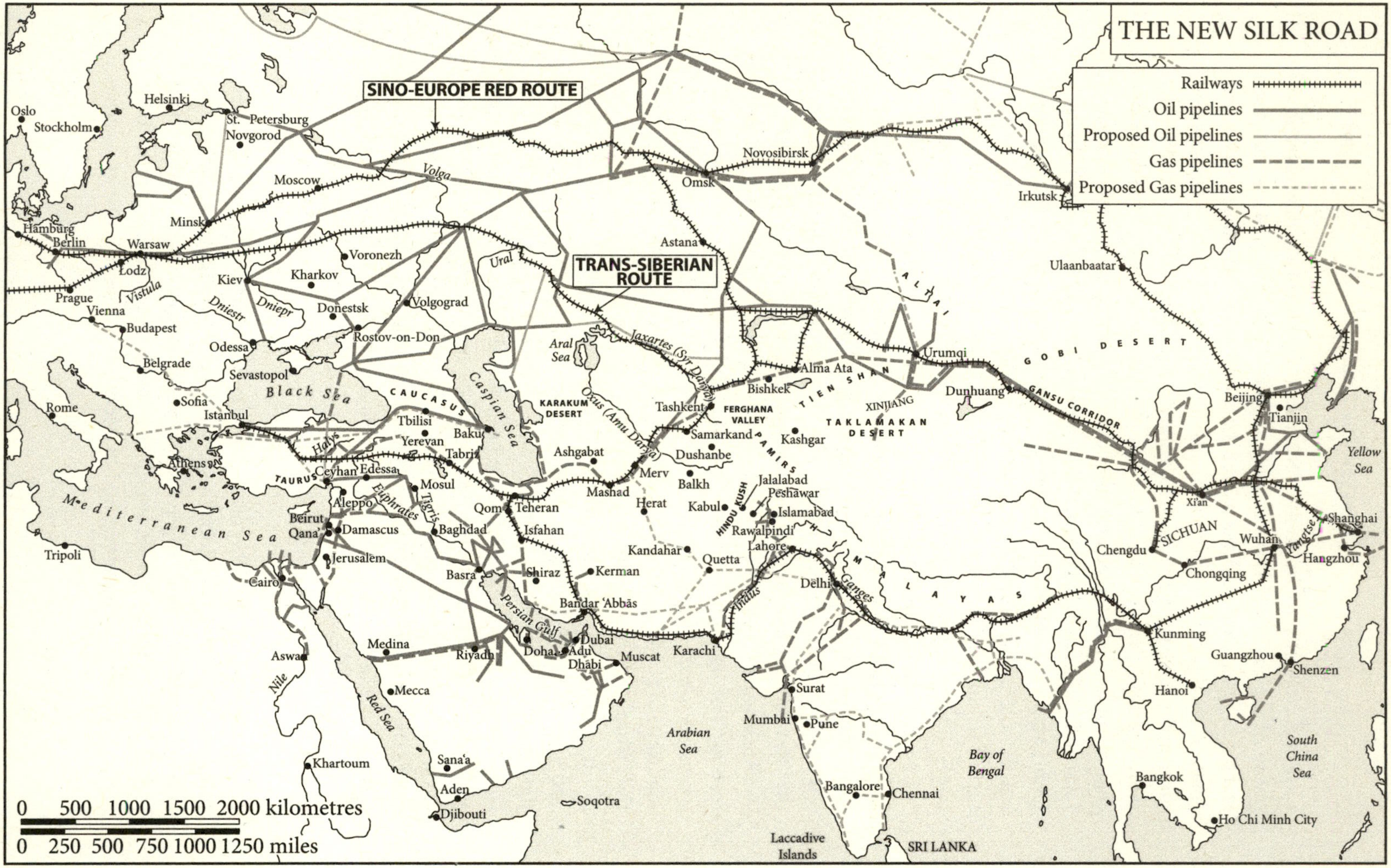
THE NEW SILK ROAD
Railways
Oil pipelines
Proposed Oil pipelines
Gas pipelines
Proposed Gas pipelines
SINO-EUROPE RED ROUTE
TRANS-SIBERIAN ROUTE
Oslo
Stockholm
Helsinki
St. Petersburg
Novgorod
Moscow
Volga
Minsk
Hamburg
Berlin
Warsaw
Lodz
Vistula
Prague
Vienna
Budapest
Belgrade
Kiev
Dniestr
Dniepr
Kharkov
Voronezh
Donestsk
Volgograd
Rostov-on-Don
Odessa
Sevastopol
Black Sea
Sofia
Istanbul
Athens
Rome
Tripoli
Mediterranean Sea
Cairo
Aswa
Nile
Khartoum
Novosibirsk
Omsk
Irkutsk
Astana
Ural
Ulaanbaatar
ALTAI
GOBI DESERT
GANSU CORRIDOR
Urumqi
Dunhuang
Alma Ata
Bishkek
TIEN SHAN
XINJIANG
TAKLAMAKAN DESERT
Kashgar
Aral Sea
Jaxartes (Syr Darya)
Oxus (Amu Darya)
KARAKUM DESERT
Tashkent
FERGHANA VALLEY
Samarkand
PAMIRS
Dushanbe
Balkh
Merv
Ashgabat
Mashad
Herat
Kabul
HINDU KUSH
Jalalabad
Peshawar
Islamabad
Rawalpindi
Lahore
Kandahar
Quetta
Delhi
Ganges
HIMALAYAS
Indus
Karachi
Surat
Mumbai
Pune
Bangalore
Chennai
SRI LANKA
Laccadive Islands
Arabian Sea
Bay of Bengal
CAUCASUS
Caspian Sea
Tbilisi
Yerevan
Baku
Tabriz
Halys
TAURUS
Ceyhan
Edessa
Mosul
Tigris
Euphrates
Aleppo
Beirut
Qana
Damascus
Jerusalem
Baghdad
Qom
Teheran
Isfahan
Shiraz
Kerman
Basra
Bandar 'Abbās
Persian Gulf
Doha
Dubai
Adu Dhabi
Muscat
Riyadh
Medina
Mecca
Red Sea
Sana'a
Aden
Djibouti
Soqotra
Beijing
Tianjin
Yellow Sea
Xi'an
SICHUAN
Chengdu
Chongqing
Wuhan
Yangtse
Shanghai
Hangzhou
Kunming
Hanoi
Guangzhou
Shenzen
South China Sea
Bangkok
Ho Chi Minh City
0 500 1000 1500 2000 kilometres
0 250 500 750 1000 1250 miles

yet to turn their attention to the riches that lie in or under the soil, beneath the waters or buried in the mountains of the belts linking the Black Sea, Asia Minor and the Levant with the Himalayas. Instead they have focused on groups of countries with no historical connections but superficially similar measurable data, like the BRICS (Brazil, Russia, India, China and South Africa), often now voguishly replaced by MIST countries (Malaysia, Indonesia, South Korea and Turkey).[11] In fact, it is the true Mediterranean—the "centre of the world"—to which we should be looking. This is no Wild East, no New World waiting to be discovered—but a region and a series of connections re-emerging in front of our eyes.

Cities are booming, with new airports, tourism resorts, luxury hotels and landmark buildings springing up in countries that find themselves with enormous sums at their disposal to indulge their fantasies. Ashgabat in Turkmenistan has had a new presidential palace and indoor winter sports arena built at the cost of hundreds of millions of dollars, while conservative estimates suggest that the Avaza tourist region on the eastern coast of the Caspian Sea has already had more than $2 billion lavished on it. The modern terminal at Heydar Aliyev international airport in Baku, with its giant wooden cocoons and concave glass walls, leaves travellers arriving in oil-soaked Azerbaijan with little doubt about the country's ambition and wealth, as does the Crystal Hall, a concert venue constructed to host the Eurovision Song Contest in 2012. As Baku has boomed, so have the choices available to the international traveller, who for overnight stays in Azerbaijan's capital is now able to choose between the Hilton, Kempinski, Radisson, Ramada, Sheraton and Hyatt Regency, as well as a new crop of boutique hotels. And this is just the start: in 2011 alone, the number of hotel rooms in the city doubled, with the expectation that the figure will have doubled again over the following four years.[12] Or there is Erbil, unknown to many outside the oil industry, but the main city in Iraqi Kurdistan. There, the rates at the new Erbil Rotana hotel are higher than in most of the capitals of Europe and many major cities in the United States: basic rooms start at $290 per night—which includes breakfast and use of the spa (but not wi-fi).[13]

Major new urban centres have been founded, even including a new capital city—Astana in Kazakhstan, which has risen from the dust in less than twenty years. It is now home to a spectacular Palace of Peace and Reconciliation, designed by Norman Foster, as well as Bayterek, a 330-foot-tall tower in the shape of a tree in which nestles a golden egg, where visitors are encouraged to place their hand in an imprint formed by the President of Kazakhstan and make a wish. To the untrained eye, this looks like a new frontier-land, a place whose billionaires appear from nowhere to buy the finest works of art in the auction houses of London, New York and Paris, and are happy to acquire the best real estate on the globe at prices that are scarcely believable to long-term residents: in the London property market the average spend of buyers from the former Soviet republics is nearly three times higher than that of buyers from the United States or China, and four times higher than that of local purchasers.[14] One after another, exclusive private homes and landmark buildings in Manhattan, Mayfair, Knightsbridge and the South of France are bought by Uzbek copper magnates, by tycoons who have made their fortunes in the potash business in the Urals or by oil moguls from Kazakhstan who pay top dollar—and usually in cash. Some lavish their fortunes on world-famous footballers, such as Samuel Eto'o, bought by an oligarch from the Caspian Sea to play for Anzhi Makhachkala, a club based in Dagestan—and who was at one point the highest-paid footballer in the world; others spare no expense in building their country's profile, with Baku's hosting of the women's Under-17 football World Cup marked by Jennifer Lopez's performance at the opening ceremony—a sharp difference from the ten-minute grand opening for the event two years earlier when it was held in Trinidad and Tobago, when a small dance troupe was watched by a few hundred spectators.[15]

New connections are springing up across the spine of Asia, linking this key region to the north, south, east and west, and taking many different routes, shapes and forms—just as they have done for millennia. These have been supplemented by new kinds of arteries, such as the Northern Distribution Network, a series of transit corridors for the delivery of "non-lethal goods" to U.S. and coalition forces in Afghanistan through Russia, Uzbekistan, Kazakhstan, Kyrgyzstan and Tajikistan—with several making use of infrastructure set up by the USSR in the 1980s during the Soviet occupation.[16]

Then, of course, there are the oil and gas pipelines that bring energy to consumers willing and able to pay for them in Europe, India, China and beyond. Pipelines criss-cross the region in every direction, linking to the port of Ceyhan in south-eastern Turkey or sprawling across Central Asia to fulfil the need for fossil fuels in China as the economy grows. New markets too are being opened up and tied together, prompting close co-operation between Afghanistan, Pakistan and India, whose interests align closely when it comes to accessing more plentiful and cheaper energy via a new pipeline that will have a capacity of 950 billion cubic feet of natural gas per year. The route—following the highway from the gasfields of Turkmenistan towards Herat to Kandahar, and then on to Quetta and Multan—would have been as familiar to Sogdian traders active 2,000 years ago as to seventeenth-century horse dealers, as recognisable to British railway planners and strategists in the Victorian era as to poets travelling to work at the medieval Ghaznavid court.

Existing and proposed pipelines connect Europe to the oil and gas reserves in the centre of the world as well—raising the political, economic and strategic importance not only of the exporter states but also of those whose territories the pipelines cross: as Russia has already shown, energy supplies can be used as a weapon, whether through price hikes or simply by turning off supplies to Ukraine. With many countries in Europe heavily dependent on Russian gas, and many more on companies where the Kremlin-backed Gazprom holds a strategic or even a controlling stake, the use of energy, resources and pipelines as economic, diplomatic and political weapons is likely to be an issue in the twenty-first century. It is perhaps an ominous sign that President Putin's PhD dissertation was concerned with strategic planning and the uses of Russian mineral resources—even though some have cast doubt on the originality of the thesis, and even on the veracity of the award of a doctorate.[17]

To the east, these pipelines are bringing the lifeblood of tomorrow as China buys forward gas supplies on a thirty-year contract, worth $400 billion over its lifetime. This giant sum, partly to be paid in advance, gives Beijing the energy security it craves, while more than justifying the estimated $22 billion cost of a new pipeline, and providing Moscow freedom and additional confidence in how it deals with its neighbours and its rivals. It is no surprise then that China was the only member of the UN Security Council not to rebuke Russia for its actions during the Ukraine crisis of 2014; the cold reality of mutually beneficial trade is far more compelling than the political brinkmanship of the west.

Transport links as well as pipelines have expanded dramatically in the last three decades. Major investment in transcontinental railway lines has already opened up freight routes along the 7,000-mile Yuxinou International Railway that runs from China to a major distribution centre near Duisburg in Germany—visited by President Xi Jinping in person in 2014. Trains half a mile long have started carrying millions of laptops, shoes, clothes and other non-perishable items in one direction and electronics, car parts and medical equipment in the other on a journey that takes sixteen days—considerably faster than the sea route from China's Pacific ports.

With $43 billion of investment in improving rail links already announced, some predict that the number of containers being transported by train each year will rise from 7,500 in 2012 to 7.5 million by 2020.[18] This is just the beginning; railway lines are being planned that will pass through Iran, Turkey, the Balkans and Siberia to Moscow, Berlin and Paris, and new routes will link Beijing with Pakistan, Kazakhstan with India. There is even talk of a tunnel 200 miles long being built under the Bering strait that will allow trains to pass from China through Alaska and Canada and into the continental United States.[19]

The Chinese government is building networks carefully and deliberately to connect to minerals, energy sources and access to cities, harbours and oceans. Barely a month goes by without the announcement of funding on a massive scale to either upgrade or build from scratch infrastructure that will enable volumes and velocities of exchange to rise sharply. It does so in partnership with countries whose status is raised from "iron friends" to relationships than can survive in "all-weather" conditions.[20]

These changes have already led to the re-emergence of China's western provinces. With labour cheaper deep in the interior than on the coast, many businesses have started to relocate to cities close to the Dzungarian gate—the ancient entry point in the country's west through which modern trains now pass. Hewlett Packard has moved production from Shanghai to Chongqing in the south-west, where it now produces 20 million laptops and 15 million printers per year, shipping millions of units by train to markets in the west. Others, like the Ford Motor Company, have followed suit. Or there is Foxconn, a leading IT manufacturer and key Apple supplier that has built up its presence in Chengdu at the expense of its former facilities in Shenzhen.[21]

Other transport networks have also burst into life. Five flights a day take businessmen and tourists from China to Almaty in Kazakhstan; Baku in Azerbaijan sends thirty-five plane loads a week to and from Istanbul, and many more to cities across Russia. Arrival and departure schedules for airports such as Ashgabat, Teheran, Astana and Tashkent show a vast and growing transport mesh between the cities of this region—while also showing how light the contact is with Europe, from where inbound flights are a rarity, especially compared with flights to the Gulf, India and China.

New intellectual centres of excellence are also emerging in a region that at one time produced the world's most outstanding scholars. Campuses have been springing up across the Persian Gulf that have been endowed by local rulers and magnates and administered by Yale, Columbia and others; and there are the Confucius Institutes, non-profit cultural centres promoting Chinese language and culture, that have been established in every one of the countries between China and the Mediterranean to display the generosity and goodwill of Beijing.

New centres for the arts are likewise being built, from the extraordinary National Museum of Qatar to the Guggenheim Museum in Abu Dhabi, to the Baku Museum of Modern Art—or imposing new buildings like the National Library in Tashkent or the Sameba Cathedral in Tblisi, paid for by the Georgian tycoon Bidzina Ivanishvili who bought Picasso's *Dora Maar* for $95 million at auction in 2006. This is a region being revived and restored to former glory.

Western fashion houses like Prada, Burberry and Louis Vuitton are building huge new stores and seeing spectacular sales figures across the Persian Gulf, Russia, China and the Far East (so that, with delicious irony, fine fabrics and silks are being sold back to the place where silk and fine fabrics originated).[22] Clothing has always been a marker of social differentiation, from Xiongnu chieftains 2,000 years ago to the men and women of the Renaissance five centuries ago. Today's ravenous appetites for the most exclusive brands have a rich historical pedigree—and are an obvious indicator of the emerging new elites in countries whose wealth and importance are rising.

For those with more exotic and malign tastes, there is the encrypted website where weapons, drugs and more can be traded anonymously—and whose name was chosen deliberately to evoke the communication networks and trade emporia of the past: the Silk Road. While law-enforcement agencies engage in constant games of cat and mouse with those developing new technologies and for control of the future, the battle for the past is also becoming an increasingly important part of the new era that we are heading into.

It is not just that history will be re-examined and re-evaluated for its own sake—although this will happen too as the new universities and campuses blossom and grow. But the past is very much a live subject across the Silk Roads. The battle for the soul of Islam, between rival sects, rival leaders and rival doctrines, is as intense as in the first century that followed the death of the Prophet Muḥammad, with much depending on interpretations of the past; the relationships between Russia and its neighbours on the one hand, and with the western world on the other, likewise have proved volatile and intense. Old rivalries and enmities can be stirred up—or soothed—with carefully chosen examples from history where scores were settled, or were set to one side. Establishing how useful and important old connections were in the past can be very helpful for the future—one reason why China is investing so heavily in bonding itself to the Silk Roads that lie to the west, precisely by asserting a common heritage of commercial and intellectual exchange.

Indeed, China has been at the forefront of the telecoms revolution across the region, pushing the construction of fixed-line cables, together with data transmitters that allow some of the fastest download speeds in the world. Much of this has been built by Huawei and ZTE, companies with close links to the People's Liberation Army of China, with soft loans provided by the China Development Bank or in the form of intergovernmental aid, enabling the construction of state-of-the-art facilities in Tajikistan, Kyrgyzstan, Uzbekistan and Turkmenistan—countries where China is keen on building long-term futures because of the regional stability and above all the mineral wealth. Concern about these telecoms companies was enough to prompt U.S. congressional hearings which concluded that Huawei and ZTE "cannot be trusted" on the basis that they are too close to Chinese "state influence and thus pose a security threat to the United States"—paradoxical given the subsequent revelation that the National Security Agency set up a clandestine programme named Operation Shotgiant to infiltrate and hack Huawei's servers.[23]

The west's growing preoccupation with China is not surprising, for a new Chinese network is in the process of being built that extends across the globe. As late as the middle of the twentieth century, it was possible to sail from Southampton, London or Liverpool to the other side of the world without leaving British territory, putting in at Gibraltar and then Malta before Port Said; from there to Aden, Bombay and Colombo, pausing in the Malay peninsula and finally reaching Hong Kong. Today, it is the Chinese who can do something similar. Chinese investment in the Caribbean rose more than four-fold between 2004 and 2009, while across the Pacific region roads, sports stadia and gleaming government buildings are being constructed with the help of aid, soft loans or direct investment from China. Africa too has seen a heavy intensification of activity as China builds a series of footholds to help it get ahead in the range of Great Games that are under way—part of the competition for energy, mineral resources, food supplies and political influence at a time when environmental change is likely to have a significant impact on each.

The age of the west is at a crossroads, if not at an end. In the opening statement of a review prepared by the U.S. Department of Defense in 2012, President Obama's first sentence spells out the long-term perception of the future in no uncertain terms: "Our Nation is at a moment of transition." The world is transforming before our eyes, the President continued, something that "demands our leadership [so that] the United States of America will remain the greatest force for freedom and security that the world has ever known."[24] In practice, as the review makes clear, this means nothing less than the complete reorientation of the United States. "We will of necessity," it explained, "rebalance towards the Asia-Pacific region." Despite budget cuts of $500 billion to defence spending already planned over the next decade and with further reductions likely, President Obama took pains to stress that these "will not come at the expense of this critical [Asia-Pacific] region."[25] If one may brutally paraphrase the report, for a hundred years the U.S. has directed much of its attention to its special relationships with countries in western Europe; it is now time to look elsewhere.

The same conclusion has been reached separately by the Ministry of Defence in London, whose own recent report likewise accepted that the world is going through a period of turbulence and transformation. The period up to 2040 "will be a time of transition," noted the authors of the study, with the understatement so characteristic of the British civil service. Among the challenges to be faced in the coming decades, it declared, are "the reality of a changing climate, rapid population growth, resource scarcity, resurgence in ideology, and shifts in power from West to East."[26]

As the heart of the world takes shape, institutions and organisations that formalise relations across this pivotal region are also coming into being. Originally set up to facilitate political, economic and military collaboration between Russia, Kazakhstan, Kyrgyzstan, Tajikistan, Uzbekistan and China, the Shanghai Co-Operation Organisation (SCO) is becoming increasingly influential and gradually turning into a viable alternative to the European Union. Although some decry the association as "a vehicle for human rights violations," highlighting the failure of member states to respect the UN convention on torture and their flagrant lack of protection for minorities, others see it as the future, with countries like Belarus and Sri Lanka granted formal permission to attend meetings as observers.[27] That is not enough for Turkey, which has clamoured to join as a full member—and to reorient away from Europe. The country would turn its back on its protracted and frustrating application to join the European Union, the Turkish Prime Minister announced in a television interview in 2013, and look to the east; the SCO, he stated, is "better and more powerful and we have values in common."[28]

These comments should perhaps not be taken entirely at face value, for the countries and peoples in this part of the world have long been used to playing two sides against each other and juggling competing interests to their own benefit. Nevertheless, it is no coincidence that, as thoughts turn to the emerging new world order, the same conclusions are being drawn in Washington, Beijing, Moscow and elsewhere. It is time, the U.S. Secretary of State said in 2011, to "set our sights on a new Silk Road" that will help the region as a whole to flourish.[29]

It is a theme taken up by the Chinese President, Xi Jinping. For more than 2,000 years, he announced in Astana during a major tour of the centre of Asia in the autumn of 2013, the peoples who live in the region that connects east and west have been able to coexist, co-operate and flourish despite "differences in race, belief and cultural background." It is a "foreign policy priority," he went on, "for China to develop friendly co-operative relations with the Central Asian countries." The time has come, he went on, to make economic ties closer, improve communication, encourage trade and enhance monetary circulation. The time has come, he said, for a "Silk Road Economic Belt" to be built—in other words, a New Silk Road.[30]

The world is changing around us. As we move into an era where the political, military and economic dominance of the west is coming under pressure, the sense of uncertainty is unsettling. The false dawn of an "Arab Spring" which promised a wave of liberalism and a surge of democracy has given way to intolerance, suffering and fear across the region and beyond, as "Islamic State in Iraq and Syria" and its adherents seek to take control of territory, oil and the mind of its victims. Few doubt there is more turbulence to come, not least because of the dramatic fall in the price of oil, which threatens to have an impact on the stability of states across the Persian Gulf, Arabian Peninsula, and Central Asia who find themselves struggling to balance their budgets and being forced to introduce austerity measures after generations of living off rich deposits of oil and gas. Economic compression and political volatility go hand in hand—and rarely resolve quickly and easily.

To the north of the Black Sea, Russia's absorption of the Crimea and its involvement in Ukraine have destabilised relations between Moscow and Washington, as well as with the European Union—in direct contrast to the trajectory of Iran, long a pariah state, but now seemingly reverting to its traditional role of an anchor from which peace and prosperity might spread. And then of course there is China, clearly entering a phase of transition, where the breakneck speed of economic growth of the last two decades is slowing to a pace widely referred to as a "new normal"—consistent, but not dramatic. How China engages with its neighbours and near-neighbours, and the role it plays on the global stage, will help shape the twenty-first century.

The immense resources being ploughed into the One Belt, One Road vision set out by Xi Jinping in 2013 strongly suggest that China is planning for the future. Elsewhere, the traumas and difficulties, the challenges and problems, seem to be birthing pains—signs of a new world emerging before our eyes. While we ponder where the next threat might come from, how best to deal with religious extremism, how to negotiate with states who seem willing to disregard international law, and how to build relations with peoples, cultures and regions about whom we have spent little or no time trying to understand, networks and connections are quietly being knitted together across the spine of Asia; or rather, they are being restored. The Silk Roads are rising again.

Acknowledgements

There is no finer place in the world for a historian to work than Oxford. The libraries and collections are second to none, while the librarians are brilliant in their resourcefulness in tracking down materials. I am particularly grateful to the Bodleian Library, the Oriental Institute Library, the Sackler Library, the Taylor Slavonic and Modern Greek Library and the Middle Eastern Library at St. Antony's College, and to all their staff. I could not have written this book without the use of the astonishing resources of Oxford University, and without the support and patience of those who look after them.

I spent much time at the National Archives in Kew reading letters, telegrams and memos held in Foreign Office records, working through minutes of Cabinet meetings, or examining Ministry of Defence proposals—all of which reached me within forty minutes. I am thankful for the efficiency and courtesy of all those who work there.

The University Library in Cambridge allowed me to consult the papers of Lord Hardinge, while the Churchill Archives Centre at Churchill College, Cambridge, kindly let me read the private diaries of Maurice (Lord) Hankey and also gave me access to the remarkable archive of the Propaganda Research Section Papers assembled by Mark Abrams. I must thank the BP Archive at the University of Warwick and Peter Housego, the Archive Manager, for digging out a large number of files relating to BP and its predecessors, the Anglo-Persian and Anglo-Iranian Oil Companies.

I am also grateful to the National Security Archive at George Washington University, a non-governmental collection of declassified documents relating to international affairs and, above all, to the history of the United States in the twentieth and twenty-first centuries. This is a treasure trove of important source material from recent decades. Being able to find so many documents in one place saved me repeated journeys across the Atlantic that would have been frustrating and time-consuming.

I should thank the Provost and Fellows of Worcester College, Oxford, who have been wonderfully and consistently kind since I came to the college as a Junior Research Fellow nearly twenty years ago. I am fortunate to work alongside a remarkable group of scholars at the Oxford Centre for Byzantine Research, where Mark Whittow in particular has been a never-ending source of inspiration and encouragement. Conversations and discussions with colleagues and friends in Oxford and elsewhere and in travels across Britain, Europe, Asia and Africa have helped refine good ideas, and sometimes prompted bad ones to be discarded.

Several colleagues and friends read chapters of the book, and I owe each a debt of gratitude. Paul Cartledge, Averil Cameron, Christopher Tyerman, Marek Jankowiak, Dominic Parviz Brookshaw, Lisa Jardine, Mary Laven, Seena Fazel, Colin Greenwood, Anthony McGowan and Nicholas Windsor all read sections of this book, and made helpful and incisive comments that helped make it better than it otherwise would have been. I am thankful to Angela McLean for pointing me towards the latest research on plague and the spread of infectious disease in Central Asia.

In recent years, history books have tended to focus on increasingly narrow subject matter over ever shortening timeframes; I am thrilled that Bloomsbury and Knopf were keen to provide a home for an ambitious book that spans centuries, continents and cultures. My editor Michael Fishwick has been a pillar of support from the outset, urging me to cast my horizons wide, and then waiting patiently as I did so. His good humour, sharp eye and unswerving backing were as reliable as they were invaluable. I am grateful too to Andrew Miller at Knopf for astute observations, questions and ideas that were both helpful and well-timed.

There are many at Bloomsbury that I should thank. Anna Simpson played the role of circus master with exemplary charm, ensuring everything was in the right place and in good order—from typeface to maps, from images to pagination—to turn a computer document into a beautiful real-life book. Peter James worked through the manuscript more than once and made elegant suggestions on how and where the book could be improved; his good judgement was much appreciated. Catherine Best did a wonderful job as the proofreader, picking up problems that I had never even noticed, while David Atkinson heroically produced the index. The maps were made by Martin Lubikowski, whose skill was matched by his patience, while Phil Beresford helped bring all the lovely images together. Chip Kidd is responsible for a jacket design that is simply stunning. I am grateful to Brittany Morrongiello and Danielle Plafsky for helping to encourage people to read what I have written.

I owe a particular debt of gratitude, however, to Catherine Clarke who, over lunch in Oxford several years ago, told me she thought I might be able to pull multiple strands together in a single work, something I found dubious at the time. Those doubts re-appeared often while I was writing, usually late at night; I am grateful for her advice, support and encouragement, as I am to the tireless Zoe Pagnamenta, my champion in New York. Chloe Campbell was my guardian angel, reading all the chapters of the draft, and ironing out niggles and bad habits gracefully and diplomatically.

My parents like to remind me that they taught me to walk and talk. It was they who gave me my prized map of the world when I was a boy and allowed me to put it on my bedroom wall (though they never gave me permission to use sticky tape, nor to paste Star Wars stickers on the open oceans). They taught me to think for myself and to challenge what I heard and read. My siblings and I were lucky to be brought up in a household where a multitude of languages could be heard at the dinner table, and where we were expected to follow the conversation and chip in. The lesson of learning to understand what other people said, but also to work out what they really meant, has proved invaluable. I am thankful to my brothers and sisters, my best friends since the nursery, for setting high standards and for being my toughest critics; they are the only people I know who think studying the past is easy.

My wife Jessica has been alongside me for twenty-five years, inspiring me since we were earnest undergraduates together, when we debated the meaning of life, talked about the importance of tribal peoples and danced in the cellars of the Cambridge colleges. I have to pinch myself every day how lucky I am. *The Silk Roads* could not have been written without her.

But this book is dedicated to our four children, who have watched, listened and asked increasingly good questions as I emerged from my study, or re-appeared from air-conditioned or exotic archives to ponder the problem of the day. Katarina, Flora, Francis and Luke: you are my pride and joy. Now the book is finished, I can finally play with you in the garden for as long as you like.

Notes

PREFACE

1. E. Wolf, *Europe and the People without History* (Berkeley, 1982), p. 5.
2. A. Herrman, "Die älteste türkische Weltkarte (1076 n. Chr)," *Imago Mundi* 1.1 (1935), 21–8, and also Maḥmud al-Kashghari, *Dīwān lughāt al-turk: Compendium of the Turkic Dialects*, ed. and tr. R. Dankhoff and J. Kelly, 3 vols (Cambridge, MA, 1982–85), 1, pp. 82–3. For the city's location, V. Goryacheva, *Srednevekoviye gorodskie tsentry i arkhitekturnye ansambli Kirgizii* (Frunze, 1983), esp. pp. 54–61.
3. For rising Chinese demand for luxury goods, see for example, Credit Lyonnais Securities Asia, *Dipped in Gold: Luxury Lifestyles in China* (2011); for India, see Ministry of Home Affairs, *Houselisting and Housing Census Data* (New Delhi, 2012).
4. See for example, Transparency International, *Corruption Perception Index 2013* (www.transparency.org); Reporters without Borders, *World Press Freedom Index 2013–2014* (www.rsf.org); Human Rights Watch, *World Report 2014* (www.hrw.org).
5. Genesis 2:8–9. For perceptions on the location of the Garden of Eden, J. Dulumeau, *History of Paradise: The Garden of Eden in Myth and Tradition* (New York, 1995).
6. For Mohenjo-daro and others, see J. Kenoyer, *Ancient Cities of the Indus Valley* (Oxford, 1998).
7. *Records of the Grand Historian by Sima Qian, Han Dynasty*, tr. B. Watson, 2 vols (rev. edn, New York, 1971), 123, 2, pp. 234–5.
8. F. von Richthofen, "Über die zentralasiatischen Seidenstrassen bis zum 2. Jahrhundert. n. Chr.," *Verhandlungen der Gesellschaft für Erdkunde zu Berlin* 4 (1877), 96–122.
9. E. Said, *Orientalism* (New York, 1978). Also note the overwhelmingly positive and highly romanticised reaction of French thinkers like Foucault, Sartre and Godard to the east and to China in particular, R. Wolin, *French Intellectuals, the Cultural Revolution and the Legacy of the 1960s: The Wind from the East* (Princeton, 2010).
10. Bābur-Nāma, tr. W. Thackston, *Memoirs of Babur, Prince and Emperor* (London, 2006), pp. 173–4.

11. W. Thackston, "Treatise on Calligraphic Arts: A Disquisition on Paper, Colors, Inks and Pens by Simi of Nishapur," in M. Mazzaoui and V. Moreen (eds), *Intellectual Studies on Islam: Essays Written in Honor of Martin B. Dickinson* (Salt Lake City, 1990), p. 219.
12. Al-Muqaddasī, *Aḥsanu-t-taqāsīm fī ma'rifati-l-aqālīm*, tr. B. Collins, *Best Division of Knowledge* (Reading, 2001), p. 252; Ibn al-Faqīh, *Kitāb al-buldān*, tr. P. Lunde and C. Stone, "Book of Countries," in *Ibn Fadlan and the Land of Darkness: Arab Travellers in the Far North* (London, 2011), p. 113.
13. Cited by N. di Cosmo, *Ancient China and its Enemies: The Rise of Nomadic Power in East Asian History* (Cambridge, 2002), p. 137.
14. For example, S. Freud, *The Interpretation of Dreams*, ed. J. Strachey (New York, 1965), p. 564; J. Derrida, *Résistances de la psychanalyse* (Paris, 1996), pp. 8–14.

CHAPTER 1—THE CREATION OF THE SILK ROAD

1. C. Renfrew, "Inception of Agriculture and Rearing in the Middle East," *C.R. Palevol* 5 (2006), 395–404; G. Algaze, *Ancient Mesopotamia at the Dawn of Civilization: The Evolution of an Urban Landscape* (Chicago, 2008).
2. Herodotus, *Historiai*, 1.135, in *Herodotus: The Histories*, ed. and tr. A. Godley, 4 vols (Cambridge, MA, 1982), 1, pp. 174–6.
3. See in general J. Curtis and St. J. Simpson (eds), *The World of Achaemenid Persia: History, Art and Society in Iran and the Ancient Near East* (London, 2010).
4. Herodotus, *Historiai*, 8.98, 4, p. 96; D. Graf, "The Persian Royal Road System," in H. Sancisi-Weerdenburg, A. Kuhrt and M. Root (eds), *Continuity and Change* (Leiden, 1994), pp. 167–89.
5. H. Rawlinson, "The Persian Cuneiform Inscription at Behistun, Decyphered and Translated," *Journal of the Royal Asiatic Society* 11 (1849), 1–192.
6. Ezra, 1:2. Also see Isaiah, 44:24, 45:3.
7. R. Kent, *Old Persian Grammar, Texts, Lexicon* (New Haven, 1953), pp. 142–4.
8. Herodotus, *Historiai*, 1.135, 1, pp. 174–6.
9. Ibid., 1.214, 1, p. 268.
10. Aeschylus, *The Persians*. Also note more ambivalent attitudes, P. Briant, "History and Ideology: The Greeks and 'Persian Decadence,'" in T. Harrison (ed.), *Greeks and Barbarians* (New York, 2002), pp. 193–210.
11. Euripides, *Bakhai*, in *Euripides: Bacchae, Iphigenia at Aulis, Rhesus*, ed. and trans. D. Kovacs (Cambridge, MA, 2003), p. 13.
12. Plutarch, *Bioi Paralleloi: Alexandros*, 32–3, in *Plutarch's Lives*, ed. and tr. B. Perrin, 11 vols (Cambridge, MA, 1914–26), 7, pp. 318–26. He was wearing a lucky outfit to judge from a famous mosaic that adorned the grandest house in Pompeii, A. Cohen, *Alexander Mosaic: Stories of Victory and Defeat* (Cambridge, 1996).
13. Quintus Curtius Rufus, *Historiae Alexandri Magni Macedonis*, 5.1, in *Quintus Curtius Rufus: History of Alexander*, ed. and tr. J. Rolfe, 2 vols (Cambridge, MA, 1946), 1, pp. 332–4.
14. M. Beard, "Was Alexander the Great a Slav?," *Times Literary Supplement*, 3 July 2009.

15. Arrian, *Anabasis*, 6.29, in *Arrian: History of Alexander and Indica*, ed. and tr. P. Brunt, 2 vols (Cambridge, MA, 1976–83), 2, pp. 192–4; Plutarch also talks of the importance of Alexander's pacific and generous approach, *Alexandros*, 59, 1, p. 392.
16. Arrian, *Anabasis*, 3.22, 1, p. 300.
17. Quintus Curtius Rufus, *Historiae*, 8.8, 2, p. 298.
18. A. Shahbazi, "Iranians and Alexander," *American Journal of Ancient History* 2.1 (2003), 5–38. Also see here M. Olbryct, *Aleksander Wielki i swiat iranski* (Gdansk, 2004); M. Brosius, "Alexander and the Persians," in J. Roitman (ed.), *Alexander the Great* (Leiden, 2003), pp. 169–93.
19. See above all P. Briant, *Darius dans l'ombre d'Alexandre* (Paris, 2003).
20. For Huaxia, see C. Holcombe, *A History of East Asia: From the Origins of Civilization to the Twenty-First Century* (Cambridge, 2010); for the wall, A. Waldron, "The Problem of the Great Wall of China," *Harvard Journal of Asiatic Studies* 43.2 (1983), 643–63, and above all di Cosmo, *Ancient China and its Enemies.*
21. See most recently J. Romm, *Ghost on the Throne: The Death of Alexander the Great and the War for Crown and Empire* (New York, 2011). It has been variously argued that Alexander died from typhoid, malaria, leukaemia, alcohol poisoning (or related illness) or infection from a wound; some contend that he was murdered, A. Bosworth, "Alexander's Death: The Poisoning Rumors," in J. Romm (ed.), *The Landmark Arrian: The Campaigns of Alexander* (New York, 2010), pp. 407–11.
22. See R. Waterfield, *Dividing the Spoils: The War for Alexander the Great's Empire* (Oxford, 2011).
23. K. Sheedy, "Magically Back to Life: Some Thoughts on Ancient Coins and the Study of Hellenistic Royal Portraits," in K. Sheedy (ed.), *Alexander and the Hellenistic Kingdoms: Coins, Image and the Creation of Identity* (Sydney, 2007), pp. 11–16; K. Erickson and N. Wright, "The 'Royal Archer' and Apollo in the East: Greco-Persian Iconography in the Seleukid Empire," in N. Holmes (ed.), *Proceedings of the XIVth International Numismatic Congress* (Glasgow, 2011), pp. 163–8.
24. L. Robert, "De Delphes à l'Oxus: inscriptions grecques nouvelles de la Bactriane," *Comptes Rendus de l'Académie des Inscriptions* (1968), 416–57. Translation here is by F. Holt, *Thundering Zeus: The Making of Hellenistic Bactria* (London, 1999), p. 175.
25. J. Jakobsson, "Who Founded the Indo-Greek Era of 186/5 BCE?," *Classical Quarterly* 59.2 (2009), 505–10.
26. D. Sick, "When Socrates Met the Buddha: Greek and Indian Dialectic in Hellenistic Bactria and India," *Journal of the Royal Asiatic Society* 17.3 (2007), 253–4.
27. J. Derrett, "Early Buddhist Use of Two Western Themes," *Journal of the Royal Asiatic Society* 12.3 (2002), 343–55.
28. B. Litvinsky, "Ancient Tajikistan: Studies in History, Archaeology and Culture (1980–1991)," *Ancient Civilisations* 1.3 (1994), 295.
29. S. Nath Sen, *Ancient Indian History and Civilisation* (Delhi, 1988), p. 184. Also see R. Jairazbhoy, *Foreign Influence in Ancient India* (New York, 1963), pp. 48–109.

30. Plutarch, *Peri tes Alexandrou tukhes he arête*, 5.4 in *Plutarch: Moralia*, ed. and tr. F. Babitt et al., 15 vols (Cambridge, MA, 1927–76), 4, pp. 392–6; J. Derrett, "Homer in India: The Birth of the Buddha," *Journal of the Royal Asiatic Society* 2.1 (1992), 47–57.
31. J. Frazer, *The Fasti of Ovid* (London, 1929); J. Lallemant, "Une Source de l'Enéide: le Mahabharata," *Latomus* 18 (1959), 262–87; Jairazbhoy, *Foreign Influence*, p. 99.
32. C. Baumer, *The History of Central Asia: The Age of the Steppe Warriors* (London, 2012), pp. 290–5.
33. V. Hansen, *The Silk Road* (Oxford, 2012), pp. 9–10.
34. Sima Qian, *Records of the Grand Historian of China*, 123, 2, p. 238.
35. Ibid., 129, 2, p. 440.
36. H. Creel, "The Role of the Horse in Chinese History," *American Historical Review* 70 (1965), 647–72. The Dunhuang caves have many celestial horses painted on their walls, T. Chang, *Dunhuang Art through the Eyes of Duan Wenjie* (New Delhi, 1994), pp. 27–8.
37. Recent excavations of the Emperor Wu's mausoleum in Xi'an in 2011, *Xinhua*, 21 February 2011.
38. Huan Kuan, *Yan Tie Lun*, cited by Y. Yu, *Trade and Expansion in Han China: A Study in the Structure of Sino-Barbarian Economic Relations* (Berkeley, 1967), p. 40.
39. For example, Sima Qian, *Records of the Grand Historian of China*, 110, 2, pp. 145–6. For some comments on Xiongnu education, customs and fashions, pp. 129–30.
40. See Yu, *Trade and Expansion in Han China*, pp. 48–54.
41. Ibid., p. 47, n. 33; also here see R. McLaughlin, *Rome and the Distant East: Trade Routes to the Ancient Lands of Arabia, India and China* (London, 2010), pp. 83–5.
42. Sima Qian, *Records of the Grand Historian of China*, 110, 2, p. 143.
43. S. Durrant, *The Cloudy Mirror: Tension and Conflict in the Writings of Sima Qian* (Albany, NY, 1995), pp. 8–10.
44. Sima Qian, *Records of the Grand Historian of China*, 123, 2, p. 235.
45. E. Schafer, *The Golden Peaches of Samarkand: A Study of Tang Exotics* (Berkeley, 1963), pp. 13–14.
46. Hansen, *Silk Road*, p. 14.
47. T. Burrow, *A Translation of Kharoshthi Documents from Chinese Turkestan* (London, 1940), p. 95.
48. Hansen, *Silk Road*, p. 17.
49. R. de Crespigny, *Biographical Dictionary of Later Han to the Three Kingdoms (23–220 AD)* (Leiden, 2007).
50. M. R. Shayegan, *Arsacids and Sasanians: Political Ideology in Post-Hellenistic and Late Antique Persia* (Cambridge, 2011).
51. N. Rosenstein, *Imperatores victi: Military Defeat and Aristocratic Competition in the Middle and Late Republic* (Berkeley, 1990); also S. Phang, *Roman Military Service: Ideologies of Discipline in the Late Republic and Early Principate* (Cambridge, 2008).

52. P. Heather, *The Fall of the Roman Empire: A New History of Rome and the Barbarians* (Oxford, 2006), p. 6. For the prohibition on marriage, see above all S. Phang, *Marriage of Roman Soldiers (13 BC–AD 235): Law and Family in the Imperial Army* (Leiden, 2001).
53. C. Howgego, "The Supply and Use of Money in the Roman World 200 B.C. TO A.D. 300," *Journal of Roman Studies* 82 (1992), 4–5.
54. A. Bowman, *Life and Letters from the Roman Frontier: Vindolanda and its People* (London, 1994).
55. Diodorus Siculus, *Bibliotheke Historike*, 17.52, in *The Library of History of Diodorus of Sicily*, ed. and tr. C. Oldfather, 12 vols (Cambridge, MA, 1933–67), 7, p. 268. Modern scholars estimate Alexandria's population to have been as high as half a million, for example R. Bagnall and B. Frier, *The Demography of Roman Egypt* (Cambridge, 1994), pp. 54, 104.
56. D. Thompson, "Nile Grain Transport under the Ptolemies," in P. Garnsey, K. Hopkins and C. Whittaker (eds), *Trade in the Ancient Economy* (Berkeley, 1983), pp. 70–1.
57. Strabo, *Geographika*, 17.1, in *The Geography of Strabo*, ed. and tr. H. Jones, 8 vols (Cambridge, MA, 1917–32), 8, p. 42.
58. Cassius Dio, *Historia Romana*, 51.21, in *Dio's Roman History*, ed. and tr. E. Cary, 9 vols (Cambridge, MA, 1914–27), 6, p. 60; Suetonius, *De Vita Cesarum. Divus Augustus*, 41, in *Suetonius: Lives of the Caesars*, ed. and tr. J. Rolfe, 2 vols (Cambridge, MA, 1997–98), 41, 1, p. 212; R. Duncan-Jones, *Money and Government in the Roman Empire* (Cambridge, 1994), p. 21; M. Fitzpatrick, "Provincializing Rome: The Indian Ocean Trade Network and Roman Imperialism," *Journal of World History* 22.1 (2011), 34.
59. Suetonius, *Divus Augustus*, 41, 1, pp. 212–14.
60. Ibid., 28, 1, p. 192; Augustus' claim is supported by the archaeological record, P. Zanker, *The Power of Images in the Age of Augustus* (Ann Arbor, 1989).
61. For taxes on the caravan routes: J. Thorley, "The Development of Trade between the Roman Empire and the East under Augustus," *Greece and Rome* 16.2 (1969), 211. Jones, *History of Rome*, pp. 256–7, 259–60; R. Ritner, "Egypt under Roman Rule: The Legacy of Ancient Egypt," in *Cambridge History of Egypt*, 1, p. 10; N. Lewis, *Life in Egypt under Roman Rule* (Oxford, 1983), p. 180.
62. See Lewis, *Life in Egypt*, pp. 33–4; Ritner, "Egypt under Roman Rule," in *Cambridge History of Egypt*, 1, pp. 7–8; A. Bowman, *Egypt after the Pharaohs 332 BC–AD 642: From Alexander to the Arab Conquest* (Berkeley, 1986), pp. 92–3.
63. For the registration of births and deaths in Roman Egypt, R. Ritner, "Poll Tax on the Dead," *Enchoria* 15 (1988), 205–7. For the census, including its date, see J. Rist, "Luke 2:2: Making Sense of the Date of Jesus' Birth," *Journal of Theological Studies* 56.2 (2005), 489–91.
64. Cicero, *Pro lege Manilia*, 6, in *Cicero: The Speeches*, ed. and tr. H. Grose Hodge (Cambridge, MA, 1927), p. 26.
65. Sallust, *Bellum Catilinae*, 11.5–6, in *Sallust*, ed. and tr. J. Rolfe (Cambridge, MA, 1931), p. 20; A. Dalby, *Empire of Pleasures: Luxury and Indulgence in the Roman World* (London, 2000), p. 162.
66. F. Hoffman, M. Minas-Nerpel and S. Pfeiffer, *Die dreisprachige Stele des C. Cor-*

nelius Gallus. Übersetzung und Kommentar (Berlin, 2009), pp. 5ff. G. Bowersock, "A Report on Arabia Provincia," *Journal of Roman Studies* 61 (1971), 227.

67. W. Schoff, *Parthian Stations of Isidore of Charax: An Account of the Overland Trade between the Levant and India in the First Century* BC (Philadelphia, 1914). The text has often been seen as being concerned with trade routes; Millar shows that this is incorrect, "Caravan Cities," 119ff. For the identification of Alexandropolis, see P. Fraser, *Cities of Alexander the Great* (Oxford, 1996), pp. 132–40.
68. Strabo, *Geographica*, 2.5, 1, p. 454; Parker, "Ex Oriente," pp. 64–6; Fitzpatrick, "Provincializing Rome," 49–50.
69. Parker, "Ex Oriente," 64–6; M. Vickers, "Nabataea, India, Gaul, and Carthage: Reflections on Hellenistic and Roman Gold Vessels and Red-Gloss Pottery," *American Journal of Archaeology* 98 (1994), 242; E. Lo Cascio, "State and Coinage in the Late Republic and Early Empire," *Journal of Roman Studies* 81 (1981), 82.
70. Cited by G. Parker, *The Making of Roman India* (Cambridge, 2008), p. 173.
71. In H. Kulke and D. Rothermund, *A History of India* (London, 2004), 107–8.
72. L. Casson (ed.), *The Periplus Maris Erythraei: Text with Introduction, Translation and Commentary* (Princeton, 1989), 48–9, p. 80; 56, p. 84.
73. W. Wendrich, R. Tomber, S. Sidebotham, J. Harrell, R. Cappers and R. Bagnall, "Berenike Crossroads: The Integration of Information," *Journal of the Economic and Social History of the Orient* 46.1 (2003), 59–62.
74. V. Begley, "Arikamedu Reconsidered," *American Journal of Archaeology* 87.4 (1983), 461–81; Parker, "Ex Oriente," 47–8.
75. See T. Power, *The Red Sea from Byzantium to the Caliphate, AD 500–1000* (Cairo, 2012).
76. Tacitus, *Annales*, ed. H. Heubner (Stuttgart, 1983), 2.33, p. 63.
77. Petronius, *Satyricon*, ed. K. Müller (Munich, 2003), 30–8, pp. 23–31; 55, p. 49.
78. Martial, *Epigrams*, 5.37, in *Martial: Epigrams*, ed. and tr. D. Shackleton Bailey, 3 vols (Cambridge, MA, 1993), 1, p. 388.
79. *Talmud Bavli*, cited by Dalby, *Empire of Pleasures*, p. 266.
80. Juvenal, *Satire* 3, in *Juvenal and Persius*, ed. and tr. S. Braund (Cambridge, MA, 2004), pp. 172–4.
81. Casson, *Periplus Maris Erythraei*, 49, p. 80; 56, p. 84; 64, p. 90.
82. Seneca, *De Beneficiis*, 7.9, in *Seneca: Moral Essays*, ed. and tr. J. Basore, 3 vols (Cambridge, MA, 1928–35), 3, p. 478.
83. Tacitus, *Annales*, 2.33, p. 63.
84. Pliny the Elder, *Naturalis Historia*, 6.20, in *Pliny: The Natural History*, ed. and tr. H. Rackham, 10 vols (Cambridge, MA, 1947–52), 2, p. 378.
85. Ibid., 6.26, p. 414.
86. Ibid., 12.49, p. 62.
87. H. Harrauer and P. Sijpesteijn, "Ein neues Dokument zu Roms Indienhandel, P. Vindob. G40822," *Anzeiger der Österreichischen Akademie der Wissenschaften, phil.-hist.Kl.122* (1985), 124–55; also see L. Casson, "New Light on Maritime Loans: P. Vindob. G 40822," *Zeitschrift für Papyrologie und Epigraphik* 84 (1990),

195–206, and F. Millar, "Looking East from the Classical World," *International History Review* 20.3 (1998), 507–31.

88. Casson, *Periplus Maris Erythraei*, 39, p. 74.
89. J. Teixidor, *Un Port roman du désert: Palmyre et son commerce d'Auguste à Caracalla* (Paris, 1984); E. Will, *Les Palmyréniens, la Venise des sables (Ier siècle avant–IIIème siècle après J.-C.)* (Paris, 1992).
90. Ammianus Marcellinus, *Rerum Gestarum Libri Qui Supersunt*, 14.3, in *Ammianus Marcellinus*, ed. and tr. J. Rolfe, 3 vols (Cambridge, MA, 1935–40), 1, p. 24.
91. J. Cribb, "The Heraus Coins: Their Attribution to the Kushan King Kujula Kadphises, c. AD 30–80," in M. Price, A. Burnett and R. Bland (eds), *Essays in Honour of Robert Carson and Kenneth Jenkins* (London, 1993), pp. 107–34.
92. Casson, *Periplus Maris Erythraei*, 43, pp. 76–8; 46, pp. 78–80.
93. Ibid., 39, p. 76; 48–9, p. 81. For the Kushans, see the collection of essays in V. Masson, B. Puris, C. Bosworth et al. (eds), *History of Civilizations of Central Asia*, 6 vols (Paris, 1992–), 2, pp. 247–396.
94. D. Leslie and K. Gardiner, *The Roman Empire in Chinese Sources* (Rome, 1996), esp. pp. 131–62; also see R. Kauz and L. Yingsheng, "Armenia in Chinese Sources," *Iran and the Caucasus* 12 (2008), 157–90.
95. Sima Qian, *Records of the Grand Historian of China*, 123, 2, p. 241.
96. Still see B. Laufer, *Sino-Iranica: Chinese Contributions to the History of Civilisation in Ancient Iran* (Chicago, 1919), and R. Ghirshman, *Iran: From the Earliest Times to the Islamic Conquest* (Harmondsworth, 1954).
97. Power, *Red Sea*, p. 58.
98. Schafer, *Golden Peaches of Samarkand*, p. 1.
99. That the embassy brought tortoiseshell, rhinoceros horn and ivory suggests that the envoys had been well briefed on Chinese tastes, F. Hirth, *China and the Roman Orient* (Leipzig, 1885), pp. 42, 94. See here R. McLaughlin, *Rome and the Distant East: Trade Routes to the Ancient Lands of Arabia, India and China* (London, 2010).
100. Fitzpatrick, "Provincializing Rome," 36; Horace, *Odes*, 1.12, in *Horace: Odes and Epodes*, ed. and tr. N. Rudd (Cambridge, MA, 2004), p. 48.
101. B. Isaac, *The Limits of Empire: The Roman Army in the East* (Oxford, 1990), p. 43; S. Mattern, *Rome and the Enemy: Imperial Strategy in the Principate* (Berkeley, 1999), p. 37.
102. Cassius Dio, 68.29, 8, pp. 414–16; H. Mattingly (ed.), *A Catalogue of the Coins of the Roman Empire in the British Museum*, 6 vols (London, 1940–62), 3, p. 606. For Trajan's campaign, see J. Bennett, *Trajan: Optimus Princeps* (London, 1997), pp. 183–204.
103. Jordanes, *Romana*, in *Iordanis Romana et Getica*, pp. 34–5.
104. Lactantius, *De Mortibus Persecutorum*, ed. and tr. J. Creed (Oxford, 1984), 5, p. 11.
105. A. Invernizzi, "Arsacid Palaces," in I. Nielsen (ed.), *The Royal Palace Institution in the First Millennium BC* (Athens, 2001), pp. 295–312; idem, "The Culture of Nisa, between Steppe and Empire," in J. Cribb and G. Herrmann (eds), *After Alexander: Central Asia before Islam: Themes in the History and Archaeology of*

Western Central Asia (Oxford, 2007), pp. 163–77. Long-forgotten Nisa is home to many magnificent examples of Hellenistic art forms. V. Pilipko, *Rospisi Staroi Nisy* (Tashkent, 1992); P. Bernard and F. Grenet (eds), *Histoire des cultes de l'Asie Centrale préislamique* (Paris, 1991).

106. For Characene, L. Gregoratti, "A Parthian Port on the Persian Gulf: Characene and its Trade," *Anabasis* 2 (2011), 209–29. For pottery, see for example H. Schenk, "Parthian Glazed Pottery from Sri Lanka and the Indian Ocean Trade," *Zeitschrift für Archäologie Außereuropäischer Kulturen* 2 (2007), 57–90.
107. F. Rahimi-Laridjani, *Die Entwicklung der Bewässerungslandwirtschaft im Iran bis in Sasanidisch-frühislamische Zeit* (Weisbaden, 1988); R. Gyselen, *La Géographie administrative de l'empire sasanide: les témoignages sigilographiques* (Paris, 1989).
108. A. Taffazoli, "List of Trades and Crafts in the Sassanian Period," *Archaeologische Mitteilungen aus Iran* 7 (1974), 192–6.
109. T. Daryaee, *Šahrestānīhā-ī Ērānšahr: A Middle Persian Text on Late Antique Geography, Epic, and History* (Costa Mesa, CA, 2002).
110. M. Morony, "Land Use and Settlement Patterns in Late Sasanian and Early Islamic Iraq," in A. Cameron, G. King and J. Haldon (eds), *The Byzantine and Early Islamic Near East*, 3 vols (Princeton, 1992–6), 2, pp. 221–9.
111. R. Frye, "Sasanian Seal Inscriptions," in R. Stiehl and H. Stier (eds), *Beiträge zur alten Geschichte und deren Nachleben*, 2 vols (Berlin, 1969–70), 1, pp. 77–84; J. Choksy, "Loan and Sales Contracts in Ancient and Early Medieval Iran," *Indo-Iranian Journal* 31 (1988), 120.
112. T. Daryaee, "The Persian Gulf Trade in Late Antiquity," *Journal of World History* 14.1 (2003), 1–16.
113. Lactantius, *De Mortibus Persecutorum*, 7, p. 11.
114. Ibid., 23, p. 36.
115. Bodrum Museum of Underwater Archaeology. As far as I am aware, the inscription, discovered in 2011, is yet to be published.
116. Pseudo-Aurelius Victor, *Epitome de Caesaribus*, ed. M. Festy, *Pseudo-Aurelius Victor. Abrégé de Césars* (Paris, 1999), 39, p. 41.
117. Suetonius, *Divus Julius*, 79, in *Lives of the Caesars*, 1, p. 132.
118. Libanius, *Antioch as a Centre of Hellenic Culture as Observed by Libanius*, tr. A. Norman (Liverpool, 2001), pp. 145–67.
119. For a stern dismissal of the "myth of *translatio imperii*," see L. Grig and G. Kelly (eds), *Two Romes: Rome and Constantinople in Late Antiquity* (Cambridge, 2012).

CHAPTER 2—THE ROAD OF FAITHS

1. H. Falk, *Asókan Sites and Artefacts: A Source-book with Bibliography* (Mainz, 2006), p. 13; E. Seldeslachts, "Greece, the Final Frontier?—The Westward Spread of Buddhism," in A. Heirman and S. Bumbacher (eds), *The Spread of Buddhism* (Leiden, 2007), esp. pp. 158–60.
2. Sick, "When Socrates Met the Buddha," 271; for the contemporary Pali literature, T. Hinüber, *A Handbook of Pali Literature* (Berlin, 1996).

3. G. Fussman, "The Mat *Devakula*: A New Approach to its Understanding," in D. Srivasan (ed.), *Mathurā: The Cultural Heritage* (New Delhi, 1989), pp. 193–9.
4. For example, P. Rao Bandela, *Coin Splendour: A Journey into the Past* (New Delhi, 2003), pp. 32–5.
5. D. MacDowall, "Soter Megas, the King of Kings, the Kushana," *Journal of the Numismatic Society of India* (1968), 28–48.
6. Note for example the description in the Book of Psalms as "the God of God . . . the Lord of Lords" (Ps. 136:2–3), or "God of gods and Lord of lords" (Deut. 10:17). The Book of Revelation tells how the beast will be defeated, because the Lamb is "the Lord of Lords and King of Kings" (Rev. 17:14).
7. *The Lotus of the Wonderful Law or The Lotus Gospel: Saddharma Pundarīka Sūtra Miao-Fa Lin Hua Chung*, tr. W. Soothill (London, 1987), p. 77.
8. X. Liu, *Ancient India and Ancient China: Trade and Religious Exchanges AD 1–600* (Oxford, 1988), p. 102.
9. *Sukhāvatī-vyūha: Description of Sukhāvatī, the Land of Bliss*, tr. F. Müller (Oxford, 1883), pp. 33–4; *Lotus of the Wonderful Law*, pp. 107, 114.
10. D. Schlumberger, M. Le Berre and G. Fussman (eds), *Surkh Kotal en Bactriane*, vol. 1: *Les Temples: architecture, sculpture, inscriptions* (Paris, 1983); V. Gaibov, "Ancient Tajikistan Studies in History, Archaeology and Culture (1980–1991)," *Ancient Civilizations from Scythia to Siberia* 1.3 (1995), 289–304.
11. R. Salomon, *Ancient Buddhist Scrolls from Gandhara* (Seattle, 1999).
12. J. Harle, *The Art and Architecture of the Indian Subcontinent* (New Haven, 1994), pp. 43–57.
13. See above all E. de la Vaissière, *Sogdian Traders: A History* (Leiden, 2005).
14. K. Jettmar, "Sogdians in the Indus Valley," in P. Bertrand and F. Grenet (eds), *Histoire des cultes de l'Asie centrale préislamique* (Paris, 1991), pp. 251–3.
15. C. Huart, *Le Livre de Gerchāsp, poème persan d'Asadī junior de Toūs*, 2 vols (Paris, 1926–9), 2, p. 111.
16. R. Giès, G. Feugère and A. Coutin (eds), *Painted Buddhas of Xinjiang: Hidden Treasures from the Silk Road* (London, 2002); T. Higuchi and G. Barnes, "Bamiyan: Buddhist Cave Temples in Afghanistan," *World Archaeology* 27.2 (1995), 282ff.
17. M. Rhie, *Early Buddhist Art of China and Central Asia*, vol. 1 (Leiden, 1999); R. Wei, *Ancient Chinese Architecture: Buddhist Buildings* (Vienna, 2000).
18. G. Koshelenko, "The Beginnings of Buddhism in Margiana," *Acta Antiqua Academiae Scientiarum Hungaricae* 14 (1966), 175–83; R. Foltz, *Religions of the Silk Road: Premodern Patterns of Globalization* (2nd edn, Basingstoke, 2010), pp. 47–8; idem, "Buddhism in the Iranian World," *Muslim World* 100.2–3 (2010), 204–14.
19. N. Sims-Williams, "Indian Elements in Parthian and Sogdian," in R. Röhrborn and W. Veenker (eds), *Sprachen des Buddhismus in Zentralasien* (Wiesbaden, 1983), pp. 132–41; W. Sundermann, "Die Bedeutung des Parthischen für die Verbreitung buddhistischer Wörter indischer Herkunft," *Altorientalische Forschungen* 9 (1982), 99–113.
20. W. Ball, "How Far Did Buddhism Spread West?," *Al-Rāfidān* 10 (1989), 1–11.

21. T. Daryaee, *Sasanian Persia: The Rise and Fall of an Empire* (London, 2009), pp. 2–5.
22. Many scholars have written on the question of continuity and change. See here M. Canepa, *The Two Eyes of the Earth: Art and Ritual of Kingship between Rome and Sasanian Iran* (Berkeley, 2009).
23. M. Canepa, "Technologies of Memory in Early Sasanian Iran: Achaemenid Sites and Sasanian Identity," *American Journal of Archaeology* 114.4 (2010), 563–96; U. Weber, "Wahram II: König der Könige von Eran und Aneran," *Iranica Antiqua* 44 (2009), 559–643.
24. For Sasanian coinage in general, R. Göbl, *Sasanian Numismatics* (Brunswick, 1971).
25. M. Boyce, *Zoroastrians: Their Religious Beliefs and Practices* (London, 1979).
26. R. Foltz, "Zoroastrian Attitudes toward Animals," *Society and Animals* 18 (2010), 367–78.
27. *The Book of the Counsel of Zartusht*, 2–8, in R. Zaehner, *The Teachings of the Magi: A Compendium of Zoroastrian Beliefs* (New York, 1956), pp. 21–2. Also see here M. Boyce, *Textual Sources for the Study of Zoroastrianism* (Manchester, 1984).
28. See for example M. Boyce, *Textual Sources for the Study of Zoroastrianism* (Manchester, 1984), pp. 104–6.
29. M. Boyce and F. Grenet, *A History of Zoroastrianism* (Leiden, 1991), pp. 30–3. For Zoroastrian beliefs, including prayers and creed, see Boyce, *Textual Sources*, pp. 53–61; for rituals and practices, pp. 61–70.
30. J. Harmatta, "Late Bactrian Inscriptions," *Acta Antiqua Hungaricae* 17 (1969), 386–8.
31. M. Back, "Die sassanidischen Staatsinschriften," *Acta Iranica* 18 (1978), 287–8.
32. S. Shaked, "Administrative Functions of Priests in the Sasanian Period," in G. Gnoli and A. Panaino (eds), *Proceedings of the First European Conference of Iranian Studies*, 2 vols (Rome, 1991), 1, pp. 261–73; T. Daryaee, "Memory and History: The Construction of the Past in Late Antiquity," *Name-ye Iran-e Bastan* 1.2 (2001–2), 1–14.
33. Back, "Sassanidischen Staatsinschriften," 384. For the full inscription, M.-L. Chaumont, "L'Inscription de Kartir à la Kaʿbah de Zoroastre: text, traduction et commentaire," *Journal Asiatique* 248 (1960), 339–80.
34. M.-L. Chaumont, *La Christianisation de l'empire iranien, des origines aux grandes persécutions du IV siècle* (Louvain, 1988), p. 111; G. Fowden, *Empire to Commonwealth: Consequences of Monotheism in Late Antiquity* (Princeton, 1993), pp. 28–9.
35. R. Merkelbach, *Mani und sein Religionssystem* (Opladen, 1986); J. Russell, "Kartir and Mani: A Shamanistic Model of their Conflict," *Iranica Varia: Papers in Honor of Professor Ehsan Yarshater* (Leiden, 1990), pp. 180–93; S. Lieu, *History of Manicheanism in the Later Roman Empire and Medieval China: A Historical Survey* (Manchester, 1985). For Shāpūr and Mani, see M. Hutter, "Manichaeism in the early Sasanian Empire," *Numen* 40 (1993), 2–15.
36. P. Gigoux (ed. and tr.), *Les Quatre Inscriptions du mage Kirdir, textes et concordances* (Paris, 1991). Also C. Jullien and F. Jullien, "Aux frontières de l'iranité:

'nasraye' et 'kristyone' des inscriptions du mobad Kirdir: enquête littéraire et historique," *Numen* 49.3 (2002), 282–335; F. de Blois, "*Naṣrānī* (Ναζωραῖος) and *ḥanīf* (ἐθνικός): Studies on the Religious Vocabulary of Christianity and of Islam," *Bulletin of the School of Oriental and African Studies* 65 (2002), 7–8.

37. S. Lieu, "Captives, Refugees and Exiles: A Study of Cross-Frontier Civilian Movements and Contacts between Rome and Persia from Valerian to Jovian," in P. Freeman and D. Kennedy (eds), *The Defence of the Roman and Byzantine East* (Oxford, 1986), pp. 475–505.
38. A. Kitchen, C. Ehret, S. Assefa and C. Mulligan, "Bayesian Phylogenetic Analysis of Semitic Languages Identifies an Early Bronze Age Origin of Semitic in the Near East," *Proceedings of the Royal Society B*, 276.1668 (2009), 2702–10. Some scholars suggest a North African origin for Semitic languages, e.g. D. McCall, "The Afroasiatic Language Phylum: African in Origin, or Asian?," *Current Anthropology* 39.1 (1998), 139–44.
39. R. Stark, *The Rise of Christianity: A Sociologist Reconsiders History* (Princeton, 1996), and idem, *Cities of God: The Real Story of How Christianity Became an Urban Movement and Conquered Rome* (San Francisco, 2006). Stark's views and methodologies have proved controversial, see *Journal of Early Christian Studies* 6.2 (1998).
40. Pliny the Younger, Letter 96, ed. and tr. B. Radice, *Letters and Panegyricus*, 2 vols (Cambridge, MA, 1969), 2, pp. 284–6.
41. Ibid., Letter 97, 2, pp. 290–2.
42. J. Helgeland, R. Daly and P. Patout Burns (eds), *Christians and the Military: The Early Experience* (Philadelphia, 1985).
43. M. Roberts, *Poetry and the Cult of the Martyrs* (Ann Arbor, 1993); G. de Ste. Croix, *Christian Persecution, Martyrdom and Orthodoxy* (Oxford, 2006).
44. Tertullian, *Apologia ad Nationes*, 42, in *Tertullian: Apology: De Spectaculis*, ed. and tr. T. Glover (London, 1931), p. 190; G. Stoumsa, *Barbarian Philosophy: The Religious Revolution of Early Christianity* (Tübingen, 1999), pp. 69–70.
45. Tertullian, *Apologia*, 8, p. 44.
46. W. Baum and D. Winkler, *Die Apostolische Kirche des Ostens* (Klagenfurt, 2000), pp. 13–17.
47. S. Rose, *Roman Edessa: Politics and Culture on the Eastern Fringes of the Roman Empire, 114–242 CE* (London, 2001).
48. T. Mgaloblishvili and I. Gagoshidze, "The Jewish Diaspora and Early Christianity in Georgia," in T. Mgaloblishvili (ed.), *Ancient Christianity in the Caucasus* (London, 1998), pp. 39–48.
49. J. Bowman, "The Sassanian Church in the Kharg Island," *Acta Iranica* 1 (1974), 217–20.
50. *The Book of the Laws of the Countries: Dialogue on the Fate of Bardaisan of Edessa*, tr. H. Drijvers (Assen, 1965), p. 61.
51. J. Asmussen, "Christians in Iran," in *The Cambridge History of Iran: The Seleucid, Parthian and Sasanian Periods* (Cambridge, 1983), 3.2, pp. 929–30.
52. S. Brock, "A Martyr at the Sasanid Court under Vahran II: Candida," *Analecta Bollandiana* 96.2 (1978), 167–81.
53. Eusebius, *Evaggelike Proparaskeus*, ed. K. Mras, *Eusebius Werke: Die Praepara-*

tio Evangelica (Berlin, 1954), 1.4, p. 16; A. Johnson, "Eusebius' *Praeparatio Evangelica* as Literary Experiment," in S. Johnson (ed.), *Greek Literature in Late Antiquity: Dynamism, Didacticism, Classicism* (Aldershot, 2006), p. 85.

54. P. Brown, *The Body and Society: Men, Women and Sexual Renunciation in Early Christianity* (London, 1988); C. Wickham, *The Inheritance of Rome: A History of Europe from 400 to 1000* (London, 2009), pp. 55–6.
55. B. Dignas and E. Winter, *Rome and Persia in Late Antiquity* (Cambridge, 2007), pp. 210–32.
56. See A. Sterk, "Mission from Below: Captive Women and Conversion on the East Roman Frontiers," *Church History* 79.1 (2010), 1–39.
57. For the conversion R. Thomson (ed. and tr.), *The Lives of St. Gregory: The Armenian, Greek, Arabic and Syriac Versions of the History Attributed to Agathaneglos* (Ann Arbor, 2010). For the much debated date, W. Seibt, *Die Christianisierung des Kaukasus: The Christianisation of Caucasus (Armenia, Georgia, Albania)* (Vienna, 2002), and M.-L. Chaumont, *Recherches sur l'histoire d'Arménie, de l'avènement des Sassanides à la conversion du royaume* (Paris, 1969), pp. 131–46.
58. Eusebius of Caesarea, *Bios tou megalou Konstantinou*, ed. F. Winkelmann, *Über das Leben des Kaisers Konstantin* (Berlin, 1992), 1.28–30, pp. 29–30. For Constantine's conversion and in general, see the collection of essays in N. Lenski (ed.), *The Cambridge Companion to the Age of Constantine* (rev. edn, Cambridge, 2012).
59. Sozomen, *Ekklesiastike Historia*, ed. J. Bidez, *Sozomenus: Kirchengeschichte* (Berlin, 1995), 2.3, p. 52.
60. Eusebius, *Bios tou megalou Konstantinou*, 2.44, p. 66.
61. A. Lee, "Traditional Religions," in Lenski, *Age of Constantine*, pp. 159–80.
62. *Codex Theodosianus*, tr. C. Pharr, *The Theodosian Code and Novels and the Simondian Constitutions* (Princeton, 1952), 15.12, p. 436.
63. Eusebius, *Bios tou megalou Konstantinou*, 3.27–8, p. 96.
64. Ibid., 3.31–2, p. 99.
65. P. Sarris, *Empires of Faith* (Oxford, 2012), pp. 22–3.
66. Eusebius, *Vita Constantini*, 4.13, p. 125; translation in Dodgeon and Lieu (eds), *The Roman Eastern Frontier and the Persian Wars A. D. 226–363: A Documentary History* (London, 1991), p. 152. For the date, G. Fowden, *Empire to Commonwealth: Consequences of Monotheism in Late Antiquity* (Princeton, 1993), pp. 94–9.
67. J. Eadie, "The Transformation of the Eastern Frontier 260–305," in R. Mathisen and H. Sivan (eds), *Shifting Frontiers in Late Antiquity* (Aldershot, 1996), pp. 72–82; M. Konrad, "Research on the Roman and Early Byzantine Frontier in North Syria," *Journal of Roman Archaeology* 12 (1999), 392–410.
68. Sterk, "Mission from Below," 10–11.
69. Eusebius, *Vita Constantini*, 5.56, p. 143; 5.62, pp. 145–6.
70. T. Barnes, "Constantine and the Christians of Persia," *Journal of Roman Studies* 75 (1985), 132.
71. Aphrahat, *Demonstrations*, M.-J. Pierre, *Aphraate le sage person: les exposés* (Paris, 1988–1989), no. 5.

72. J. Walker, *The Legend of Mar Qardagh: Narrative and Christian Heroism in Late Antique Iraq* (Berkeley, 2006), 6, p. 22.
73. See in general J. Rist, "Die Verfolgung der Christen im spätkirchen Sasanidenreich: Ursachen, Verlauf, und Folgen," *Oriens Christianus* 80 (1996), 17–42. The evidence is not without problems of interpretation, S. Brock, "Saints in Syriac: A Little-Tapped Resource," *Journal of East Christian Studies* 16.2 (2008), esp. 184–6.
74. J. Wiesehöfer, *Ancient Persia, 500 BC to 650 AD* (London, 2001), p. 202.

CHAPTER 3—THE ROAD TO A CHRISTIAN EAST

1. O. Knottnerus, "Malaria in den Nordseemarschen: Gedanken über Mensch und Umwelt," in M. Jakubowski-Tiessen and J. Lorenzen-Schmidt, *Dünger und Dynamit: Beiträge zur Umweltgeschichte Schleswig-Holsteins und Dänemarks* (Neumünster, 1999), pp. 25–39; P. Sorrel et al., "Climate Variability in the Aral Sea Basin (Central Asia) during the Late Holocene Based on Vegetation Changes," *Quaternary Research* 67.3 (2007), 357–70; H. Oberhänsli et al., "Variability in Precipitation, Temperature and River Runoff in W. Central Asia during the Past ~2000 Yrs," *Global and Planetary Change* 76 (2011), 95–104; O. Savoskul and O. Solomina, "Late-Holocene Glacier Variations in the Frontal and Inner Ranges of the Tian Shan, Central Asia," *Holocene* 6.1 (1996), 25–35.
2. N. Sims-Williams, "Sogdian Ancient Letter II," in A. Juliano and J. Lerner (eds), *Monks and Merchants: Silk Road Treasures from Northern China: Gansu and Ningxia 4th–7th Century* (New York, 2001), pp. 47–9. Also see F. Grenet and N. Sims-Williams, "The Historical Context of the Sogdian Ancient Letters," *Transition Periods in Iranian History*, *Studia Iranica* 5 (1987), 101–22; N. Sims-Williams, "Towards a New Edition of the Sogdian Letters," in E. Trembert and E. de la Vaissière (eds), *Les Sogdiens en Chine* (Paris, 2005), pp. 181–93.
3. E. de la Vaissière, "Huns et Xiongnu," *Central Asiatic Journal* 49.1 (2005), 3–26.
4. P. Heather, *Empires and Barbarians* (London, 2009), pp. 151–88; A. Poulter, "Cataclysm on the Lower Danube: The Destruction of a Complex Roman Landscape," in N. Christie (ed.), *Landscapes of Change: Rural Evolutions in Late Antiquity and the Early Middle Ages* (Aldershot, 2004), pp. 223–54.
5. See F. Grenet, "Crise et sortie de crise en Bactriane-Sogdiane aux IVe–Ve s de n.è.: de l'héritage antique à l'adoption de modèles sassanides," in *La Persia e l'Asia Centrale da Alessandro al X secolo. Atti dei Convegni Lincei* 127 (Rome, 1996), pp. 367–90; de la Vaissière, *Sogdian Traders*, pp. 97–103.
6. G. Greatrex and S. Lieu, *The Roman Eastern Frontier and the Persian Wars, Part II, AD 363–630* (London, 2002), pp. 17–19; O. Maenchen-Helfen, *The World of the Huns* (Los Angeles, 1973), p. 58.
7. Although scholars have long debated possible dating of this construction, recent advances in radiocarbon dating and optically simulated luminescence dating now securely place the erection of this huge fortification to this period, J. Nokandeh et al., "Linear Barriers of Northern Iran: The Great Wall of Gorgan and the Wall of Tammishe," *Iran* 44 (2006), 121–73.

8. J. Howard-Johnston, "The Two Great Powers in Late Antiquity: A Comparison," in A. Cameron, G. King and J. Haldon (eds), *The Byzantine and Early Islamic Near East*, 3 vols (Princeton, 1992–6), 3, pp. 190–7.
9. R. Blockley, "Subsidies and Diplomacy: Rome and Persia in Late Antiquity," *Phoenix* 39 (1985), 66–7.
10. Greatrex and Lieu, *Roman Eastern Frontier*, pp. 32–3.
11. See Heather, *Fall of the Roman Empire*, pp. 191–250.
12. St. Jerome, "Ad Principiam," *Select Letters of St. Jerome*, ed. and tr. F. Wright (Cambridge, MA, 1933), 127, p. 462.
13. Jordanes, *Getica*, 30, in *Iordanis Romana et Getica*, ed. T. Mommsen (Berlin, 1882), pp. 98–9.
14. J. Hill, *Through the Jade Gate to Rome: A Study of the Silk Routes during the Late Han Dynasty, 1st to 2nd Centuries* CE*: An Annotated Translation of the Chronicle of the "Western Regions" from the Hou Hanshu* (Charleston, NC, 2009).
15. Sarris, *Empires of Faith*, pp. 41–3.
16. A document from the early fourth century lists the tribes that had poured into the Roman Empire, A. Riese (ed.), *Geographi latini minores* (Hildesheim, 1964), pp. 1280–9. For another example, Sidonius Apollinaris, "Panegyric on Avitus," in *Sidonius Apollinaris: Poems and Letters*, ed. and tr. W. Anderson, 2 vols (Cambridge, MA, 1935–56), 1, p. 146.
17. Ammianus Marcellinus, *Rerum Gestarum Libri XXX*, 31.2, 3, p. 382.
18. Priscus, *Testimonia*, fragment 49, ed. and tr. R. Blockley, *The Fragmentary Classicising Historians of the Later Roman Empire: Eunapius, Olympiodorus, Priscus, and Malchus*, 2 vols (Liverpool, 1981–3), 2, p. 356.
19. Ammianus Marcellinus, *Rerum Gestarum Libri XXX*, 31.2, 3, p. 380.
20. D. Pany and K. Wiltschke-Schrotta, "Artificial Cranial Deformation in a Migration Period Burial of Schwarzenbach, Central Austria," *VIAVIAS* 2 (2008), 18–23.
21. Priscus, *Testimonia*, fragment 24, 2, pp. 316–17. For the Huns' successes, Heather, *Fall of the Roman Empire*, pp. 300–48.
22. B. Ward-Perkins, *The Fall of Rome and the End of Civilization* (Oxford, 2005), pp. 91ff.
23. Salvian, *Œuvres*, ed. and tr. C. Lagarrigue, 2 vols (Paris, 1971–5), 2, 4.12. Translation from E. Sanford (tr.), *The Government of God* (New York, 1930), p. 118.
24. Zosimus, *Historias Neas*, ed. and tr. F. Paschoud, *Zosime, Histoire nouvelle*, 3 vols (Paris, 2000), 2.7, 1, pp. 77–9.
25. Asmussen, "Christians in Iran," pp. 929–30.
26. S. Brock, "The Church of the East in the Sasanian Empire up to the Sixth Century and its Absence from the Councils in the Roman Empire," *Syriac Dialogue: First Non-Official Consultation on Dialogue within the Syriac Tradition* (Vienna, 1994), 71.
27. A. Cameron and R. Hoyland (eds), *Doctrine and Debate in the East Christian World 300–1500* (Farnham, 2011), p. xi.
28. W. Barnstone, *The Restored New Testament: A New Translation with Commentary, Including the Gnostic Gospels of Thomas, Mary and Judas* (New York, 2009).

29. N. Tanner, *The Decrees of the Ecumenical Councils*, 2 vols (Washington, DC, 1990), 1; A. Cameron, *The Later Roman Empire, AD 284–430* (London, 1993), pp. 59–70.
30. See P. Wood, *The Chronicle of Seert. Christian Historical Imagination in Late Antique Iraq* (Oxford, 2013), pp. 23–4.
31. S. Brock, "The Christology of the Church of the East in the Synods of the Fifth to Early Seventh Centuries: Preliminary Considerations and Materials," in G. Dagras (ed.), *A Festschrift for Archbishop Methodios of Thyateira and Great Britain* (Athens, 1985), pp. 125–42.
32. Baum and Winkler, *Apostolische Kirche*, pp. 19–25.
33. Synod of Dadjesus, *Synodicon orientale, ou Recueil de synods nestoriens*, ed. J. Chabot (Paris, 1902), pp. 285–98; Brock, "Christology of the Church of the East," pp. 125–42; Brock, "Church of the East," 73–4.
34. Wood, *Chronicle of Seert*, pp. 32–7.
35. Gregory of Nazianzus, *De Vita Sua*, in D. Meehan (tr.), *Saint Gregory of Nazianzus: Three Poems* (Washington, DC, 1987), pp. 133–5.
36. St. Cyril of Alexandria, Letter to Paul the Prefect, in J. McEnerney (tr.), *Letters of St. Cyril of Alexandria*, 2 vols (Washington, DC, 1985–87), 2, 96, pp. 151–3.
37. S. Brock, "From Antagonism to Assimilation: Syriac Attitudes to Greek Learning," in N. Garsoian, T. Mathews and T. Thomson (eds), *East of Byzantium: Syria and Armenia in the Formative Period* (Washington, DC, 1982), pp. 17–34; also idem, "Christology of the Church of the East," pp. 165–73.
38. R. Norris, *The Christological Controversy* (Philadelphia, 1980), pp. 156–7.
39. Brock, "Christology of the Church of the East," pp. 125–42; also see Baum and Winkler, *Apostolische Kirche*, pp. 31–4.
40. F.-C. Andreas, "Bruchstücke einer Pehlevi-Übersetzung der Psalmen aus der Sassanidenzeit," *Sitzungsberichte der Berliner Akademie der Wissenschaften* (1910), 869–72; J. Asmussen, "The Sogdian and Uighur-Turkish Christian Literature in Central Asia before the Real Rise of Islam: A Survey," in L. Hercus, F. Kuiper, T. Rajapatirana and E. Skrzypczak (eds), *Indological and Buddhist Studies: Volume in Honour of Professor J. W. de Jong on his Sixtieth Birthday* (Canberra, 1982), pp. 11–29.
41. Sarris, *Empires of Faith*, p. 153.
42. For the Council of 553, R. Price, *The Acts of the Council of Constantinople of 553: Edited with an introduction and notes*, 2 vols (Liverpool, 2009). For the Syriac text, with translation, S. Brock, "The Conversations with the Syrian Orthodox under Justinian (532)," *Orientalia Christiana Periodica* 47 (1981), 87–121, and idem, "Some New Letters of the Patriarch Severus," *Studia Patristica* 12 (1975), 17–24.
43. Evagrius Scholasticus, *Ekklesiastike historia*, 5.1, *Ecclesiastical History of Evagrius Scholasticus*, tr. M. Whitby (Liverpool, 2005), p. 254.
44. For the compilation of the text and its date, see R. Lim, *Public Disputation: Power and Social Order in Late Antiquity* (Berkeley, 1991), p. 227.
45. Sterk, "Mission from Below," 10–12.
46. For the 300 martyrs of Najran, I. Shahid, "The Martyrdom of Early Arab Christians: Sixth Century Najran," in G. Corey, P. Gillquist, M. Mackoul et al.

(eds), *The First One Hundred Years: A Centennial Anthology Celebrating Antiochian Orthodoxy in North America* (Englewood, NJ, 1996), pp. 177–80. For the journey of Cosmas Indicopleustes, see S. Faller, *Taprobane im Wandel der Zeit* (Stuttgart, 2000); H. Schneider, "Kosmas Indikopleustes, Christliche Topographie: Probleme der Überlieferung und Editionsgeschichte," *Byzantinische Zeitschrift* 99.2 (2006), 605–14.

47. *The History of Theophylact Simocatta: An English Translation with Introduction and Notes*, ed. and tr. M. Whitby and M. Whitby (Oxford, 1986), 5.10, p. 147.
48. See Wood, *Chronicle of Seert*, p. 23.
49. B. Spuler, *Iran in früh-Islamischer Zeit* (Wiesbaden, 1952), pp. 210–13; P. Jenkins, *The Lost History of Christianity* (Oxford, 2008), pp. 14, 53; Also see S. Moffett, *A History of Christianity in Asia*, 2 vols (San Francisco, 1998); J. Asmussen, "Christians in Iran," pp. 924–48.
50. A. Atiya, *A History of Eastern Christianity* (London, 1968), pp. 239ff.
51. Agathias, *Historion*, 2.28, *Agathias: Histories*, tr. J. Frendo (Berlin, 1975), p. 77.
52. For the prayers, Brock, "Church of the East," 76; for the election, Synod of Mar Gregory I, *Synodicon orientale*, p. 471.
53. T. Daryaee (ed. and tr.), *Šahrestānīhā-ī Ērānšahr: A Middle Persian Text on Late Antique Geography, Epic and History* (Costa Mesa, CA, 2002).
54. M. Morony, "Land Use and Settlement Patterns in Late Sasanian and Early Islamic Iraq," in Cameron, King and Haldon, *The Byzantine and Early Islamic Near East*, 2, pp. 221–9; F. Rahimi-Laridjani, *Die Entwicklung der Bewässerungslandwirtschaft im Iran bis Sasanidisch-frühislamische zeit* (Weisbaden, 1988); R. Gyselen, *La géographie administrative de l'empire sasanide: les témoignages sigilographiques* (Paris, 1989).
55. P. Pourshariati, *Decline and Fall of the Sasanian Empire: The Sasanian–Parthian Confederacy and the Arab Conquest of Iran* (London, 2009), pp. 33–60. Also see Z. Rubin, "The Reforms of Khusro Anushirwān," in Cameron, *Islamic Near East*, 3, pp. 225–97.
56. A. Taffazoli, "List of Trades and Crafts in the Sassanian Period," *Archaeologische Mitteilungen aus Iran* 7 (1974), 192–6.
57. R. Frye, "Sasanian Seal Inscriptions," in R. Stiehl and H. Stier, *Beiträge zur alten Gesichte und deren Nachleben*, 2 vols (Berlin, 1969–70), 1, pp. 79–84; J. Choksy, "Loan and Sales Contracts in Ancient and Early Medieval Iran," *Indo-Iranian Journal* 31 (1988), 120.
58. Daryaee, "Persian Gulf Trade," 1–16.
59. E. de la Vaissière, *Histoire des marchands sogdiens* (Paris, 2002), pp. 155–61, 179–231. N. Sims-Williams, "The Sogdian Merchants in China and India," in A. Cadonna and L. Lanciotti (eds), *Cina e Iran: da Alessandro Magno alla dinastia Tang* (Florence, 1996), pp. 45–67; J. Rose, "The Sogdians: Prime Movers between Boundaries," *Comparative Studies of South Asia, Africa and the Middle East* 30.3 (2010), 410–19.
60. F. Thierry and C. Morrisson, "Sur les monnaies Byzantines trouvés en Chine," *Revue numismatique* 36 (1994), 109–45; L. Yin, "Western Turks and Byzantine Gold Coins Found in China," *Transoxiana* 6 (2003); B. Marshak and

W. Anazawa, "Some Notes on the Tomb of Li Xian and his Wife under the Northern Zhou Dynasty at Guyuan, Ningxia and its Gold-Gilt Silver Ewer with Greek Mythological Scenes Unearthed There," *Cultura Antiqua* 41.4 (1989), 54–7.

61. D. Shepherd, "Sasanian Art," in *Cambridge History of Iran*, 3.2, pp. 1085–6.
62. For Easter, Eusebius, *Vita Constantini*, 3.18, p. 90. For examples of legislation against intermarriage, *Codex Theodosianus*, 16.7, p. 466; 16.8, pp. 467–8.
63. L. Feldman, "Proselytism by Jews in the Third, Fourth and Fifth Centuries," *Journal for the Study of Judaism* 24.1 (1993), 9–10.
64. Ibid., 46.
65. P. Schäfer, *Jesus in the Talmud* (Princeton, 2007); P. Schäfer, M. Meerson and Y. Deutsch (eds), *Toledot Yeshu ("The Life Story of Jesus") Revisited* (Tübingen, 2011).
66. G. Bowersock, "The New Greek Inscription from South Yemen," in A. Sedov and J.-F. Salles (eds), *Qāni': le port antique du Ḥaḍramawt entre la Méditerranée, l'Afrique et l'Inde: fouilles russes 1972, 1985–89, 1991, 1993–94* (Turnhout, 2013), pp. 393–6.
67. J. Beaucamp, F. Briquel-Chatonnet and C. Robin (eds), *Juifs et chrétiens en Arabie aux Ve et VIe siècles: regards croisés sur les sources* (Paris, 2010); C. Robin, "Joseph, dernier roi de Himyar (de 522 à 525, ou une des années suivantes)," *Jerusalem Studies in Arabic and Islam* 34 (2008), 1–124.
68. G. Bowersock, *The Throne of Adulis: Red Sea Wars on the Eve of Islam* (Oxford, 2013), pp. 78–91.
69. Brock, "Church of the East," 73.
70. Walker, *The Legend of Mar Qardagh*; text, pp. 19–69.
71. Y. Saeki, *The Nestorian Documents and Relics in China* (2nd edn, Tokyo, 1951), pp. 126–7; D. Scott, "Christian Responses to Buddhism in Pre-Medieval Times," *Numen* 32.1 (1985), 91–2.
72. See E. Pagels, *The Gnostic Gospels* (New York, 1979); H.-J. Klimkeit, *Gnosis on the Silk Road: Gnostic Texts from Central Asia* (San Francisco, 1993); K. King, *What is Gnosticism?* (Cambridge, MA, 2003).
73. P. Crone, "Zoroastrian Communism," *Comparative Studies in Society and History* 36.4 (1994), 447–62; G. Gnoli, "Nuovi studi sul Mazdakismo," in *Convegno internazionale: la Persia e Bisanzio* (Rome, 2004), pp. 439–56.
74. Hui Li, *Life of Hiuen-tsang*, tr. Samuel Beal (Westport, CT, 1973), p. 45.
75. Ibid., p. 46; R. Foltz, "When was Central Asia Zoroastrian?," *Mankind Quarterly* (1988), 189–200.
76. S. Beal, *Buddhist Records of the Western World* (New Delhi, 1969), pp. 44–6.
77. G. Mitchell and S. Johar, "The Maratha Complex at Ellora," *Modern Asian Studies* 28.1 (2012), 69–88.
78. Excavations and surveys were conducted in the 1970s by joint teams from Japan and Afghanistan. See T. Higuchi, *Japan–Afghanistan Joint Archaeological Survey 1974, 1976, 1978* (Kyoto, 1976–80).
79. For the dating of the Bamiyan complex to *c.* 600, see D. Klimburg-Salter, "Buddhist Painting in the Hindu Kush *c.* VIIth to Xth Centuries: Reflections

of the Co-existence of Pre-Islamic and Islamic Artistic Cultures during the Early Centuries of the Islamic Era," in E. de la Vaissière, *Islamisation de l'Asie Centrale: processus locaux d'acculturation du VIIe au XIe siècle* (Paris, 2008), pp. 140–2; also see F. Flood, "Between Cult and Culture: Bamiyan, Islamic Iconoclasm, and the Museum," *Art Bulletin* 84.4 (2002), 641ff. Also see here L. Morgan, *The Buddhas of Bamiyan* (London, 2012).

80. Cited by Power, *Red Sea*, p. 58.
81. I. Gillman and H.-J. Klimkeit, *Christians in Asia before 1500* (Ann Arbor, 1999), pp. 265–305.
82. G. Stroumsa, *Barbarian Philosophy: The Religious Revolution of Early Christianity* (Tübingen, 1999), pp. 80, 274–81.
83. J. Choksy, "Hagiography and Monotheism in History: Doctrinal Encounters between Zoroastrianism, Judaism and Christianity," *Islam and Christian–Muslim Relations* 14.4 (2010), 407–21.

CHAPTER 4—THE ROAD TO REVOLUTION

1. Pseudo-Dionysius of Tel Mahre, *Chronicle (Known Also as the Chronicle of Zuqnin), Part III*, tr. W. Witaksowski (Liverpool, 1996), p. 77.
2. Procopius, *Hyper ton polemon*, 2.22–3, in *History of the Wars, Secret History, Buildings*, ed. and tr. H. Dewing, 7 vols (Cambridge, MA), 1, pp. 450–72.
3. M. Morony, "'For Whom Does the Writer Write?': The First Bubonic Plague Pandemic According to Syriac Sources," in K. Lester (ed.), *Plague and the End of Antiquity: The Pandemic of 541–750* (Cambridge, 2007), p. 64; D. Twitchett, "Population and Pestilence in T'ang China," in W. Bauer (ed.), *Studia Sino-Mongolica* (Wiesbaden, 1979), 42, 62.
4. P. Sarris, *Economy and Society in the Age of Justinian* (Cambridge, 2006); idem, "Plague in Byzantium: The Evidence of Non-Literary Sources," in Lester, *Plague and the End of Antiquity*, pp. 119–34; A. Cameron, *The Mediterranean World in Late Antiquity: AD 395–700* (London, 1993), pp. 113ff.; D. Stathakopoulos, *Famine and Pestilence in the Late Roman and Early Byzantine Empire: A Systematic Survey of Subsistence Crises and Epidemics* (Birmingham, 2004), pp. 110–65.
5. Sarris, *Empires of Faith*, pp. 145ff.
6. Procopius, *The Secret History*, tr. P. Sarris (London, 2007), p. 80.
7. John of Ephesus, *Ecclesiastical History*, 6.24, tr. R. P. Smith (1860), p. 429.
8. M.-T. Liu, *Die chinesischen Nachrichten zur Geschichte der Ost-Türken (T'u-küe)*, 2 vols (Wiesbaden, 2009), 1, p. 87. Also J. Banaji, "Precious-Metal Coinages and Monetary Expansion in Late Antiquity," in F. De Romanis and S. Sorda (eds), *Dal denarius al dinar: l'oriente e la monetà romana* (Rome, 2006), pp. 265–303.
9. *The History of Menander the Guardsman*, tr. R. Blockley (Liverpool, 1985), pp. 121–3.
10. Ibid., pp. 110–7.
11. Sarris, *Empires of Faith*, pp. 230–1.

12. *Menander the Guardsman*, pp. 173–5.
13. For the sources here, Greatrex and Lieu, *Roman Eastern Frontier, Part II*, pp. 153–8.
14. R. Thomson, *The Armenian History Attributed to Sebeos. Part I: Translation and Notes* (Liverpool, 1999), 8, p. 9.
15. Agathias, *Historion*, 2.24, p. 72.
16. G. Fisher, "From Mavia to al-Mundhir: Arab Christians and Arab Tribes in the Late Antique Roman East," in I. Toral-Niehoff and K. Dimitriev (eds), *Religious Culture in Late Antique Arabia* (Leiden, 2012), p. x; M. Maas, "'Delivered from their Ancient Customs': Christianity and the Question of Cultural Change in Early Byzantine Ethnography," in K. Mills and A. Grafton (eds), *Conversion in Late Antiquity and the Early Middle Ages* (Rochester, NY, 2003), pp. 152–88.
17. R. Hoyland, "Arab Kings, Arab Tribes and the Beginnings of Arab Historical Memory in Late Roman Epigraphy," in H. Cotton, R. Hoyland, J. Price and D. Wasserstein (eds), *From Hellenism to Islam: Cultural and Linguistic Change in the Roman Near East* (Cambridge, 2009), pp. 374–400.
18. M. Whittow, "Rome and the Jafnids: Writing the History of a Sixth-Century Tribal Dynasty," in J. Humphrey (ed.), *The Roman and Byzantine Near East: Some Recent Archaeological Research* (Ann Arbor, 1999), pp. 215–33.
19. K. ʿAtahmina, "The Tribal Kings in Pre-Islamic Arabia: A Study of the Epithet *malik* or *dhū al-tāj* in Early Arabic Traditions," *al-Qanṭara* 19 (1998), 35; M. Morony, "The Late Sasanian Economic Impact on the Arabian Peninsula," *Nāme-ye Irān-e Bāstān* 1.2 (201/2), 35–6; I. Shahid, *Byzantium and the Arabs in the Sixth Century*, 2 vols (Washington, DC, 1995–2009), 2.2, pp. 53–4.
20. Sarris, *Empires of Faith*, pp. 234–6.
21. Procopius, *Buildings*, 3.3, 7, pp. 192–4.
22. J. Howard-Johnston, *Witnesses to a World Crisis: Historians and Histories of the Middle East in the Seventh Century* (Oxford, 2010), pp. 438–9.
23. Synod of Mar Gregory I, *Synodicon orientale*, p. 471. Also see Walker, *Mar Qardagh*, pp. 87–9.
24. F. Conybeare, "Antiochos Strategos' Account of the Sack of Jerusalem in AD 614," *English Historical Review* 25 (1910), 506–8, but see Howard-Johnston, *Witnesses to a World Crisis*, pp. 164–5. For the propaganda, J. Howard-Johnston, "Heraclius' Persian Campaigns and the Revival of the Roman Empire," *War in History* 6 (1999), 36–9.
25. *Chronicon Paschale*, tr. M. Whitby and M. Whitby (Liverpool, 1989), pp. 161–2; Howard-Johnston, "Heraclius' Persian Campaigns," 3; Sarris, *Empires of Faith*, p. 248.
26. *Chronicon Paschale*, pp. 158, 164.
27. Howard-Johnston, "Heraclius' Persian Campaigns," 37.
28. The precise date is contentious; R. Altheim-Stiehl, "Würde Alexandreia im Juni 619 n. Chr. durch die Perser Erobert?," *Tyche* 6 (1991), 3–16.
29. J. Howard-Johnston, "The Siege of Constantinople in 626," in C. Mango and G. Dagron (eds), *Constantinople and its Hinterland* (Aldershot, 1995), pp. 131–42.

30. Howard-Johnston, "Heraclius' Persian Campaigns," 23–4; C. Zuckerman, "La Petite Augusta et le Turc: Epiphania-Eudocie sur les monnaies d'Héraclius," *Revue Numismatique* 150 (1995), 113–26.
31. See N. Oikonomides, "Correspondence between Heraclius and Kavadh-Siroe in the *Paschal Chronicle (628)*," *Byzantion* 41 (1971), 269–81.
32. Sebeos, *Armenian History*, 40, pp. 86–7; Theophanes, *The Chronicle of Theophanes Confessor: Byzantine and Near Eastern History, AD 284–813*, tr. C. Mango and R. Scott (Oxford, 1997), pp. 455–6.
33. *Chronicon Paschale*, pp. 166–7; Sebeos, *Armenian History*, 38, pp. 79–81.
34. G. Dagron and V. Déroche, "Juifs et chrétiens en Orient byzantin," *Travaux et Mémoires* 11 (1994), 28ff.
35. Cameron and Hoyland, *Doctrine and Debate*, pp. xxi–xxii.
36. Letter of the Bishops of Persia, *Synodicon orientale*, pp. 584–5.
37. Theophanes, *Chronicle*, p. 459; Mango, "Deux études sur Byzance et la Perse sassanide," *Travaux et Mémoires* 9 (1985), 117.
38. B. Dols, "Plague in Early Islamic History," *Journal of the American Oriental Society* 94.3 (1974), 376; P. Sarris, "The Justinianic Plague: Origins and Effects," *Continuity and Change* 17.2 (2002), 171.
39. Bowersock, *Throne of Adulis*, pp. 106–33. Also G. Lüling, *Die Wiederentdeckung des Propheten Muhammad: eine Kritik am "christlichen" Abendland* (Erlangen, 1981).
40. C. Robin, "Arabia and Ethiopia," in S. Johnson (ed.), *Oxford Handbook of Late Antiquity* (Oxford, 2012), p. 302.
41. *Qur'ān*, 96.1, ed. and tr. N. Dawood, *The Koran: With a Parallel Translation of the Arabic Text* (London, 2014).
42. Ibn Hisham, *Sīrat rasūl Allāh*, tr. A. Guillaume, *The Life of Muhammad: A Translation of Isḥāq's Sīrat rasūl Allāh* (Oxford, 1955), p. 106; *Qur'ān*, 81.23, p. 586.
43. See H. Motzki, "The Collection of the *Qur'ān*: A Reconsideration of Western Views in Light of Recent Methodological Developments," *Der Islam* 78 (2001), 1–34, and also A. Neuwirth, N. Sinai and M. Marx (eds), *The Qur'ān in Context: Historical and Literary Investigations into the Qur'ānic Milieu* (Leiden, 2010).
44. *Qur'ān*, 18.56, p. 299.
45. *Qur'ān*, 16.98–9, p. 277.
46. For example, *Qur'ān*, 2.165; 2.197; 2.211.
47. See above all F. Donner, *Narratives of Islamic Origins: The Beginnings of Islamic Historical Writing* (Princeton, 1998). Also, for example, T. Holland, *In the Shadow of the Sword: The Battle for Global Empire and the End of the Ancient World* (London, 2012).
48. E. El Badawi, *The Qur'ān and the Aramaic Gospel Traditions* (London, 2013).
49. P. Crone, *Meccan Trade and the Rise of Islam* (Princeton, 1977); also R. Serjeant, "Meccan Trade and the Rise of Islam: Misconceptions and Flawed Polemics," *Journal of the American Oriental Society* 110.3 (1990), 472–3.
50. C. Robinson, "The Rise of Islam," in M. Cook et al. (eds), *The New Cambridge History of Islam*, 6 vols (Cambridge, 2010), pp. 180–1; M. Kister, "The Struggle

against Musaylima and the Conquest of Yamāma," *Jerusalem Studies in Arabic and Islam* 27 (2002), 1–56.

51. G. Heck, "'Arabia without Spices': An Alternative Hypothesis: The Issue of 'Makkan Trade and the Rise of Islam,'" *Journal of the American Oriental Society* 123.3 (2003), 547–76; J. Schiettecatte and C. Robin, *L'Arabie à la veille de l'Islam: un bilan clinique* (Paris, 2009).
52. P. Crone, "Quraysh and the Roman Army: Making Sense of the Meccan Leather Trade," *Bulletin of the School of Oriental and African Studies* 70.1 (2007), 63–88.
53. Ibn al-Kalbī, *Kitāb al-aṣnām*, tr. N. Faris, *The Book of Idols Being a Translation from the Arabic of the Kitāb al-aṣnām* (Princeton, 1952), pp. 23–4.
54. *Qur'ān*, 36.33–6, p. 441; G. Reinink, "Heraclius, the New Alexander: Apocalyptic Prophecies during the Reign of Heraclius," pp. 81–94; W. E. Kaegi Jr., "New Evidence on the Early Reign of Heraclius," *Byzantinische Zeitschrift* 66 (1973), 308–30.
55. *Qur'ān*, 47.15, p. 507.
56. *Qur'ān*, 5.33, p. 112.
57. *Qur'ān*, 4.56, p. 86. Also W. Shepard, *Sayyid Qutb and Islamic Activism: A Translation and Critical Analysis of Social Justice in Islam* (Leiden, 2010). Also note the important observations about gender and social justice in early Islam, A. Wahud, *Qur'ān and Woman: Rereading the Sacred Text from a Woman's Perspective* (Oxford, 1999).
58. *Qur'ān*, 47.15, p. 507.
59. P. Crone, "The Religion of the Qur'ānic Pagans: God and the Lesser Deities," *Arabica* 57 (2010), 151–200.
60. R. Hoyland, "New Documentary Texts and the Early Islamic State," *Bulletin of the School of Oriental and African Studies* 69.3 (2006), 395–416. For the date of Muḥammad's flight, A. Noth, *The Early Arabic Historical Tradition: A Source Critical Study* (Princeton, 1994), p. 40; M. Cook and P. Crone, *Hagarism: The Making of the Islamic World* (Cambridge, 1977), pp. 24, 157.
61. Nikephoros of Constantinople, *Chronographikon syntomon*, ed. and tr. C. Mango, *Short History* (Washington, DC, 1990), pp. 68–9; Theophylact Simokatta, *History*, 3.17. For Arab "identity" before the rise of Islam, A. Al-Azmeh, *The Emergence of Islam in Late Antiquity* (Oxford, 2014), p. 147; also see W. Kaegi, "Reconceptualizing Byzantium's Eastern Frontiers," in Mathisen and Sivan, *Shifting Frontiers*, p. 88.
62. *Qur'ān*, 43.3, p. 488.
63. C. Robinson, "Rise of Islam," p. 181.
64. Mālik records two similar variants, presumably reflecting the comment's pedigree, Mālik ibn Anas, *al-Muwaṭṭa*, 45.5, tr. A. 'Abdarahman and Y. Johnson (Norwich, 1982), p. 429.
65. *Qur'ān*, 2.143–4, p. 21; also al-Azmeh, *Emergence of Islam*, p. 419.
66. *Qur'ān*, 22.27–9, pp. 334–5.
67. R. Frye, "The Political History of Iran under the Sasanians," in *Cambridge History of Iran*, 3.1, p. 178; Tabarī, *The Battle of al-Qādisiyyah and the Conquest of Syria and Palestine*, tr. Y. Friedmann (Albany, NY, 1992), pp. 45–6.
68. H. Kennedy, *The Great Arab Conquests* (London, 2007), pp. 103–5.

69. Tabarī, *Battle of al-Qādisiyyah*, p. 63.
70. Ibid.
71. *Qur'ān*, 29.1–5, p. 395.
72. Crone, *Meccan Trade*, p. 245.
73. C. Robinson, *The First Islamic Empire*, in J. Arnason and K. Raaflaub (eds), *The Roman Empire in Context: Historical and Comparative Perspectives* (Oxford, 2010), p. 239; G.-R. Puin, *Der Dīwān von 'Umar Ibn al-Ḥattab* (Bonn, 1970); F. Donner, *The Early Islamic Conquests* (Princeton, 1981), pp. 231–2, 261–3.
74. Pourshariati, *Decline and Fall of the Sasanian Empire*, pp. 161ff. Also here Donner, *Early Islamic Conquests*, pp. 176–90; Kennedy, *Arab Conquests*, pp. 105–7.
75. For the date of the conquest of Jerusalem, P. Booth, *Crisis of Empire: Doctrine and Dissent at the End of Late Antiquity* (Berkeley, 2014), p. 243.
76. Sebeos, *Armenian History*, 42, p. 98.
77. See Howard-Johnston, *Witnesses to a World Crisis*, pp. 373–5.

CHAPTER 5—THE ROAD TO CONCORD

1. For the text, F. Donner, *Muhammad and the Believers: At the Origins of Islam* (Cambridge, MA, 2010), pp. 228–32. Also M. Lecker, *The "Constitution of Medina": Muhammad's First Legal Document* (Princeton, 2004).
2. See the important collection of essays in M. Goodman, G. van Kooten and J. van Ruiten, *Abraham, the Nations and the Hagarites: Jewish, Christian and Islamic Perspectives on Kinship with Abraham* (Leiden, 2010).
3. *Doctrina Iacobi* in Dagron and Déroche, "Juifs et chrétiens," 209. Translation here by R. Hoyland, *Seeing Islam as Others Saw It: A Survey and Evaluation of Christian, Jewish and Zoroastrian Writings on Early Islam* (Princeton, 1997), p. 57.
4. Note therefore W. van Bekkum, "Jewish Messianic Expectations in the Age of Heraclius," in G. Reinink and H. Stolte (eds), *The Reign of Heraclius (610–641): Crisis and Confrontation* (Leuven, 2002), pp. 95–112.
5. Dagron and Déroche, "Juifs et chrétiens," 240–7. For the reliability of much of the information in the text, Howard-Johnston, *Witnesses to a World Crisis*, pp. 155–7; for the likely audience and purpose of the text, D. Olster, *Roman Defeat, Christian Response and the Literary Construction of the Jew* (Philadelphia, 1994). Above all here, Hoyland, *Seeing Islam as Others Saw It*.
6. J. Reeves, *Trajectories in Near Eastern Apocalyptic: A Postrabbinic Jewish Apocalypse Reader* (Leiden, 2006), pp. 78–89; B. Lewis, "An Apocalyptic Vision of Islamic History," *Bulletin of the School of Oriental and African Studies* 13 (1950), 321–30. Also see S. Shoemaker, *The Death of a Prophet: The End of Muhammad's Life and the Beginnings of Islam* (Philadelphia, 2012), pp. 28–33.
7. *Canonici Hebronensis Tractatus de invention sanctorum patriarchum Abraham, Ysaac et Yacob*, in *Recueil des Historiens des Croisades: Historiens Occidentaux* 1, p. 309; translation by N. Stillman, *The Jews of Arab Lands: A History and Source Book* (Philadelphia, 1979), p. 152.
8. M. Conterno, "'L'abominio della desolazione nel luogo santo': l'ingresso di

'Umar I a Gerusalemme nella *Cronografia* de Teofane Confessore e in tre cronache siriache," in *Quaderni di storia religiosa* 17 (2010), pp. 9–24.

9. J. Binns, *Ascetics and Ambassadors of Christ: The Monasteries of Palestine 314–631* (Oxford, 1994); B. Horn, *Asceticism and Christological Controversy in Fifth-Century Palestine: The Career of Peter the Iberian* (Oxford, 2006); Cameron and Hoyland, *Doctrine and Debate*, p. xxix.
10. S. Brock, "North Mesopotamia in the Late Seventh Century: Book XV of John Bar Penkaye's Rish Melle," *Jerusalem Studies in Arabic and Islam* 9 (1987), 65.
11. *Corpus Scriptorum Christianorum Orientalium*, Series 3, 64, pp. 248–51; Donner, *Muhammad and the Believers*, p. 114.
12. *Qur'ān*, 2.87, p. 12.
13. *Qur'ān*, 3.3, p. 49.
14. *Qur'ān*, 2.42–3, p. 54.
15. Cameron and Hoyland, *Doctrine and Debate*, p. xxxii.
16. *Qur'ān*, 3.65, p. 57.
17. *Qur'ān*, 3.103; 105, p. 62.
18. *Qur'ān*, 2.62, p. 9, 5.69, p. 118.
19. R. Hoyland, *In God's Path: The Arab Conquests and the Creation of an Islamic Empire* (Oxford, 2015), pp. 224–9.
20. Robinson, "The Rise of Islam," p. 186.
21. C. Luxenburg, *The Syro-Aramaic Reading of the Koran: A Contribution to the Decoding of the Language of the Koran* (Berlin, 2007); see here D. King, "A Christian Qur'ān? A Study in the Syriac background to the language of the Qur'ān as presented in the work of Christoph Luxenberg," *Journal for Late Antique Religion and Culture* 3 (2009), 44–71.
22. *Qur'ān*, 30.2–4, p. 403.
23. *Qur'ān*, 30.6, p. 404.
24. T. Sizgorich, *Violence and Belief in Late Antiquity: Militant Devotion in Christianity and Islam* (Philadelphia, 2009), pp. 160–1.
25. R. Finn, *Asceticism in the Graeco-Roman World* (Cambridge, 2009).
26. *Qur'ān*, 3.84, p. 60.
27. *Qur'ān*, 10.19, p. 209.
28. Shoemaker, *Death of a Prophet*, pp. 18–72. Also R. Hoyland, "The Earliest Christian Writings on Muhammad: An Appraisal," in H. Motzki (ed.), *The Biography of Muhammad: The Issue of the Sources* (Leiden, 2000), esp. pp. 277–81; Cook, "Muhammad," 75–6.
29. Sophronius of Jerusalem, "Logos eis to hagion baptisma," in A. Papadopoulos-Kermeus, "Tou en hagiois patros hemon Sophroniou archiepiskopou Hierosolymon logos eis to hagion baptisma," *Analekta Hierosolymitikes Stakhiologias* 5 (St. Petersburg, 1898), 166–7.
30. G. Anvil, *The Byzantine–Islamic Transition in Palestine: An Archaeological Approach* (Oxford, 2014); R. Schick, *The Christian Communities of Palestine from Byzantine to Islamic Rule* (Princeton, 1995).
31. al-Balādhurī, *Kitâb futûḥ al-buldân*, tr. P. Hitti, *The Origins of the Islamic State* (New York, 1916), 8, p. 187.

32. John of Nikiu, *Khronike*, tr. R. Charles, *The Chronicle of John of Nikiu* (London, 1916), 120.17–28, pp. 193–4.
33. G. Garitte, "'Histoires édifiantes' géorgiennes," *Byzantion* 36 (1966), 414–16; Hoyland, *Seeing Islam*, p. 63.
34. Robinson, *First Islamic Empire*, pp. 239ff.
35. W. Kubiak, *Al-Fustiat, Its Foundation and Early Urban Development* (Cairo, 1987); N. Luz, "The Construction of an Islamic City in Palestine: The Case of Umayyad al-Ramla," *Journal of the Royal Asiatic Society* 7.1 (1997), 27–54; H. Djaït, *Al-Kūfa: naissance de la ville islamique* (Paris, 1986); D. Whitcomb, "The Misr of Ayla: New Evidence for the Early Islamic City," in G. Bisheh (ed.), *Studies in the History and Archaeology of Jordan* (Amman, 1995), pp. 277–88.
36. J. Conant, *Staying Roman: Conquest and Identity in Africa and the Mediterranean, 439–700* (Cambridge, 2012), pp. 362–70. Also P. Grossman, D. Brooks-Hedstrom and M. Abdal-Rassul, "The Excavation in the Monastery of Apa Shnute (Dayr Anba Shinuda) at Suhag," *Dumbarton Oaks Papers* 58 (2004), 371–82; E. Bolman, S. Davis and G. Pyke, "Shenoute and a Recently Discovered Tomb Chapel at the White Monastery," *Journal of Early Christian Studies* 18.3 (2010), 453–62; for Palestine, L. di Segni, "Greek Inscriptions in Transition from the Byzantine to the Early Islamic Period," in Hoyland, *Hellenism to Islam*, pp. 352–73.
37. N. Green, "The Survival of Zoroastrianism in Yazd," *Iran* 28 (2000), 115–22.
38. A. Tritton, *The Caliphs and their Non-Muslim Subjects: A Critical Study of the Covenant of Umar* (London, 1970); Hoyland, *God's Path*, esp. pp. 207–31.
39. N. Khairy and A.-J. ʿAmr, "Early Islamic Inscribed Pottery Lamps from Jordan," *Levant* 18 (1986), 152.
40. G. Bardy, "Les Trophées de Damas: controverse judéo-chrétienne du VIIe siècle," *Patrologia Orientalis* 15 (1921), 222.
41. J. Johns, "Archaeology and the History of Early Islam: The First Seventy Years," *Journal of the Economic and Social History of the Orient* 46.4 (2003), 411–36; A. Oddy, "The Christian Coinage of Early Muslim Syria," *ARAM* 15 (2003), 185–96.
42. E. Whelan, "Forgotten Witnesses: Evidence for the Early Codification of the Qur'an," *Journal of the American Oriental Society* 118.1 (1998), 1–14; W. Graham and N. Kermani, "Recitation and Aesthetic Reception," in J. McAuliffe (ed.), *The Cambridge Companion to the Qur'ān* (Cambridge, 2005), pp. 115–43; S. Blair, "Transcribing God's Word: Qur'an Codices in Context," *Journal of Qur'anic Studies* 10.1 (2008), 72–97.
43. R. Hoyland, "Jacob of Edessa on Islam," in G. Reinink and A. Cornelis Klugkist (eds), *After Bardasian: Studies on Continuity and Change in Syriac Christianity* (Leuven, 1999), pp. 158–9.
44. M. Whittow, *The Making of Orthodox Byzantium, 600–1025* (London, 1996), pp. 141–2.
45. R. Hoyland, "Writing the Biography of the Prophet Muhammad: Problems and Sources," *History Compass* 5.2 (2007), 593–6. Also see I. and W. Schulze, "The Standing Caliph Coins of al-Jazīra: Some Problems and Suggestions,"

Numismatic Chronicle 170 (2010), 331–53; S. Heidemann, "The Evolving Representation of the Early Islamic Empire and its Religion on Coin Imagery," in A. Neuwirth, N. Sinai and M. Marx (eds), *The Qurʾān in Context: Historical and Literary Investigations into the Qurʾānic Milieu* (Leiden, 2010), pp. 149–95.

46. B. Flood, *The Great Mosque of Damascus: Studies on the Makings of an Umayyad Visual Culture* (Leiden, 2001).
47. Johns, "Archaeology and History of Early Islam," 424–5. Also see Hoyland, *Seeing Islam*, esp. pp. 550–3, 694–5, and in general P. Crone and M. Hinds, *God's Caliph: Religious Authority in the First Centuries of Islam* (Cambridge, 1986).
48. O. Grabar, *The Dome of the Rock* (Cambridge, MA, 2006), pp. 91–2.
49. John of Damascus, *On Heresies*, tr. F. Chase, *The Fathers of the Church* (Washington, DC, 1958), 101, p. 153; Sarris, *Empires of Faith*, p. 266.
50. For example, M. Bennett, *Fighting Techniques of the Medieval World AD 500–AD 1500: Equipment, Combat Skills and Tactics* (Staplehurst, 2005).
51. P. Reynolds, *Trade in the Western Mediterranean, AD 400–700: The Ceramic Evidence* (Oxford, 1995); S. Kinsley, "Mapping Trade by Shipwrecks," in M. Mundell Mango (ed.), *Byzantine Trade, 4th–12th Centuries* (Farnham, 2009), pp. 31–6. See M. McCormick, *Origins of the European Economy: Communications and Commerce, AD 300–900* (Cambridge, 2001); Wickham, *Inheritance of Rome*, esp. pp. 255ff.
52. de la Vaissière, *Sogdian Traders*, pp. 279–86.
53. al-Yaʿqūbī and al-Balādhurī cited by J. Banaji, "Islam, the Mediterranean and the Rise of Capitalism," *Historical Materialism* 15 (2007), 47–74, esp. 59–60.
54. For the loose structures across the Sogdian world at this time, de la Vaissière, *Marchands sogdiens*, pp. 144–76.
55. See here F. Grenet and E. de la Vaissière, "The Last Days of Panjikent," *Silk Road Art and Archaeology* 8 (2002), 155–96.
56. See here J. Karam Skaff, *Sui-Tang China and Its Turko-Mongol Neighbours: Culture, Power, and Connections, 580–800* (Oxford, 2012).
57. D. Graff, "Strategy and Contingency in the Tang Defeat of the Eastern Turks, 629–30," in N. di Cosmo (ed.), *Warfare in Inner Asian History, 500–1800* (Leiden, 2002), pp. 33–72.
58. de la Vaissière, *Sogdian Traders*, pp. 217–20.
59. C. Mackerras, *The Uighur Empire According to the T'ang Dynastic Histories* (Canberra, 1972); T. Allsen, *Commodity and Exchange in the Mongol Empire: A Cultural History of Islamic Textiles* (Cambridge, 1997), p. 65.
60. C. Beckwith, "The Impact of Horse and Silk Trade on the Economics of T'ang China and the Uighur Empire: On the Importance of International Commerce in the Early Middle Ages," *Journal of the Economic and Social History of the Orient* 34 (1991), 183–98.
61. J. Kolbas, "Khukh Ordung: A Uighur Palace Complex of the Seventh Century," *Journal of the Royal Asiatic Society* 15.3 (2005), 303–27.
62. L. Albaum, *Balalyk-Tepe: k istorii material'noĭ kul'tury i iskusstva Tokharistana* (Tashkent, 1960); F. Starr, *Lost Enlightenment: Central Asia's Golden Age from the Arab Conquest to Tamerlane* (Princeton, 2014), p. 104.

63. A. Walmsley and K. Damgaard, "The Umayyad Congregational Mosque of Jerash in Jordan and its Relationship to Early Mosques," *Antiquity* 79 (2005), 362–78; I. Roll and E. Ayalon, "The Market Street at Apollonia—Arsuf," *BASOR* 267 (1987), 61–76; K. al-As'ad and Stepniowski, "The Umayyad *suq* in Palmyra," *Damazener Mitteilungen* 4 (1989), 205–23; R. Hillenbrand, "Anjar and Early Islamic Urbanism," in G.-P. Brogiolo and B. Ward-Perkins (eds), *The Idea and Ideal of the Town between Late Antiquity and the Early Middle Ages* (Leiden, 1999), pp. 59–98.
64. Hilāl al-Ṣābi', *Rusūm dār al-khilāfah*, in *The Rules and Regulations of the Abbasid Court*, tr. E. Salem (Beirut, 1977), pp. 21–2.
65. Ibn al-Zubayr, *Kitāb al-hadāyā wa al-tuḥaf*, in *Book of Gifts and Rarities: Selections Compiled in the Fifteenth Century from an Eleventh-Century Manuscript on Gifts and Treasures*, tr. G. al-Qaddūmī (Cambridge, MA, 1996), pp. 121–2.
66. B. Lewis, *Islam: From the Prophet Muhammad to the Capture of Constantinople* (New York, 1987), pp. 140–1.
67. Muqaddasī, *Best Divisions for Knowledge*, p. 60.
68. Ibid., pp. 107, 117, 263.
69. J. Bloom, *Paper before Print: The History and Impact of Paper in the Islamic World* (New Haven, 2001).
70. Muqaddasī, *Best Divisions for Knowledge*, pp. 6, 133–4, 141.
71. *Two Arabic travel books: Accounts of China and India*, ed. and trans. T. Mackintosh-Smith and J. Montgomery (New York, 2014), p. 37.
72. Ibid., pp. 59, 63.
73. J. Stargardt, "Indian Ocean Trade in the Ninth and Tenth Centuries: Demand, Distance, and Profit," *South Asian Studies* 30.1 (2014), 35–55.
74. A. Northedge, "Thoughts on the Introduction of Polychrome Glazed Pottery in the Middle East," in E. Villeneuve and P. Watson (eds), *La Céramique byzantine et proto-islamique en Syrie-Jordanie (IVe–VIIIe siècles apr. J.-C.)* (Beirut, 2001), pp. 207–14; R. Mason, *Shine Like the Sun: Lustre-Painted and Associated Pottery from the Medieval Middle East* (Toronto, 2004); M. Milwright, *An Introduction to Islamic Archaeology* (Edinburgh, 2010), pp. 48–9.
75. H. Khalileh, *Admiralty and Maritime Laws in the Mediterranean Sea (ca. 800–1050): The Kitāb Akriyat al Sufun vis-à-vis the Nomos Rhodion Nautikos* (Leiden, 2006), pp. 212–14.
76. Muqaddasī, *Best Divisions for Knowledge*, p. 347.
77. Daryaee, "Persian Gulf Trade," 1–16; Banaji, "Islam, the Mediterranean and the Rise of Capitalism," 61–2.
78. E. Grube, *Cobalt and Lustre: The First Centuries of Islamic Pottery* (London, 1994); O. Watson, *Ceramics from Islamic Lands* (London, 2004).
79. Du Huan, Jinxing Ji, cited by X. Liu, *The Silk Road in World History* (Oxford, 2010), p. 101.
80. *Kitāb al-Tāj (fī akhlāq al-mulūk)* in *Le Livre de la couronne: ouvrage attribute à Ğahiz*, tr. C. Pellat (Paris, 1954), p. 101.
81. For borrowing from Sasanian ideals, Walker, *Qardagh*, p. 139. For hunting scenes from a group of palaces near Teheran, D. Thompson, *Stucco from Chal-Tarkhan-Eshqabad near Rayy* (Warminster, 1976), pp. 9–24.

82. D. Gutas, *Greek Thought, Arabic Culture: The Graeco-Arabic Translation Movement in Baghdad and Early ʿAbbasid Society (2nd–4th/8th–10th Centuries)* (London, 1998); R. Hoyland, "Theonmestus of Magnesia, Hunayn ibn Ishaq and the Beginnings of Islamic Veterinary Science," in R. Hoyland and P. Kennedy (eds), *Islamic Reflections, Arabic Musings* (Oxford, 2004), pp. 150–69; A. McCabe, *A Byzantine Encyclopedia of Horse Medicine* (Oxford, 2007), pp. 182–4.
83. V. van Bladel, "The Bactrian Background of the Barmakids," in A. Akasoy, C. Burnett and R. Yoeli-Tialim, *Islam and Tibet: Interactions along the Musk Route* (Farnham, 2011), pp. 82–3; Gutas, *Greek Thought, Arabic Culture*, p. 13.
84. See P. Pormann and E. Savage-Smith, *Medieval Islamic Medicine* (Edinburgh, 2007); Y. Tabbaa, "The Functional Aspects of Medieval Islamic Hospitals," in M. Boner, M. Ener and A. Singer (eds), *Poverty and Charity in Middle Eastern Contexts* (Albany, NY, 2003), pp. 97–8.
85. Pormann and Savage-Smith, *Medieval Islamic Medicine*, p. 55.
86. E. Lev and L. Chipman, "A Fragment of a Judaeo-Arabic Manuscript of Sābūr b. Sahl's Al-Aqrābādhīn al-Ṣaghīr Found in the Taylor-Schechter Cairo Genizah Collection," *Medieval Encounters* 13 (2007), 347–62.
87. Ibn al-Haytham, *The Optics of Ibn al-Haytham, Books I–III: On Direct Vision*, tr. A. Sabra, 2 vols (London, 1989).
88. W. Gohlman, *The Life of Ibn Sina: A Critical Edition and Annotated Translation* (New York, 1974), p. 35.
89. al-Jāḥiẓ, *Kitāb al-Ḥayawān*, cited by Pormann and Savage-Smith, *Medieval Islamic Medicine*, p. 23.
90. Mahsatī, *Mahsati Ganjavi: la luna e le perle*, tr. R. Bargigli (Milan, 1999); also F. Bagherzadeh, "Mahsati Ganjavi et les potiers de Rey," in *Varia Turcica* 19 (1992), 161–76.
91. Augustine, *The Confessions of St. Augustine*, tr. F. Sheed (New York, 1942), p. 247.
92. al-Masʿūdī, cited by Gutas, *Greek Thought, Arabic Culture*, p. 89.
93. Muqaddasī, *Best Divisions for Knowledge*, p. 8.
94. M. Barrucand and A. Bednorz, *Moorish Architecture in Andalusia* (Cologne, 1999), p. 40.
95. See for example M. Dickens, "Patriarch Timothy II and the Metropolitan of the Turks," *Journal of the Royal Asiatic Society* 20.2 (2010), 117–39.
96. Conant, *Staying Roman*, pp. 362–70.
97. Narshakhī, *The History of Bukhara: Translated from a Persian Abridgement of the Arabic Original by Narshakhī*, tr. N. Frye (Cambridge, MA, 1954), pp. 48–9.
98. A. Watson, *Agricultural Innovation in the Early Islamic World* (Cambridge, 1983); T. Glick, "Hydraulic Technology in al-Andalus," in M. Morony (ed.), *Production and the Exploitation of Resources* (Aldershot, 2002), pp. 327–39.

CHAPTER 6—THE ROAD OF FURS

1. W. Davis, *Readings in Ancient History: Illustrative Extracts from the Sources*, 2 vols (Boston, 1912–1913), 2, pp. 365–7.

2. Ibn Khurradādhbih, *Kitāb al-masālik wa-l-mamālik*, tr. Lunde and Stone, "Book of Roads and Kingdoms," in *Ibn Fadlan and the Land of Darkness*, pp. 99–104.
3. E. van Donzel and A. Schmidt, *Gog and Magog in Early Christian and Islamic Sources: Sallam's Quest for Alexander's Wall* (Leiden, 2010); also note here F. Sezgin, *Anthropogeographie* (Frankfurt, 2010), pp. 95–7; I. Krachovskii, *Arabskaya geographitcheskaya literatura* (Moscow, 2004), esp. pp. 138–41.
4. A. Gow, "Gog and Magog on *Mappaemundi* and Early Printed World Maps: Orientalizing Ethnography in the Apocalyptic Tradition," *Journal of Early Modern History* 2.1 (1998), 61–2.
5. Ibn Faḍlān, *Book of Ahmad ibn Faḍlān*, tr. Lunde and Stone, *Land of Darkness*, p. 12.
6. Ibid., pp. 23–4.
7. Ibid., p. 12; for Tengri, see U. Harva, *Die Religiösen Vorstellungen der altaischen Völker* (Helsinki, 1938), pp. 140–53.
8. R. Mason, "The Religious Beliefs of the Khazars," *Ukrainian Quarterly* 51.4 (1995), 383–415.
9. Note therefore a recent contrary argument that decouples Sufism and the nomad world, J. Paul, "Islamizing Sufis in Pre-Mongol Central Asia," in de la Vaissière, *Islamisation de l'Asie Centrale*, pp. 297–317.
10. Abū Hāmid al-Gharnātī, *Tuḥfat al-albāb wa-nukhbat al-iʿjāb wa-Riḥlah ilá Ūrubbah wa-Āsiyah*, tr. Lunde and Stone, "The Travels," in *Land of Darkness*, p. 68.
11. A. Khazanov, "The Spread of World Religions in Medieval Nomadic Societies of the Eurasian Steppes," in M. Gervers and W. Schlepp (eds), *Nomadic Diplomacy, Destruction and Religion from the Pacific to the Adriatic* (Toronto, 1994), pp. 11–34.
12. E. Seldeslachts, "Greece, the Final Frontier? The Westward Spread of Buddhism," in A. Heirman and S. Bumbacher (eds), *The Spread of Buddhism* (Leiden, 2007); R. Bulliet, "Naw Bahar and the Survival of Iranian Buddhism," *Iran* 14 (1976), 144–5; Narshakhī, *History of Bukhara*, p. 49.
13. Constantine Porphyrogenitus, *De Administrando Imperio*, ed. G. Moravcsik, tr. R. Jenkins (Washington, DC, 1967), 37, pp. 166–70.
14. Ibn Faḍlān, "Book of Ahmad ibn Faḍlān," p. 22. Some scholars play down the significance of pastoral nomadism on the steppe, e.g. B. Zakhoder, *Kaspiiskii svod svedenii o Vostochnoi Evrope*, 2 vols (Moscow, 1962), 1, pp. 139–40.
15. D. Dunlop, *The History of the Jewish Khazars* (Princeton, 1954), p. 83; L. Baranov, *Tavrika v epokhu rannego srednevekov'ia (saltovo-maiatskaia kul'tura)* (Kiev, 1990), pp. 76–9.
16. A. Martinez, "Gardīzī's Two Chapters on the Turks," *Archivum Eurasiae Medii Aevi* 2 (1982), 155; T. Noonan, "Some Observations on the Economy of the Khazar Khaganate," in P. Golden, H. Ben-Shammai and A. Róna-Tas (eds), *The World of the Khazars* (Leiden, 2007), pp. 214–15.
17. Baranov, *Tavrika*, pp. 72–6.
18. Al-Muqaddasī, in *Land of Darkness*, pp. 169–70.

19. Abū Hāmid, "Travels," p. 67.
20. McCormick, *Origins of the European Economy*, pp. 369–84.
21. J. Howard-Johnston, "Trading in Fur, from Classical Antiquity to the Early Middle Ages," in E. Cameron (ed.), *Leather and Fur: Aspects of Early Medieval Trade and Technology* (London, 1998), pp. 65–79.
22. Mas'ūdī, *Kitāb al-tanbīh wa-al-ishrāf*, tr. Lunde and Stone, "The Meadows of Gold and Mines of Precious Gems," *Land of Darkness*, p. 161.
23. Muqaddasī, *Aḥsanu-t-taqāsīm fī ma'rifati-l-aqālīm*, tr. Lunde and Stone, "Best Divisions for the Knowledge of the Provinces," *Land of Darkness*, p. 169.
24. Abū Hāmid, "Travels," p. 75.
25. R. Kovalev, "The Infrastructure of the Northern Part of the 'Fur Road' between the Middle Volga and the East during the Middle Ages," *Archivum Eurasiae Medii Aevi* 11 (2000–1), 25–64.
26. Muqaddasī, *Best Division of Knowledge*, p. 252.
27. Ibn al-Faqīh, *Land of Darkness*, p. 113.
28. al-Muqaddasī, *Best Division of Knowledge*, p. 245.
29. For a recent overview, G. Mako, "The Possible Reasons for the Arab–Khazar Wars," *Archivum Eurasiae Medii Aevi* 17 (2010), 45–57.
30. R.-J. Lilie, *Die byzantinische Reaktion auf die Ausbreitung der Araber. Studien zur Strukturwandlung des byzantinischen Staates im 7. und 8. Jahrhundert* (Munich, 1976), pp. 157–60; J. Howard-Johnston, "Byzantine Sources for Khazar History," in Golden, Ben-Shammai and Róna-Tas, *World of the Khazars*, pp. 163–94.
31. The marriage of the daughter of the Emperor Heraclius with the Türk *khagan* at the height of the confrontation with the Persians in the early seventh century was the only exception, C. Zuckermann, "La Petite Augusta et le Turc: Epiphania-Eudocie sur les monnaies d'Héraclius," *Revue numismatique* 150 (1995), 113–26.
32. Ibn Faḍlān, "Book of Ahmad ibn Faḍlān," p. 56.
33. Dunlop, *History of the Jewish Khazars*, p. 141.
34. See P. Golden, "The Peoples of the South Russian Steppes," in *The Cambridge History of Early Inner Asia* (Cambridge, 1990), pp. 256–84; A. Novosel'tsev, *Khazarskoye gosudarstvo i ego rol' v istorii Vostochnoy Evropy i Kavkaza* (Moscow, 1990).
35. P. Golden, "Irano-Turcica: The Khazar Sacral Kingship," *Acta Orientalia* 60.2 (2007), 161–94. Some scholars interpret the change in the nature of the role of the *khagan* as resulting from a shift in religious beliefs and practices during this period. See for example J. Olsson, "Coup d'état, Coronation and Conversion: Some Reflections on the Adoption of Judaism by the Khazar Khaganate," *Journal of the Royal Asiatic Society* 23.4 (2013), 495–526.
36. R. Kovalev, "Commerce and Caravan Routes along the Northern Silk Road (Sixth–Ninth Centuries). Part I: The Western Sector," *Archivum Eurasiae Medii Aevi* 14 (2005), 55–105.
37. Mas'ūdī, "Meadows of Gold," pp. 131, 133; Noonan, "Economy of the Khazar Khaganate," p. 211.

38. Istakhrī, *Kitāb suwar al-aqalīm*, tr. Lunde and Stone, "Book of Roads and Kingdoms," in *Land of Darkness*, pp. 153–5.
39. J. Darrouzès, *Notitiae Episcopatuum Ecclesiae Constantinopolitanae* (Paris, 1981), pp. 31–2, 241–2, 245.
40. Istakhrī, "Book of Roads and Kingdoms," pp. 154–5.
41. Mason, "The Religious Beliefs of the Khazars," 411.
42. C. Zuckerman, "On the Date of the Khazars' Conversion to Judaism and the Chronology of the Kings of the Rus' Oleg and Igor: A Study of the Anonymous Khazar Letter from the Genizah of Cairo," *Revue des Etudes Byzantines* 53 (1995), 245.
43. Ibid., 243–4. For borrowings from Constantine's writing, P. Meyvaert and P. Devos, "Trois énigmes cyrillo-méthodiennes de la 'Légende Italique' résolues grâce à un document inédit," *Analecta Bollandiana* 75 (1955), 433–40.
44. P. Lavrov (ed.), *Materialy po istorii vozniknoveniya drevnishei slavyanskoi pis'mennosti* (Leningrad, 1930), p. 21; F. Butler, "The Representation of Oral Culture in the *Vita Constantini*," *Slavic and East European Review* 39.3 (1995), 372.
45. "The Letter of Rabbi Hasdai," in J. Rader Marcus (ed.), *The Jew in the Medieval World* (Cincinnati, 1999), pp. 227–8. Also here see N. Golb and O. Pritsak (eds), *Khazarian Hebrew Documents of the Tenth Century* (London, 1982).
46. "The Letter of Joseph the King," in J. Rader Marcus (ed.), *The Jew in the Medieval World*, p. 300. For a discussion of the date and context, P. Golden, "The Conversion of the Khazars to Judaism," in Golden, Ben-Shammai and Róna-Tas, *World of the Khazars*, pp. 123–62.
47. R. Kovalev, "Creating 'Khazar Identity' through Coins—the 'Special Issue' Dirhams of 837/8," in F. Curta (ed.), *East Central and Eastern Europe in the Early Middle Ages* (Ann Arbor, 2005), pp. 220–53. For the change in burial practices, V. Petrukhin, "The Decline and Legacy of Khazaria," in P. Urbanczyk (ed.), *Europe around the Year 1000* (Warsaw, 2001), pp. 109–22.
48. *Qur'ān*, 2.285, p. 48; 3.84, p. 60.
49. Zuckerman, "On the Date of the Khazars' Conversion," 241. Also Golb and Pritsak, *Khazarian Hebrew Documents*, p. 130.
50. Mas'ūdī, "Meadows of Gold," p. 132; for elite Judaism, Mason, "The Religious Beliefs of the Khazars," 383–415.
51. Pritsak and Golb, *Khazarian Hebrew Documents*; Mas'ūdī, "Meadows of Gold," p. 133; Istakhrī, "Book of Roads and Kingdoms," p. 154.
52. Ibn Khurradādhbih, "Book of Roads and Kingdoms," p. 110.
53. Ibid., pp. 111–12.
54. Ibid., p. 112.
55. Ibn al-Faqīh, "Book of Countries," p. 114.
56. Liudprand of Cremona, a visitor to Constantinople in the tenth century, thought the name for the Rus' came from the Greek word *rousios*, or red, because of their distinctive hair colour, *The Complete Works of Liudprand of Cremona*, tr. P. Squatriti (Washington, DC, 2007), 5.15, p. 179. In fact, the word comes from Scandinavian words *roþrsmenn* and *roðr* meaning to row. S. Ekbo, "Finnish Ruotsi and Swedish Roslagen—What Sort of Connection?," *Medieval*

Scandinavia 13 (2000), 64–9; W. Duczko, *Viking Rus: Studies on the Presence of Scandinavians in Eastern Europe* (Leiden, 2004), pp. 22–3.

57. S. Franklin and J. Shepard, *The Emergence of Rus' 750–1200* (London, 1996).
58. Constantine Porphyrogenitus, *De Administrando Imperio*, 9, pp. 58–62.
59. *De Administrando Imperio*, 9, p. 60.
60. Ibn Rusta, *Kitāb al-a'lāq an-nafīsa*, tr. Lunde and Stone, "Book of Precious Gems," in *Land of Darkness*, p. 127.
61. Ibn Faḍlān, "Book of Ahmad ibn Faḍlān," p. 45.
62. Ibn Rusta, "Book of Precious Gems," p. 127.
63. Ibn Faḍlān, "Book of Ahmad ibn Faḍlān," pp. 46–9.
64. A. Winroth, *The Conversion of Scandinavia* (New Haven, 2012), pp. 78–9.
65. M. Bogucki, "The Beginning of the Dirham Import to the Baltic Sea and the Question of the Early Emporia," in A. Bitner-Wróblewska and U. Lund-Hansen (eds), *Worlds Apart? Contacts across the Baltic Sea in the Iron Age: Network Denmark–Poland 2005–2008* (Copenhagen, 2010), pp. 351–61. For Sweden, I. Hammarberg, *Byzantine Coin Finds in Sweden* (1989); C. von Heijne, *Särpräglat. Vikingatida och tidigmedeltida myntfynd från Danmark, Skåne, Blekinge och Halland (ca. 800–1130)* (Stockholm, 2004).
66. T. Noonan, "Why Dirhams First Reached Russia: The Role of Arab–Khazar Relations in the Development of the Earliest Islamic Trade with Eastern Europe," *Archivum Eurasiae Medii Aevi* 4 (1984), 151–82, and above all idem, "Dirham Exports to the Baltic in the Viking Age," in K. Jonsson and B. Malmer (eds), *Sigtuna Papers: Proceedings of the Sigtuna Symposium on Viking-Age Coinage 1–4 June 1989* (Stockholm, 1990), pp. 251–7.

CHAPTER 7—THE SLAVE ROAD

1. Ibn Rusta, "Book of Precious Gems," pp. 126–7.
2. Ibid.
3. *De Administrando Imperio*, 9, p. 60.
4. Ibn Faḍlān, "Book of Ahmad ibn Faḍlān," p. 47.
5. D. Wyatt, *Slaves and Warriors in Medieval Britain and Ireland, 800–1200* (Leiden, 2009).
6. L. Delisle (ed.), *Littérature latine et histoire du moyen âge* (Paris, 1890), p. 17.
7. See J. Henning, "Strong Rulers—Weak Economy? Rome, the Carolingians and the Archaeology of Slavery in the First Millennium AD," in J. Davis and M. McCormick (eds), *The Long Morning of Medieval Europe: New Directions in Early Medieval Studies* (Aldershot, 2008), pp. 33–53; for Novgorod, see H. Birnbaum, "Medieval Novgorod: Political, Social and Cultural Life in an Old Russian Urban Community," *California Slavic Studies* (1992), 14, p. 11.
8. Adam of Bremen, *History of the Archbishops of Hamburg Bremen*, ed. and tr. F. Tschan (New York, 1959), 4.6, p. 190.
9. B. Hudson, *Viking Pirates and Christian Princes: Dynasty, Religion and Empire in the North Atlantic* (Oxford, 2005), p. 41; in general, also see S. Brink, *Vikingarnas slavar: den nordiska träldomen under yngre järnålder och äldsta medeltid* (Stockholm, 2012).

10. T. Noonan, "Early Abbasid Mint Output," *Journal of Economic and Social History* 29 (1986), 113–75; R. Kovalev, "Dirham Mint Output of Samanid Samarqand and its Connection to the Beginnings of Trade with Northern Europe (10th Century)," *Histoire & Mesure* 17.3–4 (2002), 197–216; T. Noonan and R. Kovalev, "The Dirham Output and Monetary Circulation of a Secondary Samanid Mint: A Case Study of Balkh," in R. Kiernowski (ed.), *Moneta Mediævalis: Studia numizmatyczne i historyczne ofiarowane Profesorowi Stanisławowi Suchodolskiemu w 65. rocznicę urodzin* (Warsaw, 2002), pp. 163–74.
11. R. Segal, *Islam's Black Slaves: The Other Black Diaspora* (New York, 2001), p. 121.
12. Ibn Ḥawqal, *Kītāb ṣūrat al-ard*, cited by D. Ayalon, "The Mamluks of the Seljuks: Islam's Military Might at the Crossroads," *Journal of the Royal Asiatic Society* 6.3 (1996), 312. From this point, I switch from Türk to Turk to distinguish between peoples of the steppes and the ancestors of modern Turkey.
13. W. Scheidel, "The Roman Slave Supply," in K. Bradley, P. Cartledge, D. Eltis and S. Engerman (eds), *The Cambridge World History of Slavery*, 3 vols (Cambridge, 2011–), 1, pp. 287–310.
14. See F. Caswell, *The Slave Girls of Baghdad. The Qiyan in the Early Abbasid Era* (London, 2011), p. 13.
15. Tacitus, *Annals*, 15.69, p. 384.
16. Ibn Buṭlān, *Taqwīm al-ṣiḥḥa*, cited by G. Vantini, *Oriental Sources concerning Nubia* (Heidelberg, 1975), pp. 238–9.
17. Kaykāvūs ibn Iskandar ibn Qābūs, ed. and tr. R. Levy, *Naṣīḥat-nāma known as Qābūs-nāma*, (London, 1951), p. 102.
18. Ibid.
19. D. Abulafia, "Asia, Africa and the Trade of Medieval Europe," in M. Postan, E. Miller and C. Postan (eds), *Cambridge Economic History of Europe: Trade and Industry in the Middle Ages* (2nd edn, Cambridge, 1987), p. 417. Also see D. Mishin, "The Saqaliba Slaves in the Aghlabid State," in M. Sebök (ed.), *Annual of Medieval Studies at CEU 1996/1997* (Budapest, 1998), pp. 236–44.
20. Ibrāhīm ibn Ya'qūb, tr. Lunde and Stone, in *Land of Darkness*, pp. 164–5. For Prague's role as a slave centre, D. Třeštík, "'Eine große Stadt der Slawen namens Prag': Staaten und Sklaven in Mitteleuropa im 10. Jahrhundert," in P. Sommer (ed.), *Boleslav II: der tschechische Staat um das Jahr 1000* (Prague, 2001), pp. 93–138.
21. Ibn al-Zubayr, *Book of Gifts and Rarities*, pp. 91–2. See A. Christys, "The Queen of the Franks Offers Gifts to the Caliph Al-Muktafi," in W. Davies and P. Fouracre (eds), *The Languages of Gift in the Early Middle Ages* (Cambridge, 2010), pp. 140–71.
22. Ibrāhīm ibn Ya'qūb, pp. 162–3.
23. R. Naismith, "Islamic Coins from Early Medieval England," *Numismatic Chronicle* 165 (2005), 193–222; idem, "The Coinage of Offa Revisited," *British Numismatic Journal* 80 (2010), 76–106.
24. M. McCormick, "New Light on the 'Dark Ages': How the Slave Trade Fuelled the Carolingian Economy," *Past & Present* 177 (2002), 17–54; also J. Henning, "Slavery or Freedom? The Causes of Early Medieval Europe's Economic Advancement," *Early Medieval Europe* 12.3 (2003), 269–77.

25. Ibn Khurradādhbih, "Book of Roads and Kingdoms," p. 111.
26. Ibn Ḥawqal, *Kītāb ṣūrat al-ard*, tr. Lunde and Stone, "Book of the Configuration of the Earth," in *Land of Darkness*, p. 173.
27. Ibid. Also Al-Muqaddasī, *Land of Darkness*, p. 170.
28. al-Jāḥiẓ, *Kitāb al-Ḥayawān*, cited in C. Verlinden, *L'Esclavage dans l'Europe mediévale*, 2 vols (Bruges, 1955–77), 1, p. 213.
29. Ibid.
30. Verlinden, *Esclavage*, 2, pp. 218–30, 731–2; W. Phillips, *Slavery from Roman Times to the Early Transatlantic Trade* (Manchester, 1985), p. 62.
31. H. Loyn and R. Percival (eds), *The Reign of Charlemagne: Documents on Carolingian Government and Administration* (London, 1975), p. 129.
32. In Germany, it used to be common to do the same, with "Servus" a regular greeting.
33. Adam of Bremen, *Gesta Hammaburgensis ecclesiae pontificum*, tr. T. Reuter, *History of the Archbishops of Hamburg-Bremen* (New York, 2002), I.39–41.
34. *Pactum Hlotharii I*, in McCormick, "Carolingian Economy," 47.
35. G. Luzzato, *An Economic History of Italy from the Fall of the Roman Empire to the Sixteenth Century*, tr. P. Jones (London, 1961), pp. 35, 51–3; Phillips, *Slavery*, p. 63.
36. McCormick, "Carolingian Economy," 48–9.
37. *Hudūd al-ʿĀlam*, in *The Regions of the World: A Persian Geography 372 AH–982 AD*, tr. V. Minorsky, ed. C. Bosworth (London, 1970), pp. 161–2.
38. Ibn Faḍlān, "Book of Ahmad ibn Faḍlān," p. 44; Ibn Khurradādhbih, "Book of Roads and Kingdoms," p. 12; Martinez, "Gardīzī's Two Chapters on the Turks," pp. 153–4.
39. *Russian Primary Chronicle*, tr. S. Cross and O. Sherbowitz-Wetzor (Cambridge, MA, 1953), p. 61.
40. *Annales Bertiniani*, ed. G. Waitz (Hanover, 1885), p. 35.
41. Masʿūdī, "Meadows of Gold," pp. 145–6; Ibn Ḥawqal, "Book of the Configuration of the Earth," p. 175.
42. Ibn Ḥawqal, "Book of the Configuration of the Earth," p. 178.
43. R. Kovalev, "Mint Output in Tenth Century Bukhara: A Case Study of Dirham Production with Monetary Circulation in Northern Europe," *Russian History/Histoire Russe* 28 (2001), 250–9.
44. *Russian Primary Chronicle*, p. 86.
45. Ibid., p. 90.
46. H. Halm, *Das Reich des Mahdi. Der Aufstieg der Fatimiden (875–973)* (Munich, 1991); F. Akbar, "The Secular Roots of Religious Dissidence in Early Islam: The Case of the Qaramita of Sawad Al-Kufa," *Journal of the Institute of Muslim Minority Affairs* 12.2 (1991), 376–90. For the breakdown of the caliphate in this period, see M. van Berkel, N. El Cheikh, H. Kennedy and L. Osti, *Crisis and Continuity at the Abbasid Court: Formal and Informal Politics in the Caliphate of al-Muqtadir* (Leiden, 2013).
47. Bar Hebraeus, *Ktābā d-maktbānūt zabnē*, E. Budge (ed. and tr.), *The Chronography of Gregory Abul Faraj*, 2 vols (Oxford, 1932), 1, p. 164.
48. Matthew of Edessa, *The Chronicle of Matthew of Edessa*, tr. A. Dostourian

(Lanham, 1993), I.1, p. 19; M. Canard, "Baghdad au IVe siècle de l'Hégire (Xe siècle de l'ère chrétienne)," *Arabica* 9 (1962), 282–3. See here R. Bulliet, *Cotton, Climate, and Camels in Early Islamic Iran: A Moment in World History* (New York, 2009), pp. 79–81; R. Ellenblum, *The Collapse of the Eastern Mediterranean: Climate Change and the Decline of the East, 950–1072* (Cambridge, 2012), pp. 32–6.

49. Ellenblum, *Collapse of the Eastern Mediterranean*, pp. 41–3.
50. C. Mango, *The Homilies of Photius Patriarch of Constantinople* (Cambridge, MA, 1958), pp. 88–9.
51. *Russian Primary Chronicle*, pp. 74–5.
52. Shepard, "The Viking Rus' and Byzantium," in S. Brink and N. Price (eds), *The Viking World* (Abingdon, 2008), pp. 498–501.
53. See for example A. Poppe, "The Building of the Church of St. Sophia in Kiev," *Journal of Medieval History* 7.1 (1981), 15–66.
54. Shepard, "Viking Rus'," p. 510.
55. T. Noonan and R. Kovalev, "Prayer, Illumination and Good Times: The Export of Byzantine Wine and Oil to the North of Russia in Pre-Mongol Times," *Byzantium and the North. Acta Fennica* 8 (1997), 73–96; M. Roslund, "Brosamen vom Tisch der Reichen. Byzantinische Funde aus Lund und Sigtuna (ca. 980–1250)," in M. Müller-Wille (ed.), *Rom und Byzanz im Nordern. Mission und Glaubensweschel im Ostseeraum während des 8–14 Jahrhunderts* (Stuttgart, 1997), 2, pp. 325–85.
56. L. Golombek, "The Draped Universe of Islam," in P. Parsons Soucek (ed.), *Content and Context of Visual Arts in the Islamic World: Papers from a Colloquium in Memory of Richard Ettinghausen* (University Park, PA, 1988), pp. 97–114. For Antioch's textile production after 1098, see T. Vorderstrasse, "Trade and Textiles from Medieval Antioch," *Al-Masāq* 22.2 (2010), 151–71.
57. D. Jacoby, "Byzantine Trade with Egypt from the Mid-Tenth Century to the Fourth Crusade," *Thesaurismata* 30 (2000), 36.
58. V. Piacentini, "Merchant Families in the Gulf: A Mercantile and Cosmopolitan Dimension: The Written Evidence," *ARAM* 11–12 (1999–2000), 145–8.
59. D. Goitein, *A Mediterranean Society: The Jewish Communities of the Arab World as Portrayed in the Documents of the Cairo Geniza*, 6 vols (Berkeley, 1967–93), 4, p. 168; Jacoby, "Byzantine Trade with Egypt," 41–3.
60. Nāṣir-i Khusraw, *Safarnāma*, tr. W. Thackston, *Nāṣer-e Khosraw's Book of Travels* (Albany, NY, 1986), pp. 39–40.
61. Jacoby, "Byzantine Trade with Egypt," 42; S. Simonsohn, *The Jews of Sicily 383–1300* (Leiden, 1997), pp. 314–16.
62. M. Vedeler, *Silk for the Vikings* (Oxford, 2014).
63. E. Brate and E. Wessén, *Sveriges Runinskrifter: Södermanlands Runinskrifter* (Stockholm, 1924–36), p. 154.
64. S. Jansson, *Västmanlands runinskrifter* (Stockholm, 1964), pp. 6–9.
65. G. Isitt, "Vikings in the Persian Gulf," *Journal of the Royal Asiatic Society* 17.4 (2007), 389–406.
66. P. Frankopan, "Levels of Contact between West and East: Pilgrims and Visitors

to Constantinople and Jerusalem in the 9th–12th Centuries," in S. Searight and M. Wagstaff (eds), *Travellers in the Levant: Voyagers and Visionaries* (Durham, 2001), pp. 87–108.

67. See J. Wortley, *Studies on the Cult of Relics in Byzantium up to 1204* (Farnham, 2009).
68. S. Blöndal, *The Varangians of Byzantium*, tr. B. Benedikz (Cambridge, 1978); J. Shepard, "The Uses of the Franks in 11th-Century Byzantium," *Anglo-Norman Studies* 15 (1992), 275–305.
69. P. Frankopan, *The First Crusade: The Call from the East* (London, 2012), pp. 87–8.
70. H. Hoffmann, "Die Anfänge der Normannen in Süditalien," *Quellen und Forschungen aus Italienischen Archiven und Bibiliotheken* 47 (1967), 95–144; G. Loud, *The Age of Robert Guiscard: Southern Italy and the Norman Conquest* (Singapore, 2000).
71. al-ʿUtbī, *Kitāb-i Yamīnī*, tr. J. Reynolds, *Historical memoirs of the amír Sabaktagín, and the sultán Mahmúd of Ghazna* (London, 1868), p. 140. See in general C. Bosworth, *The Ghaznavids, 994–1040* (Cambridge, 1963).
72. A. Shapur Shahbāzī, *Ferdowsī: A Critical Biography* (Costa Mesa, CA, 1991), esp. pp. 91–3; also G. Dabiri, "The Shahnama: Between the Samanids and the Ghaznavids," *Iranian Studies* 43.1 (2010), 13–28.
73. Y. Bregel, "Turko-Mongol Influences in Central Asia," in R. Canfield (ed.), *Turko-Persia in Historical Perspective* (Cambridge, 1991), pp. 53ff.
74. Herrman, "Die älteste türkische Weltkarte," 21–8.
75. Yūsuf Khāṣṣ Ḥājib, *Kutadgu Bilig*, tr. R. Dankoff, *Wisdom of Royal Glory (Kutadgu Bilig): A Turko-Islamic Mirror for Princes* (Chicago, 1983), p. 192.
76. For the rise of the Seljuks, see C. Lange and S. Mecit (eds), *The Seljuqs: Politics, Society and Culture* (Edinburgh, 2011).
77. For a discussion on some contradictions in the sources here, see O. Safi, *Politics of Knowledge in Pre-Modern Islam: Negotiating Ideology and Religious Inquiry* (Chapel Hill, NC, 2006), pp. 35–6.
78. Dunlop, *History of the Jewish Khazars*, p. 260; A. Peacock, *Early Seljuq History: A New Interpretation* (Abingdon, 2010), pp. 33–4; Dickens, "Patriarch Timothy," 117–39.
79. Aristakes of Lastivert, *Patmutʿiwn Aristakeay Vardapeti Lastivertts ʿwoy*, tr. R. Bedrosian, *Aristakēs Lastivertcʿi's History* (New York, 1985), p. 64.
80. For a collection of the sources for the battle of Manzikert, see C. Hillenbrand, *Turkish Myth and Muslim Symbol* (Edinburgh, 2007), pp. 26ff.
81. Frankopan, *First Crusade*, pp. 57–86.
82. Ibid., pp. 13–25.
83. Bernold of Constance, *Die Chroniken Bertholds von Reichenau und Bernolds von Konstanz*, ed. I. Robinson (Hanover, 2003), p. 520.
84. Frankopan, *First Crusade*, pp. 1–3, 101–13.
85. Ibid., passim. For the fear of the Apocalypse, see J. Rubenstein, *Armies of Heaven: The First Crusade and the Quest for Apocalypse* (New York, 2011).

CHAPTER 8—THE ROAD TO HEAVEN

1. Albert of Aachen, *Historia Iherosolimitana*, ed. and tr. S. Edgington (Oxford, 2007), 5.45, p. 402; Frankopan, *First Crusade*, p. 173.
2. Raymond of Aguilers, *Historia Francorum qui ceperunt Jerusalem*, tr. J. Hill and L. Hill, *Le "Liber" de Raymond d'Aguilers* (Paris, 1969), 14, p. 127. For the expedition and the Crusades in general, C. Tyerman, *God's War: A New History of the Crusades* (London, 2006).
3. Fulcher of Chartres, *Gesta Francorum Iherusalem Peregrinantium*, tr. F. Ryan, *A History of the Expedition to Jerusalem 1095–1127* (Knoxville, 1969), I.27, p. 122. There is much to be learnt from current research on the relationship between mental health and extreme violence in combat. For example, R. Ursano et al., "Posttraumatic Stress Disorder and Traumatic Stress: From Bench to Bedside, from War to Disaster," *Annals of the New York Academy of Sciences* 1208 (2010), 72–81.
4. Anna Komnene, *Alexias*, tr. P. Frankopan, *Alexiad* (London, 2009), 13.11, pp. 383–4; for Bohemond's return to Europe, L. Russo, "Il viaggio di Boemundo d'Altavilla in Francia," *Archivio storico italiano* 603 (2005), pp. 3–42; Frankopan, *First Crusade*, pp. 188–9.
5. R. Chazan, "'Let Not a Remnant or a Residue Escape': Millenarian Enthusiasm in the First Crusade," *Speculum* 84 (2009), 289–313.
6. al-Harawī, *Kitāb al-ishārāt ilā ma'rifat al-ziyārāt* in A. Maalouf, *The Crusade through Arab Eyes* (London, 1984), p. xiii. Also note Ibn al-Jawzī,' *al-Muntaẓam fī tārīkh al-mulūk wa-al-umam*, in C. Hillenbrand, *The Crusades: Islamic Perspectives* (Edinburgh, 1999), p. 78. In general here, see P. Cobb, *The Race for Paradise: An Islamic History of the Crusades* (Oxford, 2014).
7. For accounts of the suffering, S. Eidelberg (tr.), *The Jews and the Crusaders* (Madison, 1977). See M. Gabriele, "Against the Enemies of Christ: The Role of Count Emicho in the Anti-Jewish Violence of the First Crusade," in M. Frassetto (ed.), *Christian Attitudes towards the Jews in the Middle Ages: A Casebook* (Abingdon, 2007), pp. 61–82.
8. Frankopan, *First Crusade*, pp. 133–5, 167–71; J. Pryor, "The Oath of the Leaders of the Crusade to the Emperor Alexius Comnenus: Fealty, Homage," *Parergon*, New Series 2 (1984), 111–41.
9. Raymond of Aguilers, *Le "Liber,"* 10, pp. 74–5.
10. Frankopan, *First Crusade*, esp. pp. 186ff.
11. Ibn al-Athīr, *al-Kāmil fī l-ta'rīkh*, tr. D. Richards, *The Chronicle of Ibn al-Athir for the Crusading Period from al-Kāmil fī'l-ta'rīkh* (Aldershot, 2006), p. 13.
12. Jacoby, "Byzantine Trade with Egypt," 44–5.
13. S. Goitein, *A Mediterranean Society*, 1, p. 45.
14. A. Greif, "Reputation and Coalitions in Medieval Trade: Evidence on the Maghribi Traders," *Journal of Economic History* 49.4 (1989), 861.
15. Ibn Khaldūn, *Dīwān al-mubtada'*, tr. V. Monteil, *Discours sur l'histoire universelle (al-Muqaddima)*, (Paris, 1978), p. 522.
16. Frankopan, *First Crusade*, pp. 29–30.

17. E. Occhipinti, *Italia dei communi. Secoli XI–XIII* (2000), pp. 20–1.
18. J. Riley-Smith, *The First Crusaders, 1095–1131* (Cambridge, 1997), p. 17.
19. The Monk of the Lido, *Monachi Anonymi Littorensis Historia de Translatio Sanctorum Magni Nicolai*, in *Recueil des Historiens des Croisades: Historiens Occidentaux* 5, pp. 272–5; J. Prawer, *The Crusaders' Kingdom: European Colonialism in the Middle Ages* (London, 2001), p. 489.
20. *Codice diplomatico della repubblica di Genova*, 3 vols (Rome, 1859–1940), 1, p. 20.
21. B. Kedar, "Genoa's Golden Inscription in the Church of the Holy Sepulchre: A Case for the Defence," in G. Airaldi and B. Kedar (eds), *I comuni italiani nel regno crociato di Gerusalemme* (Genoa, 1986), pp. 317–35. Also see M.-L. Favreau-Lilie, who argues that this document may have been tampered with at a later date, *Die Italiener im Heiligen Land vom ersten Kreuzzug bis zum Tode Heinrichs von Champagne (1098–1197)* (Amsterdam, 1989), p. 328.
22. Dandolo, *Chronica per extensum descripta*, *Rerum Italicarum Scriptores*, 25 vols (Bologna, 1938–58), 12, p. 221. Also here see Monk of the Lido, *Monachi Anonymi*, pp. 258–9.
23. M. Pozza and G. Ravegnani, *I Trattati con Bisanzio 992–1198* (Venice, 1993), pp. 38–45. For the date of the concessions, which have long been dated to the 1080s, see P. Frankopan, "Byzantine Trade Privileges to Venice in the Eleventh Century: The Chrysobull of 1092," *Journal of Medieval History* 30 (2004), 135–60.
24. Monk of the Lido, *Monachi Anonymi*, pp. 258–9; Dandolo, *Chronica*, p. 221. Also see D. Queller and I. Katele, "Venice and the Conquest of the Latin Kingdom of Jerusalem," *Studi Veneziani* 21 (1986), 21.
25. F. Miklosich and J. Müller, *Acta et Diplomata graeca medii aevi sacra et profana*, 6 vols (Venice, 1860–90), 3, pp. 9–13.
26. R.-J. Lilie, *Byzantium and the Crusader States, 1096–1204*, tr. J. Morris and J. Ridings (Oxford, 1993), pp. 87–94; "Noch einmal zu den Thema 'Byzanz und die Kreuzfahrerstaaten,'" *Poikila Byzantina* 4 (1984), 121–74. Treaty of Devol, *Alexiad*, XII.24, pp. 385–96.
27. S. Epstein, *Genoa and the Genoese: 958–1528* (Chapel Hill, NC, 1996), pp. 40–1; D. Abulafia, "Southern Italy, Sicily and Sardinia in the Medieval Mediterranean Economy," in idem, *Commerce and Conquest in the Mediterranean* (Aldershot, 1993), 1, pp. 24–7.
28. T. Asbridge, "The Significance and Causes of the Battle of the Field of Blood," *Journal of Medieval History* 23.4 (1997), 301–16.
29. Fulcher of Chartres, *Gesta Francorum*, p. 238.
30. G. Tafel and G. Thomas, *Urkunden zur älteren handels und Staatsgeschichte der Republik Venedig*, 3 vols (Vienna, 1857), 1, p. 78; Queller and Katele, "Venice and the Conquest," 29–30.
31. Tafel and Thomas, *Urkunden*, 1, pp. 95–8; Lilie, *Byzantium and the Crusader States*, pp. 96–100; T. Devaney, "'Like an Ember Buried in Ashes': The Byzantine–Venetian Conflict of 1119–1126," in T. Madden, J. Naus and V. Ryan (eds), *Crusades—Medieval Worlds in Conflict* (Farnham, 2010), pp. 127–47.

32. Tafel and Thomas, *Urkunden*, 1, pp. 84–9. Also here J. Prawer, "The Italians in the Latin Kingdom" in idem, *Crusader Institutions* (Oxford, 1980), p. 224; M. Barber, *The Crusader States* (London, 2012), pp. 139–42; J. Riley-Smith, "The Venetian Crusade of 1122–1124," in Airaldi and Kedar, *I Comuni Italiani*, pp. 339–50.
33. G. Bresc-Bautier, *Le Cartulaire du chapitre du Saint-Sépulcre de Jérusalem* (Paris, 1984), pp. 51–2.
34. Bernard of Clairvaux, *The Letters of St. Bernard of Clairvaux*, ed. and tr. B. James and B. Kienzle (Stroud, 1998), p. 391.
35. *Annali Genovesi de Caffaro e dei suoi Continutatori, 1099–1240*, 5 vols (Genoa, 1890–1929) 1, p. 48.
36. D. Abulafia, *The Great Sea: A Human History of the Mediterranean* (London, 2011), p. 298. Also see idem, "Christian Merchants in the Almohad Cities," *Journal of Medieval Iberian Studies* 2 (2010), 251–7; O. Constable, *Housing the Stranger in the Mediterranean World: Lodging, Trade and Travel in Late Antiquity and the Middle Ages* (Cambridge, 2003), p. 278.
37. P. Jones, *The Italian City State: From Commune to Signoria* (Oxford, 1997). Also M. Ginatempo and L. Sandri, *L'Italia delle città: il popolamento urbano tra Medioevo e Rinascimento (secoli XIII–XVI)* (Florence, 1990).
38. Usāma b. Munqidh, *Kitāb al-i'tibār*, tr. P. Cobb, *The Book of Contemplation: Islam and the Crusades* (London, 2008), p. 153.
39. V. Lagardère, *Histoire et société en Occident musulman: analyse du Mi'yar d'al-Wansharisi* (Madrid, 1995), p. 128; D. Valérian, "Ifrīqiyan Muslim Merchants in the Mediterranean at the End of the Middle Ages," *Mediterranean Historical Review* 14.2 (2008), 50.
40. *Gesta Francorum et aliorum Hierosolimitanorum*, ed. and tr. R. Hill (London, 1962), 3, p. 21.
41. See C. Burnett (ed.), *Adelard of Bath: An English Scientist and Arabist of the Early Twelfth Century* (London, 1987); L. Cochrane, *Adelard of Bath: The First English Scientist* (London, 1994).
42. Adelard of Bath, *Adelard of Bath, Conversations with his Nephew: On the Same and the Different, Questions on Natural Science and on Birds*, ed. and tr. C. Burnett (Cambridge, 1998), p. 83.
43. A. Pym, *Negotiating the Frontier: Translators and Intercultures in Hispanic History* (Manchester, 2000), p. 41.
44. T. Burman, *Reading the Qur'ān in Latin Christendom, 1140–1560* (Philadelphia, 2007).
45. P. Frankopan, "The Literary, Cultural and Political Context for the Twelfth-Century Commentary on the *Nicomachean Ethics*," in C. Barber (ed.), *Medieval Greek Commentaries on the Nicomachean Ethics* (Leiden, 2009), pp. 45–62.
46. Abulafia, *Great Sea*, p. 298.
47. A. Shalem, *Islam Christianised: Islamic Portable Objects in the Medieval Church Treasuries of the Latin West* (Frankfurt-am-Main, 1998).
48. Vorderstrasse, "Trade and Textiles from Medieval Antioch," 168–71; M. Meuwese, "Antioch and the Crusaders in Western Art," in *East and West in the Medieval Mediterranean* (Leuven, 2006), pp. 337–55.

49. R. Falkner, "Taxes of the Kingdom of Jerusalem," in *Statistical Documents of the Middle Ages: Translations and Reprints from the Original Sources of European History* 3:2 (Philadelphia, 1907), 19–23.
50. C. Cahen, *Makhzumiyyat: études sur l'histoire économique et financière de l'Egypte médiévale* (Leiden, 1977); Abulafia, "Africa, Asia and the Trade of Medieval Europe," pp. 402–73.
51. S. Stern, "Ramisht of Siraf: A Merchant Millionaire of the Twelfth Century," *Journal of the Royal Asiatic Society of Great Britain and Ireland* 1.2 (1967), 10–14.
52. T. Madden, "Venice and Constantinople in 1171 and 1172: Enrico Dandolo's Attitudes towards Byzantium," *Mediterranean Historical Review* 8.2 (1993), 166–85.
53. D. Nicol, *Byzantium and Venice: A Study in Diplomatic and Cultural Relations* (Cambridge, 1988), p. 107.
54. P. Magdalino, "Isaac II, Saladin and Venice," in J. Shepard (ed.), *The Expansion of Orthodox Europe: Byzantium, the Balkans and Russia* (Aldershot, 2007), pp. 93–106.
55. Ibn Shaddād, *Life of Saladin by Baha ad-Din* (London, 1897), pp. 121–2; G. Anderson, "Islamic Spaces and Diplomacy in Constantinople (Tenth to Thirteenth Centuries C.E.)," *Medieval Encounters* 15 (2009), 104–5.
56. Anna Komnene, *Alexiad*, X.5, p. 277.
57. Ibn Jubayr, *Riḥlat Ibn Jubayr*, tr. R. Broadhurst, *The Travels of Ibn Jubayr* (London, 1952), p. 315.
58. Ibid. Also C. Chism, "Memory, Wonder and Desire in the Travels of Ibn Jubayr and Ibn Battuta," in N. Paul and S. Yeager (eds), *Remembering the Crusades: Myth, Image and Identity* (Cambridge, 2012), pp. 35–6.
59. Ibn al-Athīr, *Chronicle*, pp. 289–90; Barber, *Crusader States*, p. 284.
60. Barber, *Crusader States*, pp. 296–7; Imād al-Dīn, *al-Fatḥ al-qussī fī l-fatḥ al-qudsī*, tr. H. Massé, *Conquête de la Syrie et de la Palestine par Saladin* (Paris, 1972), pp. 27–8.
61. Barber, *Crusader States*, pp. 305–13; T. Asbridge, *The Crusades: The War for the Holy Land* (London, 2010), pp. 342–64.
62. J. Riley-Smith, *The Crusades: A History* (London, 1987), p. 137.
63. J. Phillips, *The Crusades 1095–1197* (London, 2002), pp. 146–50; J. Phillips, *Holy Warriors: A Modern History of the Crusades* (London, 2009), pp. 136–65.
64. Geoffrey of Villehardouin, "The Conquest of Constantinople," in *Chronicles of the Crusades*, tr. M. Shaw (London, 1963), p. 35.
65. William of Tyre, *Chronicon*, ed. R. Huygens, 2 vols (Turnhout, 1986), 2, p. 408; J. Phillips, *The Fourth Crusade and the Sack of Constantinople* (London, 2004), pp. 67–8.
66. D. Queller and T. Madden, "Some Further Arguments in Defence of the Venetians on the Fourth Crusade," *Byzantion* 62 (1992), 438.
67. T. Madden, "Venice, the Papacy and the Crusades before 1204," in S. Ridyard (ed.), *The Medieval Crusade* (Woodbridge, 2004), pp. 85–95.
68. D. Queller and T. Madden, *The Fourth Crusade: The Conquest of Constantinople* (Philadelphia, 1997), pp. 55ff.
69. Tafel and Thomas, *Urkunden*, 1, pp. 444–52.

70. Robert of Clari, *La Conquête de Constantinople*, ed. P. Lauer (Paris, 1924), 72–3, pp. 71–2.
71. Niketas Khoniates, *Khronike diegesis*, ed. J. van Dieten, *Nicetae Choniatae Historia* (New York, 1975), pp. 568–77.
72. P. Riant, *Exuviae sacrae constantinopolitanae*, 2 vols (Geneva, 1876), 1, pp. 104–5.
73. Khoniates, *Khronike*, p. 591. For an important reassessment of the damage to the city, T. Madden, "The Fires of the Fourth Crusade in Constantinople, 1203–1204: A Damage Assessment," *Byzantinische Zeitschrift* 84/85 (1992), 72–93.
74. See M. Angold, *The Fourth Crusade* (2003), pp. 219–67; also D. Perry, "The *Translatio Symonensis* and the Seven Thieves: Venetian Fourth Crusade *Furta Sacra* Narrative and the Looting of Constantinople," in T. Madden (ed.), *The Fourth Crusade: Event, Aftermath and Perceptions* (Aldershot, 2008), pp. 89–112.
75. R. Gallo, "La tomba di Enrico Dandolo in Santa Sofia a Constantinople," *Rivista Mensile della Città di Venezia* 6 (1927), 270–83; T. Madden, *Enrico Dandolo and the Rise of Venice* (Baltimore, 2003), pp. 193–4.
76. Michael Khoniates, *Michaelis Choniatae Epistulae*, ed. F. Kolovou (Berlin, 2001), Letters 145, 165, 100; T. Shawcross, "The Lost Generation (c. 1204–c. 1222): Political Allegiance and Local Interests under the Impact of the Fourth Crusade," in J. Herrin and G. Saint-Guillain (eds), *Identities and Allegiances in the Eastern Mediterranean after 1204* (Farnham, 2011), pp. 9–45.
77. Tafel and Thomas, *Urkunden*, 1, pp. 464–88; N. Oikonomides, "La Decomposition de l'Empire byzantin à la veille de 1204 et les origines de l'Empire de Nicée: à propos de la 'Partitio Romaniae,'" in *XV Congrès international d'études byzantines* (Athens, 1976), 1, pp. 3–22.
78. C. Otten-Froux, "Identities and Allegiances: The Perspective of Genoa and Pisa," in Herrin and Saint-Guillan, *Identities and Allegiances*, pp. 265ff.; also G. Jehei, "The Struggle for Hegemony in the Eastern Mediterranean: An Episode in the Relations between Venice and Genoa According to the Chronicles of Ogerio Pane," *Mediterranean Historical Review* 11.2 (1996), 196–207.
79. F. Van Tricht, *The Latin Renovatio of Byzantium: The Empire of Constantinople (1204–1228)* (Leiden, 2011), esp. pp. 157ff.
80. See S. McMichael, "Francis and the Encounter with the Sultan [1219]," in *The Cambridge Companion to Francis of Assisi*, ed. M. Robson (Cambridge, 2012), pp. 127–42; J. Tolan, *Saint Francis and the Sultan: The Curious History of a Christian–Muslim Encounter* (Oxford, 2009).
81. Dulumeau, *History of Paradise*, pp. 71–96.
82. M. Gosman, "La Légende du Prêtre Jean et la propagande auprès des croisés devant Damiette (1228–1221)," in D. Buschinger (ed.), *La Croisade: réalités et fictions. Actes du colloque d'Amiens 18–22 mars 1987* (Göppinger, 1989), pp. 133–42; J. Valtrovà, "Beyond the Horizons of Legends: Traditional Imagery and Direct Experience in Medieval Accounts of Asia," *Numen* 57 (2010), 166–7.
83. C. Beckingham, "The Achievements of Prester John," in C. Beckingham and B. Hamilton (eds), *Prester John, the Mongols and the Ten Lost Tribes* (Aldershot, 1996), pp. 1–22; P. Jackson, *The Mongols and the West* (London, 2005), pp. 20–1.

84. F. Zarncke, "Der Priester Johannes II," *Abhandlungen der Königlich Sächsischen Gesellschaft der Wissenschaften, Phil.-hist. Kl.* 8 (1876), 9.
85. Jackson, *Mongols and the West*, pp. 48–9.

CHAPTER 9—THE ROAD TO HELL

1. Het'um, *Patmich' T'at'arats'*, *La flor des estoires de la terre d'Orient*, in *Recueil des Historiens des Croisades: Historiens Arméniens* 1, p. x.
2. 'Ata-Malik Juvaynī, *Ta'rīx-i Jahān-Gušā*, tr. J. Boyle, *Genghis Khan: The History of the World-Conqueror*, 2 vols (Cambridge, MA, 1958), 1, 1, pp. 21–2.
3. For the meaning of Činggis as a title, see I. de Rachewiltz, "The Title Činggis Qan/Qayan Re-examined," in W. Hessig and K. Sangster (eds), *Gedanke und Wirkung* (Wiesbaden, 1989), pp. 282–8; T. Allsen, "The Rise of the Mongolian Empire and Mongolian Rule in North China," in *The Cambridge History of China*, 15 vols (Cambridge, 1978–), 6, pp. 321ff.
4. *The Secret History of the Mongols*, tr. I. de Rachewiltz, 2 vols (Leiden, 2004), 1, p. 13.
5. Allsen, "Rise of the Mongolian Empire," pp. 321ff.; G. Németh, "Wanderungen des mongolischen Wortes *Nökür* 'Genosse,'" *Acta Orientalia Academiae Scientiarum Hungaricae* 3 (1952), 1–23.
6. T. Allsen, "The Yüan Dynasty and the Uighurs of Turfan in the 13th Century," in M. Rossabi (ed.), *China among Equals: The Middle Kingdom and its Neighbors, 10th–14th Centuries* (Berkeley, 1983), pp. 246–8.
7. P. Golden, "'I Will Give the People unto Thee': The Činggisid Conquests and their Aftermath in the Turkic World," *Journal of the Royal Asiatic Society* 10.1 (2000), 27.
8. Z. Bunyatov, *Gosudarstvo Khorezmshakhov-Anushteginidov* (Moscow, 1986), pp. 128–32; Golden, "Činggisid Conquests," 29.
9. Juvaynī, *History of the World Conqueror*, 16, 1, p. 107.
10. Ibn al-Athīr, in B. Spuler, *History of the Mongols* (London, 1972), p. 30.
11. D. Morgan, *The Mongols* (Oxford, 1986), p. 74.
12. Nasawī, *Sīrat al-ṣultān Jalāl al-Dīn Mangubirtī*, tr. O. Houdas, *Histoire du sultan Djelāl ed-Dīn Mankobirti prince du Khārezm* (Paris, 1891), 16, p. 63.
13. K. Raphael, "Mongol Siege Warfare on the Banks of the Euphrates and the Question of Gunpowder (1260–1312)," *Journal of the Royal Asiatic Society*, 19.3 (2009), 355–70.
14. A. Waley (tr.), *The Travels of an Alchemist: The Journey of the Taoist, Ch'ang-ch'un, from China to the Hindukush at the Summons of Chingiz Khan, Recorded by his Disciple, Li Chih-ch'ang* (London, 1931), pp. 92–3.
15. See the pioneering work by Allsen, *Commodity and Exchange*, and G. Lane, *Early Mongol Rule in Thirteenth-Century Iran: A Persian Renaissance* (London, 2003).
16. Juvaynī, *History of the World Conqueror*, 27, 1, pp. 161–4.
17. J. Smith, "Demographic Considerations in Mongol Siege Warfare," *Archivum Ottomanicum* 13 (1994), 329–34; idem, "Mongol Manpower and Persian Popu-

lation," *Journal of Economic and Social History of the Orient* 18.3 (1975), 271–99; D. Morgan, "The Mongol Armies in Persia," *Der Islam* 56.1 (2009), 81–96.

18. *Novgorodskaya Pervaya Letopis' starshego i mladshego isvodov*, ed. A. Nasonov (Leningrad, 1950), p. 61.
19. Ibid., pp. 74–7.
20. E. Petrukhov, *Serapion Vladimirskii, russkii propovedenik XIII veka* (St. Petersburg, 1888), Appendix, p. 8.
21. Although medieval commentators made a link between Tatars and Tartarus, the former term was in use across the steppes as a reference to nomadic tribesmen, likely derived from the Tungusic word "*ta-ta*," meaning to drag or pull. See S. Akiner, *Religious Language of a Belarusian Tatar Kitab* (Wiesbaden, 2009), pp. 13–14.
22. Jackson, *Mongols and the West*, pp. 59–60; D. Sinor, "The Mongols in the West," *Journal of Asian History* 33.1 (1999), 1–44.
23. C. Rodenburg (ed.), *MGH Epistulae saeculi XIII e regestis pontificum Romanorum selectae*, 3 vols (Berlin, 1883–94), 1, p. 723; Jackson, *Mongols and the West*, pp. 65–9.
24. P. Jackson, "The Crusade against the Mongols (1241)," *Journal of Ecclesiastical History* 42 (1991), 1–18.
25. H. Dörrie, "Drei Texte zur Gesichte der Ungarn und Mongolen. Die Missionreisen des fr. Julianus O.P. ins Ural-Gebiet (1234/5) und nach Rußland (1237) und der Bericht des Erzbischofs Peter über die Tataren," *Nachrichten der Akademie der Wissenschaften in Göttingen, phil-hist. Klasse* (1956) 6, 179; also Jackson, *Mongols and the West*, p. 61.
26. Thomas the Archdeacon, *Historia Salonitanorum atque Spalatinorum pontificum*, ed. and trans. D. Krabić, M. Sokol and J. Sweeney (Budapest, 2006), p. 302; Jackson, *Mongols and the West*, p. 65.
27. Copies of two of these letters survive, C. Rodenberg (ed.), *Epistolae saeculi XII e regestis pontificum romanorum*, 3 vols (Berlin, 1883–94), 2, pp. 72; 3, p. 75.
28. Valtrovà, "Beyond the Horizons of Legends," 154–85.
29. William of Rubruck, *The Mission of Friar William of Rubruck*, tr. P. Jackson, ed. D. Morgan (London, 1990), 28, p. 177.
30. Ibid., 2, pp. 72, 76; 13, p. 108; Jackson, *Mongols and the West*, p. 140.
31. John of Plano Carpini, *Sinica Franciscana: Itinera et relationes fratrum minorum saeculi XVII et XIV*, ed. A. van den Wyngaert, 5 vols (Florence, 1929), 1, pp. 60, 73–5.
32. John of Plano Carpini, *Ystoria Mongolarum*, ed. A. van den Wyngaert (Florence, 1929), pp. 89–90.
33. "Letter of the Great Khan Güyüg to Pope Innocent IV (1246)," in I. de Rachewiltz, *Papal Envoys to the Great Khans* (Stanford, 1971), p. 214 (with differences).
34. C. Dawson, *Mongol Mission: Narratives and Letters of the Franciscan Missionaries in Mongolia and China in the Thirteenth and Fourteenth Centuries* (London, 1955), pp. 44–5.
35. P. Jackson, "World-Conquest and Local Accommodation: Threat and Blandishment in Mongol Diplomacy," in J. Woods, J. Pfeiffer, S. Quinn and E. Tucker

(eds), *History and Historiography of Post-Mongol Central Asia and the Middle East: Studies in Honor of John E. Woods* (Wiesbaden, 2006), pp. 3–22.

36. R. Thomson, "The Eastern Mediterranean in the Thirteenth Century: Identities and Allegiances. The Peripheries; Armenia," in Herrin and Saint-Gobain, *Identities and Allegiances*, pp. 202–4.
37. J.-L. van Dieten, "Das Lateinische Kaiserreich von Konstantinopel und die Verhandlungen über kirchliche Wiedervereinigung," in V. van Aalst and K. Ciggaar (eds), *The Latin Empire: Some Contributions* (Hernen, 1990), pp. 93–125.
38. Wiliam of Rubruck, *Mission of Friar William*, 33, p. 227.
39. George Pachymeres, *Chronicon*, ed. and tr. A. Faillier, *Relations historiques*, 2 vols (Paris, 1984), 2, pp. 108–9; J. Langdon, "Byzantium's Initial Encounter with the Chinggisids: An Introduction to the Byzantino-Mongolica," *Viator* 29 (1998), 130–3.
40. ʿAbdallāh b. Faḍlallāh Waṣṣāf, *Tarjiyat al-amṣār wa-tajziyat al-aʿṣār*, in Spuler, *History of the Mongols*, pp. 120–1.
41. Allsen, *Commodity and Exchange*, pp. 28–9.
42. J. Richard, "Une Ambassade mongole à Paris en 1262," *Journal des Savants* 4 (1979), 295–303; Jackson, *Mongols and the West*, p. 123.
43. N. Nobutaka, "The Rank and Status of Military Refugees in the Mamluk Army: A Reconsideration of the *Wāfidīyah*," *Mamluk Studies Review* 10.1 (2006), 55–81; R. Amitai-Preiss, "The Remaking of the Military Elite of Mamluk Egypt by al-Nāṣir Muḥammad b. Qalāwūn," *Studia Islamica* 72 (1990), 148–50.
44. P. Jackson, "The Crisis in the Holy Land in 1260," *English Historical Review* 95 (1980), 481–513.
45. R. Amitai-Preiss, *Mongols and Mamluks: The Mamluk–Ilkhanid War, 1260–1281* (Cambridge, 1995).
46. Jūzjānī, *Tabaḳāt-i-Nāṣirī*, tr. H. Raverty, *A general history of the Muhammadan dynasties of Asia, including Hindūstān, from 810 A.D. to 1260 A.D., and the irruption of the infidel Mughals into Islam* (Calcutta, 1881), 23.3–4, pp. 1104, 1144–5.
47. L. Lockhart, "The Relations between Edward I and Edward II of England and the Mongol Il-Khans of Persia," *Iran* 6 (1968), 23. For the expedition, C. Tyerman, *England and the Crusades, 1095–1588* (London, 1988), pp. 124–32.
48. W. Budge, *The Monks of Kublai Khan, Emperor of China* (London, 1928), pp. 186–7.
49. S. Schein, "Gesta Dei per Mongolos 1300: The Genesis of a Non-Event," *English Historical Review* 94.272 (1979), 805–19.
50. R. Amitai, "Whither the Ilkhanid Army? Ghazan's First Campaign into Syria (1299–1300)," in di Cosmo, *Warfare in Inner Asian History*, pp. 221–64.
51. William Blake, "Jerusalem." Legends about Joseph of Arimathea visiting the British Isles had circulated in England since the Middle Ages, W. Lyons, *Joseph of Arimathea: A Study in Reception History* (Oxford, 2014), pp. 72–104.

CHAPTER 10—THE ROAD OF DEATH AND DESTRUCTION

1. S. Karpov, "The Grain Trade in the Southern Black Sea Region: The Thirteenth to the Fifteenth Century," *Mediterranean Historical Review* 8.1 (1993), 55–73.

2. A. Ehrenkreutz, "Strategic Implications of the Slave Trade between Genoa and Mamluk Egypt in the Second Half of the Thirteenth Century," in A. Udovitch (ed.), *The Islamic Middle East, 700–1900* (Princeton, 1981), pp. 335–43.
3. G. Lorenzi, *Monumenti per servire alla storia del Palazzo Ducale di Venezia. Parte I: dal 1253 al 1600* (Venice, 1868), p. 7.
4. "Anonimo genovese," in G. Contini (ed.), *Poeti del Duecento*, 2 vols (Milan, 1960), 1, pp. 751–9.
5. V. Cilocitan, *The Mongols and the Black Sea Trade in the Thirteenth and Fourteenth Centuries* (Leiden, 2012), pp. 16, 21; S. Labib, "Egyptian Commercial Policy in the Middle Ages," in M. Cook (ed.), *Studies in the Economic History of the Middle East* (London, 1970), p. 74.
6. See D. Morgan, "Mongol or Persian: The Government of Īl-khānid Iran," *Harvard Middle Eastern and Islamic Review* 3 (1996), 62–76, and above all Lane, *Early Mongol Rule in Thirteenth-Century Iran.*
7. G. Alef, "The Origin and Development of the Muscovite Postal System," *Jahrbücher für Geschichte Osteuropas* 15 (1967), 1–15.
8. Morgan, *The Mongols*, pp. 88–90; Golden, "Činggisid Conquests," 38–40; T. Allsen, *Mongol Imperialism: The Policies of the Grand Qan Möngke in China, Russia and the Islamic Lands, 1251–1259* (Berkeley, 1987), pp. 189–216.
9. Juvaynī, *History of the World Conqueror*, 3, 1, p. 26.
10. This process had already started by the middle of the thirteenth century, as accounts by missionaries and envoys show, G. Guzman, "European Clerical Envoys to the Mongols: Reports of Western Merchants in Eastern Europe and Central Asia, 1231–1255," *Journal of Medieval History* 22.1 (1996), 57–67.
11. William of Rubruck, *Mission of Friar William*, 35, pp. 241–2.
12. J. Ryan, "Preaching Christianity along the Silk Route: Missionary Outposts in the Tartar 'Middle Kingdom' in the Fourteenth Century," *Journal of Early Modern History* 2.4 (1998), 350–73. For Persia, R. Lopez, "Nuove luci sugli italiani in Estremo Oriente prima di Colombo," *Studi Colombiani* 3 (1952), 337–98.
13. Dawson, *Mission to Asia*, pp. 224–6; de Rachewiltz, *Papal Envoys*, pp. 160–78; also J. Richard, *La Papauté et les missions d'Orient au moyen age (XIIIe–XVe siècles)* (Rome, 1977), pp. 144ff. John blames the Nestorians for the fact that not more were converted, saying that they accused him of being a spy and a magician: rivalries between Christians played out in China, just as they had done in Persia and elsewhere.
14. P. Jackson, "Hülegü Khan and the Christians: The Making of a Myth," in J. Phillips and P. Edbury (eds), *The Experience of Crusading*, 2 vols (Cambridge, 2003), 2, pp. 196–213; S. Grupper, "The Buddhist Sanctuary-Vihara of Labnasagut and the Il-qan Hülegü: An Overview of Il-Qanid Buddhism and Related Matters," *Archivum Eurasiae Medii Aevi* 13 (2004), 5–77; Foltz, *Religions of the Silk Road*, p. 122.
15. S. Hackel, "Under Pressure from the Pagans?—The Mongols and the Russian Church," in J. Breck and J. Meyendorff (eds), *The Legacy of St. Vladimir: Byzantium, Russia, America* (Crestwood, NY, 1990), pp. 47–56; C. Halperin, "Know Thy Enemy: Medieval Russian Familiarity with the Mongols of the Golden Horde," *Jahrbücher für Geschichte Osteuropas* 30 (1982), 161–75.

16. D. Ostrowski, *Muscovy and the Mongols: Cross-Cultural Influences on the Steppe Frontier, 1304–1589* (Cambridge, 1998); M. Bilz-Leonardt, "Deconstructing the Myth of the Tartar Yoke," *Central Asian Survey* 27.1 (2008), 35–6.
17. R. Hartwell, "Demographic, Political and Social Transformations of China, 750–1550," *Harvard Journal of Asiatic Studies* 42.2 (1982), 366–9; R. von Glahn, "Revisiting the Song Monetary Revolution: A Review Essay," *International Journal of Asian Studies* 1.1 (2004), 159.
18. See for example G. Wade, "An Early Age of Commerce in Southeast Asia, 900–1300 CE," *Journal of Southeast Asia Studies* 40.2 (2009), 221–65.
19. S. Kumar, "The Ignored Elites: Turks, Mongols and a Persian Secretarial Class in the Early Delhi Sultanate," *Modern Asian Studies* 43.1 (2009), 72–6.
20. P. Buell, E. Anderson and C. Perry, *A Soup for the Qan: Chinese Dietary Medicine of the Mongol Era as Seen in Hu Szu-hui's Yin-shan Cheng-yao* (London, 2000).
21. P. Buell, "Steppe Foodways and History," *Asian Medicine, Tradition and Modernity* 2.2 (2006), 179–80, 190.
22. P. Buell, "Mongolian Empire and Turkization: The Evidence of Food and Foodways," in R. Amitai-Preiss (ed.), *The Mongol Empire and its Legacy* (Leiden, 1999), pp. 200–23.
23. Allsen, *Commodity and Exchange*, pp. 1–2, 18; J. Paviot, "England and the Mongols (c. 1260–1330)," *Journal of the Royal Asiatic Society* 10.3 (2000), 317–18.
24. P. Freedman, "Spices and Late-Medieval European Ideas of Scarcity and Value," *Speculum* 80.4 (2005), 1209–27.
25. S. Halikowski-Smith, "The Mystification of Spices in the Western Tradition," *European Review of History: Revue Européenne d'Histoire* 8.2 (2001), 119–25.
26. A. Appadurai, "Introduction: Commodities and the Politics of Value," in A. Appadurai (ed.), *The Social Life of Things: Commodities in Cultural Perspective* (Cambridge, 1986), pp. 3–63.
27. Francesco Pegolotti, *Libro di divisamenti di paesi (e di misure di mercatantie)*, tr. H. Yule, *Cathay and the Way Thither*, 4 vols (London, 1913–16), 3, pp. 151–5. Also here see J. Aurell, "Reading Renaissance Merchants' Handbooks: Confronting Professional Ethics and Social Identity," in J. Ehmer and C. Lis (eds), *The Idea of Work in Europe from Antiquity to Modern Times* (Farnham, 2009), pp. 75–7.
28. R. Prazniak, "Siena on the Silk Roads: Ambrozio Lorenzetti and the Mongol Global Century, 1250–1350," *Journal of World History* 21.2 (2010), 179–81; M. Kupfer, "The Lost Wheel Map of Ambrogio Lorenzetti," *Art Bulletin* 78.2 (1996), 286–310.
29. Ibn Baṭṭūṭa, *al-Riḥla*, tr. H. Gibb, *The Travels of Ibn Battuta*, 4 vols (Cambridge, 1994), 4, 22, pp. 893–4.
30. E. Endicott-West, "The Yuan Government and Society," *Cambridge History of China*, 6, pp. 599–60.
31. Allsen, *Commodity and Exchange*, pp. 31–9.
32. C. Salmon, "Les Persans à l'extrémité orientale de la route maritime (IIe A.E.–XVIIe siècle)," *Archipel* 68 (2004), 23–58; also L. Yingsheng, "A Lingua Franca along the Silk Road: Persian Language in China between the 14th and the 16th

Centuries," in R. Kauz (ed.), *Aspects of the Maritime Silk Road from the Persian Gulf to the East China Sea* (Wiesbaden, 2010), pp. 87–95.

33. F. Hirth and W. Rockhill, *Chau Ju-Kua: His Work on the Chinese and Arab Trade in the Twelfth and Thirteenth Centuries, Entitled Chu-fan-chi* (St. Petersburg, 1911), pp. 124–5, 151, 142–3.
34. See R. Kauz, "The Maritime Trade of Kish during the Mongol Period," in L. Komaroff (ed.), *Beyond the Legacy of Genghis Khan* (Leiden, 2006), pp. 51–67.
35. Marco Polo, *Le Devisament dou monde*, tr. A. Moule and P. Pelliot, *The Description of the World*, 2 vols (London, 1938); Ibn Baṭṭūṭa, 22, *Travels*, 4, p. 894.
36. For Marco Polo, see J. Critchley, *Marco Polo's Book* (Aldershot, 1992), and now see H. Vogel, *Marco Polo was in China: New Evidence from Currencies, Salts and Revenues* (Leiden, 2013).
37. C. Wake, "The Great Ocean-Going Ships of Southern China in the Age of Chinese Maritime Voyaging to India, Twelfth to Fifteenth Centuries," *International Journal of Maritime History* 9.2 (1997), 51–81.
38. E. Schafer, "Tang," in K. Chang (ed.), *Food in Chinese Culture: Anthropological and Historical Perspective* (New Haven, 1977), pp. 85–140.
39. V. Tomalin, V. Sevakumar, M. Nair and P. Gopi, "The Thaikkal-Kadakkarapally Boat: An Archaeological Example of Medieval Ship Building in the Western Indian Ocean," *International Journal of Nautical Archaeology* 33.2 (2004), 253–63.
40. R. von Glahn, *Fountain of Fortune: Money and Monetary Policy in China 1000–1700* (Berkeley, 1996), p. 48.
41. A. Watson, "Back to Gold—and Silver," *Economic History Review* 20.1 (1967), 26–7; I. Blanchard, *Mining, Metallurgy and Minting in the Middle Age: Continuing Afro-European Supremacy, 1250–1450* (Stuttgart, 2001), 3, pp. 945–8.
42. T. Sargent and F. Velde, *The Big Problem of Small Change* (Princeton, 2002), p. 166; J. Deyell, "The China Connection: Problems of Silver Supply in Medieval Bengal," in J. Richards (ed.), *Precious Metals in the Later Medieval and Early Modern World* (Durham, NC, 1983); M. Allen, "The Volume of the English Currency, 1158–1470," *Economic History Review* 54.4 (2001), 606–7.
43. This is clearly shown from the case of Japan in the fourteenth century, A. Kuroda, "The Eurasian Silver Century, 1276–1359: Commensurability and Multiplicity," *Journal of Global History* 4 (2009), 245–69.
44. V. Fedorov, "Plague in Camels and its Prevention in the USSR," *Bulletin of the World Health Organisation* 23 (1960), 275–81. For earlier experiments, see for example A. Tseiss, "Infektsionnye zabolevaniia u verbliudov, neizvestnogo do sik por poriskhozdeniia," *Vestnik mikrobiologii, epidemiologii i parazitologii* 7.1 (1928), 98–105.
45. Boccaccio, *Decamerone*, tr. G. McWilliam, *Decameron* (London, 2003), p. 51.
46. T. Ben-Ari, S. Neerinckx, K. Gage, K. Kreppel, A. Laudisoit et al., "Plague and Climate: Scales Matter," *PLoS Pathog* 7.9 (2011), 1–6. Also B. Krasnov, I. Khokhlova, L. Fielden and N. Burdelova, "Effect of Air Temperature and Humidity on the Survival of Pre-Imaginal Stages of Two Flea Species (Siphonaptera: Pulicidae)," *Journal of Medical Entomology* 38 (2001), 629–37; K. Gage,

T. Burkot, R. Eisen and E. Hayes, "Climate and Vector-Borne Diseases," *American Journal of Preventive Medicine* 35 (2008), 436–50.

47. N. Stenseth, N. Samia, H. Viljugrein, K. Kausrud, M. Begon et al., "Plague Dynamics are Driven by Climate Variation," *Proceedings of the National Academy of Sciences of the United States of America* 103 (2006), 13110–15.
48. Some scholars suggest the earliest identification may come from tombstones in a cemetery in eastern Kyrgyzstan dating from the 1330s, S. Berry and N. Gulade, "La Peste noire dans l'Occident chrétien et musulman, 1347–1353," *Canadian Bulletin of Medical History* 25.2 (2008), 466. However, this is based on a misunderstanding. See J. Norris, "East or West? The Geographic Origin of the Black Death," *Bulletin of the History of Medicine* 51 (1977), 1–24.
49. Gabriele de' Mussis, *Historia de Morbo*, in *The Black Death*, tr. R. Horrox (Manchester, 2001), pp. 14–17; M. Wheelis, "Biological Warfare at the 1346 Siege of Caffa," *Emerging Infectious Diseases* 8.9 (2002), 971–5.
50. M. de Piazza, *Chronica*, in Horrox, *Black Death*, pp. 35–41.
51. *Anonimalle Chronicle*, in Horrox, *Black Death*, p. 62.
52. John of Reading, *Chronica*, in Horrox, *Black Death*, p. 74.
53. Ibn al-Wardī, *Risālat al-nabaʾ ʿan al-wabaʾ*, cited by B. Dols, *The Black Death in the Middle East* (Princeton, 1977), pp. 57–63.
54. M. Dods, "Ibn al-Wardi's 'Risalah al-naba' an al-waba,'" in D. Kouymjian (ed.), *Near Eastern Numismatics, Iconography, Epigraphy and History* (Beirut, 1974), p. 454.
55. B. Dols, *Black Death in the Middle East*, pp. 160–1.
56. Boccaccio, *Decameron*, p. 50.
57. de' Mussis, *Historia de Morbo*, p. 20; "Continuation Novimontensis," in *Monumenta Germaniae Historica, Scriptores*, 9, p. 675.
58. John Clynn, *Annalium Hibernae Chronicon*, in Horrox, *Black Death*, p. 82.
59. Louis Heylgen, *Breve Chronicon Clerici Anonymi*, in Horrox, *Black Death*, pp. 41–2.
60. Horrox, *Black Death*, pp. 44, 117–18; Dols, *Black Death in the Middle East*, p. 126.
61. Bengt Knutsson, *A Little Book for the Pestilence*, in Horrox, *Black Death*, p. 176; John of Reading, *Chronica*, pp. 133–4.
62. S. Simonsohn (ed.), *The Apostolic See and the Jews: Documents, 492–1404* (Toronto, 1988), 1, no. 373.
63. In general here see O. Benedictow, *The Black Death, 1346–1353: The Complete History* (Woodbridge, 2004), pp. 380ff.
64. O. Benedictow, "Morbidity in Historical Plague Epidemics," *Population Studies* 41 (1987), 401–31; idem, *What Disease was Plague? On the Controversy over the Microbiological Identity of Plague Epidemics of the Past* (Leiden, 2010), esp. 289ff.
65. Petrarch, *Epistolae*, in Horrox, *Black Death*, p. 248.
66. *Historia Roffensis*, in Horrox, *Black Death*, p. 70.
67. S. Pamuk, "Urban Real Wages around the Eastern Mediterranean in Comparative Perspective, 1100–2000," *Research in Economic History* 12 (2005), 213–32.
68. S. Pamuk, "The Black Death and the Origins of the 'Great Divergence' across

Europe, 1300–1600," *European Review of Economic History* 11 (2007), 308–9; S. Epstein, *Freedom and Growth: The Rise of States and Markets in Europe, 1300–1750* (London, 2000), pp. 19–26. Also M. Bailey, "Demographic Decline in Late Medieval England: Some Thoughts on Recent Research," *Economic History Review* 49 (1996), 1–19.

69. H. Miskimin, *The Economy of Early Renaissance Europe, 1300–1460* (Cambridge, 1975); D. Herlihy, *The Black Death and the Transformation of the West* (Cambridge, 1997).
70. D. Herlihy, "The Generation in Medieval History," *Viator* 5 (1974), 347–64.
71. For the contraction in Egypt and the Levant, A. Sabra, *Poverty and Charity in Medieval Islam: Mamluk Egypt 1250–1517* (Cambridge, 2000).
72. S. DeWitte, "Mortality Risk and Survival in the Aftermath of the Medieval Black Death," *Plos One* 9.5 (2014), 1–8. For improved diets, T. Stone, "The Consumption of Field Crops in Late Medieval England," in C. Woolgar, D. Serjeantson and T. Waldron (eds), *Food in Medieval England: Diet and Nutrition* (Oxford, 2006), pp. 11–26.
73. Epstein, *Freedom and Growth*, pp. 49–68; van Bavel, "People and Land: Rural Population Developments and Property Structures in the Low Countries, c. 1300–c. 1600," *Continuity and Change* 17 (2002), 9–37.
74. Pamuk, "Urban Real Wages," 310–11.
75. Anna Bijns, "Unyoked is Best! Happy the Woman without a Man," in K. Wilson, *Women Writers of the Renaissance and Reformation* (Athens, 1987), p. 382. See here T. de Moor and J. Luiten van Zanden, "Girl Power: The European Marriage Pattern and Labour Markets in the North Sea Region in the Late Medieval and Early Modern Period," *Economic History Review* (2009), 1–33.
76. J. de Vries, "The Industrial Revolution and the Industrious Revolution," *Journal of Economic History* 54.2 (1994), 249–70; J. Luiten van Zanden, "The 'Revolt of the Early Modernists' and the 'First Modern Economy': An Assessment," *Economic History Review* 55 (2002), 619–41.
77. E. Ashtor, "The Volume of Mediaeval Spice Trade," *Journal of European Economic History* 9 (1980), 753–7; idem, "Profits from Trade with the Levant in the Fifteenth Century," *Bulletin of the School of Oriental and African Studies* 38 (1975), 256–87; Freedman, "Spices and Late Medieval European Ideas," 1212–15.
78. For Venetian imports of pigments, see L. Matthew, "'Vendecolori a Venezia': The Reconstruction of a Profession," *Burlington Magazine* 114.1196 (2002), 680–6.
79. Marin Sanudo, "Laus Urbis Venetae," in A. Aricò (ed.), *La città di Venetia (De origine, situ et magistratibus Urbis Venetae) 1493–1530* (Milan, 1980), pp. 21–3; for changes to internal space in this period, see R. Good, "Double Staircases and the Vertical Distribution of Housing in Venice 1450–1600," *Architectural Research Quarterly* 39.1 (2009), 73–86.
80. B. Krekic, "L'Abolition de l'esclavage à Dubrovnik (Raguse) au XVe siècle: mythe ou réalité?," *Byzantinische Forschungen* 12 (1987), 309–17.
81. S. Mosher Stuard, "Dowry Increase and Increment in Wealth in Medieval Ragusa (Dubrovnik)," *Journal of Economic History* 41.4 (1981), 795–811.

82. M. Abraham, *Two Medieval Merchant Guilds of South India* (New Delhi, 1988).
83. Ma Huan, *Ying-yai sheng-lan*, tr. J. Mills, *The Overall Survey of the Ocean's Shores* (Cambridge, 1970), p. 140.
84. T. Sen, "The Formation of Chinese Maritime Networks to Southern Asia, 1200–1450," *Journal of the Economic and Social History of the Orient*, 49.4 (2006), 427, 439–40; H. Ray, *Trade and Trade Routes between India and China, c. 140 BC–AD 1500* (Kolkata, 2003), pp. 177–205.
85. H. Tsai, *The Eunuchs in the Ming Dynasty* (New York, 1996), p. 148; T. Ju-kang, "Cheng Ho's Voyages and the Distribution of Pepper in China," *Journal of the Royal Asiatic Society* 2 (1981), 186–97.
86. W. Atwell, "Time, Money and the Weather: Ming China and the 'Great Depression' of the Mid-Fifteenth Century," *Journal of Asia Studies* 61.1 (2002), 86.
87. T. Brook, *The Troubled Empire: China in the Yuan and Ming Dynasties* (Cambridge, MA, 2010), pp. 107–9.
88. Ruy González de Clavijo, *Embajada a Tamorlán*, tr. G. Le Strange, *Embassy to Tamerlane 1403–1406* (London, 1928), 11, pp. 208–9.
89. Ibid., 14, p. 270.
90. Ibid., pp. 291–2. For the dissemination of the Timurid vision in art and architecture, see T. Lentz and G. Lowry, *Timur and the Princely Vision: Persian Art and Culture in the Fifteenth Century* (Los Angeles, 1989), pp. 159–232.
91. Khvānd Mīr, *Habibu's-siyar*, Tome Three, ed. and tr. W. Thackston, *The Reign of the Mongol and the Turk*, 2 vols (Cambridge, MA, 1994), 1, p. 294; D. Roxburgh, "The 'Journal' of Ghiyath al-Din Naqqash, Timurid Envoy to Khan Balïgh, and Chinese Art and Architecture," in L. Saurma-Jeltsch and A. Eisenbeiss (eds), *The Power of Things and the Flow of Cultural Transformations: Art and Culture between Europe and Asia* (Berlin, 2010), p. 90.
92. R. Lopez, H. Miskimin and A. Udovitch, "England to Egypt, 1350–1500: Long-Term Trends and Long-Distance Trade," in M. Cook (ed.), *Studies in the Economic History of the Middle East from the Rise of Islam to the Present Day* (London, 1970), pp. 93–128. J. Day, "The Great Bullion Famine," *Past & Present* 79 (1978), 3–54, J. Munro, "Bullion Flows and Monetary Contraction in Late-Medieval England and the Low Countries," in J. Richards (ed.), *Precious Metals in the Later Medieval and Early Modern Worlds* (Durham, NC, 1983), pp. 97–158.
93. R. Huang, *Taxation and Governmental Finance in Sixteenth-Century Ming China* (Cambridge, 1974), pp. 48–51.
94. T. Brook, *The Confusions of Pleasure: Commerce and Culture in Ming China* (Berkeley, 1998).
95. N. Sussman, "Debasements, Royal Revenues and Inflation in France during the Hundred Years War, 1415–1422," *Journal of Economic History* 53.1 (1993), 44–70; idem, "The Late Medieval Bullion Famine Reconsidered," *Journal of Economic History* 58.1 (1998), 126–54.
96. R. Wicks, "Monetary Developments in Java between the Ninth and Sixteenth Centuries: A Numismatic Perspective," *Indonesia* 42 (1986), 59–65; J. Whitmore, "Vietnam and the Monetary Flow of Eastern Asia, Thirteenth to Eighteenth

Centuries," in Richards, *Precious Metal*, pp. 363–93; J. Deyell, "The China Connection: Problems of Silver Supply in Medieval Bengal," in Richards, *Precious Metal*, pp. 207–27.

97. Atwell, "Time, Money and the Weather," 92–6.
98. A. Vasil'ev, "Medieval Ideas of the End of the World: West and East," *Byzantion* 16 (1942–3), 497–9; D. Strémooukhoff, "Moscow the Third Rome: Sources of the Doctrine," *Speculum* (1953), 89; "Drevnie russkie paskhalii na os'muiu tysiachu let ot sotvereniia mira," *Pravoslavnyi Sobesednik* 3 (1860), 333–4.
99. A. Bernáldez, *Memorías de los reyes católicos*, ed. M. Gómez-Moreno and J. Carriazo (Madrid, 1962), p. 254.
100. I. Aboab, *Nomologia, o Discursos legales compuestos* (Amsterdam, 1629), p. 195; D. Altabé, *Spanish and Portuguese Jewry before and after 1492* (Brooklyn, 1983), p. 45.
101. Freedman, "Spices and Late Medieval European Ideas," 1220–7.
102. V. Flint, *The Imaginative Landscape of Christopher Columbus* (Princeton, 1992), pp. 47–64.
103. C. Delaney, "Columbus's Ultimate Goal: Jerusalem," *Comparative Studies in Society and History* 48 (2006), 260–2.
104. Ibid., 264–5; M. Menocal, *The Arabic Role in Medieval Literary History: A Forgotten Heritage* (Philadelphia, 1987), p. 12. For the text of the letters of introduction, S. Morison, *Journals and Other Documents on the Life and Voyages of Christopher Columbus* (New York, 1963), p. 30.

CHAPTER 11—THE ROAD OF GOLD

1. O. Dunn and J. Kelley (ed. and tr.), *The Diario of Christopher Columbus' First Voyage to America, 1492–1493* (Norman, OK, 1989), p. 19.
2. Ibn al-Faqīh, in N. Levtzion and J. Hopkins (eds), *Corpus of Early Arabic Sources for West African History* (Cambridge, 1981), p. 28.
3. R. Messier, *The Almoravids and the Meanings of Jihad* (Santa Barbara, 2010), pp. 21–34. Also see idem, "The Almoravids: West African Gold and the Gold Currency of the Mediterranean Basin," *Journal of the Economic and Social History of the Orient* 17 (1974), 31–47.
4. V. Monteil, "Routier de l'Afrique blanche et noire du Nord-Ouest: al-Bakri (cordue 1068)," *Bulletin de l'Institut Fondamental d'Afrique Noire* 30.1 (1968), 74; I. Wilks, "Wangara, Akan and Portuguese in the Fifteenth and Sixteenth Centuries. 1. The Matter of Bitu," *Journal of African History* 23.3 (1982), 333–4.
5. N. Levtzion, "Islam in West Africa," in W. Kasinec and M. Polushin (eds), *Expanding Empires: Cultural Interaction and Exchange in World Societies from Ancient to Early Modern Times* (Wilmington, 2002), pp. 103–14; T. Lewicki, "The Role of the Sahara and Saharians in the Relationship between North and South," in M. El Fasi (ed.), *Africa from the Seventh to Eleventh Centuries* (London, 1988), pp. 276–313.
6. S. Mody Cissoko, "L'Intelligentsia de Tombouctou aux 15e et 16e siècles," *Présence Africaine* 72 (1969), 48–72. These manuscripts were catalogued in the sixteenth century by Muḥammad al-Wangarī and formed part of the mag-

nificent collection that belong to his descendants to the present day; initial reports indicating that the documents had been destroyed by the Tuareg in 2012 proved to be wrong.

7. Ibn Faḍl Allāh al-ʿUmarī, *Masālik al-abṣār fī mamālik al-amṣār*, tr. Levtzion and Hopkins, *Corpus of Early Arabic Sources*, pp. 270–1. The depression in the value of gold is widely noted by modern commentators; for a more sceptical view, see W. Schultz, "Mansa Musa's Gold in Mamluk Cairo: A Reappraisal of a World Civilizations Anecdote," in J. Pfeiffer and S. Quinn (eds), *History and Historiography of Post-Mongol Central Asia and the Middle East: Studies in Honor of John E. Woods* (Wiesbaden, 2006), pp. 451–7.
8. Ibn Baṭṭūṭa, *Travels*, 25, 4, p. 957.
9. B. Kreutz, "Ghost Ships and Phantom Cargoes: Reconstructing Early Amalfitan Trade," *Journal of Medieval History* 20 (1994), 347–57; A. Fromherz, "North Africa and the Twelfth-Century Renaissance: Christian Europe and the Almohad Islamic Empire," *Islam and Christian Muslim Relations* 20.1 (2009), 43–59; D. Abulafia, "The Role of Trade in Muslim–Christian Contact during the Middle Ages," in D. Agius and R. Hitchcock (eds), *The Arab Influence in Medieval Europe* (Reading, 1994), pp. 1–24.
10. See the pioneering work of M. Horton, *Shanga: The Archaeology of a Muslim Trading Community on the Coast of East Africa* (London, 1996); also S. Guérin, "Forgotten Routes? Italy, Ifriqiya and the Trans-Saharan Ivory Trade," *Al-Masāq* 25.1 (2013), 70–91.
11. D. Dwyer, *Fact and Legend in the Catalan Atlas of 1375* (Chicago, 1997); J. Messing, "Observations and Beliefs: The World of the Catalan Atlas," in J. Levenson (ed.), *Circa 1492: Art in the Age of Exploration* (New Haven, 1991), p. 27.
12. S. Halikowski Smith, "The Mid-Atlantic Islands: A Theatre of Early Modern Ecocide," *International Review of Social History* 65 (2010), 51–77; J. Lúcio de Azevedo, *Epocas de Portugal Económico* (Lisbon, 1973), pp. 222–3.
13. F. Barata, "Portugal and the Mediterranean Trade: A Prelude to the Discovery of the 'New World,'" *Al-Masāq* 17.2 (2005), 205–19.
14. Letter of King Dinis of Portugal, 1293, J. Marques, *Descobrimentos Portugueses—Documentos para a sua História*, 3 vols (Lisbon, 1944–71), 1, no. 29; for the Mediterranean routes see C.-E. Dufourcq, "Les Communications entre les royaumes chrétiens et les pays de l'Occident musulman dans les derniers siècles du Moyen Age," *Les Communications dans la Péninsule Ibérique au Moyen Age. Actes du Colloque* (Paris, 1981), pp. 30–1.
15. Gomes Eanes de Zurara, *Crónica da Tomada de Ceuta* (Lisbon, 1992), pp. 271–6; A. da Sousa, "Portugal," in P. Fouracre et al. (eds), *The New Cambridge Medieval History*, 7 vols (Cambridge, 1995–2005), 7, pp. 636–7.
16. A. Dinis (ed.), *Monumenta Henricina*, 15 vols (Lisbon, 1960–74), 12, pp. 73–4, tr. P. Russell, *Prince Henry the Navigator: A Life* (New Haven, 2000), p. 121.
17. P. Hair, *The Founding of the Castelo de São Jorge da Mina: An Analysis of the Sources* (Madison, 1994).
18. J. Dias, "As primeiras penetrações portuguesas em África," in L. de Albequerque (ed.), *Portugal no Mundo*, 6 vols (Lisbon, 1989), 1, pp. 281–9.
19. M.-T. Seabra, *Perspectives da colonização portuguesa na costa occidental Afri-*

cana: análise organizacional de S. Jorge da Mina (Lisbon, 2000), pp. 80–93; Z. Cohen, "Administração das ilhas de Cabo Verde e seu Distrito no Segundo Século de Colonização (1560–1640)," in M. Santos (ed.), *Historia Geral de Cabo Verde*, 2 vols (1991), 2, pp. 189–224.

20. L. McAlister, *Spain and Portugal in the New World, 1492–1700* (Minneapolis, MN, 1984), pp. 60–3; J. O'Callaghan, "Castile, Portugal, and the Canary Islands: Claims and Counterclaims," *Viator* 24 (1993), 287–310.
21. Gomes Eanes de Zuara, *Crónica de Guiné*, tr. C. Beazley, *The chronicle of the discovery and conquest of Guinea*, 2 vols (London, 1896–9), 18, 1, p. 61. For Portugal in this period, M.-J. Tavares, *Estudos de História Monetária Portuguesa (1383–1438)* (Lisbon, 1974); F. Barata, *Navegação, comércio e relações politicas: os portugueses no Mediterrâneo occidental (1385–1466)* (Lisbon, 1998).
22. Gomes Eanes de Zurara, *Chronicle*, 25, 1, pp. 81–2. For some comments about this complex source, L. Barreto, "Gomes Eanes de Zurara e o problema da Crónica da Guiné," *Studia* 47 (1989), 311–69.
23. A. Saunders, *A Social History of Black Slaves and Freemen in Portugal, 1441–1555* (Cambridge, 1982); T. Coates, *Convicts and Orphans: Forces and State-Sponsored Colonizers in the Portuguese Empire, 1550–1755* (Stanford, 2001).
24. Gomes Eanes de Zurara, *Chronicle*, 87, 2, p. 259.
25. Ibid., 18, 1, p. 62.
26. H. Hart, *Sea Road to the Indies: An Account of the Voyages and Exploits of the Portuguese Navigators, Together with the Life and Times of Dom Vasco da Gama, Capitão Mór, Viceroy of India and Count of Vidigueira* (New York, 1950), pp. 44–5.
27. Gomes Eanes de Zurara, *Chronicle*, 87, 2, p. 259.
28. J. Cortés López, "El tiempo africano de Cristóbal Colón," *Studia Historica* 8 (1990), 313–26.
29. A. Brásio, *Monumenta Missionaria Africana*, 15 vols (Lisbon, 1952), 1, pp. 84–5.
30. Ferdinand Columbus, *The Life of the Admiral Christopher Columbus by his Son Ferdinand*, tr. B. Keen (New Brunswick, NJ, 1992), p. 35; C. Delaney, *Columbus and the Quest for Jerusalem* (London, 2012), pp. 48–9.
31. C. Jane (ed. and tr.), *Select Documents Illustrating the Four Voyages of Columbus*, 2 vols (London, 1930–1931), 1, pp. 2–19.
32. O. Dunn and J. Kelley (eds and trs), *The Diario of Christopher Columbus's First Voyage to America, 1492–3* (Norman, OK, 1989), p. 67.
33. Ibid., pp. 143–5.
34. W. Phillips and C. Rahn Phillips, *Worlds of Christopher Columbus* (Cambridge, 1992), p. 185. For the publication of the letter across Europe, R. Hirsch, "Printed Reports on the Early Discoveries and their Reception," in M. Allen and R. Benson (eds), *First Images of America: The Impact of the New World on the Old* (New York, 1974), pp. 90–1.
35. M. Zamora, "Christopher Columbus' 'Letter to the Sovereigns': Announcing the Discovery," in S. Greenblatt (ed.), *New World Encounters* (Berkeley, 1993), p. 7.
36. Delaney, *Columbus and the Quest for Jerusalem*, p. 144.
37. Bartolomé de las Casas, *Historia de las Indias*, 1.92, tr. P. Sullivan, *Indian*

Freedom: The Cause of Bartolomé de las Casas, 1484–1566 (Kansas City, 1995), pp. 33–4.

38. E. Vilches, "Columbus' Gift: Representations of Grace and Wealth and the Enterprise of the Indies," *Modern Language Notes* 119.2 (2004), 213–14.
39. C. Sauer, *The Early Spanish Main* (Berkeley, 1966), p. 109.
40. L. Formisano (ed.), *Letters from a New World: Amerigo Vespucci's Discovery of America* (New York, 1992), p. 84; M. Perri, "'Ruined and Lost': Spanish Destruction of the Pearl Coast in the Early Sixteenth Century," *Environment and History* 15 (2009), 132–4.
41. Dunn and Kelley, *The Diario of Christopher Columbus's First Voyage*, p. 235.
42. Ibid., pp. 285–7.
43. Ibid., pp. 235–7.
44. Bartolomé de las Casas, *Historia*, 3.29, p. 146.
45. Francisco López de Gómara, *Cortés: The Life of the Conqueror by his Secretary*, tr. L. Byrd Simpson (Berkeley, 1964), 27, p. 58.
46. Bernardino de Sahagún, *Florentine Codex: General History of the Things of New Spain. Book 12*, tr. A. Anderson and C. Dibble (Santa Fe, NM, 1975), p. 45; R. Wright (tr.), *Stolen Continents: Five Hundred Years of Conquest and Resistance in the Americas* (New York, 1992), p. 29.
47. S. Gillespie, *The Aztec Kings: The Construction of Rulership in Mexican History* (Tucson, AZ, 1989), pp. 173–207; C. Townsend, "Burying the White Gods: New Perspectives on the Conquest of Mexico," *American Historical Review* 108.3 (2003), 659–87.
48. An image now held in the Huntington Art Gallery in Austin, Texas, shows Cortés greeting Xicoténcatl, leader of the Tlaxcala, who saw an opportunity to take advantage of the new arrivals to strengthen his own position in Central America.
49. J. Ginés de Sepúlveda, *Demócrates Segundo o de la Justas causas de la Guerra contra los indios*, ed. A. Losada (Madrid, 1951), pp. 35, 33. The comparison with monkeys was erased from the manuscript used by Losada, A. Pagden, *Natural Fall of Man: The American Indian and the Origins of Comparative Ethnology* (Cambridge, 1982), p. 231, n. 45.
50. Sahagún, *Florentine Codex*, 12, p. 49; Wright (tr.), *Stolen Continents*, pp. 37–8.
51. Sahagún, *Florentine Codex*, 12, pp. 55–6.
52. I. Rouse, *The Tainos: Rise and Decline of the People who Greeted Columbus* (New Haven, 1992); N. D. Cook, *Born to Die: Disease and New World Conquest, 1492–1650* (Cambridge, 1998).
53. R. McCaa, "Spanish and Nahuatl Views on Smallpox and Demographic Catastrophe in Mexico," *Journal of Interdisciplinary History* 25 (1995), 397–431. In general, see A. Crosby, *The Columbian Exchange: Biological and Cultural Consequences of 1492* (Westport, CT, 2003).
54. Bernardino de Sahagún, *Historia general de las cosas de Nueva España* (Mexico City, 1992), p. 491; López de Gómara, *Life of the Conqueror*, 141–2, pp. 285–7.
55. Cook, *Born to Die*, pp. 15–59. Also Crosby, *Columbian Exchange*, pp. 56, 58; C. Merbs, "A New World of Infectious Disease," *Yearbook of Physical Anthropology* 35.3 (1993), 4.

56. Fernández de Enciso, *Suma de geografía*, cited by E. Vilches, *New World Gold: Cultural Anxiety and Monetary Disorder in Early Modern Spain* (Chicago, 2010), p. 24.
57. V. von Hagen, *The Aztec: Man and Tribe* (New York, 1961), p. 155.
58. P. Cieza de León, *Crónica del Perú*, tr. A. Cook and N. Cook, *The Discovery and Conquest of Peru* (Durham, NC, 1998), p. 361.
59. For Diego de Ordás, see C. García, *Vida del Comendador Diego de Ordaz, Descubridor del Orinoco* (Mexico City, 1952).
60. A. Barrera, "Empire and Knowledge: Reporting from the New World," *Colonial Latin American Review* 15.1 (2006), 40–1.
61. H. Rabe, *Deutsche Geschichte 1500–1600. Das Jahrhundert der Glaubensspaltung* (Munich, 1991), pp. 149–53.
62. Letter of Pietro Pasqualigo, in J. Brewer (ed.), *Letters and Papers, Foreign and Domestic, of the Reign of Henry VIII*, 23 vols (London, 1867), 1.1, pp. 116–17.
63. For Anne Boleyn, in *Calendar of State Papers and Manuscripts, Relating to English Affairs, Existing in the Archives and Collections of Venice, and in Other Libraries of Northern Italy*, ed. R. Brown et al., 38 vols (London, 1970), 4, p. 824.
64. Francisco López de Gómara, *Historia general de las Indias*, ed. J. Gurría Lacroix (Caracas, 1979), 1, p. 7.
65. Pedro Mexía, *Historia del emperador Carlos V*, ed. J. de Mata Carrizo (Madrid, 1945), p. 543. Also here Vilches, *New World Gold*, p. 26.
66. F. Ribeiro da Silva, *Dutch and Portuguese in Western Africa: Empires, Merchants and the Atlantic System, 1580–1674* (Leiden, 2011), pp. 116–17; Coates, *Convicts and Orphans*, pp. 42–62.
67. E. Donnan (ed.), *Documents Illustrative of the History of the Slave Trade to America*, 4 vols (Washington, DC, 1930), 1, pp. 41–2.
68. B. Davidson, *The Africa Past: Chronicles from Antiquity to Modern Times* (Boston, 1964), pp. 194–7.
69. Brásio, *Missionaria Africana*, 1, pp. 521–7.
70. A. Pagden, *Spanish Imperialism and the Political Imagination: Studies in European and Spanish-American Social and Political Theory, 1513–1830* (New Haven, 1990).
71. Letter of Manoel da Nóbrega, cited by T. Botelho, "Labour Ideologies and Labour Relations in Colonial Portuguese America, 1500–1700," *International Review of Social History* 56 (2011), 288.
72. M. Cortés, *Breve compendio de la sphere y el arte de navegar*, cited by Vilches, *New World Gold*, pp. 24–5.
73. R. Pieper, *Die Vermittlung einer neuen Welt: Amerika im Nachrichtennetz des Habsburgischen Imperiums, 1493–1598* (Mainz, 2000), pp. 162–210.
74. Diego de Haëdo, *Topografía e historia general de Arge*, tr. H. de Grammont, *Histoire des rois d'Alger* (Paris, 1998), 1, p. 18.
75. E. Lyon, *The Enterprise of Florida: Pedro Menéndez de Avilés and the Spanish Conquest of 1565–1568* (Gainesville, FL, 1986), pp. 9–10.
76. Jose de Acosta, *Historia natural y moral de las Indias*, in Vilches, *New World Gold*, p. 27.

CHAPTER 12—THE ROAD OF SILVER

1. H. Miskimin, *The Economy of Later Renaissance Europe, 1460–1600* (Cambridge, 1977), p. 32; J. Munro, "Precious Metals and the Origins of the Price Revolution Reconsidered: The Conjecture of Monetary and Real Forces in the European Inflation of the Early to Mid-16th Century," in C. Núñez (ed.), *Monetary History in Global Perspective, 1500–1808* (Seville, 1998), pp. 35–50; H. İnalcık, "The Ottoman State: Economy and Society, 1300–1600," in H. İnalcık and D. Quataert (eds), *An Economic and Social History of the Ottoman Empire, 1300–1914* (Cambridge, 1994), pp. 58–60.
2. P. Spufford, *Money and its Use in Medieval Europe* (Cambridge, 1988), p. 377.
3. Ch'oe P'u, *Ch'oe P'u's Diary: A Record of Drifting Across the Sea*, tr. J. Meskill (Tucson, AZ, 1965), pp. 93–4.
4. Vélez de Guevara, *El diablo conjuelo*, cited by R. Pike, "Seville in the Sixteenth Century," *Hispanic American Historical Review* 41.1 (1961), 6.
5. Francisco de Ariño, *Sucesos de Sevilla de 1592 a 1604*, in ibid., 12–13; Vilches, *New World Gold*, pp. 25–6.
6. G. de Correa, *Lendas de India*, 4 vols (Lisbon, 1858–64), 1, p. 7; A. Baião and K. Cintra, *Ásia de João de Barros: dos feitos que os portugueses fizeram no descombrimento e conquista dos mares e terras do Oriente*, 4 vols (Lisbon, 1988–), 1, pp. 1–2.
7. A. Velho, *Roteiro da Primeira Viagem de Vasco da Gama*, ed. N. Águas (Lisbon, 1987), p. 22.
8. S. Subrahmanyam, *The Career and Legend of Vasco da Gama* (Cambridge, 1997), pp. 79–163.
9. Velho, *Roteiro de Vasco da Gama*, pp. 54–5.
10. Ibid., p. 58.
11. S. Subrahmanyam, "The Birth-Pangs of Portuguese Asia: Revisiting the Fateful 'Long Decade' 1498–1509," *Journal of Global History* 2 (2007), 262.
12. Velho, *Roteiro de Vasco da Gama*, p. 60.
13. See Subrahmanyam, *Vasco da Gama*, pp. 162–3, pp. 194–5.
14. Letter of King Manuel, cited by Subrahmanyam, *Vasco da Gama*, p. 165.
15. B. Diffie and G. Winius, *Foundations of the Portuguese Empire, 1415–1580* (Oxford, 1977), pp. 172–4; M. Newitt, *Portugal in European and World History* (2009), pp. 62–5; Delaney, *Columbus and the Quest for Jerusalem*, pp. 124–5; J. Brotton, *Trading Territories: Mapping the Early Modern World* (London, 1997), pp. 71–2.
16. M. Guedes, "Estreito de Magelhães," in L. Albuquerque and F. Domingues (eds), *Dictionário de história dos descobrimentos portugueses*, 2 vols (Lisbon, 1994), 2, pp. 640–4.
17. M. Newitt, *A History of Portuguese Overseas Expansion, 1400–1668* (London, 2005), pp. 54–7; A. Teixeira da Mota (ed.), *A viagem de Fernão de Magalhães e a questão das Molucas* (Lisbon, 1975).
18. R. Finlay, "Crisis and Crusade in the Mediterranean: Venice, Portugal, and the Cape Route to India (1498–1509)," *Studi Veneziani* 28 (1994), 45–90.

19. Girolamo Priuli, *I Diarii di Girolamo Priuli*, tr. D. Weinstein, *Ambassador from Venice* (Minneapolis, 1960), pp. 29–30.
20. "La lettre de Guido Detti," in P. Teyssier and P. Valentin, *Voyages de Vasco da Gama: Relations des expeditions de 1497–1499 et 1502–3* (Paris, 1995), pp. 183–8.
21. "Relazione delle Indie Orientali di Vicenzo Quirini nel 1506," in E. Albèri, *Le relazioni degli Ambasciatori Veneti al Senato durante il secolo decimosesto*, 15 vols (Florence, 1839–63), 15, pp. 3–19; Subrahmanyam, "Birth-Pangs of Portuguese Asia," 265.
22. P. Johnson Brummett, *Ottoman Seapower and Levantine Diplomacy in the Age of Discovery* (Albany, NY, 1994), pp. 33–6; Subrahmanyam, "Birth-Pangs of Portuguese Asia," 274.
23. G. Ramusio, "Navigazione verso le Indie Orientali di Tomé Lopez," in M. Milanesi (ed.), *Navigazioni e viaggi* (Turin, 1978), pp. 683–73; Subrahmanyam, *Vasco da Gama*, p. 205.
24. D. Agius, "Qalhat: A Port of Embarkation for India," in S. Leder, H. Kilpatrick, B. Martel-Thoumian and H. Schönig (eds), *Studies in Arabic and Islam* (Leuven, 2002), p. 278.
25. C. Silva, *O Fundador do "Estado Português da Índia," D. Francisco de Almeida, 1457(?)–1510* (Lisbon, 1996), p. 284.
26. J. Aubin, "Un Nouveau Classique: l'anonyme du British Museum," in J. Aubin (ed.), *Le Latin et l'astrolabe: recherches sur le Portugal de la Renaissance, son expansion en Asie et les relations internationales* (Lisbon, 1996), 2, p. 553; S. Subrahmanyam, "Letters from a Sinking Sultan," in L. Thomasz (ed.), *Aquém e Além da Taprobana: Estudos Luso-Orientais à Memória de Jean Aubin e Denys Lombard* (Lisbon, 2002), pp. 239–69.
27. Silva, *Fundador do "Estado Português da Índia,"* pp. 387–8. For Portuguese aims and policies in the Atlantic, Persian Gulf, Indian Ocean and beyond, see F. Bethencourt and D. Curto, *Portuguese Oceanic Expansion, 1400–1800* (Cambridge, 2007).
28. G. Scammell, *The First Imperial Age: European Overseas Expansion, c. 1400–1715* (London, 1989), p. 79.
29. A. Hamdani, "An Islamic Background to the Voyages of Discovery," in S. Khadra Jayyusi (ed.), *The Legacy of Muslim Spain* (Leiden, 1992), p. 288. For Malacca's importance before the Portuguese conquest, K. Hall, "Local and International Trade and Traders in the Straits of Melaka Region: 600–1500," *Journal of Economic and Social History of the Orient* 47.2 (2004), 213–60.
30. S. Subrahmanyam, "Commerce and Conflict: Two Views of Portuguese Melaka in the 1620s," *Journal of Southeast Asian Studies* 19.1 (1988), 62–79.
31. Atwell, "Time, Money and the Weather," 100.
32. P. de Vos, "The Science of Spices: Empiricism and Economic Botany in the Early Spanish Empire," *Journal of World History* 17.4 (2006), 410.
33. ʿUmar ibn Muḥammad, *Rawḍ al-ʿāṭir fī nuzʹhat al-khāṭir*, tr. R. Burton, *The Perfumed Garden of the Shaykh Nefzawi* (New York, 1964), p. 117.
34. F. Lane, "The Mediterranean Spice Trade: Further Evidence of its Revival in the Sixteenth Century," *American Historical Review* 45.3 (1940), 584–5; M. Pearson, *Spices in the Indian Ocean World* (Aldershot, 1998), p. 117.

35. Lane, "Mediterranean Spice Trade," 582–3.
36. S. Halikowski Smith, "'Profits Sprout Like Tropical Plants': A Fresh Look at What Went Wrong with the Eurasian Spice Trade, c. 1550–1800," *Journal of Global History* 3 (2008), 390–1.
37. Letter of Alberto da Carpi, in K. Setton, *The Papacy and the Levant, 1204–1571*, 4 vols (Philadelphia, 1976–84), 3, p. 172, n. 3.
38. P. Allen, *Opus Epistolarum Desiderii Erasmi Roterodami*, 12 vols (Oxford, 1906–58), 9, p. 254; J. Tracy, *Emperor Charles V, Impresario of War* (Cambridge, 2002), p. 27.
39. A. Clot, *Suleiman the Magnificent: The Man, his Life, his Epoch*, tr. M. Reisz (New York, 1992), p. 79. Also R. Finlay, "Prophecy and Politics in Istanbul: Charles V, Sultan Suleyman and the Habsburg Embassy of 1533–1534," *Journal of Modern History* 3 (1998), 249–72.
40. G. Casale, "The Ottoman Administration of the Spice Trade in the Sixteenth Century Red Sea and Persian Gulf," *Journal of the Economic and Social History of the Orient* 49.2 (2006), 170–98.
41. L. Riberio, "O Primeiro Cerco de Diu," *Studia* 1 (1958), 201–95; G. Casale, *The Ottoman Age of Exploration* (Oxford, 2010), pp. 56–75.
42. G. Casale, "Ottoman *Guerre de Course* and the Indian Ocean Spice Trade: The Career of Sefer Reis," *Itinerario* 32.1 (2008), 66–7.
43. *Corpo diplomatico portuguez*, ed. J. da Silva Mendes Leal and J. de Freitas Moniz, 14 vols (Lisbon, 1862–1910), 9, pp. 110–11.
44. Halikowski Smith, "Eurasian Spice Trade," 411; J. Boyajian, *Portuguese Trade in Asia under the Habsburgs, 1580–1640* (Baltimore, 1993), pp. 43–4, and Table 3.
45. Casale, "Ottoman Administration of the Spice Trade," 170–98; also see here N. Stensgaard, *The Asian Trade Revolution of the Seventeenth Century: The East India Companies and the Decline of Caravan Trade* (Chicago, 1974).
46. S. Subrahmanyam, "The Trading World of the Western Indian Ocean, 1546–1565: A Political Interpretation," in A. de Matos and L. Thomasz (eds), *A Carreira da India e as Rotas dos Estreitos* (Braga, 1998), pp. 207–29.
47. S. Pamuk, "In the Absence of Domestic Currency: Debased European Coinage in the Seventeenth-Century Ottoman Empire," *Journal of Economic History* 57.2 (1997), 352–3.
48. H. Crane, E. Akin and G. Necipoğlu, *Sinan's Autobiographies: Five Sixteenth-Century Texts* (Leiden, 2006), p. 130.
49. R. McChesney, "Four Sources on Shah ʿAbbas's Building of Isfahan," *Muqarnas* 5 (1988), 103–34; Iskandar Munshī, *ʿTārīk-e ʿālamārā-ye ʿAbbāsī*, tr. R. Savory, *History of Shah ʿAbbas the Great*, 3 vols (Boulder, CO, 1978), p. 1038; S. Blake, "Shah ʿAbbās and the Transfer of the Safavid Capital from Qazvin to Isfahan," in A. Newman (ed.), *Society and Culture in the Early Modern Middle East: Studies on Iran in the Safavid Period* (Leiden, 2003), pp. 145–64.
50. M. Dickson, "The Canons of Painting by Ṣādiqī Bek," in M. Dickson and S. Cary Welch (eds), *The Houghton Shahnameh*, 2 vols (Cambridge, MA, 1989), 1, p. 262.
51. A. Taylor, *Book Arts of Isfahan: Diversity and Identity in Seventeenth-Century Persia* (Malibu, 1995).

52. H. Cross, "South American Bullion Production and Export, 1550–1750," in Richards, *Precious Metals*, pp. 402–4.
53. A. Jara, "Economia minera e historia economica hispano-americana," in *Tres ensayos sobre economia minera hispano-americana* (Santiago, 1966).
54. A. Attman, *American Bullion in European World Trade, 1600–1800* (Gothenburg, 1986), pp. 6, 81; H-Sh. Chuan, "The Inflow of American Silver into China from the Late Ming to the Mid-Ch'ing Period," *Journal of the Institute of Chinese Studies of the Chinese University of Hong Kong* 2 (1969), 61–75.
55. B. Karl, "'Galanterie di cose rare . . .': Filippo Sassetti's Indian Shopping List for the Medici Grand Duke Francesco and his Brother Cardinal Ferdinando," *Itinerario* 32.3 (2008), 23–41. For a contemporary account of Aztec society, Diego Durán, *Book of the Gods and Rites and the Ancient Calendar*, tr. F. Horcasitas and D. Heyden (1971), pp. 273–4.
56. J. Richards, *The Mughal Empire* (Cambridge, 1993), pp. 6–8.
57. *Bābur-Nāma*, pp. 173–4. Also D. F. Ruggles, *Islamic Gardens and Landscapes* (Philadelphia, PA, 2008), p. 70.
58. *Bābur-Nāma*, p. 359.
59. Ibn Baṭṭūṭa, *Travels*, 8, 2, p. 478.
60. J. Gommans, *Mughal Warfare: Indian Frontiers and High Roads to Empire, 1500–1700* (London, 2002), pp. 112–13. For the size of Indian horses, J. Tavernier, *Travels in India*, ed. V. Ball, 2 vols (London, 1889), 2, p. 263. For Central Asian horses, see J. Masson Smith, "Mongol Society and Military in the Middle East: Antecedents and Adaptations," in Y. Lev (ed.), *War and Society in the Eastern Mediterranean, 7th–15th Centuries* (Leiden, 1997), pp. 247–64.
61. L. Jardine and J. Brotton, *Global Interests: Renaissance Art between East and West* (London, 2005), pp. 146–8.
62. J. Gommans, "Warhorse and Post-Nomadic Empire in Asia, c. 1000–1800," *Journal of Global History* 2 (2007), 1–21.
63. See S. Dale, *Indian Merchants and Eurasian Trade, 1600–1750* (Cambridge, 1994), pp. 41–2.
64. Cited by M. Alam, "Trade, State Policy and Regional Change: Aspects of Mughal–Uzbek Commercial Relations, c. 1550–1750," *Journal of the Economic and Social History of the Orient* 37.3 (1994), 221; also see here C. Singh, *Region and Empire: Punjab in the Seventeenth Century* (New Delhi, 1991), pp. 173–203.
65. J. Gommans, *Mughal Warfare: Indian Frontiers and High Roads to Empire, 1500–1700* (London, 2002), p. 116.
66. D. Washbrook, "India in the Early Modern World Economy: Modes of Production, Reproduction and Exchange," *Journal of Global History* 2 (2007), 92–3.
67. Letter of Duarte de Sande, in *Documenta Indica*, ed. J. Wicki and J. Gomes, 18 vols (Rome, 1948–88), 9, p. 676.
68. R. Foltz, "Cultural Contacts between Central Asia and Mughal India," in S. Levi (ed.), *India and Central Asia* (New Delhi, 2007), pp. 155–75.
69. M. Subtelny, "Mirak-i Sayyid Ghiyas and the Timurid Tradition of Landscape Architecture," *Studia Iranica* 24.1 (1995), 19–60.
70. J. Westcoat, "Gardens of Conquest and Transformation: Lessons from the Earli-

est Mughal Gardens in India," *Landscape Journal* 10.2 (1991), 105–14; F. Ruggles, "Humayun's Tomb and Garden: Typologies and Visual Order," in A. Petruccioli (ed.), *Gardens in the Time of the Great Muslim Empires* (Leiden, 1997), pp. 173–86. For Central Asia's influence, see above all M. Subtelny, "A Medieval Persian Agricultural Manual in Context: The Irshad al-Zira'a in Late Timurid and Early Safavid Khorasan," *Studia Iranica* 22.2 (1993), 167–217.

71. J. Westcoat, M. Brand and N. Mir, "The Shedara Gardens of Lahore: Site Documentation and Spatial Analysis," *Pakistan Archaeology* 25 (1993), 333–66.
72. M. Brand and G. Lowry (eds), *Fatephur Sikri* (Bombay, 1987).
73. *The Shah Jahan Nama of 'Inayat Khan*, ed. and tr. W. Begley and Z. Desai (Delhi, 1990), pp. 70–1.
74. J. Hoil, *The Book of Chilam Balam of Chumayel*, tr. R. Roys (Washington, DC, 1967), pp. 19–20.
75. Letter of John Newbery, in J. Courtney Locke (ed.), *The First Englishmen in India* (London, 1930), p. 42.
76. Samuel Purchas, *Hakluytus posthumus, or, Purchas His Pilgrimes*, 20 vols (Glasgow, 1905–7), 3, p. 93; G. Scammell, "European Exiles, Renegades and Outlaws and the Maritime Economy of Asia, c.1500–1750," *Modern Asian Studies* 26.4 (1992), 641–61.
77. L. Newsom, "Disease and Immunity in the Pre-Spanish Philippines," *Social Science & Medicine* 48 (1999), 1833–50; idem, "Conquest, Pestilence and Demographic Collapse in the Early Spanish Philippines," *Journal of Historical Geography* 32 (2006), 3–20.
78. Antonio de Morga, in W. Schurz, *The Manila Galleon* (New York, 1959), pp. 69–75; also see Brook, *Confusions of Pleasure*, pp. 205–6.
79. D. Irving, *Colonial Counterpoint: Music from Early Modern Manila* (Oxford, 2010), p. 19.
80. For the Ottoman crisis, Pamuk, "In the Absence of Domestic Currency," 353–8.
81. W. Barrett, "World Bullion Flows, 1450–1800," in J. Tracy (ed.), *The Rise of Merchant Empires: Long-Distance Trade in the Early Modern Worlds, 1350–1750* (Cambridge, 1990), pp. 236–7; D. Flynn and A Giráldez, "Born with a 'Silver Spoon': The Origin of World Trade in 1571," *Journal of World History* 6.2 (1995), 201–21; J. TePaske, "New World Silver, Castile, and the Philippines, 1590–1800," in Richards, *Precious Metals*, p. 439.
82. P. D'Elia, *Documenti originali concernenti Matteo Ricci e la storia delle prime relazioni tra l'Europa e la Cina (1579–1615)*, 4 vols (Rome, 1942), 1, p. 91.
83. Brook, *Confusions of Pleasure*, pp. 225–6. For Chinese attitudes to antiquities and to the past, C. Clunas, *Superfluous Things: Material Culture and Social Status in Early Modern China* (Cambridge, 1991), pp. 91–115.
84. W. Atwell, "International Bullion Flows and the Chinese Economy *circa* 1530–1650," *Past & Present* 95 (1982), 86.
85. Richard Hakluyt, *The Principal Navigation, Voyages, Traffiques, & Discoveries of the English Nations*, 12 vols (Glasgow, 1903–5), 5, p. 498.
86. C. Boxer, *The Christian Century in Japan, 1549–1650* (Berkeley, 1951), pp. 425–7. Above all, see here R. von Glahn, "Myth and Reality of China's Seventeenth-

Century Monetary Crisis," *Journal of Economic History* 56.2 (1996), 429–54; D. Flynn and A Giráldez, "Arbitrage, China and World Trade in the Early Modern Period," *Journal of the Economic and Social History of the Orient* 6.2 (1995), 201–21.

87. C. Clunas, *Empire of Great Brightness: Visual and Material Cultures of Ming China, 1368–1644* (London, 2007); Brook, *Confusions of Pleasure*.
88. *The Plum in the Golden Vase, or, Chin P'ing Mei*, tr. D. Roy, 5 vols (Princeton, 1993–2013). See here N. Ding, *Obscene Things: Sexual Politics in Jin Ping Mei* (Durham, NC, 2002).
89. C. Cullen, "The Science/Technology Interface in Seventeenth-Century China: Song Yingxing on *Qi* and the *Wu Xing*," *Bulletin of the School of Oriental and African Studies* 53.2 (1990), 295–318.
90. W. de Bary, "Neo-Confucian Cultivation and the Seventeenth-Century Enlightenment," in de Bary (ed.), *The Unfolding of Neo-Confucianism* (New York, 1975), pp. 141–216.
91. The Selden Map itself may have been captured in this way, R. Batchelor, "The Selden Map Rediscovered: A Chinese Map of East Asian Shipping Routes, c. 1619," *Imago Mundi: The International Journal for the History of Cartography* 65.1 (2013), 37–63.
92. W. Atwell, "Ming Observations of Ming Decline: Some Chinese Views on the 'Seventeenth Century Crisis' in Comparative Perspective," *Journal of the Royal Asiatic Society* 2 (1988), 316–48.
93. A. Smith, *An Inquiry into the Nature and Causes of the Wealth of Nations*, 4.7, ed. R. Campbell and A. Skinner, 2 vols (Oxford, 1976), 2, p. 626.

CHAPTER 13—THE ROAD TO NORTHERN EUROPE

1. José de Acosta, *Historia natural y moral de las Indias*, tr. E. Mangan, *Natural and Moral History of the Indies* (Durham, NC, 2002), p. 179.
2. *Regnans in excelsis*, in R. Miola (ed.), *Early Modern Catholicism: An Anthology of Primary Sources* (Oxford, 2007), pp. 486–8; see P. Holmes, *Resistance and Compromise: The Political Thought of the Elizabethan Catholics* (Cambridge, 2009).
3. D. Loades, *The Making of the Elizabethan Navy 1540–1590: From the Solent to the Armada* (London, 2009).
4. C. Knighton, "A Century on: Pepys and the Elizabethan Navy," *Transactions of the Royal Historical Society* 14 (2004), pp. 143–4; R. Barker, "Fragments from the Pepysian Library," *Revista da Universidade de Coimbra* 32 (1986), 161–78.
5. M. Oppenheim, *A History of the Administration of the Royal Navy, 1509–1660* (London, 1896), pp. 172–4; N. Williams, *The Maritime Trade of the East Anglian Ports, 1550–1590* (Oxford, 1988), pp. 220–1.
6. C. Martin and G. Parker, *The Spanish Armada* (Manchester, 1988); G. Mattingly, *The Armada* (New York, 2005).
7. E. Bovill, "The *Madre de Dios*," *Mariner's Mirror* 54 (1968), 129–52; G. Scammell, "England, Portugal and the Estado da India, c. 1500–1635," *Modern Asian Studies* 16.2 (1982), 180.

8. *The Portable Hakluyt's Voyages*, ed. R. Blacker (New York, 1967), p. 516; J. Parker, *Books to Build an Empire* (Amsterdam, 1965), p. 131; N. Matar, *Turks, Moors, and Englishmen in the Age of Discovery* (New York, 1999).
9. N. Matar, *Britain and Barbary, 1589–1689* (Gainesville, FL, 2005), p. 21; *Merchant of Venice*, I.1.
10. C. Dionisotti, "Lepanto nella cultura italiana del tempo," in G. Benzoni (ed.), *Il Mediterraneo nella seconda metà del '500 alla luce di Pepanto* (Florence, 1974), pp. 127–51; I. Fenlon, "'In destructione Turcharum': The Victory of Lepanto in Sixteenth-Century Music and Letters," in E. Degreda (ed.), *Andrea Gabrieli e il suo tempo: Atti del Convengo internazionale (Venezia 16–18 settembre 1985)* (Florence, 1987), pp. 293–317; I. Fenlon, "Lepanto: The Arts of Celebration in Renaissance Venice," *Proceedings of the British Academy* 73 (1988), 201–36.
11. S. Skilliter, "Three Letters from the Ottoman 'Sultana' Safiye to Queen Elizabeth I," in S. Stern (ed.), *Documents from Islamic Chanceries* (Cambridge, MA, 1965), pp. 119–57.
12. G. Maclean, *The Rise of Oriental Travel: English Visitors to the Ottoman Empire, 1580–1720* (London, 2004), pp. 1–47; L. Jardine, "Gloriana Rules the Waves: Or, the Advantage of Being Excommunicated (and a Woman)," *Transactions of the Royal Historical Society* 14 (2004), 209–22.
13. A. Artner (ed.), *Hungary as "Propugnaculum" of Western Christianity: Documents from the Vatican Secret Archives (ca. 1214–1606)* (Budapest, 2004), p. 112.
14. Jardine, "Gloriana Rules the Waves," 210.
15. S. Skilliter, *William Harborne and the Trade with Turkey 1578–1582: A Documentary Study of the First Anglo-Ottoman Relations* (Oxford, 1977), p. 69.
16. Ibid., p. 37.
17. L. Jardine, *Worldly Goods: A New History of the Renaissance* (London, 1996), pp. 373–6.
18. *Merchant of Venice*, II.7; *Othello*, I.3.
19. J. Grogan, *The Persian Empire in English Renaissance Writing, 1549–1622* (London, 2014).
20. A. Kapr, *Johannes Gutenberg: Persönlichkeit und Leistung* (Munich, 1987).
21. E. Shaksan Bumas, "The Cannibal Butcher Shop: Protestant Uses of Las Casas's 'Brevísima Relación' in Europe and the American Colonies," *Early American Literature* 35.2 (2000), 107–36.
22. A. Hadfield, "Late Elizabethan Protestantism, Colonialism and the Fear of the Apocalypse," *Reformation* 3 (1998), 311–20.
23. R. Hakluyt, "A Discourse on Western Planting, 1584," in *The Original Writings and Correspondence of the Two Richard Hakluyts*, ed. E. Taylor, 2 vols (London, 1935), 2, pp. 211–326.
24. M. van Gelderen, *The Political Thought of the Dutch Revolt, 1555–1590* (Cambridge, 2002).
25. "The First Voyage of the right worshipfull and valiant knight, Sir John Hawkins," in *The Hawkins Voyages*, ed. C. Markham (London, 1878), p. 5. Also here Kelsey, *Sir John Hawkins*, pp. 52–69.
26. Hakluyt, "A Discourse on Western Planting," 20, p. 315.
27. See J. McDermott, *Martin Frobisher: Elizabethan Privateer* (New Haven, 2001).

28. *Calendar of State Papers and Manuscripts, Venice*, 6.i, p. 240.
29. P. Bushev, *Istoriya posol'tv i diplomaticheskikh otnoshenii russkogo i iranskogo gosudarstv v 1586–1612 gg* (Moscow, 1976), pp. 37–62.
30. R. Hakluyt, *The principal navigations, voyages, traffiques and discoveries of the English nations*, 12 vols (Glasgow, 1903–5), 3, pp. 15–16; R. Ferrier, "The Terms and Conditions under which English Trade was Transacted with Safavid Persia," *Bulletin of the School of Oriental and African Studies* 49.1 (1986), 50–1; K. Meshkat, "The Journey of Master Anthony Jenkinson to Persia, 1562–1563," *Journal of Early Modern History* 13 (2009), 209–28.
31. S. Cabot, "Ordinances, instructions and aduertisements of and for the direction of the intended voyage for Cathaye," 22, in Hakluyt, *Principal navigations*, 2, p. 202.
32. Vilches, *New World Gold*, p. 27.
33. A. Romero, S. Chilbert and M. Eisenhart, "Cubagua's Pearl-Oyster Beds: The First Depletion of a Natural Resource Caused by Europeans in the American Continent," *Journal of Political Ecology* 6 (1999), 57–78.
34. M. Drelichman and H.-J. Voth, "The Sustainable Debts of Philip II: A Reconstruction of Spain's Fiscal Position, 1560–1598," *Centre for Economic Policy Research*, Discussion Paper DP6611 (2007).
35. D. Fischer, *The Great Wave: Price Revolutions and the Rhythm of History* (Oxford, 1996). Also D. Flynn, "Sixteenth-Century Inflation from a Production Point of View," in E. Marcus and N. Smukler (eds), *Inflation through the Ages: Economic, Social, Psychological, and Historical Aspects* (New York, 1983), pp. 157–69.
36. O. Gelderblom, *Cities of Commerce: The Institutional Foundations of International Trade in the Low Countries, 1250–1650* (Princeton, 2013).
37. J. Tracy, *A Financial Revolution in the Habsburg Netherlands: Renten and Renteniers in the County of Holland, 1515–1565* (Berkeley, 1985).
38. O. van Nimwegen, *"Deser landen crijchsvolck." Het Staatse leger en de militarie revoluties 1588–1688* (Amsterdam, 2006).
39. J. Israel, *The Dutch Republic: Its Rise, Greatness and Fall 1477–1806* (Oxford, 1995), pp. 308–12.
40. W. Fritschy, "The Efficiency of Taxation in Holland," in O. Gelderblom (ed.), *The Political Economy of the Dutch Republic* (2003), pp. 55–84.
41. C. Koot, *Empire at the Periphery: British Colonists, Anglo-Dutch Trade, and the Development of the British Atlantic, 1621–1713* (New York, 2011), pp. 19–22; E. Sluitter, "Dutch–Spanish Rivalry in the Caribbean Area," *Hispanic American Historical Review* 28.2 (1948), 173–8.
42. Israel, *Dutch Republic*, pp. 320–1.
43. M. Echevarría Bacigalupe, "Un notable episodio en la guerra económica hispano-holandesa: El decreto Guana 1603," *Hispania: Revista española de historia* 162 (1986), 57–97; J. Israel, *Empires and Entrepots: The Dutch, the Spanish Monarchy and the Jews, 1585–1713* (London, 1990), p. 200.
44. R. Unger, "Dutch Ship Design in the Fifteenth and Sixteenth Centuries," *Viator* 4 (1973), 387–415.

45. A. Saldanha, "The Itineraries of Geography: Jan Huygen van Linschoten's Itinerario and Dutch Expeditions to the Indian Ocean, 1594–1602," *Annals of the Association of American Geographers* 101.1 (2011), 149–77.
46. K. Zandvliet, *Mapping for Money: Maps, Plans and Topographic Paintings and their Role in Dutch Overseas Expansion during the 16th and 17th Centuries* (Amsterdam, 1998), pp. 37–49, 164–89.
47. E. Beekman, *Paradijzen van Weeler. Koloniale Literatuur uit Nederlands-Indië, 1600–1950* (Amsterdam, 1988), p. 72.
48. D. Lach, *Asia in the Making of Europe*, 3 vols (Chicago, 1977), 2, 492–545.
49. O. Gelderblom, "The Organization of Long-Distance Trade in England and the Dutch Republic, 1550–1650," in Gelderblom, *Political Economy of the Dutch Republic*, pp. 223–54.
50. J.-W. Veluwenkamp, "Merchant Colonies in the Dutch Trade System (1550–1750)," in K. Davids, J. Fritschy and P. Klein (eds), *Kapitaal, ondernemerschap en beleid. Studies over economie en politiek in Nederland, Europe en Azië van 1500 tot heden* (Amsterdam, 1996), pp. 141–64.
51. Cited by C. Boxer, *The Dutch in Brazil 1624–1654* (Oxford, 1957), pp. 2–3.
52. For Goa at the start of the seventeenth century, A. Gray and H. Bell (eds), *The Voyage of François Pyrard of Laval to the East Indies, the Maldives, the Moluccas and Brazil*, 2 vols (London, 1888), 2, pp. 2–139.
53. J. de Jong, *De waaier van het fortuin. De Nederlands in Asië de Indonesiche archipel, 1595–1950* (Zoetermeer, 1998), p. 48.
54. K. Zandvliet, *The Dutch Encounter with Asia, 1600–1950* (Amsterdam, 2002), p. 152.
55. See here the collection of essays in J. Postma (ed.), *Riches from Atlantic Commerce: Dutch Transatlantic Trade and Shipping, 1585–1817* (Leiden, 2003).
56. J. van Dam, *Gedateerd Delfts aardwek* (Amsterdam, 1991); idem, *Dutch Delftware 1620–1850* (Amsterdam, 2004).
57. A. van der Woude, "The Volume and Value of Paintings in Holland at the Time of the Dutch Republic," in J. de Vries and D. Freedberg (eds), *Art in History, History in Art: Studies in Seventeenth-Century Dutch Culture* (Santa Monica, 1991), pp. 285–330.
58. See in general S. Schama, *The Embarrassment of Riches* (New York, 1985); S. Slive, *Dutch Painting, 1600–1800* (New Haven, 1995).
59. T. Brook, *Vermeer's Hat: The Seventeenth Century and the Dawn of the Global World* (London, 2008), pp. 5–83.
60. *The Travels of Peter Mundy in Europe and Asia, 1608–1667*, ed. R. Temple, 5 vols (Cambridge, 1907–36), pp. 70–1; J. de Vries, *The Industrious Revolution: Consumer Behavior and the Household Economy, 1650 to the Present* (Cambridge, 2008), p. 54.
61. J. Evelyn, *Diary of John Evelyn*, ed. E. de Beer, 6 vols (Oxford, 1955), 1, pp. 39–40.
62. See here C. van Strien, *British Travellers in Holland during the Stuart Period: Edward Browne and John Locke as Tourists in the United Provinces* (Leiden, 1993).
63. G. Scammell, "After da Gama: Europe and Asia since 1498," *Modern Asian Studies* 34.3 (2000), 516.

64. Pedro de Cieza de Léon, *The Incas of Pedro de Cieza de Léon*, tr. H de Onis (1959), 52, p. 171.
65. Ibid., 55, pp. 177–8.
66. S. Hill (ed.), *Bengal in 1756–7: A Selection of Public and Private Papers Dealing with the Affairs of the British in Bengal during the Reign of Siraj-uddaula*, 3 vols (London, 1905), 1, pp. 3–5.
67. P. Perdue, "Empire and Nation in Comparative Perspective: Frontier Administration in Eighteenth-Century China," *Journal of Early Modern History* 5.4 (2001), 282; C. Tilly (ed.), *The Formation of National States in Western Europe* (Princeton, 1975), p. 15.
68. P. Hoffman, "Prices, the Military Revolution, and Western Europe's Comparative Advantage in Violence," *Economic History Review*, 64.1 (2011), 49–51.
69. See, for example, A. Hall, *Isaac Newton: Adventurer in Thought* (Cambridge, 1992), pp. 152, 164–6, 212–16; L. Debnath, *The Legacy of Leonhard Euler: A Tricentennial Tribute* (London, 2010), pp. 353–8; P-L. Rose, "Galileo's Theory of Ballistics," *The British Journal for the History of Science* 4.2 (1968), 156–9, and in general S. Drake, *Galileo at work: His Scientific Biography* (Chicago, 1978).
70. T. Hobbes, *Leviathan*, ed. N. Malcolm (Oxford, 2012).
71. A. Carlos and L. Neal, "Amsterdam and London as Financial Centers in the Eighteenth Century," *Financial History Review* 18.1 (2011), 21–7.
72. M. Bosker, E. Buringh and J. van Zanden, "From Baghdad to London: The Dynamics of Urban Growth and the Arab World, 800–1800," *Centre for Economic Policy Research*, Paper 6833 (2009), 1–38; W. Fritschy, "State Formation and Urbanization Trajectories: State Finance in the Ottoman Empire before 1800, as Seen from a Dutch Perspective," *Journal of Global History* 4 (2009), 421–2.
73. E. Kuipers, *Migrantenstad: Immigratie en Sociale Verboudingen in 17e-Eeuws Amsterdam* (Hilversum, 2005).
74. W. Fritschy, "A 'Financial Revolution' Reconsidered: Public Finance in Holland during the Dutch Revolt, 1568–1648," *Economic History Review* 56.1 (2003), 57–89; L. Neal, *The Rise of Financial Capitalism: International Capitalism in the Age of Reason* (Cambridge, 1990).
75. P. Malanima, *L'economia italiana: dalla crescita medievale alla crescita contemporanea* (Bologna, 2002); idem, "The Long Decline of a Leading Economy: GDP in Central and Northern Italy, 1300–1913," *European Review of Economic History* 15 (2010), 169–219.
76. S. Broadberry and B. Gupta, "The Early Modern Great Divergence: Wages, Prices and Economic Development in Europe and Asia, 1500–1800," *Economic History Review* 59.1 (2006), 2–31; J. van Zanden, "Wages and the Standard of Living in Europe, 1500–1800," *European Review of Economic History* 3 (1999), 175–97.
77. Sir Dudley Carleton, "The English Ambassador's Notes, 1612," in D. Chambers and B. Pullan (eds), *Venice: A Documentary History, 1450–1630* (Oxford, 1992), pp. 3–4.
78. G. Bistort (ed.), *Il magistrato alle pompe nella repubblica di Venezia* (Venice, 1912), pp. 403–5, 378–81.

79. E. Chaney, *The Evolution of the Grand Tour: Anglo-Italian Cultural Relations since the Renaissance* (Portland, OR, 1998). For art prices, see F. Etro and L. Pagani, "The Market for Paintings in Italy during the Seventeenth Century," *Journal of Economic History* 72.2 (2012), 414–38.
80. See for example C. Vout, "Treasure, Not Trash: The Disney Sculpture and its Place in the History of Collecting," *Journal of the History of Collections* 24.3 (2012), 309–26. Also here V. Coltman, *Classical Sculpture and the Culture of Collecting in Britain since 1760* (Oxford, 2009).
81. C. Hanson, *The English Virtuoso: Art, Medicine and Antiquarianism in the Age of Empiricism* (Chicago, 2009).
82. See in general P. Ayres, *Classical Culture and the Ideas of Rome in Eighteenth-Century England* (Cambridge, 1997).

CHAPTER 14—THE ROAD TO EMPIRE

1. D. Panzac, "International and Domestic Maritime Trade in the Ottoman Empire during the 18th Century," *International Journal of Middle East Studies* 24.2 (1992), 189–206; M. Genç, "A Study of the Feasibility of Using Eighteenth-Century Ottoman Financial Records as an Indicator of Economic Activity," in H. İslamoğlu-İnan (ed.), *The Ottoman Empire and the World-Economy* (Cambridge, 1987), pp. 345–73.
2. See here S. White, *The Climate of Rebellion in the Early Modern Ottoman Empire* (Cambridge, 2011).
3. T. Kuran, "The Islamic Commercial Crisis: Institutional Roots of Economic Underdevelopment in the Middle East," *Journal of Economic History* 63.2 (2003), 428–31.
4. M. Kunt, *The Sultan's Servants: The Transformation of Ottoman Provincial Government, 1550–1650* (New York, 1983), pp. 44–56.
5. Schama, *Embarrassment of Riches*, pp. 330–5.
6. Thomas Mun, *England's Treasure by Foreign Trade* (London, 1664), cited by de Vries, *Industrious Revolution*, p. 44.
7. C. Parker, *The Reformation of Community: Social Welfare and Calvinist Charity in Holland, 1572–1620* (Cambridge, 1998).
8. S. Pierson, "The Movement of Chinese Ceramics: Appropriation in Global History," *Journal of World History* 23.1 (2012), 9–39; S. Iwanisziw, "Intermarriage in Late-Eighteenth-Century British Literature: Currents in Assimilation and Exclusion," *Eighteenth-Century Life* 31.2 (2007), 56–82; F. Dabhoiwala, *The Origins of Sex: A History of the First Sexual Revolution* (London, 2012).
9. W. Bradford, *History of Plymouth Plantation, 1606–1646*, ed. W. Davis (New York, 1909), pp. 46–7.
10. For the exodus to North America, A. Zakai, *Exile and Kingdom: History and Apocalypse in the Puritan Migration to America* (Cambridge, 1992); for debate about the origins of Thanksgiving, G. Hodgson, *A Great and Godly Adventure: The Pilgrims and the Myth of the First Thanksgiving* (New York, 2006).
11. K. Chaudhari, *The Trading World of Asia and the English East India Company* (Cambridge, 2006).

12. Gelderblom, "The Organization of Long-Distance Trade," 232–4.
13. S. Groenveld, "The English Civil Wars as a Cause of the First Anglo-Dutch War, 1640–1652," *Historical Journal* 30.3 (1987), 541–66. For Anglo-Dutch rivalry in this period, see L. Jardine, *Going Dutch: How England Plundered Holland's Glory* (London, 2008).
14. S. Pincus, *Protestantism and Patriotism: Ideologies and the Making of English Foreign Policy, 1650–1668* (Cambridge, 1996). Also C. Wilson, *Profit and Power: A Study of England and the Dutch Wars* (London, 1957).
15. J. Davies, *Gentlemen and Tarpaulins: The Officers and Men of the Restoration Navy* (Oxford, 1991), p. 15.
16. J. Glete, *Navies and Nations: Warships, Navies and State Building in Europe and America, 1500–1860*, 2 vols (Stockholm, 1993), pp. 192–5.
17. Witsen's book, *Aeloude en Hedendaegsche Scheeps-bouw en Bestier*, published in 1671, was the most influential volume of its day. For Pepys's copy, N. Smith et al., *Catalogue of the Pepys Library at Magdalene College, Cambridge*, vol. 1 (1978), p. 193. The diarist played a prominent role setting up Christ's Hospital, which remains one of Britain's leading schools, E. Pearce, *Annals of Christ's Hospital* (London, 1901), pp. 99–126; for new designs, see B. Lavery (ed.), *Deane's Doctrine of Naval Architecture, 1670* (London, 1981).
18. D. Benjamin and A. Tifrea, "Learning by Dying: Combat Performance in the Age of Sail," *Journal of Economic History* 67.4 (2007), 968–1000.
19. E. Lazear and S. Rosen, "Rank-Order Tournaments as Optimum Labor Contracts," *Journal of Political Economy* 89.5 (1981), 841–64; also see D. Benjamin and C. Thornberg, "Comment: Rules, Monitoring and Incentives in the Age of Sail," *Explorations in Economic History* 44.2 (2003), 195–211.
20. J. Robertson, "The Caribbean Islands: British Trade, Settlement, and Colonization," in L. Breen (ed.), *Converging Worlds: Communities and Cultures in Colonial America* (Abingdon, 2012), pp. 176–217.
21. P. Stern, "Rethinking Institutional Transformation in the Making of Empire: The East India Company in Madras," *Journal of Colonialism and Colonial History* 9.2 (2008), 1–15.
22. H. Bowen, *The Business of Empire: The East India Company and Imperial Britain, 1756–1833* (Cambridge, 2006).
23. H. Bingham, "Elihu Yale, Governor, Collector and Benefactor," *American Antiquarian Society. Proceedings* 47 (1937), 93–144; idem, *Elihu Yale: The American Nabob of Queen Square* (New York, 1939).
24. J. Osterhammel, *China und die Weltgesellschaft* (1989), p. 112.
25. See for example F. Perkins, *Leibniz and China: A Commerce of Light* (Cambridge, 2004).
26. Cited by S. Mentz, *The English Gentleman Merchant at Work: Madras and the City of London 1660–1740* (Copenhagen, 2005), p. 162.
27. Procopius, *The Wars*, 8.20, 5, pp. 264–6.
28. K. Matthews, "Britannus/Britto: Roman Ethnographies, Native Identities, Labels and Folk Devils," in A. Leslie, *Theoretical Roman Archaeology and Architecture: The Third Conference Proceedings* (1999), p. 15.

29. R. Fogel, "Economic Growth, Population Theory, and Physiology: The Bearing of Long-Term Processes on the Making of Economic Policy," *American Economic Review* 84.3 (1994), 369–95; J. Mokyr, "Why was the Industrial Revolution a European Phenomenon?," *Supreme Court Economic Review* 10 (2003), 27–63.
30. J. de Vries, "Between Purchasing Power and the World of Goods: Understanding the Household Economy in Early Modern Europe," in J. Brewer and R. Porter (eds), *Consumption and the World of Goods* (1993), pp. 85–132; idem, *The Industrious Revolution*; H.-J. Voth, "Time and Work in Eighteenth-Century London," *Journal of Economic History* 58 (1998), 29–58.
31. N. Voigtländer and H.-J. Voth, "Why England? Demographic Factors, Structural Change and Physical Capital Accumulation during the Industrial Revolution," *Journal of Economic Growth* 11 (2006), 319–61; L. Stone, "Social Mobility in England, 1500–1700," *Past & Present* 33 (1966), 16–55; also see P. Fichtner, *Protestantism and Primogeniture in Early Modern Germany* (London, 1989), for an assessment of the connection between religion and primogeniture.
32. K. Karaman and S. Pamuk, "Ottoman State Finances in European Perspective, 1500–1914," *Journal of Economic History* 70.3 (2010), 611–12.
33. G. Ames, "The Role of Religion in the Transfer and Rise of Bombay," *Historical Journal* 46.2 (2003), 317–40.
34. J. Flores, "The Sea and the World of the Mutasaddi: A Profile of Port Officials from Mughal Gujarat (c.1600–1650)," *Journal of the Royal Asiatic Society* 3.21 (2011), 55–71.
35. *Tūzuk-i-Jahāngīrī*, tr. W. Thackston, *The Jahangirnama: Memoirs of Jahangir, Emperor of India* (Oxford, 1999), p. 108.
36. A. Loomba, "Of Gifts, Ambassadors, and Copy-cats: Diplomacy, Exchange and Difference in Early Modern India," in B. Charry and G. Shahani (eds), *Emissaries in Early Modern Literature and Culture: Mediation, Transmission, Traffic, 1550–1700* (Aldershot, 2009), pp. 43–5 and passim.
37. Rev. E. Terry, *A Voyage to East India* (London, 1655), p. 397, cited by T. Foster, *The Embassy of Sir Thomas Roe to India* (London, 1926), pp. 225–6, n. 1. The traveller Peter Mundy saw two dodos when he visited Surat, which may also have been presents from merchants eager to win Jahangir's favour, *Travels of Peter Mundy*, 2, p. 318.
38. L. Blussé, *Tribuut aan China. Vier eeuwen Nederlands–Chinese betrekkingen* (Amsterdam, 1989), pp. 84–7.
39. For the list of gifts, J. Vogel (ed.), *Journaal van Ketelaar's hofreis naar den Groot Mogol te Lahore* (The Hague, 1937), pp. 357–93; A. Topsfield, "Ketelaar's Embassy and the Farengi Theme in the Art of Udaipur," *Oriental Art* 30.4 (1985), 350–67.
40. For details of the weighing, see *Shah Jahan Nama*, p. 28; Jean de Thévenot, who travelled to India in the seventeenth century, provides a vivid account of the weighing ceremony, in S. Sen, *Indian Travels of Thevenot and Careri* (New Delhi, 1949), 26, pp. 66–7.
41. P. Mundy, *Travels*, pp. 298–300.

42. N. Manucci, *A Pepys of Mogul India, 1653–1708: Being an Abridged Edition of the "Storia do Mogor" of Niccolao Manucci* (New Delhi, 1991), pp. 197, 189.
43. J. Gommans, "Mughal India and Central Asia in the Eighteenth Century: An Introduction to a Wider Perspective," *Itinerario* 15.1 (1991), 51–70. For tribute payments, see J. Spain, *The Pathan Borderland* (The Hague, 1963), pp. 32–4; also see C. Noelle, *State and Tribe in Nineteenth-Century Afghanistan: The Reign of Amir Dost Muhamad Khan (1826–1863)* (London, 1997), p. 164.
44. S. Levi, "The Ferghana Valley at the Crossroads of World History: The Rise of Khoqand 1709–1822," *Journal of Global History* 2 (2007), 213–32.
45. S. Levi, "India, Russia and the Eighteenth-Century Transformation of the Central Asian Caravan Trade," *Journal of the Economic and Social History of the Orient* 42.4 (1999), 519–48.
46. See I. McCabe, *Shah's Silk for Europe's Silver: The Eurasian Trade of the Julfa Armenians in Safavid Iran and India, 1530–1750* (Atlanta, 1999). Also see B. Bhattacharya, "Armenian European Relationship in India, 1500–1800: No Armenian Foundation for European Empire?," *Journal of the Economic and Social History of the Orient* 48.2 (2005), 277–322.
47. S. Delgoda, "'Nabob, Historian and Orientalist': Robert Orme: The Life and Career of an East India Company Servant (1728–1801)," *Journal of the Royal Asiatic Society* 2.3 (1992), 363–4.
48. Cited by T. Nechtman, "A Jewel in the Crown? Indian Wealth in Domestic Britain in the Late Eighteenth Century," *Eighteenth-Century Studies* 41.1 (2007), 73.
49. A. Bewell, *Romanticism and Colonial Disease* (Baltimore, 1999), p. 13.
50. T. Bowrey, *Geographical Account of Countries around the Bay of Bengal 1669 to 1679*, ed. R. Temple (London, 1905), pp. 80–1.
51. C. Smylitopoulos, "Rewritten and Reused: Imagining the Nabob through 'Upstart Iconography,'" *Eighteenth-Century Life* 32.2 (2008), 39–59.
52. P. Lawson, *The East India Company: A History* (London, 1993), p. 120.
53. Nechtman, "Indian Wealth in Domestic Britain," 76.
54. E. Burke, *The Writings and Speeches of Edmund Burke*, ed. W. Todd, 9 vols (Oxford, 2000), 5, p. 403.
55. D. Forrest, *Tea for the British: The Social and Economic History of a Famous Trade* (London, 1973), Tea Consumption in Britain, Appendix II, Table 1, p. 284.
56. For Bengal, R. Datta, *Society, Economy and the Market: Commercialization in Rural Bengal, c. 1760–1800* (New Delhi, 2000); R. Harvey, *Clive: The Life and Death of a British Emperor* (London, 1998).
57. P. Marshall, *East India Fortunes: The British in Bengal in the Eighteenth Century* (Oxford, 1976), p. 179.
58. J. McLane, *Land and Local Kingship in Eighteenth-Century Bengal* (Cambridge, 1993), pp. 194–207.
59. See N. Dirks, *Scandal of Empire: India and the Creation of Imperial Britain* (Cambridge, MA, 2006), pp. 15–17.
60. P. Lawson, *The East India Company: A History* (New York, 1993).
61. J. Fichter, *So Great a Proffit: How the East Indies Trade Transformed Anglo-American Capitalism* (Cambridge, MA, 2010), pp. 7–30.

62. Letters from inhabitants of Boston complained for months afterwards about "the taste of their fish being altered," raising fears that the tea "may have so contaminated the water in the Harbour that the fish may have contracted a disorder, not unlike the nervous complaints of the human Body," *Virginia Gazette*, 5 May 1774.
63. Cited by Dirks, *Scandal*, p. 17.

CHAPTER 15—THE ROAD TO CRISIS

1. K. Marx, *Secret Diplomatic History of the Eighteenth Century*, ed. L. Hutchinson (London, 1969).
2. A. Kappeler, "Czarist Policy toward the Muslims of the Russian Empire," in A. Kappeler, G. Simon and G. Brunner (eds), *Muslim Communities Reemerge: Historical Perspectives on Nationality, Politics, and Opposition in the Former Soviet Union and Yugoslavia* (Durham, NC, 1994), pp. 141–56; also D. Brower and E. Lazzerini, *Russia's Orient: Imperial Borderlands and Peoples, 1700–1917* (Bloomington, IN, 1997).
3. The best general surveys of Russia's expansion are M. Khodarkovsky, *Russia's Steppe Frontier: The Making of a Colonial Empire, 1500–1800* (Bloomington, IN, 2002); J. Kusber, "'Entdecker' und 'Entdeckte': Zum Selbstverständnis von Zar und Elite im frühneuzeitlichen Moskauer Reich zwischen Europa und Asien," *Zeitschrift für Historische Forschung* 34 (2005), 97–115.
4. J. Bell, *Travels from St. Petersburg in Russia to Various Parts of Asia* (Glasgow, 1764), p. 29; M. Khodarkovsky, *Where Two Worlds Met: The Russian State and the Kalmyk Nomads 1600–1771* (London, 1992).
5. A. Kahan, "Natural Calamities and their Effect upon the Food Supply in Russia," *Jahrbücher für Geschichte Osteuropas* 16 (1968), 353–77; J. Hittle, *The Service City: State and Townsmen in Russia, 1600–1800* (Cambridge, MA, 1979), pp. 3–16; P. Brown, "How Muscovy Governed: Seventeenth-Century Russian Central Administration," *Russian History* 36 (2009), 467–8.
6. L. de Bourrienne, *Memoirs of Napoleon Bonaparte*, ed. R. Phipps, 4 vols (New York, 1892), 1, p. 179.
7. J. Cole, *Napoleon's Egypt: Invading the Middle East* (New York, 2007), pp. 213–15.
8. C. de Gardane, *Mission du Général Gardane en Perse* (Paris, 1865). For France and Persia in this period in general, and the attempt to use it as a bridge to India, I. Amini, *Napoléon et la Perse: les relations franco-persanes sous le Premier Empire dans le contexte des rivalités entre la France et la Russie* (Paris, 1995).
9. Ouseley to Wellesley, 30 April 1810, FO 60/4.
10. Ouseley to Wellesley, 30 November 1811, FO 60/6.
11. For this episode see A. Barrett, "A Memoir of Lieutenant-Colonel Joseph d'Arcy, R.A., 1780–1848," *Iran* 43 (2005), 241–7.
12. Ibid., 248–53.
13. Ouseley to Castlereagh, 16 January 1813, FO 60/8.
14. Abul Hassan to Castlereagh, 6 June 1816, FO 60/11.
15. A. Postnikov, "The First Russian Voyage around the World and its Influence

on the Exploration and Development of Russian America," *Terrae Incognitae* 37 (2005), 60–1.

16. S. Fedorovna, *Russkaya Amerika v "zapiskakh" K. T. Khlebnikova* (Moscow, 1985).
17. M. Gammer, "Russian Strategy in the Conquest of Chechnya and Dagestan, 1825–59," in M. Broxup (ed.), *The North Caucasus Barrier: The Russian Advance towards the Muslim World* (New York, 1992), pp. 47–61; for Shamil, S. Kaziev, *Imam Shamil* (Moscow, 2001).
18. For translations of the poems, see M. Pushkin, *Eugene Onegin and Four Tales from Russia's Southern Frontier*, tr. R. Clark (London, 2005), pp. 131–40; L. Kelly, *Lermontov: Tragedy in the Caucasus* (London, 2003), pp. 207–8.
19. M. Orlov, *Kapituliatsiia Parizha. Politicheskie sochinenniia. Pis'ma* (Moscow, 1963), p. 47.
20. P. Chaadev, *Lettres philosophiques*, 3 vols (Paris, 1970), pp. 48–57.
21. S. Becker, "Russia between East and West: The Intelligentsia, Russian National Identity and the Asian Borderlands," *Central Asian Survey* 10.4 (1991), 51–2.
22. T. Levin, *The Hundred Thousand Fools of God: Musical Travels in Central Asia* (Bloomington, IN, 1996), pp. 13–15; Borodin's symphonic poem is usually rendered in English as "In the Steppes of Central Asia."
23. J. MacKenzie, *Orientalism: History, Theory and the Arts* (Manchester, 1995), pp. 154–6.
24. F. Dostoevskii, *What is Asia to Us?*, ed. and tr. M. Hauner (London, 1992), p. 1.
25. Broxup, *North Caucasus Barrier*, p. 47; J. Baddeley, *The Russian Conquest of the Caucasus* (London, 1908), pp. 152–63.
26. L. Kelly, *Diplomacy and Murder in Teheran: Alexandre Griboyedov and Imperial Russia's Mission to the Shah of Persia* (London, 2002). For Griboyedov's views, see S. Shostakovich, *Diplomatischeskaia deiatel'nost'* (Moscow, 1960).
27. "Peridskoe posol'stvo v Rossii 1828 goda," *Russkii Arkhiv* 1 (1889), 209–60.
28. Cited by W. Dalrymple, *Return of a King: The Battle for Afghanistan* (London, 2013), pp. 50–1.
29. J. Norris, *The First Afghan War 1838–42* (Cambridge, 1967); M. Yapp, *Strategies of British India: Britain, Iran and Afghanistan 1798–1850* (Oxford, 1980), pp. 96–152; C. Allworth, *Central Asia: A Century of Russian Rule* (New York, 1967), pp. 12–24.
30. Palmerston to Lamb, 22 May 1838, Beauvale Papers, MS 60466; D. Brown, *Palmerston: A Biography* (London, 2010), p. 216.
31. Palmerston to Lamb, 22 May 1838, cited in D. Brown, *Palmerston: A Biography* (London, 2010), p. 216.
32. Palmerston to Lamb, 23 June 1838, in ibid., pp. 216–7.
33. S. David, *Victoria's Wars: The Rise of Empire* (London, 2006), pp. 15–47; A. Burnes, *Travels into Bokhara. Being an account of a Journey from India to Cabool, Tartary and Persia*, 3 vols (London 1834). For Burnes's murder, Dalrymple, *Return of a King*, pp. 30–5.
34. W. Yapp, "Disturbances in Eastern Afghanistan, 1839–42," *Bulletin of the School of Oriental and African Studies* 25.1 (1962), 499–523; idem, "Disturbances in

Western Afghanistan, 1839–42," *Bulletin of the School of Oriental and African Studies* 26.2 (1963), 288–313; Dalrymple, *Return of a King*, pp. 378–88.

35. A. Conoly to Rawlinson 1839; see S. Brysac and K. Mayer, *Tournament of Shadows: The Great Game and the Race for Empire in Asia* (London, 2006).
36. "Proceedings of the Twentieth Anniversary Meeting of the Society," *Journal of the Royal Asiatic Society* 7 (1843), x–xi. For Stoddart, Conolly and others like them, P. Hopkirk, *The Great Game: On Secret Service in High Asia* (London, 2001).
37. H. Hopkins, *Charles Simeon of Cambridge* (London, 1977), p. 79.
38. J. Wolff, *Narrative of a Mission to Bokhara: In the Years 1843–1845*, 2 vols (London, 1845); for Wolff himself, H. Hopkins, *Sublime Vagabond: The Life of Joseph Wolff—Missionary Extraordinary* (Worthing, 1984), pp. 286–322.
39. A. Levshin, *Opisanie Kirgiz-Kazach'ikh, ili Kirgiz-kaisatskikh, ord i stepei* (Almaty, 1996) 13, p. 297.
40. Burnes, *Travels into Bokhara*, 11, 2, p. 381.
41. R. Shukla, *Britain, India and the Turkish Empire, 1853–1882* (New Delhi, 1973), p. 27.
42. O. Figes, *Crimea: The Last Crusade* (London, 2010), p. 52.
43. For France, see M. Racagni, "The French Economic Interests in the Ottoman Empire," *International Journal of Middle East Studies* 11.3 (1980), 339–76.
44. W. Baumgart, *The Peace of Paris 1856: Studies in War, Diplomacy and Peacemaking*, tr. A. Pottinger Saab (Oxford, 1981), pp. 113–16, 191–4.
45. K. Marx, *The Eastern Question: A Reprint of Letters Written 1853–1856 Dealing with the Events of the Crimean War* (London, 1969); idem, *Dispatches for the New York Tribune: Selected Journalism of Karl Marx*, ed. F. Wheen and J. Ledbetter (London, 2007).
46. G. Ameil, I. Nathan and G.-H. Soutou, *Le Congrès de Paris (1856): un événement fondateur* (Brussels, 2009).
47. P. Levi, "Il monumento dell'unità Italiana," *La Lettura*, 4 April 1904; T. Kirk, "The Political Topography of Modern Rome, 1870–1936: Via XX Septembre to Via dell'Impero," in D. Caldwell and L. Caldwell (eds), *Rome: Continuing Encounters between Past and Present* (Farnham, 2011), pp. 101–28.
48. Figes, *Crimea*, pp. 411–24; Baumgart, *Peace of Paris*, pp. 113–16.
49. D. Moon, *The Abolition of Serfdom in Russia, 1762–1907* (London, 2001), p. 54.
50. E. Brooks, "Reform in the Russian Army, 1856–1861," *Slavic Review* 43.1 (1984), 63–82.
51. For serfdom in Russia, see T. Dennison, *The Institutional Framework of Russian Serfdom* (Cambridge, 2011). For the banking crisis, S. Hoch, "Bankovskii krizis, krest'ianskaya reforma i vykupnaya operatsiya v Rossii, 1857–1861," in L. Zakharova, B. Eklof and J. Bushnell (eds), *Velikie reformy v Rossii, 1856–1874* (Moscow, 1991), pp. 95–105.
52. Nikolai Miliutin, Assistant Minister of the Interior, had warned in 1856 that the abolition of serfdom was not just a priority but a necessity: there would be unrest and possibly revolution in the countryside if action was not taken, *Gosudarstvennyi arkhiv Rossiiskoi Federatsii*, 722, op. 1, d. 230, cited by L. Zakha-

rova, "The Reign of Alexander II: A Watershed?," in *The Cambridge History of Russia*, ed. D. Lieven (Cambridge, 2006), p. 595.

53. V. Fedorov, *Istoriya Rossii XIX–nachala XX v.* (Moscow, 1998), p. 295; P. Gatrell, "The Meaning of the Great Reforms in Russian Economic History," in B. Eklof, J. Bushnell and L. Zakharovna (eds), *Russia's Great Reforms, 1855–1881* (Bloomington, IN, 1994), p. 99.
54. N. Ignat'ev, *Missiya v' Khivu i Bukharu v' 1858 godu* (St. Petersburg, 1897), p. 2.
55. Ibid.
56. Alcock to Russell, 2 August 1861, FO Confidential Print 1009 (3), FO 881/1009.
57. A. Grinev, "Russian Politarism as the Main Reason for the Selling of Alaska," in K. Matsuzato (ed.), *Imperiology: From Empirical Knowledge to Discussing the Russian Empire* (Sapporo, 2007), pp. 245–58.

CHAPTER 16—THE ROAD TO WAR

1. W. Mosse, "The End of the Crimean System: England, Russia and the Neutrality of the Black Sea, 1870–1," *Historical Journal* 4.2 (1961), 164–72.
2. *Spectator*, 14 November 1870.
3. W. Mosse, "Public Opinion and Foreign Policy: The British Public and the War-Scare of November 1870," *Historical Journal* 6.1 (1963), 38–58.
4. Rumbold to Granville, 19 March 1871, FO 65/820, no. 28, p. 226; Mosse, "End to the Crimean System," 187.
5. Lord Granville, House of Lords, 8 February 1876, Hansard, 227, 19.
6. Queen Victoria to Disraeli, Hughenden Papers, 23 July 1877; L. Knight, "The Royal Titles Act and India," *Historical Journal* 11.3 (1968), 493.
7. Robert Lowe, House of Commons, 23 March 1876, Hansard, 228, 515–16.
8. Sir William Fraser, House of Commons, 16 March 1876, Hansard, 228, 111; Benjamin Disraeli, House of Commons, 23 March, Hansard, 227, 500.
9. Knight, "Royal Titles Act," 494.
10. L. Morris, "British Secret Service Activity in Khorasan, 1887–1908," *Historical Journal* 27.3 (1984), 662–70.
11. Disraeli to Salisbury, 1 April 1877, W. Monypenny and G. Buckle (eds), *The Life of Benjamin Disraeli, Earl of Beaconsfield* (London, 1910–20), 6, p. 379.
12. B. Hopkins, "The Bounds of Identity: The Goldsmid Mission and Delineation of the Perso-Afghan Border in the Nineteenth Century," *Journal of Global History* 2.2 (2007), 233–54.
13. R. Johnson, "'Russians at the Gates of India'? Planning the Defence of India, 1885–1900," *Journal of Military History* 67.3 (2003), 705.
14. Ibid., 714–18.
15. General Kuropatkin's Scheme for a Russian Advance Upon India, June 1886, CID 7D, CAB 6/1.
16. Johnson, "'Russians at the Gates of India,'" 734–9.
17. G. Curzon, *Russia in Central Asia in 1889 and the Anglo-Russian Question* (London, 1889), pp. 314–15.
18. A. Morrison, "Russian Rule in Turkestan and the Example of British India, c. 1860–1917," *Slavonic and East European Review* 84.4 (2006), 674–6.

19. B. Penati, "Notes on the Birth of Russian Turkestan's Fiscal System: A View from the Fergana *Oblast'*," *Journal of the Economic and Social History of the Orient* 53 (2010), 739–69.
20. D. Brower, "Russian Roads to Mecca: Religious Tolerance and Muslim Pilgrimage in the Russian Empire," *Slavic Review* 55.3 (1996), 569–70.
21. M. Terent'ev, *Rossiya i Angliya v Srednei Azii* (St. Petersburg, 1875), p. 361.
22. Morrison, "Russian Rule in Turkestan," 666–707.
23. *Dnevnik P. A. Valueva, ministra vnutrennikh del*, ed. P. Zaionchkovskii, 2 vols (Moscow, 1961), 2, pp. 60–1.
24. M. Sladkovskii, *History of Economic Relations between Russia and China: From Modernization to Maoism* (New Brunswick, 2008), pp. 119–29; C. Paine, *Imperial Rivals: China, Russia and their Disputed Frontier, 1858–1924* (New York, 1996), p. 178.
25. B. Anan'ich and S. Beliaev, "St. Petersburg: Banking Center of the Russian Empire," in W. Brumfield, B. Anan'ich and Y. Petrov (eds), *Commerce in Russian Urban Culture, 1861–1914* (Washington, DC, 2001), pp. 15–17.
26. P. Stolypin, *Rechy v Gosudarstvennoy Dume (1906–11)* (Petrograd, 1916), p. 132.
27. E. Backhouse and J. Blood, *Annals and Memoirs of the Court of Peking* (Boston, 1913), pp. 322–31.
28. M. Mosca, *From Frontier Policy to Foreign Policy: The Question of India and the Transformation of Geopolitics in Qing China* (Stanford, CA, 2013).
29. R. Newman, "Opium Smoking in Late Imperial China: A Reconsideration," *Modern Asian Studies* 29.4 (1995), 765–94.
30. J. Polachek, *The Inner Opium War* (Cambridge, MA, 1991).
31. C. Pagani, "Objects and the Press: Images of China in Nineteenth-Century Britain," in J. Codell (ed.), *Imperial Co-Histories: National Identities and the British and Colonial Press* (Madison, NJ, 2003), p. 160.
32. Memorandum by Lord Northbrook for the Cabinet, 20 May 1885, FO 881/5207, no. 29, p. 11. See here I. Nish, "Politics, Trade and Communications in East Asia: Thoughts on Anglo-Russian Relations, 1861–1907," *Modern Asian Studies* 21.4 (1987), 667–78.
33. D. Drube, *Russo-Indian Relations, 1466–1917* (New York, 1970), pp. 215–16.
34. Lord Roberts, "The North-West Frontier of India. An Address Delivered to the Officers of the Eastern Command on 17th November, 1905," *Royal United Services Institution Journal* 49.334 (1905), 1355.
35. Summary of Rittich Pamphlet on "Railways in Persia," Part I, p. 2, Sir Charles Scott to the Marquess of Salisbury, St. Petersburg, 2 May 1900, FO 65/1599. Also here P. Kennedy and J. Siegel, *Endgame: Britain, Russia and the Final Struggle for Central Asia* (London, 2002), p. 4.
36. "Memorandum by Mr. Charles Hardinge," p. 9, to the Marquess of Salisbury, St. Petersburg, 2 May 1900, FO 65/1599.
37. Foreign Secretary, Simla, to Political Resident, Persian Gulf, July 1899, FO 60/615.
38. R. Greaves, "British Policy in Persia, 1892–1903 II," Bulletin of the School of Oriental and African Studies 28.2 (1965), 284–8.
39. Durand to Salisbury, 27 January 1900, FO 60/630.

40. Minute by the Viceroy on Seistan, 4 September 1899, FO 60/615, p. 7. For the proposed new communication networks, "Report on preliminary survey of the Route of a telegraph line from Quetta to the Persian frontier," 1899, FO 60/615.
41. R. Greaves, "Sistan in British Indian Frontier Policy," *Bulletin of the School of Oriental and African Studies* 49.1 (1986), 90–1.
42. Lord Curzon to Lord Lansdowne, 15 June 1901, Lansdowne Papers, cited by Greaves, "British Policy in Persia," 295.
43. Lord Salisbury to Lord Lansdowne, 18 October 1901, Lansdowne Papers, cited by Greaves, "British Policy in Persia," 298.
44. Lord Ellenborough, House of Lords, 5 May 1903, Hansard, 121, 1341.
45. Lord Lansdowne, House of Lords, 5 May 1903, Hansard, 121, 1348.
46. Greaves, "Sistan in British Indian Frontier Policy," 90–102.
47. British Interests in Persia, 22 January 1902, Hansard, 101, 574–628; Earl of Ronaldshay, House of Commons, 17 February 1908, Hansard, 184, 500–1.
48. King Edward VII to Lansdowne, 20 October 1901, cited by S. Lee, *King Edward VII*, 2 vols (New York, 1935–7), 2, pp. 154–5.
49. S. Gwynn, *The Letters and Friendships of Sir Cecil Spring-Rice*, 2 vols (Boston, 1929), 2, p. 85; M. Habibi, "France and the Anglo-Russian Accords: The Discreet Missing Link," *Iran* 41 (2003), 292.
50. Report of a Committee Appointed to Consider the Military Defence of India, 24 December 1901, CAB 6/1; K. Neilson, *Britain and the Last Tsar: British Policy and Russia, 1894–1917* (Oxford, 1995), p. 124.
51. Stevens to Lansdowne, 12 March 1901, FO 248/733.
52. Morley to Minto, 12 March 1908, cited by S. Wolpert, *Morley and India, 1906–1910* (Berkeley, 1967), p. 80.
53. W. Robertson to DGMI, secret, 10 November 1902, Robertson Papers, I/2/4, in Neilson, *Britain and the Last Tsar*, p. 124.
54. S. Cohen, "Mesopotamia in British Strategy, 1903–1914," *International Journal of Middle East Studies* 9.2 (1978), 171–4.
55. Neilson, *Britain and the Last Tsar*, pp. 134–5.
56. *The Times*, 21 October 1905.
57. H.-U. Wehler, *Deutsche Gesellschaftsgeschichte*, 5 vols (Munich, 2008), 3, pp. 610–12.
58. C. Clark, *The Sleepwalkers: How Europe Went to War in 1914* (London, 2012), p. 130.
59. F. Tomaszewski, *A Great Russia: Russia and the Triple Entente, 1905–1914* (Westport, CT, 2002); M. Soroka, *Britain, Russia and the Road to the First World War: The Fateful Embassy of Count Aleksandr Benckendorff (1903–16)* (Farnham, 2011).
60. Minute of Grey, FO 371/371/26042.
61. G. Trevelyan, *Grey of Fallodon* (London, 1937), p. 193.
62. Hardinge to de Salis, 29 December 1908, Hardinge MSS, vol. 30.
63. K. Wilson, "Imperial Interests in the British Decision for War, 1914: The Defence of India in Central Asia," *Review of International Studies* 10 (1984), 190–2.

64. Nicolson to Hardinge, 18 April 1912, Hardinge MSS, vol. 92.
65. Grey to Nicholson, 19 March 1907; Memorandum, Sir Edward Grey, 15 March 1907, FO 418/38.
66. Clark, *Sleepwalkers*, pp. 85, 188; H. Afflerbach, *Der Dreibund. Europäische Grossmacht- und Allianz-politik vor dem Ersten Weltkrieg* (Vienna, 2002), pp. 628–32.
67. Grey to Nicolson, 18 April 1910, in G. Gooch and H. Temperley (eds), *British Documents on the Origins of the War, 1898–1914*, 11 vols (London, 1926–38), 6, p. 461.
68. Cited by B. de Siebert, *Entente Diplomacy and the World* (New York, 1921), p. 99.
69. I. Klein, "The Anglo-Russian Convention and the Problem of Central Asia, 1907–1914," *Journal of British Studies* 11.1 (1971), esp. 140–3.
70. Grey to Buchanan, 18 March 1914, Grey MSS, FO 800/74, pp. 272–3.
71. Nicolson to Grey, 24 March 1909, FO 800/337, p. 312; K. Wilson, *The Policy of the Entente: Essays on the Determinants of British Foreign Policy* (Cambridge, 1985), p. 38.
72. Nicolson to Grey, 24 March 1909, FO 800/337, p. 312.
73. Cited by N. Ferguson, *The Pity of War* (London, 1998), p. 73.
74. Cited by K. Wilson, *Empire and Continent: Studies in British Foreign Policy from the 1880s to the First World War* (London, 1987), pp. 144–5; G. Schmidt, "Contradictory Postures and Conflicting Objectives: The July Crisis," in G. Schöllgen, *Escape into War? The Foreign Policy of Imperial Germany* (Oxford, 1990), p. 139.
75. Cited by R. MacDaniel, *The Shuster Mission and the Persian Constitutional Revolution* (Minneapolis, 1974), p. 108.
76. T. Otte, *The Foreign Office Mind: The Making of British Foreign Policy, 1865–1914* (Cambridge, 2011), p. 352.
77. Bertie to Mallet, 11 June 1904 replying to Mallet to Bertie, 2 June 1904, FO 800/176.
78. The Schlieffen plan is controversial—in its context and precise date of composition, and in its use in the build-up to the First World War. See G. Gross, "There was a Schlieffen Plan: New Sources on the History of German Military Planning," *War in History* 15 (2008), 389–431; T. Zuber, *Inventing the Schlieffen Plan* (Oxford, 2002); and idem, *The Real German War Plan* (Stroud, 2011).
79. J. Sanborn, *Imperial Apocalypse: The Great War and the Destruction of the Russian Empire* (Oxford, 2014), p. 25. For Plan 19 and its variants, also see I. Rostunov, *Russki front pervoi mirovoi voiny* (Moscow, 1976), pp. 91–2.
80. Kaiser Wilhelm to Morley, 3 November 1907, cited by Cohen, "British Strategy in Mesopotamia," 176. For the Kaiser's involvement in the railway, see J. Röhl, *Wilhelm II: Into the Abyss of War and Exile, 1900–1941*, tr. S. de Bellaigue and R. Bridge (Cambridge, 2014), pp. 90–5.
81. R. Zilch, *Die Reichsbank und die finanzielle Kriegsvorbereitung 1907 bis 1914* (Berlin, 1987), pp. 83–8.
82. A. Hitler, *Mein Kampf* (London, repr. 2007), p. 22. See here, B. Rubin and W. Schwanitz, *Nazis, Islamists, and the Making of the Modern Middle East* (New Haven, 2014), pp. 22–5.

83. D. Hoffmann, *Der Sprung ins Dunkle oder wie der I. Weltkrieg entfesselt wurde* (Leipzig, 2010), pp. 325–30; also A. Mombauer, *Helmuth von Moltke and the Origins of the First World War* (Cambridge, 2001), pp. 172–4.
84. R. Musil, "Europäertum, Krieg, Deutschtum," *Die neue Rundschau* 25 (1914), 1303.
85. W. Le Queux, *The Invasion of 1910* (London, 1906); Andrew, *Defence of the Realm*, p. 8; Ferguson, *Pity of War*, pp. 1–11.
86. "Britain scared by Russo-German deal," *New York Times*, 15 January 1911. Also see D. Lee, *Europe's Crucial Years: The Diplomatic Background of World War 1, 1902–1914* (Hanover, NH, 1974), pp. 217–20.
87. A. Mombauer, *Helmuth von Moltke and the Origins of the First World War* (Cambridge, 2001), p. 120.
88. R. Bobroff, *Roads to Glory: Late Imperial Russia and the Turkish Straits* (London, 2006), pp. 52–5.
89. Grigorevich to Sazonov, 19 January 1914, in *Die Internationalen Beziehungen im Zeitalter des Imperialismus*, 8 vols (Berlin, 1931–43), Series 3, 1, pp. 45–7, cited by Clark, *Sleepwalkers*, p. 485. Also see M. Aksakal, *The Ottoman Road to War in 1914: The Ottoman Empire and the First World War* (Cambridge, 2008), pp. 42–56.
90. S. McMeekin, *The Russian Origins of the First World War* (Cambridge, MA, 2011), pp. 29, 36–8.
91. Girs to Sazonov, 13 November 1913, cited by McMeekin, *Russian Origins*, pp. 30–1.
92. W. Kampen, *Studien zur deutschen Türkeipolitik in der Zeit Wilhelms II* (Kiel, 1968), 39–57; M. Fuhrmann, *Der Traum vom deutschen Orient: Zwei deutsche Kolonien im Osmanischen Reich*, 1851–1918 (Frankfurt-am-Main, 2006).
93. See J. Röhl, *The Kaiser and his Court: Wilhelm II and the Government of Germany*, tr. T. Cole (Cambridge, 1996), pp. 162–89.
94. Nicolson to Goschen, 5 May 1914, FO 800/374.
95. For the transfusion, A. Hustin, "Principe d'une nouvelle méthode de transfusion muqueuse," *Journal Médical de Bruxelles* 2 (1914), 436; for forest fires, Z. Frenkel, "Zapiski o zhiznennom puti," *Voprosy istorii* 1 (2007), 79; for the German football, C. Bausenwein, *Was ist Was: Fußballbuch* (Nuremberg, 2008), p. 60; A. Meynell, "Summer in England, 1914," in *The Poems of Alice Meynell: Complete Edition* (Oxford, 1940), p. 100.
96. H. Pogge von Strandmann, "Germany and the Coming of War," in R. Evans and H. Pogge von Strandmann (eds), *The Coming of the First World War* (Oxford, 2001), pp. 87–8.
97. T. Ashton and B. Harrison (eds), *The History of the University of Oxford*, 8 vols (Oxford, 1994), 8, pp. 3–4.
98. For the details of the assassins' training, the attempts on Franz Ferdinand's life and his murder, see the court documents concerning the trial of Princip and his accomplices, *The Austro-Hungarian Red Book*, Section II, Appendices 1-13, nos. 20–34 (1914–15).
99. Clark, *Sleepwalkers*, p. 562.

100. E. Grey, *Twenty-Five Years, 1892–1916* (New York, 1925), p. 20.
101. I. Hull, "Kaiser Wilhelm II and the 'Liebenberg Circle,'" in J. Röhl and N. Sombart (eds), *Kaiser Wilhelm II: New Interpretations* (Cambridge, 1982), pp. 193–220; H. Herwig, "Germany," in R. Hamilton and H. Herwig, *The Origins of the First World War* (Cambridge, 2003), pp. 150–87.
102. Conversation with Sazonov, reported by V. Kokovtsov, *Out of my Past: The Memoirs of Count Kokovtsov, Russian Minister of Finance, 1904–1914*, ed. H. Fisher (Oxford, 1935), p. 348.
103. Bureau du Levant to Lecomte, 2 July 1908, *Archives des Ministres des Affaires Etrangères: correspondance politique et commerciale (nouvelle série) 1897–1918. Perse*, vol. 3, folio 191.
104. Clark, *Sleepwalkers*, pp. 325–6.
105. Clerk, "Anglo-Persian Relations in Persia," 21 July 1914, FO 371/2076/33484.
106. Buchanan to Nicolson, 16 April 1914, in Gooch and Temperley, *British Documents*, 10.2, pp. 784–5.
107. Buchanan to Grey, 25 July 1914, in Gooch and Temperley, *British Documents*, 11, p. 94.
108. "Memorandum communicated to Sir G. Buchanan by M. Sazonof," 11 July 1914, in FO 371/2076; M. Paléologue, *La Russie des tsars pendant la grande guerre*, 3 vols (Paris, 1921), 1, p. 23.
109. K. Jarausch, "The Illusion of Limited War: Bethmann Hollweg's Calculated Risk, July 1914," *Central European History* 2 (1969), 58; idem, *The Enigmatic Chancellor: Bethmann Hollweg and the Hubris of Imperial Germany* (London, 1973), p. 96.
110. J. McKay, *Pioneers for Profit: Foreign Entrepreneurship and Russian Industrialization, 1885–1913* (Chicago, 1970), pp. 28–9. Also here see D. Lieven, *Russia and the Origins of the First World War* (London, 1983); O. Figes, *A People's Tragedy: The Russian Revolution, 1891–1924* (London, 1996), esp. pp. 35–83.
111. D. Fromkin, "The Great Game in Asia," *Foreign Affairs* (1980), 951; G. D. Clayton, *Britain and the Eastern Question: Missolonghi to Gallipoli* (London, 1971), p. 139.
112. E. Vandiver, *Stand in the Trench, Achilles: Classical Receptions in British Poetry of the Great War* (Oxford, 2010), pp. 263–9.
113. H. Strachan, *The Outbreak of the First World War* (Oxford, 2004), pp. 181ff.
114. W. Churchill, *The World Crisis, 1911–1918, with New Introduction by Martin Gilbert* (New York, 2005), pp. 667–8; for the views about the Churchill family, Hardinge to O'Beirne, 9 July 1908, Hardinge MSS 30.
115. E. Campion Vaughan, *Some Desperate Glory* (Edinburgh, 1982), p. 232.
116. HM Stationery Office, *Statistics of the Military Efforts of the British Empire during the Great War, 1914–1920* (London, 1922), p. 643.
117. Grey to Goschen, 5 November 1908, FO 800/61, p. 2.
118. Rupert Brooke to Jacques Raverat, 1 August 1914, in G. Keynes (ed.), *The Letters of Rupert Brooke* (London, 1968), p. 603.
119. W. Letts, "The Spires of Oxford," in *The Spires of Oxford and Other Poems* (New York, 1917), pp. 3–4.

120. *The Treaty of Peace between the Allied and Associated Powers and Germany* (London, 1919).
121. Sanborn, *Imperial Apocalypse*, p. 233.
122. H. Strachan, *Financing the First World War* (Oxford, 2004), p. 188.
123. Ibid. Also see K. Burk, *Britain, America and the Sinews of War, 1914–1918* (Boston, 1985); M. Horn, *Britain, France and the Financing of the First World War* (Montreal, 2002), pp. 57–75.
124. Above all, Strachan, *Financing the First World War*; also see Ferguson, *Pity of War*, esp. pp. 318ff., and B. Eichengreen, *Golden Fetters: The Gold Standard and the Great Depression, 1919–1939* (Oxford, 1992).

CHAPTER 17—THE ROAD OF BLACK GOLD

1. D. Carment, "D'Arcy, William Knox," in B. Nairn and G. Serle (eds), *Australian Dictionary of Biography* (Melbourne, 1981), 8, pp. 207–8.
2. J. Banham and J. Harris (eds), *William Morris and the Middle Ages* (Manchester, 1984), pp. 187–92; L. Parry, "The Tapestries of Sir Edward Burne-Jones," *Apollo* 102 (1972), 324–8.
3. National Portrait Gallery, NPG 6251 (14), (15).
4. For the Background here see R. Ferrier and J. Bamburg, *The History of the British Petroleum Company*, 3 vols (London, 1982–2000), 1, pp. 29ff.
5. S. Cronin, "Importing Modernity: European Military Missions to Qajar Iran," *Comparative Studies in Society and History* 50.1 (2008), 197–226.
6. Lansdowne to Hardinge, 18 November 1902, in A. Hardinge, *A Diplomatist in the East* (London, 1928), pp. 286–96. Also see R. Greaves, "British Policy in Persia, 1892–1903 II," *Bulletin of the School of Oriental and African Studies* 28.2 (1965), 302–3.
7. Wolff to Kitabgi, 25 November 1900, D'Arcy Concession; Kitabgi Dossier and Correspondence regarding Kitabgi's claims, BP 69454.
8. See in general Th. Korres, *Hygron pyr: ena hoplo tes Vizantines nautikes taktikes* (Thessaloniki, 1989); J. Haldon, "A Possible Solution to the Problem of Greek Fire," *Byzantinische Zeitschrift* 70 (1977), 91–9; J. Partington, *A History of Greek Fire and Gunpowder* (Cambridge, 1960), pp. 1–41.
9. W. Loftus, "On the Geology of Portions of the Turco-Persian Frontier and of the Districts Adjoining," *Quarterly Journal of the Geological Society* 11 (1855), 247–344.
10. M. Elm, *Oil, Power, and Principle: Iran's Oil Nationalization and its Aftermath* (Syracuse, 1992), p. 2.
11. Letter of Sayyid Jamāl al-Dīn al-Afghānī to Mujtahid, in E. Browne, *The Persian Revolution of 1905–1909* (London, 1966), pp. 18–19.
12. P. Kazemzadeh, *Russia and Britain in Persia, 1864–1914: A Study in Imperialism* (New Haven, 1968), pp. 122, 127.
13. Griffin to Rosebery, 6 December 1893, FO 60/576.
14. Currie Minute, 28 October 1893, FO 60/576.

15. J. de Morgan, "Notes sur les gîtes de Naphte de Kend-e-Chirin (Gouvernement de Ser-i-Paul)," *Annales des Mines* (1892), 1–16; idem, Mission scientifique en Perse, 5 vols (Paris, 1894–1905); B. Redwood, *Petroleum: Its Production and Use* (New York, 1887); J. Thomson and B. Redwood, *Handbook on Petroleum for Inspectors under the Petroleum Acts* (London, 1901).
16. Kitabgi to Drummond-Wolff, 25 December 1900, Kitabgi Dossier and Correspondence regarding Kitabgi's claims, BP 69454.
17. Gosselin to Hardinge, 12 March 1901, FO 248/733; Marriott mentions the letter of introduction in his Diary, 17 April 1901, BP 70298.
18. Marriott Diary, pp. 16, 25, BP 70298.
19. Hardinge to Lansdowne, 12 May 1901, FO 60/640; Marriott Diary, BP 70298.
20. Marriott to Knox D'Arcy, 21 May, BP 70298; Knox D'Arcy to Marriott, 23 May, BP 70298.
21. Ferrier and Bamberg, *History of the British Petroleum Company*, pp. 33–41.
22. Ibid., Appendix 1, pp. 640–3.
23. N. Fatemi, *Oil Diplomacy: Powder Keg in Iran* (New York, 1954), p. 357.
24. Hardinge to Lansdowne, 30 May 1900, FO 60/731.
25. Marriott Diary, 23 May 1901, BP 70298.
26. Knox D'Arcy to Lansdowne, 27 June 1901, FO 60/731; Greaves, "British Policy in Persia," 296–8.
27. Hardinge to Lansdowne, 30 May 1900, FO 60/731.
28. Ferrier and Bamberg, *British Petroleum*, pp. 54–9.
29. D'Arcy to Reynolds, 15 April 1902, BP H12/24, p. 185.
30. Letter Book, Persian Concession 1901 to 1902, BP 69403.
31. Bell to Jenkin, 13 July, Cash Receipt Book, BP 69531.
32. A. Marder (ed.), *Fear God and Dread Nought: The Correspondence of Admiral the First Sea Lord Lord Fisher of Kilverstone*, 3 vols (Cambridge, MA, 1952), 1, p. 185. For this and for Britain's turn to oil before the First World War see Yergin, *The Prize*, pp. 134ff.
33. Kitabgi Dossier and Correspondence regarding Kitabgi's claims, BP 69454; Hardinge to Grey, 23 December 1905, FO 416/26; T. Corley, *A History of the Burmah Oil Company, 1886–1924* (London, 1983), pp. 95–111.
34. Ferrier and Bamberg, *British Petroleum*, pp. 86–8.
35. Ibid.
36. A. Wilson, *South West Persia: Letters and Diary of a Young Political Officer, 1907–1914* (London, 1941), p. 42.
37. Ibid.
38. Ibid., p. 103; Corley, *Burmah Oil Company*, pp. 128–45.
39. Fisher, *Fear God and Dread Nought*, 2, p. 404.
40. Churchill, *World Crisis*, pp. 75–6.
41. "Oil Fuel Supply for His Majesty's Navy," 19 June 1913, CAB 41/34.
42. Asquith to King George V, 12 July 1913, CAB 41/34.
43. Churchill, House of Commons, 17 July 1913, Hansard, 55, 1470.
44. Slade to Churchill, 8 November 1913, "Anglo-Persian Oil Company. Proposed Agreement, December 1913," ADM 116/3486.

45. Cited by D. Yergin, *The Prize: The Epic Quest for Oil, Money and Power* (3rd edn, New York, 2009), p. 167.
46. Cited by M. Aksakal, "'Holy War Made in Germany?' Ottoman Origins of the Jihad," *War in History* 18.2 (2011), 196.
47. F. Moberly, *History of the Great War Based on Official Documents: The Campaign in Mesopotamia 1914–1918*, 4 vols (London, 1923), 1, pp. 130–1.
48. Kitchener to HH The Sherif Abdalla, Enclosure in Cheetham to Grey, 13 December 1914, FO 371/1973/87396. Also here E. Karsh and I. Karsh, "Myth in the Desert, or Not the Great Arab Revolt," *Middle Eastern Studies* 33.2 (1997), 267–312.
49. J. Tomes, *Balfour and Foreign Policy: The International Thought of a Conservative Statesman* (Cambridge, 1997), p. 218.
50. Soroka, *Britain, Russia and the Road to the First World War*, pp. 201–36; Aksakal, *Ottoman Road to War*.
51. "Russian War Aims," Memo from British Embassy in Petrograd to the Russian government, 12 March 1917, in F. Golder, *Documents of Russian History 1914–1917* (New York, 1927), pp. 60–2.
52. Grey to McMahon, 8 March 1915, FO 800/48. For French investment before the war, see M. Raccagni, "The French Economic Interests in the Ottoman Empire," *International Journal of Middle East Studies* 11.3 (198), 339–76; V. Geyikdagi, "French Direct Investments in the Ottoman Empire Before World War I," *Enterprise & Society* 12.3 (2011), 525–61.
53. E. Kedourie, *In the Anglo-Arab Labyrinth: The McMahon–Husayn Correspondence and its Interpretations, 1914–1939* (Abingdon, 2000), pp. 53–5.
54. For the campaign, see P. Hart, *Gallipoli* (London, 2011).
55. *The Times*, 7 January 1918.
56. *The Times*, 12 January 1917.
57. C. Seymour (ed.), *The Intimate Papers of Colonel House*, 4 vols (Cambridge, MA, 1928), 3, p. 48.
58. Yergin, *The Prize*, pp. 169–72.
59. "Petroleum Situation in the British Empire and the Mesopotamia and Persian Oilfields," 1918, CAB 21/119.
60. Hankey to Balfour, 1 August 1918, FO 800/204.
61. Hankey to Prime Minister, 1 August 1918, CAB 23/119; V. Rothwell, "Mesopotamia in British War Aims, 1914–1918," *The Historical* Journal 13.2 (1970), 289–90.
62. War Cabinet minutes, 13 August 1918, CAB 23/42.
63. G. Jones, "The British Government and the Oil Companies 1912–24: The Search for an Oil Policy," *Historical Journal* 20.3 (1977), 655.
64. Petrol Control Committee, Second Report, 19 December 1916, Board of Trade, POWE 33/1.
65. "Reserves of Oil Fuel in U.K. and general position 1916 to 1918," minute by M. Seymour, 1 June 1917, MT 25/20; Jones, "British Government and the Oil Companies," 657.
66. B. Hendrick, *The Life and Letters of Walter H. Page*, 2 vols (London, 1930), 2, p. 288.

67. "Eastern Report, No 5," 28 February 1917, CAB 24/143.
68. Balfour to Lloyd George, 16 July 1918, Lloyd George Papers, F/3/3/18.

CHAPTER 18—THE ROAD TO COMPROMISE

1. Marling to Foreign Office, 24 December 1915, FO 371/2438/198432.
2. Hardinge to Gertrude Bell, 27 March 1917, Hardinge MSS 30.
3. Slade, "The Political Position in the Persian Gulf at the End of the War," 4 November 1916, CAB 16/36.
4. Europäische Staats und Wirtschafts Zeitung, 18 Aug 1916, CAB 16/36.
5. Hankey Papers, 20 December 1918; 4 December 1918 entry, 1/6, Churchill Archives Centre, Cambridge; E. P. Fitzgerald, "France's Middle Eastern Ambitions, the Sykes–Picot Negotiations, and the Oil Fields of Mosul, 1915–1918," *Journal of Modern History* 66.4 (1994), 694–725; D. Styan, *France and Iraq: Oil, Arms and French Policy-Making in the Middle East* (London, 2006), pp. 9–21.
6. A. Roberts, *A History of the English-Speaking Peoples since 1900* (London, 2006), p. 132.
7. *The Times*, 7 November 1917. For Samuel, see S. Huneidi, *A Broken Trust: Herbert Samuel, Zionism and the Palestinians* (London, 2001).
8. Lord Balfour, House of Lords, 21 June 1922, Hansard, 50, 1016–17.
9. "Report by the Sub-Committee," Imperial Defence, 13 June 1928, CAB 24/202.
10. *Time*, 21 April 1941; J. Barr, *A Line in the Sand: Britain, France and the Struggle that shaped the Middle East* (London, 2011), p. 163.
11. A. Arslanian, "Dunstersville's Adventures: A Reappraisal," *International Journal of Middle East Studies* 12.2 (1980), 199–216; A. Simonian, "An Episode from the History of the Armenian–Azerbaijani Confrontation (January–February 1919)," *Iran & the Caucasus* 9.1 (2005), 145–58.
12. Sanborn, *Imperial Apocalypse*, pp. 175–83.
13. Secretary of State to Viceroy, 5 January 1918, cited by L. Morris, "British Secret Missions in Turkestan, 1918–19," *Journal of Contemporary History* 12.2 (1977), 363–79.
14. See Morris, "British Secret Missions," 363–79.
15. L. Trotsky, Central Committee, Russian Communist Party, 5 August 1919, in J. Meijer (ed.), *The Trotsky Papers*, 2 vols (The Hague, 1964), 1, pp. 622, 624.
16. *Congress of the East, Baku, September 1920*, tr. B. Pearce (London, 1944), pp. 25–37.
17. L. Murawiec, *The Mind of Jihad* (Cambridge, 2008), pp. 210–23. More generally, see Ansari, "Pan-Islam and the Making of Early Indian Socialism," *Modern Asian Studies* 20 (1986), 509–37.
18. Corp. Charles Kavanagh, Unpublished diary, Cheshire Regiment Museum.
19. *Pobeda oktyabr'skoi revoliutsii v Uzbekistane: sbornik dokumentov*, 2 vols (Tashkent, 1963–72), 1, p. 571.
20. A copy of the poster appears in D. King, *Red Star over Russia: A Visual History of the Soviet Union from 1917 to the Death of Stalin* (London, 2009), p. 180.

21. M. MacMillan, *Peacemakers: Six Months that Changed the World* (London, 2001), p. 408.
22. Treaty with HM King Faisal, 20 October 1922, Command Paper 1757; Protocol of 30 April 1923 and Agreements Subsidiary to the Treaty with King Faisal, Command Paper 2120. For the new ceremonials, see E. Podeh, "From Indifference to Obsession: The Role of National State Celebrations in Iraq, 1921–2003," *British Journal of Middle Eastern Studies* 37.2 (2010), 185–6.
23. B. Busch, *Britain, India and the Arabs, 1914–1921* (Berkeley, 1971), pp. 408–10.
24. H. Katouzian, "The Campaign against the Anglo-Iranian Agreement of 1919," *British Journal of Middle Eastern Studies* 25.1 (1998), p. 10.
25. H. Katouzian, "Nationalist Trends in Iran, 1921–6," *International Journal of Middle Eastern Studies* 10.4 (1979), 539.
26. Cited by H. Katouzian, *Iranian History and Politics: The Dialectic of State and Society* (London, 2003), p. 167.
27. Curzon to Cambon, 11 March 1919, FO 371/3859.
28. See Katouzian, "The Campaign against the Anglo-Iranian Agreement," p. 17.
29. Marling to Foreign Office, 28 February 1916, FO 371/2732. Also see D. Wright, "Prince ʿAbd ul-Husayn Mirza Farman-Farma: Notes from British Sources," *Iran* 38 (2000), 107–14.
30. Loraine to Curzon, 31 January 1922, FO 371/7804.
31. M. Zirinsky, "Imperial Power and Dictatorship: Britain and the Rise of Reza Shah, 1921–1926," *International Journal of Middle East Studies* 24.4 (1992), 639–63.
32. Caldwell to Secretary of State, 5 April 1921, in M. Gholi Majd, *From Qajar to Pahlavi: Iran, 1919–1930* (Lanham, MA, 2008), pp. 96–7.
33. "Planning Committee, Office of Naval Operations to Benson," 7 October 1918, in M. Simpson (ed.), *Anglo-American Naval Relations, 1917–19* (Aldershot, 1991), pp. 542–3.
34. Cited by Yergin, *The Prize*, p. 178.
35. Cited by M. Rubin, "Stumbling through the 'Open Door': The US in Persia and the Standard–Sinclair Oil Dispute, 1920–1925," *Iranian Studies* 28.3/4 (1995), 206.
36. Ibid., 210.
37. Ibid.
38. Ibid., 209.
39. Ibid., 213.
40. M. Gilbert, *Winston S. Churchill*, 8 vols (London, 1966–88), 4, p. 638.
41. See M. Zirinsky, "Imperial Power and Dictatorship: Britain and the Rise of Reza Shah, 1921–1926," *International Journal of Middle East Studies* 24.4 (1992), 650; H. Mejcher, *Imperial Quest for Oil: Iraq 1910–1928* (London, 1976), p. 49.
42. For Egypt, see A. Maghraoui, *Liberalism without Democracy: Nationhood and Citizenship in Egypt, 1922–1936* (Durham, NC, 2006), pp. 54–5.
43. Cited by M. Fitzherbert, *The Man Who was Greenmantle: A Biography of Aubrey Herbert* (London, 1985), p. 219.
44. S. Pedersen, "Getting Out of Iraq—in 1932: The League of Nations and the

Road to Normative Statehood," *American Historical Review* 115.4 (2010), 993–1000.

45. Y. Ismael, *The Rise and Fall of the Communist Party of Iraq* (Cambridge, 2008), p. 12.
46. For the Purna Swaraj declaration, M. Gandhi, *The Collected Works of Mahatma Gandhi*, 90 vols (New Delhi, 1958–84), 48, p. 261.
47. Cited by Ferrier and Bamberg, *British Petroleum*, pp. 593–4.
48. "A Record of the Discussions Held at Lausanne on 23rd, 24th and 25th August, 1928," BP 71074.
49. Cadman to Teymourtache, 3 January 1929, BP 71074.
50. Young report of Lausanne discussions, BP H16/20; also see Ferrier and Bamberg, *British Petroleum*, pp. 601–17.
51. Vansittart minute, 29 November 1932, FO 371/16078.
52. Hoare to Foreign Office, 29 November 1932, FO 371/16078.
53. Lord Cadman's Private Diary, BP 96659/002.
54. Cadman, Notes, Geneva and Teheran, BP 96659.
55. G. Bell, *Gertrude Bell: Complete Letters* (London, 2014), p. 224.

CHAPTER 19—THE WHEAT ROAD

1. "Hitler's Mountain Home," *Homes & Gardens*, November 1938, 193–5.
2. A. Speer, *Inside the Third Reich*, tr. R. and C. Winston (New York, 1970), p. 161.
3. Ibid. For Kannenberg's accordion playing, C. Schroder, *Er War mein Chef. Aus den Nachlaß der Sekretärin von Adolf Hitler* (Munich, 1985), pp. 54, 58.
4. R. Hargreaves, *Blitzkrieg Unleashed: The German Invasion of Poland* (London, 2008), p. 66; H. Hegner, *Die Reichskanzlei 1933–1945: Anfang und Ende des Dritten Reiches* (Frankfurt-am-Main, 1959), pp. 334–7.
5. Speer, *Inside the Third Reich*, p. 162.
6. M. Muggeridge, *Ciano's Diary, 1939–1943* (London, 1947), pp. 9–10.
7. House of Commons Debate, 31 March 1939, Hansard, 345, 2415.
8. Ibid., 2416; see G. Roberts, *The Unholy Alliance: Stalin's Pact with Hitler* (London, 1989); R. Moorhouse, *The Devil's Alliance: Hitler's Pact with Stalin* (London, 2014).
9. L. Bezymenskii, *Stalin und Hitler. Pokerspiel der Diktatoren* (London, 1967), pp. 186–92.
10. J. Herf, *The Jewish Enemy: Nazi Propaganda during World War II and the Holocaust* (Cambridge, MA, 2006).
11. W. Churchill, *The Second World War*, 6 vols (London, 1948–53), 1, p. 328.
12. Bezymenskii, *Stalin und Hitler*, pp. 142, 206–9.
13. T. Snyder, *Bloodlands: Europe between Hitler and Stalin* (London, 2010), pp. 81, 93.
14. Cited by E. Jäckel and A. Kahn, *Hitler: Sämtliche Aufzeichnungen, 1905–1924* (Stuttgart, 1980), p. 186.
15. J. Weitz, *Hitler's Diplomat: The Life and Times of Joachim von Ribbentrop* (New York, 1992), p. 6.

16. S. Sebag Montefiore, *Stalin: The Court of the Red Tsar* (London, 2004), p. 317.
17. Hegner, *Die Reichskanzlei*, pp. 337–8, 342–3; for the treaty and its secret annexe, *Documents on German Foreign Policy, 1918–1945*, Series D, 13 vols (London, 1949–64), 7, pp. 245–7.
18. Sebag Montefiore, *Stalin*, p. 318.
19. N. Khrushchev, *Khrushchev Remembers*, tr. S. Talbott (Boston, MA, 1970), p. 128.
20. Besymenski, *Stalin und Hitler*, pp. 21–2; D. Volkogonov, *Stalin: Triumph and Tragedy* (New York, 1991), p. 352.
21. L. Kovalenko and V. Maniak, *33'i: Golod: Narodna kniga-memorial* (Kiev, 1991), p. 46, in Snyder, *Bloodlands*, p. 49; also see pp. 39–58.
22. For Vyshinskii and the show trials, see A. Vaksberg, *Stalin's Prosecutor: The Life of Andrei Vyshinsky* (New York, 1990), and N. Werth et al. (eds), *The Little Black Book of Communism: Crimes, Terror, Repression* (Cambridge, MA, 1999).
23. M. Jansen and N. Petrov, *Stalin's Loyal Executioner: People's Commissar Nikolai Ezhov, 1895–1940* (Stanford, 2002), p. 69.
24. V. Rogovin, *Partiya Rasstrelianykh* (Moscow, 1997), pp. 207–19; also Bezymenskii, *Stalin und Hitler*, p. 96; Volkogonov, *Stalin*, p. 368.
25. "Speech by the Führer to the Commanders in Chief," 22 August 1939, in *Documents on German Foreign Policy*, Series D, 7, pp. 200–4; I. Kershaw, *Hitler, 1936–45: Nemesis* (London, 2001), pp. 207–8.
26. "Second speech by the Führer," 22 August 1939, in *Documents on German Foreign Policy, 1918–1945*, Series D, p. 205.
27. "Speech by the Führer to the Commanders in Chief," p. 204.
28. K.-J. Müller, *Das Heer und Hitler: Armee und nationalsozialistisches Regime 1933–1940* (Stuttgart, 1969), p. 411, n. 153; Müller does not provide a supporting reference.
29. W. Baumgart, "Zur Ansprache Hitlers vor den Führern der Wehrmacht am 22. August 1939. Eine quellenkritische Untersuchung," *Viertejahreshefte für Zeitgeschichte* 16 (1968), 146; Kershaw, *Nemesis*, p. 209.
30. G. Corni, *Hitler and the Peasants: Agrarian Policy of the Third Reich, 1930–39* (New York, 1990), pp. 66–115.
31. See for example R.-D. Müller, "Die Konsequenzen der 'Volksgemeinschaft': Ernährung, Ausbeutung und Vernichtung," in W. Michalka (ed.), *Der Zweite Weltkrieg. Analysen-Grundzüge-Forschungsbilanz* (Weyarn, 1989), pp. 240–9.
32. A. Kay, *Exploitation, Resettlement, Mass Murder: Political and Economic Planning for German Occupation Policy in the Soviet Union, 1940–1941* (Oxford, 2006), p. 40.
33. A. Bondarenko (ed.), *God krizisa: 1938–1939: dokumenty i materialy v dvukh tomakh*, 2 vols (Moscow, 1990), 2, pp. 157–8.
34. E. Ericson, *Feeding the German Eagle: Soviet Economic Aid to Nazi Germany, 1933–1941* (Westport, CT, 1999), pp. 41ff.
35. A. Bullock, *Hitler: A Study in Tyranny* (London, 1964), p. 719.
36. S. Fritz, *Ostkrieg: Hitler's War of Extermination in the East* (2011), p. 39.
37. C. Browning, *The Origins of the Final Solution: The Evolution of Nazi Jewish Policy, September 1939–March 1942* (Lincoln, NE, 2004), p. 16; Snyder, *Bloodlands*, p. 126.

38. War Cabinet, 8 September 1939, CAB 65/1; A. Prazmowska, *Britain, Poland and the Eastern Front, 1939* (Cambridge, 1987), p. 182.
39. British Legation Kabul to Foreign Office London, Katodon 106, 24 September 1939, cited by M. Hauner, "The Soviet Threat to Afghanistan and India, 1938–1940," *Modern Asian Studies* 15.2 (1981), 297.
40. Hauner, "Soviet Threat to Afghanistan and India," 298.
41. Report by the Chiefs of Staff Committee, "The Military Implications of Hostilities with Russia in 1940," 8 March 1940, CAB 66/6.
42. "Appreciation of the Situation Created by the Russo-German Agreement," 6 October 1939, CAB 84/8; see here M. Hauner, *India in Axis Strategy: Germany, Japan and Indian Nationalists in the Second World War* (Stuttgart, 1981), esp. 213–37.
43. Hauner, *India in Axis Strategy*, 70–92.
44. M. Hauner, "Anspruch und Wirklichkeit: Deutschland also Dritte Macht in Afghanistan, 1915–39," in K. Kettenacker et al. (eds), *Festschrift für Paul Kluge* (Munich, 1981), pp. 222–44; idem, "Afghanistan before the Great Powers, 1938–45," *International Journal of Middle East Studies* 14.4 (1982), 481–2.
45. "Policy and the War Effort in the East," 6 January 1940, *Documents on German Foreign Policy, 1918–1945*, Series D, 8, pp. 632–3.
46. "Memorandum of the Aussenpolitisches Amt," 18 December 1939, *Documents on German Foreign Policy, 1918–1945*, Series D, 8, p. 533; Hauner, *India in Axis Strategy*, pp. 159–72.
47. M. Hauner, "One Man against the Empire: The Faqir of Ipi and the British in Central Asia on the Eve of and during the Second World War," *Journal of Contemporary History* 16.1 (1981), 183–212.
48. Rubin and Schwanitz, *Nazis, Islamists*, p. 4 n. 13.
49. S. Hauser, "German Research on the Ancient Near East and its Relation to Political and Economic Interests from Kaiserreich to World War II," in W. Schwanitz (ed.), *Germany and the Middle East, 1871–1945* (Princeton, 2004), pp. 168–9; M. Ghods, *Iran in the Twentieth Century: A Political History* (Boulder, CO, 2009), pp. 106–8.
50. Rubin and Schwanitz, *Nazis, Islamists*, p. 128.
51. Cited in ibid., p. 5.
52. T. Imlay, "A Reassessment of Anglo-French Strategy during the Phony War, 1939–1940," *English Historical Review* 119.481 (2004), 337–8.
53. First Lord's Personal Minute, 17 November 1939, ADM 205/2. See here Imlay, "Reassessment of Anglo-French Strategy," 338, 354–9.
54. Imlay, "Reassessment of Anglo-French Strategy," 364.
55. CAB 104/259, "Russia: Vulnerability of Oil Supplies," JIC (39) 29 revise, 21 November 1939; Imlay, "Reassessment of Anglo-French Strategy," 363–8.
56. For Guderian, and for Hitler's repeated loss of nerve, see K. H. Frieser, *Blitzkrieg-Legende. Der Westfeldung 1940* (Munich, 1990), pp. 240–3, 316–22.
57. See M. Hauner, "Afghanistan between the Great Powers, 1938–1945," *International Journal of Middle East Studies* 14.4 (1982), 487; for the proposed reduction in freight costs, Ministry of Economic Warfare, 9 January 1940, FO 371/24766.
58. Ericson, *Feeding the German Eagle*, pp. 109–18.

59. Fritz, *Ostkrieg*, pp. 38–41.
60. J. Förster, "Hitler's Decision in Favour of War against the Soviet Union," in H. Boog, J. Förster et al. (eds), *Germany and the Second World War*, vol. 4: *The Attack on the Soviet Union* (Oxford, 1996), p. 22; also see Kershaw, *Nemesis*, p. 307.
61. Corni, *Hitler and the Peasants*, pp. 126–7, 158–9, 257–60. Also see H. Backe, *Die Nahrungsfreiheit Europas: Großliberalismus in der Wirtschaft* (Berlin, 1938).
62. V. Gnucheva, "Materialy dlya istorii ekspeditsii nauk v XVIII i XX vekakh," *Trudy Arkhiva Akademii Nauk SSSR* 4 (Moscow, 1940), esp. 97–108.
63. M. Stroganova (ed.), *Zapovedniki evropeiskoi chasti RSFSR* (Moscow, 1989); C. Kremenetski, "Human Impact on the Holocene Vegetation of the South Russian Plain," in J. Chapman and P. Dolukhanov (eds), *Landscapes in Flux: Central and Eastern Europe in Antiquity* (Oxford, 1997), pp. 275–87.
64. H. Backe, *Die russische Getreidewirtschaft als Grundlage der Land- und Volkswirtschaft Rußlands* (Berlin, 1941).
65. Bundesarchiv-Militärarchiv, RW 19/164, fo. 126, cited by Kay, *Exploitation*, pp. 211, 50.
66. Cited by A. Hillgruber, *Hitlers Strategie: Politik und Kriegführung 1940–1941* (Frankfurt-am-Main, 1965), p. 365.
67. "Geheime Absichtserklärungen zur künftigen Ostpolitik: Auszug aus einem Aktenvermerk von Reichsleiter M. Bormann vom 16.7.1941," in G. Uebershär and W. Wette (eds), *Unternehmen Barbarossa: Der deutsche Überfall auf die Sowjetunion, 1941: Berichte, Anaylsen, Dokumente* (Paderborn, 1984), pp. 330–1.
68. G. Corni and H. Gies, *Brot—Butter—Kanonen. Die Ernährungswirtschaft in Deutschland unter der Diktatur Hitlers* (Berlin, 1997), p. 451; R.-D. Müller, "Das 'Unternehmen Barbarossa' als wirtschaftlicher Raubkrieg," in Uebershär and Wette, *Unternehmen Barbarossa*, p. 174.
69. German radio broadcast, 27 February 1941, Propaganda Research Section Papers, 6 December 1940, Abrams Papers, 3f 65; 3f 8/41.
70. *Die Tagebücher von Joseph Goebbels*, ed. E. Fröhlich, 15 vols (Munich, 1996), 28 June 1941, *Teil I*, 9, p. 409; 14 July, *Teil II*, 1, pp. 63–4.
71. Kershaw, *Nemesis*, pp. 423–4.
72. Private correspondence of Backe, cited by G. Gerhard, "Food and Genocide: Nazi Agrarian Politics in the Occupied Territories of the Soviet Union," *Contemporary European History* 18.1 (2009), 56.
73. "Aktennotiz über Ergebnis der heutigen Besprechung mit den Staatssekretären über Barbarossa," in A. Kay, "Germany's Staatssekretäre, Mass Starvation and the Meeting of 2 May 1941," *Journal of Contemporary History* 41.4 (2006), 685–6.
74. Kay, "Mass Starvation and the Meeting of 2 May 1941," 687.
75. "Wirtschaftspolitische Richtlinien für Wirtschaftsorganisation Ost, Gruppe Landwirtschaft," 23 May 1941, in *Der Prozess gegen die Hauptkriegsverbrecher vor dem Internationalen Militärgerichtshof, Nürnberg 14 November 1945—1 October 1946*, 42 vols (Nuremberg, 1947–9), 36, pp. 135–7. A similar report was issued three weeks later on 16 June, Kay, *Exploitation*, pp. 164–7.

76. Backe, *Die russische Getreidewirtschaft*, cited by Gerhard, "Food and Genocide," 57–8; also Kay, "Mass Starvation," 685–700.
77. H. Backe, "12 Gebote für das Verhalten der Deutschen im Osten und die Behandlung der Russen," in R. Rürup (ed.), *Der Krieg gegen die Sowjetunion 1941–1945: Eine Dokumentation* (Berlin, 1991), p. 46; Gerhard, "Food and Genocide," 59.
78. *Die Tagebücher von Joseph Goebbels*, 1 May 1941, *Teil I*, 9, pp. 283–4.
79. Ibid., 9 July 1941, *Teil II*, 1, pp. 33–4.
80. Russian radio broadcast, 19 June 1941, Propaganda Research Section Papers, Abrams Papers, 3f 24/41.
81. F. Halder, *The Halder War Diary*, ed. C. Burdick and H.-A. Jacobsen (London, 1988), 30 March 1941, pp. 345–6.
82. 19 May 1941, *Verbrechen der Wehrmacht: Dimensionen des Vernichtungskrieges 1941–1945. Ausstellungskatalog* (Hamburg 2002), pp. 53–5.
83. "Ausübund der Kriegsgerichtsbarkeit im Gebiet 'Barbarossa' und besondere Maßnahmen Truppe," 14 May 1941, in H. Bucheim, M. Broszat, J.-A. Jacobsen and H. Krasunick, *Anatomie des SS-Staates*, 2 vols (Olten, 1965), 2, pp. 215–18.
84. "Richtlinien für die Behandlung politischer Kommissare," 6 June 1941, in Bucheim et al., *Anatomie des SS-Staates*, pp. 225–7.

CHAPTER 20—THE ROAD TO GENOCIDE

1. C. Streit, *Keine Kameraden. Die Wehrmacht und die sowjetischen Kriegsgefangenen 1941–1945* (Stuttgart, 1978), pp. 143, 153.
2. Cited by Kershaw, *Nemesis*, p. 359.
3. Ibid., p. 360.
4. Ibid., pp. 400, 435.
5. W. Lower, *Nazi Empire Building and the Holocaust in Ukraine* (Chapel Hill, NC, 2007), pp. 171–7.
6. A. Hitler, *Monologe im Führer-Hauptquartier 1941–1944*, ed. W. Jochmann (Hamburg, 1980), 17–18 September 1941, pp. 62–3; Kershaw, *Nemesis*, p. 401.
7. Cited by Kershaw, *Nemesis*, p. 434.
8. Hitler, *Monologe*, 13 October 1941, p. 78; Kershaw, *Nemesis*, p. 434.
9. Ericson, *Feeding the German Eagle*, pp. 125ff.
10. V. Anfilov, ". . . Razgovor zakonchilsia ugrozoi Stalina," *Voenno-istoricheskiy Zhurnal* 3 (1995), 41; L. Bezymenskii, "O 'plane' Zhukova ot 15 maia 1941 g.," *Novaya Noveishaya Istoriya* 3 (2000), 61. See here E. Mawdsley, "Crossing the Rubicon: Soviet Plans for Offensive War in 1940–1941," *International History Review* 25 (2003), 853.
11. D. Murphy, *What Stalin Knew: The Enigma of Barbarossa* (New Haven, 2005).
12. R. Medvedev and Z. Medvedev, *The Unknown Stalin: His Life, Death and Legacy* (London, 2003), p. 226.
13. G. Zhukov, *Vospominaniya i rasmyshleniya*, 3 vols (Moscow, 1995), 1, p. 258.
14. Assarasson to Stockholm, 21 June 1941, cited by G. Gorodetsky, *Grand Delusion: Stalin and the German Invasion of Russia* (New Haven, 1999), p. 306.

15. *Dokumenty vneshnei politiki SSSR*, 24 vols (Moscow, 1957–), 23.2, pp. 764–5.
16. A. Tooze, *The Wages of Destruction: The Making and Breaking of the Nazi Economy* (New York, 2006), pp. 452–60; R. di Nardo, *Mechanized Juggernaut or Military Anachronism? Horses and the German Army of World War II* (Westport, CT, 1991), pp. 35–54.
17. Cited by Beevor, *Stalingrad* (London, 1998), p. 26.
18. J. Stalin, *O Velikoi Otechestvennoi voine Sovestkogo Soiuza* (Moscow, 1944), p. 11.
19. A. von Plato, A. Leh and C. Thonfeld (eds), *Hitler's Slaves: Life Stories of Forced Labourers in Nazi-Occupied Europe* (Oxford, 2010).
20. E. Radzinsky, *Stalin* (London, 1996), p. 482; N. Ponomariov, cited by I. Kershaw, *Fateful Choices: Ten Decisions that Changed the World, 1940–1941* (London, 2007), p. 290.
21. Fritz, *Ostkrieg*, p. 191.
22. H. Trevor-Roper, *Hitler's Table Talk, 1941–1944: His Private Conversations* (London, 1953), p. 28.
23. W. Lower, "'On Him Rests the Weight of the Administration': Nazi Civilian Rulers and the Holocaust in Zhytomyr," in R. Brandon and W. Lower (eds), *The Shoah in Ukraine: History, Testimony, Memorialization* (Bloomington, IN, 2008), p. 225.
24. E. Steinhart, "Policing the Boundaries of 'Germandom' in the East: SS Ethnic German Policy and Odessa's 'Volksdeutsche', 1941–1944," *Central European History* 43.1 (2010), 85–116.
25. W. Hubatsch, *Hitlers Weisungen für die Kriegführung 1939–1945. Dokumente des Oberkommandos der Wehrmacht* (Munich, 1965), pp. 139–40.
26. Rubin and Schwanitz, *Nazis, Islamists*, pp. 124, 127.
27. Ibid., p. 85; H. Lindemann, *Der Islam im Aufbruch, in Abwehr und Angriff* (Leipzig, 1941).
28. Churchill, *Second World War*, 3, p. 424.
29. A. Michie, "War in Iran: British Join Soviet Allies," *Life*, 26 January 1942, 46.
30. R. Sanghvi, *Aryamehr: The Shah of Iran: A Political Biography* (London, 1968), p. 59; H. Arfa, *Under Five Shahs* (London, 1964), p. 242.
31. Bullard to Foreign Office, 25 June 1941, in R. Bullard, *Letters from Teheran: A British Ambassador in World War II Persia*, ed. E. Hodgkin (London, 1991), p. 60.
32. Lambton to Bullard, 4 October 1941, FO 416/99.
33. Intelligence Summary for 19–30 November, 2 December 1941, FO 416/99.
34. "Minister in Iran to the Foreign Ministry," 9 July 1941, *Documents on German Foreign Policy, 1918–1945*, Series D, 13, pp. 103–4.
35. P. Dharm and B. Prasad (eds), *Official History of the Indian Armed Forces in the Second World War, 1939–1945: The Campaign in Western Asia* (Calcutta, 1957), pp. 126–8.
36. Cited by J. Connell, *Wavell: Supreme Commander* (London, 1969), pp. 23–4.
37. R. Stewart, *Sunrise at Abadan: The British and Soviet Invasions of Iran, 1941* (New York, 1988), p. 59, n. 26.
38. "Economic Assistance to the Soviet Union," *Department of State Bulletin* 5 (1942), 109.

39. R. Sherwood, *The White House Papers of Harry L. Hopkins*, 2 vols (Washington, DC, 1948), 1, pp. 306–9.
40. Michie, "War in Iran," 40–4.
41. Bullard, *Letters*, p. 80.
42. Reza Shah Pahlavi to Roosevelt, 25 August 1941; Roosevelt to Reza Shah Pahlavi, 2 September 1941, cited by M. Majd, *August 1941: The Anglo-Russian Occupation of Iran and Change of Shahs* (Lanham, MD, 2012), pp. 232–3; Stewart, *Abadan*, p. 85.
43. J. Buchan, *Days of God: The Revolution in Iran and its Consequences* (London, 2012), p. 27.
44. Military attaché, "Intelligence summary 27," 19 November 1941, FO 371 27188.
45. R. Dahl, *Going Solo* (London, 1986), p. 193.
46. F. Halder, *Kriegstagebuch: tägliche Aufzeichnungen des Chefs des Generalstabes des Heeres, 1939–1942*, ed. H.-A. Jacobson and A. Philippi, 3 vols (Stuttgart, 1964), 3, 10 September 1941, p. 220; 17 September 1941, p. 236.
47. D. Stahel, *Kiev 1941: Hitler's Battle for Supremacy in the East* (Cambridge, 2012), pp. 133–4.
48. H. Pichler, *Truppenarzt und Zeitzeuge. Mit der 4. SS-Polizei-Division an vorderster Front* (Dresden, 2006), p. 98.
49. *Die Tagebücher von Joseph Goebbels*, 27 August 1941, *Teil II*, 1, p. 316.
50. Cited by Beevor, *Stalingrad*, pp. 56–7.
51. Fritz, *Ostkrieg*, pp. 158–9.
52. A. Hillgruber, *Staatsmänner und Diplomaten bei Hitler. Vertrauliche Aufzeichungen 1939–1941* (Munich, 1969), p. 329.
53. W. Kemper, "Pervitin—Die Endsieg-Droge," in W. Pieper (ed.), *Nazis on Speed: Drogen im Dritten Reich* (Lohrbach, 2003), pp. 122–33.
54. R.-D. Müller, "The Failure of the Economic 'Blitzkrieg Strategy,'" in H. Boog et al. (eds), *The Attack on the Soviet Union*, vol. 4 of W. Deist et al. (eds), *Germany and the Second World War*, 9 vols (Oxford, 1998), pp. 1127–32; Fritz, *Ostkrieg*, p. 150.
55. M. Guglielmo, "The Contribution of Economists to Military Intelligence during World War II," *Journal of Economic History* 66.1 (2008), esp. 116–20.
56. R. Overy, *War and the Economy in the Third Reich* (Oxford, 1994), pp. 264, 278; J. Barber and M. Harrison, *The Soviet Home Front, 1941–1945: A Social and Economic History of the USSR in World War II* (New York, 1991), pp. 78–9.
57. A. Milward, *War, Economy and Society, 1939–45* (Berkeley, 1977), pp. 262–73; Tooze, *Wages of Destruction*, pp. 513–51.
58. German radio broadcast, 5 November 1941, Propaganda Research Section Papers, Abrams Papers, 3f 44/41.
59. "Gains of Germany (and her Allies) through the Occupation of Soviet Territory," in Coordinator of Information, *Research and Analysis Branch, East European Section Report*, 17 (March 1942), pp. 10–11.
60. "Reich Marshal of the Greater German Reich," 11th meeting of the General Council, 24 June 1941, cited by Müller, "Failure of the Economic 'Blitzkrieg Strategy,'" p. 1142.
61. Halder, *Kriegstagebuch*, 8 July 1941, 3, p. 53.

62. C. Streit, "The German Army and the Politics of Genocide," in G. Hirschfeld (ed.), *The Policies of Genocide: Jews and Soviet Prisoners of War in Nazi Germany* (London, 1986), pp. 8–9.
63. J. Hürter, *Hitlers Heerführer. Die deutschen Oberbefehlshaber im Krieg gegen die Sowjetunion 1941/1942* (Munich, 2006), p. 370.
64. Streit, *Keine Kameraden*, p. 128; also see Snyder, *Bloodlands*, pp. 179–84.
65. R. Overmans, "Die Kriegsgefangenenpolitik des Deutschen Reiches 1939 bis 1945," in J. Echternkamp (ed.), *Das Deutsche Reich und der Zweite Weltkrieg*, 10 vols (Munich, 1979–2008), 9.2, p. 814; Browning, *Origins of the Final Solution*, p. 357; Snyder, *Bloodlands*, pp. 185–6.
66. K. Berkhoff, "The 'Russian' Prisoners of War in Nazi-Ruled Ukraine as Victims of Genocidal Massacre," *Holocaust and Genocide Studies* 15.1 (2001), 1–32.
67. Röhl, *The Kaiser and his Court*, p. 210. For the Kaiser's attitudes to Jews, see L. Cecil, "Wilhelm II und die Juden," in W. Mosse (ed.), *Juden im Wilhelminischen Deutschland, 1890–1914* (Tübingen, 1976), pp. 313–48.
68. Hitler's speech to the Reichstag, 30 January 1939, in *Verhandlungen des Reichstags, Stenographische Berichte 4. Wahlperiode 1939–1942* (Bad Feilnbach, 1986), p. 16.
69. Rubin and Schwanitz, *Nazis, Islamists*, p. 94.
70. H. Jansen, *Der Madagaskar-Plan: Die beabsichtigte Deportation der europäischen Juden nach Madagaskar* (Munich, 1997), esp. pp. 309–11. For theories about the Malagasy, see E. Jennings, "Writing Madagascar Back into the Madagascar Plan," *Holocaust and Genocide Studies* 21.2 (2007), 191.
71. F. Nicosia, "Für den Status-Quo: Deutschland und die Palästinafrage in der Zwischenkriegszeit," in L. Schatkowski Schilcher and C. Scharf (eds), *Der Nahe Osten in der Zwischenkriegszeit 1919–1939. Die Interdependenz von Politik, Wirtschaft und Ideologie* (Stuttgart, 1989), p. 105.
72. D. Cesarani, *Eichmann: His Life and Crimes* (London, 2004), pp. 53–6.
73. Cited by D. Yisraeli, *The Palestinian Problem in German Politics, 1889–1945* (Ramat-Gan, 1974), p. 315.
74. J. Heller, *The Stern Gang: Ideology, Politics and Terror, 1940–1949* (London, 1995), pp. 85–7.
75. T. Jersak, "Blitzkrieg Revisited: A New Look at Nazi War and Extermination Planning," *Historical Journal* 43.2 (2000), 582.
76. See above all G. Aly, "'Judenumsiedlung': Überlegungen zur politischen Vorgeschichte des Holocaust," in U. Herbert (ed.), *Nationalsozialistische Vernichtungspolitik 1939–1945: neue Forschungen und Kontroversen* (Frankfurt-am-Main, 1998), pp. 67–97.
77. Streit, "The German Army and the Politics of Genocide," p. 9; Fritz, *Ostkrieg*, p. 171.
78. J.-M. Belière and L. Chabrun, *Les Policiers français sous l'Occupation, d'après les archives inédites de l'épuration* (Paris, 2001), pp. 220–4; P. Griffioen and R. Zeller, "Anti-Jewish Policy and Organization of the Deportations in France and the Netherlands, 1940–1944: A Comparative Study," *Holocaust and Genocide Studies* 20.3 (2005), 441.

79. L. de Jong, *Het Koninkrijk der Nederlanden in de Tweede Wereldoorlog*, 14 vols (The Hague, 1969–1991), 4, pp. 99–110.
80. For the Wannsee conference, C. Gerlach, "The Wannsee Conference, the Fate of German Jews, and Hitler's Decision in Principle to Exterminate All European Jews," *Journal of Modern History* 70 (1998), 759–812; Browning, *Origins of the Final Solution*, pp. 374ff.
81. R. Coakley, "The Persian Corridor as a Route for Aid to the USSR," in M. Blumenson, K. Greenfield et al., *Command Decisions* (Washington, DC, 1960), pp. 225–53; also T. Motter, *The Persian Corridor and Aid to Russia* (Washington, DC, 1952).
82. For the convoys, R. Woodman, *Arctic Convoys, 1941–1945* (London, 2004).
83. J. MacCurdy, "Analysis of Hitler's Speech on 26th April 1942," 10 June 1942, Abrams Archive, Churchill College, Cambridge.
84. E. Schwaab, *Hitler's Mind: A Plunge into Madness* (New York, 1992).
85. Rubin and Schwanitz, *Nazis, Islamists*, pp. 139–41. In general, M. Carver, *El Alamein* (London, 1962).
86. For the U.S. in the Pacific, see H. Willmott, *The Second World War in the Far East* (London, 2012); also see A. Kernan, *The Unknown Battle of Midway: The Destruction of the American Torpedo Squadrons* (New Haven, 2005).
87. Cited by Fritz, *Ostkrieg*, p. 235; for the context, pp. 231–9.
88. Ibid., pp. 261–70; Speer, *Inside the Third Reich*, p. 215.
89. For the visit to Moscow in October 1944, see CAB 120/158.
90. M. Gilbert, *Churchill: A Life* (London, 1991), p. 796; R. Edmonds, "Churchill and Stalin," in R. Blake and R. Louis (eds), *Churchill* (Oxford, 1996), p. 320. Also Churchill, *Second World War*, 6, pp. 227–8.
91. W. Churchill, "The Sinews of Peace," 5 March 1946, in J. Muller (ed.), *Churchill's "Iron Curtain" Speech Fifty Years Later* (London, 1999), pp. 8–9.
92. D. Reynolds, *From World War to Cold War: Churchill, Roosevelt, and the International History of the 1940s* (Oxford, 2006), pp. 250–3.
93. M. Hastings, *All Hell Let Loose: The World at War, 1939–1945* (London, 2011), pp. 165–82; Beevor, *Stalingrad*, passim.
94. See A. Applebaum, *Iron Curtain: The Crushing of Eastern Europe, 1944–56* (London, 2012).

CHAPTER 21—THE ROAD OF COLD WARFARE

1. A. Millspaugh, *Americans in Persia* (Washington, DC, 1946), Appendix C; B. Kuniholm, *The Origins of the Cold War in the Near East: Great Power Conflict and Diplomacy in Iran, Turkey and Greece* (Princeton, 1980), pp. 138–43.
2. The Minister in Iran (Dreyfus) to the Secretary of State, 21 August 1941, *Foreign Relations of the United States, Diplomatic Papers 1941*, 7 vols (Washington, DC, 1956–62), 3, p. 403.
3. Ali Dashti, writing in December 1928, cited by Buchan, *Days of God*, p. 73.
4. B. Schulze-Holthus, *Frührot in Persien* (Esslingen, 1952), p. 22. Schulze-Holthus was sent to Iran by the Abwehr (German military intelligence) as vice-consul

in the city of Tabriz. He remained under cover in Teheran during the war, canvassing support among anti-Allied factions. Also see here S. Seydi, "Intelligence and Counter-Intelligence Activities in Iran during the Second World War," *Middle Eastern Studies* 46.5 (2010), 733–52.

5. Bullard, *Letters*, p. 154.
6. Ibid., p. 216.
7. Ibid., p. 187.
8. C. de Bellaigue, *Patriot of Persia: Muhammad Mossadegh and a Very British Coup* (London, 2012), pp. 120–3.
9. Shepherd to Furlonge, 6 May 1951, FO 248/1514.
10. *The Observer*, 20 May 1951, FO 248/1514.
11. Cited by de Bellaigue, *Patriot of Persia*, p. 123, n. 12.
12. Buchan, *Days of God*, p. 82.
13. L. Elwell-Sutton, *Persian Oil: A Study in Power Politics* (London, 1955), p. 65.
14. Ibid.
15. C. Bayly and T. Harper, *Forgotten Armies: The Fall of British Asia, 1841–1945* (London, 2004), pp. 182, 120.
16. I. Chawla, "Wavell's Breakdown Plan, 1945–47: An Appraisal," *Journal of Punjabi Studies* 16.2 (2009), 219–34.
17. W. Churchill, House of Commons debates, 6 March 1947, Hansard, 434, 676–7.
18. See L. Chester, *Borders and Conflict in South Asia: The Radcliffe Boundary Commission and the Partition of the Punjab* (Manchester, 2009). Also A. von Tunzelmann, *Indian Summer: The Secret History of the End of an Empire* (London, 2007).
19. I. Talbot, "Safety First: The Security of Britons in India, 1946–1947," *Transactions of the RHS* 23 (2013), pp. 203–21.
20. K. Jeffrey, *MI6: The History of the Secret Intelligence Service, 1909–1949* (London, 2010), pp. 689–90.
21. N. Rose, *"A Senseless, Squalid War": Voices from Palestine 1890s–1948* (London, 2010), pp. 156–8.
22. A. Halamish, *The Exodus Affair: Holocaust Survivors and the Struggle for Palestine* (Syracuse, NY, 1998).
23. Cited by J. Glubb, *A Soldier with the Arabs* (London, 1957), pp. 63–6.
24. E. Karsh, *Rethinking the Middle East* (London, 2003), pp. 172–89.
25. F. Hadid, *Iraq's Democratic Moment* (London, 2012), pp. 126–36.
26. Beeley to Burrows, 1 November 1947, FO 371/61596/E10118.
27. Outward Saving Telegram, 29 July 1947; Busk to Burrows, 3 November 1947, FO 371/61596.
28. K. Kwarteng, *Ghosts of Empire: Britain's Legacies in the Modern World* (London, 2011), p. 50.
29. B. Uvarov and A. Waterston, "MEALU General Report of Anti-Locust Campaign, 1942–1947," 19 September 1947, FO 371/61564.
30. N. Tumarkin, "The Great Patriotic War as Myth and Memory," *European Review* 11.4 (2003), 595–7.
31. J. Stalin, "Rech na predvybornom sobranii izbiratelei Stalinskogo izbiratel'nogo

okruga goroda Moskvy," in J. Stalin, *Sochineniya*, ed. R. McNeal, 3 vols (Stanford, CA, 1967), 3, p. 2.

32. B. Pimlott (ed.), *The Second World War Diary of Hugh Dalton, 1940–45* (London, 1986), 23 February 1945, marginal insertion, p. 836, n. 1.
33. It seems these words were added by Churchill on the train on the way to Fulton, J. Ramsden, "Mr. Churchill Goes to Fulton," in Muller, *Churchill's "Iron Curtain" Speech: Fifty Years Later*, p. 42. In general, P. Wright, *Iron Curtain: From Stage to Cold War* (Oxford, 2007).
34. B. Rubin, *The Great Powers in the Middle East, 1941–1947: The Road to the Cold War* (London, 1980), pp. 73ff.
35. "Soviet Military and Political Intentions, Spring 1949," Report No. 7453, 9 December 1948.
36. K. Blake, *The US–Soviet Confrontation in Iran 1945–62: A Case in the Annals of the Cold War* (Lanham, MD, 2009), pp. 17–18.
37. "General Patrick J. Hurley, Personal Representative of President Roosevelt, to the President," 13 May 1943, *FRUS, Diplomatic Papers 1943: The Near East and Africa*, 4, pp. 363–70.
38. Millspaugh, *Americans in Persia*, p. 77.
39. A. Offner, *Another Such Victory: President Truman and the Cold War, 1945–53* (Stanford, 2002), p. 128.
40. "The Chargé in the Soviet Union (Kennan) to the Secretary of State," 22 February 1946, *FRUS 1946: Eastern Europe, the Soviet Union*, 6, pp. 696–709.
41. D. Kisatsky, "Voice of America and Iran, 1949–1953: US Liberal Developmentalism, Propaganda and the Cold War," *Intelligence and National Security* 14.3 (1999), 160.
42. "The Present Crisis in Iran, undated paper presented in the Department of State," *FRUS, 1950: The Near East, South Asia, and Africa*, 5, pp. 513, 516.
43. M. Byrne, "The Road to Intervention: Factors Influencing US Policy toward Iran, 1945–53," in M. Gasiorowski and M. Byrne (eds), *Mohammad Mosaddeq and the 1953 Coup in Iran* (Syracuse, NY, 2004), p. 201.
44. Kisatsky, "Voice of America and Iran," 167, 174.
45. M. Gasiorowski, *US Foreign Policy and the Shah: Building a Client State in Iran* (Ithaca, NY, 1991), pp. 10–19.
46. Buchan, *Days of God*, pp. 30–1.
47. Cited by Yergin, *The Prize*, p. 376.
48. A. Miller, *Search for Security: Saudi Arabian Oil and American Foreign Policy, 1939–1949* (Chapel Hill, NC, 1980), p. 131.
49. E. DeGolyer, "Preliminary Report of the Technical Oil Mission to the Middle East," *Bulletin of the American Association of Petroleum Geologists* 28 (1944), 919–23.
50. "Summary of Report on Near Eastern Oil," 3 February 1943, in Yergin, *The Prize*, p. 375.
51. Beaverbrook to Churchill, 8 February 1944, cited by K. Young, *Churchill and Beaverbrook: A Study in Friendship and Politics* (London, 1966), p. 261.
52. Foreign Office memo, February 1944, FO 371/42688.
53. Churchill to Roosevelt, 20 February 1944, FO 371/42688.

54. Halifax to Foreign Office, 20 February 1944, FO 371/42688; Z. Brzezinski, *Strategic Vision: America and the Crisis of Global Power* (New York, 2012), p. 14.
55. *Historical Statistics of the United States: Colonial Times to 1970* (Washington, DC, 1970); Yergin, *The Prize*, p. 391.
56. Yergin, *The Prize*, p. 429.
57. W. Louis, *The British Empire in the Middle East, 1945–51: Arab Nationalism, the United States and Postwar Imperialism* (Oxford, 1984), p. 647.
58. Yergin, *The Prize*, p. 433.
59. de Bellaigue, *Patriot of Persia*, p. 118. Also see here M. Crinson, "Abadan: Planning and Architecture under the Anglo-Iranian Oil Company," *Planning Perspectives* 12.3 (1997), 341–59.
60. S. Marsh, "Anglo-American Crude Diplomacy: Multinational Oil and the Iranian Oil Crisis, 1951–1953," *Contemporary British History Journal* 21.1 (2007), 28; J. Bill and W. Louis, *Musaddiq, Iranian Nationalism, and Oil* (Austin, TX, 1988), pp. 329–30.
61. "The Secretary of State to the Department of State," 10 November 1951, *FRUS, 1952–1954: Iran, 1951–1954*, 10, p. 279.
62. Ibid.
63. R. Ramazani, *Iran's Foreign Policy, 1941–1973: A Study of Foreign Policy in Modernizing Nations* (Charlottesville, 1975), p. 190.
64. In de Bellaigue, *Patriot of Persia*, p. 150.
65. Yergin, *The Prize*, p. 437.
66. Cited by J. Bill, *The Eagle and the Lion: The Tragedy of American–Iranian Relations* (New Haven, 1988), p. 84.
67. *Correspondence between His Majesty's Government in the United Kingdom and the Persian Government and Related Documents Concerning the Oil Industry in Persia, February 1951 to September 1951* (London, 1951), p. 25.
68. Shinwell, Chiefs of Staff Committee, Confidential Annex, 23 May 1951, DEFE 4/43; for the British press at this time, de Bellaigue, *Patriot of Persia*, pp. 158–9.
69. S. Arjomand, *The Turban for the Crown: The Islamic Revolution in Iran* (Oxford, 1988), pp. 92–3.
70. *Time*, 7 January 1952.
71. Elm, *Oil, Power, and Principle*, p. 122.
72. M. Holland, *America and Egypt: From Roosevelt to Eisenhower* (Westport, CT, 1996), pp. 24–5.
73. H. Wilford, *America's Great Game: The CIA's Secret Arabists and the Shaping of the Modern Middle East* (New York, 2013), p. 73.
74. Ibid., p. 96.
75. Ibid.
76. D. Wilber, *Clandestine Services History: Overthrow of Premier Mossadeq of Iran: November 1952–August 1953* (1969), p. 7, National Security Archive.
77. Ibid., pp. 22, 34, 33.
78. See S. Koch, *"Zendebad, Shah!": The Central Intelligence Agency and the Fall of Iranian Prime Minister Mohammed Mossadeq, August 1953* (1998), National Security Archive.

79. M. Gasiorowski, "The Causes of Iran's 1953 Coup: A Critique of Darioush Bayandor's Iran and the CIA," *Iranian Studies* 45.5 (2012), 671–2; W. Louis, "Britain and the Overthrow of the Mosaddeq Government," in Gasiorowski and Byrne, *Mohammad Mosaddeq*, pp. 141–2.
80. Wilber, *Overthrow of Premier Mossadeq*, p. 35.
81. Ibid., p. 19.
82. Berry to State Department, 17 August 1953, National Security Archive.
83. For the radio, see M. Roberts, "Analysis of Radio Propaganda in the 1953 Iran Coup," *Iranian Studies* 45.6 (2012), 759–77; for the press, de Bellaigue, *Patriot of Persia*, p. 232.
84. For Rome, Soraya Esfandiary Bakhtiary, *Le Palais des solitudes* (Paris, 1992), pp. 165–6. Also here Buchan, *Days of God*, p. 70.
85. de Bellaigue, *Patriot of Persia*, pp. 253–70.
86. "Substance of Discussions of State—Joint Chiefs of Staff Meeting," 12 December 1951, *FRUS, 1951: The Near East and Africa*, 5, p. 435.
87. "British-American Planning Talks, Summary Record," 10–11 October 1978, FCO 8/3216.
88. "Memorandum of Discussion at the 160th Meeting of the National Security Council, 27 August 1953," *FRUS, 1952–1954: Iran, 1951–1954*, 10, p. 773.
89. "The Ambassador in Iran (Henderson) to Department of State," 18 September 1953, *FRUS, 1952–1954: Iran, 1951–1954*, 10, p. 799.

CHAPTER 22—THE AMERICAN SILK ROAD

1. *The International Petroleum Cartel, the Iranian Consortium, and US National Security*, United States Congress, Senate (Washington, DC, 1974), pp. 57–8; Yergin, *The Prize*, p. 453.
2. Bill, *The Eagle and the Lion*, p. 88; "Memorandum of the discussion at the 180th meeting of the National Security Council," 14 January 1954, *FRUS, 1952–1954: Iran, 1951–1954*, 10, p. 898.
3. M. Gasiorowski, *US Foreign Policy and the Shah: Building a Client State in Iran* (Ithaca, NY, 1991), pp. 150–1.
4. V. Nemchenok, "'That So Fair a Thing Should Be So Frail': The Ford Foundation and the Failure of Rural Development in Iran, 1953–1964," *Middle East Journal* 63.2 (2009), 261–73.
5. Ibid., 281; Gasiorowski, *US Foreign Policy*, pp. 53, 94.
6. C. Schayegh, "Iran's Karaj Dam Affair: Emerging Mass Consumerism, the Politics of Promise, and the Cold War in the Third World," *Comparative Studies in Society and History* 54.3 (2012), 612–43.
7. "Memorandum from the Joint Chiefs of Staff," 24 March 1949, *FRUS, 1949: The Near East, South Asia, and Africa*, 6, pp. 30–1.
8. "Report by the SANACC [State-Army-Navy-Air Force Co-ordinating Committee] Subcommittee for the Near and Middle East," *FRUS, 1949: The Near East, South Asia, and Africa*, 6, p. 12.

9. In general here, B. Yesilbursa, *Baghdad Pact: Anglo-American Defence Policies in the Middle East, 1950–59* (Abingdon, 2005).
10. R. McMahon, *The Cold War on the Periphery: The United States, India and Pakistan* (New York, 1994), pp. 16–17.
11. P. Tomsen, *The Wars of Afghanistan: Messianic Terrorism, Tribal Conflicts and the Failures of the Great Powers* (New York, 2011), pp. 181–2.
12. R. McNamara, *Britain, Nasser and the Balance of Power in the Middle East, 1952–1967* (London, 2003), pp. 44–5.
13. A. Moncrieff, *Suez: Ten Years After* (New York, 1966), pp. 40–1; D. Kunz, *The Economic Diplomacy of the Suez Crisis* (Chapel Hill, NC, 1991), p. 68.
14. Eden to Eisenhower, 6 September 1956, FO 800/740.
15. M. Heikal, *Nasser: The Cairo Documents* (London, 1972), p. 88.
16. H. Macmillan, Diary, 25 August 1956, in A. Horne, *Macmillan: The Official Biography* (London, 2008), p. 447.
17. Cited by McNamara, *Britain, Nasser and the Balance of Power*, p. 46.
18. McNamara, *Britain, Nasser and the Balance of Power*, pp. 45, 47.
19. "Effects of the Closing of the Suez Canal on Sino-Soviet Bloc Trade and Transportation," Office of Research and Reports, Central Intelligence Agency, 21 February 1957, Freedom of Information Act Electronic Reading Room, Central Intelligence Agency.
20. Kirkpatrick to Makins, 10 September 1956, FO 800/740.
21. *Papers of Dwight David Eisenhower: The Presidency: The Middle Way* (Baltimore, 1970), 17, p. 2415.
22. See here W. Louis and R. Owen, *Suez 1956: The Crisis and its Consequences* (Oxford, 1989); P. Hahn, *The United States, Great Britain, and Egypt, 1945–1956: Strategy and Diplomacy in the Early Cold War* (Chapel Hill, NC, 1991).
23. Eisenhower to Dulles, 12 December 1956, in P. Hahn, "Securing the Middle East: The Eisenhower Doctrine of 1957," *Presidential Studies Quarterly* 36.1 (2006), 39.
24. Cited by Yergin, *The Prize*, p. 459.
25. Hahn, "Securing the Middle East," 40.
26. See above all S. Yaqub, *Containing Arab Nationalism: The Eisenhower Doctrine and the Middle East* (Chapel Hill, NC, 2004).
27. R. Popp, "Accommodating to a Working Relationship: Arab Nationalism and US Cold War Policies in the Middle East," *Cold War History* 10.3 (2010), 410.
28. "The Communist Threat to Iraq," 17 February 1959, *FRUS, 1958–1960: Near East Region; Iraq; Iran; Arabian Peninsula*, 12, pp. 381–8.
29. S. Blackwell, *British Military Intervention and the Struggle for Jordan: King Hussein, Nasser and the Middle East Crisis* (London, 2013), p. 176; "Memorandum of Conference with President Eisenhower," 23 July 1958, *FRUS, 1958–1960: Near East Region; Iraq; Iran; Arabian Peninsula*, 12, p. 84.
30. "Iraq: The Dissembler," *Time*, 13 April 1959.
31. "Middle East: Revolt in Baghdad," *Time*, 21 July 1958; J. Romero, *The Iraqi Revolution of 1958: A Revolutionary Quest for Unity and Security* (Lanham, MD, 2011).

32. C. Andrew and V. Mitrokhin, *The KGB and the World: The Mitrokhin Archive II* (London, 2005), pp. 273–4; W. Shawcross, *The Shah's Last Ride* (London, 1989), p. 85.
33. OIR Report, 16 January 1959, cited by Popp, "Arab Nationalism and US Cold War Policies," p. 403.
34. Yaqub, *Containing Arab Nationalism*, p. 256.
35. W. Louis and R. Owen, *A Revolutionary Year: The Middle East in 1958* (London, 2002).
36. F. Matar, *Saddam Hussein: The Man, the Cause and his Future* (London, 1981), pp. 32–44.
37. "Memorandum of Discussion at the 420th Meeting of the National Security Council," 1 October 1959, *FRUS, 1958–1960: Near East Region; Iraq; Iran; Arabian Peninsula*, 12, p. 489, n. 6.
38. This incident was revealed during investigations in 1975 into the use of assassination as a political tool by U.S. intelligence agencies. The colonel, who is not named, was apparently executed by firing squad in Baghdad before the handkerchief plan was put into action, *Alleged Assassination Plots Involving Foreign Leaders, Interim Report of the Select Committee to Study Governmental Operations with Respect to Intelligence Activities* (Washington, DC, 1975), p. 181, n. 1.
39. H. Rositzke, *The CIA's Secret Operations: Espionage, Counterespionage and Covert Action* (Boulder, CO, 1977), pp. 109–10.
40. A. Siddiqi, *Challenge to Apollo: The Soviet Union and the Space Race, 1945–1974* (Washington, DC, 2000); B. Chertok, *Rakety i lyudi: Fili Podlipki Tyuratam* (Moscow, 1996).
41. A. Siddiqi, *Sputnik and the Soviet Space Challenge* (Gainesville, FL, 2003), pp. 135–8.
42. G. Laird, *North American Air Defense: Past, Present and Future* (Maxwell, AL, 1975); S. Zaloga, "Most Secret Weapon: The Origins of Soviet Strategic Cruise Missiles, 1945–1960," *Journal of Slavic Military Studies* 6.2 (1993), 262–73.
43. D. Kux, *The United States and Pakistan, 1947–2000: Disenchanted Allies* (Washington, DC, 2001), p. 112; N. Polmar, *Spyplane: The U-2 History Declassified* (Osceola, WI, 2001), pp. 131–48.
44. Karachi to Washington DC, 31 October 1958, *FRUS, 1958–60: South and Southeast Asia*, 15, p. 682.
45. Memcon Eisenhower and Ayub, 8 December 1959, *FRUS, 1958–60: South and Southeast Asia*, 15, pp. 781–95.
46. R. Barrett, *The Greater Middle East and the Cold War: US Foreign Policy under Eisenhower and Kennedy* (London, 2007), pp. 167–8.
47. Department of State Bulletin, 21 July 1958.
48. Kux, *United States and Pakistan*, pp. 110–11.
49. V. Nemchenok, "In Search of Stability amid Chaos: US Policy toward Iran, 1961–63," *Cold War History* 10.3 (2010), 345.
50. Central Intelligence Bulletin, 7 February 1961; A. Rubinstein, *Soviet Foreign Policy toward Turkey, Iran and Afghanistan: The Dynamics of Influence* (New York, 1982), pp. 67–8.

51. National Security Council Report, Statement of U.S. Policy to Iran, 6 July 1960, *FRUS, 1958–1960: Near East Region; Iraq; Iran; Arabian Peninsula*, 12, pp. 680–8.
52. M. Momen, "The Babi and the Baha'i Community of Iran: A Case of 'Suspended Genocide'?," *Journal of Genocide Research* 7.2 (2005), 221–42.
53. E. Abrahamian, *Iran between Two Revolutions* (Princeton, 1982), pp. 421–2.
54. J. Freivalds, "Farm Corporations in Iran: An Alternative to Traditional Agriculture," *Middle East Journal* 26.2 (1972), 185–93; J. Carey and A. Carey, "Iranian Agriculture and its Development: 1952–1973," *International Journal of Middle East Studies* 7.3 (1976), 359–82.
55. H. Ruhani, *Nehzat-e Imam-e Khomeini*, 2 vols (Teheran, 1979), 1, p. 25.
56. CIA Bulletin, 5 May 1961, cited by Nemchenok, "In Search of Stability," 348.
57. *Gahnamye panjah sal Shahanshahiye Pahlavi* (Paris, 1964), 24 January 1963.
58. See D. Brumberg, *Reinventing Khomeini: The Struggle for Reform in Iran* (Chicago, 2001).
59. D. Zahedi, *The Iranian Revolution: Then and Now* (Boulder, CO, 2000), p. 156.
60. "United States Support for Nation-Building" (1968); U.S. Embassy Teheran to State Department, 4 May 1972, both cited by R. Popp, "An Application of Modernization Theory during the Cold War? The Case of Pahlavi Iran," *International History Review* 30.1 (2008), 86–7.
61. Polk to Mayer, 23 April 1965, cited by Popp, "Pahlavi Iran," 94.
62. Zahedi, *Iranian Revolution*, p. 155.
63. A. Danielsen, *The Evolution of OPEC* (New York, 1982); F. Parra, *Oil Politics: A Modern History of Petroleum* (London, 2004), pp. 89ff.
64. Above all see M. Oren, *Six Days of War: June 1967 and the Making of the Modern Middle East* (Oxford, 2002).

CHAPTER 23—THE ROAD OF SUPERPOWER RIVALRY

1. P. Pham, *Ending "East of Suez": The British Decision to Withdraw from Malaysia and Singapore, 1964–1968* (Oxford, 2010).
2. G. Stocking, *Middle East Oil: A Study in Political and Economic Controversy* (Nashville, TN, 1970), p. 282; H. Astarjian, *The Struggle for Kirkuk: The Rise of Hussein, Oil and the Death of Tolerance in Iraq* (London, 2007), p. 158.
3. "Moscow and the Persian Gulf," Intelligence Memorandum, 12 May 1972, *FRUS, 1969–1976: Documents on Iran and Iraq, 1969–72*, E-4, 307.
4. *Izvestiya*, 12 July 1969.
5. Buchan, *Days of God*, p. 129.
6. Kwarteng, *Ghosts of Empire*, pp. 72–3.
7. Department of State to Embassy in France, Davies-Lopinot talk on Iraq and Persian Gulf, 20 April 1972, *FRUS, 1969–1976: Documents on Iran and Iraq, 1969–72*, E-4, 306.
8. G. Payton, "The Somali Coup of 1969: The Case for Soviet Complicity," *Journal of Modern African Studies* 18.3 (1980), 493–508.
9. Popp, "Arab Nationalism and US Cold War Policies," 408.
10. "Soviet aid and trade activities in the Indian Ocean Area," CIA report, S-6064 (1974); V. Goshev, *SSSR i strany Persidskogo zaliva* (Moscow, 1988).

11. U.S. Arms Control and Disarmament Agency, *World Military Expenditure and Arms Transfers, 1968–1977* (Washington, DC, 1979), p. 156; R. Menon, *Soviet Power and the Third World* (New Haven, 1986), p. 173; for Iraq, A. Fedchenko, *Irak v bor'be za nezavisimost'* (Moscow, 1970).
12. S. Mehrotra, "The Political Economy of Indo-Soviet Relations," in R. Cassen (ed.), *Soviet Interests in the Third World* (London, 1985), p. 224; L. Racioppi, *Soviet Policy towards South Asia since 1970* (Cambridge, 1994), pp. 63–5.
13. L. Dupree, *Afghanistan* (Princeton, 1973), pp. 525–6.
14. "The Shah of Iran: An Interview with Mohammad Reza Pahlavi," *New Atlantic*, 1 December 1973.
15. Ibid.
16. Boardman to Douglas-Home, August 1973, FCO 55/1116. Also O. Freedman, "Soviet Policy towards Ba'athist Iraq, 1968–1979," in R. Donaldson (ed.), *The Soviet Union in the Third World* (Boulder, CO, 1981), pp. 161–91.
17. Saddam Hussein, *On Oil Nationalisation* (Baghdad, 1973), pp. 8, 10.
18. R. Bruce St. John, *Libya: From Colony to Revolution* (Oxford, 2012), pp. 138–9.
19. Gaddafi, "Address at Ţubruq," 7 November 1969, in "The Libyan Revolution in the Words of its Leaders," *Middle East Journal* 24.2 (1970), 209.
20. Ibid., 209–10; M. Ansell and M. al-Arif, *The Libyan Revolution: A Sourcebook of Legal and Historical Documents* (Stoughton, WI, 1972), p. 280; *Multinational Corporations and United States Foreign Policy*, 93rd Congressional Hearings (Washington, DC, 1975), 8, pp. 771–3, cited by Yergin, *The Prize*, p. 562.
21. F. Halliday, *Iran, Dictatorship and Development* (Harmondsworth, 1979), p. 139; Yergin, *The Prize*, p. 607.
22. P. Marr, *Modern History of Iraq* (London, 2004), p. 162.
23. Embassy in Tripoli to Washington, 5 December 1970, cited by Yergin, *The Prize*, p. 569.
24. G. Hughes, "Britain, the Transatlantic Alliance, and the Arab–Israeli War of 1973," *Journal of Cold War Studies* 10.2 (2008), 3–40.
25. "The Agranat Report: The First Partial Report," *Jerusalem Journal of International Relations* 4.1 (1979), 80. Also see here U. Bar-Joseph, *The Watchman Fell Asleep: The Surprise of Yom Kippur and its Sources* (Albany, NY, 2005), esp. pp. 174–83.
26. A. Rabinovich, *The Yom Kippur War: The Epic Encounter that Transformed the Middle East* (New York, 2004), p. 25; Andrew and Mitrokhin, *The Mitrokhin Archive II*, p. 160.
27. G. Golan, "The Soviet Union and the Yom Kippur War," in P. Kumaraswamy, *Revisiting the Yom Kippur War* (London, 2000), pp. 127–52; idem, "The Cold War and the Soviet Attitude towards the Arab–Israeli Conflict," in N. Ashton (ed.), *The Cold War in the Middle East: Regional Conflict and the Superpowers, 1967–73* (London, 2007), p. 63.
28. H. Kissinger, *Years of Upheaval* (Boston, 1982), p. 463.
29. "Address to the Nation about Policies to Deal with the Energy Shortages," 7 November 1973, *Public Papers of the Presidents of the United States* [*PPPUS*]: *Richard M. Nixon, 1973* (Washington, DC, 1975), pp. 916–17.
30. Ibid; Yergin, *The Prize*, pp. 599–601.

31. D. Tihansky, "Impact of the Energy Crisis on Traffic Accidents," *Transport Research* 8 (1974), 481–3.
32. S. Godwin and D. Kulash, "The 55 mph Speed Limit on US Roads: Issues Involved," *Transport Reviews: A Transnational Transdisciplinary Journal* 8.3 (1988), 219–35.
33. See for example R. Knowles, *Energy and Form: Approach to Urban Growth* (Cambridge, MA, 1974); P. Steadman, *Energy, Environment and Building* (Cambridge, 1975).
34. D. Rand, "Battery Systems for Electric Vehicles—a State-of-the-Art Review," *Journal of Power Sources* 4 (1979), 101–43.
35. Speech to Seminar on Energy, 21 August 1973, cited by E. S. Godbold, *Jimmy and Rosalynn Carter: The Georgian Years, 1924–1974* (Oxford, 2010), p. 239.
36. J. G. Moore, "The Role of Congress," in R. Larson and R. Vest, *Implementation of Solar Thermal Technology* (Cambridge, MA, 1996), pp. 69–118.
37. President Nixon, "Memorandum Directing Reductions in Energy Consumption by the Federal Government," 29 June 1973, *PPPUS: Nixon, 1973*, p. 630.
38. Yergin, *The Prize*, pp. 579, 607.
39. Ibid., p. 616.
40. K. Makiya, *The Monument: Art, Vulgarity, and Responsibility in Iraq* (Berkeley, 1991), pp. 20–32; R. Baudouï, "To Build a Stadium: Le Corbusier's Project for Baghdad, 1955–1973," *DC Papers, revista de crítica y teoría de la arquitectura* 1 (2008), 271–80.
41. P. Stearns, *Consumerism in World History: The Global Transformation of Desire* (London, 2001), p. 119.
42. Sreedhar and J. Cavanagh, "US Interests in Iran: Myths and Realities," *ISDA Journal* 11.4 (1979), 37–40; U.S. Arms Control and Disarmament Agency, *World Military Expenditures and Arms Transfers 1972–82* (Washington, DC, 1984), p. 30; T. Moran, "Iranian Defense Expenditures and the Social Crisis," *International Security* 3.3 (1978), 180.
43. Cited by Buchan, *Days of God*, p. 162.
44. A. Alnasrawi, *The Economy of Iraq: Oil, Wars, Destruction of Development and Prospects, 1950–2010* (Westport, CT, 1994), p. 94; C. Tripp, *A History of Iraq* (Cambridge, 2000), p. 206.
45. "Secretary Kerry's Interview on Iran with NBC's David Gregory," 10 November 2013, U.S. State Department, Embassy of the United States London, website.
46. "Past Arguments Don't Square with Current Iran Policy," *Washington Post*, 27 March 2005.
47. S. Parry-Giles, *The Rhetorical Presidency, Propaganda, and the Cold War, 1945–55* (Westport, CT, 2002), pp. 164ff.
48. Cited by Shawcross, *Shah's Last Ride*, p. 179.
49. Secretary of State Henry A. Kissinger to President Gerald R. Ford, Memorandum, 13 May 1975, in M. Hunt (ed.), *Crises in US Foreign Policy: An International History Reader* (New York, 1996), p. 398.
50. J. Abdulghani, *Iran and Iraq: The Years of Crisis* (London, 1984), pp. 152–5.
51. R. Cottam, *Iran and the United States: A Cold War Case Study* (Pittsburgh, 1988), pp. 149–51.

52. H. Kissinger, *The White House Years* (Boston, 1979), p. 1265; idem, *Years of Upheaval*; L. Meho, *The Kurdish Question in US Foreign Policy: A Documentary Sourcebook* (Westport, CT, 2004), p. 14.
53. *Power Study of Iran, 1974–75*, Report to the Imperial Government of Iran (1975), pp. 3–24, cited by B. Mossavar-Rahmani, "Iran," in J. Katz and O. Marwah (eds), *Nuclear Power in Developing Countries: An Analysis of Decision Making* (Lexington, MA, 1982), p. 205.
54. D. Poneman, *Nuclear Power in the Developing World* (London, 1982), p. 86.
55. Ibid., p. 87; J. Yaphe and C. Lutes, *Reassessing the Implications of a Nuclear-Armed Iran* (Washington, DC, 2005), p. 49.
56. B. Mossavar-Rahmani, "Iran's Nuclear Power Programme Revisited," *Energy Policy* 8.3 (1980), 193–4, and idem, *Energy Policy in Iran: Domestic Choices and International Implications* (New York, 1981).
57. S. Jones and J. Holmes, "Regime Type, Nuclear Reversals, and Nuclear Strategy: The Ambiguous Case of Iran," in T. Yoshihara and J. Holmes (eds), *Strategy in the Second Nuclear Age: Power, Ambition and the Ultimate Weapon* (Washington, DC, 2012), p. 219.
58. *Special Intelligence Estimate: Prospects for Further Proliferation of Nuclear Weapons* (1974), p. 38, National Security Archive.
59. K. Hamza with J. Stein, "Behind the Scenes with the Iraqi Nuclear Bomb," in M. Sifry and C. Cerf (eds), *The Iraq War Reader: History, Documents, Opinions* (New York, 2003), p. 191.
60. J. Snyder, "The Road to Osirak: Baghdad's Quest for the Bomb," *Middle East Journal* 37 (1983), 565–94; A. Cordesman, *Weapons of Mass Destruction in the Middle East* (London, 1992), pp. 95–102; D. Albright and M. Hibbs, "Iraq's Bomb: Blueprints and Artifacts," *Bulletin of the Atomic Scientists* (1992), 14–23.
61. A. Cordesman, *Iraq and the War of Sanctions: Conventional Threats and Weapons of Mass Destruction* (Westport, CT, 1999), pp. 603–6.
62. *Prospects for Further Proliferation*, pp. 20–6.
63. K. Mahmoud, *A Nuclear Weapons-Free Zone in the Middle East: Problems and Prospects* (New York, 1988), p. 93.
64. Wright to Parsons and Egerton, 21 November 1973, FO 55/1116.
65. F. Khan, *Eating Grass: The Making of the Pakistani Bomb* (Stanford, 2012), p. 279.
66. Dr. A. Khan, "Pakistan's Nuclear Programme: Capabilities and Potentials of the Kahuta Project," Speech to the Pakistan Institute of National Affairs, 10 September 1990, quoted in Khan, *Making of the Pakistani Bomb*, p. 158.
67. Kux, *The United States and Pakistan*, pp. 221–4.
68. Memcon, 12 May 1976, cited by R. Alvandi, *Nixon, Kissinger, and the Shah: The United States and Iran in the Cold War* (Oxford, 2014), p. 163.
69. G. Sick, *All Fall Down: America's Tragic Encounter with Iran* (New York, 1987), p. 22.
70. "Toasts of the President and the Shah at a State Dinner," 31 December 1977, *PPPUS: Jimmy Carter, 1977*, pp. 2220–2.
71. Mossaver-Rahmani, "Iran's Nuclear Power," 192.
72. Pesaran, "System of Dependent Capitalism in Pre- and Post-Revolutionary

Iran," *International Journal of Middle East Studies* 14 (1982), 507; P. Clawson, "Iran's Economy between Crisis and Collapse," *Middle East Research and Information Project Reports* 98 (1981), 11–15; K. Pollack, *Persian Puzzle: The Conflict between Iran and America* (New York, 2004), p. 113; also here N. Keddie, *Modern Iran: Roots and Results of Revolution* (New Haven, 2003), pp. 158–62.

73. M. Heikal, *Iran: The Untold Story* (New York, 1982), pp. 145–6.
74. Shawcross, *Shah's Last Ride*, p. 35.
75. J. Carter, *Keeping Faith: Memoirs of a President* (Fayetteville, AR, 1995), p. 118.
76. A. Moens, "President Carter's Advisers and the Fall of the Shah," *Political Science Quarterly* 106.2 (1980), 211–37.
77. D. Murray, *US Foreign Policy and Iran: American–Iranian Relations since the Islamic Revolution* (London, 2010), p. 20.
78. U.S. Department of Commerce, *Foreign Broadcast Service*, 6 November 1979.
79. "Afghanistan in 1977: An External Assessment," U.S. Embassy Kabul to State Department, 30 January 1978.
80. Braithwaite, *Afgantsy*, pp. 78–9; S. Coll, *Ghost Wars: The Secret History of the CIA, Afghanistan, and Bin Laden, from the Soviet Intervention to September 10, 2001* (New York, 2004), p. 48.

CHAPTER 24—THE ROAD TO CATASTROPHE

1. Andrew and Mitrokhin, *Mitrokhin Archive II*, pp. 178–80.
2. Sreedhar and Cavanagh, "US Interests in Iran," 140.
3. C. Andrew and O. Gordievsky, *KGB: The Inside Story of its Foreign Operations from Lenin to Gorbachev* (London, 1990), p. 459.
4. W. Sullivan, *Mission to Iran: The Last Ambassador* (New York, 1981), pp. 201–3, 233; also Sick, *All Fall Down*, pp. 81–7; A. Moens, "President Carter's Advisors," *Political Science Quarterly* 106.2 (1991), 244.
5. Z. Brzezinski, *Power and Principle: Memoirs of the National Security Adviser, 1977–1981* (London, 1983), p. 38.
6. "Exiled Ayatollah Khomeini returns to Iran," BBC News, 1 February 1979.
7. Sick, *All Fall Down*, pp. 154–6; D. Farber, *Taken Hostage: The Iran Hostage Crisis and America's First Encounter with Radical Islam* (Princeton, 2005), pp. 99–100, 111–13.
8. C. Vance, *Hard Choices: Critical Years in America's Foreign Policy* (New York, 1983), p. 343; B. Glad, *An Outsider in the White House: Jimmy Carter, his Advisors, and the Making of American Foreign Policy* (Ithaca, NY, 1979), p. 173.
9. *Constitution of the Islamic Republic of Iran* (Berkeley, 1980).
10. "Presidential Approval Ratings—Historical Statistics and Trends," www.gallup.com.
11. A. Cordesman, *The Iran–Iraq War and Western Security, 1984–1987* (London, 1987), p. 26. Also D. Kinsella, "Conflict in Context: Arms Transfers and Third World Rivalries during the Cold War," *American Journal of Political Science* 38.3 (1994), 573.
12. Sreedhar and Cavanagh, "US Interests in Iran," 143.

13. "Comment by Sir A. D. Parsons, Her Majesty's Ambassador, Teheran, 1974–1979," in N. Browne, *Report on British Policy on Iran, 1974–1978* (London, 1980), Annexe B.
14. R. Cottam, "US and Soviet Responses to Islamic Political Militancy," in N. Keddie and M. Gasiorowski (eds), *Neither East nor West: Iran, the Soviet Union and the United States* (New Haven, 1990), 279; A. Rubinstein, "The Soviet Union and Iran under Khomeini," *International Affairs* 57.4 (1981), 599.
15. Turner's testimony was leaked to the press, "Turner Sees a Gap in Verifying Treaty: Says Iran Bases Can't Be Replaced until '84," *New York Times*, 17 April 1979.
16. R. Gates, *From the Shadows: The Ultimate Insider's Story of Five Presidents and How They Won the Cold War* (New York, 1996). Gates says little other than that negotiations were delicate; and that Admiral Turner grew a moustache for the visit, presumably as a disguise, pp. 122–3.
17. J. Richelson, "The Wizards of Langley: The CIA's Directorate of Science and Technology," in R. Jeffreys-Jones and C. Andrew (eds), *Eternal Vigilance? 50 Years of the CIA* (London, 1997), pp. 94–5.
18. Rubinstein, "The Soviet Union and Iran under Khomeini," 599, 601.
19. Gates, *From the Shadows*, p. 132.
20. R. Braithwaite, *Afgantsy: The Russians in Afghanistan, 1979–89* (London, 2011), pp. 37–44.
21. "Main Outlines of the Revolutionary Tasks"; Braithwaite, *Afgantsy*, pp. 42–3; P. Dimitrakis, *The Secret War in Afghanistan: The Soviet Union, China and Anglo-American Intelligence in the Afghan War* (London, 2013), 1–20.
22. J. Amstutz, *Afghanistan: The First Five Years of Soviet Occupation* (Washington, DC, 1986), p. 130; H. Bradsher, *Afghanistan and the Soviet Union* (Durham, NC, 1985), p. 1010.
23. N. Newell and R. Newell, *The Struggle for Afghanistan* (Ithaca, NY, 1981), p. 86.
24. N. Misdaq, *Afghanistan: Political Frailty and External Interference* (2006), p. 108.
25. A. Assifi, "The Russian Rope: Soviet Economic Motives and the Subversion of Afghanistan," *World Affairs* 145.3 (1982–3), 257.
26. V. Bukovsky, *Reckoning with Moscow: A Dissident in the Kremlin's Archives* (London, 1998), pp. 380–2.
27. Gates, *From the Shadows*, pp. 131–2.
28. U.S. Department of State, Office of Security, *The Kidnapping and Death of Ambassador Adolph Dubs, February 14 1979* (Washington, DC, 1979).
29. D. Cordovez and S. Harrison, *Out of Afghanistan: The Inside Story of the Soviet Withdrawal* (Oxford, 1995), p. 35; D. Camp, *Boots on the Ground: The Fight to Liberate Afghanistan from Al-Qaeda and the Taliban* (Minneapolis, 2012), pp. 8–9.
30. CIA Briefing Papers, 20 August; 24 August; 11 September; 14 September, 20 September; Gates, *From the Shadows*, pp. 132–3.
31. "What Are the Soviets Doing in Afghanistan?," 17 September 1979, National Security Archive.

32. D. MacEachin, *Predicting the Soviet Invasion of Afghanistan: The Intelligence Community's Record* (Washington, DC, 2002); O. Sarin and L. Dvoretsky, *The Afghan Syndrome: The Soviet Union's Vietnam* (Novato, CA, 1993), pp. 79–84.
33. M. Brecher and J. Wilkenfeld, *A Study of Crisis* (Ann Arbor, MI, 1997), p. 357.
34. *Pravda*, 29, 30 December 1979.
35. Amstutz, *Afghanistan*, pp. 43–4. These rumours were so strong—and presumably so persuasive—that Ambassador Dubs himself had made enquiries with the CIA to check if they were true, Braithwaite, *Afgantsy*, pp. 78–9. For gossip spread locally, R. Garthoff, *Détente and Confrontation: Soviet–American Relations from Nixon to Reagan* (Washington, DC, 1985), p. 904. Also here Andrew and Mitrokhin, *Mitrokhin Archive II*, pp. 393–4.
36. A. Lyakhovskii, *Tragediya i doblest' Afgana* (Moscow, 1995), p. 102.
37. Braithwaite, *Afgantsy*, pp. 78–9, 71; Lyakhovskii, *Tragediya i doblest' Afgana*, p. 181.
38. Cited by V. Zubok, *A Failed Empire: The Soviet Union in the Cold War from Stalin to Gorbachev* (Chapel Hill, NC, 2007), p. 262; Coll, *Ghost Wars*, p. 48.
39. "Meeting of the Politburo Central Committee," 17 March 1979, pp. 142–9, in Dimitrakis, *Secret War*, p. 133.
40. Lyakhovskii, *Tragediya i doblest' Afgana*, pp. 109–12.
41. *Pravda*, 13 January 1980.
42. Braithwaite, *Afgantsy*, p. 77.
43. "The Current Digest of the Soviet Press," *American Association for the Advancement of Slavic Studies* 31 (1979), 4.
44. Zubok, *A Failed Empire*, p. 262.
45. Lyakhovskii, *Tragediya i doblest' Afgana*, p. 215.
46. *Pravda*, 13 January 1980.
47. Cited by Lyakhovskii, *Tragediya i doblest' Afgana*, p. 252.
48. Brzezinski downplays such warnings, *Power and Principle*, pp. 472–5; Vance, *Hard Choices*, pp. 372–3; Glad, *Outsider in the White House*, pp. 176–7.
49. D. Harris, *The Crisis: The President, the Prophet, and the Shah: 1979 and the Coming of Militant Islam* (New York, 2004), p. 193.
50. Ibid., pp. 199–200.
51. Farber, *Taken Hostage*, pp. 41–2.
52. Saunders, "Diplomacy and Pressure, November 1979—May 1980," in W. Christopher (ed.), *American Hostages in Iran: Conduct of a Crisis* (New Haven, 1985), pp. 78–9.
53. H. Alikhani, *Sanctioning Iran: Anatomy of a Failed Policy* (New York, 2001), p. 67.
54. "Rivals doubt Carter will retain poll gains after Iran crisis," *Washington Post*, 17 December 1979. See here C. Emery, "The Transatlantic and Cold War Dynamics of Iran Sanctions, 1979–80," *Cold War History* 10.3 (2010), 374–6.
55. "Text of Khomeini speech," 20 November 1979, NSC memo to President Carter, cited by Emery, "Iran Sanctions," 374.
56. Ibid.
57. Ibid., 375.

58. "The Hostage Situation," Memo from the Director of Central Intelligence, 9 January 1980, cited by Emery, "Iran Sanctions," 380.
59. Carter, *Keeping Faith*, p. 475.
60. Ibid. Also G. Sick, "Military Operations and Constraints," in Christopher, *American Hostages in Iran*, pp. 144–72.
61. Woodrow Wilson Center, *The Origins, Conduct, and Impact of the Iran–Iraq War, 1980–1988: A Cold War International History Project Document Reader* (Washington, DC, 2004).
62. "NSC on Afghanistan," Fritz Ermath to Brzezinski, cited by Emery, "Iran Sanctions," 379.
63. "The State of the Union. Address Delivered Before a Joint Session of the Congress," 23 January 1980, p. 197.
64. M. Bowden, *Guests of the Ayatollah: The First Battle in America's War with Militant Islam* (2006), pp. 359–61.
65. J. Kyle and J. Eidson, *The Guts to Try: The Untold Story of the Iran Hostage Rescue Mission by the On-Scene Desert Commander* (New York, 1990); also P. Ryan, *The Iranian Rescue Mission: Why It Failed* (Annapolis, 1985).
66. S. Mackey, *The Iranians: Persia, Islam and the Soul of a Nation* (New York, 1996), p. 298.
67. Brzezinski to Carter, 3 January 1980, in H. Brands, "Saddam Hussein, the United States, and the Invasion of Iran: Was There a Green Light?," *Cold War History* 12.2 (2012), 322–3; also see O. Njølstad, "Shifting Priorities: The Persian Gulf in US Strategic Planning in the Carter Years," *Cold War History* 4.3 (2004), 30–8.
68. R. Takeyh, "The Iran–Iraq War: A Reassessment," *Middle East Journal* 64 (2010), 367.
69. A. Bani-Sadr, *My Turn to Speak: Iran, the Revolution and Secret Deals with the U.S.* (Washington, DC, 1991), pp. 13, 70–1; D. Hiro, *Longest War: The Iran–Iraq Military Conflict* (New York, 1991), pp. 71–2; S. Fayazmanesh, *The United States and Iran: Sanctions, Wars and the Policy of Dual Containment* (New York, 2008), pp. 16–17.
70. Brands, "Saddam Hussein, the United States, and the Invasion of Iran," 321–37.
71. K. Woods and M. Stout, "New Sources for the Study of Iraqi Intelligence during the Saddam Era," *Intelligence and National Security* 25.4 (2010), 558.
72. "Transcript of a Meeting between Saddam Hussein and his Commanding Officers at the Armed Forces General Command," 22 November 1980, cited by H. Brands and D. Palkki, "Saddam Hussein, Israel, and the Bomb: Nuclear Alarmism Justified?," *International Security* 36.1 (2011), 145–6.
73. "Meeting between Saddam Hussein and High-Ranking Officials," 16 September 1980, in K. Woods, D. Palkki and M. Stout (eds), *The Saddam Tapes: The Inner Workings of a Tyrant's Regime* (Cambridge, 2011), p. 134.
74. Cited by Brands and Palkki, "Saddam, Israel, and the Bomb," 155.
75. "President Saddam Hussein Meets with Iraqi Officials to Discuss Political Issues," November 1979, in Woods, Palkki and Stout, *Saddam Tapes*, p. 22.
76. Cited by Brands, "Saddam Hussein, the United States, and the Invasion of

Iran," 331. For Saddam's paranoid views, see K. Woods, J. Lacey and W. Murray, "Saddam's Delusions: The View from the Inside," *Foreign Affairs* 85.3 (2006), 2–27.

77. J. Parker, *Persian Dreams: Moscow and Teheran since the Fall of the Shah* (Washington, DC, 2009), pp. 6–10.
78. Brands, "Saddam Hussein, the United States, and the Invasion of Iran," 331.
79. O. Smolansky and B. Smolansky, *The USSR and Iraq: The Soviet Quest for Influence* (Durham, NC, 1991), pp. 230–4.
80. "Military Intelligence Report about Iran," 1 July 1980, cited by Brands, "Saddam Hussein, the United States, and the Invasion of Iran," 334. Also H. Brands, "Why Did Saddam Hussein Invade Iran? New Evidence on Motives, Complexity, and the Israel Factor," *Journal of Military History* 75 (2011), 861–5; idem, "Saddam and Israel: What Do the New Iraqi Records Reveal?," *Diplomacy & Statecraft* 22.3 (2011), 500–20.
81. Brands, "Saddam Hussein, the United States, and the Invasion of Iran," 323.
82. Sick, *All Fall Down*, pp. 313–14; J. Dumbrell, *The Carter Presidency: A Re-Evaluation* (Manchester, 2005), p. 171.
83. Brzezinski, *Power and Principle*, p. 504.
84. J.-M. Xaviere (tr.), *Sayings of the Ayatollah Khomeini: Political, Philosophical, Social and Religious: Extracts from Three Major Works by the Ayatollah* (New York, 1980), pp. 8–9.
85. E. Abrahamian, *Khomeinism: Essays on the Islamic Republic* (London, 1989), p. 51.
86. T. Parsi, *The Treacherous Alliance: The Secret Dealings of Iran, Israel and the United States* (New Haven, 2007), p. 107.
87. R. Claire, *Raid on the Sun: Inside Israel's Secret Campaign that Denied Saddam Hussein the Bomb* (New York, 2004).
88. Woods, Palkki and Stout, *Saddam Tapes*, p. 79.
89. "Implications of Iran's Victory over Iraq," 8 June 1982, National Security Archive.
90. *The Times*, 14 July 1982.
91. G. Shultz, *Turmoil and Triumph: Diplomacy, Power and the Victory of the American Deal* (New York, 1993), p. 235.
92. B. Jentleson, *Friends Like These: Reagan, Bush, and Saddam, 1982–1990* (New York, 1994), p. 35; J. Hiltermann, *A Poisonous Affair: America, Iraq and the Gassing of Halabja* (Cambridge, 2007), pp. 42–4.
93. "Talking Points for Amb. Rumsfeld's Meeting with Tariq Aziz and Saddam Hussein," 14 December 1983, cited by B. Gibson, *Covert Relationship: American Foreign Policy, Intelligence and the Iran–Iraq War, 1980–1988* (Santa Barbara, 2010), pp. 111–12.
94. Cited by Gibson, *Covert Relationship*, p. 113.
95. H. Brands and D. Palkki, "Conspiring Bastards: Saddam Hussein's Strategic View of the United States," *Diplomatic History* 36.3 (2012), 625–59.
96. "Talking Points for Ambassador Rumsfeld's Meeting with Tariq Aziz and Saddam Hussein," 4 December 1983, cited by Gibson, *Covert Relationship*, p. 111.

97. Gibson, *Covert Relationship*, pp. 113–18.
98. Admiral Howe to Secretary of State, "Iraqi Use of Chemical Weapons," 1 November 1983, cited by Gibson, *Covert Relationship*, p. 107.
99. Cited by Z. Fredman, "Shoring up Iraq, 1983 to 1990: Washington and the Chemical Weapons Controversy," *Diplomacy & Statecraft* 23.3 (2012), 538.
100. The United Nations Security Council passed Resolution 540, calling for an end to military operations, but falling short of mentioning chemical weapons. According to one senior UN official, when the secretary-general, Javier Pérez de Cuéllar, raised the issue of looking into this matter, "he encountered an antarctically cold atmosphere; the Security Council wanted nothing of it." Hiltermann, *A Poisonous Affair*, p. 58. Also here see Gibson, *Covert Relationship*, pp. 108–9.
101. Fredman, "Shoring up Iraq," 539.
102. "Iraqi Use of Chemical Weapons," in Gibson, *Covert Relationship*, p. 108.
103. Fredman, "Shoring Up Iraq," 542.
104. A. Neier, "Human Rights in the Reagan Era: Acceptance by Principle," *Annals of the American Academy of Political and Social Science* 506.1 (1989), 30–41.
105. Braithwaite, *Afgantsy*, pp. 201–2, and M. Bearden and J. Risen, *Afghanistan: The Main Enemy* (New York, 2003), pp. 227, 333–6.
106. Braithwaite, *Afgantsy*, p. 214; D. Gai and V. Snegirev, *Vtorozhenie* (Moscow, 1991), p. 139.
107. Braithwaite, *Afgantsy*, pp. 228–9.
108. Ibid., p. 223.
109. J. Hershberg, "The War in Afghanistan and the Iran–Contra Affair: Missing Links?," *Cold War History* 3.3 (2003), 27.
110. National Security Decision Directive 166, 27 March 1985, National Security Archive.
111. Hershberg, "The War in Afghanistan and the Iran–Contra Affair," 28; also H. Teicher and G. Teicher, *Twin Pillars to Desert Storm: America's Flawed Vision in the Middle East from Nixon to Bush* (New York, 1993), pp. 325–6.
112. Braithwaite, *Afgantsy*, p. 215.
113. Coll, *Ghost Wars*, pp. 161–2, 71–88.
114. *Beijing Review*, 7 January 1980.
115. M. Malik, *Assessing China's Tactical Gains and Strategic Losses Post-September 11* (Carlisle Barracks, 2002), cited by S. Mahmud Ali, *US–China Cold War Collaboration: 1971–1989* (Abingdon, 2005), p. 177.
116. Braithwaite, *Afgantsy*, pp. 202–3.
117. Cited by Teicher and Teicher, *Twin Pillars to Desert Storm*, p. 328.
118. "Toward a Policy in Iran," in *The Tower Commission Report: The Full Text of the President's Special Review Board* (New York, 1987), pp. 112–15.
119. H. Brands, "Inside the Iraqi State Records: Saddam Hussein, 'Irangate' and the United States," *Journal of Strategic Studies* 34.1 (2011), 103.
120. H. Emadi, *Politics of the Dispossessed: Superpowers and Developments in the Middle East* (Westport, CT, 2001), p. 41.
121. Hershberg, "The War in Afghanistan and the Iran–Contra Affair," 30–1.

122. Ibid., 35, 37–9.
123. M. Yousaf and M. Adkin, *The Bear Trap* (London, 1992), p. 150.
124. "Memorandum of Conversation, 26 May 1986," *Tower Commission Report*, pp. 311–12; Hershberg, "The War in Afghanistan and the Iran–Contra Affair," 40, 42.
125. Cited by Hershberg, "The War in Afghanistan and the Iran–Contra Affair," 39.
126. S. Yetiv, *The Absence of Grand Strategy: The United States in the Persian Gulf, 1972–2005* (Baltimore, 2008), p. 57.
127. E. Hooglund, "The Policy of the Reagan Administration toward Iran," in Keddie and Gasiorowski, *Neither East nor West*, p. 190. For another example, see Brands, "Inside the Iraqi State Records," 100.
128. K. Woods, *Mother of All Battles: Saddam Hussein's Strategic Plan for the Persian Gulf War* (Annapolis, 2008), p. 50.
129. B. Souresrafil, *Khomeini and Israel* (London, 1988), p. 114.
130. *Report of the Congressional Committees Investigating the Iran–Contra Affair, with Supplemental, Minority, and Additional Views* (Washington, DC, 1987), p. 176.
131. For the arms sales, *Report of the Congressional Committees Investigating the Iran–Contra Affair*, passim.
132. A. Hayes, "The Boland Amendments and Foreign Affairs Deference," *Columbia Law Review* 88.7 (1988), 1534–74.
133. "Address to the Nation on the Iran Arms and Contra Aid Controversy," 13 November 1986, *PPPUS: Ronald Reagan, 1986*, p. 1546.
134. "Address to the Nation on the Iran Arms and Contra Aid Controversy," 4 March 1987, *PPPUS: Ronald Reagan, 1987*, p. 209.
135. L. Walsh, *Final Report of the Independent Counsel for Iran/Contra Matters*, 4 vols (Washington, DC, 1993).
136. G. H. W. Bush, "Grant of Executive Clemency," Proclamation 6518, 24 December 1992, *Federal Register* 57.251, pp. 62145–6.
137. "Cabinet Meeting regarding the Iran–Iraq War, mid-November 1986," and "Saddam Hussein Meeting with Ba'ath Officials," early 1987, both cited by Brands, "Inside the Iraqi State Records," 105.
138. "Saddam Hussein Meeting with Ba'ath Officials," early 1987, cited by Brands, "Inside the Iraqi State Records," 112–13.
139. Ibid., 113.
140. *Comprehensive Report of the Special Advisor to the Director of Central Intelligence on Iraq's Weapons of Mass Destruction*, 3 vols (2004), 1, p. 31; Brands, "Inside the Iraqi State Records," 113.
141. Colin Powell Notes of meeting 21 January 1987, Woodrow Wilson Center, *The Origins, Conduct, and Impact of the Iran–Iraq War*.
142. Brands, "Inside the Iraqi State Records," 112.
143. D. Neff, "The US, Iraq, Israel and Iran: Backdrop to War," *Journal of Palestinian Studies* 20.4 (1991), 35.
144. Brands and Palkki, "Conspiring Bastards," 648.
145. Fredman, "Shoring Up Iraq," 548.

146. WikiLeaks, 90 BAGHDAD 4237.
147. "Excerpts from Iraqi Document on Meeting with US Envoy," *New York Times*, 23 September 1990.

CHAPTER 25—THE ROAD TO TRAGEDY

1. Paul to Foreign & Commonwealth Office, "Saddam Hussein al-Tikriti," 20 December 1969, FCO 17/871; "Saddam Hussein," Telegram from British Embassy, Baghdad to Foreign and Commonwealth Office, London, 20 December 1969, FCO 17/871.
2. "Rumsfeld Mission: December 20 Meeting with Iraqi President Saddam Hussein," National Security Archive. For the French and Saddam, C. Saint-Prot, *Saddam Hussein: un gaullisme arabe?* (Paris, 1987); also see D. Styan, *France and Iraq: Oil, Arms and French Policy Making in the Middle East* (London, 2006).
3. "Saddam and his Senior Advisors Discussing Iraq's Historical Rights to Kuwait and the US Position," 15 December 1990, in Woods, Palkki and Stout, *Saddam Tapes*, pp. 34–5.
4. President George H. W. Bush, "National Security Directive 54. Responding to Iraqi Aggression in the Gulf," 15 January 1991, National Security Archive.
5. G. Bush, *Speaking of Freedom: The Collected Speeches of George H. W. Bush* (New York, 2009), pp. 196–7.
6. J. Woodard, *The America that Reagan Built* (Westport, CT, 2006), p. 139, n. 39.
7. President George H. W. Bush, "National Security Directive 54. Responding to Iraqi Aggression in the Gulf."
8. G. Bush and B. Scowcroft, *A World Transformed* (New York, 1998), p. 489.
9. Cited by J. Connelly, "In Northwest: Bush–Cheney Flip Flops Cost America in Blood," *Seattle Post-Intelligencer*, 29 July 2004. Also see B. Montgomery, *Richard B. Cheney and the Rise of the Imperial Vice Presidency* (Westport, CT, 2009), p. 95.
10. W. Martel, *Victory in War: Foundations of Modern Strategy* (Cambridge, 2011), p. 248.
11. President Bush, "Address before a Joint Session of the Congress on the State of the Union," 28 January 1992, *PPPUS: George Bush, 1992–1993*, p. 157.
12. For the collapse of the Soviet Union, see S. Plokhy, *The Last Empire: The Final Days of the Soviet Union* (New York, 2014); for China in this period, L. Brandt and T. Rawski (eds), *China's Great Economic Transformation* (Cambridge, 2008).
13. Bush, "State of the Union," 28 January 1992, p. 157.
14. UN Resolution 687 (1991), Clause 20.
15. S. Zahdi and M. Smith Fawzi, "Health of Baghdad's Children," *Lancet* 346.8988 (1995), 1485; C. Ronsmans et al., "Sanctions against Iraq," *Lancet* 347.8995 (1996), 198–200. The mortality figures were later revised downwards, S. Zaidi, "Child Mortality in Iraq," *Lancet* 350.9084 (1997), 1105.
16. *60 Minutes*, CBS, 12 May 1996.

17. B. Lambeth, *The Unseen War: Allied Air Power and the Takedown of Saddam Hussein* (Annapolis, 2013), p. 61.
18. For an overview here, see C. Gray, "From Unity to Polarization: International Law and the Use of Force against Iraq," *European Journal of International Law* 13.1 (2002), 1–19. Also A. Bernard, "Lessons from Iraq and Bosnia on the Theory and Practice of No-Fly Zones," *Journal of Strategic Studies* 27 (2004), 454–78.
19. Iraq Liberation Act, 31 October 1998.
20. President Clinton, "Statement on Signing the Iraq Liberation Act of 1998," 31 October 1998, *PPPUS: William J. Clinton, 1998*, pp. 1938–9.
21. S. Aubrey, *The New Dimension of International Terrorism* (Zurich, 2004), pp. 53–6; M. Ensalaco, *Middle Eastern Terrorism: From Black September to September 11* (Philadelphia, 2008), pp. 183–6; for the Dharan attack, however, note C. Shelton, "The Roots of Analytic Failure in the US Intelligence Community," *International Journal of Intelligence and CounterIntelligence* 24.4 (2011), 650–1.
22. Response to the Clinton letter, undated, 1999. Clinton Presidential Records, Near Eastern Affairs, Box 2962; Folder: Iran–U.S., National Security Archive. For Clinton's dispatch, delivered by the Foreign Minister of Oman, see "Message to President Khatami from President Clinton," undated, 1999, National Security Archive.
23. "Afghanistan: Taliban seeks low-level profile relations with [United States government]—at least for now," U.S. Embassy Islamabad, 8 October 1996, National Security Archive.
24. "Afghanistan: Jalaluddin Haqqani's emergence as a key Taliban Commander," U.S. Embassy Islamabad, 7 January 1997, National Security Archive.
25. "Usama bin Ladin: Islamic Extremist Financier," CIA biography 1996, National Security Archive.
26. "Afghanistan: Taliban agrees to visits of militant training camps, admit Bin Ladin is their guest," U.S. Consulate (Peshawar) cable, 9 January 1996, National Security Archive.
27. Ibid.
28. *National Commission on Terrorist Attacks upon the United States* (Washington, DC, 2004), pp. 113–14.
29. President Clinton, "Address to the Nation," 20 August 1998, *PPPUS: Clinton, 1998*, p. 1461. Three days earlier, the President had given his now famous testimony that the previous statement he had given, "I did not have sexual relations with that woman, Miss [Monica] Lewinsky," was truthful and that his claim that "there is not a sexual relationship, an improper sexual relationship or any other kind of improper relationship" was correct, depending "on what the meaning of the word 'is' is," *Appendices to the Referral to the US House of Representatives* (Washington, DC, 1998), 1, p. 510.
30. "Afghanistan: Reaction to US Strikes Follows Predictable Lines: Taliban Angry, their Opponents Support US," U.S. Embassy (Islamabad) cable, 21 August 1998, National Security Archive.

31. "Bin Ladin's Jihad: Political Context," U.S. Department of State, Bureau of Intelligence and Research, Intelligence Assessment, 28 August 1998, National Security Archive.
32. "Afghanistan: Taliban's Mullah Omar's 8/22 Contact with State Department," U.S. Department of State cable, 23 August 1998, National Security Archive.
33. "Osama bin Laden: Taliban Spokesman Seeks New Proposal for Resolving bin Laden Problem," U.S. Department of State cable, 28 November 1998, National Security Archive.
34. Ibid.
35. "Afghanistan: Taliban's Mullah Omar's 8/22 Contact with State Department," U.S. Department of State cable, 23 August 1998, National Security Archive.
36. Ibid.
37. For example, "Afghanistan: Tensions Reportedly Mount within Taliban as Ties with Saudi Arabia Deteriorate over Bin Ladin," U.S. Embassy (Islamabad) cable, 28 October 1998; "Usama bin Ladin: Coordinating our Efforts and Sharpening our Message on Bin Ladin," U.S. Embassy (Islamabad) cable, 19 October 1998; "Usama bin Ladin: Saudi Government Reportedly Turning the Screws on the Taliban on Visas," U.S. Embassy (Islamabad) cable, 22 December 1998, National Security Archive.
38. *Osama bin Laden: A Case Study*, Sandia Research Laboratories, 1999, National Security Archive.
39. "Afghanistan: Taleban External Ambitions," U.S. Department of State, Bureau of Intelligence and Research, 28 October 1998, National Security Archive.
40. A. Rashid, *Taliban: The Power of Militant Islam in Afghanistan and Beyond* (rev. edn, London, 2008).
41. *Osama bin Laden: A Case Study*, p. 13.
42. "Bin Ladin Determined to Strike in US," 6 August 2001, National Security Archive.
43. "Searching for the Taliban's Hidden Message," U.S. Embassy (Islamabad) cable, 19 September 2000, National Security Archive.
44. *The 9/11 Commission Report: Final Report of the National Commission on Terrorist Attacks upon the United States* (New York, 2004), p. 19.
45. Ibid., passim.
46. President George W. Bush, Address to the Nation on the Terrorist Attacks, 11 September 2001, *PPPUS: George W. Bush, 2001*, pp. 1099–100.
47. "Arafat Horrified by Attacks, But Thousands of Palestinians Celebrate; Rest of World Outraged," Fox News, 12 September 2001.
48. Statement of Abdul Salam Zaeef, Taliban ambassador to Pakistan, 12 September 2001, National Security Archive.
49. Al-Jazeera, 12 September 2001.
50. "Action Plan as of 9/13/2001, 7:55am," U.S. Department of State, 13 September 2001, National Security Archive.
51. "Deputy Secretary Armitage's Meeting with Pakistani Intel Chief Mahmud: You're Either with Us or You're Not," U.S. Department of State, 13 September 2001, National Security Archive.

52. "Message to Taliban," U.S. Department of State cable, 7 October 2001, National Security Archive.
53. "Memorandum for President Bush: Strategic Thoughts," Office of the Secretary of Defense, 30 September 2001, National Security Archive.
54. President Bush, State of the Union address, 29 January 2002, *PPPUS: Bush, 2002*, p. 131.
55. "US Strategy in Afghanistan: Draft for Discussion," National Security Council Memorandum, 16 October 2001, National Security Archive.
56. "Information Memorandum. Origins of the Iraq Regime Change Policy," U.S. Department of State, 23 January 2001, National Security Archive.
57. "Untitled," Donald Rumsfeld notes, 27 November 2001, National Security Archive.
58. Ibid.
59. "Europe: Key Views on Iraqi Threat and Next Steps," 18 December 2001; "Problems and Prospects of 'Justifying' War with Iraq," 29 August 2002. Both issued by U.S. Department of State, Bureau of Intelligence and Research Intelligence Assessment, National Security Archive. Lord Goldsmith to Prime Minister, "Iraq," 30 July 2002; "Iraq: Interpretation of Resolution 1441," Draft, 14 January 2003; "Iraq: Interpretation of Resolution 1441," Draft, 12 February 2003, The Iraq Enquiry Archive.
60. "To Ousted Boss, Arms Watchdog Was Seen as an Obstacle in Iraq," *New York Times*, 13 October 2013.
61. "Remarks to the United Nations Security Council," 5 February 2003, National Security Archive.
62. "The Status of Nuclear Weapons in Iraq," 27 January 2003, IAEA, National Security Archive.
63. "An Update on Inspection," 27 January 2003, UNMOVIC, National Security Archive.
64. Woods and Stout, "New Sources for the Study of Iraqi Intelligence," esp. 548–52.
65. "Remarks to the United Nations Security Council," 5 February 2003; cf. "Iraqi Mobile Biological Warfare Agent Production Plants," CIA report, 28 May 2003, National Security Archive.
66. "The Future of the Iraq Project," State Department, 20 April 2003, National Security Archive.
67. Ari Fleischer, Press Briefing, 18 February 2003; Paul Wolfowitz, "Testimony before House Appropriations Subcommittee on Defense," 27 March 2003.
68. "US Strategy in Afghanistan: Draft for Discussion," National Security Council Memorandum, 16 October 2001, National Security Archive.
69. Planning Group Polo Step, U.S. Central Command Slide Compilation, c. 15 August 2002, National Security Archive.
70. H. Fischer, "US Military Casualty Statistics: Operation New Dawn, Operation Iraqi Freedom and Operation Enduring Freedom," *Congressional Research Service*, RS22452 (Washington, DC, 2014).
71. Estimates of numbers of civilian casualties in Iraq and Afghanistan between 2001 and 2014 are regularly placed within the range of 170,000–220,000. See for example www.costsofwar.org.

72. L. Bilmes, "The Financial Legacy of Iraq and Afghanistan: How Wartime Spending Decisions Will Constrain Future National Security Budgets," *Harvard Kennedy School Faculty Research Working Paper Series*, March 2013.
73. R. Gates, *Memoirs of a Secretary at War* (New York, 2014), p. 577.
74. "How is Hamid Karzai Still Standing?," *New York Times*, 20 November 2013.
75. "Memorandum for President Bush: Strategic Thoughts," National Security Archive.
76. "'Rapid Reaction Media Team' Concept," U.S. Department of Defense, Office of the Assistant Secretary for Special Operations and Low-Intensity Conflict, 16 January 2003, National Security Archive.
77. M. Phillips, "Cheney Says He was Proponent for Military Action against Iran," *Wall Street Journal*, 30 August 2009.
78. "Kerry presses Iran to prove its nuclear program peaceful," Reuters, 19 November 2013.
79. "Full Text: Al-Arabiya Interview with John Kerry," 23 January 2014, www.alarabiya.com.
80. President Obama, "Remarks by the President at AIPAC Policy Conference," 4 March 2012, White House.
81. D. Sanger, "Obama Order Sped Up Wave of Cyber-Attacks against Iran," *New York Times*, 1 June 2012; idem, *Confront and Conceal: Obama's Secret Wars and Surprising Use of American Power* (New York, 2012).

CONCLUSION: THE NEW SILK ROAD

1. B. Gelb, *Caspian Oil and Gas: Production and Prospects* (2006); *BP Statistical Review of World Energy June 2006*; PennWell Publishing Company, *Oil & Gas Journal*, 19 December 2005; Energy Information Administration, *Caspian Sea Region: Survey of Key Oil and Gas Statistics and Forecasts*, July 2006; "National Oil & Gas Assessment," U.S. Geological Survey (2005).
2. T. Klett, C. Schenk, R. Charpentier, M. Brownfield, J. Pitman, T. Cook and M. Tennyson, "Assessment of Undiscovered Oil and Gas Resources of the Volga-Ural Region Province, Russia and Kazakhstan," U.S. Geological Service (2010), pp. 3095–6.
3. Zelenyi Front, "Vyvoz chernozema v Pesochine: brakon'ervy zaderrzhany," Press Release (Kharkiv, 12 June 2011).
4. World Bank, *World Price Watch* (Washington, DC, 2012).
5. Afghanistan is responsible for 74 per cent of global opium production, down from 92 per cent in 2007, *United Nations Office on Drugs and Crime—World Drug Report 2011* (Vienna, 2011), p. 20. Ironically, as local opium prices show, the more effective the campaign to reduce opium production, the higher the prices—and hence the more lucrative cultivation and trafficking become. For some recent figures, see *Afghanistan Opium Price Monitoring: Monthly Report* (Ministry of Counter Narcotics, Islamic Republic of Afghanistan, Kabul, and United Nations Office on Drugs and Crime, Kabul, March 2010).
6. "Lifestyles of the Kazakhstani leadership," U.S. diplomatic cable, EO 12958, 17 April 2008, WikiLeaks.

7. *Guardian*, 20 April 2015.
8. "President Ilham Aliyev—Michael (Corleone) on the Outside, Sonny on the Inside," U.S. diplomatic cable, 18 September 2009, WikiLeaks EO 12958; for Aliyev's property holding in Dubai, *Washington Post*, 5 March 2010.
9. Quoted in "HIV created by West to enfeeble third world, claims Mahmoud Ahmadinejad," *Daily Telegraph*, 18 January 2012.
10. Hillary Clinton, "Remarks at the New Silk Road Ministerial Meeting," New York, 22 September 2011, U.S. State Department.
11. J. O'Neill, *Building with Better BRICS*, Global Economics Paper, No. 66, Goldman Sachs (2003); R. Sharma, *Breakout Nations: In Pursuit of the Next Economic Miracles* (London, 2012); J. O'Neill, *The Growth Map: Economic Opportunity in the BRICs and Beyond* (London, 2011).
12. Jones Lang Lasalle, *Central Asia: Emerging Markets with High Growth Potential* (February 2012).
13. www.rotana.com/erbilrotana.
14. *The World in London: How London's Residential Resale Market Attracts Capital from across the Globe*, Savills Research (2011).
15. The Cameroon international star, Samuel Eto'o, signed from Barcelona in 2011, Associated Press, 23 August 2011. The opening of the 2010 Under-17 Women's World Cup was marked by a ten-minute opening ceremony featuring "award-winning dance group Shiv Shakit," "Grand Opening: Trinbagonian treat in store for U-17 Women's World Cup," *Trinidad Express*, 27 August 2010.
16. T. Kutchins, T. Sanderson and D. Gordon, *The Northern Distribution Network and the Modern Silk Road: Planning for Afghanistan's Future*, Center for Strategic and International Studies (Washington, DC, 2009).
17. I. Danchenko and C. Gaddy, "The Mystery of Vladimir Putin's Dissertation," edited version of presentations by the authors at a Brookings Institution Foreign Policy Program panel, 30 March 2006.
18. "Putin pledges $43 billion for infrastructure," Associated Press, 21 June 2013. For estimates, see International Association "Coordinating Council on Trans-Siberian Transportation," "Transsib: Current Situation and New Business Perspectives in Europe–Asian Traffic," UNECE Workgroup, 9 September 2013.
19. See for example the *Beijing Times*, 8 May 2014.
20. "Hauling New Treasure along Silk Road," *New York Times*, 20 July 2013.
21. For a report on China's impact on retail gold prices, World Gold Council, *China's Gold Market: Progress and Prospects* (2014). Sales in China of Prada and related companies rose by 40 per cent in 2011 alone, *Annual Report, Prada Group* (2011). By the end of 2013, Prada Group's revenues in Greater China were almost double those of North and South America combined, *Annual Report* (2014).
22. See for example the recent announcement of a $46bn investment to build the China–Pakistan Economic Corridor, Xinhua, 21 April 2015.
23. *Investigative Report on the US National Security Issues Posed by Chinese Telecommunications Companies Huawei and ZTE*, U.S. House of Representatives Report, 8 October 2012.

24. Department of Defense, *Sustaining US Global Leadership: Priorities for 21st Century Defense* (Washington, DC, 2012).
25. President Obama, "Remarks by the President on the Defense Strategic Review," 5 January 2012, White House.
26. Ministry of Defence, *Strategic Trends Programme: Global Strategic Trends—Out to 2040* (London, 2010), p. 10.
27. International Federation for Human Rights, *Shanghai Cooperation Organisation: A Vehicle for Human Rights Violations* (Paris, 2012).
28. "Erdoğan's Shanghai Organization remarks lead to confusion, concern," *Today's Zaman*, 28 January 2013.
29. Hillary Clinton, "Remarks at the New Silk Road Ministerial Meeting," 22 September 2011, New York City.
30. President Xi Jinping, "Promote People-to-People Friendship and Create a Better Future," 7 September 2013, Xinhua.

Index